Walking in
AUSTRALIA

Sandra Bardwell
Matthew Fletcher
Glenn van der Knijff
Greg Caire
Gareth McCormack
Simon Richmond
Grant Dixon

LONELY PLANET PUBLICATIONS
Melbourne • Oakland • London • Paris

AUSTRALIA

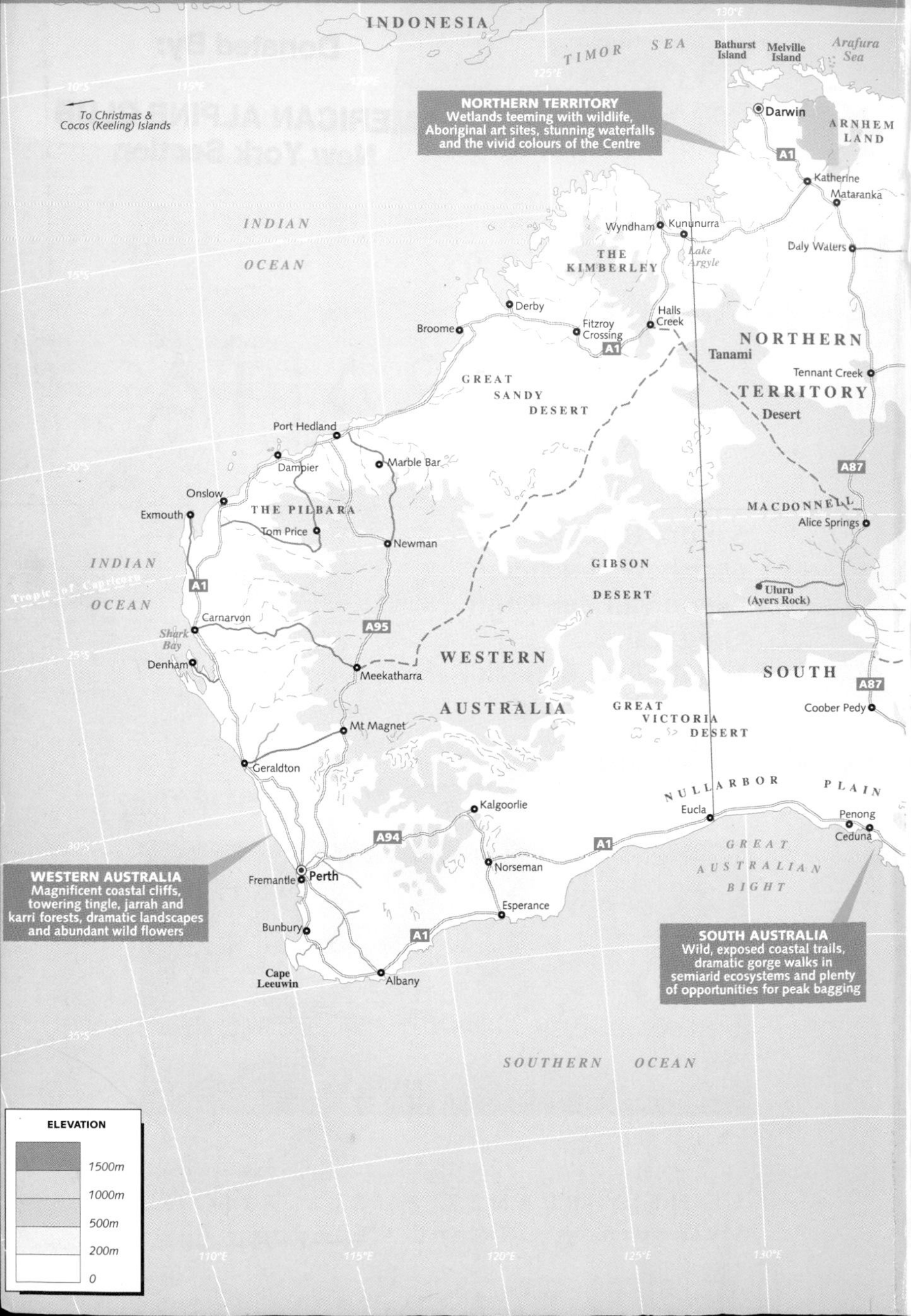

INDONESIA
TIMOR SEA
Bathurst Island
Melville Island
Arafura Sea
To Christmas & Cocos (Keeling) Islands
NORTHERN TERRITORY
Wetlands teeming with wildlife, Aboriginal art sites, stunning waterfalls and the vivid colours of the Centre
Darwin
ARNHEM LAND
A1
Katherine
Mataranka
INDIAN OCEAN
Wyndham
Kununurra
Lake Argyle
Daly Waters
THE KIMBERLEY
Derby
Broome
Fitzroy Crossing
Halls Creek
A1
NORTHERN TERRITORY
Tanami Desert
Tennant Creek
GREAT SANDY DESERT
Port Hedland
Marble Bar
Dampier
A87
Onslow
Exmouth
THE PILBARA
Tom Price
Newman
MACDONNELL
Alice Springs
INDIAN OCEAN
Tropic of Capricorn
A1
GIBSON DESERT
Uluru (Ayers Rock)
Carnarvon
A95
Shark Bay
Denham
WESTERN AUSTRALIA
Meekatharra
SOUTH
A87
Coober Pedy
GREAT VICTORIA DESERT
Mt Magnet
Geraldton
NULLARBOR PLAIN
Kalgoorlie
Eucla
Penong
Ceduna
A94
A1
GREAT AUSTRALIAN BIGHT
Norseman
Perth
Fremantle
WESTERN AUSTRALIA
Magnificent coastal cliffs, towering tingle, jarrah and karri forests, dramatic landscapes and abundant wild flowers
Esperance
Bunbury
A1
SOUTH AUSTRALIA
Wild, exposed coastal trails, dramatic gorge walks in semiarid ecosystems and plenty of opportunities for peak bagging
Cape Leeuwin
Albany
SOUTHERN OCEAN
ELEVATION
1500m
1000m
500m
200m
0
110°E
115°E
120°E
125°E
130°E
10°S
15°S
20°S
25°S
30°S
35°S

AUSTRALIA

QUEENSLAND
Challenging peaks, sandy islands and the chance to walk through unique tropical rainforest

NEW SOUTH WALES
Magnificent walking country: Blue Mountains escarpment, glacial lakes, rolling alpine plains, limestone gorges, hidden coastal valleys, imposing volcanic buttresses and World Heritage List rainforests

SYDNEY REGION
Sandy beaches, a palm jungle, swimming holes in remote creeks, all within cooee of one of the world's most vibrant cities

AUSTRALIAN CAPITAL TERRITORY
Grassy subalpine valleys, rugged rocky ridges and the serenity of the Murrumbidgee River valley

MELBOURNE REGION
Cool temperate rainforest, spectacular rocky gorges, mountain forests and river red gum woodlands

VICTORIA
A region of contrasts, from the sand dunes and sparse mallee woodlands of the interior to snow plains, alpine peaks and long, unspoiled beaches

TASMANIA
Some of the most challenging walks in Australia, with craggy peaks, glacial lakes, pristine wilderness areas and an untamed coastline

0   250   500km
0   125   250mi
1:21,500,000

Torres Strait

PAPUA NEW GUINEA

Thursday Island · Cape York

Weipa

Groote Eylandt

GULF OF CARPENTARIA

Coen

Cape York Peninsula

Cooktown

CORAL SEA

Mossman

Cairns

ATHERTON TABLELAND

Borroloola

Mornington Island

Normanton

Townsville

Whitsunday Islands

GREAT BARRIER REEF

GREAT DIVIDING RANGE

BARKLY TABLELAND

Mount Isa

Cloncurry

Hughenden

Mackay

QUEENSLAND

RANGES

Boulia

Winton

Longreach

Rockhampton

CHANNEL COUNTRY

SIMPSON DESERT

Birdsville

Tropic of Capricorn

STURT STONY DESERT

SOUTH AUSTRALIA

Lake Eyre

Charleville

Maryborough

Fraser Island

PACIFIC OCEAN

Cunnamulla

DARLING DOWNS

Toowoomba

Noosa

Brisbane

Goondiwindi

Surfers Paradise

Byron Bay

Woomera

Bourke

Moree

Grafton

NEW SOUTH WALES

Broken Hill

Port Augusta

Port Pirie

Dubbo

Port Macquarie

Lord Howe Island

Adelaide

Mildura

Hay

Newcastle

Kangaroo Island

Wagga Wagga

Sydney

Wollongong

Bendigo

Echuca

Albury

CANBERRA

Mount Gambier

Ballarat

Geelong

VICTORIA

Kosciuszko

Bega

Portland

Melbourne

Sale

The Grampians

Apollo Bay

Wilsons Promontory

BASS STRAIT

King Island

Flinders Island

TASMAN SEA

Burnie

Devonport

Launceston

Queenstown

Hobart

Bruny Island

TASMANIA

Murray River

Walking in Australia
4th edition – January 2001
First published – May 1988

Published by
Lonely Planet Publications Pty Ltd ABN 36 005 607 983
90 Maribyrnong St, Footscray, Victoria 3011, Australia

Lonely Planet Offices
Australia Locked Bag 1, Footscray, Victoria 3011
USA 150 Linden St, Oakland, CA 94607
UK 10a Spring Place, London NW5 3BH
France 1 rue du Dahomey, 75011 Paris

Photographs
Many of the images in this guide are available for licensing from
Lonely Planet Images.
email: lpi@lonelyplanet.com.au

Main front cover photograph
Tidal River rock formations at Wilsons Promontory, Victoria (Karen Trist)

Small front cover photograph
Hiking through Gastrolobium Saddle, Larapinta Trail, Northern Territory
(Matthew Fletcher)

ISBN 0 86442 669 0

Printed by Colorcraft Ltd, Hong Kong

Although the authors and Lonely Planet try to make the information as accurate as possible, we accept no responsibility for any loss, injury or inconvenience sustained by anyone using this book.

Contents

GETTING AROUND

AUSTRALIAN CAPITAL TERRITORY

SYDNEY REGION

NEW SOUTH WALES

NORTHERN TERRITORY

QUEENSLAND

SOUTH AUSTRALIA

The Walks	Duration	Standard	Transport
Australian Capital Territory			
Grassy Creek	5–6 hours	medium	no
Tidbinbilla Ridge	7–7½ hours	hard	no
Kambah Pool	5½–6 hours	easy-medium	yes
Sydney Region			
Bouddi Coast	5 hours	medium	no
Mt Wondabyne	4½–5 hours	easy-medium	no
Cowan to Brooklyn	4 hours	easy-medium	yes
Red Hands Cave	4–4½ hours	easy-medium	yes
Forest Path	3½–4 hours	easy-medium	yes
Palm Jungle	4–4½ hours	medium	yes
New South Wales			
Wentworth Falls & the Valley of the Waters	5½–7 hours	easy-medium	yes
Blue Gum Forest	2 days	medium	yes
Six Foot Track	3 days	medium	yes
Mt Kosciuszko & the Main Range	3 days	medium	yes
The Chimneys	5–6 hours	easy-medium	yes
Mt Jagungal	3–4 days	medium	yes
Cooleman Plain	5–6 hours	medium	yes
Corang Peak to the Castle	3 days	medium-hard	yes
Pigeon House Mountain	3 hours	medium	yes
Bungonia Gorge	2 days	medium-hard	no
Warrumbungles Grand High Tops	2–3 days	medium	no
Wonga Walk	3 hours	easy	no
Never Never Circuit	4 hours	medium	no
Washpool Rainforest	3 hours	easy	no
Northern Territory			
Tabletop Range	2 days	medium	yes
Barrk Sandstone Bushwalk	4½–5 hours	medium	no
Jatbula Trail	4–5 days	medium	yes
Ormiston Gorge & Pound	4½–5 hours	easy-medium	no
Larapinta Trail Highlight	3 days	medium	no
Queensland			
Green Mountains	2 days	medium hard	yes
Ships Stern & Dave's Creek Circuit	2 days	easy-medium	yes
Fraser Island Lakes Circuit	4 days	medium	yes
Thorsborne Trail	4 days	easy-medium	yes
Mt Bartle Frere	2 days	hard	yes

The Walks *continued*	Duration	Standard	Transport
South Australia			
Morialta Circuit	4½–5 hours	easy-medium	yes
West Coast Circuit	2 days	medium	no
Rocky River	6 hours	medium	no
Mt Remarkable Gorges	2 days	medium	yes
Wilpena Pound	2 days	easy-medium	yes
Tasmania			
Mt Wellington	6–7 hours	medium	yes
The Organ Pipes	3–4 hours	easy	yes
Mt Field National Park	5–6 hours	medium	seasonal
Mt Anne Circuit	3 days	hard	seasonal
Overland Track	7 days	medium	yes
Walls of Jerusalem	2 days	easy-medium	seasonal
South Coast Track	7 days	medium-hard	seasonal
Freycinet Peninsula	2 days	easy-medium	yes
Maria Island	4 hours	easy-medium	yes
Cape Pillar	3 days	medium	no
Melbourne Region			
Brisbane Ranges Traverse	3 days	medium	no
Werribee Gorge	3½–4 hours	medium	no
Macedon Ranges Trail Highlight	5½–6 hours	medium	no
Gellibrand Hill	3–3½ hours	easy	yes
Sherbrooke Forest	3½–4 hours	easy-medium	yes
Main Creek	4–4½ hours	medium	no
Victoria			
Hattah–Kulkyne Tour	3 days	easy-medium	yes
Mt Rosea	3–3½ hours	medium	no
Mt Stapylton	4½–5 hours	medium-hard	no
Cape Bridgewater	4¾–5 hours	easy-medium	no
Cape Otway	2 days	medium	no
Mt Bogong	2 days	medium-hard	no
Huts of the Bogong High Plains	3½–4½ hours	medium	no
Mt Feathertop & the Razorback	2 days	hard	no
Mt Speculation & Mt Howitt	2 days	medium-hard	no
The Bluff	5–6 hours	medium	no
Mt Buffalo Plateau	5–6 hours	medium	no
Sealers Cove	2 days	medium	no
Croajingolong Coast Walk	5 days	easy-medium	no
Western Australia			
Cape to Cape Walk Highlight	5½–6 hours	medium	no
Bluff Knoll	3–3½ hours	medium	no
Toolbrunup Peak	3 hours	medium-hard	no
Lowlands Beach to Cosy Corner	5¾–6¼ hours	medium	no
Walpole to Peaceful Bay	4 days	medium	no

Best Time	Features	Page
May–Oct	Marked trails winding through a landscape of forests and gorges	269
Aug–Oct	A walk along Kangaroo Island's wild west coast to picturesque West Bay	273
Aug–Oct	A traverse of the limestone cliffs of Kangaroo Island's west coast	276
Aug–Oct	A walk through flood plains and mixed forest to ferny gorges	278
May–Oct	Circuiting the ancient peaks of an oasis-like natural amphitheatre	282
Oct–April	Good tracks lead to an alpine area with great views of Hobart	295
all year	Easy tracks pass a waterfall to the base of huge dolerite columns	297
Oct–April	Fantastic alpine walking with great views of Tasmania's wilderness	299
Oct–April	A challenging ridge circuit with spectacular alpine scenery	303
Oct–Apri	A classic walk through rugged alpine scenery and dense forest	308
Oct–April	A walk through an alpine area of tarns and pencil pine groves	323
all year	A remote wilderness walk taking in wild coast and inland peaks	327
all year	Easy coastal walking with beautiful bays and beaches	335
all year	An easy outing on a historic island, with views of the east coast	339
all year	Good tracks along the highest sea cliffs in Australia	342
Aug–Nov	A remote walk close to Melbourne, featuring gold-mining relics	353
Sept–Nov	A scrambly walk with rock hopping through the sheer-walled gorge	357
all year	A historic walk through tall mountain forest with panoramic views	361
March–Nov	A walk featuring river red gums and an early colonial homestead	363
Aug–Nov	A stroll through towering mountain ash forest and fern gullies	366
all year	A good track through woodland to sea cliffs and a secluded beach	368
May–Nov	Camp among river red gums beside the mighty Murray River	376
Aug–Nov	Superb views from a great, high mountain climb in the Grampians	381
Aug–Nov	Spectacular mountain scenery and exhilarating rock hopping	382
Oct–March	Superlative coast walking, including Victoria's highest sea cliff	384
Nov–April	Superb walking along coastal cliffs and unspoilt beaches	391
Nov–April	Victoria's highest summit with panoramic views and a waterfall	398
Nov–April	Old cattlemen's huts, grassy snow plains and expansive views	403
Nov–April	An impressive pointed summit with wild flowers and views	406
Nov–April	High summits, wonderful views and a spectacular camp site	410
Nov–April	A classic cliff-bordered summit with rocky crags and grassy moors	414
Oct–May	A beautiful snow plain and forest walk with plenty of wildlife	416
all year	A scenic walk linking the best of the Prom's world-class beaches	423
all year	A wilderness walk along some of Victoria's unspoilt coastline	428
Sept–Dec	A walk through coastal heathland with places for whale watching	445
Sept–Dec	A good track to the south-west's highest peak with great views	450
Sept–Dec	A steep, rocky climb to a fantastic vista of mountains and plains	451
Sept–Dec	A walk round West Cape Howe, near the state's southernmost point	454
Oct–Nov	A walk through giant tingle and karri forests to a sandy bay	457

The Maps

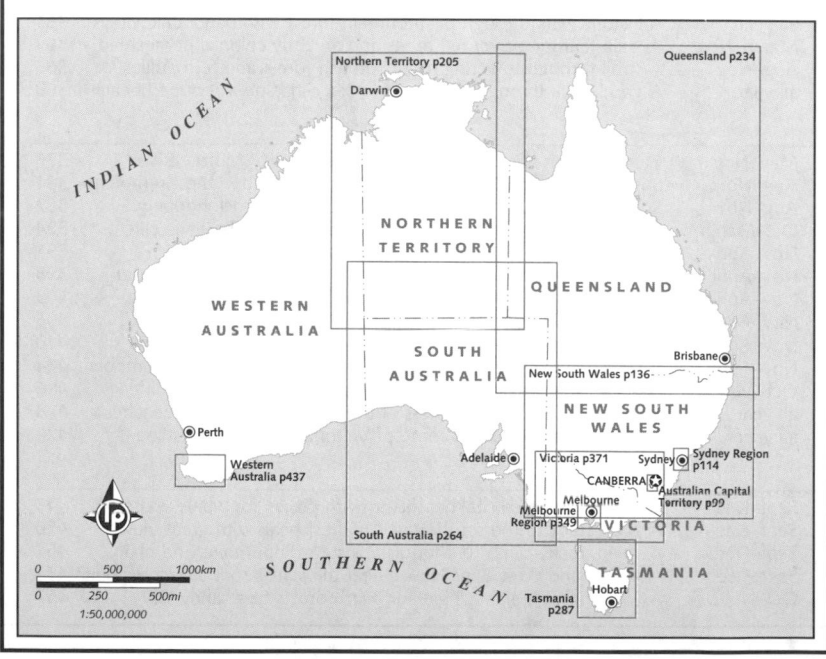

The Authors

Sandra Bardwell
After graduating with a thesis on the history of national parks in Victoria, Sandra worked as an archivist and then as historian for the National Parks Service and its successors. She has been a dedicated walker since joining a bushwalking club in the early 1960s and became well known through her column in the Melbourne *Age* and as the author of several guidebooks on the subject. In 1989 Sandra and her husband Hal retired to the Highlands of Scotland where they live in a village near Loch Ness. She has walked extensively in Australia and Britain, and for Lonely Planet in Italy, Ireland and France, and now even more extensively in Australia.

Matthew Fletcher
After four years at art college Matt traded a damp flat and the hills of south-west England for camp sites under African skies and peaks over 500m. Mt Kenya, the Maralal International Camel Derby and northern coast of Mozambique provided inspiration for a writing career. A brief incarnation as a staff writer on an adventure sports magazine soon passed on and Matt has been freelancing ever since, travelling and trekking in the UK, Europe and Africa, his articles appearing in magazines ranging from *Trail* to *Feng Shui for Modern Living*. Matt is also a contributor to Lonely Planet's *Walking in Spain*, *Kenya* and *East Africa* guides.

Glenn van der Knijff
Glenn's first bushwalk was over 20 years ago and he has enjoyed an outdoor life ever since. He grew up in Bright (at the foot of the Victorian high country), completed a degree in cartography in Melbourne, then tried his hand at garbage collecting. But his first real job, though short-lived, was for a small 'back yard' map publishing company. He then did everything from Subscription Manager to Assistant Editor at *Wild* and *Rock* magazines, before joining Lonely Planet in 1997. His increasing passion for both downhill and cross-country skiing has seen him jet to North America on two separate occasions, and he dreams of skiing all the major resorts of Europe.

Greg Caire
Greg has been walking and climbing since being introduced to the outdoors at high school. After completing a degree and entering professional employment, he quit a promising career for the wilds of Brazil, here learning the joys of climbing in a foreign land and *cachaca* – Brazilian rum. Since then, he has climbed in Thailand, New Zealand and the UK, sea kayaked and paraglided in Australia, walked in Japan and cycled through Pakistan, China and Western Tibet.

Greg's photographs and articles appear in numerous publications worldwide. Photographic contributions to Lonely Planet guidebooks include *Brazil*, *Karakoram Highway*, *Pakistan* and *Tibet*.

He now resides in Melbourne, splitting his time between a successful food industry marketing career and his first loves: climbing and outdoor photography.

Gareth McCormack

After finishing a degree in law in 1995 Gareth travelled, walked and climbed his way across Asia, Australia and New Zealand for 18 months. This trip inspired a radical career turnaround and he is now a writer and photographer based in Ireland. He is a regular contributor to the magazine *Walking World Ireland* and co-authored Lonely Planet's *Walking in Ireland* and *Walking in France*. Every year he tries to spend several months photographing wild and beautiful parts of the world.

Simon Richmond

Simon Richmond's first experience of the great outdoors was probably toddling along the Prom in his hometown of Blackpool. He has since tackled more rugged trails in the UK, Japan, South-East Asia and South America, as well as Australia, where he sometimes stops travelling long enough to call Sydney home. Simon has also contributed to Lonely Planet's *Central Asia*, the *Out to Eat* guides to Sydney and London and the new *Istanbul to Kathmandu* shoestring guide.

Grant Dixon

Grant works part-time for the Tasmanian Parks and Wildlife Service and spends much of the rest of his time exploring and photographing remote parts of the world. He is a native Tasmanian and is always drawn home to the wild natural landscapes of south-west Tasmania, a region he knows a lifetime won't be long enough to fully explore.

FROM THE AUTHORS

Sandra Bardwell The warm hospitality of family and friends in Sydney, Canberra and Melbourne was deeply appreciated. The staff at many visitor centres were most helpful: Busselton, Manjimup, Mt Barker, Albany, Denmark, Walpole, Margaret River, Sydney, Glenbrook, Canberra, Dromana, Dandenong Ranges, Horsham, Portland and Apollo Bay. Many conservation agency people provided advice: CALM staff at Como, Busselton and Albany, especially John Watson and Annie Keating; NSW NPSW staff at Hurstville, Bobbin Head and Audley; Environment ACT staff; Parks Victoria people at Brisbane Ranges, Grampians, Otway, Hattah–Kulkyne and Lower Glenelg National Parks; Brambuk Aboriginal Cultural Centre, and Friends of the Bibbulmun Track.

At Lonely Planet, I'm indebted to Sue Galley for tempting me originally, to Nick, Lindsay and Teresa for advice and support, Emily for good fellowship during editing and Glenn for design.

At home, we're grateful to friends and neighbours for looking after our interests while we were away.

Without Hal's unfailing companionship and advice, it would have been a long, lonely track indeed.

Matthew Fletcher Thanks to Clare Irvin who helped in many ways with my contribution, Tricky Dicky and Marlon Bando who made us feel right at home in Sydney, David and Robyn for hospitality and handy hints, 'the folks' for putting us up when we were homeless, Helen O'Callaghan and Russell Willis for some good pointers and the outdoor types at LP for sorting out such a great job. Also thanks to Nita Buick, Jacqui Blackeby, Fiona Gill on Kangaroo Island, Michael Holton and Michael Wigg at Mt Remarkable, Katherine and the staff at Wilpena Pound Resort, Charlie at Trek Larapinta, Chris Day, Michelle Cox, Anthony Stephens, Michael Barritt at Litchfield National Park, Andrew and Steve at Nitmiluk National Park, Jacques Marcelis, Jeanette Rosendale at Kakadu National Park, Julie Balley and Felicity Chapman at Cardwell Reef and Rainforest Centre, Sue Olsson, Robyn Towne at Kingfisher Bay Tourism, Michelle at Nature Walks, Andy Quick, Nicola Bryden, John Lane of Cairns Bushwalking Club and many, many more.

Glenn van der Knijff Glenn would like to thank the National Library of Australia; Nat Webb for use of his historical photo of the Chalet; and Nick, Chris and the crew at Lonely Planet for giving him this assignment.

Greg Caire Thanks to Ian Sheiffer for transport to Bungonia, excellent Arabic coffee, and for spotting a tree blown off the gorge rim that nearly squished us. Thanks to Wade Stevens and Nina for use of their car, and Wade's tolerance at being shuffled around the Warrumbungles in snow and rain.

To the fantastic Parks staff at Croajingolong, a big thanks (particularly Brooke Connor and Bob Fisher). Michael Hampton and Kim deserve mention for agreeing to be dragged through Croajingolong, and forgiving me for eating all their scroggin on the first night. Thanks to the park staff at Bungonia for their assistance.

Finally, special thanks to Matilda Schmitt for a mammoth effort, organising last-minute flights under great duress for the Dorrigo and Washpool sections.

Gareth McCormack Thanks to those in Tasmania who gave valuable advice, including the staff of the Parks & Wildlife Service and Carl and Cathy at the Backpackers Barn. Special thanks to three surfers who put on their walking boots (and may never do so again!) to keep me company for an epic outing on the Mt Anne Circuit. They are Michael Thornhill, Eoghan 'Yogi' Mullan and Daniel Kavanagh. Thanks also to Helen who bravely undertook the task of organising my slides while I was away.

Simon Richmond Many thanks to Aine Gliddon for courteously answering my many queries, and to Meredith for her knowledge and enthusiasm while guiding me along the Six Foot Track.

This Book

The first three editions of Lonely Planet's *Bushwalking in Australia* were written by John & Monica Chapman. For this 4th, retitled edition, a team of writers revised and expanded the selection of walks and thoroughly rewrote the text. Sandra Bardwell was co-ordinating author, and wrote the introductory chapters, the Australian Capital Territory, Sydney Region, Melbourne Region, Western Australia and the first half of the Victoria chapter. Matthew Fletcher wrote the Northern Territory, Queensland and South Australia chapters, Glenn van der Knijff wrote the Victorian Alps and Kosciuszko National Park sections, and Greg Caire walked and wrote up the Croajingolong Wilderness Coast Track and much of the New South Wales chapter. Simon Richmond provided the introduction to New South Wales and researched the Blue Mountains. Gareth McCormack wrote most of the Tasmania, with assistance from Grant Dixon, who researched and wrote up the South Coast Track. Emily Coles wrote the Wilsons Promontory National Park section.

Material from the 3rd edition of Lonely Planet's *New South Wales* guide by Paul Harding, Sally Webb, Michelle Bennett and Andrew Draffen was used in the book.

From the Publisher

Walking in Australia is proudly brought to you by Emily Coles (coordinating editor) and Glenn van der Knijff (coordinating designer) in Lonely Planet's Melbourne office. Anne Mulvaney edited and proofed much of the book, Lindsay Brown edited the Fauna & Flora section and Janet Brunckhorst assisted Emily with editing and proofing. Glenn masterminded the climate charts and mapping, with assistance from Paul Piaia, Maree Styles, Andrew Smith and Chris Klep. Matt King, Martin Harris and Kate Nolan provided illustrations and Jamieson Gross designed the cover. Thanks to Glenn Tempest for the author photo of Greg Caire.

Thanks to Senior Editor Lindsay Brown and Senior Designer Michael Blore for their valuable input, Chris Klep for planning and reading assistance, Leonie Mugavin for checking the Getting There & Away chapter, Annie Horner for assistance with slides, Tim Uden for his layout wisdom, David Burnett for sharing his historical and geological knowledge, Sean Pywell and Lindsay Brown for their wildlife expertise and Sally Dillon for checking the cycling section.

Thanks

Thanks to all the readers who wrote in with their interesting anec-dotes and useful comments on *Bushwalking in Australia*:

Rob & Marina Caron, Sarah Dunlop, Michael Green, Andrew Hazel, Barrett Higman, Mary Hunt, Susan Jack, Ben Kefford, Beth Little, Fran Lynch, Stephen Proctor, Servane Rangehead, Andrew Roberts, Derek Tole, Margaret Toohey, John Ward and Daniel Wurm.

Foreword

ABOUT LONELY PLANET GUIDEBOOKS

The story begins with a classic travel adventure: Tony and Maureen Wheeler's 1972 journey across Europe and Asia to Australia. Useful information about the overland trail did not exist at that time, so Tony and Maureen published the first Lonely Planet guidebook to meet a growing need.

From a kitchen table, then from a tiny office in Melbourne (Australia), Lonely Planet has become the largest independent travel publisher in the world, an international company with offices in Melbourne, Oakland (USA), London (UK) and Paris (France).

Today Lonely Planet guidebooks cover the globe. There is an ever-growing list of books and there's information in a variety of forms and media. Some things haven't changed. The main aim is still to help make it possible for adventurous travellers to get out there – to explore and better understand the world.

At Lonely Planet we believe travellers can make a positive contribution to the countries they visit – if they respect their host communities and spend their money wisely. Since 1986 a percentage of the income from each book has been donated to aid projects and human rights campaigns.

Updates Lonely Planet thoroughly updates each guidebook as often as possible. This usually means there are around two years between editions, although for more unusual or more stable destinations the gap can be longer. Check the imprint page (following the colour map at the beginning of the book) for publication dates.

Between editions up-to-date information is available in two free newsletters – the paper *Planet Talk* and email *Comet* (to subscribe, contact any Lonely Planet office) – and on our Web site at www.lonelyplanet.com. The *Upgrades* section of the Web site covers a number of important and volatile destinations and is regularly updated by Lonely Planet authors. *Scoop* covers news and current affairs relevant to travellers. And, lastly, the *Thorn Tree* bulletin board and *Postcards* section of the site carry unverified, but fascinating, reports from travellers.

Correspondence The process of creating new editions begins with the letters, postcards and emails received from travellers. This correspondence often includes suggestions, criticisms and comments about the current editions. Interesting excerpts are immediately passed on via newsletters and the Web site, and everything goes to our authors to be verified when they're researching on the road. We're keen to get more feedback from organisations or individuals who represent communities visited by travellers.

> Lonely Planet gathers information for everyone who's curious about the planet – and especially for those who explore it first-hand. Through guidebooks, phrasebooks, activity guides, maps, literature, newsletters, image library, TV series and Web site we act as an information exchange for a worldwide community of travellers.

Research Authors aim to gather sufficient practical information to enable travellers to make informed choices and to make the mechanics of a journey run smoothly. They also research historical and cultural background to help enrich the travel experience and allow travellers to understand and respond appropriately to cultural and environmental issues.

Authors don't stay in every hotel because that would mean spending a couple of months in each medium-sized city and, no, they don't eat at every restaurant because that would mean stretching belts beyond capacity. They do visit hotels and restaurants to check standards and prices, but feedback based on readers' direct experiences can be very helpful.

Many of our authors work undercover, others aren't so secretive. None of them accept freebies in exchange for positive write-ups. And none of our guidebooks contain any advertising.

Production Authors submit their raw manuscripts and maps to offices in Australia, USA, UK or France. Editors and cartographers – all experienced travellers themselves – then begin the process of assembling the pieces. When the book finally hits the shops, some things are already out of date, we start getting feedback from readers and the process begins again …

WARNING & REQUEST

Things change – prices go up, schedules change, good places go bad and bad places go bankrupt – nothing stays the same. So, if you find things better or worse, recently opened or long since closed, please tell us and help make the next edition even more accurate and useful. We genuinely value all the feedback we receive. Julie Young coordinates a well travelled team that reads and acknowledges every letter, postcard and email and ensures that every morsel of information finds its way to the appropriate authors, editors and cartographers for verification.

Everyone who writes to us will find their name in the next edition of the appropriate guidebook. They will also receive the latest issue of *Planet Talk*, our quarterly printed newsletter, or *Comet*, our monthly email newsletter. Subscriptions to both newsletters are free. The very best contributions will be rewarded with a free guidebook.

Excerpts from your correspondence may appear in new editions of Lonely Planet guidebooks, the Lonely Planet Web site, *Planet Talk* or *Comet*, so please let us know if you *don't* want your letter published or your name acknowledged.

Send all correspondence to the Lonely Planet office closest to you:

Australia: Locked Bag 1, Footscray, Victoria 3011
USA: 150 Linden St, Oakland, CA 94607
UK: 10A Spring Place, London NW5 3BH
France: 1 rue du Dahomey, 75011 Paris

Or email us at: talk2us@lonelyplanet.com.au

For news, views and updates see our Web site: www.lonelyplanet.com

Introduction

Australia has vast expanses of natural open space endowed with magnificent scenery and unique wildlife. With these attributes, plus a great tradition of bushwalking, this isolated continent beckons anyone who would explore it on foot.

The variety of landscapes is almost unimaginably broad: tropical rainforests, the arid and harshly beautiful Centre, long pristine beaches in the south-west and rugged mountain ranges in Tasmania. There are unusual islands in Queensland, ephemeral waterways lined with majestic eucalyptuses in the dry interior, and spacious snow plains and summits in the High Country. Even on the doorsteps of the nation's capital and its largest cities there's beautiful bushland, rocky coasts, mountains and river valleys.

When to enjoy all this? Well, the walking season is year-round in Australia – spring, summer, autumn or winter you can enjoy walking somewhere.

Enticing walks are found in Australia's outstanding national parks and conservation reserves. Hundreds of natural areas from one end of the country to the other protect the finest landscapes and a multitude of ecosystems. In some parks, you can learn first-hand about the beliefs and customs of Australia's Aboriginal people and their harmonious relationships with the land.

Walking tracks reach far and wide and can be followed for a day, a week, a month or more. There are walks for everyone, from easy strolls to challenging expeditions in remote country demanding high levels of fitness and self-sufficiency. There are areas

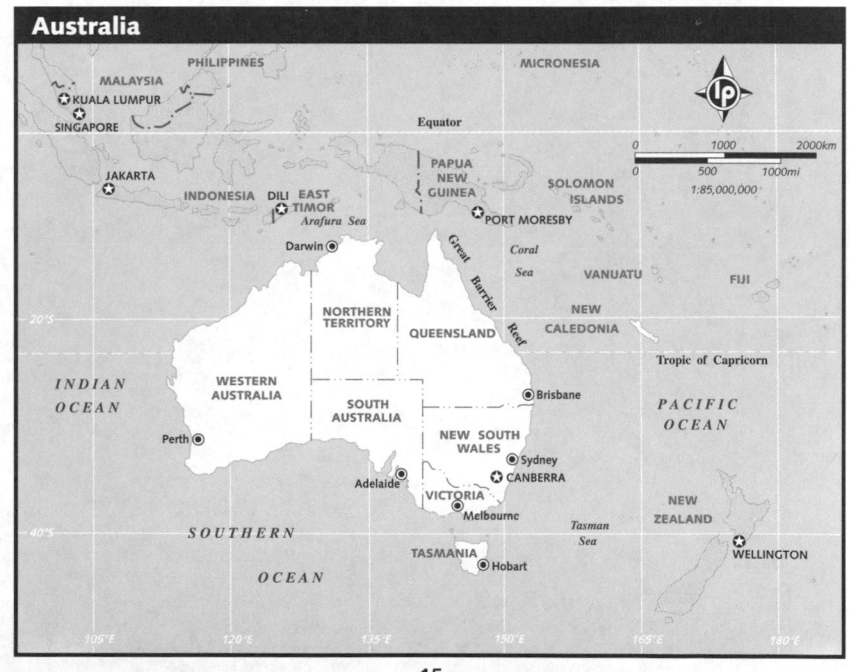

where tracks are few and faint, and where skills in route finding and bushcraft are really put to the test.

Many national parks have camping grounds with simple facilities, some accessible on wheels, others only on foot. Camping can be the ideal way to savour the space and remoteness of Down Under and to encounter wildlife. If you prefer the shelter of a solid roof, many parks aren't too far from towns, with plenty of reasonably priced accommodation that can be enjoyed at the beginning or end of your walk.

Walking in national parks is the best way to see and appreciate its fascinating fauna and flora – even the names are intriguing: quolls, bandicoots, galahs, perenties, grevilleas, pandanis, mallee eucalyptuses, kookaburras. They're colourful, noisy, prickly, elusive, but only a few are downright threatening. In fact, the most dangerous encounter in the bush could be the falling branch of a river red gum.

In some very remote areas, you might go for a few days without seeing another soul, but in other places meeting fellow walkers at camp sites and on mountain tops is part of the fun. In fact, meeting Aussies anywhere is a great experience – you'd have to go a long way to find friendlier people.

If the thought of all this walking brings food and drink to mind, you won't be disappointed. Australia is a veritable cornucopia of locally grown foods, delectable wines and thirst-quenching beers. What's more, restaurants offering imaginative, inexpensive fare aren't confined to the big cities. Sampling their menus can be a most enjoyable introduction to contemporary Australia's richly multicultural society.

Once you've sampled a couple of the walks in this book, the temptation will be there to explore further. Australia is like that – ceaselessly fascinating, immensely rewarding and addictive.

Facts about Australia

HISTORY

c. 60,000 BC – Probable first human settlement of the Australian continent from South-East Asia (the exact date is still hotly contested); Aboriginal (indigenous) people gradually settled the continent.

24,000 BC – Centre of the continent settled.

20,000 BC – Probable date of some of the oldest archaeological remains, at Lake Mungo, New South Wales (NSW).

AD 1616 – First European landing on the west coast of Australia.

1642 – Dutch navigator Abel Tasman named Van Diemen's Land (VDL; later renamed Tasmania).

1688 – William Dampier, British adventurer, investigated Shark Bay on Western Australian (WA) coast.

1770 – James Cook explored the east coast and claimed the continent for Britain, naming it New South Wales; about 300,000 Aboriginal people living on the continent.

1788 – Convicts, sailors and soldiers of the First Fleet under Arthur Phillip established a settlement at Sydney Cove.

1791 – European population reached about 4000.

1798 – George Bass and Matthew Flinders circumnavigated VDL.

1804 – First settlement near Hobart, Tasmania.

1813 – First crossing of the Blue Mountains, west of Sydney.

1824 – Hume and Hovell made the first overland journey from Sydney to Port Phillip Bay, in present-day Victoria.

1825 – Settlement established on the Brisbane River, Queensland.

1826 – First settlement in the west, at Albany, WA.

1829 – Settlement founded on the Swan River, later named Perth, in WA; Charles Sturt discovered that the Murrumbidgee and Darling Rivers join the Murray River; he also found the mouth of the Murray.

1834 – Portland, on the west coast, became Victoria's first settlement.

1835 – Settlement established at Port Phillip Bay, which became Melbourne, Victoria.

1836 – Thomas Mitchell travelled from southern NSW through western Victoria to the coast; Adelaide, South Australia (SA), founded as a convict-free settlement.

1840 – Total population of Australia about 190,000.

1850s – Railways built in most colonies.

1851 – Major gold discovery at Ballarat, Victoria; Australia's population 2.25 million, the majority Australian-born.

1854 – Eureka Rebellion at Ballarat, fought for the miners' right to vote and purchase land.

1856 – People of VDL changed the colony's name to Tasmania.

1860 – Twenty million sheep in Australia; a severely reduced Aboriginal population.

1861 – Gold discovered in Queensland.

1862 – John McDouall Stuart completed the first south to north crossing of the continent, from Adelaide (SA) to near Darwin, in the Northern Territory (NT).

1865 – Legislation passed ensuring that colonial laws couldn't be overridden by UK laws.

1869 – Settlement successfully set up at the site of Darwin, after several failures.

1872 – Overland Telegraph completed from near Darwin to the site of Alice Springs, NT.

1879 – Australia's first national park created south of Sydney (later named Royal National Park).

1893 – Gold discovered at Kalgoorlie, WA.

1895 – AB Patterson wrote 'Waltzing Matilda', Australia's unofficial national anthem.

1901 – Commonwealth of Australia established; the colonies became states and a Federal parliament was set up, with Melbourne the capital and seat of Federal government; Australia's population 3.77 million.

1902 – Women gained the vote.

1908 – Site selected for a national capital between Sydney and Melbourne.

1911 – Commonwealth purchased land for the Australian Capital Territory (ACT); the name 'Canberra' chosen for the national capital two years later.

1914 – Australia entered WWI.

1915 – Australian troops landed at Gallipoli, the origin of Anzac Day.

1919 – First aeroplane from overseas landed in Australia, at Darwin.

1920s – Scientific exploration expeditions travelled through the NT's Arnhem Land.

1921 – Australia's population 5.4 million.

1923 – Rich deposits of copper, lead, silver and zinc discovered at Mt Isa, Queensland.

1927 – Federal parliament sat for the first time in Canberra.

1928 – First Flying Doctor base opened, at Cloncurry, Queensland, to provide medical services to the Outback.

1930s – Simpson Desert explored, the last major area to be explored on foot.

1931 – Beginning of the Depression, with unemployment soon at 30%.

1932 – Sydney Harbour Bridge opened.

1938 – Airmail service inaugurated between the capital cities.

1939 – Australia joined the Allies at outbreak of WWII; Australia's population seven million.

1942 – Darwin and some settlements in north-west WA bombed.

1947 – Major postwar migration from Britain and Europe started.

1949 – Snowy Mountains Hydroelectric Scheme launched to harness the power of the Murray and Snowy Rivers.

1950s – Woomera Rocket Range opened in SA; atomic bombs tested on sites at Maralinga and Emu Junction.

1953 – First oil strike made on Australian territory, in WA.

1956 – Olympic Games held in Melbourne; National Parks Act passed in Victoria, the first specialised legislation for national parks in Australia.

1961 – Australia's population 10.5 million.

1965 – Metric system adopted.

1967 – Citizenship granted to Aboriginal people and Torres Strait Islanders at a referendum by white Australians.

1971 – Yirrkala Land Case in which Australian courts upheld the principle of *terra nullius*, ie, that Australia was unoccupied in 1788.

1972 – Lake Pedder in south-west Tasmania was flooded despite a landmark conservation campaign, leading to the formation of the United Tasmania Group, which became the world's first Green Party.

1973 – Sydney Opera House opened.

1974 – Striking on Christmas Eve, Cyclone Tracey destroyed 95% of Darwin's buildings.

1976 – Australia's population 13.56 million.

1978 – Self-government granted to the NT.

1982 – World Heritage listing for south-west Tasmania; it now covers 1.38 million hectares.

1983 – Franklin River in south-west Tasmania saved from flooding.

1986 – World Heritage listing for Kakadu.

1988 – Nationwide celebrations marked 200 years of European settlement.

1992 – Mabo Land Case, in which the High Court rejected *terra nullius* and recognised that a principle of native title existed before British settlers arrived.

1996 – Census revealed that 240 languages other than English were spoken in the home, including about 50 indigenous languages; Australia's population 18 million.

1997 – Constitutional Convention set up to produce recommendations for a republican form of government.

1999 – Federal government's proposals for a republican constitution and government rejected in referendum.

2000 – Olympic Games held in Sydney.

History of Walking

During the first century of European settlement, Australia was explored on foot or on horseback and many people moved about the vast country on foot. At the end of the 19th century, as more and more people crowded into the cities, it was natural that some looked to the bush for recreation, and by 1900 at least three walking clubs had been set up: the Wallaby Club and the Melbourne Amateur Walking & Touring Club (later the Melbourne Walking Club, or MWC) in 1894 in Victoria, and the Warragamba Walking Club in 1895 in Sydney. They were open to men only (the MWC remains so). The MWC was soon venturing far beyond the fringes of Melbourne into the ranges, its members lugging heavy swags in best Australian style – bed rolls and camping gear slung over their shoulders. The Mountain Trails Club was founded in Sydney on the eve of WWI by Myles Dunphy, who became the inspirational leader of the bushwalking conservation movement in the 1930s.

Soon after the war, Melbourne's women, determined not to be left at home, established

Hume and Hovell crossing the Murray River in 1825. Wood engraving by FA Sleap.

BY PERMISSION OF THE NATIONAL LIBRARY OF AUSTRALIA

the Melbourne Women's Walking Club, and were soon organising adventurous expeditions into the mountains. Australia's oldest mixed club, Sydney Bushwalkers, was founded in 1927; its name is believed to be the first public use of this uniquely Australian term. Two years later, the Hobart Walking Club was set up for both men and women. Members made the first ascent of Frenchmans Cap in the early 1930s and actively campaigned for national parks. Throughout the 1930s walking enjoyed a boom, and clubs sprang up all over the place. Organised mass walks were popular, and strongly promoted by the railway authorities and newspapers.

Bushwalkers' close involvement with conservation campaigns, particularly for the creation and protection of national parks, began about this time. In NSW, Myles Dunphy's National Parks and Primitive Areas Council, and the emergence of a threat to the magnificent Blue Gum Forest in the Blue Mountains, spurred the foundation of the NSW Federation of Bushwalking Clubs, with nine member clubs, in 1932. Victoria set up its Federation of Walking Clubs (FVWC) in 1934, with eight clubs; within a few years it was lobbying the state government for the creation of 'primitive' (or wilderness) areas. In Queensland, the National Parks Association, established in 1930, had a strong bushwalking flavour, although its sights were mainly set on creating more parks.

The 1930s also marked two more significant events. Australia's first bushwalking gear manufacturing business was launched by Paddy Pallin in Sydney (see the boxed text 'Australia's Bushwalking Gear Pioneer' in the Facts for the Walker chapter). Dunphy published the first of his maps for bushwalkers, and these intricate, reliable maps were still being used well into the 1980s.

After WWII bushwalking took a few steps backwards, the number of clubs growing fairly slowly until the mid-1970s. A search and rescue group was set up within the FVWC in the late 1940s, following the example of NSW; both groups still participate in or organise searches for lost walkers and others. Victoria's answer to Dunphy's

maps first appeared in 1950 over the signature of Stuart Brookes, whose maps are still being updated.

In 1955 the Hobart Walking Club persuaded the Tasmanian government to set aside a national park around Lake Pedder – only to see it flooded in 1972. The Adelaide Bushwalkers were also very concerned with conservation issues.

Federation Peak, the most formidable of south-west Tasmania's challenging peaks, was first climbed by a Victorian party in 1949, but as late as 1960 barely 100 Europeans had set foot in the south-west; this number did not start to grow until the 1970s.

Matching the rapid growth of interest in conservation issues from the 1970s onwards, people took to the bush in ever greater numbers. In 1974 Victoria's federation had 30 member clubs, and by the late 1990s more than 60. Federations of bushwalking clubs had also been set up in SA and Queensland.

Ethical issues and matters of good bushwalking practice have long exercised walkers' minds. A bushwalking code, covering every aspect of the activity, was originated by the Victorian and NSW Federations and is now widely promoted by national parks agencies across the country.

Specialised walking guidebooks began to appear, and have proved very popular. Outdoor gear shops have proliferated and more Australian-based manufacturers have become established. *Wild* magazine was first published in 1981 and is now a widely read, outspoken advocate for bushwalking and kindred activities and related conservation and park management issues.

Australia has taken very enthusiastically to electronic communications and there are several bushwalking Web sites. Perhaps virtual bushwalking will be the next big outdoor development!

GEOGRAPHY

A clutch of statistics sums up Australia's immensity: it's the world's sixth-largest country, with an area of 7,682,300 sq km, about half as large again as Europe, and it occupies 5.7% of the world's land surface. About 4000km separate the eastern and

A Flat Continent?

Australia may be the flattest continent in the world, but the highest peaks in each state are still quite respectable.

In Kosciuszko National Park, a few summits exceed 2000m and several others rise above 1500m. Similarly, in the Victorian Alps some peaks top 1800m. In the ACT, along and near the NSW border, numerous summits rise above 1500m, the highest of which, Bimberi Peak (1911m), is right on the border. Queensland has a fairly large number of mountains over 1100m, while SA's share of high mountains (1000m-plus) is concentrated in the Musgrave and Mann Ranges near the NT border, including some over 1200m; there are also a few high ones farther south in the Flinders Ranges. Most of WA's major peaks are in the north, in the Hammersley Range and Pilbara, although the Stirling Range, with a handful of summits around 1000m, isn't far behind. Tasmania has numerous peaks over 1200m in the south-west. In the NT, the major summits are in the Western MacDonnell Ranges and in several other ranges north and north-east of Alice Springs.

Highest Peaks State by State

NSW	Mt Kosciuszko	2228m
Victoria	Mt Bogong	1986m
ACT	Bimberi Peak	1911m
Queensland	Mt Bartle Frere	1622m
Tasmania	Mt Ossa	1617m
NT	Mt Ziel	1531m
SA	Mt Woodroffe	1440m
WA	Mt Meharry	1245m

western extremities, and it's 3180km from north to south. The coastline (including the island state of Tasmania) stretches for 36,735km. Australia is the lowest-lying and flattest of the earth's continents; the average elevation is only 300m, and the lowest point is Lake Eyre in the Centre, at 18m below sea level, although these facts conceal a surprisingly mountain-strewn landscape.

The west coast faces the Indian Ocean, and the east the Pacific Ocean and Tasman Sea.

The Southern Ocean is to the south; Tasmania is separated from the continent's south-east coast by Bass Strait. Along the north coast are the Timor Sea and Torres Strait.

The eastern coastline is fringed by a coastal plain of varying width, from which rises the Great Dividing Range. This vast chain of mountain ranges and high tablelands extends from Cape York in the north, through Queensland and NSW, to the Grampians in western Victoria. Dozens of rivers flow east and south from the range to the sea. From its sprawling north-west and western slopes, watercourses fan out; some enter the Gulf of Carpentaria, others disappear into the desert, while others reach the maze-like Channel country leading towards Lake Eyre. Other rivers rising west of the Great Dividing Range become part of Australia's largest river system, the Murray–Darling. The Murray River enters the sea on SA's south-east coast.

Much of the western half of the country is a huge plateau (300m to 400m high), dotted with mountain ranges and part-time lakes. The coastal plain is generally narrow and confined to the south-west. This is backed by hilly country that rises farther east to the Stirling and Porongurup Ranges.

The centre of the continent, although arid, is anything but monotonous. The vast Great Sandy, Great Victoria, Sturt Stony and Simpson Deserts, and the Nullarbor Plain, are an intricate mosaic of dunes, sand ridges, rock outcrops and lake beds. There are also many mountain ranges, notably the MacDonnell Ranges straddling the heart of the continent, the Musgrave and Flinders Ranges in SA, and the Pilbara and Hammersley Range in WA. Uluru–Kata Tjuta, the Bungle Bungles, Mt Augustus and Mt Connor are among the extraordinary mountains of rock rising from the deserts.

Natural permanent lakes of any size are relatively few; Lake Eyre (9700 sq km) only fills after prolonged flooding of its many tributaries. The largest lakes are artificial, created for crop irrigation or to power hydroelectricity projects.

Tasmania, the island state, is more compactly rugged than the mainland. It is a green land with lots of craggy mountains concentrated in the western half of the state and, most famously for bushwalkers, the southwest in particular.

The enormously long Australian coastline is extremely varied: towering cliffs, massive headlands, mudflats, huge sand dunes and long sandy beaches. The most accessible cliff-lined coasts are in NSW just south of Sydney, along Victoria's Otway coast and in south-eastern Tasmania. Some of the most spectacular coast (best seen from the air between Perth and the east) is along the Great Australian Bight. The longest stretch of cliff coast is in the rugged Kimberley region of far north-western WA, with innumerable deep inlets. Some of the longest beaches are found in western Victoria, north and eastern Tasmania and south-west WA.

The largest Australian offshore islands are SA's Kangaroo Island, Bathurst and Melville Islands in the north, and Flinders and King Islands in Bass Strait. Queensland has the most unusual and famous offshore features: sand islands (notably Fraser Island), continental islands, including Hinchinbrook, and the mighty Great Barrier Reef.

GEOLOGY

Australia is partly built of some of the oldest rocks on earth, formed thousands of millions of years ago. The continent only began to acquire its present shape, however, about 130 million years ago. The supercontinent of Gondwanaland started to pull apart and the Australian chunk broke off. During the next 50 million years or so, three major events happened. The Tasman Sea filled as the New Zealand and Lord Howe Island blocks floated away; Antarctica drifted southwards and the Southern Ocean opened up; ocean levels subsided and the Australian landmass emerged high and dry. By then, the mountain ranges in the Centre and central west (including the MacDonnell Ranges, the Kimberleys and the Hammersley Range) had been thrust up from the earth's core and worn down again. Extensive areas of limestone were formed in warm shallow seas, and for eons an ice cap blanketed almost the entire area that is now Australia.

The Tasmanian mountains were formed about 165 million years ago, mainly of dolerite, a volcanic rock, creating the typically rugged peaks. The deep gorges in western Tasmania have been cut through much softer quartzite. Tasmania broke free of the continental mainland 25 million years ago, opening up Bass Strait.

Some of Australia's major landforms are much newer. The Eastern Highlands, which include the Bass Strait and Torres Strait islands, were originally pushed up about 65 million years ago; tablelands along the east coast took shape even more recently when a huge area in the continent's interior slumped.

RICHARD I'ANSON

Cradle Mountain dominates the scene from Lake Dove, Cradle Mountain–Lake St Clair National Park

In the west, the 1000km-long Darling Scarp formed – the sharply defined edge of an ancient rock mass. These mountain-building processes were relatively slow and gentle compared with the forces at work in, say, New Zealand, explaining why Australia has few sharp, alpine-looking peaks.

Volcanoes (all extinct) are quite a common feature, mainly on the Queensland–NSW border and in the Warrumbungles to the south-west. Mt Warning, near the NSW coast, is the core of the largest – fragments of its 40km-diameter rim make up three mountain ranges. It rumbled away for about three million years. The volcanic era lasted until about six million years ago, with activity in the later stages mainly in western Victoria and on the northern Queensland tablelands.

The last ice age began about 18,000 years ago. Its effects are most evident in southwest Tasmania and to a lesser extent in the Mt Kosciuszko area, creating tarns, moraine heaps and aretes. Sea levels were lowered by as much as 120m and Bass Strait became a land bridge. When the ice melted, 8000 to 10,000 years ago, sea levels rose, flooding coastal river valleys (most notably forming Sydney Harbour), reopening Bass Strait and once again separating Tasmania from the continental mainland.

CLIMATE

Australian seasons are the inverse of those in Europe and North America. December is hot, while July and August are relatively cold. Spring starts in September, summer in December, autumn in March and winter in June.

Generally, the climate is pleasantly livable most of the year – 40% of the continent lies north of the Tropic of Capricorn, where seasonal temperatures don't vary greatly.

The major influence on Australia's climate is a broad belt of high pressure, made up of a nearly unbroken chain of cells of air that move from west to east across the continent under clear skies. Slipping between the cells are lows (troughs), which bring cool changes and some rain every so often. To the north of this belt, breezes drift from the south-east, and to the south, winds blow from the west and south-west. In winter, this belt sits across the centre of the country. Northwards, conditions are dry and mainly sunny. To the south, the westerly winds accelerate and bring plentiful rain; very cold air dragged up from the Antarctic drops snow over high ground.

The pattern is more or less reversed in summer as the belt shifts south to lie over Bass Strait. With hot, moist air coming down from equatorial regions, the north is drenched almost daily during what's known as the Wet. Occasional tropical cyclones (hurricanes) hit the coast with violent winds and torrential rains. The gales soon die, but the downpour can last for several days, often spreading far inland and southwards. Eastern areas of Queensland are frequently cloudy and wet, thanks to inflows of tropical air from the Pacific Ocean. Down south, conditions are comparatively dry except along the east coast where easterly winds prevail. Spells of fine, warm to hot weather are usually separated by strong, cool changes from the south-west. The coast and mountain ranges are cooler, thanks to onshore sea breezes and elevation.

Generally Australia is a warm country compared with other landmasses at the same latitude. This is mainly because the prevailing winds flow for long distances over land and are warmed on the way. Even Hobart, the most southerly capital, can endure summer heat waves, when the temperature rises above 38°C for at least three days in succession. Shade temperatures above 45°C are not uncommon inland.

During winter, the south-westerlies are cooled as they rise over high ground and they then condense into snow that covers the Alps and Tasmanian mountains from mid-June to mid-September. Elsewhere frosts are common; Alice Springs wakes to more frosty mornings than all of the southern cities except Canberra.

Australia is the driest continent; more than half has less than 300mm of rain annually. The highest average rainfalls are 4000mm on the north-east coast of Queensland, 3600mm in western Tasmania and 3200mm in the Snowy Mountains. Elsewhere, rainfall decreases steadily away from the coast; a large part of the inland has 100mm or less per year.

Fauna & Flora of Australia

The Australian landmass is one of the most ancient on earth. Cut off from other continents by the sea for more than 50 million years, its indigenous plants and animals have evolved in isolation over an unusually long period.

About 55 million years ago, Australia was completely covered by cool-climate rainforest. As the continent then drifted northwards, it gradually dried out. The rainforests retreated, wattles, eucalyptuses and other plants took over and grasslands expanded, producing the distinctive habitats we see today (see Ecosystems later).

FAUNA

Australia has some of the most fascinating native fauna in the world. Many creatures are unique survivors from ancient times and are superbly adapted to the often harsh Australian environment. For a comprehensive guide to wildlife-spotting techniques, locations and identification, see Lonely Planet's *Watching Wildlife Australia*.

MONOTREMES

Although the monotremes retain some intriguing characteristics from their reptile ancestors, such as laying eggs, they possess a distinct mammalian lineage and are not a primitive stage in the evolution of mammals. There are just two of them: the platypus, found only in Australia, and the echidna, also found in the highlands of Papua New Guinea. The newly hatched young are suckled on milk.

Platypus

The platypus (*Ornithorhynchus anatinus*) is well equipped for its semi-aquatic life. It has a softish, duck-like bill, short legs, webbed feet and a short, thick, beaver-like tail. Adult males reach 50cm in length, plus 10cm to 13cm of tail, and weigh about 2kg; the females are slightly smaller.

A platypus spends most of its time in the extensive burrows it digs along river banks, or in the water, foraging for small crustaceans, worms and tadpoles with its super-sensitive bill, and occasionally basking in the sun.

The platypus is confined to the eastern mainland of Australia and Tasmania.

RICHARD I'ANSON

Karri forest, Western Australia

SIMON FOALE

Platypus

Title page: The yellow-footed rock-wallaby inhabits rocky outcrops in semiarid regions. Photograph by Mitch Reardon.

Echidna

The short-beaked echidna (or spiny anteater; *Tachyglosus aculeatus*) has a coat of long spines on its back and a furry belly. Fully grown it weighs about 4.5kg and is 45cm long. The elongated, beak-like snout measures about 7.5cm; its sticky tongue can whip some 15cm beyond the end of the snout – perfect for catching ants and termites, its main food. At the first sign of danger, the echidna rapidly burrows into the ground, leaving only its formidable spines exposed.

Short-beaked echidnas are found everywhere from hot, dry deserts up to around 1800m in alpine areas.

MARSUPIALS

Marsupials are mammals that raise their young in a pouch, or *marsupium*. They are largely confined to Australia and include around 120 species, including the familiar kangaroos, koalas and possums as well as some less well-known ones such as bandicoots and quolls.

Marsupial young are tiny at birth and spend a good deal of time developing in the pouch before they can live independently of their mother.

Echidna

Kangaroos & Wallabies

The kangaroo and its kindred belong to a family whose name, Macropodidae, means 'big foot', the hind foot in fact, which in kangaroos and wallaroos is more than 25cm long. They feed on grasses, leaves and bark, and are never far from water. There are about 50 species in all.

There are now more kangaroos in Australia than there were when Europeans arrived, thanks to farm dams and the creation of grasslands for sheep and cattle. However, loss of habitat and predation by foxes and feral cats threaten some species with extinction. Nevertheless about three million kangaroos are culled legally each year and many more are killed for 'sport' or by farmers who believe the cull doesn't protect their paddocks from overgrazing.

Red Kangaroo The distinctive red kangaroo (*Macropus rufus*) is the largest and most widespread macropod. A fully grown male can stand 2m high and measure 2.4m in length. In western areas both sexes are brick-red coloured, while in the east this colouring is usually confined to the males; females are smaller and often blue-grey. They range over the saltbush and grass plains in most of arid Australia.

Red kangaroos

FAUNA & FLORA OF AUSTRALIA

Grey Kangaroo The eastern grey kangaroo *(M. giganteus)* is about the same size as the red, and is found in eucalyptus forests from Queensland to Tasmania. The western grey *(M. fuliginosus)* is darker in colour and is common in southern Western Australia (WA) and South Australia (SA), central and western New South Wales (NSW) and western Victoria.

Wallabies Wallabies come in a variety of shapes and sizes. The most commonly seen are the red-necked *(M. rufogriseus)* in the eastern states and Tasmania, the agile *(M. agilis)* in the Northern Territory's (NT's) Top End, and the swamp wallaby *(Wallabia bicolor)* along the east coast, all of which are about 1.7m long fully grown. Their hind feet are generally less than 12cm long.

Rock-wallabies are small (about 1m long) and found on cliffs and rocky habitats where they can perform acrobatic leaps to scale difficult inclines. The brush-tailed rock-wallaby *(Petrogale penicillata)*, once widespread along the Great Dividing Range in the eastern states, is now confined to a few locations and is classed as vulnerable.

Common Wallaroo The common wallaroo or euro *(M. robustus)* is more solidly built and has a rougher, shaggier coat than the red or grey kangaroo. The males' colouring varies from grey-black to reddish-brown to fawn while the females are usually smaller and paler in colour. They range widely, throughout Queensland, NSW, SA and WA.

Tree Kangaroos Two species are found in Australia: Bennett's *(Dendrolagus bennettianus)* and Lumholtz's *(D. lumholtzi).* Although they live in trees and have strong forelimbs, they are not graceful climbers. Both species are found only in north Queensland rainforests, where logging has made serious inroads on their habitat.

Bandicoots & Bilbies

Small, rat like bandicoots are largely nocturnal, but are occasionally seen scampering through the bush. Insects are their main food, varied occasionally with plant material.

One of the most common is the southern brown bandicoot *(Isoodon obesulus)*, found in eastern and western Australia.

Eastern grey kangaroo

CHRIS MELOR

Black-footed rock-wallaby (and joey)

MITCH REARDON

Western barred bandicoot

MITCH REARDON

Brushtail possum

Koala

Common wombat

The rare bilby *(Macrotis lagotis)* lives mainly in the NT. With rabbit-like ears, it has been promoted as Australia's answer to the Easter Bunny (rabbits having a pretty poor reputation here). A concerted campaign has been launched to ensure its survival.

Possums & Gliders

Possums (or phalangers) are very numerous and widespread. You'll even find them in city parks and suburban gardens. They often besiege campsites in timbered country and will steal any unguarded food.

The most familiar are the common brushtail *(Trichosurus vulpecula)*, which is found throughout the mainland and in Tasmania, and the common ringtail *(Pseudocheirus laniginosus)*, whose prehensile tail is used for climbing.

The sugar glider *(Petaurus breviceps)* has membranes between its front and back legs. These are spread and used for gliding from the top of one tree to the base of the next, covering up to 100m in a single swoop – an amazing sight.

Koala

Fully grown koalas *(Phascolarctos cinereus)* measure about 70cm and weigh around 10kg. They have round, tufted ears and a hard, black nose. The Aboriginal name *koala* means 'no water', referring to the idea that koalas get all their moisture from gum leaves, although they do drink occasionally.

Koalas are very selective feeders, preferring mainly manna gum in Victoria and blue and grey gums in NSW; they are particularly sensitive to changes in their habitat. They are found from around Townsville in Queensland south to Melbourne and have been reintroduced to SA where they had become extinct.

Wombats

Wombats are slow, powerfully built marsupials with broad heads and short legs. Adults reach about 1m in length and weigh up to 35kg. Their strong forelegs are excellent digging tools used to construct their extensive burrows. They live on grasses, roots and tree bark. The female has a backward-facing pouch so she doesn't cover her young with soil.

The most numerous of the three species is the common wombat *(Vombatus ursinus)*, found throughout the south-eastern forests and up to the tree line in mountainous country.

Dasyuroids

These are predatory marsupials mainly distinguished by their pointy, elongated snouts. They include the nocturnal, voracious quolls – very efficient hunters – and the endangered numbat (*Myrmecobius fasciatus*), whose diet consists almost entirely of termites. It is now confined to the forests of south-west WA.

Tasmanian Devil The carnivorous Tasmanian devil (*Sarcophilus harrisii*) is the largest of the dasyuroids and very fierce-looking and sounding. Of solitary and nocturnal habits, it has a black body with a white stripe across the chest. It measures around 60cm in length with another 25cm of tail. It feeds on small birds and mammals, insects and carrion and its habitat is confined to Tasmania.

Tasmanian devil

MITCH REARDON

EUTHERIANS

Eutherians, or placental mammals, are the largest mammalian group on earth. Australia's native eutherians include marine mammals, numerous species of bats and rodents and the native dog or dingo.

Dingo

The dingo (*Canis lupus dingo*), Australia's native dog, probably arrived about 4000 years ago, introduced by Asian seafarers. It howls rather than barks and breeds only once a year, rather than twice. It is widespread and common in many parts of the Outback. Dingos prey mainly on rabbits, rats and mice, although when food is scarce they may attack stock.

Dingo

CHRIS MELLOR

Marine Mammals

Humpback Whale A regular visitor to the east and west coasts, this massive mammal (*Megaptera novaeangliae*) is a delight to watch, especially its spectacular breaching. In winter it migrates from Antarctic feeding grounds to breed in subtropical waters. Adults range from 14m to 19m in length and can live for more than 30 years.

Southern Right Whale The southern right whale (*Eubalaena australis*) – so called because it was the 'right' one to kill – was hunted almost to extinction, but is now returning to Australian waters. It is recognised by its down-turned mouth lined with balleen plates with which it filters prey from the sea. It grows to 18m and travels alone or in small family groups.

Humpback whale

BOB CHARLTON

Australian fur seal

Emu

Blue-winged kookaburra

Australian Fur Seal One of two species of fur seal in Australian waters, the Australian fur seal (*Arctocephalus pusillus*) was nearly killed off by fur hunters in early colonial times. It's now quite common along the south-eastern coast and Bass Strait Islands. Generally black in colour when wet, the males measure about 2m in length, the females slightly less. They live in large colonies on the coast or offshore islands where the young are born in late spring.

BIRDS

Australia's birdlife is as beautiful as it is varied, with over 750 recorded species, many of them endemic. Birds are most active in the early morning and you will have a better chance of seeing a good variety if you set off early. Birds are generally unconcerned with the activities of walkers; many species are inquisitive and others see people as a meal ticket because they stir up insects as they walk. Nonetheless, if you walk and talk quietly you will see more birds (and other creatures). A light pair of binoculars will be handy for closer views, and will help you appreciate the subtleties of plumage colouration.

The Royal Australasian Ornithologists Union runs bird observatories in NSW, Victoria and WA, which provide accommodation and guides. Contact the RAOU (☎ 03-9882 2622) at 415 Riversdale Rd, Hawthorn East, Victoria 3123.

Emu

The emu (*Dromaius novaehollandiae*) is a shaggy, flightless bird that stands 2m high. The only bird larger than the emu is the African ostrich. Emus are nomadic, and are found across the country in areas away from human habitation. They are efficient sprinters, reaching speeds of up to 50km/h. After the female lays her six to 12 large, dark green eggs the male hatches them and raises the young.

Kookaburra

The laughing kookaburra (*Dacelo novaeguinae*) is common throughout coastal Australia, but particularly in the east and south-west of the country. The blue-winged kookaburra (*D. leachii*) is found in northern coastal woodlands. Kookaburras are the largest members of the kingfisher family. The kookaburra is heard as much as it is seen – you can't miss its loud, cackling laugh.

Bowerbird

The stocky, stout-billed bowerbird, of which there are at least half a dozen species, is best known for its unique mating practice. The brightly coloured male builds a bower that he decorates with various coloured objects to attract the less showy female. The female is impressed by the male's neatly built bower and attractively displayed treasures, but once they've mated all the hard work is left to her.

The three most common species are the great (*Chlamydera nuchalis*), the spotted (*C. maculata*) and the satin (*Ptilonorhynchus violaceus*).

Magpie

The black-and-white magpie (*Gymnorhina* spp) is one of the most widespread birds in Australia, being found virtually throughout the country. One of the most distinctive sounds of the Australian bush is the melodious song of the magpie, which is heard at any time of day, but especially at dawn. One of the magpie's less endearing traits is the way it swoops at people who approach its nest too closely in spring. The several geographic species of magpie all look much alike to the untrained eye but differ in the arrangement of their black and white markings.

Wedge-Tailed Eagle

The wedge-tailed eagle (*Aquila audax*) is Australia's largest bird of prey. It has a wing span of up to 2m, and is easily identified in flight by its distinctive wedge-shaped tail. 'Wedgies' are often seen in Outback Australia, either soaring to great heights or feeding on road-kill carcasses.

Parrots, Rosellas, Lorikeets & Cockatoos

There is an amazing variety of these vividly colourful birds throughout Australia.

Rosella There are a number of species of rosella (*Platycercus* spp), most of them brilliantly coloured. The mainly red, yellow and blue eastern rosella (*P. eximius*) is the most widespread and is found throughout rural south-eastern Australia. They are not at all backward about taking a free feed from humans.

Galah The pink and grey galah (*Cacatua roseicapilla*) is one of the most common cockatoos, and is often sighted scratching for seeds on the roadside.

Magpie

DAVID CURL

Wedge-tailed eagle

JASON EDWARDS

Galah

CHRIS MELLOR

Rainbow lorikeet

Superb lyrebird

Black-necked stork, or jabiru

Rainbow Lorikeet The rainbow lorikeet (*Trichoglossus haematodus*) is so extravagantly colourful that it is hard to imagine until you've seen one, with its blue head, orange breast and green body. Lorikeets have a brush-like tongue for extracting nectar from flowers.

Budgerigar Budgies (*Melopsittacus undulatus*) are widespread over inland Australia where they can be seen in flocks of thousands flying in tight formation. Budgies are probably the most widely kept cage bird in the world.

Black-Cockatoo There are six species of black-cockatoo, the most widespread being the large red-tailed black-cockatoo (*Calyptorhynchus magnificus*) and the yellow-tailed black-cockatoo (*C. funereus*).

Sulphur-Crested Cockatoo This noisy cocky (*Cacatua galerita*), often seen in large, raucous flocks, is found throughout eastern and northern Australia. When the flock is feeding on the ground, several individuals will fly to a high vantage point to watch over the flock and signal if there is any danger.

Lyrebird

The shy superb lyrebird (*Menura novaehollandiae*) is a ground-dwelling rainforest bird found in south-eastern Australia. The male has tail feathers that form a lyre shape when displayed to attract a mate. The similar Albert's lyrebird (*M. alberti*) is found in the rainforests of southern Queensland and northern NSW. Lyrebirds have a beautiful song and are also clever mimics.

Black-Necked Stork

The black-necked stork (or jabiru, *Xenorhynchus asiaticus*) is found throughout northern and eastern Australia, although it is not often seen. It stands over 1m high, and has an almost iridescent green-black neck, black and white body, and orange legs.

Magpie Goose

The magpie (or pied) goose (*Anseranas semipalmata*) is commonly seen in the tropical wetlands of northern Australia – indeed when water becomes scarce towards the end of the Dry season (October) they often gather in huge numbers on the retreating wetlands.

Brolga

Another bird commonly seen in wetland areas of northern and, to a lesser extent, eastern Australia, is the tall crane known as the brolga *(Grus rubicundus)*. They stand over one metre high, are grey in colour and have a distinctive red head colouring.

Black Swan

Commonly seen on stretches of water from the Top End to Tasmania are black swans *(Cygnus atratus)*. They are usually seen in large flocks near fresh or brackish water. Black swans nest among reeds or on islands in lakes and both parents take on nesting duties.

Black swan

MITCH REARDON

REPTILES

Snakes

Australia's 140 species of snakes are mostly shy and steer clear of humans. Of the deadly species, the most dangerous are the taipan, tiger snake and death adder, followed by the copperhead, brown snake and red-bellied black snake. Pythons, found mainly in northern regions, are beautifully patterned and generally large; harmless to humans, they feed on small mammals, which they crush to death then swallow whole.

Crocodiles

It's important to be able to tell the difference between Australia's two species of crocodile – one is dangerous, the other less aggressive, and they're both common in the north.

Saltwater crocodile

MITCH REARDON

Saltwater Crocodile Commonly known as 'salties', saltwater crocodiles *(Crocodylus porosus)* can grow to 7m and will attack and kill humans. They inhabit estuaries and may be found far from the coast after floods, or in permanent fresh water more than 100km inland.

Freshwater crocodile

DAVID CURL

Freshwater Crocodile Smaller than salties, freshwater crocodiles *(C. johnstoni)*, or 'freshies', are always less than 4m long, have much narrower snouts and smaller teeth than salties. Although unlikely to go after human prey, they have been known to bite in defence of their nests.

Lizards

Goanna The dozen or so species of goanna (monitor) are large lizards up to 2.5m long. With forked

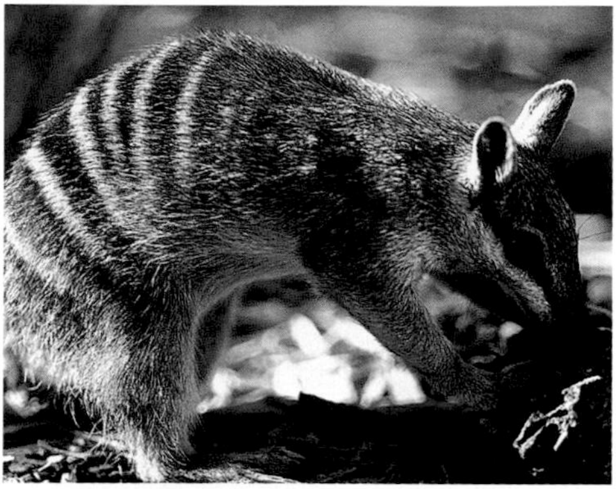

DAVID CURL

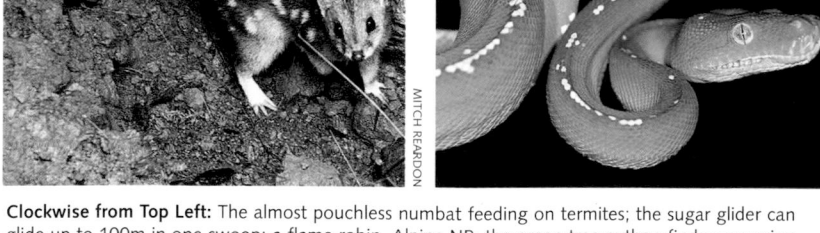

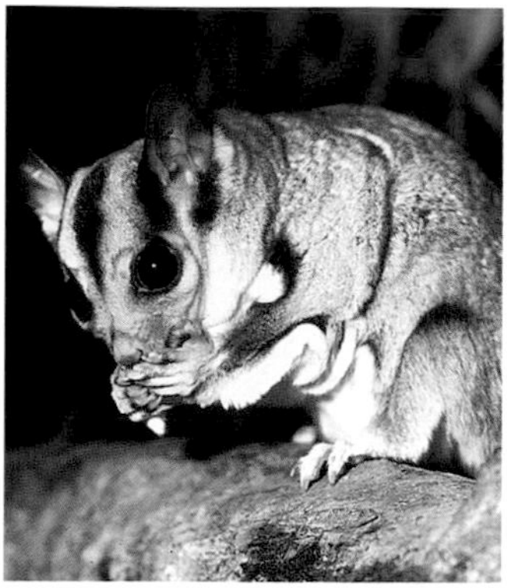

DAVID CURL

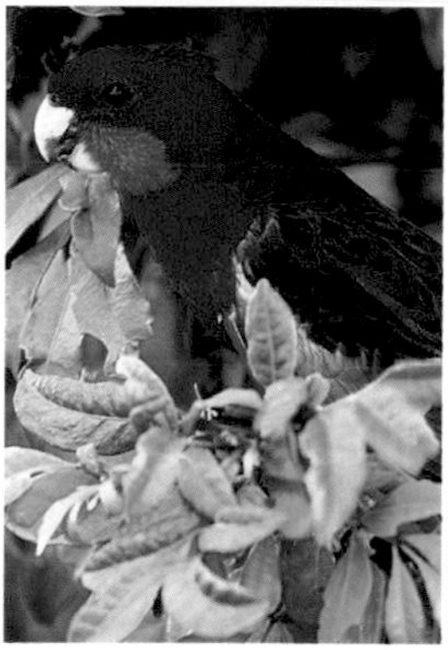

MITCH REARDON

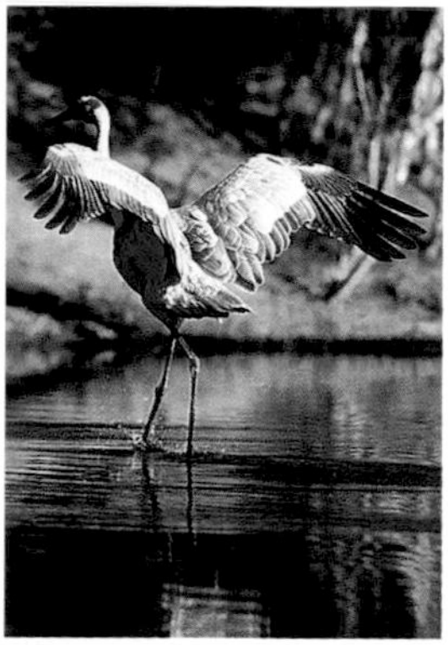

DAVID CURL

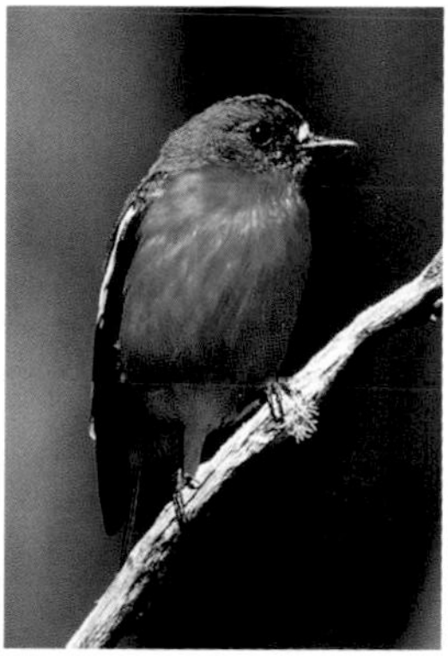

ROB DRUMMOND

MITCH REARDON

MARTIN COHEN

Clockwise from Top Left: The almost pouchless numbat feeding on termites; the sugar glider can glide up to 100m in one swoop; a flame robin, Alpine NP; the green tree python finds prey using heat sensors on its lips; an eastern quoll, Cradle Mountain–Lake St Clair NP; the gregarious crimson rosella lives along the edges of eucalyptus forests and woodlands; a dancing brolga, Kakadu NP.

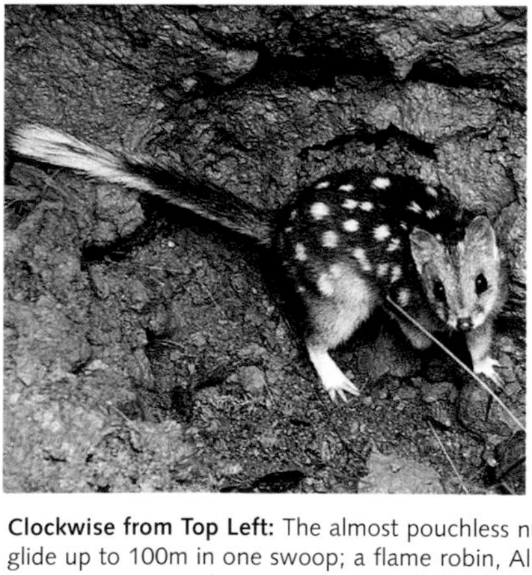

Clockwise from Top Left: the delicate stamens of the red-flowering gum; majestic native mountain ashes rising out of an understorey of tree ferns, Dandenong Ranges NP, Victoria; pencil pine, Southwest NP, Tasmania; a plain of hardy spinifex grass, Central Australia; ghost gum, West MacDonnell Ranges; snow gum, gnarled and stunted by cold winters and alpine winds, Alpine NP, Victoria.

DAVID CURL

Sand Monitor

MARTIN COHEN

Frilled lizard

tongues and a loud hiss, they can be quite formidable and are best left alone as they will stand their ground. The largest goanna is the carnivorous perentie *(Varanus giganteus)*, which lives in sandy deserts.

Frilled Lizard The frilled lizard *(Chlamydosaurus kingii)* is commonly seen in eastern and northern bushland areas. The frill is a loose flap of skin that normally hangs flat around the neck. When the lizard is upset or threatened, it raises the flap and opens its mouth wide to make it look more ferocious; it may rise up on its hind legs and make off at high speed.

SPIDERS

The redback *(Latrodectus hasselti)* is Australia's most notorious spider. It is generally glossy black with a red streak down its back. It's fond of woodheaps and garden sheds and its bite can be fatal. The potentially lethal Sydney funnel-web *(Atrax robustus)* is a large, aggressive, ground-dwelling spider restricted to a 200km radius of Sydney.

FLORA

Together with about 11,000 species of flowering plants, Australia has hundreds of ferns, mosses, fungi and conifers. Forests cover about 5% of the land surface and plants can be found even in the arid Centre, although many grow and flower only after heavy rains.

NATIVE GRASSES

Australia has more than 700 species of native grass, occurring in a variety of habitats. Land clearing has removed many species from the south-east, where native grasslands are now quite rare.

Spinifex

The hardiest and most common desert plants belong to the group of grasses commonly called spinifex *(Triodia* spp and *Plectrachne* spp). They are dense, dome-shaped clumps of long, needle-like leaves up to 2m high, found on sandy soils and rocky ground in semiarid and arid areas. Individual clumps can spread across several metres. Spinifex grasslands host large populations of reptiles and small mammals. True spinifex *(Spinifex* spp) grows on coastal sand dunes where its roots stabilise the shifting sands.

Buttongrass

Largely confined to poorly drained plains in south-west Tasmania, buttongrass (*Gymnoschoenus sphaerocephalus*) grows in tall tussocks, separated by patches of bare bog, and is notorious among walkers. Leaping from tussock to tussock with a heavy pack can be very tiring. Its leaves are tough and the flower for which it is named is a small cluster of white spikelets.

Buttongrass plain, south-west Tasmania

SHRUBS & FLOWERS

Callistemons

Callistemons, or bottlebrushes (after the brush-like flowers), are found right across the country, but especially in NSW, on rocky or sandy ground or near watercourses. They are hardy plants and attract many species of native birds. There are about 25 species, ranging in height from 1m to 10m. Some of the most common are the crimson bottlebrush (*Callistemon citrinus*) along the east coast, the weeping bottlebrush (*C. viminalis*) in NSW and Queensland and, found along inland river systems, the prickly bottlebrush (*C. brachycandrus*).

Grevilleas

Of the 250 or more varieties of this major family of shrubs, all but 20 are native to Australia. They come in various sizes and flower colours and are found in the Australian Alps, forests, semi-arid country and near the coast. Most are small to medium in size, although the silky oak (*Grevillea robusta*) can grow to 30m and, covered with golden-brown flowers, is one of Australia's most beautiful trees.

Grevillea tetragonaloba, Western Australia

Leptospermums

Leptospermums, or tea-trees (*Leptospermum* spp) are widespread in the east, south-east and Tasmania, from the coast to alpine regions. Most species are large, usually dense bushes rather than trees; the name comes from early settlers' attempts to brew tea using the leaves. Flowers are mainly white and the leaves, of various shapes, are small. Among the most common are the aptly named prickly tea-tree (*L. juniperum*) and woolly tea-tree (*L. lanigerum*).

Pandani

The tallest heath plant in the world, pandani (*Richea pandanifolia*) looks more like a tropical palm. It can reach a height of 12m with a crown of stiff leathery

Pandani, Franklin–Gordon Wild Rivers National Park, Tasmania

ROB BLAKERS

Pandani in the Tasmanian highlands

leaves 1.5m long. Old, dead leaves or fronds can form a huge skirt around the lower trunk. Pandanis are fairly common throughout the west and south-west of Tasmania.

Another of the richeas, alpine richea *(Richea scoparia)*, grows in dense bushes in upland areas of Tasmania. Contact with its rigid prickly leaves can be quite painful; it does, however, produce beautiful crimson flowers in early summer.

CYCADS & FERNS
Cycads
The MacDonnell Ranges cycad *(Macrozamia macdonnelli)* is one of Australia's 18 species of the ancient cycad family. It is very slow-growing, often found high on rocky hillsides and in gorges. Seed cones grow at the tip of the short trunk on female plants and the male cones carry the pollen; the seeds are poisonous.

The burrawang *(Macrozamia communis)* grows along the NSW coast on sandy soils. The 2m-long palm-like fronds grow from ground level; its red seeds are also poisonous.

DAN HARLEY

Soft tree fern

Tree Ferns
The beautifully ornate rough tree fern (*Cyathea* spp) and the soft tree fern *(Dicksonia antarctica)* are found in the temperate rainforests of eastern Australia. Some reach a height of 20m and all are capped by a crown of green fronds.

TREES
Cabbage Palms
Among Australia's 40 palm species is the well-known cabbage palm *(Livistona mariae)* of Finke Gorge National Park near Alice Springs. The tree grows to 30m high and is confined to this area. The growing tip of the tree consists of tender green leaves, which were a source of food to Aboriginal people.

The cabbage fan-palm *(L. australis)* reaches the same height and grows along the NSW coast and in far eastern Victoria. The tree is topped with fan-shaped leaves up to 2m across, divided into numerous radiating strands.

Acacias
The Australian species of the genus *Acacia* are commonly know as wattles and more than 660 species

PAUL SINCLAIR

Cabbage palm

have been recorded. They vary from small shrubs to the towering blackwoods. The flowers come in all shades of yellow; most species flower during late winter and spring, bringing brilliant splashes of colour to the bush.

Blackwood The largest of the acacias, blackwood (*A. melanoxylon*), can reach 30m and more in good deep soil and has pale creamy flowers. It is widely distributed on the eastern and southern ranges.

Mulga The mulga (*A. aneura*) is extremely widespread across the arid inland in dense thickets or open woodland. It has adapted to the dry climate with hairy, resin-covered leaves; many branches rise from or just above the ground and shed water onto the base of the trunk, where its roots are most dense.

Golden Wattle Australia's floral emblem, the golden wattle (*A. pycnantha*) grows best in hot arid areas but is common throughout the south-east. During spring it's a magnificent sight – masses of golden flowers against dark green foliage.

Banksias

Banksias (*Banksia* spp) take their name from Sir Joseph Banks, the botanist who accompanied Captain James Cook on his exploration of eastern Australia. Numbering about 60 species, and confined to Australia, they are common on sandy soils. Most of them sport upright cylindrical flower spikes up to 30cm long, covered with vibrant orange, red or yellow flowers. As the flowers die, the woody fruits appear, giving the cylinder a rather comical appearance. Aboriginal people dipped the banksia spikes in water to make a sweet drink. One of the most striking is the scarlet banksia (*B. coccinea*) found in sandy soils on the south coast of WA.

Casuarinas

Also known as she-oaks, these hardy trees are almost as much a part of the Australian landscape as eucalyptuses. They are characterised by feathery 'leaves' that are actually small branches; the true leaves are small scales clustered in whorls at intervals along the branchlets. Casuarinas produce distinctive small knobbly cones. They are widely distributed from the desert to the coast.

Saw banksia

SARA-JANE CELAND

RICHARD I'ANSON

Desert oaks, Uluru, Northern Territory

Desert Oak Its height, broad shady crown, dark weeping foliage and the sighing sound of the winds in its leaves make the desert oak *(Allocasuarina decaisneana)* a memorable feature of the sand plains. It is confined to the western part of the arid Centre and is common around Uluru and near Alice Springs.

River She-oak The tall river she-oak *(Casuarina cunninghamania)*, found mainly in eastern NSW, is highly valued because its roots bind river banks, greatly reducing erosion.

Scrub She-oak Common in heathlands of the south-east and Tasmania, and in western arid areas, scrub she-oak *(C. paludosa)* grows to about 3m and has grey-green foliage.

Eucalyptuses

The eucalyptus (*Eucalyptus* spp) or gum tree is ubiquitous in Australia except in the deepest rainforests and most arid regions. Of the 700 species, 95% occur naturally in Australia; the timber of many is highly prized for a variety of uses. Gum trees vary in form and height from the tall, straight jarrah and karri (confined to WA) and the towering mountain ash, to the twisted snow gums of alpine areas and the hardy ironbarks.

PAUL SINCLAIR

River red gums along the Murray River

River Red Gum River red gums *(E. camaldulensis)* typically line watercourses, permanent or ephemeral, where their deep roots tap underground water reserves. The most widespread eucalyptus, these massive, spreading trees grow to 45m high and can live for hundreds of years.

Mallee Eucalyptuses These hardy, shrub-like eucalyptuses are widespread where SA, Victoria and NSW meet, and west of Adelaide to beyond Kalgoorlie in WA. There are more than 100 species of these ground-branching trees, which grow from a massive underground root (lignotuber) that enables them to survive fire.

COLIN K BARNES

Snow gum in the NSW High Country

Snow Gum The snowgum *(E. pauciflora)* flourishes higher than any other eucalyptus – up to 1700m in the Australian Alps and in the Tasmanian highlands. A low-branching tree, it ranges from 1m to 20m in height and has smooth whitish bark, sometimes splashed with greens and reds.

Melaleucas

Melaleucas (paperbarks or honey-myrtles) are easily recognised by their pale papery bark, which peels from the trunk in thin sheets. They are widespread on rocky ground, from the coast to semiarid inland areas. The flower spikes consist of many tiny filaments and range from cream through crimson to purple.

Common varieties include the swamp paperbark (*Melaleuca ericifolia*) with creamy flowers, and giant (or bracelet) honey-myrtle (*M. armillaris*), which can reach 14m in height.

Conifers

Australia has several families of native conifers, but they rarely dominate the vegetation as some pines and spruces do in the northern hemisphere.

Pencil Pine Endemic to Tasmania, the pencil pine (*Athrotaxis cupressoides*) is found in areas of high rainfall – the central plateau and the south-west. A graceful tree, it usually grows to a height of about 15m.

Oyster Bay Pine Growing in coastal areas and inland semi-arid country in all states except WA, the Oyster Bay pine (*Callitris rhomboidea*) has distinctive segmented cones and reaches a height of 6m. Foliage is typical of the *Callitris* family – tiny scaly leaves arranged along thin branchlets.

Grass Trees

The unusual looking grass trees (*Xanthorrhoea* spp) are widespread in south-eastern and south-western Australia, mainly on sandy soils. They have very thin long leaves, a short thick trunk, and a distinctive flower spike up to 3m tall, with tiny flowers massed along the upper half of a long stem.

Mangroves

Australia has about 50 species of mangroves – trees and shrubs adapted to daily flooding by salt water. Along northern coasts and estuaries various species grow to around 30m, while at the southern limit of their distribution, in Victoria, they rarely exceed 5m. Mangroves have various ways of coping with inundation – some breathe through aerial roots, which are exposed at low tide. They help to stabilise shorelines and are homes for fish, birds, crabs, prawns and other wildlife.

ROB BLAKERS

Pencil pine, Cradle Mountain–Lake St Clair National Park, Tasmania

DAVID CURL

Grass tree in the Northern Territory

Endangered Species

It's easy to think that Australia has a wealth of wildlife when you're confronted with mobs of kangaroos, huge flocks of cockatoos, and extensive eucalyptus bushland. Indeed, with thousands of unique plants and animals, Australia is one of the 12 most biologically diverse countries in the world. However, in little more than two centuries of European settlement an alarming number of species has been lost or threatened.

Cassowary

Loss of habitat continues to be crucial for the survival of wildlife. Since 1788, 70% of all native vegetation has been lost due to land clearing, including 40% of forests and 75% of rainforests. Land clearing for farming continues and old-growth forests are still being logged. Loss of species inevitably follows loss of habitat. Ten of the 120 or so species of marsupials have gone and many other animals and plants are either endangered, ie, in urgent need of conservation to ensure their survival, or vulnerable, ie, likely to become endangered with further loss of habitat. The introduction of alien (non-native) species has also had a drastic impact, not the least in Central Australia (see the boxed text 'Driven to Extinction' in the Northern Territory chapter).

The creation of national parks and conservation reserves goes some way to protecting endangered species. However, this is the responsibility of the states, so doesn't necessarily come about uniformly. The Federal government has taken a lead in focusing on the plight of endangered species with its Environment Protection & Biodiversity Conservation Act 1999. The Act provides for the preparation of national recovery plans and wildlife conservation plans for endangered and vulnerable species in Commonwealth areas. It also enables the Commonwealth to join with the states in national environment protection schemes, especially for the conservation of biodiversity, or to try to save species from extinction.

Bilby

The Act includes lists of endangered and vulnerable species of flora and fauna. The endangered list runs to 618 species, about 75% of which are plants. There are 28 fish and amphibians; 12 reptiles; and 33 bird species, including parrots, honeyeaters, cockatoos and the southern cassowary. Endangered mammals (29 species) include species of bandicoots, potoroos and dunnarts, Leadbeater's possum and the southern right whale. The list of vulnerable species runs to 824.

Southern right whale

ECOLOGY & ENVIRONMENT

Humans have been living in and changing Australia's physical environment for at least 50,000 years, but it is only since European settlement 200 years ago that dramatic and often harmful changes have happened.

Clearing of the native bush has caused the loss or severe alteration of 70% of all native vegetation. Land clearing continues at an alarming rate as marginal land is cleared for precarious farming and old growth forests are logged for timber. As well as causing loss of biodiversity (see the section on Endangered Species in the Fauna & Flora special section), land clearing contributes significantly to salinity, degradation of inland waterways, erosion and increases in greenhouse-gas emisssions. Biodiversity pressure also results from pollution, mining and the proliferation of introduced plants and animals and the diseases they can carry. Tourism is another guilty party – large numbers of visitors are in some cases damaging the very thing they have come to see.

The news is not all bad and Australia compares favourably with many other industrialised countries. It is a large, sparsely populated country, with a highly urbanised population, and extensive areas are still in good condition, pollution is still relatively low and general environmental awareness has grown dramatically.

Ecosystems

The huge island continent embraces a variety of ecosystems: dynamic interactions of the physical environment and living organisms. Tropical rainforests and wetlands are found in the north, eucalyptus forests dominate the south-east and south-west, and deserts and arid lands characterise the vast Centre. Mountain uplands are confined to the alpine regions of the south-east and Tasmania, and the whole country is surrounded by a diverse coastline. The following descriptions, divided into temperate rainforest, wet and dry eucalyptus forests, and sandy and rocky coasts, are a general guide – the categories are very broad and there are many variants.

Tropical Wetland Life here is governed by the annual cycle of wet and dry. Towards the end of the Dry, retreating swamps and lagoons attract thousands of water birds. Noisy flocks of whistling ducks and magpie geese are joined by fish-hunting jabiru and pied herons. By the end of December heavy rains have arrived, and estuarine crocodiles begin to nest and antilopine wallaroos are forced to higher ground. Plant growth is rapid, and many water birds nest among the rushes and wild rice. Storms flatten the tall grasses; by about May the Wet is finished. As the land dries, natural fires continue to shape the environment.

Tropical Rainforest The tree canopy filters sunlight and resounds to the calls of birds and fruit bats. Lichens, ferns and orchids festoon tree trunks and the forest floor is carpeted with palms and a deep layer of forest litter. Pythons, bandicoots, cassowaries and native mice are the largest inhabitants of the forest floor; possums, tree kangaroos and cuscuses clamber among the branches. Brightly coloured birds are often seen near water and in patches of sunlight.

Eucalyptus Forest Among the 600-plus species of eucalyptus there is great variety: mountain ashes (the world's tallest flowering plant), stunted alpine gums, wiry ironbarks and hardy mallee eucalyptuses. Understoreys range from damp ferns to dry acacias and grasses. Koalas are found in only a few species, while brushtail and ringtail possums are less choosy. The kookaburra hunts lizards, snakes, frogs and small mammals; noisy cockatoos and parrots squabble and dart about. Grey kangaroos and wallabies move into open forest in the evenings to browse in shrubs and graze on grasses.

Mountain Uplands Small clumps of hardy snow gums and black sallees fringe extensive open plains carpeted with a large variety of stunted plants. Once the snow has thawed by mid-November, the High Country bursts into life with a wealth of wild flowers – candle heaths, peas, everlastings, snow daisies and mint bushes. In poorly drained hollows thick clumps of sphagnum moss shelter frogs and insects. Few birds or mammals live here year-round, although wombats are quite at home shuffling about in snow. During spring and summer, currawongs, flame robins and cockatoos arrive from the lowlands, together with wallabies and kangaroos, and clouds of Bogong moths gather on rocky summits.

Arid Lands Life is most conspicuous in shaded gorges and along dry river courses where river red gums, home to colourful cockatoos, tap deep water reserves. Sparse vegetation and red sandy soils are rarely and briefly transformed by rain into a carpet of wild flowers. Clumps of spinifex grass provide shelter for small marsupials and mice. A few lizards venture out in the daytime heat to feed on ants. Tall brick-red kangaroos shelter among the scattered mulga and desert oak, but emus continue to forage for seeds and fruit. Rock wallabies emerge to feed in the cool evenings.

The Coast Salt and wind are the key factors governing the make-up of plant communities in three broad types of coast. Sand dunes, whether they are shifting or stabilised, are held together with marram grass in exposed areas. Elsewhere tea-tree, wattles, banksias, she-oaks and peppermint gums provide good shelter for many small birds, rodents and bandicoots. In more open heathlands, wind-pruned wild flowers are prolific – daisy bushes, rice flowers and everlastings. On the cliffs, cushion bush or everlastings cling to tiny pockets of soil. Reeds and grasses, saltbushes and the unusual mangroves fringe estuaries and mudflats rich in bird life – waders, ducks and stately pelicans. Sandpipers and dotterels skitter along the beaches, oystercatchers poke about among rocks where pools teem with marine life. Gulls, terns and cormorants cruise inshore. Out to sea, gannets dive for fish, and seals, porpoises, dolphins and whales come and go according to the season.

Conservation

Australia has a dynamic and often very effective conservation movement, operating on three broad fronts. More than 300,000 people belong to 'green' groups across the country. There are the major national organisations and their high-profile public campaigns; the Australian Conservation Foundation (ACF) and The Wilderness Society (TWS) in particular are leaders in issues of direct concern to walkers, such as protection and expansion of national parks and wilderness areas. Other well-known national organisations include Greenpeace and Friends of the Earth, campaigning on environmental issues such as water and air quality, global warming and genetic engineering (which are also on the agendas of the ACF and TWS).

Then there are numerous state-based organisations, which mainly deal with issues confined to their own states. Campaigns include those in Victoria and NSW to keep private commercial developments for tourism and recreation out of flagship parks such as Wilsons Promontory, Kosciuszko and Blue Mountains National Parks.

Thirdly, there is a host of 'grass roots' groups working away on local, often practical projects, protecting both urban and rural environments, eg, Friends of National Parks and LandCare groups.

The conservation movement has grown from disparate campaigns by field naturalists and others for the creation of national parks and protection of wildlife at the beginning of the 20th century. Then came organisations such as the first National Parks Association (in Queensland) and the NSW National Parks and Primitive Areas Council in the 1930s, and, much later, the ACF in 1965. The flooding of Tasmania's Lake Pedder in 1972 dramatically raised public awareness of conservation issues. This led directly to the formation of what is now TWS; it also gave birth to Tasmania's Green Party, which has become a significant force in that state's politics.

Key issues have become protection of World Heritage List areas from logging, flooding, mining and other inappropriate developments, and the role for parks in saving threatened species of flora and fauna from extinction. Just as important is the campaign for nationwide protection of wilderness areas.

Membership of conservation groups declined generally during the early 1990s, but there was a resurgence later that decade. The ACF recorded its highest-ever membership in 1999, and many organisations involved more young people in their work. It now counts more than 60,000 people in its supporter base.

Despite ongoing setbacks, achievements since the 1980s have been impressive. Tasmania's Gordon and Franklin Rivers and WA's Fitzroy River were saved from damming, and several outstanding areas, such as Queensland's Daintree Rainforest and Fraser Island, were protected from logging by the creation of national parks or their inclusion on the World Heritage List. Part of the largest area of temperate rainforest remaining in the southern hemisphere, the Tarkine, was saved from logging by the creation of Savage River National Park. A historic agreement in 1999 ended all old-growth and wilderness logging in Queensland, thereby protecting nearly half a million hectares of forest. Many wilderness areas have been declared in NSW, Victoria, SA and Queensland. These include the Starcke area in Cape York (far northern Queensland), where the land was saved from sale to overseas interests; the wilderness park is now managed by its traditional owners. Aboriginal people are partners in the management of several other parks, notably Uluru–Kata Tjuta in the NT.

Protection from mining has been much more elusive. There have been some victories in the Kakadu area, in Queensland (Shoalwater Bay), Tasmania (Exit Cave) and South Australia (Yombarra wilderness). However, mining for uranium in central Australia, and particularly in the World Heritage Kakadu National Park, promises to be one of the major battlegrounds for conservationists early this century.

Logging of old-growth forests in and near parks continues to cause confrontation, sometimes violently in the Otway and East Gippsland areas in Victoria. In WA, harvesting of karri and jarrah forests, and the intensive logging methods used by both private industry and the government's Department of Conservation and Land Management (CALM), have met with strong opposition, including from the tourism industry. Only about 350,000 hectares of unlogged, old growth forest is left in WA, and about 40% of that is available for logging. Apart from the loss of irreplaceable natural assets, the fact that much of the output from logging nationwide is destined for overseas markets has aroused considerable passion.

NATIONAL PARKS & RESERVES

Australia has more than 500 national parks, and many more conservation reserves (with various titles); these are nonurban, legally protected, natural areas of outstanding importance for their flora, fauna and scenic landscapes. Each state creates and manages its own national parks, but the principles are broadly in line across the country. National parks are as diverse as the land and its ecosystems, protecting rainforest, semiarid desert, the coast and rugged mountain ranges. They vary in size from mere dots on the map to areas covering hundreds of thousands of hectares. Most national parks are essentially uninhabited, except for some in central Australia that embrace tribal lands of indigenous peoples. In many parks there are also small enclaves where parks staff live and work. During the 1990s, a few states created wilderness parks or areas, or set aside wilderness zones within existing national parks. The criteria for these reservations is even more demanding in the degree of naturalness required. The great majority of walks in this book are within national parks.

Several parks have been added to the United Nations World Heritage List, joining more than 400 other natural or cultural places of world significance that would be an irreplaceable loss to the planet if they were altered. Four of these parks (Kakadu, Uluru–Kata Tjuta, Willandra Lakes and Tasmania's World Heritage Area) have achieved the very unusual distinction of meeting both natural and cultural criteria for listing, and Tasmania's World Heritage Area was ac-

Myles Dunphy, Wilderness Advocate

Protection of wilderness became a major conservation issue during the 1990s and is at the top of The Wilderness Society's agenda for the years beyond 2000. Yet the idea of wilderness – pristine natural areas, invaluable for ecological reasons and the supreme challenge for self-sufficient walkers – has been around in Australia since the 1920s.

The idealistic and adventurous Myles Dunphy (1891–1985) set up the Mountain Trails Club in Sydney in 1914, as a 'bush brotherhood' of men dedicated to self-sufficient expeditions into remote bushland. Inspired by wilderness area campaigners in the US, Dunphy began work on proposals for a Greater Blue Mountains National Park, based on his expeditions with fellow 'Trailers'.

Dunphy was one of the founders of Sydney Bushwalkers in 1927 and the guiding light of the National Parks & Primitive Areas Council from the 1930s. With Dunphy in the driving seat, the council promoted his Blue Mountains plan and the first of several reservations soon followed. His ideals were far-sighted: 'Somewhere handy to the various heavily populated districts of our continent there must be wilderness and plenty of it'. He believed deeply in people's 'moral right to the use of Crown (public) lands for bushland recreation' and in bushwalking as a self-reliant 'rational way of living'.

Integral to Dunphy's meticulous plans were his superlative, painstakingly compiled maps, many of the 30 or more replete with information for bushwalkers. He had a seemingly inexhaustible capacity for work and spent enormous amounts of time meeting senior officials and taking part in public meetings. By the 1960s, his methods of achieving results – personal lobbying and working behind the scenes – had had their day as more aggressive tactics were adopted by conservation bodies. One of the leading figures in this new wave was Dunphy's son, Milo, a charismatic figure until his untimely death in 1998.

It's a fitting tribute that a great many bushwalkers still uphold the ideas that Myles Dunphy first expressed more than 75 years ago.

MARTIN HARRIS

cepted on the basis of satisfying a record seven out of 10 possible Unesco criteria.

State governments have authority over their own national parks, and the Federal government is responsible for ensuring that Australia meets its international treaty obligations. In any dispute arising from a related conflict between a state and the Federal government, the latter can override the state. Thus, the Federal government can force a state to protect an area with World Heritage listing, as it did in the early 1980s when the Tasmanian government proposed to dam the Gordon River in the state's south-west and thereby flood much of the wild Franklin River. However, the Federal government is also a law unto itself and in 1998 approved development of a new uranium mine in Kakadu National Park, despite the opposition of the traditional Mirrar owners. The UN considered downgrading the park's World Heritage listing, but decided against it and instead has threatened to put Kakadu on the ignominious list of

Threatened World Heritage Areas. Mining can continue at the Ranger site until 2009 and can start at Jabiluka in 2001.

National park agency addresses are listed under Useful Organisations in the Facts for the Walker chapter.

History

Australia's first national park was set aside in 1879, only a few years after Yellowstone in the USA, the world's first. An area of sandstone bushland just south of Sydney was reserved by the colonial government mainly to provide the people of the city with somewhere safe for healthy outdoor recreation. It was known simply as The National Park until 1954, when it became Royal National Park to mark the visit of Queen Elizabeth II. The idea of keeping the park in a wilderness condition didn't occur to the park's early trustees; walking tracks, roads and a guesthouse were built and exotic trees planted.

Other parks soon followed – Belair in SA in 1891 and others in NSW and WA – and were managed in much the same way. The colonists' urge to tame the wilderness was stubbornly strong.

However, field naturalists began to draw attention to Australia's unique flora and fauna and campaigned for large national parks where development would be minimal or absent and natural features protected. Early successes included Wilsons Promontory and Mt Buffalo in Victoria and Cradle Mountain in Tasmania. By the mid-1920s, there were national parks in each state and two fauna and flora reserves in the NT. These parks included John Forrest in WA, Bunya Mountains in Queensland, Ku-ring-gai in NSW and Freycinet in Tasmania. Within a decade, a wholly new philosophy about national parks had gained strong support among NSW bushwalkers and conservationists. Led by the tireless campaigner Myles Dunphy, they promoted the concept of wilderness and its protection by the creation of large, development-free parks. Dunphy's proposals were directly responsible for the creation of Blue Mountains National Park in 1932, Kosciusko National Park in 1944 and others (see also History of Walking earlier).

From the late 1940s national park campaigners began to lobby for legislation specifically for national parks. They deplored inappropriate developments and the lack of permanent protection from alien activities. They also agitated for the establishment of dedicated national park agencies.

Victoria led the way with a National Parks Act in 1956. In 1965 NSW gained a National Parks & Wildlife Service and special legislation, and Tasmania, SA and Queensland followed in the 1970s. WA has had a national parks board, but parks are now managed by Conservation & Land Management (CALM). The ACT's one national park (Namadgi) was set aside in 1981 and, with its other reserves, is looked after by the Parks & Wildlife Service. Generally, these arrangements have changed little since.

POPULATION & PEOPLE

Australia's population is about 19.1 million. The most populous states are NSW (6.5 million) and Victoria (4.8 million), which also have the two largest cities, Sydney (four million) and Melbourne (3.3 million). The population is crowded along the east and south-east coasts from Cairns to Adelaide, and there is a small cluster in the south-west corner of WA. The inland areas are very sparsely populated.

Until the late 1940s, most Australians were of British and Irish descent, but large-scale immigration has since radically changed the make-up of society. There are now substantial numbers of people from Greece and Italy, as well as Germany, the Netherlands, Malta, Yugoslavia, Lebanon, Turkey and other countries. More recently, there have been large influxes of Vietnamese and other South-East Asian people. On the whole, 'new Australians' have been accepted readily enough, and a certain pride is taken in the multicultural character of the country.

At the 1996 census around 350,000 people identified themselves as Aboriginal or Torres Strait Islander. This is a large increase on previous such counts, indicating perhaps that people are more willing to declare their indigenous origins. Most Aboriginal people live in northern and central Australia.

ABORIGINAL CULTURE
Traditional Society

Australia's Aboriginal people were tribal, living in extended family groups, or clans, whose members descended from a common ancestral being. Tradition, rituals and laws linked each clan to the land they occupied and each clan had sites of spiritual significance to which their spirits would return when they died. Clan members performed rituals to honour their ancestral spirits. These beliefs underlay the Aboriginal peoples' ties to the land in which they lived.

Many Aboriginal communities were seminomadic, others sedentary, depending on the availability of food and water. Wisdom and skills, accumulated over millennia, enabled them to live in harmony with their environment. Their intimate knowledge of animals' behaviour and of the best time to harvest plants ensured that food shortages were rare. Their only modification of the landscape was selective burning of forest undergrowth and of dead grass on the plains. This encouraged new growth and attracted game animals. There was a lively trade in goods and implements via a wide-ranging network of trade routes across the country. Large numbers of people would meet for 'exchange ceremonies' where not only goods but also songs and dances were passed on.

Beliefs & Ceremonies

Religion, history, law and art are integrated in complex ceremonies depicting the activities of ancestral beings, and prescribing codes of behaviour and responsibilities for looking after the land and all living things. Songs explain that the landscape contains their powerful creator ancestors who can exert a benign or malevolent influence. They also tell of the best places and times to hunt, where to find water in drought times, and can specify kinship relationships and identify correct marriage partners.

Ceremonies are still performed in many areas; many sacred sites are believed to be dangerous and entry is prohibited under traditional Aboriginal law. This restriction may also have another basis, such as the presence of poisonous wildlife.

Experiencing Sacred Sites

Access to sacred sites is overseen by the area's traditional owners, and in some cases is also regulated legally by the relevant state government. It is important to ensure that sites are always treated with respect, and not disturbed or damaged in any way. In some cases, an uninitiated person merely entering the site (eg, swimming in a waterhole) may have serious repercussions for the site's custodians (see also the boxed text 'Bushwalking & Aboriginal Land' in the Northern Territory chapter).

Sacred sites can be viewed in every state, although the best known examples of rock art are in the NT. Walks in this guide that take in sacred sites include:

- Red Hands Cave, Blue Mountains National Park, in the Sydney Region

- Jatbula Trail in Nitmiluk (Katherine Gorge) National park, in the Northern Territory

- Barrk Sandstone Bushwalk, in Kakadu

- Thorsborne Trail, on Queensland's Hinchinbrook Island

Sacred Sites

Aboriginal religious beliefs centre on the continuing existence of spirit beings that lived on earth during the Dreamtime, before the arrival of humans. These beings created all the features of the natural world and were the ancestors of all living things. They took different forms, but behaved as people do, and left signs to show where they had passed on their travels. Eventually the ancestors returned to the sleep from which they had awoken at the dawn of time. Here their spirits remain as eternal forces that breathe life into the newborn and influence natural events. Each ancestor's spiritual energy flows along the path it followed during the Dreamtime and is strongest at the points where it left evidence of its activities – a tree, hill or claypan. These features are sacred sites.

Every person, animal and plant is believed to have a mortal and an immortal soul. The immortal soul is part of a particular ancestral spirit and returns to the sacred sites of that ancestor after death; the mortal soul simply fades into oblivion. Each person is spiritually bound to the sacred sites that mark the land associated with his or her ancestor. Each individual must help care for these sites by performing the necessary rituals and singing the songs telling of the ancestor's deeds. The order created by that ancestor is thus maintained. Traditional punishments for neglect of these duties can still be severe.

Aboriginal sacred sites cannot be 'de-sanctified' (as can a Christian church) before bulldozers move in. Nor can they be bought, sold or transferred. In Aboriginal society, land belongs to the community; damaging or destroying a sacred site threatens both the living and the spirit inhabitants of the land.

LANGUAGE

The Australian version of the English language includes many peculiarly Australian words and phrases. Some have completely different meanings than they do in other English-speaking countries; commonly used words and names are routinely shortened to mysterious monosyllables. Others are derived from Aboriginal languages or from the slang used by early British and Irish convict settlers. The accent varies slightly between regions – most noticeably in Queensland, where speech is even more nasal. The difference between country and city is mainly a matter of speed. Some of the most famous words are scarcely used – few people have 'cobbers' these days, but nearly everyone has 'mates'.

Lonely Planet publishes an *Australian phrasebook*, which is an introduction to Australian English and to Aboriginal languages. The Glossary at the end of this book comprises mainly specialist words relating to bushwalking and camping, as well as a small selection of other odd words that commonly arise.

Facts for the Walker

SUGGESTED ITINERARIES

Deciding on an itinerary for a visit to Australia will be an exercise in making extremely difficult choices from a huge array of possibilities. For a short (one-month) visit, the timing will automatically rule out some destinations and point unwaveringly to others. September or October, for example, is ideal for south-west Western Australia (WA), the Centre and most of Queensland, but unsuitable for the Australian Alps and most of Tasmania where there will probably still be some snow on the ground and the weather can often be bad.

It's most important to keep in mind that Australia is very big (at least by European standards) – the whole of Britain fits into the state of Victoria, which occupies only a

---

Highlights

- **Surprising** grazing herds of eastern grey kangaroos in Namadgi National Park

- **Exploring** the surreal subtropical, microclimate world of Burning Palms in Sydney's Royal National Park

- **Diving** into the emerald sea of the Grose Valley to discover Blue Gum Forest

- **Discovering** the untamed beauty of the High Country in Kosciuszko National Park

- **Resting** at Crystal Shower Falls, under the tangled canopy of one of the finest tropical rainforests in the world

- **Gazing** on flocks of red-tailed black cockatoos taking flight in Nitmiluk National Park

- **Joining** the excellent ranger-led walk through historic Ubirr Art Site in Kakadu National Park

- **Sitting out** the heat of the day by Fish Hole in West MacDonnell Ranges National Park

- **Finally being told** the secret to leech-free walking – halfway up Mt Bartle Frere

- **Plunging** into a pool at the base of Zoe Falls on Hinchinbrook Island

- **Walking** through Alligator Gorge, Mt Remarkable National Park, with the calm of evening approaching

- **Climbing** St Mary Peak in Wilpena Pound to spectacular views across the ancient Flinders Ranges

- **Experiencing** that dizzy feeling at Cape Pillar, on the edge of the highest sea cliffs in Australia

- **Strolling** through stands of mountain ash and lush tree ferns in Dandenong Ranges National Park

- **Encountering** blowholes, spectacular headlands and seal colonies on the Great South West Walk

- **Scrambling** up to the summit of Mt Anne – one of the most challenging mountain walks in Tasmania

- **Taking in** the view of the south coast and offshore islands of Tasmania from the Ironbound Range on the South Coast Track

- **Being given** a lesson in the Koori history of the Grampians at the Brambuk Aboriginal Cultural Centre near Halls Gap

- **Trekking** in the Victorian Alps with their exposed peaks, rocky crags and wind-swept snow gums

- **Swimming** in the sheltered, blue waters of Refuge Cove, Wilsons Promontory

- **Gazing** with awe at the magnificent, gnarled trunks of red tingle trees and majestic karri forests in Walpole–Nornalup National Park

- **Making camp** with views of endless beaches stretching to the horizon on the Bibbulmun Track

small part of Australia's total land area – and distances between major centres are measured in hundreds, if not thousands, of kilometres.

For a short visit, the most sensible way of travelling within the country is generally to fly between state capitals and to use hire cars to reach the walking areas. However, if you are in the country for several months you can travel more widely by car, and use public transport here and there.

The following suggestions, which allow for some ordinary sightseeing, are based on the walks described in detail in this book, but can be varied by including some of the many other walks also outlined at the end of the chapter.

One Month

Divide your time between two states; otherwise you'll be spending too much time just getting around. Also, concentrate on doing a selection of shorter walks that will provide a greater range of contrasts. The following suggestions cover spring (September to November), summer (December to February), winter (June to August) and from late winter to spring.

Spring

Western Australia Leeuwin–Naturaliste, Stirling Range and Walpole–Nornalup National Parks

New South Wales Royal National Park, Blue Mountains National Park, and either the Australian Capital Territory (ACT) or Kosciuszko National Park

Victoria Grampians National Park and Great South West Walk

South Australia Mount Remarkable National Park and Flinders Chase National Park

Summer

Tasmania Overland Track, Mt Field National Park and Freycinet Peninsula

Victoria Alpine National Park and walks in the Melbourne Region

Winter

Northern Territory Kakadu National Park, Western MacDonnell Ranges and Katherine Gorge National Parks

South Australia Flinders Ranges National Park

Victoria Hattah–Kulkyne National Park

Late Winter to Spring

Queensland Lamington National Park, Fraser Island and Hinchinbrook Island

New South Wales Warrumbungle National Park or other northern New South Wales (NSW) parks plus walks in the Sydney Region

Three Months

It wouldn't be unrealistic to visit four states and to do some of the extended walks. The following suggestions are based on the conventional timing of the seasons, but they could be split to make different combinations such as late winter and early spring. The autumn months are March to May.

Spring

Western Australia Leeuwin–Naturaliste, Walpole–Nornalup and Stirling Range National Parks

South Australia Morialta Conservation Park, Mt Remarkable Gorges and Flinders Chase National Park

Victoria Hattah–Kulkyne and Grampians National Parks, Otway National Park and walks in the Melbourne Region

New South Wales Walks in the Sydney Region and Blue Mountains National Park

Australian Capital Territory Tidbinbilla and walks around Canberra

Summer

Tasmania South Coast Track, Walls of Jerusalem and, near Hobart, Mt Wellington and the Organ Pipes

Victoria Wilsons Promontory and Croajingolong National Parks

Victoria, New South Wales & Australian Capital Territory Australian Alps

Autumn

Northern Territory Western MacDonnell Ranges, Katherine Gorge, Litchfield and Kakadu National Parks

Queensland Lamington National Park

New South Wales Dorrigo and Washpool National Parks

Victoria Mt Buffalo National Park and Great South West Walk

Winter

South Australia Flinders Ranges National Park

Victoria Hattah–Kulkyne National Park

Northern Territory The Top End

Queensland Mt Bartle Frere, Hinchinbrook Island and Fraser Island

Six Months

You should be able to sample the entire range of walks presented in this book starting, for example, between late May and early summer. This avoids the hottest months and most of the Wet season (summer) in the north and the hottest months elsewhere, although Tasmania can offer some temperate weather in high summer.

PLANNING
When to Walk

Every month of the year is suitable for walking somewhere in Australia. Summer is the time to be in Tasmania, most of Victoria and southern WA, as well as the Australian Alps. The walking season for the Northern Territory (NT) starts around March, the beginning of the Dry season, and lasts until November or early December, the beginning of the Wet. Anywhere in Queensland and northern NSW is generally best during this time too.

During winter, snow and severe weather can make walking hazardous if not impossible in much of Tasmania, and snow covers most of the high ground in the Australian Alps. However, this is the ideal time for the inland areas of Victoria, NSW and South Australia (SA). Spring means wild flowers, particularly in south-west WA, western Victoria, the Sydney Region and the Blue Mountains; this is also an ideal time to visit the ACT and Melbourne Region.

What Kind of Walk?

Bushwalking in Australia can be what you'd like it to be, with a theme of self-contained

Long-Distance Walking in Australia

Because of Australia's vast and frequently harsh landscape, there are still many areas that simply are not accessible except on foot. This gives walkers the opportunity to reach country that is untouched by towns, roads and pastoral land, even on relatively short walks. However, it is long-distance walking that really gives walkers the opportunity to explore Australia's wild places. Whether it be walking for a week in Tasmania's pristine wilderness, or undertaking one of the long tracks that wind across the country, linking towns via mountain ranges and tracts of bushland, long-distance walks are a unique way to experience the country.

While few of them are described in detail in this book (Tasmania's Overland and South Coast Tracks being the exceptions), there are many starting points provided for the bolder adventurer. Short sections of the Great South West Walk, the Larapinta Trail and the Bibbulman Track are included, along with information and resources for those interested in more extended journeys. Other long-distance walks are outlined, with some planning information, in boxed texts (highlighted with the icon shown at the beginning of this text); the table below is an easy-find reference.

walk title	region	distance	duration	page
Great North Walk	NSW	250km	14 days	123
Hume & Hovell Walking Track	NSW	450km	20 days	185
Larapinta Trail*	NT	220km	14 days	226
Heysen Trail	SA	1200km	60 days	266
Overland Track	Tasmania	81km	5–8 days	308
South Coast Track	Tasmania	86km	7 days	327
Great South West Walk	Victoria	250km	12–14 days	386
Australian Alps Walking Track	Victoria, NSW & ACT	750km	45 days	397
Bibbulmun Track	WA	964km	50 days	452

* The Larapinta Trail was not completed at the time of writing; times and distances refer to the entire proposed route.

travel on foot in the bush. The majority of walks described in this book are from one to eight days long, so they involve camping in the bush, for which a lightweight tent is essential. There are huts or shelters in several areas, but it's unwise to depend on space being available. However, there are also innumerable opportunities for day walks from a base camp in a national park (for example) or from more substantial accommodation, especially near the major cities and some larger towns.

The type of country you can walk through is almost infinitely varied – from semiarid desert to luxuriant tropical rainforest, from the coast to the Australian Alps and other mountainous areas, from temperate rainforest to open grasslands.

Reliable maps, well-marked walking tracks and good track notes make independent walking almost always entirely safe, even if you have no previous experience of the Australian bush. However, if you'd like a change from doing all the organising, the chance to walk with like-minded people and to benefit from the knowledge of experienced guides (especially in more remote areas such as far north-west WA), numerous tour companies run programs of guided walks throughout the country. A selection is listed under Guided Walks later in this chapter, with suggestions of where to find out about others.

Maps
Small-Scale Maps A car touring atlas, such as the Penguin *Explore Australia* or Steve Parish's *Australian Handy Atlas*, will greatly assist in planning trips around the country. Lonely Planet's *Australia Travel Atlas* is another option, with maps at various scales, including detailed city maps of Canberra and the state capitals.

Auslig, Australia's national mapping agency, publishes topographical maps at the useful scale of 1:250,000 for the whole country (more than 530 sheets).

There are numerous very good state and regional maps produced by major commercial publishers such as Gregory's, HEMA and UBD. These are covered in more detail in individual walks chapters. The state automobile associations also produce excellent maps for car travel.

City street directories, also listed in the walks chapters, cover areas beyond the major cities to varying degrees, and are virtually essential for access to and within the larger capitals.

Large-Scale Maps Auslig's 1:100,000 colour topographical series covers the entire coast and hinterland, but not the more remote Outback areas. It lacks the detail needed for reliable route finding, so is useful only for general orientation and identification of major landscape features.

Truly large-scale topographical maps (1:50,000 and 1:25,000) are available for most walking areas. Defence Mapping's 1:50,000 series mainly covers the northern half of the country; coverage in the south is sporadic and often very dated. Most states have an official mapping agency that produces large-scale colour topographical maps suitable for bushwalking (contact details are given in individual walks chapters). There are also excellent maps of national parks and popular walking areas produced specifically for walkers and obtainable at specialist map shops, outdoor gear shops and some park visitor centres.

For information on the custom-drawn walkers' maps in this book, see the Maps in This Book section under Walks in this Book later in this chapter.

Buying Maps There are specialist map shops in the capital cities, and outdoor gear shops usually carry at least some of the main topographical map series for the state in which they're located.

Auslig's Web site at 🖳 www.auslig.gov.au is useful for identifying which small-scale maps you might need; you can also order maps through this site.

Email ordering services at the Melbourne Map Centre (🖲 info@ melbmap.com.au) and Perth Map Centre (🖲 sales@perthmap .com.au) are especially useful if you want to obtain maps before arriving in the country (see the Melbourne Region and Western

Australia chapters for more information on these map centres). Another alternative, the privately maintained map ordering service (🖳 www.aussiemaps.com) has more than 6000 maps in stock.

What to Bring

Clothing See the boxed text 'Equipment Check List' for a list of essential items to bring. Remember that all your protective gear, a spare warm jacket, spare socks and gloves, emergency food, a torch (flashlight)

and a whistle should be carried on all walks of more than a couple of hours.

Your waterproof jacket should be in good condition and a proven performer in wet weather, especially if you're going to southern Tasmania, where it can be very wet at any time of the year. The ideal specifications are a breathable, waterproof fabric, a roomy hood, capacious map pocket, good-quality, heavy gauge zips and a minimum of fiddly draw cords; make sure the sleeves are long enough to cover warm clothes underneath

---

Equipment Check List

This list is a general guide to the things you might take on a walk. Your list will vary depending on the kind of walking you want to do, whether you're camping or planning on staying in hostels or B&Bs, and on the terrain, weather conditions and time of year.

Equipment
- [ ] **backpack** with waterproof liner
- [ ] **camera** and spare film
- [ ] **emergency, high-energy food**
- [ ] **map, compass and guidebook**
- [ ] **medical kit***, toiletries and insect repellent
- [ ] **pocket knife** (with corkscrew)
- [ ] **repair kit**
- [ ] **sleeping sheet**
- [ ] **small towel**
- [ ] **sunglasses and sunscreen**
- [ ] **survival bag or blanket**
- [ ] **torch** (flashlight) with spare batteries and globe
- [ ] **water containers**
- [ ] **water purification tablets, iodine or filter**
- [ ] **whistle** (for emergencies)

Clothes
- [ ] **gaiters**
- [ ] **runners** (training shoes) **or sandals**
- [ ] **shorts and trousers**
- [ ] **socks and underwear**
- [ ] **sunhat**
- [ ] **sweater, fleece or windproof jacket**
- [ ] **thermal underwear**
- [ ] **T-shirt and long-sleeved shirt** with collar

- [ ] **walking boots** and spare laces
- [ ] **warm hat, scarf and gloves**
- [ ] **waterproof jacket or cape**
- [ ] **waterproof overtrousers**

Camping
- [ ] **cooking, eating and drinking utensils**
- [ ] **dishwashing items**
- [ ] **insulating mat**
- [ ] **matches, lighter and candle**
- [ ] **portable stove and fuel**
- [ ] **sleeping bag**
- [ ] **spare cord**
- [ ] **tent** (check pegs and poles)
- [ ] **toilet paper and toilet trowel**

Optional Items
- [ ] **altimeter**
- [ ] **binoculars**
- [ ] **day-pack**
- [ ] **emergency distress beacon****
- [ ] **GPS receiver****
- [ ] **lightweight groundsheet**
- [ ] **mobile phone****
- [ ] **mosquito net**
- [ ] **swimming costume**
- [ ] **walking poles or stick**
- [ ] **waterproof, slip-on backpack cover**
- [ ] **notebook and pencil**

* see the Medical Kit Check List in Health & Safety for a list of contents

** see Safety on the Walk in Health & Safety for a discussion of communications equipment

and that the overall length allows you to sit down on the jacket.

Overpants will be welcome during cooler weather, but at other times it's debatable whether you're wetter with or without them. Gaiters go a long way to keeping your feet dry and provide better protection against mud, abrasive vegetation and invasive wildlife. Look for those made of strong synthetic fabric, with a robust zip, protected by a flap, and with an easy-to-undo method of securing around the foot.

Protection against the wind will be very welcome along exposed coasts, so a windproof fleece or tightly woven polycotton jacket is handy in such areas.

Underneath, it's more a matter of personal preference; consider a long-sleeved shirt if you're fair-skinned. A cotton garment will take longer to dry than one made of a synthetic fabric and is not necessarily cooler in the heat. For warmth, wear garments of wool or fleece; one or two thin layers of thermal underwear may be more versatile than a single thick one. Absolutely essential are a broad-brimmed hat and sunglasses with UV lenses.

While shorts are worn universally during summer, there are times when long trousers are preferable, eg, in leech-infested country and for protection against the sun. Polycotton is a suitable material, and the garment should be of a looser fit than you might normally wear, to allow freedom of movement and to minimise the risk of chafing.

Keep the contents of your pack dry by putting everything in a large heavy-duty plastic bag inside the pack.

Footwear Many Australian walkers would not be seen dead in anything other than runners (training shoes), wherever they're walking. Runners are certainly lighter than many walking boots, although they lack the same ankle support. Unless your feet are used to training shoes, especially over rough ground, it's better to wear boots.

If you've never bought a pair of walking boots before, go for a walk before you visit your chosen shop, so that your feet can expand slightly, as they would do in the bush.

Buy the best you can afford that suits your style of walking; some rigidity in the sole is helpful on rough ground. Gore-Tex lined boots are more expensive and as nothing will keep out persistent rain (let alone the water and mud on such walks as Tasmania's South Coast Track), they might not be worth the cost. Make a point of wearing your new boots a few times before you set out on your first serious walk.

There's no need to wear two pairs of socks for warmth, although a double layer cushions the foot's impact on the ground. There are several good brands of walkers' socks made of a hard-wearing wool-synthetic mix, free of ridged seams in the wrong places.

Equipment The accompanying check list covers the gear you will need for walking and camping. Your backpack must be hardwearing and weatherproof. Make sure it sits comfortably on your back when loaded and that you know how to adjust the harness. Even if the manufacturer claims it's waterproof, use heavy-duty liners (garden refuse bags are ideal, or custom-made sacks are also available); external pack covers can easily catch the wind and fly off or be ripped to shreds by overhanging scrub. Take a small pack for day walks, or use spare liners to store unwanted gear during the day.

When choosing a tent, ease of pitching is an important consideration so that you can put it up quickly in bad weather. Carry a tube of seam sealer for emergencies. Adequate headroom is also a valuable feature if you are tent-bound in bad weather, as is space to stow your gear.

Protection against mosquitoes is absolutely essential for your comfort and sanity during summer, and at most times in the north of the country. Make sure your tent zips up completely, and if you're intending to sleep outside or in accommodation along the way, take along a mosquito net.

A sleeping mat ensures a good night's rest and puts a layer of insulation between you and the cold and/or wet ground. Compact self-inflating mats are far better than bulky rolls of foam that can be torn apart on the scrub bordering tracks.

Australia's Bushwalking Gear Pioneer

Australia's thriving bushwalking gear industry was born in 1930 in a Sydney suburban bedroom belonging to Paddy Pallin, who had migrated to Australia from northern England a few years earlier. A keen walker, he soon began exploring the bushland on the fringes of Sydney and in the still largely unexplored Blue Mountains.

Losing his hated office job at the start of the Depression, he seized the chance to turn his recreation into an income earner, and set about designing and making lightweight bushwalking gear in his home, very much aware that equipment for extended bushwalking trips was virtually nonexistent. Meantime his wife, May, worked to earn enough to keep them afloat. He was firmly established in small city premises by 1934, the year in which the first edition of his manual *Bushwalking & Camping* was published; it's still regularly updated.

After a disastrous fire in his shop and factory in the early 1950s, the business went from strength to strength, with its own city shop in the 1970s, and expanded state-wide and interstate during the 1980s. 'Paddymade' gear in those days covered the full range: rucksacks (as they were called), sleeping bags, tents, clothing and camping equipment. Many innovative items were developed – double sleeping bags, H-frame packs, self-standing lightweight water buckets and even highly prized pink wool socks, known as 'Paddy's Pinkies'.

Paddy himself remained active throughout his life, learning to cross-country ski in his 50s and trekking in Nepal in his 70th year; he died aged 91 in 1991. His autobiography *Never Truly Lost* is a fascinating account of bushwalking in a bygone era and of his personal – and timeless – philosophy.

Paddy Pallin is still a family business, although the range of Paddymade gear has narrowed and other reputable brands are sold in its many shops. The company actively supports environmental and community conservation programs and runs its own Don't Bag the Environment scheme to reduce the amount of packaging used in its shops.

MARTIN HARRIS

An inner sheet with your sleeping bag keeps it clean and adds an extra insulating later. They must be used at youth hostels, although sheets can usually be hired and sleeping bags may not be allowed. Subzero overnight temperatures are quite likely during winter in many parts of Australia.

As a general guideline, the fuel stove you choose needs to be stable when sitting on the ground and to have a good wind shield. Make sure you take the instructions for use and a small repair kit. Fuel stoves fall roughly into three categories: multifuel, methylated spirits (ethyl alcohol) or Shellite (white spirits), and butane gas.

Multifuel stoves are small, very efficient and are ideal for places where a reliable supply of fuel is hard to find. They tend to be noisy and sooty, however, and require some maintenance.

Stoves running on methylated spirits or Shellite are slower and less efficient, but are safe, clean and easy to use.

Butane gas stoves are commonly sold in camping shops around the world. Although clean and reliable, however, they can be slow, and the gas canisters can be awkward to carry and a potential litter problem. They are also more wasteful of resources than liquid fuel.

If you're not taking a butane gas stove, you'll need a clearly labelled aluminium or purpose-built plastic bottle to carry fuel – the plastic containers in which it's sold are too flimsy for safety. None of these items can be carried when travelling by air, however.

If you plan to stay in national park camping grounds where timber is provided for fires, a packet of firelighters will be handy – the timber is usually large logs that don't catch fire readily. Rather than use kindling that's lying about, firelighters will speed up the business of getting the fire lit, especially if it's wet.

For a discussion of the pros and cons of including a mobile phone, GPS navigation system or emergency beacon in your backpack, see Safety on the Walk in the Health & Safety chapter.

Buying & Hiring Locally You'll find outdoor gear shops, including branches of major national chains, in each capital. Such shops in other cities and towns are listed in the walks chapters. *Wild* magazine has a comprehensive directory of outdoor gear shops (also online; see Newspapers & Magazines later).

Australian designers and manufacturers of bushwalking gear include: Paddy Pallin (see the boxed text 'Australia's Bushwalking Gear Pioneer' earlier), Adventure Designs, Mountain Designs, Snowgum, Summit, Wilderness Equipment, Wilderness Wear and One Planet. All have good reputations.

Outdoor gear shops carry stocks of various brands of gas canisters. Shellite, kerosene and methylated spirits are often also stocked; if not, try a supermarket or hardware shop.

Facilities for hiring gear are very limited – Paddy Pallin offers this service in some states, as do some of the smaller shops. However, it isn't cheap and you're probably better off buying what you need – Australian gear is world-class.

Physical Preparation

Some of the walks in this book are physically demanding and most require a basic level of fitness. Whatever standard of walk you tackle, it pays to be moderately fit at the start of your trip rather than launch straight into it after months of fairly sedentary living.

Unless you're a regular walker, aim to begin your get-fit campaign about a month before your trip. Take a vigorous walk of about an hour two or three times per week, and gradually extend the duration of your outings as the departure date nears. If you plan to carry a full backpack on any walks, carry a loaded pack sometimes as well. Walkers over the age of 55 with little previous experience should have a medical checkup beforehand.

WALKS IN THIS BOOK

All the walks described are summarised in the Walks Table at the beginning of the book, which outlines the essential information you'll need to identify the walks that suit you best.

Route Descriptions

Each walk description is organised around day-long stages. At the end of each day of a multi-day walk there should be somewhere to spend the night, such as a camp site, hut or shelter, equipped with, at the very least, a water supply.

Places passed during a day's walk where you could stop overnight are also mentioned, giving you the scope to extend or shorten the daily stages. Side trips to worthwhile places are outlined at the end of each day's stage.

Along the route, features of interest are highlighted in bold in the walk description; water sources are also noted.

Each walk is prefaced with a short discussion of its main features, track conditions and opportunities for variations (such as doing the walk in the opposite direction to that described). The Planning section of each walk includes the best time to do the walk and any special equipment needed.

Standards

The walks are graded into five categories: easy, easy-medium, medium, medium-hard and hard. These are based on daily distance, the amount of ascent and descent, the quality of the tracks (rough, well formed, clear, vague), navigational difficulty, and any other factors, such as rock scrambling. The grades are for people of average ability, ie, neither rank beginners nor extremely fit and experienced types.

Easy Routes are on good, well-signposted tracks, strictly walking-only (no scrambling) with minimal climbing, and are comfortably within the abilities of a family with children aged over 10.

Medium Walks are accessible to anyone of average fitness, with a little effort. The upgrade from easy reflects one or more factors, such as climbing, greater distance, rougher or less clear tracks, or the need for route finding using a map and compass.

Hard Walks are physically challenging in terms of their length and/or duration, terrain and navigation.

Times & Distances

The times noted for walks in this book are the actual times taken and do not include any rest stops. In most cases a range is given (eg, 5½ to 6 hours) to allow for different walking speeds. The authors have provided an average time, irrespective of how long they each took to do the walk. Allowance has been made for rocky, sandy or boggy ground. Those walks involving long ascents (more than 500m) assume a climbing rate of roughly 300m per hour.

The walk descriptions also include intermediary times, eg, from the start to the first landmark, from there to a lunch spot, and so on. Distances between significant points, especially short ones between track junctions, are also given. These can be crucial in places such as heavily tracked areas where track markers can disappear overnight and may not be replaced immediately.

Overall distances for walks are either those given by the responsible agencies or have been carefully measured by the authors.

Maps in This Book

The maps in this book are intended to show the general route of a walk and to be used in conjunction with the maps recommended in the Planning section for each walk or national park. Every effort has been made to ensure that these walk maps are accurate and up to date. They are drawn to a metric scale with varying contour intervals.

A wide band of brown stipple shows the main route covered by the text; alternative routes are marked with a dashed brown stipple line and side trips are shown with a dotted stipple line. Start and finish points are marked with boxes, and camp sites, lookout points, roads, tracks, park boundaries and nearby accommodation, ie, all the features mentioned in the walk descriptions, are also indicated. A wide band of grey stipple shows land boundaries and borders, and the coverage of any adjoining or overlapping maps is shown, along with their page numbers.

Each chapter has a regional map showing the gateway towns or cities, principal transport routes and starting and finishing points of the walks fully described.

Altitude Measurements

Heights of mountains and cliffs are taken from official topographical maps, most of which are liberally sprinkled with summit and spot heights. Where an amount of ascent or descent is quoted, it has been derived by counting contours on the maps.

Place Names & Terminology

Australian place names are a fascinating mix of Aboriginal and European words, reflecting the country's many different tribal languages (such as the prevalence of names ending in '-up' in WA) and the many home countries of European explorers and settlers (eg, Stirling Range, Wilsons Promontory and Freycinet Peninsula).

Most state governments have place names and mapping authorities that work closely together, so names are generally consistent, although the spelling of Aboriginal names can vary.

'Track' is commonly used in Australia to describe formed ways: walking tracks for pedestrians and unsealed 4WD or management tracks for wheeled vehicles. 'Trail' is also used and has the same meaning as walking track.

Public & Private Property

Most of the walks in this book are on public land, ie, land 'owned' by the government, in national parks and other conservation reserves. This was originally called Crown land, meaning land ultimately owned by the sovereign of the UK, but the more neutral term is now used.

Some of the Northern Territory walks are in national parks to which Aboriginal people hold title and for which it's essential to obtain an entry permit beforehand. Where short sections of a very few walks cross other private land, access has been granted after negotiations between the owner and a government agency, usually national parks management, and is subject to strict conditions, such as closing gates and keeping to a defined route.

There are no legal public rights of way across private land in Australia; generally private property is very private, and you'll often see large 'Trespassers Prosecuted' signs on fences and gates.

Describing which side of a creek you should be on can be confusing. In some places a compass direction is used in this book (eg, the northern side of the creek). Alternatively, the 'true' right or left bank means the right/left side as you face downstream.

Other common Australian terms, including the distinctive words for a watercourse (creek, gully), are explained in the Glossary at the back of the book.

PERMITS

General access to national parks is unrestricted, so permits aren't required, but an entry fee is charged for many of them. Fees may be collected at a staffed entrance gate, or you can obtain passes at park offices. Fees are also charged for the use of camp sites in the majority of national parks. Details of the various state systems are given in the walks chapters.

Walking Permits

Permits are required where numbers at camp sites may be limited for environmental

reasons. An outline of requirements follows, and details of where to apply are given in the walks chapters. The permit system makes more sense if you recognise that the great majority of walks in Australia are on public land, or on land to which Aboriginal people hold the title (see the boxed text 'Public & Private Property').

You must obtain a permit for overnight walks in the NT – most aren't readily available over the counter, so apply well in advance. A permit is required for overnight walks in Victoria's Wilsons Promontory National Park. All overnight walks in Queensland are subject to permits, and for at least two you need to apply well in advance. Permits are also required in SA's Flinders Ranges and Mt Remarkable National Parks. A permit system is being proposed for Tasmania's World Heritage Area (see the boxed text 'A Permit System for the WHA?' in the Tasmania chapter).

GUIDED WALKS

Several reputable, highly experienced companies run guided walks in the major national parks and into some of the more remote areas. Including a guided walk in your visit to Australia can be a way of reaching far-flung places and enjoying the benefits of experienced guides, organised transport and the company of like-minded people. Here is a selection of nationwide operators. There are also many smaller outfits in each state; *Wild* magazine, the Bushwalking in Australia Web site at 🖳 www .bushwalking.org.au (maintained by the Confederation of Bushwalking Clubs NSW) and local tourist offices are good sources of more information.

Auswalk (☎ 02-6457 2220, fax 6457 2206, 🄯 mon ica@ auswalk.com.au) PO Box 516, Jindabyne NSW 2627. Offers centre-based holidays including the Snowy Mountains (six days, $240), easy-going hotel-to-hotel tours through several areas such as the Blue Mountains (seven days, $1120) and self-guided tours with booked accommodation and detailed notes detailed track notes compiled by Auswalk, eg, The Best of Tasmania (eight days, $1250). Guided walking trips can also be arranged.

Ecotrek: Bogong Jack Adventures (☎ 08-8383 7198, fax 8383 7377, ✉ ecotrek@ozemail.com.au, 🖥 www.ecotrek.com.au) PO Box 4, Kangarilla, SA 5157. Has a wide-ranging program including the Flinders Ranges and the Heysen Trail (seven days, $985), the Gammon Ranges (seven days, $860) both in SA, the Grampians in Victoria (six days, $860) and Kosciuszko Explorer (seven days, $1180) in NSW.

The Adventure Company (☎ 03-9662 2700, fax 9662 2422, ✉ travelcentre@peregrine.net.au) Peregrine Travel Centre, 258 Lonsdale St, Melbourne, Victoria 3000. Runs adventure walks to Mt Bartle Frere (four days, $500) in Queensland, Croajingolong National Park (10 days, around $1900) in Victoria and Freycinet Peninsula (three days, $430) in Tasmania. Combination trips involving walking, rafting, cycling and canoeing are a company speciality.

World Expeditions (☎ 1300 720 000, fax 02-9261 1974, ✉ enquiries@worldexpeditions.com.au, 🖥 www.worldexpeditions.com.au) Level 3, 441 Kent St, Sydney, NSW 2000. Has an established program, including Katherine Gorge (three days, $429) and the Larapinta Trail (eight days, $1419) in the NT, and Cradle Mountain (eight days, $1095) in Tasmania.

RESPONSIBLE WALKING

The bush is a fragile place and hordes of bushwalkers tramping around can easily upset the delicate ecological balance. Here are some guidelines for 'minimal impact' bushwalking – to help walkers minimise harmful impacts and reduce the need to restrict numbers and close tracks. These guidelines are closely based on the Minimal Impact Bushwalking Code, adopted by Australian national parks agencies. (For a discussion of safety in the bush, see Safety on the Walk in the Health & Safety chapter.)

Rubbish

- Remove all surplus food packaging and put small-portion packages in a single container before your trip. Ideally, buy in bulk to minimise packaging.
- Don't rely on bottled water; use a water purifier instead. If you can't survive without a beer, keep it to a minimum.
- Burying rubbish is out. Digging disturbs soil and ground cover and encourages erosion and weed growth. Buried rubbish takes years to decompose and will probably be dug up by wild animals who may be injured or poisoned by it.

- If you've carried it in, you can carry it out – everything, including silver paper, citrus peel, cigarette butts and plastic wrappers. Empty packaging is lightweight and should be stored in a dedicated rubbish bag. Make an effort to pick up rubbish left by others.
- Sanitary napkins, tampons and condoms don't burn or decompose readily, so carry them out, whatever the inconvenience.

Human Waste Disposal

- If a toilet is provided at a camp site, please use it.
- Where there isn't one, bury your waste. Dig a small hole 15cm deep and at least 100m from any watercourse and the camp site. Take a lightweight trowel or large tent peg for this purpose. Cover the waste and paper with soil.
- Contamination of water sources by human faeces can lead to the transmission of giardia, a human bacterial parasite; gastroenteritis in popular walking areas is probably caused by exposed human faecal waste.

Feeding Animals

- Not only is it important to secure rubbish and food from maurauding beasties, it is also vital that you do not feed native animals, no matter how tame and cute they are. Feeding makes wild creatures dependent on humans for food and can cause them to develop diseases such as lumpy jaw – a fatal condition found in marsupials, causing them to starve to death.

Washing

- Don't use detergents or toothpaste in or near watercourses; even if they are biodegradable they can harm fish and wildlife.
- To wash yourself, use biodegradable soap and a water container at least 50m from the watercourse. Disperse the waste water widely so it filters through the soil before finally returning to the creek.
- Wash cooking utensils 50m from watercourses using a scourer or gritty sand instead of detergent.
- Strain food scraps from dishwashing water and carry them out in your rubbish bag.

Fires & Low-Impact Cooking

- Campfires are not allowed in fuel-stove-only areas, mainly in the Australian Alps and Tasmania's World Heritage Area.
- Fires of any kind (including fuel stoves) are prohibited on days of Total Fire Ban. In remote areas, regard any hot, dry, windy day as a fire ban day.

- Don't depend on open fires for cooking. Use a lightweight kerosene or Shellite stove rather than one powered by disposable gas canisters. They're easier to use in wet weather.
- Fires may be OK below the tree line in little-visited areas. Use a safe existing fireplace rather than make a new one. Don't surround it with rocks – they're just another visual scar – but clear away all flammable material for at least 2m. Keep the fire small (under 1 sq metre), and use the minimum of dead fallen wood.
- Be absolutely certain the fire is extinguished. Spread the embers and drown them with water. A fire is only safe to leave when you can comfortably put your hand on it. Scatter the charcoal and cover the fire site with soil and leaves.

Camping
- Use an existing camp site rather than create a new one. Avoid grassed areas and go for sandy or hard surfaces; keep at least 30m from watercourses and tracks. Move on after a night or two.
- If the tent is carefully sited, it won't be necessary to dig damaging trenches when it rains heavily.

Low-Impact Walking
- It's important to stick to existing tracks and to avoid short cuts bypassing zigzags. New trails straight down slopes will turn into watercourses after the next heavy rain and cause soil loss and erosion.
- Walk through muddy patches or pools; walking around the edge only increases the size of the patch or pool.
- Avoid removing plants that anchor the topsoil and steer clear of sensitive vegetation that is destroyed by trampling. Stick to rocks and hard ground wherever possible.

Huts
- Don't depend on huts – always carry a tent.
- Huts are available on a first-come, first-served basis; some huts in Victoria are not available for public use.
- Keep fires small, and within existing fireplaces.
- If there's a log book, fill in details of your trip and party – this may help with search and rescue.
- Don't leave food behind, as wildlife will surely find it.
- When you leave, tidy up, ensure the fire is out, replace kindling and firewood and close the windows and door properly.

WOMEN WALKERS
Australia is generally a safe place for women travellers, including women bushwalkers. As a walker, you'll most likely be accepted as a walker first and as a woman second. Nevertheless, it's worth remembering that historically, bushwalking has been regarded as a predominantly male activity. Australia's oldest bushwalking club was founded as and remains men-only, although other clubs have had women members since the 1920s. Virtually all other bushwalking clubs are open to women and men alike. (See the History of Walking section in Facts about Australia.)

Sexual harassment still occurs too frequently, and more so in country than city areas. Female hitchers should take care at all times (see Hitching in the Getting Around chapter).

In a country where shorts are almost universally worn during summer (and for longer in northern areas), you certainly won't encounter any censorious looks for wearing shorts in the bush.

WALKING WITH CHILDREN
Bushwalking certainly isn't an adults-only activity; introducing children to walking at a fairly early age can set them on the track to a lifetime's enjoyment. However, you will need to put a lot of thought into planning walks with kids.

The distance and duration have to be well within their proven capabilities. As a guide, most 10-year-olds should be able to cover 5km to 8km on good tracks with no more than 200m of climbing in a comfortable day's outing. It's important to have a set plan, so you can tell them what's coming next. Be aware of the point of no return (beyond which the end is nearer than the start) and, ideally, have an escape route for emergencies.

Trees and flowers may have little appeal, but kangaroos, wallabies and emus should. Panoramic views may be largely lost on young people and they'll be more interested in unusual rock formations to scramble around and small caves to explore. Incorporate plenty of stops into the estimated time and consider organising an activity at lunchtime (related to the local wildlife, what they've seen and so on).

Suitable clothing and good equipment are very important – children will feel the cold sooner and more keenly than you will, and their tolerance of sore feet, for example, will probably be pretty low. Getting children to carry a pack is not a bad idea, especially to encourage a sense of participation, but not one that upsets balance or normal gait.

Carry plenty of food and drinks, including as many of their favourites as possible. Having friends along could be a good idea, if they're of much the same ability and suitably equipped.

Of the walks described and outlined in this book, those suitable for children include:

Australian Capital Territory
Orroral Valley, Gibraltar Rocks
Sydney Region
Bouddi Coast, Red Hands Cave, Burning Palms
New South Wales
Wentworth Falls & the Valley of the Waters, Wonga Walk, Never Never Circuit, Washpool Rainforest
Northern Territory
Barrk Sandstone Bushwalk
South Australia
Morialta Circuit
Tasmania
The Organ Pipes, Maria Island
Melbourne Region
Main Creek, Gellibrand Hill, Werribee Gorge
Victoria
Hattah–Kulkyne Tour, Wonderland, Cape Otway, Huts of the Bogong High Plains
Western Australia
Cape Naturaliste walks, Lowlands Beach to Cosy Corner, Porongurup National Park

As far as travelling is concerned, child concessions for accommodation and transport are often available. Discounts may be up to 50% of the adult rate, although the definition of 'child' varies from under 12 to under 18 years. Lonely Planet's *Travel with Children* contains plenty of useful information.

USEFUL ORGANISATIONS
National Parks Agencies

The Commonwealth government, through Environment Australia's Biodiversity Group, manages six national parks, notably three in partnership with their Aboriginal owners: Kakadu and Uluru–Kata Tjuta (NT) and Booderee (NSW).

All other national parks and conservation reserves are managed by the various state government agencies (see National Parks & Reserves in the Facts about Australia chapter for a discussion of their role). The main addresses for information are:

Australian Capital Territory
Environment ACT (☎ 02-6207 9777, ☐ www.act.gov.au/environ) 12 Wattle St, Lyneham, ACT 2602
Commonwealth Government
Environment Australia (☎ 02-6274 1111, fax 6247 1123, ☐ www.ea.gov.au) John Gorton Building, King Edward Terrace, Parkes, ACT 2600 (GPO Box 787, ACT 2601)
New South Wales
New South Wales National Parks & Wildlife Service (☎ 02-9585 6333, fax 9585 6527, ☐ www.npws.nsw.gov.au) Level 1, 43 Bridge St (PO Box 1967), Hurstville, NSW 2220
Northern Territory
Parks & Wildlife Commission of the Northern Territory (☎ 08-8999 5511, fax 8999 4558, ☐ www.nt.gov.au/paw) 25 Chung Wah Terrace, Palmerston, NT 0830 (PO Box 496, Palmerston, NT 0831)
Parks Australia North (arm of Environment Australia; ☎ 08-8946 4300, fax 8981 3497) 80 Mitchell St, Darwin, NT 0800 (PO Box 1260, Darwin, NT 0801)
Queensland
Queensland Parks & Wildlife Service (☎ 07-3227 8186, fax 3227 8749, ☐ www.env.qld.gov.au) 160 Ann St, Brisbane, Queensland 4000 (PO Box 155, Albert St, Brisbane, Queensland 4002)
South Australia
National Parks & Wildlife South Australia (☎ 08-8204 1910, fax 8204 1919) The Environment Shop, 77 Grenfell St, Adelaide, SA 5000 (GPO Box 1047, Adelaide, SA 5001)
Tasmania
Parks & Wildlife Service (☎ 03-6233 6191, fax 6233 2158, ☐ www.parks.tas.gov.au) 134 Macquarie St, Hobart, Tasmania 7000 (PO Box 44A, Hobart, Tasmania 7001)
Victoria
Parks Victoria (☎ 13 1963, ☐ www.park web.vic.gov.au) 378 Cotham Rd, Kew, Victoria 3101
Western Australia
Department of Conservation & Land Management (☎ 08-9334 0333, fax 9334 0498, ☐ www.calm.wa.gov.au) 50 Hayman Rd, Como, Perth, WA 6152 (Locked Bag 104, Bentley DC, WA 6983)

Conservation Organisations

There are several other large national conservation and heritage organisations, including the Australian Conservation Foundation, the Wilderness Society and the Australian Trust for Conservation Volunteers, as well as many state-wide conservation groups campaigning on a host of environmental issues. (Notice boards at the major national bodies, listed earlier in this section under National Parks Agencies, are a good way of making contact.)

Australian Conservation Foundation

The Australian Conseravtion Foundation (ACF; ☎ 03-9416 1166, fax 9416 0767, ⌨ www.acfonline.org.au), 340 Gore St, Fitzroy, Victoria 3065, is the largest nongovernment conservation organisation in Australia. It covers a wide range of issues, including mining in world heritage areas, the greenhouse effect and depletion of the ozone layer, sustainable agriculture, healthy rivers and problems of land degradation. The ACF publishes an excellent magazine, *Habitat*, and a newsletter for young people. Its library in Melbourne is open to all during office hours.

The Wilderness Society

The Wilderness Society (TWS; ☎ 1800 030 641, fax 03-6224 1497, ⌨ www.wilderness.org.au), 130 Davey St, Hobart, Tasmania 7000, was originally formed by conservationists who, unsuccessful in preventing the damming of Lake Pedder in south-western Tasmania, were determined to protect the south-west wilderness from further damming. The society's campaign to save the wild Franklin River from being dammed was one of Australia's first major conservation confrontations, and ended successfully in 1983 when the Australian High Court ruled against damming the river.

TWS now campaigns to protect Australia's wilderness reserves and for the restoration of degraded wilderness areas; particular issues include forest management and mining. All its income is derived from memberships, donations and merchandising – there are TWS shops in most states where you can buy books, T-shirts, posters, badges etc.

Australian Trust for Conservation Volunteers

The Australian Trust for Conservation Volunteers (ACTV; ☎ 03-5333 1483, fax 5333 2166, ⌨ www.atcv.com.au), PO Box 423, Ballarat, Victoria 3350, is a nonprofit group that organises practical conservation projects for local volunteers and overseas visitors. Typical projects are tree planting, walking track construction, fencing and weed control. This is an excellent way of getting involved with the conservation movement, meeting like-minded people and visiting some fantastic places such as the Barossa Valley (SA), Kakadu (NT) and Fraser Island (Queensland).

Projects usually run for a weekend or a week; all food, transport and accommodation are supplied in return for a small contribution to help cover costs. Most travellers who take part in the ATCV join a Conservation Experience package that lasts six weeks and includes up to six different projects. The cost is $840, and further days/weeks can be added for $20/140.

Walking Clubs

Australia has a large number of walking clubs, most of which are regionally based. Organisations such as the Confederation of Bushwalking Clubs NSW, the Federation of Victorian Walking Clubs and the Queensland Federation of Bushwalking Clubs can be a very useful first point of contact, maintaining Web sites with excellent bushwalking information and links to member clubs. The contact details for clubs are included in the relevant walks chapters.

Gay & Lesbian Organisations

Most of the major cities have gay and lesbian walking groups. The best way to find these is to check the community listings in local gay and lesbian street press and publications.

In Victoria, you could contact the ALSO Foundation (☎ 03-9510 5569, fax 9510 5699, ⌨ www.also.org.au), which has an extensive directory of gay and lesbian organisations and businesses.

Out Touring (⌨ www.internetnorth.com .au/~shar/) is a useful resource for gay and lesbian travellers to North Queensland.

Listed below are two walking clubs that welcome visitors:

Southern Cross Outdoors Group (☎ 02-9907 9144, @ scog@pinkboard.com.au, ☐ www.pinkboard.com.au/~scog/) PO Box 411, Dee Why 2099. Runs outdoor activities, including a day walks program, in NSW.

Wayward Women Walkers (☎ 03-9888 8306, 9818 7317). A Melbourne-based bushwalking club with an active walks program.

Other Organisations

For details of the Youth Hostels Association and other backpackers organisations, see Accommodation later in this chapter.

TOURIST OFFICES

Tourist offices are a useful first port of call in familiarising yourself with the country, but beware of being overloaded with shoals of brochures, booklets and maps.

Local Tourist Offices

Each state and territory has a tourist agency and you will find information about them in the relevant walks chapters. Apart from main offices in the capital cities, they often have regional offices in major tourist centres and in other states.

As well as supplying brochures, price lists, maps and other information, staff will often book transport and accommodation. They usually have some basic information about national parks, which are generally the main walking areas. The principal offices are:

Australian Capital Territory
Canberra Visitors Centre (☎ 02-6205 0044, 1800 026 166, fax 02-6205 0776, ☐ www.canberratourism.com.au) 330 Northbourne Ave (PO Box 673), Dickson, ACT 2602

New South Wales
Sydney Visitor Centre (☎ 13 2077, ☐ www.tourism.nsw.gov.au) 106 George St, The Rocks, NSW 2000

Northern Territory
Northern Territory Holiday Centre (☎ 1800 621 336, ☐ www.nttc.com.au) PO Box 2532, Alice Springs, NT 0871

Queensland
Queensland Government Travel Centre (☎ 13 1801, 07-3874 2800, fax 3221 5320, ☐ www.qttc.com.au) 243 Edward St (GPO Box 9958), Brisbane, Queensland 4001

South Australia
South Australian Travel Centre (☎ 08-8303 2033, 1300 366 770, fax 08-8303 2231, ☐ www.tourism.sa.gov.au) 1 King William St (PO Box 1972), Adelaide, SA 5000

Tasmania
Tasmanian Travel & Information Centre (☎ 03-6230 8233, fax 6224 0289, ☐ www.tourism.tas.gov.au) Cnr Davey and Elizabeth Sts, Hobart, Tasmania 7000

Victoria
Victorian Tourism Information Service (☎ 13 2842, fax 03-9653 9744, ☐ www.tourism.vic.gov.au) GPO Box 2219T, Melbourne, Victoria 3001

Western Australia
Western Australian Tourist Centre (☎ 1800 812 808, fax 08-9481 0190, ☐ www.westernaustralia.net) Forrest Place, Perth, WA 6000

A great number of towns maintain regional tourist offices, many of which are excellent, with much local information, including walking guides and maps not readily available from the state offices.

Tourist Offices Abroad

The Australian Tourist Commission (ATC) is a government body that provides information about the country for potential visitors. ATC offices overseas have a free magazine-style periodical booklet called *Australia Travellers' Guide: Australia Unplugged*, which is a good introduction for young travellers, giving general information about the country and snapshots of major cities.

The ATC also publishes 'Fact Sheets' on various topics such as camping and national parks, which can be a useful starting point. A handy map of the country is available for a small fee. This literature is for distribution overseas only; if you want copies, you'll find them on the Web at ☐ www.australia.com, or contact a travel agent specialising in marketing Australia to international visitors. Contact details for some agencies can be found on the ATC's Web site, ☐ www.atc.net.au. Some ATC helpline telephone numbers are:

Germany	☎ 069-274 0060
Japan	☎ 03-5214 0720
New Zealand	☎ 09-379 9594
UK	☎ 020-8780 2229
USA	☎ 310-229 4870

VISAS & DOCUMENTS

All important documents (passport data and visa pages, credit cards, travel insurance policy, air/bus/train tickets, driving licence etc) should be photocopied before you leave home. Leave one copy with someone at home and keep another with you, separate from the originals.

It's also a good idea to store details of your vital travel documents in Lonely Planet's free online Travel Vault in case you lose the photocopies or can't be bothered with them. Your password-protected Travel Vault is accessible online anywhere in the world; create it at ▣ www.ekno.lonelyplanet.com.

Visas

All visitors to Australia need a visa, except New Zealand nationals, and even they receive a 'special category' visa on arrival. Check the Department of Immigration & Multicultural Affairs (DIMA) Web site at ▣ www.immi.gov.au for predeparture information on visas, customs and health issues. Helpfully, it includes *An Australian Government Guide to Visiting Australia*. The type of visa you need depends on the reason for your visit. (Check also with DIMA about eligibility and conditions of Working Holiday Visas.)

Tourist Visa This is issued by Australian diplomatic missions abroad for a stay of up to six months and costs $50. The visa is valid for use within 12 months of the date of issue and can be used to enter and leave Australia several times within that 12 months. Extensions may be granted, up to a maximum stay of 12 months.

You can also apply for a long-stay visa, which is a multiple-entry, four-year visa allowing stays of up to six months on each visit. These also cost $50.

Electronic Travel Authority (ETA) Visitors who require a tourist visa of up to three months can get a free ETA through an International Air Transport Association (IATA)-registered travel agent abroad. This system, introduced in 1997, is so far only available to passport holders of the UK, the USA, most European and Scandinavian countries and Japan. The list is likely to grow significantly.

Visa Extensions For visa extensions, apply through DIMA offices in Australia (☎ 13 1881), preferably two or three weeks before your visa expires. The application fee is $145, but beware – you won't get your money back if your application is turned down.

Driving Licence

You can generally use your own foreign driving licence in Australia, as long as it is in English (if it's not, a certified translation must be carried). However, some states prefer that you have an International Driving Permit, supported by your home licence. To avoid potential hassles we suggest you carry both.

Travel Insurance

Residents of the UK, New Zealand, the Netherlands, Sweden and Italy are entitled to free or subsidised medical and hospital treatment. For a discussion of the Medicare health insurance scheme, see Predeparture Planning in the Health & Safety chapter.

You should seriously consider taking out a travel insurance policy to cover theft, loss and medical expenses. There's a wide variety on the market, so read the fine print carefully to make sure you know what you're buying and that it suits your needs. Some policies specifically exclude 'dangerous activities', which can include walking.

You may prefer a policy that pays doctors or hospitals direct rather than you having to pay on the spot and claim later. If you have to do this, keep all the paperwork. Some policies require you to phone a centre in your home country (reverse charges) for an immediate assessment of your problem. Check that ambulances or an emergency flight home are included in your policy.

Other Documents

An International Student Identity Card (ISIC) is invaluable for travel and accommodation discounts. You can get this from a student union or similar organisation.

Possession of a Hostelling International (HI) card opens the doors of Youth Hostel Association hostels around the country and confers eligibility for lots of discounts (see Accommodation later in this chapter).

EMBASSIES
Australian Embassies Abroad
The Department of Foreign Affairs & Trade Web site at 🖳 www.dfat.gov.au has a full listing of Australian diplomatic missions overseas. Australian embassies abroad include:

Canada (☎ 613-236 0841, fax 236 4376) Suite 710, 50 O'Connor St, Ottawa, Ontario K1P 6L2
France (☎ 01 40 59 33 00, fax 01 40 59 33 10) 4 rue Jean Rey, 75724 Cedex 15, Paris
Germany (☎ 030-888 0880, fax 880 08899) Friedrich Strasse 200, Berlin, 10117
Ireland (☎ 01-676 1517, fax 661 3576) 6 Fitzwilton House, Wilton Terrace, Dublin 2
Japan (☎ 03-5232 4111, fax 5232 4149) 2-1-14 Mita, Minato-Ku, Tokyo 108
Netherlands (☎ 070-310 8200, fax 310 7863) Carnegielaan 4, The Hague 2517 KH
New Zealand (☎ 04-473 6411, fax 498 7135) 72–78 Hobson St, Thorndon, Wellington
UK (☎ 020-7379 4334, fax 7465 8218) Australia House, The Strand, London WC2B 4LA
USA (☎ 202-797 3000, fax 797 3168) 1601 Massachusetts Ave NW, Washington, DC 20036-2273

Foreign Embassies in Australia
The principal diplomatic representatives in Australia are in Canberra. Sydney and Melbourne have nearly as many consular offices, although visa applications are usually handled in Canberra. Here is a selective list; look under Consulates & Legations in the *Yellow Pages* telephone book for more:

Canada (☎ 02-6270 4000, fax 6273 3285) Commonwealth Ave, Yarralumla, ACT 2600
France (☎ 02-6216 0100, fax 6216 0127) 6 Perth Ave, Yarralumla, ACT 2600
Germany (☎ 02-6270 1911, fax 6270 1951) 119 Empire Circuit, Yarralumla, ACT 2600
Ireland (☎ 02-6273 3022, fax 6273 3201) 20 Arkana St, Yarralumla, ACT 2600
Japan (☎ 02-6273 3244, 6273 1848) 112 Empire Circuit, Yarralumla, ACT 2600
Netherlands (☎ 02-6273 3111, fax 6273 3206) 120 Empire Circuit, Yarralumla, ACT 2600

New Zealand (☎ 02-6270 4211, fax 6273 3194) Commonwealth Ave, Yarralumla ACT 2601
UK (☎ 02-6270 6666, fax 6273 3236) Commonwealth Ave, Yarralumla, ACT 2600
USA (☎ 02-6214 5600, fax 6214 5970) 21 Moonah Place, Yarralumla, ACT 2600

It's important to realise what your own embassy can and can't do to help if you get into trouble. It won't be much help if the trouble you're in is remotely your own fault. Remember that while in Australia you are bound by Australian laws. In genuine emergencies you might get some assistance, but only if other channels have been exhausted. If you have all your money and documents stolen, it might assist with getting a new passport, but a loan for onward travel is out of the question.

CUSTOMS
When entering Australia you can bring most articles in free of duty provided that customs is satisfied they are for personal use and that you'll be taking them with you when you leave. There's also a duty-free, per-person quota of 1125mL of alcohol, 250 cigarettes and dutiable goods up to the value of $400.

You will be asked to declare all goods of animal or vegetable origin – wooden spoons, straw hats, jars of honey – and show them to an official. Fresh produce is also banned – meat, cheese, fruit, vegetables and flowers. The authorities are committed to preventing weeds, pests or diseases getting into the country – Australia has so far managed to escape many of the agricultural pests and diseases prevalent in other parts of the world. There are also restrictions on taking fruit and vegetables between states (see the boxed text 'Interstate Quarantine' in the Getting Around chapter). Australian customs officers and dogs are extremely efficient at finding illegal drugs; unless you want to investigate Australian jails firsthand, don't bring illegal drugs with you.

Weapons and firearms are either prohibited or require a permit and safety testing. Other restricted goods include products (such as ivory) made from protected wildlife species, unapproved telecommunications devices and live animals.

MONEY
Currency

Australia's currency is the Australian dollar, comprising 100 cents. There are 5c, 10c, 20c, 50c, $1 and $2 coins, and $5, $10, $20, $50 and $100 notes. Although the smallest coin in circulation is 5c, prices are marked in single cents, and the total price rounded to the nearest 5c when you pay.

There are no notable restrictions on importing or exporting travellers cheques. Cash of any currency exceeding the equivalent of $5000 must be declared on arrival and departure.

In this book, unless otherwise stated, all prices are given in Australian dollars.

Exchange Rates

The Australian dollar is heavily traded on the international market and fluctuates markedly against the US dollar and other currencies.

country	unit		A$
Canada	C$1	=	$1.15
Euro	€1	=	$1.55
France	FF10	=	$2.35
Germany	DM1	=	$0.80
Ireland	IR£1	=	$1.95
Japan	¥100	=	$1.55
Netherlands	fl	=	$0.70
New Zealand	NZ$1	=	$0.75
UK	UK£1	=	$2.55
USA	US$1	=	$1.70

Exchanging Money

Changing foreign currency or travellers cheques is usually not a problem at banks or licensed moneychangers such as Thomas Cook or American Express.

Travellers Cheques For a short visit, travellers cheques are the most straightforward method of carrying money, generally enjoying a better exchange rate than foreign cash. American Express, Thomas Cook and other well-known international brands are widely used. A passport is usually adequate for identification, but a driver's licence or other form of identification may also be useful.

The fees for changing foreign currency travellers cheques vary from bank to bank.

Currently, charges by the 'big four' banks (ANZ, Commonwealth, National and Westpac) range from $5 to $7 depending mainly on the amount. Buying Australian dollar travellers cheques is worth considering. These can be exchanged immediately with a bank teller without incurring commissions, fees or exchange rate fluctuations.

Credit Cards These are an alternative to carrying large numbers of travellers cheques. Visa, MasterCard, Diners Club and American Express (Amex) are all widely accepted in Australia. Cash advances from credit cards are available over the counter and from many automatic teller machines (ATMs), depending on the card.

If you're planning to rent cars, a credit card makes life much simpler; many agencies simply won't rent you a vehicle if you don't have a card. Credit cards can also be used to make telephone calls from special public telephones, found in most towns throughout the country.

Bank Accounts & ATMs

If you're planning to stay longer than a month or so, it's worth considering a more flexible and economical way of handling your money. Many travellers open a bank account that provides a cash card, which can be used to withdraw cash from ATMs all over Australia. ATMs are usually accessible day and night, and most will accept cards from other banks. There is a limit on how much you can withdraw – usually around $1000 per day. ANZ, Commonwealth, National and Westpac branches are found nationwide. However, many smaller country branches don't have ATMs, so you have to wait until the bank is open (which may not be daily; see Business Hours later in this chapter).

As an overseas visitor, you simply present your passport to open an account at an Australian bank. It's much easier if you do this within six weeks of arrival. After six weeks it's more complicated and you need more than one form of identification. If you don't have an Australian Tax File Number (TFN), interest earned from your funds will be taxed at the rate of 47%.

Top Left: Maitland Bay, Bouddi NP, NSW. **Top Right:** The 'Postbox' at Wentworth Falls, Blue Mountains NP, NSW. **Middle Left:** Bowtells Swing Bridge, Blue Mountains NP. **Middle Right:** Grose Valley from near Fortress Creek, Blue Mountains NP. **Bottom Left:** View of Mt Kosciuszko from Mt Townsend, Kosciuszko NP, NSW. **Bottom Right:** Missed the boat? Fortress Creek, Blue Mountains NP.

GLENN VAN DER KNIJFF

GLENN VAN DER KNIJFF

GLENN VAN DER KNIJFF

GLENN VAN DER KNIJFF

GREG CAIRE

Top Left: Clarke Gorge, Kosciuszko NP. **Top Right**: Massive rocky outcrops seen from the Chimneys, Kosciuszko NP. **Middle:** The glacial Blue Lake, nestled below Mt Twynam, Kosciuszko NP. **Bottom Left:** Walking along Farm Ridge Fire Trail towards Mt Jagungal. **Bottom Right:** Deep gorges and plateaus of the central Budawang Ranges seen from Pigeon House Mountain, Morton NP, NSW.

A great many businesses are linked to the Electronic Funds Transfer at Point of Sale (EFTPOS) system, through which you can use your bank cash card to pay for services or purchases direct, and often withdraw cash as well.

On the Walk

Away from large towns, replenish your cash supply whenever it starts to drop at the first available ATM, as it might be days before you find another. When you leave the last outpost of 'civilisation', all you'll probably need is cash to pay national park permits and camping fees. Likely amounts are given in the walks chapters.

Costs

Compared with the USA, Canada and Europe, Australia is cheaper in some ways and more expensive in others. Manufactured goods tend to be more expensive: if they are imported they have the additional costs of transport and duties, and if they're locally manufactured they bear the extra costs entailed in small-volume production. On the other hand, food is normally both high in quality and low in cost. You can eat well in a pub or cafe where two courses should cost around $15; add $2 or $4 for a beer or a glass of wine. Self-catering is of course much cheaper – it isn't difficult to live well for $10 per day.

Accommodation is bargain-priced and plentiful. Dorm beds in hostels cost from $12 to $17; at a caravan park a tent site for two people is around $15, an on-site van from $35 for two and a decent cabin usually starts at $45. Camping fees in national parks (where facilities are usually pretty basic) vary from state to state, but are usually no more than $10 for a site.

The biggest cost on any trip around Australia will be transport, because it's such a vast country. Costs of public transport, car hire and fuel are given in the Getting Around chapter.

Walkers will find that topographical maps are less expensive than in the UK and at least some other European countries; much the same applies to guidebooks.

Prices for liquid fuel for portable stoves vary quite widely, but expect to pay from $4 to $4.50 per litre. A 500mL gas canister costs around $12. Other costs, eg, postage, telephone and newspapers, are given elsewhere in this chapter.

GST The Goods and Services Tax (GST) was introduced on 1 July 2000. As a result, since this book was researched many services have increased in cost, while the prices of a range of goods have fallen – prices quoted here should only be used as a general guide. Price labels on goods include the GST.

International air travel to/from Australia is GST-free, as is domestic air travel when purchased outside Australia by nonresidents. If you purchase new or second-hand goods with a total minimum value of $300 from any one supplier within 28 days before departure from Australia, you are entitled to a refund of any GST paid – ring the Australian Tax Office general inquiry line on ☎ 13 6140 for details.

Tipping

In Australia it's customary to tip in more expensive restaurants if you feel it's merited – 10% of the bill is the usual amount. Taxi drivers don't expect tips but will cheerfully keep the change if you decide to leave it.

POST & COMMUNICATIONS
Postal Rates

Australia's postal services are relatively efficient and reasonably cheap. It costs 45c to send a standard letter or postcard within Australia.

Australia Post divides international destinations into Asia Pacific and Rest of the World; the minimum cost of an airmail letter is $1 and $1.50 respectively. A postcard or aerogram to any country costs $1 and 80c respectively.

Parcels Sea mail is only available to Europe and the USA, to which a 2kg parcel, for example, costs $26. Each extra 500g costs $3, up to a maximum of 20kg. Airmail is much more expensive, but is the only option to everywhere else. A 2kg parcel sent 'economy air' to New Zealand or Japan costs $22 and $26 respectively, up to a maximum weight of 20kg.

Sending & Receiving Mail

Post offices are open from 9 am to 5 pm Monday to Friday. You can buy stamps weekdays and on Saturday morning at post office agencies (operated from newsagencies) and from Australia Post shops in the major cities.

All post offices will hold mail for visitors, and some city GPOs (main post offices) have poste restante sections. You can also have mail sent to Amex offices around the country if you have an Amex card or carry Amex travellers cheques.

Telephone

Telstra provides public phones; private phones are serviced by Telstra (mostly government-owned) and Optus. These two companies also compete in the mobile phone and pay phone markets with several other companies, including Vodafone, One.Tel, Unidial, Global One and AAPT.

Pay Phones & Phonecards There's a wide range of local and international phonecards. Lonely Planet's eKno Communication Card (see the insert at the back of this book) is aimed specifically at independent travellers and provides budget international calls, a wide range of messaging services and free email.

You can join online at 🖥 www.ekno .lonelyplanet.com, or by phone from anywhere in Australia by dialling ☎ 1800 674 100. Once you have joined, you can then access the really cheap eKno local access rates from Sydney on ☎ 02-8208 3000 and from Melbourne on ☎ 03-9909 0888. If you are elsewhere in Australia, you can use eKno by dialling ☎ 1800 114 478.

For local calls, you could also consider using a local phonecard. Phonecards can be used in any Telstra public phone that accepts cards (virtually all do), or from a private phone by dialling a toll-free access number.

Long-distance calls made from pay phones are considerably more expensive than calls made from private phones. If you can't avoid using pay phones to make a large number of calls, looking into the various cards available from providers other than Telstra may save you some money.

Some public phones are designed to take only credit cards, but the cost of these calls can quickly mount up. The minimum charge is $1.20.

Local Calls Local calls from public phones cost 40c for an unlimited amount of time, while local calls from private phones cost 25c. Calls to mobile phones attract higher rates.

Long-Distance Calls & Area Codes It's also possible to make long-distance (or STD – Subscriber Trunk Dialling) calls from virtually any public phone. They are cheaper in off-peak hours (basically outside normal business hours), and different service providers have different charges.

For the purpose of area (or STD) codes, Australia is divided into four areas. All regular numbers (ie, numbers other than mobile or information service numbers) have one of four area codes followed by an eight-digit number. Long-distance calls (ie, to more than about 50km away) within these areas are charged at long-distance rates. Broadly, the 02 code covers NSW and the ACT, 03 Victoria and Tasmania, 07 Queensland and 08 SA, WA and the NT. Area code boundaries do not necessarily coincide with state borders – for example, NSW has all four codes. Generally, you don't have to dial the area code if you're calling someone with the same code as yours.

International Calls You can make ISD (International Subscriber Dialling) calls from public and most pay phones. The international dialling code will vary depending on which provider you are using.

International calls from Australia are among the cheapest you'll find anywhere. Telstra may not be the best deal, especially off peak, and special deals often bring rates down even further. Off-peak times vary depending on the destination – call ☎ 12 552 for more details.

You can make reverse-charge (collect) or credit-card calls through the Country Direct service, which gives callers in Australia direct access to operators in nearly 60 countries. For a full list of the countries hooked into this system, check the *White Pages* telephone book.

Toll-Free Calls Many businesses and some government departments operate a toll-free service (prefix 1800), so no matter where you are ringing from around the country, it's a free call. However, these numbers may not be accessible from certain areas, or from mobile phones, in which case you'll have to dial the normal number.

Many companies, such as airlines, have numbers beginning with 13 or 1300, which are charged at the local call rate. These numbers may be Australia-wide, or applicable to a specific state or STD district only. Unfortunately, as with 1800 numbers, there's no way of telling without actually ringing the number. Calls to these services still attract charges if you are calling from a mobile phone.

Information Calls Numbers starting with 190 are usually recorded information services. They're provided by private companies, and your call is charged at anything from 35c to $5 or more per minute (more from mobile and pay phones).

Mobile Phones Australia is serviced by two separate mobile networks: digital and the digitally based CDMA. The latter has replaced the old analogue network, which was phased out during 2000. Ask the carrier you use in your home country whether or not your mobile phone will work in Australia.

The two networks service more than 90% of the population, mainly along the east coast and in the south-east, but vast tracts of the country are not covered at all – the various service providers have coverage maps and you should check these before signing up. The main operators are Telstra, Optus and Vodafone. Mobile phone numbers are prefixed with 04xx or 04xxx. The caller is charged mobile rates on calls both to and from mobiles.

Fax

You can send faxes from any post office, either to another fax or to a postal address. Faxes to another fax machine in the same state cost $2 for the first page and 50c for each subsequent page; to other states $4 and $1 respectively. Faxes to postal addresses within Australia cost the same and will be delivered by Australia Post the next day. Overseas faxes cost $6 for the first page and $2 for each subsequent page.

Many business services, photocopying shops and newsagents also have fax machines and usually charge less than post offices. Faxes can be very handy for booking accommodation if the place you want does not have email or if access to the Internet is unavailable.

Email

There are plenty of Internet cafes in the capital cities and larger towns, and even in small country towns, where you can access the Net. Many hostels also have email facilities, as do all public libraries. For the latter, the service is free but you have to book a slot about 24 hours ahead.

The cheapest way to have email access while travelling is to get a free, web-based email account such as Lonely Planet's eKno (🖳 www.ekno.lonelyplanet.com), Hotmail (🖳 www.hotmail.com) or Yahoo! (🖳 www.yahoo.com). This way you can access your mail from cybercafes and other facilities anywhere in the world using a net-connected machine running a standard Web browser such as Explorer or Netscape.

INTERNET RESOURCES

At the Lonely Planet Web site (🖳 www.lonelyplanet.com) you'll find succinct information about travelling to Australia, postcards from other travellers and the Thorn Tree bulletin board, where you can ask questions before you go or dispense advice when you get back. You can also find travel news and updates to many of our most popular guidebooks; the subWWWay section links you to the most useful travel resources elsewhere on the Web.

In addition to the sites noted elsewhere in this chapter, try these useful Australian sites:

Electronic Australiana
The official site of the National Library of Australia, it has a vast number of links to books, maps, environmental information, government departments etc.
⌨ www.nla.gov.au

The Aussie Index
A fairly comprehensive list of Australian companies, educational institutions and government departments that maintain Web sites.
⌨ www.aussie.com.au

Galactic Bushwalking
Privately maintained, this site contains a huge quantity of information on walks, national parks, accommodation, clubs, equipment and outdoor gear retailers.
⌨ www.galactic.net.au

BOOKS

All good bookshops in the country have a section devoted to Australiana, with books on every Australian subject you care to mention. For specialist bushwalking publications, the outdoor gear and map shops and visitor information centres listed in the walks chapters are the best places to go (see also the outlets listed earlier under What to Bring earlier).

Lonely Planet

Lonely Planet has a long and colourful list of titles on its home country. The *Australia* guide is an obvious first reference. For more regional detail, Lonely Planet has guides by state, as well as the *Melbourne* and *Sydney* city guides. Gourmet travellers will appreciate the *Out to Eat* restaurant guides to both these cities.

If you're planning a trip into the Outback in your own vehicle, *Outback Australia* is an invaluable practical reference. For a more offbeat perspective, *Sean & David's Long Drive* by Australian author Sean Condon provides a hilarious account of road travel.

Last but not least, Lonely Planet's *Watching Wildlife Australia* provides authoritative information for a wide range of people, from those with a casual interest through to the chase-it-anywhere enthusiast. With the focus on national parks, the guide explains where and how to see wildlife, describes the various parks and provides some background information about when to go and what to take.

Travel & Exploration

The journals of the early European explorers make fascinating reading, especially if you have been walking in or near areas they passed through. Accounts of the journeys of Thomas Mitchell in south-eastern Australia are particularly pertinent.

Accounts of more recent travels in Australia include *Tracks* by Robyn Davidson, the story of a young woman who walked alone from Alice Springs to the WA coast with her camels. *The Ribbon and the Ragged Square* by Linda Christmas is a very informative account of a nine-month investigatory trip around Australia by an English journalist.

History

For a good introduction to Australian history, look for *A Short History of Australia* by the highly respected Australian historian Manning Clark, or the more recent *A Concise History of Australia* by Stuart Macintyre. Geoffrey Blainey's long-standing *The Tyranny of Distance* studies the problems of transport and how they shaped the pattern of white settlement. *Finding Australia* by Russel Ward traces the period from the first Aboriginal arrivals up to 1821 and emphasises Aborigines, women and explorers. It's intended to be the first of a series. *The Exploration of Australia* by Michael Cannon is a coffee-table book in size and price, but it's a fascinating account of the gradual uncovering of the continent by Europeans.

Books about bushwalking aren't always easy to find, but are worth the effort. *Myles and Milo* by Peter Meredith is a thoughtful account of the lives of two walkers and wilderness conservation campaigners. Myles Dunphy led the way in securing the first national park reservation in the Blue Mountains and his son Milo was a passionate campaigner for wilderness protection after him. Dorothy Butler's *The Barefoot Bush Walker* is her engaging account of her lifetime of extraordinary climbing and walking adventures, often barefoot, in wild areas of Australia, New Zealand and beyond. Several titles by Quentin Chester, including *The Wild Calling*, convey the addictive appeal of bushwalking.

Aboriginal People

Lonely Planet's *Aboriginal Australia* is a handbook introducing and explaining Aboriginal culture and heritage, due out in mid-2001. The award-winning *Triumph of the Nomads* by Geoffrey Blainey demolishes the myth that Aborigines were 'primitive' people trapped on a hostile continent and shows how they adapted superbly to the climate and seeming lack of resources.

Three titles by Henry Reynolds – *The Other Side of the Frontier*, *With the White People* and *Why Weren't We Told* – present an Aboriginal perspective on the cost of white settlement in Australia. Other worthwhile reads are *Aboriginal Australians* by Richard Broome and *The Australian Aborigines* by Kenneth Maddock.

Natural History

Australia-wide guides to flora and fauna are inevitably fairly hefty (and relatively expensive). There are thousands of species to describe across the continent, so the more localised guides recommended in the walks chapters may be better for identification on the walk. However, several titles provide a good general introduction.

For birds, there's the highly authoritative and superbly illustrated *The Graham Pizzey & Frank Knight Field Guide to the Birds of Australia* by Pizzey & Knight. In the Key Guide series, *Australian Wildflowers* and *Australian Trees*, both by Leonard Cronin, are well illustrated. Lighter-weight and more affordable is the Green Guides series, including *Birds*, *Parrots*, *Mammals*, *Snakes* and *Spiders*, each with a single identifying photo per species.

If you're ever browsing in a library, look for one of the finest examples of the art of botanical illustration ever produced in Australia – Celia Rosser's works devoted to one of the most distinctive of all Australian plant species, the banksia (however, they're rather expensive to buy).

For an interesting (and controversial) discussion of issues facing Australia's environment, look for Tim Flannery's *The Future Eaters*. Similarly, *Taming the Great South Land: A History of the Conquest of Nature in Australia* by William Lines traces Australia's sometimes appalling record of conservation since European settlement (particularly in relation to bush clearance).

NEWSPAPERS & MAGAZINES

The *Australian* is the only national daily paper. Each capital city has at least one broadsheet and a tabloid or two. The *Sydney Morning Herald* and Melbourne *Age* are the leading dailies. Most regional centres also support a regular newspaper. The widely available *Guardian Weekly* provides in-depth detail on European current affairs. Many overseas newspapers are on sale in major newsagents in the capital cities within a few days of publication, but at premium prices.

Of the bush sports magazines, *Wild* is in a class of its own, with a strong environmental line, excellent coverage of equipment and publications, and good articles about walks around the country. It's published quarterly, as is *Outdoor Australia*. Both are available from outdoor gear shops.

WEATHER INFORMATION

Comprehensive weather reports and forecasts are published in the daily newspapers and broadcast on evening TV and radio news programs. The Bureau of Meteorology has an excellent Web site (🖳 www.bom .gov.au), which includes detailed regional forecasts across the country and all kinds of warnings and statistics. Some national park visitor centres post daily weather forecasts, including temperature ranges. During summer, it's vital to keep track of bushfire alerts, and particularly of days of total fire ban, which are widely publicised in the media, in notices at visitor centres and on roadside signs in country areas.

PHOTOGRAPHY
Film & Equipment
Australian film prices are not too far out of line with those of the rest of the Western world. A roll of 36-exposure Kodachrome 64 or Fujichrome 100 slide film costs around $26, including processing. A 24-exposure Kodacolor print film costs around $6, to which you'd have to add around $8.50 for the cost of processing.

There are plenty of camera shops in all the big cities and the standard of camera service is usually good. Many places offer one-hour developing of print film.

Photography
Almost everywhere, but particularly in the Outback, you have to allow for the exceptional light intensity. For best results shoot early in the morning and late in the afternoon – colours look washed out when the sun is high. On the coast, allow for the effect of reflected light. To photograph elusive wildlife, plant yourself in a meadow or near a water source in the pre-dawn hours, or just after sunset, and be prepared to wait in one spot, camera poised, for an hour or so. A tripod will alleviate cramped neck and finger muscles.

Always protect camera lenses with a haze or ultraviolet (UV) filter. At high altitudes the UV filter may not adequately prevent washed-out photos; a polarizing filter can correct this problem and dramatically emphasise cloud formations.

Especially in summer, keep film as cool as possible, particularly after it has been exposed. Dust is a hazard for both film and camera in inland areas, as is humidity in the northern tropics.

For a thorough grounding in the tips and techniques particular to photography on the road, read Lonely Planet's *Travel Photography* by Richard I'Anson (to be published in 2000), a full-colour guide for happy-snappers and professional photographers alike. *Wilderness Light* by Robert Rankin contains excellent practical advice on Australian light conditions, although its weight and price make it more appropriate for a coffee table than a backpack.

Photographing People
As in any country, politeness goes a long way when taking photographs; ask before taking pictures of people. Many Aboriginal people don't like having their photos taken, even from a distance.

Airport Security
To be on the safe side, carry all your film in your hand luggage so you can be sure that it isn't subjected to the super-powerful X-ray machines used for baggage security.

TIME
Australia is divided into three time zones: Western Standard Time (GMT/UTC plus eight hours) covers WA; Central Standard Time (plus 9½ hours) covers the NT and SA; and Eastern Standard Time (plus 10 hours) covers Tasmania, Victoria, NSW and Queensland. When it's noon in WA, it's 1.30 pm in the NT and SA and 2 pm in the rest of the country.

Daylight saving time, for which clocks are put forward an hour, operates in NSW, Victoria and SA from late October to late March. Tasmania's daylight saving period is slightly longer, but WA, the NT and Queensland stay on standard time. It's not as confusing as it sounds once you get used to it.

ELECTRICITY
Voltage is 220V to 240V and plugs are three-pin, but different from British three-pin plugs. It's difficult to find converters to take either US flat two-pin plugs or European round two-pin plugs for electric shavers or hairdryers, except in fancy hotels. Adaptors for British plugs can be bought in good hardware and electrical goods shops.

WEIGHTS & MEASURES
Australia uses the metric system, eg, petrol and milk are sold by the litre, apples and potatoes by the kilogram, distance is measured in metres or kilometres, height in centimetres or metres and speed limits in kilometres per hour (km/h). Colloquially, distance is often measured in the time it takes to get there, rather than in kilometres, eg, Geelong is two hours' drive away.

There's a metric conversion table at the back of this book.

BUSINESS HOURS

Most shops open from 8 am onwards and close at 5 or 5.30 pm on weekdays, and at either noon or 5 pm on Saturday (although longer hours aren't unusual). Sunday trading is generally fairly common in the major cities and is steadily becoming more widespread in regional areas. In most towns there are usually one or two late shopping nights each week, mainly Thursday and/or Friday, when the doors stay open until 9 or 9.30 pm. Many places do stay open late and all weekend – milk bars, convenience stores, supermarkets, delis and city bookshops. Some supermarkets open 24 hours a day. Laws governing the sale of alcohol on Sunday vary, but generally don't expect to buy it at an independent bottle shop – you'll probably have to find a pub that's open.

Banks are open from 9.30 am to 4 pm Monday to Thursday, and until 5 pm on Friday. Some large city branches are open from 8 am to 6 pm Monday to Friday. Some are also open to 9 pm on Friday.

PUBLIC HOLIDAYS & SPECIAL EVENTS
School Holidays

The Christmas holiday season, from mid-December to late January, is part of the summer school vacation, when you are most likely to find accommodation booked out and long queues at sights. There are three other shorter school holiday periods during the year, but they vary by a week or two from state to state. They fall generally from early to mid-April, late June to mid-July, and late September to early October.

Public Holidays

Public holidays also vary quite a bit from state to state. The following is a list of the main national public holidays. Each state and territory also has its own public holidays, such as Bank Holiday, Labour Day, Show Days, commemorative days and holidays for major horse-racing events; for precise dates check locally.

New Year's Day 1 January
Australia Day 26 January
Easter March/April – Good Friday to Easter Monday inclusive
Anzac Day 25 April
Queen's Birthday second Monday in June in all states except WA, where it's held last Monday in September
Christmas Day 25 December
Boxing Day 26 December

Special Events

Some of the most enjoyable Australian festivals are, naturally, the most typically Australian ones – surf life-saving competitions on beaches all around the country during summer and Outback race meetings, which draw together isolated communities and more than a few eccentric bush characters. There are also numerous cultural and arts events, such as music and film festivals, held annually around the country – inquire at state tourist authorities for details.

ACCOMMODATION

Australia has loads of inexpensive youth hostels, backpacker hostels and caravan parks with camp sites. There are also plenty of hotels, motels, guesthouses and B&Bs, particularly in popular tourist venues.

Family rooms in hotels and motels, and caravan park cabins sleeping at least three people, are good bets for a small group travelling together. Prices are highest in the major holiday periods (Christmas and Easter). Low-season prices can be 30% less than in the high season. High-season prices are quoted in this book, unless indicated otherwise.

All visitor centres produce free accommodation guides to their areas.

In Cities & Towns

Camping & Caravanning Caravan parks are thick on the ground and, except at peak times, you'll generally find space available. Camping is the cheapest type of shelter, with nightly costs for two at around $14 and slightly more for powered sites. Not surprisingly, many caravan parks are often intended more for caravanners (house trailers in the USA) than for campers, and space for tents can be limited.

Most Australian caravan parks are well kept and excellent value – almost all have hot showers, flush toilets and a laundry. Many have on-site vans that you can rent for the night, for around $35 for two. Cabins are also widely available; the beds are either separate from the living area or at least screened off, and many have their own tiny bathroom and toilet. Much less cramped than a caravan, they're usually fully equipped and ideal for families. Prices start at about $45.

Youth Hostels The Youth Hostels Association (YHA) has over 130 hostels, which provide accommodation in small dormitories and family, twin and even single rooms. The nightly charge is usually between $15 and $18 for members; most hostels also take nonmembers, who are charged an extra $3. Accommodation can usually be booked directly with the manager or through a Membership & Travel Centre – see the YHA handbook for details.

YHA is part of the International Youth Hostel Federation (IYHF; also known as HI, Hostelling International), so if you're a YHA member at home, you can use Australian hostels. A HI card (for nonmember visitors to Australia) costs $30. Australian residents can join at any state office or hostel for $47 per year. There's also introductory membership, where you pay an additional $3 per night at any hostel and after 10 nights receive full membership. The YHA's Accommodation Packs provide prepaid accommodation at a discount: $150/280 for 10/20 nights at any of the Australian YHA hostels.

To stay in a hostel you must have a sleeping bag sheet. These can usually be hired for $3, but it's cheaper to have your own. They're on sale at YHA offices and some larger hostels. All hostels have cooking and laundry facilities and a communal area, most have 24-hour access and the larger ones a secure luggage store. The maximum length of stay is generally five to seven days. All are nonsmoking.

The annual *YHA Accommodation & Discounts Guide*, available from all local YHA offices and from some overseas offices, has comprehensive details of all hostels and of the many attractive discounts (eg, transport and car hire) available to members.

The head office is at the Australian Youth Hostels Association (☎ 02-9565 1699, fax 9565 1325, ☒ www.yha.com.au), 10 Mallett St, Camperdown, NSW 2050. The Membership & Travel Centres in all state capitals are great sources of information and travel deals. State YHAs have activity groups that organise weekend activities based at hostels for walking, cycling, canoeing and so on.

Backpackers Hostels Backpackers hostels are plentiful and standards vary enormously. Some are run-down, inner-city hotels, generally pretty gloomy and depressing; others are former motels, with well-equipped units but minimal communal and cooking facilities. The best facilities are usually in purpose-built hostels with small rooms. Some hostels are large and impersonal – the best are usually those with an owner-manager.

With intense competition, many hostels offer a free first night, or free breakfasts. The busier hostels often have courtesy buses. Prices are typically from $12 to $18 per person per night for a dorm bed.

There are a couple of backpacker hostel organisations you might consider joining. VIP Backpacker Resorts has a large number of hostels in Australia and overseas. For $25 you'll receive 12 months' membership, which entitles you to a $1 discount on accommodation and varying discounts on transport, tours and activities. You can join at VIP hostels, Greyhound Pioneer terminals, or the larger agencies dealing in backpacker travel. Alternatively, contact the VIP office (☎ 07-3395 6111, fax 3395 6222, ☒ www.backpackers.com.au) at PO Box 600, Cannon Hill, Queensland 4170.

Nomads Backpackers has around 40 hostels in Australia. Membership ($25 for 12 months) entitles you to a range of discounts. Join at any participating hostel or travel agency, or by contacting Nomads (☎ 1800 819 883, fax 08-8224 0972, ☒ www .nomads-backpackers.com) at 288 North Terrace, Adelaide, SA 5000.

Guesthouses & B&Bs These are often in out-of-the way locations and may be restored miners' cottages, rambling old guesthouses or a simple bedroom in a family home. Tariffs are typically $50 to $100 for a double room.

Hotels Most modern hotels are in the major cities and are fairly to very expensive. Relatively few old hotels in the cities have rooms to rent; most in the country do, and are usually known as 'pubs'.

Although the building itself may be very handsome, rooms in pubs can be pretty plain and heating and cooling may be inadequate or nonexistent. Twin rooms with shared facilities cost around $25 to $35 (more with a private bathroom). You can also usually get substantial meals at reasonable prices.

Motels & Holiday Flats Motels are almost always modern places; each unit is self-contained and equipped with tea and coffee-making facilities and a small fridge. Almost every town has at least one; prices vary but most are at least $50 and singles are rarely much cheaper than doubles.

A holiday flat is much like a motel unit with a kitchen or cooking facilities, but you may need your own bedding. They're usually rented on a weekly basis, but daily rates may be available.

Other Possibilities An alternative to caravan parks is the many roadside rest areas where short-term camping is permitted.

On the Walk

Camping Many walks in this book involve camping in bush areas with minimal facilities. This is one of the outstanding highlights of bushwalking in Australia – far, far from any town and often under a sky littered with bright stars. Many camp sites in national parks have a pit (no flush) toilet and fireplace; in these circumstances you need to be self-sufficient with camping gear (including a portable stove and plenty of fuel) and food. In fact, stoves are mandatory in many areas where campfires are totally

GLENN VAN DER KNIJFF

Setting up camp on Mt Cobbler, Alpine National Park. Sites like this, with sweeping views and easy access to water, are a highlight of the Australian bushwalking experience.

banned. Water is often readily available in a nearby creek, or provided in a tank (with tap), but check with the national park people before you set out about current supplies and take a large container to save trips back and forth. See Responsible Walking earlier in this chapter for a discussion on how to camp with minimal impact on the environment.

Huts In parts of the Australian Alps simple huts, usually of timber, are open to walkers, strictly on a first-come, first-served basis (see Huts under Responsible Walking earlier). Along WA's Bibbulmun Track, camp sites are spaced a day's walk apart, equipped with a roofed three-sided shelter, toilet, water tank, and at some, a fireplace. Similar facilities, minus the shelter, are available along the Great South West Walk in Victoria. The Overland Track in Tasmania has substantial huts a day's walk apart. Unlike France, Italy, Switzerland, Britain and other European countries, there are no long-distance tracks where you can stay in a town, village or remote hostel each night, although most of the long-distance routes do begin, end or pass through a small town or two.

Other Options Some of the day walks described, particularly those in the Sydney and Melbourne Regions, can be done from a base, such as an adjacent national park camping ground or nearby town, where there is a choice of accommodation.

FOOD
Eating out can be one of the real highlights of Australia, a magnificent reflection of the country's fascinating multicultural character: Greek, Yugoslav, Italian, Lebanese, Vietnamese, Indian, Thai, Malaysian, Chinese, Polynesian and more.

Although there's no specifically Australian cuisine there's a huge variety of excellent locally produced, fresh food – fruit, vegetables, cheese, meat, fish. 'Bush' foods are unique, although mainly confined to restaurant menus – try braised kangaroo tail samosas, emu pâté, gum-leaf smoked venison, salad made from Warrigal greens.

Plenty of cafes and restaurants serve 'modern Australian' dishes that borrow heavily from a wide range of foreign cuisines, but have a definite local flavour. At these places Asian-inspired curries might share the menu with Mediterranean-inspired dishes.

Your Australian gourmet experience isn't complete without sampling some other items (depending on taste, of course). The meat pie is part of Australian culture. These vary from flaky pastry filled with tender meat with palate-tickling seasoning to dreadful envelopes of rubbery pastry around dubious stringy meat. In country towns, look for the local bakery – they're bound to produce their own on the premises. There you'll also find a tempting range of cakes and pastries, including vanilla slices (more flaky pastry sandwiching rich thick custard) and lamingtons (sponge rectangles coated with chocolate icing and coconut).

Even more a part of Australian food culture is Vegemite. This dark yeast extract, similar to British Marmite, looks and spreads like dark brown tar. Australians plaster Vegemite on bread and toast and are positively addicted to the stuff.

Where to Eat
The best value is to be found at modern, casual cafes where you can get an excellent two-course meal for under $20. Alternatively, most pubs provide either bistro meals, usually in the $10 to $15 range and served in the dining room, or counter meals, substantial if basic fare, for under $10 eaten in the public bar. Vegetarians are well catered for these days, either by vegetarian dishes at most cafes, or at dedicated restaurants, mostly found in the cities and large towns.

You'll find many restaurants advertising that they're BYO (Bring Your Own). This means they're not licensed to serve alcohol but you are permitted to bring your own – much cheaper than buying wine at restaurant prices. Most BYO restaurants have a small corkage charge – typically $1 to $2 per person.

Many cafes and restaurants do not allow smoking on the premises, while others have a no-smoking area. In SA it's illegal to smoke in any confined public area where food is consumed.

Outdoor food stalls and markets are quite common. The produce is usually excellent and good value. In the north, markets can also be excellent places to sample Asian cuisines in particular.

On the Walk

For overnight walks, the quantity of fresh food you can take depends on the weight you can carry and the weather – fresh food won't survive typical summer temperatures for long. Freeze-dried and packaged meals, including sauces to add to pasta, rice or pulses, are very widely available in outdoor gear shops, supermarkets, health food shops and ethnic food shops (particularly Asian).

Muesli (branded or in bulk from health food shops) is a good starter; dried fruit is plentiful and inexpensive, as are health/snack bars, or plain or sweet biscuits, for during the day. Packet soups are a useful stand-by, but decant them from the foil bag into a less bulky plastic bag beforehand.

Wild magazine often features articles on gourmet bush cooking, so it's worth checking current and past issues for the many delicious recipes. Look out for a copy of *The Lightweight Cooks* by George Driscoll & Avis Pearce, which has about 80 recipes that can be cooked on a single-burner stove.

DRINKS
Beer

The style of Australian beer will be fairly familiar to North Americans; it's also similar to UK lager, although it tastes like lemonade to the real-ale addict. It is invariably served deeply chilled.

There's a huge array of beers. The best known are XXXX (pronounced four-ex), Tooheys, Foster's, Carlton Draught and VB (Victoria Bitter). Then there are the lower-alcohol beers such as Foster's Light Ice, and heavier styles such as Tooheys Old Black Ale. The best beer is usually produced by

---

Swinging the Billy

This isn't some arcane, inhumane rite peculiar to Australia, but a time-honoured ritual for making a cup of tea in the bush. Sadly, it has suffered at the hands of the fall from favour of cooking over an open wood fire, and the appearance of the tea bag. But, it can still be practised with only one minor compromise – the use of a portable stove to boil the water. Tea bags just will not do – using them misses the whole purpose of the ritual.

A billy is a lidded aluminium cooking pot with a loop handle across the top. Traditionally, an essential piece of equipment for cooking over an open fire is a gallows – a pair of forked sticks on either side of the fire, with a strong cross beam (stick) resting in the forks. From the beam you dangle a couple of S-shaped iron hooks. The billy is hung from one of these over the fire.

As the water in the billy comes to the boil, the thirsty walker takes a small handful of tea leaves from the tea container and, with unerring aim, throws them into the billy. The billy is immediately deftly lifted from its hook, using a 'grabber' or billy lifter. Then, the handle is grasped firmly in one hand, arm fully extended by the side. Now, vigorously rotate your fully stretched arm, billy still in hand, several times. Finish swinging as the billy passes your leg (not in mid-air), and pour the steaming, perfectly brewed tea into a mug. By a miracle of centrifuge, the tea leaves should have sunk to the billy's bottom.

How many swings? Well, it depends on the phase of the moon, the direction of the wind, the walker's thirst and on any other relevant factors, such as the number of emus seen during the day. A fairly strong tea is best (Assam, for example), and it is traditionally drunk without milk, and either without sugar or with several spoonfuls of the stuff. The wood smoke imparts a distinctive flavour (not unlike a variety tea connoisseurs will know as Lapsang Souchong), and there's nothing like it for quenching a healthy thirst.

the smaller breweries, such as Cascade (Tasmania), Boag's (Tasmania), Coopers (SA) and Matilda Bay (WA). Small 'boutique' beers are plentiful all around the country and usually outstanding, eg, Hemp Premium Ale and Dogbolter, although they're more expensive than the big brands. For the homesick Irish, Guinness is often found on tap.

Standard beer normally contains around 5% alcohol, low-alcohol brews between 2% and 3.5%. Don't forget that people who drive under the influence of alcohol risk a heavy fine and the loss of their licence (see Car in the Getting Around chapter).

Wine

Australia has a great climate for wine producing and Australian wine has an excellent international reputation. The best known wine-growing regions are the Hunter Valley in NSW; the Barossa Valley, Coonawarra, McLaren Vale and Clare Valley in SA; Rutherglen/Milawa, the Yarra Valley, the Mornington Peninsula and the Geelong area in Victoria; and Margaret River in WA. There's even a winery (albeit a modest one) in Alice Springs and a few (such as Freycinet Vineyard) in Tasmania.

Wine is reasonably cheap and readily available. For $10 to $12 you can buy a perfectly acceptable bottle; $20 gets you something very good indeed. Cask wines (boxes containing a foil bag with a tap) are excellent value for casual drinking – a better-quality 4L cask costs around $15.

Nonalcoholic Drinks

Bottled water and fruit juices are inexpensive and plentiful; pineapple juice is a sensation if you've never tried the Australian variety, and dark grape juice also has a very distinctive flavour.

On the Walk

Clearly there's a very low limit to the number of bottles or cans you can carry on an overnight walk, although just one may be very welcome at the end of the day.

So the alternative is – well, water. As discussed in the Health & Safety chapter, you may need to boil or treat water, even in remote areas. Carry tea and/or coffee and sugar in small plastic containers. Small packets of UHT (long-life) milk will keep overnight once opened. There are a host of powdered drinks on the market, but tea and coffee are just as thirst quenching.

Health & Safety

Keeping healthy during your walking holiday depends on your predeparture preparations, your daily health care while travelling and how you handle any medical problem that crops up. While the potential problems can seem rather alarming, few travellers experience anything more than an upset stomach. The following sections are recommended reading before you go.

PREDEPARTURE PLANNING
Medical Cover
Under reciprocal arrangements, residents of the UK, New Zealand, the Netherlands, Sweden and Italy are entitled to free or subsidised medical and hospital treatment under Medicare, Australia's compulsory national health insurance scheme. To enrol, you need to show your passport and healthcare card or certificate from your own country; you are then given a Medicare card. Residents of Ireland can present their passport at a public hospital and be given free medical treatment.

Visits to private doctors are also claimable under Medicare. Clinics that advertise 'bulk billing' are the easiest to use as they charge Medicare direct. For more information, phone Medicare on ☎ 13 2011.

Health Insurance
Make sure you have adequate health insurance. For a discussion of travel insurance, see Visas & Documents in the Facts for the Walker chapter.

Immunisations
No immunisations are required for entry to Australia, but before leaving home ensure you're up to date with routine vaccinations. Those for diphtheria, tetanus and polio are usually given in childhood and a booster is required every 10 years.

First Aid
It's a good idea at any time to know the appropriate responses to a major accident or illness, and this is particularly important if you'll be walking for some time in a remote area. Consider doing a recognised basic first-aid course or adding a first-aid manual to your first-aid kit. Although detailed first-aid instruction is outside the scope of this guidebook, some basic points are given under Major Accidents later in this chapter. Preventing illness or an accident is just as important (see Staying Healthy and the boxed text 'Safety on the Walk – Basic Rules' for more advice). Also make sure that you know how to summon help should a major accident or illness befall you or someone with you (see the Rescue & Evacuation section later in this chapter).

Other Preparations
It's a good idea to have a dental checkup before you leave – toothache in the bush with solace a couple of days or more away can be miserable. If you wear glasses, take a spare pair and your prescription.

If you need a particular medicine, take enough to last the trip. Take part of the packaging showing the generic name, rather than the brand, to simplify getting replacements. It also helps to have a legible prescription or letter from your doctor to prove that you legally use the medication, to avoid problems at customs.

For more advice on preparing for a walking holiday, see the Physical Preparation section in the Facts for the Walker chapter.

Travel Health Guides
If you are planning to be in remote areas for some time, consider taking a more detailed health guide. Lonely Planet's handy pocket-sized *Healthy Travel: Australia, New Zealand & the Pacific* is packed with useful information including pretrip planning, emergency first-aid, immunisation and disease information, and what to do if you fall ill. *Travel with Children* from Lonely Planet gives excellent practical advice on travel health for younger children.

Medical Kit Check List

You should consider including these items in your medical kit – consult your pharmacist for brands available in your country.

First-Aid Supplies
- [ ] adhesive tape
- [ ] blister plasters
- [ ] butterfly closure strips
- [ ] crepe bandage
- [ ] elasticised support bandage – for knees and ankles
- [ ] gauze swabs
- [ ] nonadhesive dressings
- [ ] scissors
- [ ] sterile alcohol wipes
- [ ] sticking plasters (Band-Aids)
- [ ] triangular bandages and safety pins
- [ ] tweezers

Medications
- [ ] anti-diarrhoea and anti-nausea drugs
- [ ] antibiotics – consider including these if you're travelling well off the beaten track; see your doctor, as they must be prescribed, and carry the prescription with you
- [ ] antifungal cream or powder – for fungal skin infections and thrush
- [ ] antihistamines – for allergies (eg, hay fever), to ease the itch from insect bites or stings, and to prevent motion sickness
- [ ] antiseptic (such as povidone-iodine) – for cuts and grazes
- [ ] calamine lotion, sting relief spray or aloe vera – to ease irritation from sunburn and insect bites or stings
- [ ] cold and flu tablets, throat lozenges and nasal decongestant
- [ ] painkillers (eg, aspirin or paracetamol, acetaminophen in the USA) – for pain and fever
- [ ] rehydration mixture – to prevent dehydration, eg, due to severe diarrhoea; particularly important when travelling with children

Odds & Ends
- [ ] antibacterial preparation for hand washing
- [ ] eye drops
- [ ] insect repellent
- [ ] sunscreen and lip balm
- [ ] water purification tablets or iodine

Online Resources

The comprehensive Bushwalking in Australia Web site (💻 www.bushwalking.org.au) has information on trip planning and first aid for Australian conditions. Emergency Medicine Australia (💻 www.emergencymedicine.com.au) has first-aid information, including a section on snake and spider bites.

STAYING HEALTHY
Hygiene

Make a point of washing your hands, especially before preparing food and eating. There are a number of antibacterial preparations available in outdoor gear shops, and these can be a wise investment. In areas where detergents are not allowed, tea-tree oil is a useful substitute.

Take particular care to dispose carefully of all toilet waste when you are on a walk; see Toilets under Responsible Walking in the Facts for the Walker chapter.

Nutrition

Nutrition should never be a problem in Australia. Nevertheless, once you've been walking for a week or more, you'll find your appetite is greater; increasing your intake of energy-giving carbohydrates (pasta, rice, bread) with the evening meal isn't a bad idea. The vast range of readily available fruit and vegetables should ensure a balanced diet.

Food

Stringent food hygiene regulations are in force in Australia so you should feel confident that the food you eat in cafes and such places is safe. Nevertheless, be circumspect with shellfish, which is popular everywhere.

Water

Tap water in Australia is safe to drink, except possibly in some Outback towns that rely on bore water (from underground sources), which may be unfit for human consumption. Here, make sure you use the stored rainwater the locals are drinking.

Always beware of natural sources of water. A gurgling creek in the bush may look clear but the risk of infection from human or animal sources is real (see Responsible

Walking in the Facts for the Walker chapter). For a discussion of giardiasis, see Infectious Diseases later in this chapter.

Water Purification The simplest way of purifying water is to boil it vigorously for at least five minutes. For large quantities it's more practical to use chlorine or iodine, in powder, tablet or liquid form, available from outdoor gear suppliers and pharmacies. Follow the recommended quantity and allow the water to stand for the correct length of time. Iodine is a more effective purifier than chlorine, but too much iodine (regular use for several weeks) can be harmful. Chemical solutions may not work at all if the water is dirty.

Consider buying a water filter for a long trip. Total filters remove all parasites, bacteria and viruses and make water safe to drink, although they are expensive (from $150), complicated and heavy. Simple filters, such as a nylon mesh bag, remove only dirt and larger foreign bodies, so chemical solutions are more effective. Read the specifications so that you know exactly what the filter removes and what it leaves behind.

Common Ailments
Fatigue More injuries happen later in the day than earlier when you're fresh. You should never set out on a walk that is beyond your capabilities on the day; if you feel below par, have a day off. Although tiredness can simply be a nuisance on an easy walk, it can be life-threatening on narrow exposed ridges or in bad weather. Don't try to break records – take rests every hour or two and have a half-hour lunch break. Towards the end of the day, moderate your pace and be aware that your concentration is probably wearing out. During the day replace expended energy with energy-sustaining nuts, dried fruit and chocolate.

Blisters This problem can be avoided. Make sure your walking boots are well worn in before your visit. At the very least, wear them on a few short walks before tackling longer outings. They should fit comfortably with enough room to move your toes; boots that are too big or too small will cause blisters. Similarly be sure that socks fit properly, and wear socks specifically made for walkers; even then, check to make sure that there are no seams across the widest part of your foot. Wet and muddy socks can also cause blisters, so always pack a spare pair. Keep your toenails clipped but not too short. If you feel a blister coming on, treat it immediately. Apply a sticking plaster, or preferably a special blister plaster, which acts as a second skin; follow the maker's instructions for replacement.

Knee Pain Many walkers feel the strain on long steep descents. You can't eliminate stress on the knee joints, but it can be reduced by taking shorter steps with your legs slightly bent and ensuring that your heel hits the ground before the rest of your foot. Tubular bandages or hi-tech, strap-on supports may help.

Walking poles are very effective at taking some of the weight off the knees, although you may need to adjust the length for maximum effectiveness. Poles also help to maintain balance on scree slopes and rocky ground and when crossing creeks.

MEDICAL PROBLEMS & TREATMENT
Environmental Hazards
There's no doubt that walkers are at risk from some environmental hazards. The risks, however, can be significantly reduced by using common sense.

Asthma & Hay Fever Australia has one of the world's highest incidences of asthma, the main culprits being air-borne allergens such as dust and pollen, which are also hazards for hay fever sufferers. The main danger periods are from May to late November in the south and April, May and October in the north. Inhalers (or puffers) are available without prescription at pharmacies.

Sun Protection against the sun should always be taken very seriously in Australia. Particularly during beach walks and in dry country, sunburn occurs rapidly. Slap on the

Warning

Self-diagnosis and treatment can be risky, so you should always seek medical help. The warden or owner of a B&B, hostel or hotel, or the local tourist office can usually recommend a local doctor or clinic.

We have used generic rather than brand names for drugs throughout this chapter – check with a pharmacist for brands which are locally available.

sunscreen (at least SPF 15+) and a barrier cream for your nose and lips, wear a broad-brimmed hat, cover as much skin as possible in loose clothing and protect your eyes with good-quality sunglasses with UV lenses. If you do get burnt, calamine lotion, aloe vera or other commercial sunburn relief preparations will soothe the discomfort.

Heat Treat heat with respect! Take time to adjust to high temperatures, drink sufficient liquids and don't do anything too physically demanding until you're acclimatised. See also the Hot, Dry Country section later in this chapter.

Prickly Heat This is an itchy rash caused by excessive perspiration trapped under the skin. It usually strikes people who have just arrived in a hot climate. Keeping cool, bathing often, drying the skin and using a mild talcum or prickly heat powder, or re-treating to an air-conditioned room may help.

Dehydration & Heat Exhaustion Dehydration is a potentially dangerous and generally preventable condition caused by excessive fluid loss. Sweating and inadequate fluid intake are the commonest causes among walkers; other causes are diarrhoea, vomiting and high fever – see Diarrhoea later.

Early symptoms are weakness, thirst and passing small amounts of very concentrated urine, followed by drowsiness, dizziness or fainting on standing up, and finally, coma.

It's easy to forget how much fluid you are losing through perspiration while you're walking, particularly if a breeze is drying your skin quickly. Maintain a good fluid intake – the minimum recommended is 3L per day, or more than 4L in hot, dry country (see also Hot, Dry Country later).

Dehydration and salt deficiency can cause heat exhaustion. Salt deficiency is characterised by fatigue, lethargy, headaches, giddiness and muscle cramps; salt tablets are generally unnecessary – just add extra salt to your food.

Heatstroke This serious, occasionally fatal, condition occurs if the body's effective heat-regulating mechanism breaks down and the body temperature rises to a dangerous level. Continuous prolonged exposure to high temperatures and insufficient fluids can make you vulnerable to heatstroke.

The symptoms are feeling unwell, sweating little or not at all, and a high body temperature (39°C to 41°C, or 102°F to 106°F). Skin may be cool and clammy initially, but when sweating has ceased, the skin becomes flushed and red. Severe, throbbing headaches, nausea and vomiting and lack of coordination will also occur, and the sufferer may be confused or aggressive. Eventually the victim will become delirious or convulse. Hospitalisation is essential; meantime, get the victim out of the sun, remove clothing, elevate the feet, cover with a wet sheet or towel and fan continually. Give fluids if the person is conscious.

Hypothermia Hypothermia occurs when the body loses heat faster than it can produce it and the core temperature of the body falls. It is a real and ever-present threat for walkers – people do die from it. In the mountains, always be prepared for the onset of cold, wet and windy conditions, no matter how warm and clear the weather when you set out, and always carry spare, high-energy food (see What to Bring under Planning in the Facts for the Walker chapter).

The decline from very cold to dangerously cold can happen with frightening speed if wet clothing, fatigue and hunger are combined with windy conditions. If the weather deteriorates, take precautions immediately: put on extra layers of warm clothing, a windproof and/or waterproof jacket, plus a wool or fleece hat and gloves. Have something to eat and make sure everyone in your group is fit, feeling well and alert.

Symptoms of hypothermia are, in approximate order of appearance: lethargy, exhaustion, shivering, cold extremities, blue or grey pallor, stumbling and loss of fine motor control, dizzy spells, slurred speech, irrational or violent behaviour (such as trying to take off protective clothes), violent bursts of energy and numb fingers and toes.

To treat mild hypothermia, first get the victim to the best available shelter from the wind and/or rain (pitch tents if necessary), remove their clothing if it's wet and replace it with dry, warm garments. Wrap the person in a sleeping bag or space blanket or large bivouac bag and insulate then from the ground. Have other members of your group sit or lie as close to the sufferer as possible. Do not rub victims: instead, allow them to slowly warm themselves. Give them warm, sweet fluids (*never* alcohol), and some high-energy, easily digestible food. Early recognition and treatment of mild hypothermia is the only way to prevent severe hypothermia, which is a life-threatening condition.

Infectious Diseases

Diarrhoea Simple things like a change of water, food or climate can all cause a mild bout of diarrhoea, but a few rushed toilet trips with no other symptoms is not indicative of a major problem. More serious diarrhoea is caused by infectious agents transmitted by faecal contamination of food or water, by using contaminated utensils or directly from one person's hand to another. Paying particular attention to personal hygiene, and taking care of what you eat, are important in avoiding diarrhoea.

Dehydration is the main danger, particularly in children or the elderly, as it can occur quite quickly. Fluid replacement is the most important response. Weak, black tea with a little sugar, soda water, or flat soft drinks diluted 50% with water are all good. With severe diarrhoea, a rehydrating solution is preferable to replace minerals and salts lost. Commercially available oral rehydration

Everyday Health
Normal body temperature is up to 37°C (98.6°F); more than 2°C (4°F) higher indicates a high fever. The normal adult pulse rate is 60 to 100 beats per minute (children 80 to 100, babies 100 to 140). As a general rule the pulse increases about 20 beats per minute for each 1°C (2°F) rise in fever. Respiration (breathing) rate is also an indicator of illness. Count the number of breaths per minute: between 12 and 20 is normal for adults and older children (up to 30 for younger children and 40 for babies). People with a high fever or serious respiratory illness breathe more quickly than normal. More than 40 shallow breaths per minute may indicate pneumonia.

salts (ORS) are very useful; add them to boiled water. In an emergency you can use a solution of six teaspoons of sugar and a half-teaspoon of salt to 1L of boiled water. You need to drink at least the same volume of fluid that you are losing in bowel movements and vomiting. If you pass small amounts of concentrated urine, you need to drink more. Keep drinking small amounts often and stick to a bland diet as you recover.

Gut-paralysing drugs such as diphenoxylate or loperamide can be used to bring relief from the symptoms, but they don't cure the problem. Only use these drugs if you don't have access to toilets, eg, if you *must* travel; they are not recommended for children under 12 years, or if you have a high fever or are severely dehydrated.

Seek medical advice if you pass blood or mucus, are feverish, or suffer persistent or severe diarrhoea.

Giardiasis This intestinal disorder is contracted by drinking water contaminated with the Giardia parasite. The symptoms are stomach cramps, nausea, a bloated stomach, watery and foul-smelling diarrhoea, and frequent gas. Giardiasis can appear several weeks after you have been exposed to the parasite. The symptoms may disappear for a few days and then return; this can go on for several weeks. You should seek medical advice if you think you have giardiasis, but where this is not possible, tinidazole or metronidazole are the recommended drugs. Treatment is a 2g single dose of tinidazole or 250mg of metronidazole three times daily for five to 10 days.

Fungal Infections Sweating liberally, probably washing less than usual and going longer without a change of clothes mean that long-distance walkers risk picking up a fungal infection, which, while an unpleasant irritant, presents no danger.

Fungal infections are encouraged by moisture, so wear loose and comfortable clothes, wash whenever you can and dry yourself thoroughly. Try to expose the infected area to air or sunlight as much as possible and apply an antifungal cream or powder like tolnaftate.

Tetanus This disease is caused by a germ that lives in soil and in the faeces of animals, particularly horses. It enters the body via breaks in the skin. The first symptom may be discomfort in swallowing, or stiffening of the jaw and neck; this is followed by painful convulsions of the jaw and whole body. The disease can be fatal. It can be prevented by vaccination, so make sure you are up to date with this vaccination before you leave home.

Insect-Borne Diseases

Ross River Fever This viral disease, properly known as epidemic polyarthritis, is transmitted by some species of mosquito. The disease is more common in northern Australia where outbreaks are most likely to occur in January and February. Cases have also been recorded in south-west Western Australia and in coastal NSW. Flu-like symptoms (muscle and joint pain, rashes, fever, headache and tiredness) are possible indicators, but blood tests are necessary for a positive diagnosis. Risk of infection for travellers is usually very low.

Unfortunately, there is no treatment for Ross River fever, although the symptoms can be relieved. The symptoms do not usually last for more than a few months, but some people still feel the effects, mainly chronic fatigue, for some years. Avoiding mosquito bites is the best preventive.

Traumatic Injuries

Sprains Ankle and knee sprains are common injuries, particularly among walkers crossing rough ground. To help prevent ankle sprains, you should wear boots that have adequate ankle support. If you do suffer a sprain, immobilise the joint with a firm bandage; relieve pain and swelling by keeping it elevated for the first 24 hours and, where possible, by applying ice or cold water to the swollen joint. Distribute the contents of the pack among your group. Take simple painkillers to ease the discomfort. If the sprain is mild, you may be able to continue your walk after a couple of days. For more severe sprains, seek medical attention as an X-ray may be needed to find out whether a bone has been broken.

Major Accidents Falling or having something fall on you, resulting in head injuries or fractures, is always possible, especially if you're crossing steep slopes or unstable terrain. Here is some basic advice on what to do if a major accident happens; detailed first-aid instruction is outside the scope of this guidebook (see the First Aid section earlier for more advice). If someone suffers a bad fall:

- Make sure you and your companions are not in danger
- Assess the injured person's condition
- Stabilise any injuries, such as bleeding wounds or broken bones
- Seek medical help – see the Rescue & Evacuation section later

If the person is unconscious, immediately check their breathing – clear the airway if it is blocked – and check their pulse by feeling the side of the neck rather than the wrist. If there is a pulse but no breathing, start mouth-to-mouth resuscitation immediately. In these circumstances the patient should be moved as little as possible in case the neck or back is broken. Keep the person warm by covering with a space blanket, sleeping bag or dry clothing; insulate from the ground if possible.

Check for wounds and broken bones; if the victim is conscious ask where pain is felt. Otherwise gently inspect the body *in situ* as far as you feel you can with safety. Control any bleeding by applying firm pressure to the wound. Bleeding from the nose or ear may indicate a fractured skull. Don't give the person anything by mouth, especially if they are unconscious. Anyone who has been knocked unconscious should be watched closely. Note any signs of deterioration (eg, change in breathing patterns) to report to the rescuers.

Indications of a fracture (broken bone) are pain, swelling and discolouration, loss of function or deformity of a limb. Unless you know exactly what you're doing, you shouldn't try to straighten an obviously displaced broken bone. To protect from further injury, immobilise a nondisplaced fracture by splinting it; if the thigh bone is broken, strap it to the good leg to hold it in place. Check the splinted limb frequently to ensure the splint hasn't cut off circulation. Broken ribs are painful but usually heal by themselves and do not need splinting. If breathing becomes difficult, or the person coughs up blood, a lung may be punctured, so medical attention should be sought urgently. Simple fractures take several weeks to heal and may not require urgent medical attention.

Fractures associated with open wounds (compound fractures) require more urgent treatment than simple fractures as there is a risk of infection. Dislocations – where the bone has come out of the joint – are very painful, and should be set as soon as possible by a medical professional. Attempting to replace a dislocation yourself can lead to soft tissue and nerve damage.

Internal injuries are more difficult to detect, and cannot usually be treated in the bush. Watch for shock, a specific medical condition associated with failure to maintain circulating blood volume. Signs include a rapid pulse and cold, clammy extremities. A person in shock requires urgent medical attention.

Cuts & Scratches

Any cut or graze should be washed thoroughly and treated with an antiseptic such

as povidone-iodine. Dry wounds heal more quickly, so avoid bandages and dressing strips, unless required to control bleeding, as they inhibit drying. Infection is present if the skin margins become red, painful, swollen and hot to touch. More serious infection can cause swelling of the whole limb and of the lymph glands, and a fever may develop; medical attention should be obtained immediately.

Burns

Immerse the burnt area in cold water as soon as possible, then cover it with a clean, dry sterile dressing. Keep this in place with plasters for a day or so in the case of a small, mild burn, but longer for more extensive injuries. Medical help should be sought for severe and extensive burns.

Bites & Stings

Bees & Wasps These are usually painful rather than dangerous. However, anyone allergic to these bites can suffer severe breathing difficulties and will need urgent medical attention. Calamine lotion or a commercial sting relief spray will ease discomfort, and ice packs will reduce the pain and swelling.

Leeches Leeches are almost inseparable from damp rainforest; they attach themselves to your skin to suck your blood. Salt or a lighted cigarette end will dislodge them. Do not pull them off, as the bite is then more likely to become infected. Clean it and apply pressure if the bite is bleeding.

See the boxed text 'Beat the Leech' in the Queensland chapter for some handy tips on outsmarting leeches.

Snakes To minimise your chances of being bitten, wear boots, socks and long trousers when walking through undergrowth where snakes may be present. Don't put your hands into holes and crevices, and be careful when collecting firewood as snakes like to hide among dry branches.

Snake bites do not cause instantaneous death and antivenins are usually available. Immediately wrap the bitten limb tightly, beginning at the bite area and moving up to cover as much of the limb as possible, then down again if the length of the bandage permits. Attach a splint to immobilise the limb. Keep the victim still and calm and seek medical assistance. It may help if you can describe the offending reptile, but ensuring that venom remains on the victim's skin or clothing (eg, by covering the bite site with a sticking plaster before bandaging) is a more reliable method. The trusty old methods of tourniquets and sucking out the poison have now been comprehensively discredited.

Spiders & Scorpions Most Australian spiders bite but very few are dangerous, although the funnel-web spider is widespread and extremely poisonous, and a redback bite is potentially serious. If bitten by a funnel-web, treat as for snake bite and seek urgent medical attention (it is a good idea to capture a specimen for identification if possible). If bitten by a red-back, apply ice to the area (it is not necessary to bandage as for snake bite) and seek medical attention immediately. For other spider bites (eg, white-tail or huntsman), ice the area and seek medical attention if symptoms persist or worsen.

Scorpion stings are notoriously painful but not very venomous compared with overseas species. Scorpions like sheltering in boots or clothing.

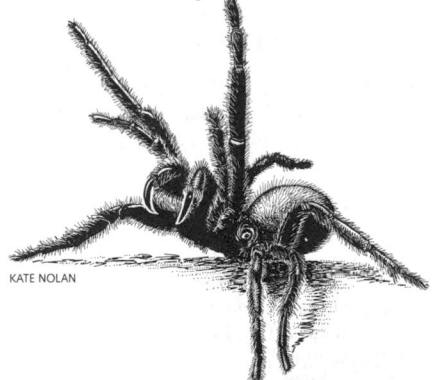

KATE NOLAN

The funnel web is one of Australia's – and the world's – most deadly spiders.

Ticks Ticks can cause skin infections and more serious diseases, so you should always check all over your body if you have been walking through a potentially tick-infested area. They are most active from spring to autumn, and usually lurk in overhanging vegetation.

If you find a tick, press down around its head with tweezers, grab the head and gently pull upwards. Avoid pulling the rear of the body as this may squeeze the tick's gut contents through the attached mouth parts into your skin, increasing the risk of infection and disease. Smearing chemicals on the tick will not dislodge it and is not recommended.

Women's Health
Gynaecological Problems Antibiotic use, synthetic underwear, sweating and contraceptive pills can lead to fungal vaginal infections (thrush), especially when travelling in hot climates. Fungal infections are characterised by a rash, itch and discharge and are usually treated by nystatin, miconazole or clotrimazole pessaries or vaginal cream. If these are not available, a vinegar or lemon-juice douche can also help. Maintaining good personal hygiene, eating natural yoghurt and wearing loose-fitting clothes and cotton underwear may help prevent these infections.

Urinary Tract Infection Cystitis, or inflammation of the bladder, is a common condition in women. Symptoms include burning when urinating and having to urinate frequently and urgently. Blood can sometimes be passed in the urine. Sexual activity with a new partner or with a partner who has been away for a while can trigger an infection.

Drinking plenty of fluids may resolve the problem. Single dose (nonantibiotic) treatments may be effective in the early stages of mild cystitis. If symptoms persist, you need to seek medical attention because a simple infection can spread to the kidneys, causing a more severe illness.

SAFETY ON THE WALK
By taking a few simple precautions, you'll reduce significantly the odds of getting into

Safety on the Walk – Basic Rules

- Allow plenty of time to complete a walk before dark, particularly when daylight hours are shorter.
- Don't overestimate your capabilities. Study the route carefully, noting the point of no return (where it takes less time to continue than to turn back). Identify escape routes in case you need to abandon the walk. Monitor your progress against the time estimated for the walk and keep an eye on the weather.
- Be aware of, and prepared for, any special demands the route makes, eg, rock scrambling or river crossings.
- Unless you're very experienced, it's wise not to walk alone. Always leave details of your intended route, the number of people in your group and expected return time, with someone responsible before you set off, and let them know when you return.
- Before setting off, make sure you have the relevant map, compass, whistle, spare clothing, water-proof matches, adequate food and water, and that you know the local weather forecast for the next 24 hours.
- If you do get lost, remain in a sheltered place and signal with a whistle or torch. See the Rescue & Evacuation section at the end of this chapter for standard emergency signals.

trouble; these are listed in the boxed text 'Safety on the Walk – Basic Rules'. A list of the clothes and equipment you should take on a walk appears in under What to Bring in the Facts for the Walker chapter.

Crossing Rivers

Sudden downpours can turn a small creek into a raging torrent very quickly. If you're in any doubt about the safety of a crossing, look for a safer passage upstream or wait; if the rain is short-lived it should subside quickly. If you decide it's essential to cross (late in the day, for example), try to find a wide shallow stretch of the river/creek rather than a bend. Take off your trousers and socks, but keep boots on – your feet could easily be injured on the creek bed. Put dry, warm clothes and a towel near the top of your pack. Undo the chest strap and hip belt of your pack and secure them out of the way, in case you have to off-load the pack in deep water. Use walking poles or go arm in arm with a companion, holding at the wrist, and cross side-on to the flow, taking short steps.

Lightning

If a storm brews, avoid exposed areas. Lightning seeks out crests, lone trees, small depressions, gullies, caves, hut doorways and wet ground. If you are caught out in the open, curl up as tightly as possible with your feet together and keep a layer of insulation between you and the ground. Put metal objects such as framed backpacks and walking poles well clear of you.

Hot, Dry Country

Several walks in this book are in areas where it's usually hot and (in north-western Victoria and northern New South Wales) very dry between mid-November and early March (late spring to early autumn). It's best to steer clear of these areas during these months and plan your visit for winter and spring.

However, if you do visit arid areas in hot weather, plan your days to avoid walking between about 10 am and 4 pm. Drink as much as you can (more than 4L per day when walking), and use the colour of your urine as a guide: if it's clear, you're probably drinking enough, but if it's dark you need to drink more. People who first arrive in a hot climate may not feel thirsty when they should; the body and 'thirst mechanisms' often need a few days to adjust. Wear a broad-brimmed hat, sunglasses and cool, loose-fitting clothes. Generally moderate your walking pace and rest briefly and often.

Surviving a Bushfire

Bushfires occur every summer in national parks and bushland areas. Although the chances of getting caught are slight, it's wise to be familiar with the precautions.

Before leaving on a walk during summer, check the weather report; fire danger warnings are usually publicised by national parks agencies, at visitor centres and possibly on Web sites. Remember that on Total Fire Ban days, even the use of a fuel stove is banned.

If you are caught in a fire, don't start running unless there's a clear escape route. Remember that fire travels faster uphill than downhill.

Seek shelter in a creek, wet gully, roadside drainage line, deep wheel rut, under a concrete bridge, in a rocky outcrop, an open area with little or no vegetation or a recently burnt area. Do not enter still water as there's a danger of being boiled alive. Clear the area around your shelter of leaves, twigs or flammable material. Cover exposed skin with clothing (preferably woollen), soft earth or anything that will give protection from the heat. Keep low and breathe air close to the ground where it's cooler and there's less smoke. Don't leave the shelter until the fire has passed.

The chances of surviving an intense fire without shelter are minimal. In this case, try to move away from the hottest part of the fire. As a last resort, walk briskly through the least intense heat and flames to a burnt area.

Don't drive along a road obscured by fire and smoke, and don't leave your vehicle either. Park as far as possible from any flammable material. Close all windows and vents and turn on the headlights. Lie on the floor and cover yourself with a blanket or any cloth that will shield you from the heat. Stay in the car until the fire has passed. If you must continue, drive slowly with headlights on and watch out for fallen trees, firefighting vehicles and firefighters.

Communications & Equipment

Mobile Phones Mobile (cell) phones don't work unless you have line of sight to a phone tower – highly unlikely in remote areas, but possible closer to a town. However, the recently established Code Division Multiple Access (CDMA) network offers improved coverage in regional and rural areas, and clear reception in rugged terrain. Unfortunately, the network is unlikely to be accessible to phones purchased outside the country.

There's also the risk of the battery going flat, and of losing the thing anyway. Even if you do establish contact, mobiles should be used to summon assistance *only* for severe injuries or illness where immediate help is a matter of life and death. If you do decide to take a mobile phone into the bush, ask at the local ranger station whether you will be in a useable range.

GPS Receivers Global Positioning System receivers use microwave signals from satellites to accurately fix the user's position on the ground. They are fallible and expensive, and are not substitutes for a map and compass. Dense vegetation and nearby mountains can render them almost useless in exactly the type of country where navigation could be tricky. Several types are available in Australian bushwalking gear shops (from around $300). Considerations to weigh up before buying or using one in the bush include: does the unit offer Australian map grid coordinates, is the unit right up to date, and can you understand the manual? While GPS receivers may be useful for extended trips in remote, poorly mapped country, all the walks in this book are along recognised routes for which adequate maps are available.

Emergency Beacons Emergency Position Indicating Radio Beacons (EPIRB) transmit a signal when activated that is picked up by a satellite, which then transmits the beacon's position to an emergency service. Emergency satellite beacons are not frequently used by walkers in Australia. However, after a series of fatal accidents, the Kosciuszko National Park management now hires out emergency beacons from its visitor centres, as do some outdoor gear shops. (See Information under Kosciuszko National Park in the NSW chapter for more details.)

Rescue & Evacuation

If someone in your group is injured or falls ill and can't move, leave somebody with the injured person while another party member, or a pair, goes for help, taking clear written details of the location (a grid reference of at least eight figures), condition of the victim and helicopter landing conditions. If there are only two of you, leave the injured person with as much warm clothing, food and water as it's sensible to spare, plus a whistle and torch. Mark the position with something conspicuous – an orange bivvy bag, or perhaps a large stone cross on the ground.

If you need to call for help, use the internationally recognised emergency signals. Give six short signals (whistle blasts, shouts or light flashes) at 10-second intervals, followed by a one-minute pause. Repeat the sequence until you get a response. If the responder knows the signals, this will be three signals at 20-second intervals, followed by a one-minute pause and a repetition of the same sequence.

Be ready to explain where the accident occurred, how many people are injured and the injuries sustained. If a helicopter needs to come in, describe the terrain and weather conditions at the place of the accident.

Search & Rescue Organisations Search and rescue operations in Australia are the responsibility of the police force in each state, with the assistance of various professional and voluntary organisations. The latter usually include experienced and trained bushwalkers. To obtain help, call ☎ 000 from any telephone and the operator will connect you with the police.

In NSW only, you can contact Bushwalkers Wilderness Rescue, a community service provided by the Confederation of Bushwalking Clubs, a member squad of the NSW Volunteer Rescue Association; call the Rescue Pager ☎ 016020 #277321.

Helicopter Rescue & Evacuation The conventional signals to helicopter crews are, standing face-on to the aircraft:

- Arms up in the shape of a letter 'V' means 'I/We need help'
- Arms in a straight diagonal line (one arm of a letter X) means 'All OK'

To land, a helicopter needs a cleared space of 25m x 25m, with a flat landing pad area of 6m x 6m. It will fly into the wind when landing. In extreme emergencies, where there's nowhere to land, a person or harness might be lowered. Take extreme care to avoid the rotors when approaching a landed helicopter.

Getting There & Away

AIR

Australia is a long way from most of the rest of the world, so flying is the only practical way of getting there. Competition between the many airlines serving the country is fierce and all kinds of fares are available. Flights are often heavily booked, particularly at popular times of the year such as midsummer, so you need to plan well ahead. The high season generally coincides with summer (December to February) and the low season with winter (June to August).

Of the several international airports, Sydney and Melbourne are the busiest, although many flights from Asia, Europe and New Zealand go directly to Perth. The other international gateways are Adelaide, Darwin, Cairns and Brisbane; Hobart is linked only to New Zealand. Surprisingly, you can't fly directly to Canberra, the national capital, from overseas. Sydney airport is chaotic and flights are frequently delayed. All other major airports (with spacious modern terminals) operate smoothly and there are good transport links to the city centres.

Both Australian airlines, Qantas and Ansett, operate from Europe, North America and New Zealand to all the Australian gateway airports.

The fares quoted in this book are simply a guide to the scale of costs involved. They are approximate and based on the rates advertised by travel agents at the time of going to press. The precise timing of the high and low seasons varies from airline to airline; as a guide, low can mean April to June, and high may be July to September and December to January. Quoted fares do not necessarily suggest a recommendation for the carrier.

Buying Tickets

The plane ticket will probably be the single most expensive item in your budget, and buying it can be an intimidating experience. There's a bewildering array of fares, alluring airline ads and dozens of agents offering attractive deals; a few hours surveying the market is time well spent. Start early – some of the cheapest tickets have to be bought months in advance, and some popular flights sell out early. Ads in newspapers and magazines are useful – watch for special offers. Phone a few travel agents for bargains. There are several specialising in travel to Australia; find out fares, routes, the duration of stopovers and any restrictions on the various tickets. There are significant differences in prices between airlines – generally, the most well known are the most expensive. Airlines themselves can supply information on routes and timetables, but usually don't sell the cheapest tickets.

Don't be pushed into buying a ticket by over-eager agents, and avoid airlines with bad safety records and any routes that involve interminable waits at awful airports. If you are travelling from the UK or the USA, you will probably find that the cheapest flights are advertised by obscure 'bucket

> ### Warning
>
> The information in this chapter is particularly vulnerable to change – prices for international travel are volatile, routes are introduced and cancelled, schedules change, rules are amended, special deals come and go. Airlines and governments seem to take a perverse pleasure in making price structures and regulations as complicated as possible: you should check directly with the airline or travel agent to make sure you understand how a fare (and any ticket you may buy) works. In addition, the travel industry is highly competitive and there are many lurks and perks.
>
> The upshot of this is that you should get quotes and advice from as many airlines and travel agents as possible before you part with your hard-earned cash. The details given in this chapter should be regarded only as pointers and cannot be any substitute for your own careful, up-to-date research.

shops'. Many such firms are honest and solvent, but there are rogues who will take your money and disappear, to reopen elsewhere a month or two later under a new name. If you feel suspicious about a firm, especially if it insists on cash in advance, go somewhere else. There's much to be said for the safety of a better-known travel agent. Firms such as STA Travel, which has offices worldwide, Trailfinders in the UK, Council Travel in the USA or Travel CUTS in Canada are not going to disappear overnight, and offer good prices to most destinations.

Once you have the ticket, ring the airline to confirm that you are actually booked on the flight. Keep a note of the ticket number, the flight number and other details separately. This will help with getting a replacement if the ticket is lost or stolen. It's sensible to buy travel insurance as early as possible. If you leave it until the week before you fly, you may find, for example, that you're not covered for delays to your flight caused by industrial action.

Round-the-World Tickets Round-the-world (RTW) tickets are often real bargains. They are usually put together by two airlines and allow you to fly anywhere on their route systems provided you don't backtrack. There may be restrictions on the number of stops allowed; the tickets are usually valid from 90 days up to a year. The cost of a South Pacific RTW ticket including Australia is typically in the US$2100 to US$4400 range.

Another type of RTW ticket is one put together by a travel agent using a combination of discounted tickets. A good UK agent like Trailfinders can put together interesting London-to-London RTW combinations that include Australia (along with some internal stopovers) for UK£970 to UK£1550. The Global Explorer, an RTW ticket put together by Qantas, British Airways, American Airlines and several others, is worth investigating; the number of stops is normally limited to six, including three in Australia, and conditions include an overall mileage limit. The low-season price of UK£1000 rockets to UK£2044 in the high season.

Circle Pacific Tickets These tickets use a combination of airlines to circle the Pacific, taking in Australia, New Zealand, North America and Asia. Advance purchase restrictions and limits on the number of stopovers apply but the fare is likely to be around 15% cheaper than an RTW ticket.

Departure Tax
Departure tax of A$30 is levied on travellers leaving Australia, but this is incorporated into the price of your air ticket.

Travellers with Special Needs
If you have a special need of any sort, eg, you've broken a leg, you're vegetarian, taking a baby, terrified of flying, you should let the airline know as soon as possible so it can make suitable arrangements. You should remind it when you reconfirm your booking (at least 72 hours before departure) and again when you check in at the airport.

Children under two travel for 10% of the standard fare (free on some airlines) as long as they don't occupy a seat. They don't get a baggage allowance either. 'Skycots' should be provided by the airline if requested in advance; these will take a child weighing up to about 10kg. Children between two and 12 can usually occupy a seat for half to two-thirds of the full fare and do get a baggage allowance. Pushchairs can often be taken on as hand luggage.

The UK & Continental Europe
Trailfinders in West London produces an illustrated brochure that includes air fare details. The Sunday papers and *Exchange & Mart* are good places to look for ads.

Most British travel agents are registered with the Association of British Travel Agents (ABTA). If you buy a ticket from an ABTA-registered agent that then goes out of business, ABTA will guarantee a refund or an alternative. Dealing with unregistered bucket shops is therefore chancy, but can sometimes be cheaper.

Good, reliable agents for cheap tickets include Trailfinders (☎ 020-7938 3366), at 194 Kensington High St, London W8 7RC, and STA Travel (☎ 020-7581 4132), with branches at 86 Old Brompton Rd, London SW7 3LQ, and (☎ 020-7465 0484) 117 Euston Rd, London NW1 2SX.

Typical direct fares from London to Sydney or Perth (there's virtually no difference between the two) are UK£325/567 one way/return during the low season (March to June), including tax. In September and mid-December, fares go up by as much as 30%. Typical direct high-season fares are UK£400/705 one way/return, including tax.

Generally, there's not a large difference between fares from various continental European cities to Australia. A standard low-season return ticket from Paris costs around 5600FF, rising to 6500FF in the high season.

The USA

There are various paths across the Pacific from Los Angeles and San Francisco to Australia, including direct flights, flights via New Zealand, island-hopping routes and more circuitous Pacific Rim routes via Asian nations. Qantas, Air New Zealand and United Airlines fly USA-Australia.

The *New York Times*, the *LA Times*, the *Chicago Tribune* and the *San Francisco Examiner* all produce weekly travel sections in which you'll find dozens of travel agents' ads. The magazine *Travel Unlimited* publishes details of the cheapest air fares for destinations all over the world from the USA. Council Travel and STA Travel have offices in major cities nationwide.

Typically a one-way/return ticket from the west coast costs US$888/961 in the low season, US$1360/1378 in the high season, or from the east coast, US$1262/1836 in the low season and US$1736/2150 in the high season.

Canada

To find good fares to Australia check the travel sections of the Toronto *Globe & Mail* and the *Vancouver Sun*. Travel CUTS has offices in all major cities. Qantas, Air New Zealand, Japan Airlines and Canadian Airlines International all fly Canada–Australia.

Fares out of Vancouver will be slightly more expensive than those from the US west coast. From Toronto, fares go from around

C$1410 return during the low season and C$2000 in the high season.

New Zealand

Air New Zealand, Ansett and Qantas operate trans-Tasman flights linking Auckland, Wellington and Christchurch with most major Australian gateway cities. STA Travel and Flight Centres International are among the major travel agents.

From Auckland to Sydney you're looking at around NZ$385/519 one way/return in the low season and NZ$425/619 in the high season – it costs a little more to Melbourne. There is a lot of competition on these routes, so there are bound to be some good discounts.

SEA

The best source of information about container ship routes and the lines plying them is the *OAG Cruise & Ferry Guide* published quarterly by the Reed Travel Group in the UK. Your travel agent might have a copy.

A few companies take bookings for freighter travel – the best way of organising such a trip.

Freighter World Cruises (☎ 818-449 3106) 180 South Lake Ave, Suite 335, Pasadena CA 91101, USA
Strand Cruise & Travel Centre (☎ 020-7836 6363) Charing Cross Shopping Centre Concourse, London WC2N 4HZ, UK
Sydney International Travel Centre (☎ 02-9229 8000) Level 8, 75 King St, NSW 2000, Australia

ORGANISED WALKS

This is a small selection of companies who run or organise guided and self-guided walking holidays in Australia.

The UK & Continental Europe

High Places (☎ 0114-275 7500, fax 275 3870, ✆ highpl@globalnet.co.uk, ⌨ www.highplaces. co.uk) The Globe Centre, Penistone Rd, Sheffield S6 3AE. Runs a 25-day Australian Contrasts trip comprising adventurous day walks in Lamington and Blue Mountains National Parks, the Snowy Mountains, the Cradle Mountain area and the Tasman Peninsula. Accommodation is in lodges and guesthouses. The all-inclusive price is UK£2780.

Ramblers Holidays (☎ 01707-331133, fax 333276, ✉ ramhols@dial.pipex.com) PO Box 43, Welwyn Garden City AL8 6PQ. Offers two trips. Flowers of Western Australia is a 19-day tour including Stirling Range National Park, Kalgoorlie and Kalbarri National Park. The all-inclusive cost is UK£1990. The highlights of Journey in the South-East are Kosciusko, Blue Mountains and Fraser Island National Parks. The all-inclusive cost for 26 days is UK£2640.

Travelbag Adventures (☎ 01420-541007, fax 541022, ✉ info@travelbag-adventures.co.uk, ✉ www.travelbag-adventures.co.uk) 15 Turk St (WA), Alton GU34 1AG. Has two trips with walking as a significant component. The 12-day Queensland Adventure includes a climb of Mt Bartle Frere (UK£1075 land-only). The West Coast and Gibb River Tour comprises 12 days from Perth to Broome, including the Pinnacles and Kalbarri (UK£677 land-only), and 10 days from Broome to Darwin, walking in Karijini National Park and Windjana Gorge (UK£507 land-only).

Walks Worldwide (☎ 01332-230883, fax 360851, ✉ WAB@walksworldwide.com, ✉ www.walks worldwide.com) 25 Mount Carmel St, Derby DE23 6TB). Runs a fully guided six-day trip along Tasmania's Overland Track (UK£790 land-only). It also organises self-guided tours in Victoria and New South Wales, providing all accommodation, travel and necessary information; one itinerary could comprise Grampians National Park and a self-drive tour from Melbourne to Sydney, the all-inclusive cost for 23 days being UK£2390.

Active Tours (☎ 8374-5899 525, fax 5899 530, ✉ info@activetours.de, ✉ www.activetours.de) Alpenrosenweg 20 87463 Dietmannsried. A German operation that runs general tours, such as the Naturwunder Australien, with some day walks included.

The USA

As well as the companies listed below, take a look at the Adventureseek.com Web site (✉ www.adventureseek.com), which lists activity-specific trips run by companies such as REI, Outer Edge and World Expeditions. Away.com (✉ www.away.com) has a similar search engine with a range of action-packed multiactivity trips and an emphasis on nature observation and ecotourism.

The Adventure Company, USA (☎ 800-388 7333, fax 617-4051 4888, ✉ adventures@adventures.com.au). Offers walks of varying standards, from day walks to eight-day trips. The Bartle Frere Wilderness Walk, in Queensland, is US$380/$340 per adult/child for 3 nights; a half-day guided rainforest walk is US$47/$28 and a nine-day Wilderness Coast Walk in Croajingolong National Park, Victoria, is US$1278 per person.

Great Outdoors Recreation Pages (GORP; ☎ 1877-440 4677, fax 303-444 3999, ✉ info@gorptravel.com, ✉ www.gorp.com) PO Box 1486 Boulder, Colorado 80306. Offers two four-day walking trips suitable for children. The Great Northern Safari incoporates 4WD transport with easy walking and costs US$575; the Wilderness Coast Walks tour from Melbourne to Wingan, in Victoria, costs US$555 (both prices land-only). Check the GORP Web site for other tour options.

Wilderness Travel (☎ 800-368 2794, fax 510 558 2489, ✉ info@wildernesstravel.com, ✉ www .wildernesstravel.com) 1102 Ninth St, Berkeley, California 94710-1211. Operates a 12-day Wild Tasmania easy-to-moderate walking trip to destinations including Cradle Mountain, Mt Field and Freycinet National Parks. Accommodation is in lodges, cabins and hotels. The land cost is US$2795 (for a small group).

New Zealand

Active New Zealand Touring (☎ 09-480 4477, fax 480 4478, ✉ nzactive@nzactive.com) PO Box 100 518 NSMC, Auckland. Offers small-group walking, paddling and cycling guided trips in Australia and New Zealand. The Gumtree trip is a 10-day driving and walking tour of NSW and Tasmania, with walks in the Blue Mountains, Snowy Mountains, Cradle Valley and Freycinet. The tour cost is NZ$1799.

Getting Around

AIR

Australia is so vast that unless your time is unlimited you will probably take a flight at least once. The major domestic carriers are Qantas Airways ☎ 13 1313 and Ansett Australia ☎ 13 1300 whose Web sites are 🖳 www.qantas.com.au and 🖳 www.ansett .com.au, respectively. All domestic flights are nonsmoking.

Cheap Fares

On virtually any Ansett or Qantas route the full economy fare won't be the cheapest. Discounts are generally greater for return than for one-way travel. However, discounted tickets are constantly changing, so full economy fares are listed in this book.

If you're planning a return trip you can save around 55% by travelling Apex – booking and paying at least 21 days ahead. Lower savings are available for booking 14 and five days in advance; various conditions are attached to Apex tickets.

Interstate Quarantine

Travelling around Australia, by land or air, you'll come across signs in airports, interstate train stations and at state borders warning against carrying fruit, plants and vegetables from one area to another. Certain pests and diseases (fruit fly, cucurbit thrips, grape phylloxera and potato cyst nematodes, to name a few) are prevalent in some areas but not in others, so the authorities are trying to keep them contained.

There are quarantine inspection posts on some state borders and other locations. Quarantine control relies partly on honesty, but many posts are staffed and the officers are entitled to search your car for undeclared items. Generally they'll confiscate all fresh fruit and vegetables, so it's best to leave shopping for these items until the first town past the inspection point.

University or other higher-education students under 26 can get a 25% discount on the regular economy fare. Australian students need an airline tertiary concession card (available from the airlines); overseas students can use their International Student Identity Card.

Nonresident international travellers can get a 30% discount on an unlimited number of internal Qantas and Ansett flights by presenting their international ticket, whatever the airline, when booking. However, other available discounts are often cheaper. It's worth exploring the market before you buy.

Any airport landing tax is usually incorporated into the ticket price, but may not be included in the price quoted by the airlines.

Air Passes

Qantas' **Boomerang Pass** can only be purchased overseas and involves buying coupons for short-haul flights for $250 one way, or $365 for long-haul sectors. You must purchase a minimum of two coupons before arriving in Australia, and once here you can buy up to eight more.

The Qantas **Backpackers Pass** can only be bought in Australia, with proof of membership of the YHA or other acceptable travellers organisations. You must purchase a minimum of three sectors for a journey of at least seven days initially, and you can buy two to six coupons afterwards. Using this pass, the fare from Sydney to Adelaide, for example, is $240 one way, against the full economy fare of $391.

Ansett's **Kangaroo Airpass**, available only in Australia, gives two options: 6000km with two to three stopovers for $949; and 10,000km with three to seven stopovers for $1499. Restrictions include the location and duration of stopovers. This pass gives savings close to 50%, especially when cheaper fares may be unavailable.

The **See Australia Pass** is available overseas and within Australia, but only to holders of international tickets into Australia. The pass costs $1278 and allows you to fly on any Ansett domestic route. The **Backpackers Fare**, available only to YHA and travellers club members, offers between 50% to 60% savings on the full economy fare, subject to various restrictions.

The **Ansett G'day Airpass** can only be purchased in some overseas countries. You must buy two coupons overseas, and optionally up to nine more in Australia. Each sector is classified as Zone 1 ($240) or Zone 2 ($300). Savings are very good: eg, the regular fare for the Perth–Cairns sector (Zone 2) is around $700.

Other Airlines

Impulse Airlines (☎ 13 1381, 🖥 www.impulseairlines.com.au) and Virgin Blue (☎ 13 6789, 🖥 www.virginblue.com.au) are new competitors (as of 2000) in the domestic market that may well prove cheaper than the main carriers.

Kendell Airlines services country areas of New South Wales (NSW), Victoria, South Australia (SA) and Tasmania. Sunstate operates services in Queensland including to some of the islands, and south to Mildura and Broken Hill. Skywest flies several routes within Western Australia (WA). Eastern Australia Airlines serves the NSW coast and far west, and Airnorth connects Darwin and Alice Springs with small towns in the Northern Territory (NT). These airlines are mostly affiliated with either Qantas or Ansett, and their flights can be booked through their affiliate (see the contact numbers at the beginning of this chapter).

All major country airports have either shuttle bus or taxi connections to town. In some places you have to ring for a taxi – free telephones are often provided.

Airport Transport

All major airports have either shuttle bus or taxi connections to town. In some places you will have to ring for a taxi – free telephones are often provided for this purpose.

BUS

Bus is generally the cheapest means of travel. There is only one national network –

Greyhound Pioneer Australia (☎ 13 2030, 🖥 www.greyhound.com.au). McCafferty's (☎ 13 1499, 🖥 www.mccaffertys.com.au) has services in all mainland states except WA. Both give a 10% discount to members of the YHA and other approved travellers organisations.

Many other bus companies operate locally or specialise in one or two main inter-city routes, such as Murrays and Firefly. In SA, Premier Stateliner operates within the state. Westrail in WA and V/Line in Victoria operate services where trains used to go. Long-haul buses are equipped with air-conditioning, toilets and videos. Smoking is not permitted. See the walks chapters for contact details.

Greyhound Pioneer Passes

The **Aussie Kilometre Pass** gives a specified amount of travel to be completed within 12 months, from 2000km ($215) up to 20,000km ($1540). This pass is valid for 12 months; you can travel wherever you like and stop as often as you like. The **Aussie Explorer Pass** gives you from two to 12 months to cover a set route – the validity period depends on distance. It lacks the flexibility of the Kilometre Pass but may be cheaper. See the Greyhound Web site for details of these and other passes.

McCafferty's Passes

The **Australian Roamer Pass** enables you to travel from 2000km ($192) to 15,000km ($1072). With the **Travel Australia Pass** you choose from various set-route passes, valid for between three and 12 months. The Best of the East & Centre, for example, costs $915. Check the McCafferty's Web site for full details.

Other Buses

The Wayward Bus (☎ 1800 882 823, 🖥 www.waywardbus.com.au) offers several trips, most of which allow you to get on or off wherever you like, and it passes areas featured in this book. Its trips include Face the Outback, an eight-day run from Adelaide to Alice Springs via Wilpena Pound for $670 including meals, accommodation charges and national park entry fees. The Classic Coast is a three-day trip along the Great Ocean Rd between Adelaide and Melbourne ($180 including lunches).

Qantas and Oz Experience (☎ 02-9221 4711 in Sydney, 1300 30 1359 elsewhere, ⌨ www.ozexperience.com) offer an Air-Bus Pass, available for more than 25 routes all over the country with Oz Experience buses and Qantas flights. For example, for $715 you can bus from Sydney to Cairns (with unlimited stops) and fly from Cairns to Perth. Conditions mainly cover the duration of the pass. Savings on separate fares are from $125.

Details of smaller operators within each state are given in the walks chapters.

TRAIN

Rail travel in Australia is generally not the fastest or most economical way to get around. Discounts of up to 40% may be available, making prices comparable to the private bus lines; Australian students get a 50% discount on economy fares. Discount tickets are offered on a first-come, first-served quota basis; book in advance to be sure. On interstate journeys you can make free stopovers, but only on economy and student tickets.

Three major interstate services (the *Ghan* from Sydney and Melbourne to Alice Springs via Adelaide, the *Indian-Pacific* between Sydney and Perth, and the *Overland* between Melbourne and Adelaide) are operated by Great Southern Railway (☎ 13 2147). Countrylink (☎ 13 2232) operates services to regional towns between Melbourne, Sydney and Brisbane.

Rail services within each state are run by that state's rail organisation.

Rail Passes

With the **Austrail Pass** you can travel economy class anywhere on the Australian rail network during a set period; the 30-day pass, for example, costs $900.

The **Austrail Flexipass** allows a set number of economy-class travelling days within a six-month period. Prices are from $475 for eight days of travel up to $1250 for 29 days.

The eight-day pass cannot be used for travel between Adelaide and Perth or on *The Ghan*.

These passes are available only to holders of non-Australian passports and must be purchased before arrival in Australia. Countrylink's Web site (⌨ www.countrylink.nsw .gov.au) lists relevant overseas agents.

Bookings can be made at any station (including major metropolitan stations) for any journey throughout the country; call Countrylink on ☎ 13 2232 during office hours.

CAR & MOTORCYCLE

A car is the most practical means of transport for a walking holiday in Australia. Public transport will take you to some larger country towns but they're mostly a long way from walking areas. See Visas & Documents in the Facts for the Walker chapter for information on driving licences.

Road Rules

Australians drive on the left-hand side of the road as in the UK and Japan. An important road rule is 'give way to the right' – if an intersection is uncontrolled, you must give way to vehicles entering the intersection from your right.

The speed limit in built-up areas is up to 60km/h and on the open highway 100km/h or 110km/h; in the NT there is no speed limit outside built-up areas. Far from the cities where traffic is light, speed limits tend to get ignored. However, police regularly use speed radar guns and cameras from concealed locations. Oncoming drivers who flash their lights may be giving a friendly warning of a speed camera ahead – or they may be telling you that your headlights are on (or off!). It's always polite to wave back.

All new cars in Australia have seat belts both in the back and front, which must be worn – you're likely to get a fine if you don't. Small children must be belted into an approved safety seat.

Drink-driving is a problem, especially in the country. Random breath tests are not uncommon in built-up areas. If you're caught driving with a blood-alcohol level of more than 0.05%, be prepared to pay a hefty fine and to lose your licence.

On the Road

Multilane highways are relatively few, but these days all major routes are sealed and have two lanes. The starting points of several walks are on unsealed roads – some gravel road driving is inevitable when travelling around Australia. Always carry spare parts, such as fan belts and radiator hoses, if you're going into remote areas where traffic is light and garages scarce.

Prices of super grade, diesel and unleaded fuel vary from place to place, but in the cities generally cost from 79c to 82c per litre. Away from the major cities, however, prices are closer to 90c or way beyond.

Hazards

Kangaroos are a common hazard on country roads and can cause a lot of damage if you hit one. They are most active at dawn and dusk, and often travel in groups. If one hops across the road in front of you, slow right down – its mates may be close behind. Many Australians avoid travelling after dark because of the hazards posed by animals.

Away from the cities you'll also meet road trains. These are huge trucks (a prime mover plus two or three trailers) up to 50m long, so you need about 1km to overtake one. When a road train approaches on a narrow bitumen road, slow down and pull over – if it has to put its wheels off the road to pass, the shower of stones thrown up could shatter your windscreen.

If you want to explore Outback Australia, there are plenty of challenging routes off the bitumen. Lonely Planet's *Outback Australia* contains all the information you'll need for safe travel.

Rental

The three main companies, Budget, Hertz and Avis, have offices in most major towns. A fourth company, Thrifty, is also widely represented. There are also hundreds of local firms, or firms with outlets in a few locations. The big operators generally charge higher rates than the local firms, but check the fine print for hidden extras.

The big firms (and some others) are represented at all the country's entry airports, so these are convenient places to pick up or leave a car. You can arrange one-way rentals with the major players, eg, picking up a car in Sydney and leaving it in Melbourne, but check for extra charges. One-way rentals

Distances by Road (km)

	Adelaide	Alice Springs	Brisbane	Broome	Cairns	Canberra	Darwin	Melbourne	Perth
Alice Springs	1690								
Brisbane	2130	3060							
Broome	4035	2770	4320						
Cairns	2865	2418	1840	4126					
Canberra	1210	2755	1295	5100	3140				
Darwin	3215	1525	3495	1965	2795	4230			
Melbourne	755	2435	1735	4780	3235	655	3960		
Perth	2750	3770	4390	2415	6015	3815	4345	3495	
Sydney	1430	2930	1030	4885	2870	305	4060	895	3990

These are the shortest distances by road; other routes may be considerably longer. For distances by coach, check the companies' leaflets.

into or out of the NT or WA may be subject to a large relocation fee.

The major companies offer either unlimited kilometres or a flat charge plus so many cents per kilometre. Daily rates are typically about $50 a day for a small car (such as a Ford Festiva), $75 a day for a medium car (Mitsubishi Magna) or $100 a day for a big vehicle (Ford Falcon), all including insurance. Rates are much lower for long-term rentals. You must be at least 21 years old to hire from most firms; if you're under 25 you may only be able to hire a small car.

Travel on unsealed (gravel) roads is not usually covered by insurance. If you have an accident you'll be liable for all the costs; make absolutely sure you know exactly what your liability is. Rather than risk the huge expenses, you can take out your own comprehensive insurance on the car, or pay an additional daily amount to the renter for an 'insurance excess reduction' policy.

The major companies also rent 4WD vehicles, at higher rates than for big cars, but still a reasonable proposition for a group of travellers. The insurance conditions, especially the excess, can be onerous, although this can often be reduced by paying an additional daily charge. Most companies' insurance does not cover damage caused when travelling off-road, ie, anywhere that is not a maintained bitumen or dirt road.

Britz:Australia (☎ 1800 331 454, 💻 www .britz.com) hires campervans and 4WDs fitted out as campervans. As a guide to rates, a three-berth campervan costs $98 per day for three to four weeks' hire. One-way rentals are possible.

Buying & Selling
Another possibility is to buy a second-hand car, which can be reasonably cheap, but you need to have time to shop around and to familiarise yourself with the red tape.

Car Connection Australia (☎ 03-5473 4469, fax 5473 4520, 💻 www.carconnec tion.com.au) runs a sell/buy-back rental scheme, which involves buying back cars at fixed rates without hidden extras. You could buy a used Ford Falcon station wagon for $2000 and use it for up to six months. In

Europe, information and car bookings are handled by its agent Travel Action GmbH (☎ 0276-47824, fax 0276-47938), Einsiedeleiweg 16, 57399 Kirchhundem.

The state automobile associations (see the following section) can advise you about local regulations, give general guidelines about buying and selling and, for a fee (around $100 for members), will check a used car and report on its condition before you buy it. They also offer car insurance to members.

Automobile Associations
State automobile associations provide emergency breakdown services, excellent touring maps and accommodation guides. Each also has reciprocal arrangements with other Australian states and with similar organisations overseas. If you're a member of the AAA in the USA or the RAC or AA in the UK, you can use the state organisations' facilities (bring proof of membership with you). Your home organisation will be able to supply contact details.

Motorcycle
Australia's long, open roads are ideal for large-capacity machines. If you want to bring your own motorcycle into Australia you'll need a *carnet de passages*. Shipping from almost anywhere is expensive.

The best deal is a buy-back arrangement from a large motorcycle dealer in a major city. Around $8000 cash should secure an excellent second-hand road bike with a written guarantee that it will be bought back (in good condition) less about $2000. You'll need a rider's licence and a helmet.

BICYCLE
Australia is a great place for cycling, and a walking–cycling visit offers freedom and flexibility – there are thousands of kilometres of good, quiet roads and a bike can get you to places not accessble by public transport.

If you haven't brought a bike and don't want to buy one, you might be able to hire one for a few days at a tourist centre (usually mountain bikes); equipment and spare parts are easy to come by. Most people carry camping equipment, but in much of

Victoria, coastal NSW, the south-east corner of Queensland and in south-west WA, you could travel from town to town staying in hostels, hotels or on-site vans. Auslig maps at 1:250,000 are ideal for medium-range trips and are available from specialist map shops. Extended tours need to be planned with water supplies, the weather and prevailing winds in mind. Bicycle helmets are compulsory everywhere, as are front and rear lights after dark.

Look out for Lonely Planet's *Cycling Australia* for all the information you'll need to plan cycling tours. As well as route notes, cue sheets and detailed maps for 31 of the best routes in the country, it contains accommodation and sightseeing advice, as well as comprehensive sections on maintenance and health and safety.

HITCHING

Hitching is not a safe practice in Australia and we don't recommend it. Travellers who decide to hitch should understand that they are taking a potentially serious risk. Queensland especially is notorious for attacks on women hitchhikers, and there have been plenty of attacks in other states as well.

Before deciding to hitch, talk to local people about the dangers. If you do decide to go ahead, the following advice should help to make your journey reasonably safe.

Solo hitching is unwise for men or women. Two women hitching together may be vulnerable, while two men can expect long waits. The best combination is a woman and a man hitching together.

Always be prepared to abandon a ride if you begin to feel uneasy for any reason. Make an excuse and get out at the first opportunity. Don't accept rides that are going to drop you in the middle of nowhere – travel from town to town, or roadhouse to roadhouse.

Just as hitchers should be wary when accepting lifts, drivers who pick up fellow travellers to share costs should also think about the risks involved.

BOAT

The *Spirit of Tasmania* car ferry between Melbourne and Devonport and the *DevilCat* catamaran between Melbourne and George Town (between the mainland and Tasmania) are the only regular passenger services. The contact number for both is ☎ 13 2010.

LOCAL TRANSPORT

Details of suburban train and bus services are given where necessary in the walks chapters.

Australian Capital Territory

Not only does the Australian Capital Territory (ACT) contain Canberra, the nation's capital city, it also justifiably lays claim to being the bush capital of Australia. More than half the ACT's area is preserved in nature reserves and a national park. Variety is the essence, from subalpine summits in Namadgi National Park and Tidbinbilla Nature Reserve to the broad Murrumbidgee River and the grasslands and woodlands of Canberra Nature Park. None of these areas is more than 1½ hours' drive from the city centre and a few are accessible by public transport. A network of more than 200km of walking tracks includes many informative nature trails. 'Walkers' paradise' is not too extravagant a title.

INFORMATION
Maps

Auslig's 1:100,000 *Australian Capital Territory*, a topographical map, is a handy guide for getting around Canberra and to walking areas farther afield. However, Auslig maps at that scale are not the best buys as walking maps. Gregory's *Canberra in Your Pocket* map No 248 is excellent for finding your way about the city and suburbs. The UBD *City Link* street directory includes all Canberra's suburbs and access to all the parks and reserves.

The Central Mapping Authority of NSW (CMA), now called Land & Property Information New South Wales (LPINSW), publishes 1:25,000 and 1:50,000 topographical maps for the ACT; details are given under Planning for each walk.

Buying Maps Canberra's Auslig Map Shop (☎ 1800 800 173, fax 6201 4381, ✉ map sales@auslig.gov.au), in the Scrivener Bldg, Dunlop Court, Fern Hill Park (off Haydon Drive) in Bruce, is open weekdays but is not the easiest place to get to. (By public transport you will need to take the Action bus No 34 from Civic or Belconnen bus terminals.) Although payment must be made by

Highlights

Australia's Parliament House dominates the skyline of Canberra, the gateway to walks in the Australian Capital Territory

- Cliffs, rapids and large swimming holes on the Murrumbidgee, one of Australia's major rivers

- A challenging, spectacular ridge walk with abundant wildlife in Tidbinbilla Nature Reserve

- Historic settlers' huts, beautiful high, open valleys and snow gum groves in Namadgi National Park

telephone, Auslig maps can also be ordered through its Web site (🖳 www.auslig.gov.au).

Guidepost Travel (☎ 02-6249 6006, fax 6257 4446, ✉ guidepostcbr@bigpond.com), in the Jolimont Tourist Centre at 65 Northbourne Ave, Canberra City, is open daily. It's more central, but its collection of topographical maps for the ACT is rather patchy. Outdoor gear shops stock maps for walkers; Paddy Pallin and Camping World have good selections.

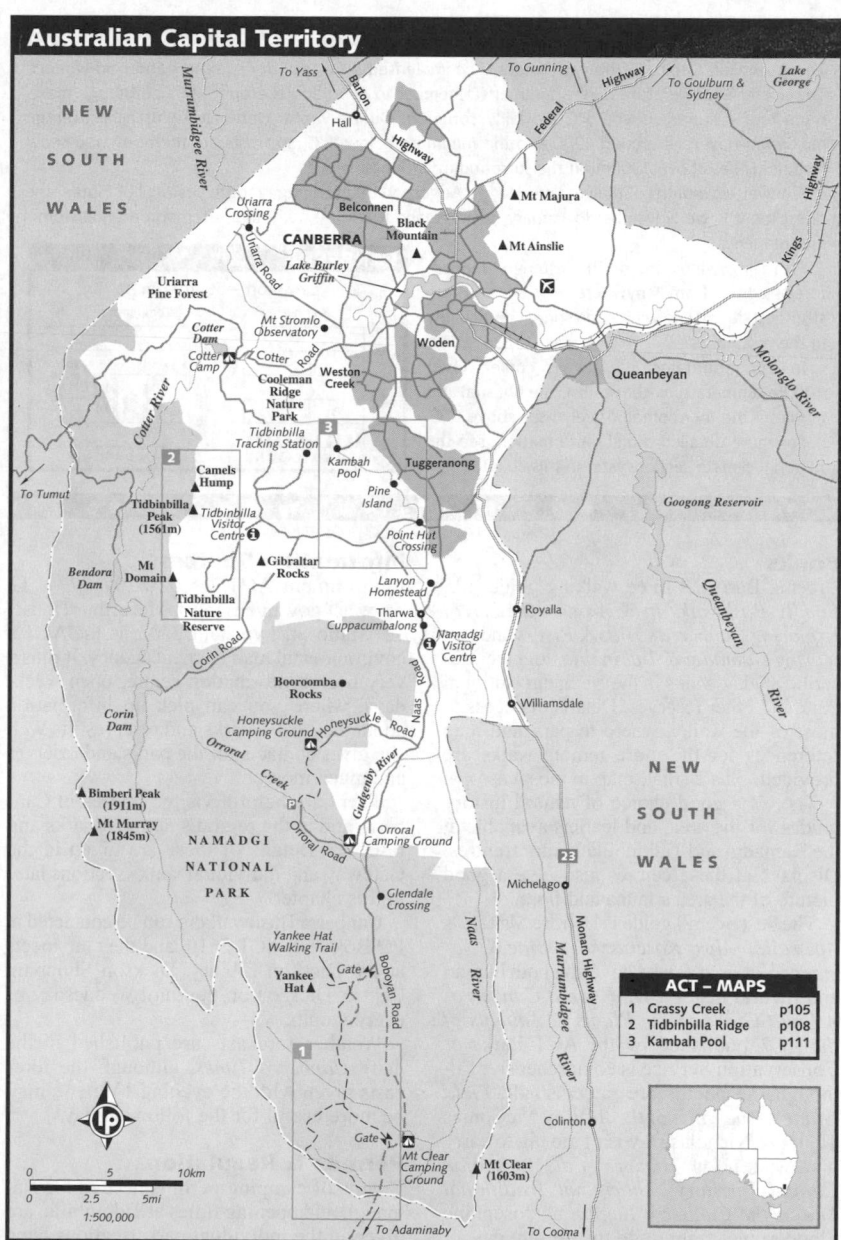

Australian Capital Territory

To Yass
Barton Highway
To Gunning
Federal Highway
To Goulburn & Sydney
Lake George
Kings Highway

NEW SOUTH WALES

Murrumbidgee River
Uriarra Crossing
Hall
Highway
Belconnen
CANBERRA
Black Mountain
Lake Burley Griffin
▲ Mt Majura
▲ Mt Ainslie

Uriarra Pine Forest
Uriarra Road
Mt Stromlo Observatory
Woden
Queanbeyan
Molonglo River

Cotter River
Cotter Dam
Cotter Camp
Cotter Road
Cooleman Ridge Nature Park
Weston Creek

Tidbinbilla Tracking Station
3
Kambah Pool
Tuggeranong
Pine Island
Googong Reservoir

2
Camels Hump
Tidbinbilla Peak (1561m) ▲
Tidbinbilla Visitor Centre ❶
Point Hut Crossing
Queanbeyan River

To Tumut

Bendora Dam
Mt Domain ▲
▲ Gibraltar Rocks
Tidbinbilla Nature Reserve
Lanyon Homestead
Tharwa
Cuppacumbalong
Namadgi Visitor Centre ❶
Royalla

Corin Road
Booroomba Rocks
Naas Road
Williamsdale

Corin Dam
Honeysuckle Camping Ground
Honeysuckle Road
Orroral Creek
Gudgenby River

▲ Bimberi Peak (1911m)
▲ Mt Murray (1845m)
Orroral Road
Orroral Camping Ground
23

NEW SOUTH WALES

NAMADGI NATIONAL PARK
Glendale Crossing
Naas River
Michelago
Monaro Highway
Murrumbidgee River

Yankee Hat Walking Trail
Yankee Hat ▲
Gate
Baboyan Road

1
Colinton

Gate
Mt Clear Camping Ground
Mt Clear (1603m) ▲

ACT – MAPS	
1 Grassy Creek	p105
2 Tidbinbilla Ridge	p108
3 Kambah Pool	p111

0   5   10km
0   2.5   5mi
1:500,000

To Adaminaby
To Cooma

The Climate of the Australian Capital Territory

The Australian Capital Territory's climate is characterised by warm, dry summers and cold winters. The average temperature during summer (December to February) is around 27°C, although maximum temperatures above 35°C are fairly common. During winter (June to August) the average maximum hovers at around 12°C and the minimum below 1°C, so frosts are the norm and snow frequently lies above 1200m on the surrounding mountains.

The wettest months of the year are May to August, with an average monthly rainfall of 82mm; the driest months are November to January (average about 60mm), although afternoon thunderstorms are frequent.

Prevailing winds are north-westerly – indeed, rarely come from anywhere else – and are strongest during late winter and spring, particularly in the mountains.

In the mountains, it's always cooler. Over 1000m temperatures above 25°C are unusual and in winter the thermometer rarely rises above 5°C.

For more detailed climate information, see the regional climate sections later in this chapter.

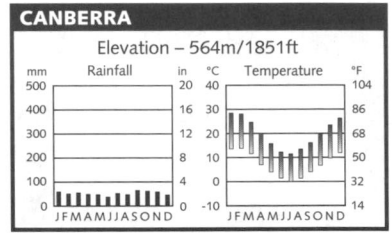

CANBERRA
Elevation – 564m/1851ft

Books

Graeme Barrow's three walking guides, *25 Family Bushwalks In & Around Canberra*, *Exploring Canberra's Hills & Rivers* and *Exploring Namadgi & Tidbinbilla*, together describe 80 day walks in the Namadgi National Park and other reserves. Details of access to most of the walks, where to park and map references for the more remote walks are provided, plus a small map in most cases.

There's a good choice of natural history guides for the area, and leaflets available at the Namadgi and Tidbinbilla Visitor Centres. Displays at these centres also give a good picture of the area's fauna and flora.

The best overall guide is Deirdre Slattery's *Australian Alps: Kosciuszko, Alpine & Namadgi National Parks*, covering both human and natural history. *Wild About Canberra: A Field Guide to the Plants & Animals of the ACT* published by the ACT Parks & Conservation Service is comprehensive, although the photos are rather small. *Field Guide to the Birds of the ACT* by McComas Taylor & Nicholas Day isn't too big to carry on a walk. *Moth Hunters of the Australian Capital Territory: Aboriginal Traditional Life in the Canberra Region* by Josephine Flood ranges right up to the present day.

Information Sources

Environment ACT (☎ 02-6207 9777, 🖳 www.act.gov.au/environ), Macarthur House, 12 Wattle St, Lyneham 2602, is the ACT's environmental management agency. It runs a very useful information centre, open weekdays, where you can pick up information about the ACT's parks and reserves. Its Web site gives contacts for the parks and reserves and much more.

There are helpful visitor centres in Canberra and at the region's national parks and reserves. Details of these are given in the Gateway and individual walks sections later in this chapter.

Canberra Bushwalkers can be contacted at PO Box 160, ACT 2610, and the club meets at the Dickson Library, Dickson Shopping Centre, Dickson on the third Wednesday of every month.

Weather forecasts are published in the daily *Canberra Times*, although the forecasts given with the evening TV news may be more useful for the following day.

Permits & Regulations

Details of camping permits needed for Namadgi, and opening times at Tidbinbilla, are given in the individual parks sections later.

In both reserves, you are encouraged to use the registers at the start of many walking tracks to enter walk details and, if possible, your time of return.

All fires, including campfires, are regulated by law in the ACT. It's OK to use an officially built fireplace at a camp site or picnic area, although a fuel stove is more environmentally friendly, as well as being obligatory near walking tracks and close to environmentally sensitive areas. See Responsible Walking in the Facts for the Walker chapter for further suggestions on how to minimise your environmental impact.

On days of Total Fire Ban, all fires are forbidden, even fuel stoves. If you are caught with an open fire on these days, you are not only endangering yourself and the environment, but you can also cop a hefty fine and/or prison sentence. Contact the ACT Bushfire Service (☎ 02-6207 8333) for more information and for emergencies.

GATEWAY
Canberra

Canberra is a spacious, orderly city surrounded by hills. Despite its image as a dull, urban centre overflowing with bureaucrats, it is well worth visiting. Lonely Planet's *Australia* guide has a chapter on Canberra.

Information The Canberra Visitor Centre (☎ 02-6205 0693, fax 6205 0776, ☺ can berravisitorscentre@msn.com.au, 🖳 www .canberratourism.com.au), 330 Northbourne Ave, Dickson 2602 (2km north of the city centre), is open daily. The helpful staff can fill you in about accommodation and local attractions and some maps and guidebooks are available. Its Web site is worth checking for places to stay, restaurants and travel.

For Internet access there's a Telstra Bigpond coin-operated machine in the Jolimont Tourist Centre, outside the Countrylink office. Community libraries of the ACT Library Service provide free Internet access, but you must book in advance. Hours vary but the central Civic Library (☎ 02-6207 5155), in East Row (near London Circuit), is open from around 10 am to 5 pm Monday to Saturday (to 7.30 pm Friday).

Supplies & Equipment Most of the major national chains of outdoor gear shops have branches in Canberra. All are open daily, with fairly short hours on Sunday, and all sell a wide range of camping equipment, walking guides, gas canisters and liquid fuel for stoves.

Of the lightweight equipment specialists, Paddy Pallin (☎ 02-6257 3883), 11 Lonsdale St, Braddon, and Mountain Designs (☎ 02-6247 7488), 6 Lonsdale St, Braddon, are centrally located. Out of the city centre and with more emphasis on gear for car-based camping are Tuggeranong Camping World (☎ 02-6293 3963), Homeworld Town Centre, Tuggeranong, and CSE's Great Outdoors Centre (☎ 02-6282 3424), 18–24 Townshend St, Phillip.

Places to Stay The *Canberra YHA (☎ 02-6248 9155, fax 6249 1731, ☺ canberra @yhansw.org.au, 191 Dryandra St, O'Connor)* has twins, doubles, quads and dorms from $18 per night. It's in a quiet setting, with a small kiosk and self-catering facilities.

City Walk Hotel (☎ 02-6257 0124, fax 6257 0116, ☺ citywalk@ozemail.com.au, 2 Mort St, Canberra City) is close to the Jolimont Tourist Centre and has a great range of accommodation from en suite singles ($55) to dorms ($20).

One of the more central camping areas is *Canberra South Motor Park (☎ 02-6280 6176, fax 6239 2250, ☺ csmp@dynamite .com.au, Canberra Ave, Fyshwick)*, with a budget motel ($65 per double), cabins ($55 a double) and tent sites ($15 for two).

Places to Eat Canberra is a very cosmopolitan place for dining and the choice is vast. The visitor centre produces a general guide.

In the city centre, on the southern end of the Melbourne Building, *Lemon Grass* is an award-winning Thai restaurant with seafood mains for $14 and a good selection of vegetarian dishes for $11. *Little Saigon*, on the corner of Alinga St and Northbourne Ave, has main courses for $8, seafood meals for $12 and a $5 lunchbox.

The excellent *Fringe Benefits (54 Marcus Clarke St)*, north-west of Civic, is a more upmarket brasserie with main courses for around $20. Nearby at No 60, *Psychedeli* has good coffee, foccacia and pizza.

Most *supermarkets* in the large town centres (such as Woden and Tuggeranong) and in the smaller suburban shopping centres are open daily until around 8 pm and later on Friday.

Getting There & Away Canberra is 306km from Sydney via the Hume Fwy and the Federal Hwy, and 655km from Melbourne via the Hume Fwy and Barton Hwy.

Air Qantas (☎ 13 1313) and Ansett (☎ 13 1300) and their various partner airlines operate flights to Canberra from all state capitals and many regional centres around Australia. A standard one-way fare from Sydney (50 minutes) is $113 and from Melbourne (one hour) $158. Tickets purchased in advance are much cheaper.

Train Countrylink (☎ 13 2232) trains arrive in Canberra from Sydney three times daily. The journey time is just over four hours and a one-way adult economy fare is $45. From Melbourne, there's one daily service but you have to change to a bus at Cootamundra or Yass Junction; the journey takes eight hours ($49).

Bus Greyhound (☎ 13 2030) buses arrive at the Jolimont Tourist Centre on Northbourne Ave. The single adult fare from Sydney is $28 (four hours), and from Melbourne $54 (eight hours for the daytime service).

Murrays Coaches (☎ 13 2251) also operates out of the Jolimont Tourist Centre. As well as the Sydney service (three daily, 3½ hours, $28), it operates from Wollongong and the New South Wales (NSW) south coast.

McCafferty's Coaches (☎ 02-6249 6006), in the Jolimont Tourist Centre, also serves the major capitals, with similar fares and journey times to the other main operators, and has good regional centre connections in NSW and Victoria.

Car Rental All the major national car rental companies have offices in Canberra. Of the locally based operators, Rumbles (☎ 02-6280 7444), 11 Paragon Mall, Gladstone St, Fyshwick, offers new and used cars; there's also Capital Car Rentals (☎ 02-6282 7272), 1 Dundas Court, Phillip.

Getting Around Canberra airport is 7km south-east of the city centre. Speedy Shuttle Bus Service (☎ 02-6294 3171) links the Jolimont Tourist Centre and various hotels with the airport ($6 one way).

The Action bus network (☎ 13 1710) serves the city and suburbs; daily tickets are purchased on board ($7).

Namadgi National Park

For walkers, the biggest attraction of the ACT is Namadgi National Park, its 106,000 hectares of bushland accounting for 45% of the territory's area. The park adjoins NSW's Kosciuszko National Park in the southwest, and is the northernmost park in the vast network of Australian Alps national parks, which extends from central eastern Victoria. Namadgi, usually pronounced 'nam-a-gee', is the Aboriginal name for the mountainous area.

The park, established in 1984 after nearly 30 years of campaigning by local conservation groups, was extended to its present area in 1991. It protects the only subalpine Aboriginal rock art site in Australia, subalpine heaths, open grassland and tall eucalyptus forests. The tallest mountains stand along the NSW border: Bimberi Peak (1911m) and Mts Gingera, Murray and Kelly (all above 1800m). There are several historic sites, associated with early settlement and with space satellite tracking stations. The Cotter River flows through the park and provides nearly all Canberra's (and nearby Queanbeyan's) water.

The numerous marked tracks cover a total distance of 160km. One day walk in the far south of the park is described in detail, and others are outlined under Other Walks at the end of the chapter.

Early Days in the High Country

European settlers looking for extensive cattle grazing lands first ventured into the High Country close to the present-day ACT–NSW border in the 1830s. Within a decade the Naas, Orroral, Gudgenby and Cotter Valleys were occupied, displacing (although not often violently) the Ngunnawal Aboriginal people. Unfortunately, several of the homesteads built by the settlers, the area's most tangible European heritage, have been demolished or destroyed since the 1960s. The Grassy Creek walk passes two of the surviving buildings and the ruins of two others; the Orroral Valley heritage walk (see Other Walks) visits another survivor.

Brayshaws Hut, near the Adaminaby road, was built of timber slabs in 1903 by the Brayshaw brothers – Edward was a skilled carpenter; the shingle roof was later covered with iron. The hut was extended during the 1930s and 1940s to accommodate later owners, but some of these additions have been removed. The original structure is still intact, thanks to restoration work by the volunteer Kosciuszko Huts Association (KHA).

Westermans Hut, close to Grassy Creek, was built in 1916 for a newly married couple. The five-room weatherboard building with its solid stone chimneys, lined ceilings and plaster walls stands on a stone foundation. Again, the KHA is mainly responsible for its well-preserved state.

Lone Pine, above Sheep Station Creek, dates from the early 20th century. A small weatherboard building, it was bulldozed in the 1950s. Boboyan, in the Naas Valley, is a few decades older and was originally the home of members of the Brayshaw family. A fine six-room building, it eventually fell prey to vandals and all but one chimney was demolished by later owners in 1971.

Orroral Homestead, in the valley of the same name, was built in the 1860s and was rescued from the brink of collapse in the 1990s by the KHA and other volunteers. Interpretive on-site signs describe its history.

Cattle, the last living link with the agrarian past, were removed from the area when, in 1984, the Namadgi National Park was established.

NATURAL HISTORY

Broadly, the rock in the western parts of Namadgi is granite with rounded tors on many summits, while the eastern areas are based on sandstones and shales.

The highest ground is treeless, but the herb fields and heaths are rich in wild flowers, notably snow daisies and billy buttons. Moving down, snow gums with their contorted, colourful trunks are the hardiest trees. Broad-leaved peppermints and candlebarks are the most common of the eucalyptuses in the lower open forest. In sheltered areas, ribbon gums line the streams and tall alpine ash clothe the slopes. Lyrebirds are quite common in ferny gullies.

Several of the wider valleys support open grasslands, which were extended by the early settlers, in areas where it's too cold for substantial tree growth. Here you'll see large herds of grey kangaroos resting under the sparse black sallee eucalyptuses. Birds most likely to be seen are mainly the larger species, including the wedge-tailed eagles, pied currawongs, gang-gang cockatoos and crimson rosellas.

PLANNING

The High Country can be very warm and dry during midsummer (see Climate earlier), so October to December is the best time to be there. The weather is always very changeable, so take clothing and equipment for both extremes.

Maps & Books

The *Namadgi Guide* published by Environment ACT has a good clear planimetric map and lots of practical information. Graeme Barrow's *Exploring Namadgi & Tidbinbilla* includes descriptions of 21 day walks in the park. The Australian Alps Walking Track (see Other Walks in the Victoria chapter) goes through Namadgi from Murray Gap north-eastwards to its official northern terminus at Namadgi Visitor Centre. John Siseman's authoritative *Australian Alps Walking Track* is the best source of information about the track.

Information Sources

Namadgi Visitor Centre (☎ 02-6207 2900, fax 6207 2901, ✆ namadgi_national_park @dpa.act.gov.au), Naas Rd, Tharwa 2620, is 37km from the centre of Canberra via Tuggeranong Parkway, Drakewood Drive and Tharwa Drive, and is open daily. This is where you pick up camping permits; the centre has displays about natural and cultural history and park management and sells books and maps. Descriptive leaflets are available for several marked walking tracks, including to the Yankee Hat Aboriginal rock paintings. Illustrated talks and special exhibitions are organised at the centre – a detailed program is available. Ranger-guided walks to historic features of the park are provided on Sunday; reserve a place by calling ☎ 02-6207 2900 between 9 am and 4 pm. The fee is $4 per adult, $2 concession or $10 per family.

Permits & Regulations

You'll need a permit to stay at the three Namadgi camping grounds: Honeysuckle, Orroral and Mt Clear. A permit is required for bush camping in the upper Cotter River catchment where numbers are limited to 24 people at any one time; contact the Namadgi Visitor Centre for advice (see Information Sources). Camping is not permitted in the middle and lower Cotter catchments.

There is no restriction on walking off tracks in the more remote parts of the park, although walkers are encouraged to enter details of their trips in the bushwalking registers at the visitor centre or at the start of the various tracks.

NEAREST TOWN & FACILITIES
Tharwa

The village of Tharwa, about 35km south of Canberra City at the junction of Tharwa

---

Thieving Magpies

When you arrive at the Orroral camping ground it seems to be a wonderfully peaceful place. Although it's beside a road, traffic is infrequent and the most audible sounds are the wind in the trees, the bubbling Orroral Creek and the eerie creaking of a nearby ageing wind-powered pump.

But the local wildlife soon begin to announce their presence. The day will have started with a dawn chorus of particularly enthusiastic kookaburras, whose laughter is just as joyful at dusk. Soulful ravens wheel about in the trees, and honeyeaters provide more tuneful background music.

Soon the sharp-eyed magpies arrive, boldly landing on the nearest picnic table, and find your food with unerring aim even if it's quite securely packed. Any unguarded morsel – even an entire slice of bread – will become air cargo.

During the night, pots and pans left lying about may be upturned by possums in their relentless search for food. Fortunately, the largest residents, the eastern grey kangaroos, are perfectly content to graze naturally.

Drive and the Tidbinbilla road, is the last outpost before the park. The *general store*, post office and petrol outlet are open daily. The shop has a small range of supplies, wines, beer and 'the best pies in Tharwa'.

Namadgi National Park

Honeysuckle, the closest camp site to the visitor centre, is used mainly by large groups. *Orroral*, on the bank of the creek of the same name, has wood barbecues (for which firewood is provided), tables, toilets and water; the fee is $3 per person per night. *Mt Clear*, the most remote (but closest to the Grassy Creek walk described in this chapter), has wood barbecues, firewood and pit toilets; the fee is $2.50 per night per person.

Getting There & Away All directions are from Namadgi Visitor Centre. For Honeysuckle Creek, turn off Naas Rd 8km south of the visitor centre onto sealed Honeysuckle Creek Rd; the camp site is 10km away. To reach the Orroral camping ground, drive south from the visitor centre for 16km along Naas Rd and turn right onto Orroral Rd (sealed); the camp site is 3.2km away. For Mt Clear, follow Naas Rd south for 44.5km (the bitumen ends 30km from the visitor centre) to the signposted turn-off – the camp site is about 1km along.

Grassy Creek

Distance	25km
Duration	5–6 hours
Standard	medium
Start/Finish	Old Boboyan Rd car park
Nearest Town	Tharwa
Public Transport	no

Summary A classic high-country walk across snow plains, through woodlands and open valleys and past some early settlers' huts.

This is a classic High Country walk in the far south of the park, through the beautiful open valleys of Grassy and Naas Creeks, and eucalyptus woodlands with relics of early settlement – ground-level building ruins and superbly preserved timber huts.

From the starting point at Old Boboyan Rd car park, it's necessary to walk 1km to the Boboyan Rd and 4km south along it to Grassy Creek Trail to make a round walk. Although this road walk can be avoided if two cars are available, there is very little parking space near the start of the trail.

The walk follows fire trails (closed to public vehicles), mostly well defined although faint in places, and the route is track-marked with arrowheads on low posts and metal stakes. The water in the streams should be safe to drink. Be prepared for sudden changes in the weather – most of the walk is above 1200m.

PLANNING

For information on when to walk and what to bring, see Planning in the introduction to Namadgi National Park.

Maps

The CMA 1:25,000 *Yaouk* and *Shannons Flat* maps are suitable for the walk but are extremely dated.

GETTING TO/FROM THE WALK

To reach Old Boboyan Rd car park, turn off Naas or Boboyan Rds 45.5km south of the Namadgi Visitor Centre (29.5km south of the Orroral Rd junction); the car park is just 1km down this steep, narrow gravel road.

THE WALK

Walk up the road from the car park to Boboyan Rd and follow it south for 4km, past **Brayshaws Hut** (see the boxed text 'Early Days in the High Country') to a stile over the fence beside a gate on the right. Climb the stile and follow the fire trail up and diagonally left, across a beautiful rolling valley. After about 25 minutes, a clump of eucalyptuses and exotic trees marks the location of **Westermans Hut**.

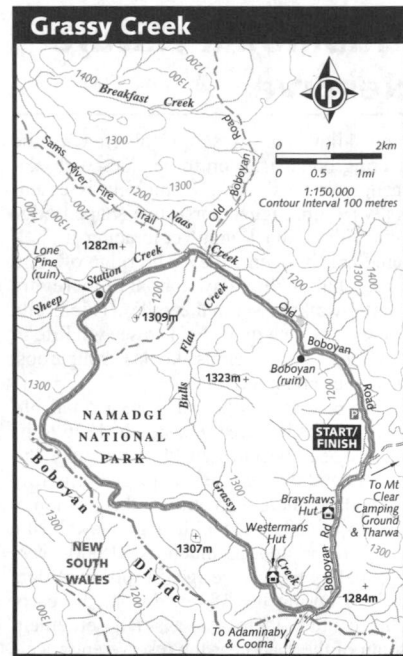

Grassy Creek

The track continues across the creek but then fades – bend left 150m beyond the creek, up past a lone tall snow gum, and continue up, then veer right into a small grove of snow gums. The track soon becomes clear in open grassland and leads generally north-westwards up the valley through some snow gum woodland. About 1½ hours from Westermans Hut, the track crosses Grassy Creek and turns north-eastwards; after about 30 minutes you descend steeply into the valley of **Sheep Station Creek**.

Soon you pass the remains of **Lone Pine Homestead**, almost buried under tall poplars and eucalyptuses. The track leads into the open along the edge of the wide valley, and about 20 minutes from the homestead you reach a track junction in **Naas Creek** valley. Continue towards Old Boboyan Rd and, a little farther on, turn right. From here it's about an hour's walk down the wide flat valley, past the massive stone chimney of the Boboyan homestead, to the car park.

Tidbinbilla Nature Reserve

Only 44km south-west of Canberra City and sharing boundaries on three sides with Namadgi National Park, Tidbinbilla is essentially a high, rugged horseshoe-shaped ridge (the Tidbinbilla Range) embracing a sheltered, partly open valley. The ridge offers a fine, challenging day out and there are shorter walks lower in the valley. Tidbinbilla is the best place in the ACT to see wildlife in a natural setting: emus, koalas, kangaroos, wallabies and many birds.

The reserve has grown from a small nucleus of 328 hectares set aside in 1936 to its present 5515 hectares. Just like Namadgi National Park, the reserve is managed primarily for conservation, recreation and education.

Aboriginal people of the Ngunnawal tribe lived in the area as much as 21,000 years ago, before the last ice age. European settlers arrived during the 1830s, and in the early 20th century there was a small settlement south of the road near the reserve entrance.

For visitors wanting to learn more about the reserve, ranger-guided activities, such as guided walks to spot wildlife, are a regular feature at Tidbinbilla. Bookings are essential – phone ☎ 02-6205 1233 between 10 am and 4 pm.

The classic Tidbinbilla Ridge walk is described here and the scenic Gibraltar Rocks walk is outlined under Other Walks at the end of the chapter.

NATURAL HISTORY

Tidbinbilla's landscape consists of sandstone, limestone and shale (known as Tidbinbilla quartzite) along the crest of the range, and granite in the valley and on the Gibraltar Range on the eastern side of the reserve. This coarse-grained rock occurs as huge rounded and columnar tors, some balanced precariously on large slabs. An excellent leaflet about the reserve's geology is available from the Tidbinbilla Visitor Centre.

Snow gums cover the upper reaches of the Tidbinbilla Range, while lower down, the open forest is dominated by scribbly gums and stringybarks. In gullies and east-facing slopes, the peppermint and ribbon gum forests are more luxuriant. More than 170 species of birds are known in the reserve and many may be seen in and around the valley. As well as the more prominent emus, kookaburras and sulphur-crested cockatoos, there are wedge-tailed eagles, crimson and eastern rosellas, honeyeaters, thornbills and robins; the wetlands are alive with geese, herons, ducks, black swans and many other water birds.

PLANNING

Spring and early summer (September to early December) are the best months for Tidbinbilla; the reserve may be closed on extreme fire danger days. The entrance gate is open from 9 am to 6 pm daily and until 8 pm during daylight saving time (end of October to late March). Walkers are encouraged to register details of longer walks in logbooks near the starting points of the tracks.

You'll need to carry water for any but the shortest walks in the reserve. The visitor centre has all you'll need for a day's visit.

Maps & Books

The *Namadgi National Park Map & Guide* includes Tidbinbilla and is useful for access to the reserve. Graeme Barrow's guide *Exploring Namadgi & Tidbinbilla* includes four walks in the reserve. Specifically for the walk detailed here, the CMA 1:25,000 *Tidbinbilla* sheet is indispensable.

Leaflets about the reserve's birds and geology, a sheet with maps of the marked walking tracks and wildlife enclosures, and many other maps and guides are available at the Tidbinbilla Visitor Centre (see Information Sources).

Information Sources

Tidbinbilla Visitor Centre (☎ 02-6205 1233, fax 6205 1232), RMB 141, Tharwa 2620, at the entrance to the reserve, is open daily and houses displays about the park's wildlife and history. There is a cafe where you can have lunch or buy snacks and drinks.

Regulations

An entry fee of $8 is charged for the reserve. Camping is not permitted. A speed limit of 35km/h is in force throughout the reserve – kangaroos and other wildlife have poor road sense.

Getting There & Away

The reserve is 44km from Canberra City via Commonwealth Ave, Cotter Rd and Paddys River Rd.

Tidbinbilla Ridge

Duration	7–7½ hours
Distance	19km
Standard	hard
Start	Mountain Creek car park
Finish	Fishing Gap Trail car park
Nearest Town	Canberra City
Public Transport	no

Summary A challenging and dramatic walk on a high, partly trackless ridge with magnificent panoramic views.

This is a challenging, strenuous and very rewarding ridge walk, high above the western side of the Tidbinbilla River valley from Mountain Creek, up to near Camels Hump, along to Mt Domain and down to Fishing Gap. A more or less continuous foot track can be followed from near Camels Hump, at the northern end, to Tidbinbilla Mountain, and from Mt Domain down to Fishing Gap Rd at the southern end. In between, the track is faint in many places, mainly on the steep descents, and considerable care is needed to keep on the ridge. Thus a map and compass are essential, plus some experience in walking over rough ground. Carry water – the ridge is quite dry.

If organising transport at each end is a problem, and walking the extra 4.3km back to the start is unappealing, there are alternatives. You could climb as far as Tidbinbilla Mountain, and return to the start, a greater distance (21km) than the through walk, but with 850m less climbing and easier walking (seven hours). An ascent of Mt Domain (650m) from Fishing Gap is straightforward, if steep, but worth it for the views; allow about 4½ hours for the 12km walk.

The panoramic views from the summits along the ridge take in just about the whole of the ACT. Snow gum woodland covers much of the ridge, with a few small natural clearings and plenty of rocky outcrops.

GETTING TO/FROM THE WALK
To the Start

About 2km north of the visitor centre, turn right along Tidbinbilla Scenic Drive in the direction of the koala wildlife enclosures and nature trails. At a junction 1.5km along, continue towards the nature trails on a narrow gravel road to a car park (another 2km). The Camelback Ridge Trail (and four nature trails) starts here.

From the Finish

The walk ends at the Fishing Gap Trail car park beside Tidbinbilla Scenic Drive, close to where it crosses the Tidbinbilla River, 2.3km south of the turn-off to the start of the walk.

THE WALK

Follow the Camelback Ridge Trail from the car park, as it climbs steadily up the side of

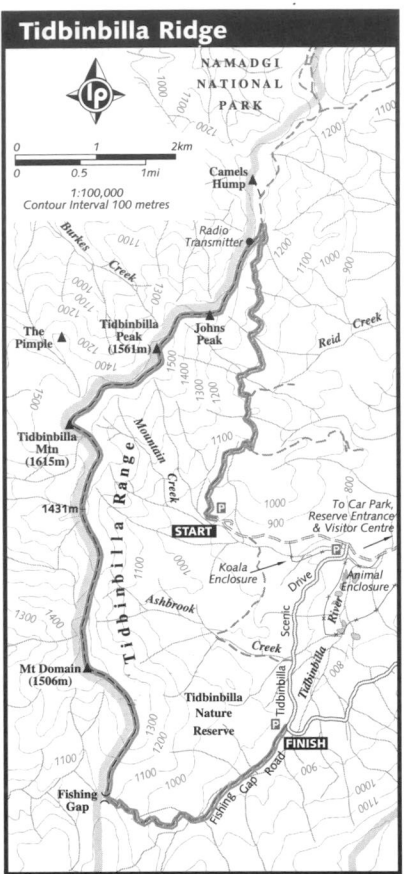

Tidbinbilla Ridge

NAMADGI NATIONAL PARK

0   1   2km
0   0.5   1mi
1:100,000
Contour Interval 100 metres

Burkes Creek

Camels Hump

Radio Transmitter

The Pimple

Tidbinbilla Peak (1561m)

Johns Peak

Reid

Creek

Tidbinbilla Mtn (1615m)

Tidbinbilla Range

Mountain Creek

1431m

START

To Car Park, Reserve Entrance & Visitor Centre

Koala Enclosure

Ashbrook

Scenic Drive

Animal Enclosure

River

Creek

Mt Domain (1506m)

Tidbinbilla Nature Reserve

Tidbinbilla

FINISH

Fishing Gap

Fishing Gap Road

the ridge, through tall open forest and across deep gullies. Pass two signposted junctions on the right as you continue up to 'Camelback Ridge', at the foot of a steep climb to the **Camels Hump** (about 1½ hours from the start).

To begin walking along the ridge from the Camels Hump, go back down the fire trail for about 225m to a faint 4WD track, or simply follow the ridge from a point where the track starts to drop steeply, and soon you'll come to a radio transmitter, well hidden in the bush. The foot track leads off quite clearly from here, climbing

fairly steeply to a rocky knob. Skirt this to the left (or scramble over the top), then head left around another rock outcrop and along the narrow open ridge to the foot of the first serious climb. Soon dramatic views of the imposing cliffs of Johns Peak open up. Go directly up, via a minor scramble either on the right or left, to the summit of **Johns Peak** (about 45 minutes from the fire trail), with excellent panoramic views of much of Canberra.

Descend steeply then continue along the rocky ridge; the path is almost invariably on or to the left of the crest. Cross a small snow plain and go to the left through some rocks. Continue up over rocky ground to the summit of **Tidbinbilla Peak** (1561m; about 30 minutes from Johns Peak). The view is more mountainous, towards the peaks of Namadgi National Park.

Continue southwards briefly, taking care to find the cairn that marks the point where the ridge swings sharply south-westwards. Cross a succession of rocky knobs, then a patch of snow gum woodland. The track switches from right to left and back again, over a minor summit on the eastern side. Beyond a very narrow band of tea-trees, then more snow gums, **Tidbinbilla Mountain** (1615m) looms impressively ahead. A pleasant stretch of relatively easy, open going leads to the start of a steep climb up through rocks, then to the left, to the open summit (about 50 minutes from Tidbinbilla Peak). Among many features, the fountain on Lake Burley Griffin, to the north-east, and Corin Dam, to the south, are clearly visible on a good day.

Then the fun starts. Some care is needed to begin the descent from the flat rocks at the northern end of the summit. Descend south-eastwards through thickish scrub; the track becomes clear farther down over open ground. Negotiate a line of cliffs via a clear break on the right. Take great care here as the ridge swings round to lead southwards. Once this change in direction is behind you, the route is a little clearer, especially where the ridge narrows sharply. Cross an open rocky summit (about 1¼ hours from Tidbinbilla Mountain), then another minor bump and descend steeply to a gap, distinguished by heaps of dead blackberry plants.

The track leads on, just on the western side of the ridge, then mainly on the crest, steeply up to a small, rocky and lightly timbered summit. Cross a narrow section and climb over scree to the top of **Mt Domain** (an hour from the rocky summit); the best views are at the northern end.

The route detours briefly to the west, then back onto the ridge. The steep descent starts abruptly on a clear track, bypassing small crags. It crosses a patch of snow gum woodland then follows the crest of the spur, in the lower reaches switching back and forth to bypass rocky obstacles. About 45 minutes from Mt Domain you reach Fishing Gap Rd; follow it down to Tidbinbilla Scenic Drive, another 45 minutes' walk. The car park is nearby to the left.

Murrumbidgee Corridor

The Murrumbidgee is one of Australia's longest rivers, flowing for 1600km from the Kosciuszko High Country to meet the Murray River in south-western NSW. In the ACT, the river's 66km are protected in a collection of nature reserves, a conservation zone and leased grazing country known as the Murrumbidgee Corridor, up to 4km wide in places.

Murrumbidgee is an Aboriginal word meaning 'Big Water'. The junction of the river and the Cotter River (west of the city centre) was the site of an important Aboriginal camp, which was the base for tracks into the High Country.

The river meanders through open woodland, grassland and scenic gorges. The outer southern suburbs of Canberra almost nudge the river, but for the greater part of its length the corridor is peaceful and seemingly remote. A marked walking track links several picnic areas, most overlooking large pools popular for swimming in summer.

The walk described here is from Point Hut Crossing to Kambah Pool and back, and covers the best section of the track. The scenic 14km section north from Kambah Pool to Casuarina Sands was partly overgrown, obscure and generally infuriatingly difficult to follow at the end of 1999. Contact Environment ACT (☎ 02-6207 2425 weekdays, ☎ 6205 1233 weekends) for up-to-date information about the condition of this track.

PLANNING

Spring or early summer are the best times for this walk, before the grassland dries out, although it should be warm enough for a swim. You'll need to carry drinking water as the river water is unfit for drinking. Gaiters and/or long trousers are recommended to protect your socks and legs from prickly grass seeds.

If you suffer from hay fever, don't forget your remedy – extensive areas of grassland are part of this walk, and the pollen is at its worst during spring and summer.

Maps & Books

The CMA 1:25,000 *Tuggeranong* map covers the walk, but does not show any walking tracks or picnic areas. Two leaflets published by the ACT Parks & Conservation Service in its Murrumbidgee River Corridor series, *Pine Island and Point Hut Crossing* and *Kambah Pool*, are useful resources, although they don't cover the 7km between Pine Island and Kambah Pool. Graeme Barrow, in his *Walking Canberra's Hills & Rivers*, describes this walk as three separate outings.

Regulations

Camping and fires are prohibited in the Murrumbidgee Corridor.

> ### Warning
>
> The Murrumbidgee River swells rapidly after heavy rain, and can be more dangerous than it appears. It may seem to be flowing sluggishly, but this can be deceptive, especially near rocks. *Never* dive into a pool – the opaque water may conceal rocks or logs.

AUSTRALIAN CAPITAL TERRITORY

Kambah Pool

Duration	5½–6 hours
Distance	18km
Standard	easy-medium
Start/Finish	Point Hut Crossing
Nearest Town	Tuggeranong
Public Transport	yes

Summary A rare chance to walk along one of Australia's major rivers, through grasslands and open woodland to a popular swimming pool. The return gives quite different views from the outward walk.

The distance and duration of this extremely scenic walk are for the return excursion from Point Hut Crossing picnic area, which is accessible by public transport. If two vehicles are available, it can be a really easy-going one-way walk, with plenty of time left for swimming.

The walking track generally keeps quite high above the river, and for much of the distance crosses open grassland. If the track has been mown regularly, it should be easy to follow. Without mowing, however, route finding could be a problem, so it would be worth checking with Environment ACT on the state of the track.

The scenic highlight is Red Rocks Gorge, perhaps not a true gorge with the impressive cliffs on the western side of the river only, but still very photogenic. Elsewhere, the Murrumbidgee is broad and sinuous, tumbling lazily over rocky bars and meandering through boulders and past clumps of black cypress pines and river oaks.

In Tuggeranong, the nearest suburb to this walk, the large shopping centre has plenty of *cafes*, *takeaways* and *shops* where you can buy the ingredients for a picnic at Kambah Pool.

GETTING TO/FROM THE WALK

By car, join Tuggeranong Parkway leading south from either Parkes Way or Hindmarsh Drive, west of the city centre. The Parkway becomes Drakeford Drive between the suburbs of Fisher and Kambah. Then, at the roundabout junction with Johnson Drive (to the east, or left) and Woodcock Drive (to the south-west, or right), turn into the latter and follow it for nearly 2km to Jim Pike Ave on the right (also signposted to Point Hut Crossing). Continue along this road for 1km to the crossing and the picnic area on the right, where there's plenty of parking space.

To reach Kambah Pool, turn right (west) off Tuggeranong Parkway at the Sulwood Drive traffic lights; Kambah Pool Rd is the first on the left, 500m along. The picnic area is 5km away.

By bus, the most convenient route for Point Hut crossing is Action bus No 85 (City–Gordon–Banks–Conder); alight at the stop near the corner of Lewis Luxton Ave and Woodcock Drive. Walk north-west along Woodcock Drive for 200m to Jim Pike Ave; turn left and go on down to Point Hut Crossing picnic area. A daily all-zone ticket costs $7; an off-peak daily ticket costs $4.

THE WALK

Walk through the picnic area, across a causeway on the right and up to the left through a step-through stile in a gate. A sign points the way to Pine Island along the Murrumbidgee River Walking Track. The grassy track climbs beside a fence to a junction – turn right then left and about 60m farther on, at a three-way junction, go to the left. The track then drops down to a footbridge across a small creek, close to the Murrumbidgee itself, and leads on, never far from the river.

About 45 minutes' walking brings you to the southern edge of the extensive **Pine Island picnic areas**. Climb through a stile in a gate and part of the way across the parking area, go left down a flight of steps and cross a broad grassed area between the river and the car park. At the end of this open area, follow the road for about 150m to another car park and turn left. Leave the bitumen as soon as possible and go down to another open grassed area. Continue in the downstream direction, past numerous barbecues and picnic tables, and look for a vertical signpost 'Pine Island North 400m'. Posts with arrowhead markers should show the way from here, through the grass and

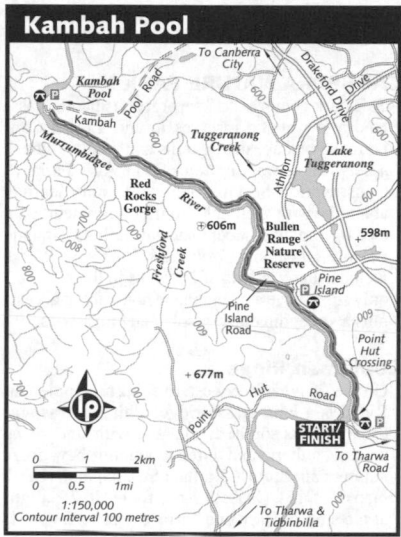

Kambah Pool

0 1 2km
0 0.5 1mi
1:150,000
Contour Interval 100 metres

into a pine plantation. At a T-junction with a vertical sign indicating the distance to Kambah Pool (7.6km), resist the temptation to go left and make your way to the nearby picnic area. Pick up a fence on the river side of the picnic area and follow it until it comes to an end, then continue on a track past a picnic shelter to a wide track junction. Turn left and descend to a Murrumbidgee River Walking Track signboard – about 45 minutes from your first encounter with the Pine Island picnic area.

Soon the track leads into the **Bullen Range Nature Reserve**, well above the river. Beyond a large pool on a very wide bend in the river below, climb a stile and turn left at a track junction towards Kambah Pool. Shortly, close to an old **stone wall** (built between 1867 and 1875), turn right then left through a gateway. Follow the centre path from here, up and over a low spur. Then, at a T-junction continue straight ahead to cross **Tuggeranong Creek** on rough stepping stones. If the creek is too deep, turn right at the T-junction to reach a bridge over the creek. Having crossed the stepping stones, climb up the bank, go through a stile and turn left along a wide track. The track

swings to the right, away from the creek; bear left through a stile in a gate. The track continues across the grassy hillside, then through scattered eucalyptuses.

A few hundred metres farther on, the cliffs of **Red Rocks Gorge** appear ahead. The track crosses a wide gully, then a broad open spur and another smaller creek. A side track down to the edge of the gorge is marked by an arrowhead on a post, but the better route is from a point about 50m farther on, at the end of the fence on your left. A narrow path descends to low cliffs overlooking the gorge (about 1½ hours from Pine Island).

Return to the main track. Soon a signposted **lookout** 100m to the left gives a fine view upstream to the gorge and beyond. The track continues across a pine-filled gully and shortly later meets a fire trail. Follow this for no more than 100m, then climb steeply on a foot track to cross an open slope. The gradual descent then begins; a lookout to the left provides a superb view of huge **Kambah Pool**. At a track junction, turn left and go through a stile and down stone steps to another junction. The pool and its sandy beach are on the left and the car park is on the right (30 minutes from the first lookout).

Other Walks

NAMADGI NATIONAL PARK
Orroral Valley

The Orroral Valley, in the central eastern part of the park, has a diverse history. No doubt visited by Aboriginal people during summer, it was settled in the 1860s – Orroral homestead is the oldest building in the park. For two decades from 1965 the valley was occupied by Australian scientists monitoring the passage of satellites. The defunct space tracking station was demolished and virtually all that's left are a few exotic trees. Interpretive signs at the homestead, the nearby shearing shed, and at the tracking station site explain their histories. A well-marked 6km walking track links these sites and Orroral camping ground. The walk can be done in either direction, from the station site or from the camp site; the latter is recommended for the manner in which the walk unfolds and changes as you progress up the valley. Carry water – there's a large kangaroo population in the valley. The

CMA 1:25,000 *Rendezvous Creek* map covers the area but is extremely out of date. Allow 3½ to four hours for this 12km return walk.

Bimberi & Murray

Bimberi Peak (1911m), the highest mountain in Namadgi, is on the NSW border. It can be climbed during a walk of three or four days, starting from the Orroral Valley car park. The climb is often coupled with an ascent of nearby Mt Murray (1845m). The best approach to Bimberi is via the Australian Alps Walking Track from where it crosses Murrays Gap; the summit is about 2.5km north along a fairly broad ridge. Mt Murray is about 1km south of the gap. You will first need to obtain a camping permit from Namadgi Visitor Centre (see the Namadgi National Park section earlier). The CMA 1:25,000 *Rendezvous Creek* map covers the area; John Siseman's *Australian Alps Walking Track* is invaluable.

TIDBINBILLA NATURE RESERVE

Camels Hump

This is a prominent feature on the ridge to the north of Tidbinbilla Mountain and offers similar views but with less climbing and a better track. From Mountain Creek car park follow the fire trail to the gap at the foot of the hump and continue to the top on the foot track. The distance is 12.5km; you'll climb 540m and take around five hours.

Gibraltar Rocks

This fantastic cluster of huge granite tors crowns a small hill on the ridge forming the eastern side of the Tidbinbilla River valley. From the old visitor centre car park, a walking track leads to a fire trail, which takes you to the foot of the rocks; a fairly well-used track snakes up through the boulders to the summit. Rather than retracing your steps to the start, a more adventurous alternative route is south-east along the trackless ridge to Devils Gap. The take-off point for this is about 600m south along the fire trail from the summit track, where the trail turns westwards. An old fence provides a useful guide most of the way. From Devils Gap a fire trail descends to Tidbinbilla Scenic Drive about 2km south of the starting point. The CMA 1:25,000 *Tidbinbilla* map covers the walk, but doesn't show all the tracks; also, the pine plantation south of the ridge has expanded since the map was published. Allow 3½ hours for the 10km route via Devils Gap.

CANBERRA NATURE PARK

This park comprises 27 separate bushland, grassland and wetland reserves in and around Canberra; some have nature trails and nearly all have a network of walking tracks. The ACT Parks & Conservation Service publishes some leaflets about the park, available from Environment ACT (see Information under Gateway earlier). Graeme Barrow's *Walking Canberra's Hills and Rivers* includes descriptions of 20 walks in the reserves; only some have a map, but the notes about access, plus a street directory, resolve any mysteries.

Cooleman Ridge

On the fringe of the western suburbs, Cooleman Ridge is a long grassy ridge, with Mt Arawang (765m) at its southern end, and with fine views across Canberra and to the mountains beyond. A nature walk starts at Kathner St, Chapman (UBD map 66, N16). On Action bus route No 26, alight at the stop in Darwinia Terrace near Kathner St. It's possible to extend the nature walk southwards, along the western flank of the ridge to Mt Arawang, and back along the eastern side. This makes a fine walk of nearly 11km; allow about three hours.

Black Mountain

Black Mountain, topped by the prominent communications tower, is one of the most distinctive features of the ACT landscape. Despite its proximity to the city and to busy highways, the extensive reserve, between Parkes and Belconnen Ways and Barry and Caswell Drives, has a remarkably natural feel about it. A dense web of walking and 4WD tracks enables many long and short walks, all featuring wide views and almost-guaranteed sightings of kangaroos and many native birds. A comprehensive leaflet (available from Environment ACT) includes a map showing the walking tracks and outlining the Woodland, Forest and Summit Trails. Separate leaflets are available for springtime wild-flower walks. The three main access points are Rani Rd (in the south-west corner, off Caswell Drive), Frith Rd (on the eastern side via Barry Drive) and Black Mountain Drive (to the summit car park adjacent to the tower).

Sydney Region

In the midst of the towering buildings of central Sydney it's difficult to believe that within 100km are several national parks where you can feel remote and where lyrebirds and kangaroos are common sightings. The parks protect temperate rainforest, eucalyptus bushland, unspoilt beaches, coastal cliffs and rock platforms dotted with deep pools. It says much for the community's commitment to national parks that these have survived intact for as long as 120 years, resisting Sydney's relentless urban sprawl. A variety of day walks in five parks are described in this chapter – just a sample of the wealth of opportunities on offer.

INFORMATION
Maps
A good street directory is indispensable for getting around the Sydney Region, especially by car. The weighty UBD *City Link* guide (published annually) covers nearly the entire area between Wollongong, the Blue Mountains and Newcastle in detail, and is well worth its not inconsiderable price. Lonely Planet's *Sydney City Map* is a portable and easy-to-use map of the city centre.

For general planning, there's not much difference between HEMA and Gregory's regional tourist maps. Gregory's maps include a detailed regional map, town maps and practical information.

The New South Wales (NSW) government's Central Mapping Authority (CMA) tourist maps are generally less up to date. The CMA's 1:25,000 series (recommended for walks in this chapter) is fine for topographic detail, but less useful for track information. The CMA has recently become the Land & Property Information New South Wales (LPINSW), which will produce new editions of the old CMA maps.

For maps covering individual walks, see Planning in the introduction to each walk.

Buying Maps Map World (☎/fax 02-9261 3601), 371 Pitt St, Sydney (open Monday to

RICHARD I'ANSON

Highlights

The Harbour Bridge from Circular Quay, at the centre of the gateway city of Sydney

- Wandering along Bouddi's sandy beaches; beautiful wind-fretted rock formations and coastal cliffs

- Enjoying the peace and seclusion of Kariong Pool and the seasonal wild flowers in Brisbane Water National Park

- Taking an invigorating dip in Crayfish Pool and viewing the ancient artistry of the Blue Mountains' Red Hands Cave

- Imagining you're in the tropics in Royal National Park's Palm Jungle

Saturday), and the Map Shop (☎ 02-9228 6111, @ maps@lic.gov.au), 23 Bridge St, Sydney, both stock a large range of topographical maps and walking guides. For LPINSW map sales, call ☎ 02-9228 6315.

Books
Several books describing walks in and around Sydney are available. The most

Sydney Region

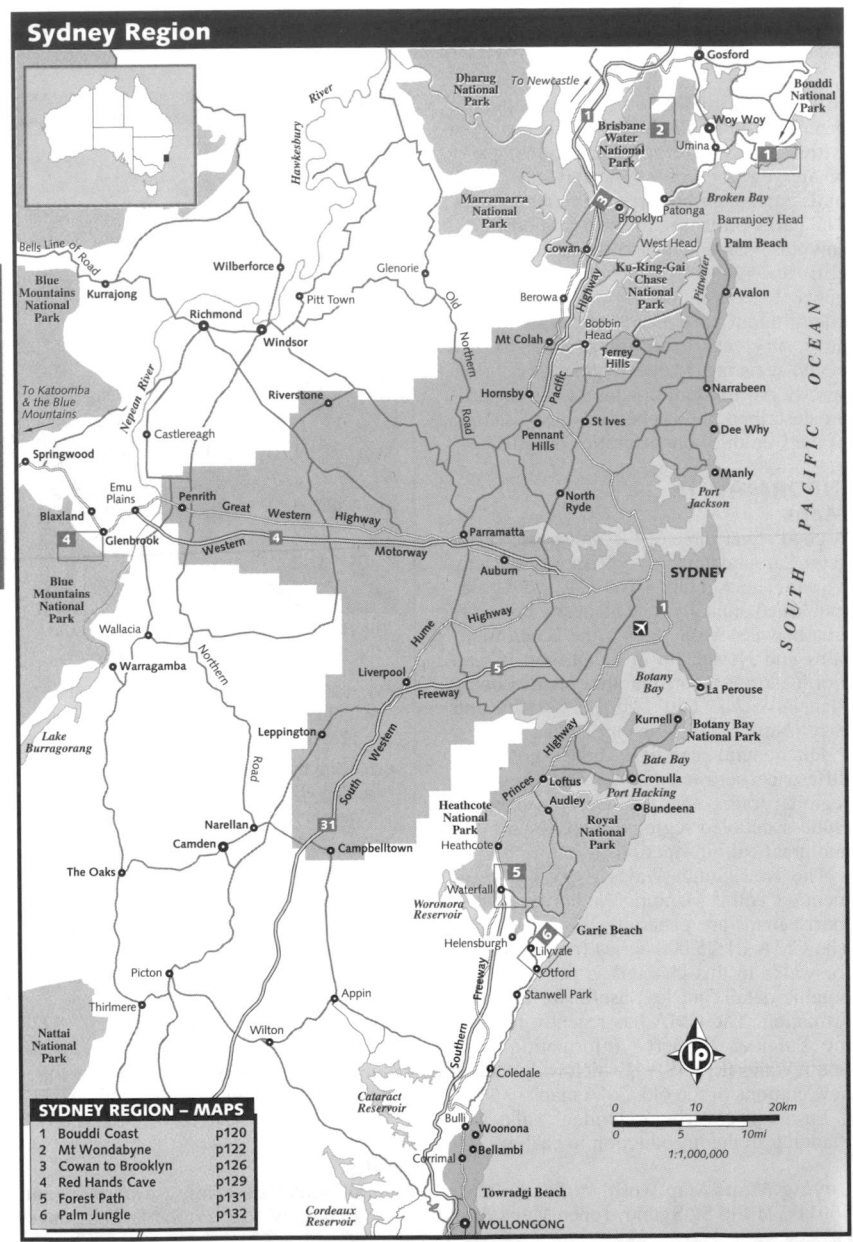

comprehensive and detailed are *Bushwalks in the Sydney Region,* Volumes 1 and 2, edited by S Lord & G Daniel and published by the National Parks Association of NSW. They describe 166 walks in all. The contributors are all active bushwalkers; the maps are almost good enough to use on the walks. *Best Sydney Bushwalks* by Neil Paton describes 60 walks from two hours' to two days' duration, most in national parks.

Gregory's *National Parks of NSW* covers 140 areas throughout the state, and would be an invaluable guide for an extended visit.

Of the many natural history books, two stand out for their clear illustrations and concise descriptions: *Common Native Plants of South Sydney* and *Common Native Plants of North Sydney*, both by Rodger Elliot & Trevor Blake.

Lonely Planet has two guides to Sydney to choose from: *Sydney* and *Sydney Condensed.*

Information Sources

The NSW National Parks & Wildlife Service (NPWS) is the prime source of information about walking in the Sydney Region. Its head office (☎ 02-9585 6444) is rather inconveniently located at 43 Bridge St, Hurstville (about 15 minutes' walk from Hurstville station). The information centre there is open weekdays and carries a comprehensive range of parks information and CMA maps. The NPWS touring guide, *Sydney: City of National Parks*, is excellent for access and background details. Its Web site (🖳 www.npws.nsw.gov.au) is also a mine of information, with contact numbers for each park, details of activity programs and news of bushfires and park closures.

For information on specific parks, it's better to call the ranger or district office (contact details are listed in the Information section for each park).

The National Parks Association of NSW (☎ 02-9299 0000, fax 9290 2525, ✆ npansw @npansw.org.au), 9/91 York St, Sydney, is one of the state's leading community conservation organisations, and has a very active walks program.

The Confederation of Bushwalking Clubs NSW represents more than 60 clubs across the state and operates a volunteer wilderness search and rescue service (see Rescue Organisations in the Health & Safety chapter). Although it cannot normally be contacted for inquiries (its office bearers are volunteers), it produces an informative magazine, *The Bushwalker*. It also maintains an excellent Web site (🖳 www.bushwalking.org.au), which includes a list of clubs, addresses of shops, information about current environmental issues and a list of national parks closed by bushfires.

The *Sydney Morning Herald* and the *Australian* daily newspapers carry detailed weather reports and forecasts.

Permits & Regulations

An entry fee of $5 to $9 per day is charged for most of the parks in this chapter. If you're spending some time in NSW, an annual pass to all the parks ($60) would be a good investment; they're available from NPWS offices and visitor centres.

Camping is permitted in all the parks featured, but only at designated sites and you must obtain a permit beforehand. This rule is intended to avoid overcrowding and to protect the environment. Details are given in the walks sections. For other suggestions on how to minimise your impact on the environment, see Responsible Walking in the Facts for the Walker chapter.

SYDNEY

Information on 'City of Glamour' and its vibrant suburbs is available at the Sydney Visitors Centre (☎ 1800 067 676, 🖳 www .tourism.nsw.gov.au), 106 George St, The Rocks, open daily. Its Web site includes a large database of hostels and hotels.

There's no shortage of Internet cafes in the city, several of which are listed in Lonely Planet's *Sydney* guide. Most public libraries provide free Internet access, but it's necessary to book a slot at least 24 hours ahead.

Supplies & Equipment

In the city, branches of the main outdoor gear shops are clustered around the lower end of Kent St. Paddy Pallin (☎ 02-9264 2685), at No 507, has a hire service. A basic

The Climate of Sydney

Sydney enjoys a temperate climate. Winter is relatively mild with average minimum and maximum temperatures of 8°C and 16°C; frosts are almost unknown along the coast, but quite common inland, and light snow can decorate the higher ground of the Blue Mountains. The average summer (December to February) maximum is 26°C, although temperatures can soar to the high 30s, especially away from the coast. If this heat is coupled with high humidity, things can become oppressive.

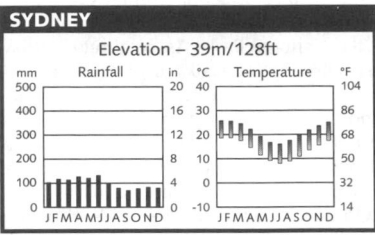

The average monthly rainfall ranges from 75mm (August to December) to 125mm (March to May); torrential downpours are fairly common between October and March.

Westerly winds prevail for most of the year, although usually becoming easterly coastal sea breezes during the afternoon. 'Southerly busters', strong cool to cold changes, are often welcomed during summer.

two-person tent can be hired for $75 for a week, and sleeping bags from $50. A deposit of $100 per item is required. Other outdoor gear shops in Kent St worth noting are Mountain Designs (☎ 02-9267 3822), at No 499, and Snowgum (☎ 02-9261 3435), at No 447.

Places to Stay & Eat

The accommodation choice in Sydney is huge and prices competitive, with good options in every price range – contact the Sydney Visitors Centre for an extensive list of accommodation options.

With great local produce, innovative chefs, inexpensive prices and BYO (Bring Your Own) alcohol licensing laws, eating out is one of the great delights of Sydney. Lonely Planet's *Out to Eat – Sydney* guide contains a lively commentary on the city's many memorable culinary highlights.

Getting There & Away

The major roads leading out of Sydney are either motorways, on which a toll is charged, or freeways. The former include the M4 from Strathfield to Emu Plains (en route to the Blue Mountains), and the latter the F3 to Newcastle (en route to Bouddi, Brisbane Water and Ku-ring-gai Chase National Parks) and the F6 from Waterfall towards Wollongong (via the Royal National Park).

Air You can fly into Sydney from all the usual international points and from all over Australia (for information on travel between Sydney and destinations outside Australia, see the Getting There & Away chapter). Both Qantas Airways (☎ 13 1313) and Ansett Australia (☎ 13 1300) have frequent flights to other capital cities and major airports, and Impulse Airlines (☎ 13 1381) flies to Sydney from several state capitals. Regional carriers, such as Eastern Australia Airlines (a subsidiary of Qantas) and Hazelton Airlines (☎ 13 1713) fly within NSW.

Bus Sydney Coach Terminal (☎ 02-9281 9366), on Eddy Ave outside Central Station, is a base for Greyhound Pioneer (☎ 13 2030) and McCafferty's (☎ 02-9361 5125). Premier (☎ 1300 368 100) and Firefly Express Coaches (☎ 02-9211 1644) have offices around the corner on Pitt St.

Train All interstate and principal regional services operate from Central Station. Call the Central Reservation Centre (☎ 13 2232) or contact a Countrylink Travel Centre (same central number). Call ☎ 13 2232 for recorded information on arrival/departure times.

Car Rental Major car-rental companies – Avis (☎ 02-9353 9000), Budget (☎ 13 2727) and Hertz (☎ 13 3039) – have offices at the airport and around the city. Thrifty Car Rental has desks at the airport (☎ 02-9669 6677) and an office (☎ 02-9380 5399) in the city at 75 William St.

Getting Around

The State Transit Authority (STA) of NSW runs most public transport in Sydney. Call ☎ 13 1500 between 6 am and 10 pm daily for information on Sydney Buses, Sydney Ferries, CityRail and Airport Express buses or visit the separate information booths at Circular Quay. Online information is available from 💻 www.131500.com.au. Also, check the front of the A–K *Yellow Pages*. Children (under 16) pay half price on STA services. It's worth trying to plan your activities to take advantage of off-peak tickets, which cost little more than a standard one-way fare for travel after 9 am on weekdays and at any time on weekends.

To/From the Airport Sydney's Kingsford Smith Airport is 10km south of the city centre. The domestic and international terminals are 4km apart. As well as a convenient free

---

Warning

During summer, the threat of bushfires in Sydney's national parks is never far away. While the proclaimed Bushfire Danger Period, usually 1 October to 31 March, is in force, no fires may be lit in the open. On days of Total Fire Ban, no fire of any kind, including cigarettes, can be lit in the open air; Total Fire Ban days are widely publicised in the news media. Electric and some gas barbecues may be used; however, part or all of any park may be closed to the public on days of extreme fire danger. Fire danger ratings are listed in the weather pages of the daily newspapers. You can also check with the local park information centre, or the National Parks & Wildlife Service of NSW (NPWS) Web site (see Information Sources).

Please make sure you're familiar with the advice on what to do if caught near a fire (see the boxed text 'Surviving a Bushfire' in the Health & Safety chapter).

---

shuttle service between the terminals (for transit ticket holders only), green-and-yellow Airport Express buses ($7/12 one way/return) travel between the domestic and international terminals and to Circular Quay (No 300), Kings Cross (No 350), and Darling Harbour and Glebe (No 352). All drop off and pick up at Eddy Ave, Central Station.

A new train service from Central Station to the airport takes 10 minutes ($12 return). These are regular commuter trains, so can get crowded and are not luggage-friendly.

Bouddi National Park

Overlooking the entrance to Broken Bay from the north, Bouddi National Park (1189 hectares) contains some superlatively beautiful, unspoiled beaches, separated by rugged cliffs and headlands. The park's great variety of vegetation ranges from dense coastal rainforest to low heathland. Created thanks to the vision of a remarkable woman (see the boxed text 'Marie Byles & Bouddi'), the park is a rarity on the NSW central coast. It is a viable (self-contained) ecosystem in an area otherwise intensively developed for housing, in which coastal views are valued in millions of dollars. The scenic Bouddi Coast walk links these features and is the focus of this section.

NATURAL HISTORY

The park's distinctive landscape of cliffs, shoreline rock platforms and the Bouddi Ridge, which rises steeply from the coast, is essentially the result of differing rates of erosion of sandstones, shales and conglomerates by wind and waves over millions of years.

Apart from coachwoods, cabbage trees and bangalow palms in the almost inaccessible rainforest, two of the trees of the open forest are particularly striking. The Sydney red gum (an angophora, a member of the same family as eucalyptuses) prefers sheltered south- or east-facing sites, and has smooth bright orange-brown or pink-brown bark. In Bouddi, scribbly gum (a eucalyptus), which is happy in more exposed

SYDNEY REGION

Marie Byles & Bouddi

Long before European settlers arrived, Aboriginal people lived in the Bouddi area; evidence of their way of life survives as rock engravings, axe-sharpening grooves and masses of discarded shells in rock shelters. For many years, dense scrub and rugged terrain kept European settlers at bay and ensured that this coast remained in its natural state.

In 1922 a remarkable young woman, Marie Byles (1900–79), ventured onto Bouddi Peninsula and was captivated by its natural beauty. Soon after, she became the first female solicitor in NSW and began her lifelong campaign for equal rights for women. Mountaineering and bushwalking were enduring passions and she was naturally drawn to the concept of national parks to preserve natural areas.

In the early 1930s Byles and a group of fellow bushwalkers campaigned for the creation of a national park at Bouddi, and in 1935 the state government set aside 263 hectares for public recreation and named the area Bouddi National Park. Its administration was in the hands of trustees, one of whom was Byles; it's almost certain that she was responsible for having the trustees' meetings on a park beach.

As Bouddi State Park, the reserve was taken over by the NSW National Parks & Wildlife Service in 1967, and in 1975 it regained national park status; the area of the park is now 1189 hectares. The park's marine extension of 287 hectares, between Gerrin and Bombi Points, was the first area of the sea bed to be given special protection in NSW.

Marie Byles was also an intrepid traveller throughout South-East Asia and a founder member of the Buddhist Society of NSW. A lookout on the Scenic Rd which overlooks Bouddi is named in her honour.

MARTIN HARRIS

places, is common in the 'mallee' form, with spindly trunks sprouting from a single set of roots. Its smooth grey or white bark is decorated with spidery crinkled lines, the trails left by the larvae of an insect. There's also the unusual burrawang (a cycad, the seeds of which are attached to cones); when mature, the seeds from the female cone fall to the ground and are toxic if eaten.

PLANNING

September to November are the best months for this walk, for the wonderfully rich displays of wild flowers. On hot summer days the several shadeless sections of the walk can be almost unbearably hot, although you can cool off with a dip at one of the beaches. There are no reliable sources of fresh water along the way, so set out with all you'll need.

Maps & Books

The CMA 1:25,000 *Broken Bay* map covers the walk described here, but does not show the full extent of the Bouddi Coast track. Gregory's *Central Coast* map is ideal for general orientation and access.

Bushwalks in the Sydney Region (see Books earlier) includes descriptions of six walks in the national park.

Information Sources

There is a park information centre beside the car park for Maitland Bay, on the Scenic Rd about 2.5km east of the Putty Beach turn-off, but it's open only at weekends. It stocks leaflets specific to the park. Alternatively, the Central Region Office of the NPWS (☎ 02-4324 4911), 207 Albany St North, Gosford, has information.

Permits & Regulations

Camping at the three bushland camping areas in the park – Tallow, Putty and Little Beaches – is by permit only; you must obtain a permit before arriving at any of the sites. Contact the NPWS Central Region Office (see Information Sources earlier). The fee for one or two people for one night is $12.50 at Tallow Beach or $17.50 at Putty and Little Beaches (additional nights cost less).

You must use a fuel or gas stove for cooking – campfires are banned. Free gas barbecues are provided at Putty and Little Beaches. Camping is not permitted elsewhere in the park. During times of extreme fire danger the park is closed to public access.

Bouddi Coast

Duration	5 hours
Distance	13.5km
Standard	medium
Start/Finish	Putty Beach
Nearest Town	Umina
Public Transport	no

Summary A varied walk along Bouddi's unspoiled coast, featuring heathland, forest, beaches, cliffs and magnificent panoramic views across Broken Bay to Sydney's northern beaches.

The Bouddi Coast walk – one of the finest of its kind in NSW – links Putty Beach (towards the western end of the park) with Little Beach, on the north-east boundary. Boardwalks, walking tracks and fire trails generally keep close to the rugged cliff-lined coast, passing through most of the different types of vegetation found in the park, from tall, cool forest in sheltered gullies to low, sparse heathland on exposed headlands.

It is described here as a return walk from Putty Beach, near Killcare, a small settlement on the shore of Brisbane Water. The medium grading is earned by the several steep ups and downs along the way, and by the occasional roughness of the track. You'll probably notice discrepancies in the distances given between places on signposts along the walk, although by no more than 1km; we've tried to reconcile these in this description.

A couple of worthwhile side trips to cliff-edge vantage points would add 1.8km and about 45 minutes. A shorter circuit, from above Maitland Bay and returning via Bouddi Lookout is outlined in Other Walks at the end of this chapter.

NEAREST TOWN & FACILITIES
Umina

Although Killcare is closer, the nearest town with a caravan park and plenty of shops is Umina, about 13km from Putty Beach. The name Umina is from an Aboriginal word meaning 'Repose'.

The nearest specialist walking gear shop stocking liquid fuel, gas canisters and CMA maps is Camping World (☎ 02-4324 6515), 188 Main St, Gosford, although the Mitre 10 hardware shop in West St carries Primus gas cylinders.

Places to Stay & Eat The *East's Ocean Beach Holiday Park* (☎ 02-4341 1522, fax 4341 4855, @ eastscp@ozemail.com), Sydney Ave, is right behind the low dunes of Umina Beach. It's large but doesn't feel too crowded. Grassed, shady tent pitches cost $16 per night. A basic cabin costs $42 per night. There are also gas barbecues, a pool and the nearby beach. The on-site shop provides room service for breakfast (mixed grill for $9) and dinner (including rump steak for $9). It also offers a huge range of takeaway food and is open until 9 pm in summer.

For somewhere to eat out, you could do far worse than *304 on West* (☎ 02-434 45433, 304 West St), open from 8.30 am to 9 pm Wednesday to Saturday; Wednesday is pasta night ($12 for pasta and sauce, salad and bread); otherwise there are main courses (Italian-style meat and fish) for $16 to $20 and daily pasta specials.

For self-catering, in West St (the main street) you'll find a *butcher*, *fresh seafood*, the unmissable *Bremen Patisserie* for bread, cakes and award-winning pies, a *health food shop* and *supermarket* (stocks liquid fuel).

Getting There & Away Umina is about 73km north of Sydney via the Sydney–Newcastle Fwy. Leave the freeway at the

Kariong and Woy Woy exit, then turn off the Pacific Hwy 1.5km south-east of the freeway along Woy Woy Rd. About 10.5km farther south, at a right bend near the shore of Woy Woy Inlet, Woy Woy Rd becomes Rawson Rd; 500m along this road turn south at a roundabout along Ocean Beach Rd. At another roundabout, 3.2km later, go right along Sydney Ave and follow the signs to the caravan park.

Although there is a good train service to Woy Woy and buses run from there to Umina, public transport is not a practical option for this particular walk in Bouddi National Park.

Putty Beach

For something a bit more natural, there's the *national park camping area* at Putty Beach (at the start of the walk), equipped with picnic tables, toilets and water. It's essential to obtain a permit first (see Permits & Regulations earlier). The nearest food shop is in the settlement of Killcare – follow the Killcare road for 400m from the junction of Putty Beach Drive and the Scenic Rd. The *Mini Market* and *bottle shop* is open daily and has a reasonable range of supplies. *Killcare*

Store opens daily; it has a small delicatessen and offers takeaway or eat-in sandwiches, pies, burgers and quiches.

GETTING TO/FROM THE WALK

From Umina, drive east along West St, then north along Barrenjoey Rd. At a roundabout 1.1km along, turn right and follow Empire Bay Drive for almost 6km, then drive south via Wards Hill Rd, which climbs very steeply up and over to the Scenic Rd. Turn right here, then take the second road on the left, signposted to Putty Beach. This partly sealed, part-gravel road ends at the beach car park, 1.1km from the Scenic Rd.

THE WALK

Walk along Putty Beach to the steps at the eastern end of the sand. Climb to an open expanse of fretted and crumbling sandstone, which leads to a long boardwalk above a fine shoreline rock platform. Soon you come to a junction where a short track leads down to small **Bullimah Beach**, which is safe only for paddling (there are many treacherous rocks just below the surface). Back on the main track, many steps take you up to **Gerrin Lookout** and fine views of

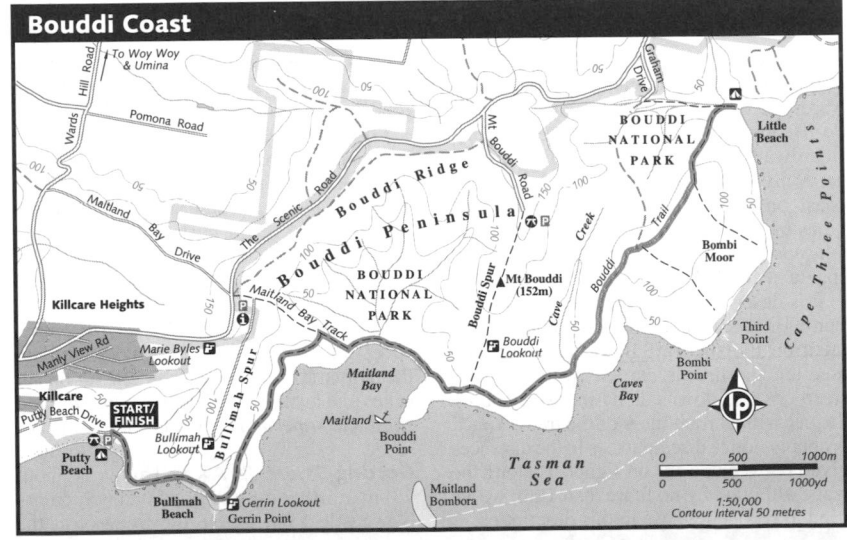

Maitland Bay, as well as the offshore rocks known as Maitland Bombora and the tall city buildings of the southern skyline. Continue through eucalyptus woodland, interspersed with some splendid burrawang palms, to a track junction; turn right to go down to **Maitland Bay** (about 1¼ hours from Putty Beach).

This beach is safe enough for swimming on a calm day. Go along to the eastern end and up the steep steps to a shallow gap on the spur leading towards Bouddi Point. There are good views of the coastal cliffs a short distance to the right; you might be able to make out the remaining fragment of the coastal paddle steamer *Maitland*, which foundered here in 1898 with the loss of about 27 lives, on the western side of Bouddi Point.

Continue along the main track up to a junction (the Mt Bouddi turn-off) and turn right towards Little Beach, with spectacular views of the Hawkesbury River estuary. The cliff-edge track, eroded in places, crosses a couple of gullies, separated by she-oak and banksia thickets, then descends to cross **Cave Creek** (about 45 minutes from Maitland Bay).

After this the way is up, via the many steps overlooking Caves Bay, to a small clearing. Turn left along a sandy 4WD track and continue climbing. Bear right at a fork and you soon come to the turn-off to Third Point on the right. There are good views of the cliffs from near the end of this track, but the next one to **Bombi Moor**, another 500m along the main track, is even more rewarding. Allow about 30 minutes for the return walk, along a fire trail that ends right on the cliff edge. The trail passes through heathland rich with wild flowers in spring. From here the magnificent views southwards include headlands of several northern Sydney beaches and the city skyscrapers.

Back on the main track, continue steadily down through varied eucalyptus woodland to a T-junction and turn right to reach **Little Beach**, a small rocky cove (about 45 minutes from Cave Creek).

The return to Putty Beach is simply a matter of retracing your steps.

Brisbane Water National Park

The deeply indented northern shores of Broken Bay, the Sydney–Newcastle Fwy and the town of Woy Woy and its satellites frame this rugged national park. Renowned for brilliant displays of wild flowers and for sweeping views of the bay, the park is endowed with plenty of walking tracks. The highlights of the walk described here are a secluded rock pool and the summit of the commanding Mt Wondabyne, close to the heart of the park.

The park was established in 1959 and covers an area of 12,000 hectares. It protects a wealth of Aboriginal cultural features, mainly rock engravings and axe-grinding grooves, created by the people of the Gurringai tribe. The Bulgandry engraving site is easily reached from the Woy Woy Rd, 2km south of the Pacific Hwy or 3km north of Staples Lookout, the starting point of the walk described.

NATURAL HISTORY

Before the last ice age, the inlets of Mooney Mooney and Mullet Creeks were river valleys; they deepened during the long cold spell and then filled when the sea level rose as the ice melted.

The sandstone plateaus in the park harbour a rich array of wild flowers. Among the most striking, especially during December, are Christmas bells, with a cluster of orange-red, yellow-edged flowers on each slender stem, and Christmas bush, a small tree covered with masses of small white or pale lilac flowers. Flannel flowers are aptly named; the bushy plants have woolly, deeply divided leaves and abundant downy, whitish flowers. White- or red-flowering hakeas have solid woody fruits and, commonly, needle-like leaves.

PLANNING

Spring is definitely the best time for this park, for the wild flowers and before the really hot weather sets in. You'll need to carry all your drinking water from the start.

Maps & Books

The CMA 1:25,000 *Gosford* map covers the walk but does not show all the tracks. The Great North Walk *Hawkesbury* map is at least as helpful. Both volumes of *Bushwalks in the Sydney Region* (see Books earlier) include walks in the park.

Mt Wondabyne

Duration	4½–5 hours
Distance	13km
Standard	easy-medium
Start/Finish	Staples Lookout, Woy Woy Rd
Nearest Town	Umina
Public Transport	no

Summary A walk that takes in one of the highest points in Brisbane Water National Park and a beautiful secluded waterfall and pool, with wild flowers everywhere in season.

Following fire trails and walking tracks, this walk takes you down into ferny Kariong Brook and up to the prominent summit of Mt Wondabyne (251m). In between, the route crosses sandstone plateaus, colourful with wild flowers in spring and early summer. For some of the distance you follow the well-signposted Great North Walk (GNW; see the boxed text 'Great North Walk'). If the day is warm, allow time for a swim in the beautiful pool in Kariong Brook.

NEAREST TOWN & FACILITIES

For a description of accommodation and other services in Umina and at Putty Beach, see Nearest Town & Facilities in the introduction to Bouddi National Park.

GETTING TO/FROM THE WALK

Staples Lookout and car park is on the eastern side of the Woy Woy Rd, 5.2km from the Sydney–Newcastle Fwy, or 6.5km from Woy Woy.

THE WALK

Walk northwards beside Woy Woy Rd from the Staples Lookout car park for about 40m, cross over to a gravel fire trail, go through a gate and then past a rehabilitated sand quarry. Turn left at a fork beneath a minor power line and, after about 200m, join a wider fire trail. Another 200m farther on, bear right along a track (also the route of the GNW). The track descends gradually with good views westwards; about 40 minutes from the start, turn right at a junction, still on the GNW, to diverge down to Kariong Brook.

After another 100m, the track bends sharply to the left across a rock slab. The descent continues quite steeply via many stone steps to the pool and waterfalls on **Kariong Brook**, beside a large stone overhang and fringed with ferns and water gums (20 minutes from the main track). Return to the main track by the same route and turn right.

The track climbs steeply, with conical Mt Wondabyne in view to the south. About 1.5km from the Kariong track junction, go left at a junction and down, with good views of the sea, to a T-junction and turn right. Continue ahead at the next intersection under

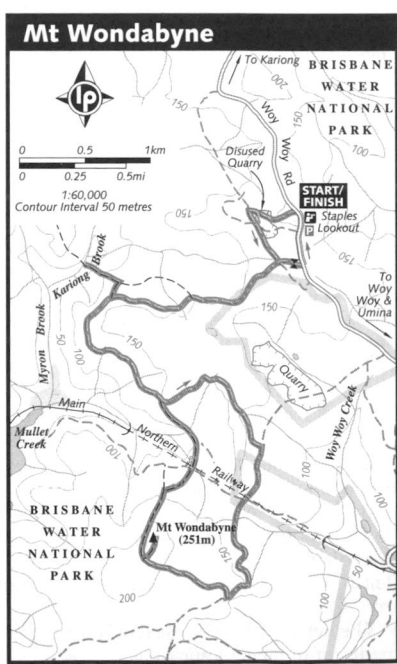

Great North Walk

One of the enduring projects celebrating the 1988 bicentenary of European settlement in Australia is the 250km Great North Walk (GNW), linking the cities of Sydney and Newcastle.

From Circular Quay, the route crosses Sydney Harbour by ferry to Valentia St wharf, goes through Lane Cove National Park, along Berowra Creek and through Ku-ring-gai Chase National Park to Broken Bay. Walkers then take a ferry ride to Brisbane Water National Park. Beyond there, the GNW traverses state forest and private land northwards to Congewoi Valley, then heads east along the Myall Range, past Lake Macquarie and on to the coast and Newcastle. The walk makes use of existing fire trails, walking tracks and some specially built sections of walking track, and is well signposted and track marked. Simple camp sites have been provided at suitable intervals, and the GNW passes

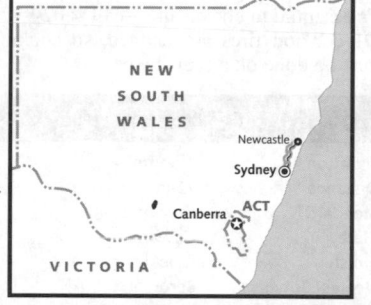

through some small towns with shops, accommodation and public transport connections in a few cases.

The recommended time for the full distance is 14 days, although this could be split into shorter journeys, mainly in the south where the route crosses the Sydney–Gosford railway line.

A set of six colour brochures, each with a topographic map showing the route of the GNW and all the necessary practical information, marketed as the Discovery Kit, is available from the Department of Land & Water Conservation (☎ 02-9228 6111), 23 Bridge St, Sydney, local tourist offices, map shops and outdoor gear suppliers.

the power lines, and soon climb to a track junction; rejoin the GNW by turning right. About 1km along this trail, diverge along a narrow track that leads up through boulders and along a rocky ridge to the summit of **Mt Wondabyne**, topped by a survey marker (nearly 1½ hours from the Kariong track junction). The fine view includes the fine spectre of Brisbane Water and the Blue Mountains on the western horizon.

Return to the main track and turn right. This track drops down across rock slabs (follow the painted arrow track markers) to a fire trail – turn right. About 400m farther on, it's left along a walking track. The route crosses expanses of sandstone patterned with water channels. At the next junction turn left, rejoining the route of the outward section of the walk. About 3.5km farther on, at the intersection beneath the power lines, continue straight ahead to a gate, beyond which is Woy Woy Rd. Turn left and walk up the cyclists' lane to Staples Lookout (almost an hour after joining the outward route).

Ku-ring-gai Chase National Park

Rising steeply from the southern shores of Broken Bay and from the long inlets of Cowan Water and Pittwater, this national park has suburbia crowding its southern boundaries and the busy Sydney–Newcastle Fwy roaring along its western side. Within its 15,000 hectares there is a huge variety of plants, from hardy banksias on the heaths and coachwoods in sheltered gullies, to the mangroves of the inlet shores.

Numerous walking tracks radiate from the main access roads into the park. The walk described here is in the north-western corner and partly follows the GNW (see the boxed text 'Great North Walk' on this page).

HISTORY

The park's name is a corruption of the name of the Aboriginal people, the Gurringai, who once roamed the area and whose culture is

SYDNEY REGION

reflected in the large numbers of rock engravings, axe-grinding grooves, middens (mounds of discarded shells and bone fragments) and examples of rock art.

The park, the second oldest in NSW, was established in 1894, thanks to the determination of one Eccleston du Faur. Despite opposition, du Faur persuaded the government of the day to realise his dream of a natural retreat free of buildings, logging and hunting. Over the years, the park's trustees fended off proposals to develop parts of the park, including a grandiose plan for the capital of the new Commonwealth of Australia at the beginning of the 20th century.

PLANNING

The best time to walk in this park is spring, for the wild flowers and before the very warm summer weather gets going. You'll need to carry all drinking water for the day as there are no reliable sources of fresh water along the way.

Maps & Books

The CMA 1:25,000 *Cowan* map shows 4WD tracks but not walking tracks. More useful is the *Benowie* map in the GNW Discovery Kit (for details see the boxed text 'Great North Walk'). The NPWS colour brochure for the park includes a map showing generalised routes of walking tracks, and much background information. This is more up to date than the CMA tourist map of the park.

Volumes 1 and 2 of *Bushwalks in the Sydney Region* (see Books at the beginning of this chapter) provide descriptions of several walks in the park.

Information Sources

The national park information centre (☎ 02-9472 8949) at Bobbin Head (about 5km from the Sydney–Newcastle Fwy via a signposted road near Mt Colah) is open daily. A wide range of publications and maps are on sale and the helpful staff can advise about track conditions in the park.

The Kalkari Visitor Centre (☎ 02-9457 9853), about 1.5km closer to the freeway, is open daily and features presentations on Aboriginal culture and Australian wildlife.

Permits & Regulations

The park entry fee is $9 per day, payable at entrance stations on the four main roads into the park (Ku-ring-gai Chase Rd, Bobbin Head Rd, West Head Rd and Coal and Candle Drive).

Camping is permitted in the park only at the Basin on the Pittwater shore in the east of the park; access is on foot down the Basin Track from West Head Rd (2.75km one way), or from Palm Beach by ferry (☎ 02-9974 5235) or water taxi (☎ 018-238 190). It's essential to book a site – call ☎ 02-9974 1011. Wood fires are banned, so cooking must be done on a fuel stove.

Cowan to Brooklyn

Duration	4 hours
Distance	12km
Standard	easy-medium
Start	Cowan
Finish	Brooklyn
Nearest Town	Berowra, Brooklyn
Public Transport	yes

Summary A very scenic stretch of the challenging Great North Walk, with mangroves, wild flowers and fern gullies.

This walk ranges from a sandstone plateau, with some good views, to the secluded shore of Jerusalem Bay and on to the waterside town of Brooklyn; the last 1km is outside the national park but is still on public land. The walk lends itself very well to public transport as both Cowan and Brooklyn, at the beginning and end of the walk, are on the railway line.

Following the GNW along walking tracks and fire trails, the route is well track marked, in places with arrows painted on rock. Steel hoops set into small cliffs make climbs or descents easier. Traffic on the freeway can be obtrusive but it's inaudible at sea level and in the deep gullies.

NEAREST TOWNS

Cowan is little more than a collection of scattered houses and a shop, about 300m north of the train station. There is a handful of places where you can have a snack or a meal at Brooklyn, but no accommodation. Berowra is the nearest place to stay, but if this doesn't appeal the walk can easily be done from a base in or nearer to the city.

Berowra

Places to Stay & Eat Between Mt Kuringgai and Berowra, *La Mancha Cara Park* (☎ *02-9456 1766, fax 9456 2067, 901 Pacific Hwy, Berowra 2081)* has a rather crowded camping ground; spaces for small tents are few, cramped and expensive ($21 for two people, charging the same price for a powered site). An on-site van ($54 per night) is preferable. Park facilities include a large campers' kitchen, swimming pool, small shop and Internet access.

At Berowra Waters Rd shopping centre (about 1km west of the Princes Hwy from a junction 1.5km north of La Mancha) are a *butcher* and *greengrocer*; 150m farther on is Berowra Market Place with a *supermarket* and *Berowra Heights Hotel,* which has a bottle shop and bistro.

Beside the highway near the Berowra Waters Rd junction is *North South Indian Restaurant* (☎ *02-9456 7033)*, open daily from 5 to 10 pm for eat-in or takeaway meals (BYO); main courses range from $7 to $14.

Getting There & Away Berowra is about 37km north of Sydney via the Pacific Hwy and Sydney–Newcastle Fwy; use the Windy Banks exit. La Mancha is about 2km south of the town and Berowra train station. Berowra, on the Gosford railway line, has a good train service from the city.

Brooklyn

Hawkesbury River Tea House (☎ *02-9985 7073)*, in a side street near the train station, is open until 3 pm (5 pm in summer) for large sandwiches, pies, Devonshire teas and drinks. There's also *JJ's Oyster Bar* opposite the station for fish and chips or oysters, and *Anglers Rest Bar & Restaurant* in the main street.

The nearest place for refreshments in the park is at Apple Tree Bay, 1km north of Bobbin Head.

GETTING TO/FROM THE WALK

If you're travelling by train, buy a return ticket to Hawkesbury River train station at Brooklyn; the standard return fare is $10.40. The journey to Cowan from the city takes 55 minutes, approximately every hour. Hawkesbury River is 11 minutes farther on.

THE WALK

At Cowan train station, walk along the southbound platform, through a gate and turn left at the bottom of the steps for about 150m, then right to a footbridge over the freeway. The track descends steeply to cross a stream and works its way farther down into a ferny gully. Traverse a rock platform, bear left then right to cross the stream again. Then it's down to the shore of **Jerusalem Bay**; mangroves line the opposite shore. The track leads generally east to some old stone steps. Continue up and across an open grassed area overlooking the bay (around 45 minutes from Cowan).

The route takes you back down to the shore via stone steps and a steel loop set into the rock. Farther on, cross a creek bed and follow the track past a large overhang and on to a cave shelter and a small stream, beyond which the climb starts. Up on the crest of the ridge, go straight on towards Brooklyn. The level going soon ends and on the way down, you come to an amazing group of **whale-backed boulders**. The marked route leads through an extremely narrow gap between two of them – you may need to detour to the left. Go down to cross Campbells Creek, then follow arrows along a convenient series of rock ledges beside low cliffs. A track then leads up towards the crest of a spur; turn left and shortly another minor climb is accomplished via steel hoops fixed into a boulder. Continue to a junction with a fire trail and turn right (about 1¼ hours from Jerusalem Bay).

About 30 minutes along the fire trail, as you round a bend, the road bridges across the scenic Hawkesbury River come into view. Then, after about 10 minutes, turn right down a steep, eroded track to another fire trail. Bear left for 130m, then right to pass through an informal *camp site*. Cross

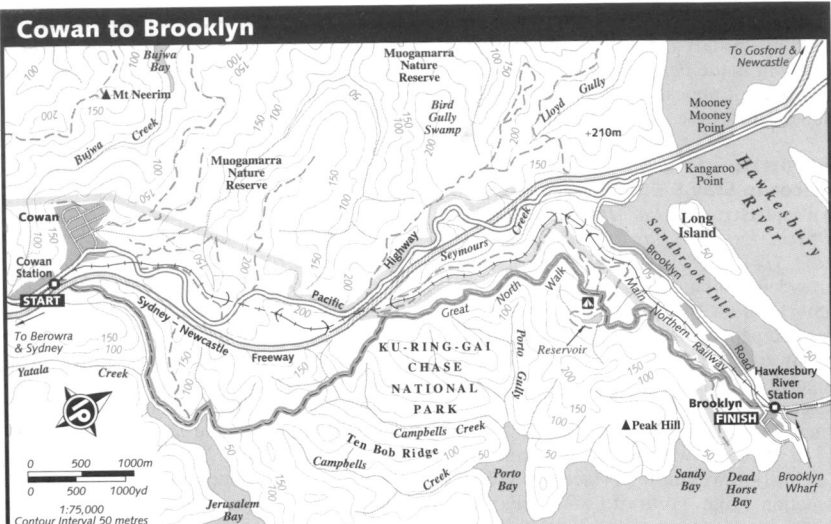

Cowan to Brooklyn

the creek flowing out of the nearby old **reservoir** and go through another *camp site*, close to the dam wall. Turn left at a fire trail and start climbing. About 15 minutes from the reservoir, turn right under a minor power line. Shortly afterwards, turn right again at a T-junction and then left, with steadily widening views of the Hawkesbury River on the steepish descent. With Brooklyn just below, turn left down a foot track, pass a pylon and keep to the left, then sharp right on a rock slab. Descend steps to near the front of a house and bear right to reach Brooklyn along the roadside path (nearly an hour from the reservoir).

Blue Mountains National Park

Among the five largest national parks in NSW, Blue Mountains National Park offers bushwalkers enough opportunities to fill a month's solid walking. Stretching west from the long escarpment overlooking Sydney's Cumberland Plain, the park, established in 1959, protects 248,146 hectares of forested sandstone ridges and deep, rugged valleys. This section focuses on the easternmost part of the park, centred on the town of Glenbrook; the area farther west is covered in the New South Wales chapter. The walk described takes in an Aboriginal rock art site and a remote swimming hole.

NATURAL HISTORY

The edge of the Blue Mountains plateau generally follows the orientation of a 100km-long fault line. Along this, about 70 million years ago, the Hawkesbury sandstone rock of the Sydney basin, laid down eons earlier, was thrust up to form the plateau to the west. Much later, streams sliced through the plateau, forming the characteristic steep-sided valleys. Euroka Clearing, a shallow basin with relatively fertile soil, is the eroded remnant of a volcanic vent that forced its way to the surface about 200 million years ago.

PLANNING

Spring is the best time for the Blue Mountains. Although the pools along the creeks are inviting in summer, this is also the season for bushfires, an ever-present risk in the area.

The water in Kanuka Brook may be safe to drink, but, to be sure, bring as much as you need for the day.

Maps & Books

The walks described in this section are covered by the CMA 1:25,000 *Penrith* map, but it does not show all the walking tracks.

For general planning, Gregory's 1:160,000 *Blue Mountains* map 238 is the most up-to-date available and includes town maps and basic walks information.

The NPWS guide *Blue Mountains National Park Walking Track & Visitor Guide: Glenbrook & the Eastern Blue Mountains* has brief track notes and information about picnic areas, lookouts and places of interest.

The two volumes of *Bushwalks in the Sydney Region* (see Books in the introduction to this chapter) contain descriptions of a good variety of walks in the area. *Native Plants of the Blue Mountains* by Margaret Baker & Robin Conningham is well illustrated, but gives only botanical (Latin) names. However, *Native Birds of the Blue Mountains* by the same authors has common names.

These publications are available at the Glenbrook Visitor Information Centre (see Information Sources).

Information Sources

The excellent NPWS Blue Mountains Heritage Centre (☎ 02-4787 8877, fax 4787 8514) is on Govetts Leap Rd near Blackheath, about 3km north of the highway. It runs ranger-guided activities and has all the information, maps and books you could need for walking in the area, plus a small selection of snacks and drinks. It's open daily from 9 am to 4.30 pm.

Closer to Sydney, the Glenbrook Visitor Information Centre (see Glenbrook for details), on the Great Western Hwy in Glenbrook, also carries a good range of maps and guides on the national park.

Permits & Regulations

The park entry fee is $5 at the entrance station 1.5km from Glenbrook. The park gates open at 8.30 am and close at 7 pm daily during summer.

Camping is permitted at Euroka Clearing, strictly by permit only; call ☎ 02-4588 5247 weekdays, 02-4739 2950 weekends for advice. Fires may be lit only in the fireplaces provided, although it's preferable to use a fuel stove.

NEAREST TOWNS
Emu Plains

On the banks of the Nepean River at the foot of the Blue Mountains escarpment, Emu Plains has the only caravan park conveniently located for walks in the lower Blue Mountains.

Places to Stay & Eat The *Nepean River Caravan Park* (☎ 02-4735 4425, fax 4735 6301), on McKellar St in Emu Plains, has plenty of space for tents, separate from the cabins and permanent homes, for $15 per night. The campers' kitchen has gas barbecues ($1 per half-hour, or $1 per 15 minutes outside). A pay phone is available during park office hours only.

O'Donoghue's Irish Pub (☎ 02-4735 5509), on the Great Western Hwy, specialises in Irish food and beer, and has a courtyard barbecue where you can cook.

For self-caterers the Lennox shopping centre beside the Great Western Hwy has stores including *supermarkets* (open daily) and *bottle shops*.

Glenbrook

Information is available from Glenbrook Visitor Information Centre (☎ 1300 653 408, @ bmta@lisp.com.au), on the Great Western Hwy, open daily. In Ross St (the road to Blue Mountains National Park) is Rocksports, open daily, where you can stock up on gas.

Places to Stay & Eat The nearest youth hostel is *Hawkesbury Heights* (☎ 02-4754 5621, 836 Hawkesbury Rd, Hawkesbury Heights). A night in this new purpose-built place costs $12 for a twin or double.

Glenbrook has two streets of shops, including a *supermarket* in Park St. For a snack or light meal try *Andra's Tea House*, *Blue Tongue Lizard* or *Syd's Caffe*.

Getting There & Away By road, Glenbrook is 65km from Sydney via the Western Motorway and the Great Western Hwy.

Train travel is a feasible option. The CityRail service runs at least hourly; the adult off-peak return fare is $8.20 (1¼ hours from Sydney Central).

Red Hands Cave

Duration	4–4½ hours
Distance	11km
Standard	easy-medium
Start/Finish	Glenbrook Causeway
Nearest Town	Glenbrook
Public Transport	yes

Summary Visit the fascinating Red Hands Cave Aboriginal rock art site, followed by an invigorating swim in a secluded creek pool.

This walk has two very different highlights: Red Hands Cave, an Aboriginal rock art site; and secluded Crayfish Pool on Kanuka Brook, a beautiful place for a swim on a warm day. The rock shelter, 'discovered' in 1913, is decorated with numerous stencils and solid images of hands, created with coloured clays (ochre) by the Daruk Aboriginal people. They roamed the area long before Europeans arrived, finding abundant supplies of food in fruits of various trees, such as the lilly-pilly and wild cherry.

The circuit walk to the cave follows well-used walking tracks up beside Red Hands Gully and down along Camp Fire Creek, with some easy rock hopping. The walk down to the pool and back is a side trip from this circuit, along a gravel road and down a steep walking track, rocky in places but generally easy to follow. If time is short, you could just concentrate on the circuit, saving about 1½ hours.

GETTING TO/FROM THE WALK

By road, the turn-off from the Great Western Hwy in Glenbrook is clearly signposted to Blue Mountains National Park. Follow Ross St to a T-junction and turn left along Burfitt Parade, which becomes Bruce Rd and leads to the park entrance.

Two car parks are convenient. One is on the right between the entrance and Glenbrook Causeway; from here walk down the road and cross the causeway – the walk starts nearby to the right. The other parking area is beside The Oaks Fire Trail, 300m up the road from the Glenbrook Causeway. From here a flight of steps leads down to the Red Hands Track beside Red Hands Gully, just up from Glenbrook Creek.

If you reach Glenbrook by train, cross the line to a footpath that parallels Burfitt Parade and Bruce Rd to the national park entrance. Walk down and across the causeway; the start of the Red Hands Track is a short distance to the right (about 1.8km from the station).

THE WALK

From the junction of Red Hands Gully and Glenbrook Creek, Red Hands Track, rocky and sandy in places, follows the gully upstream to a junction (about 40 minutes from the start). Bear right and climb through mixed forest, including bloodwoods, she-oaks and turpentines (a tall tree with dark green, glossy leaves), to **Red Hands Cave** (another 25 minutes). The cave is glassed in to protect the images; detailed interpretive signs explain its history and how the hands were created.

A broad track leads to the Red Hands Cave car park (there are toilets nearby). To continue to Crayfish Pool, turn right along the Red Hands Fire Trail. Follow this generally west for 1.3km (15 minutes); the start of the track down to the pool leads westwards between two stringybark trees and opposite a small informal car park. This excellent track makes a tortuous descent, exploiting gaps and defiles in the craggy spur. The final steep section involves a slightly awkward move down boulders using footholds in a narrow slot. Walk upstream for five minutes: go up and over a large boulder, and then down through more boulders near a sheer wall on the left to deep **Crayfish Pool**, with its sandy beach and waterfall (30 minutes from the fire trail).

Climb back up to the fire trail, turn left and return to the Red Hands car park. Follow

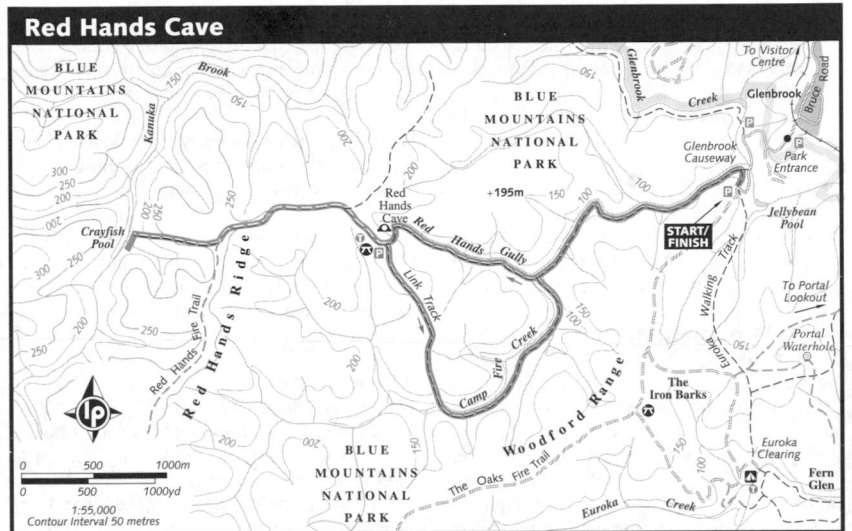

Red Hands Cave

the signposted Link Track, which descends steadily to the **Camp Fire Creek** crossing. Walk downstream beside the creek; shortly afterwards, at the first expanse of flat rock in the stream, you'll find an interpretive sign explaining how the axe-grinding grooves here were made. Another sign farther on describes the diet of the Daruk people. A little more than 1km along Camp Fire Creek, you reach Red Hands Gully and the route of the morning's walk. It's then simply a matter of going back down the track through the gully to the car parks (about an hour from Red Hands Cave car park).

Royal National Park

This is Australia's first national park, and one of *the* traditional bushwalking areas near Sydney. Within its 15,080 hectares is a wide-ranging network of walking tracks, exploring heath and open forest on the sandstone ridges, creeks in steep rugged valleys, beaches and coastal cliffs. The park is accessible by public transport and car and there's an excellent

visitor centre near Audley. Very basic bush camping is permitted at a few sites.

Two walks in the southern section of the park are described here and there are outlines of the popular long-distance Coast Track and a shorter walk linking two train stations in the Other Walks section.

PLANNING

The springtime display of wild flowers makes this the ideal season for the park; by early summer it's warm enough for a swim at the beaches or in pools along the inland creeks. To be on the safe side, carry all the drinking water you'll need for the walks.

Maps & Books

The special CMA 1:30,000 topographical map *Royal National Park, Heathcote National Park, Garawarra State Recreation Area* includes lots of background information. The CMA 1:25,000 *Appin* and *Otford* maps cover the Forest Path walk, although the Forest Path isn't shown. The NPWS provides a 1:35,000 planimetric map of the park with summary information of about 11 walks. The CMA 1:25,000 *Otford* map covers the Palm Jungle walk.

The two-volume set *Bushwalks in the Sydney Region* (see Books in the introduction to this chapter) includes descriptions of 10 walks in the park.

These publications are available from the Royal National Park Visitor Centre.

Information Sources
The Royal National Park Visitor Centre (☎ 02-9542 0648), on Farnell Ave, Audley Heights (signposted from the Princes Hwy between Loftus and Engadine), is open daily.

Permits & Regulations
An entry fee of $9 per vehicle is charged for the park. Camping is permitted only at a small number of designated sites within the park. It is essential to obtain a permit before setting out; they are available only at the visitor centre. The numbers of people using each site are strictly limited, and sites may be closed at times of high fire danger or to allow vegetation to recover. Wood fires are prohibited, so bring a portable stove for cooking. None of the camp sites is accessible by car and no facilities of any kind are provided.

It's almost certain that during 2000 some sites will be closed and fees introduced. Check with the visitor centre before making any serious plans.

NEAREST TOWN & FACILITIES
Heathcote
Although the town of Waterfall is at the start of the first walk described in this section, Heathcote (6.5km north) has a caravan park and shops.

Places to Stay & Eat Small *Heathcote Tourist Park* (☎ 02-9520 8816) is squeezed between the Princes Hwy and the railway, 400m south of the train station, so it's scarcely peaceful; however, it is conveniently located. Powered sites cost $20 per night, standard cabins for two people cost $35 nightly and en suite cabins cost $45. There are no unpowered (small tent) sites. There is an ATM in the Caltex petrol station.

In the shopping centre are a small *supermarket*, a good *bakery* and a *bottle shop*. The *Oliver Street Restaurant* (☎ 02-9520

2354), just around the corner from the highway, is open from 5.30 pm Wednesday to Sunday for mainly Mexican food, with main courses from $11.

Getting There & Away Both Waterfall and Heathcote are on the Sydney suburban Illawarra railway line. The daily half-hourly service takes 44 minutes to Heathcote ($7.60 return) and 48 minutes to Waterfall ($8.80).

By car Heathcote is 38km and Waterfall 44.5km from the city via the Princes Hwy. There are car parks close to the stations at both towns.

Garie Beach
The *Garie Beach YHA* (☎ 02-9261 1111) is small and basic (no electricity or phone), but a great base for exploring the park. Bookings are essential and you need to bring food, matches, torch (flashlight) and toilet paper; the fee is $7 per night. You can drive to the Garie Beach car park from Waterfall and then walk 1km to the hostel, or walk in from Otford or Bundeena.

Forest Path

Duration	3½–4 hours
Distance	10.5km
Standard	easy-medium
Start/Finish	Waterfall
Nearest Towns	Waterfall, Heathcote
Public Transport	yes

Summary A restored historic path through luxuriant palms and towering eucalyptuses beside tranquil Hacking River and Bola Creek.

The Forest Path is a historic and very scenic walking track circumnavigating Forest Island, a few kilometres east of Waterfall. The 'island' is a steep-sided hill, almost isolated by the Hacking River and a tributary, Bola Creek. The path, originally built in 1886 for walkers and horse riders, was restored in 1988.

The track passes through temperate and subtropical rainforest in the Hacking Valley, where the tallest trees are coachwood, sassafras, turpentine and lilly-pilly, shading luxuriant ferns and vines. The unusual cork-wood is also found in the area. Some of the finest trees were logged early in the 20th century, but public outrage ended the felling. Couranga Track, which leads down to the Hacking River from near Waterfall, follows an old logging track.

The walk as described starts and finishes at Waterfall train station (see Getting There & Away under Heathcote for transport details). Car travellers could concentrate on the Forest Path by parking at Fosters Flat beside McKell Ave (4.8km east of Waterfall), following the path from there to the Hacking River crossing and then the route described for the longer walk; the distance for this shorter walk is 5km. Crossing the Hacking River could be hazardous after heavy rain.

THE WALK

Go through a gateway in the middle of the fence along the eastern side of the Waterfall train station car park and follow a foot track to the local oval. Cross the oval to a fire trail, which leads into open heathland. About 15 minutes from the station and 40m past a memorial to bushfire fighters, turn right down the signposted **Couranga Track**.

The track loses some height along the ridge, then after about 1.4km turns sharp left and descends more steeply, following a small creek on the left into the deep, steep-sided valley of the **Hacking River**.

About 1¼ hours from Waterfall you reach a track junction (the track to the right leads to McKell Ave). Cross the river here on a line of stepping stones, go straight ahead across the sand and up steps to another track junction. Turn left along the Forest Path towards the Bola Creek rest area. The excellent track passes through the extraordinary subtropical rainforest surrounding the Hacking River. About 40 minutes from the stepping stones, the track bends to the right to follow **Bola Creek** upstream.

Another 10 minutes brings you to a simple picnic area. Go on to a fire trail, turn right and follow it southwards for about 600m, past the substantial stone pillars of an old gateway, to a car park beside the sealed Sir Bertram Stevens Drive. Take a few steps to the right down the road and continue down a track to a junction; turn left in the signposted direction of Couranga Track. Soon you are back at the stepping stones across the river. Allow about 1¼ hours for the return to Waterfall by the route you followed earlier.

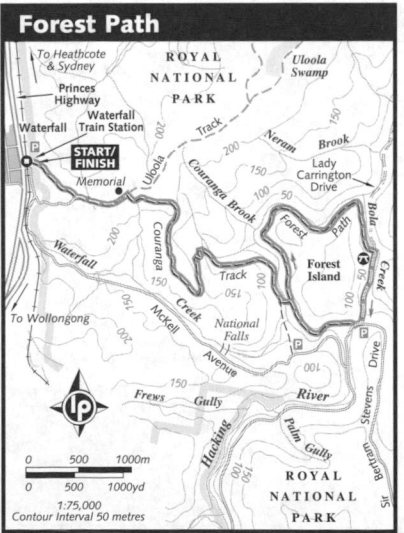

Forest Path

Palm Jungle

Duration	4–4½ hours
Distance	11km
Standard	medium
Start/Finish	Otford Lookout
Nearest Towns	Waterfall, Heathcote
Public Transport	yes

Summary A very scenic coastal walk with subtropical palm jungle, open grasslands, eucalyptus woodlands and a small historic beachside settlement.

In the south-east corner of the national park, the Garawarra Ridge falls steeply to the rocky shore. The precipitous slopes harbour an extraordinary subtropical rainforest where tall cabbage fan palms reach for the sunlight, and coachwoods, red cedars, fig trees and bird's nest ferns create the illusion of the tropics, and lyrebirds fossick in the dense undergrowth. The forest on the ridge is much more open, and here you'll see the remarkable Gymea lily with large red flowers on stems up to 3m long.

The walking track from Otford Lookout that links the ridge to the coastline through the jungle is rather faint in places. There are no markers, so be alert for traces of other walkers. The track is part of the popular long-distance Coast Walk (see Other Walks at the end of the chapter).

At Burning Palms Beach is a cluster of cabins, some of which date from the 1920s and 1930s when people settled here and supplemented the dole with fishing. The cabins are now regarded as part of the park's heritage. During summer the surf life-saving club patrols the beach. For a more secluded beach you can continue along the Coast Track from Burgh Ridge for about 1km to North Era.

Carry all the water you'll need for the day.

NEAREST TOWN & FACILITIES

For a description of accommodation and other services in Heathcote and at Garie Beach, see Nearest Town & Facilities in the introduction to the Royal National Park. The nearest shops to the walk are in Stanwell Park, on Lawrence Hargreave Drive, which is roughly 2km south of the junction with Lady Wakehurst Drive.

GETTING TO/FROM THE WALK

By road, Otford Lookout is 58km south of Sydney via the Princes Hwy and Southern Fwy. Leave the freeway about 8.5km south of Waterfall along Lawrence Hargreave Drive (this exit is due for completion in July 2000). Follow the road for nearly 3km to a junction, then continue along Lady Wakehurst Drive for 2km to Otford Lookout. There is plenty of parking space on the eastern side of the road.

Otford train station is on the Illawarra line; the relevant timetable is the CityRail Bondi Junction–Bomaderry service. The return off-peak fare is $7 ($12 standard) for the 55-minute journey from Sydney Central. Relatively few trains stop at Otford, so check the timetable beforehand; trains to Sydney Central leave Otford at 4pm and 5.15 pm. To reach Otford Lookout (the start and finish of the walk) from the train station,

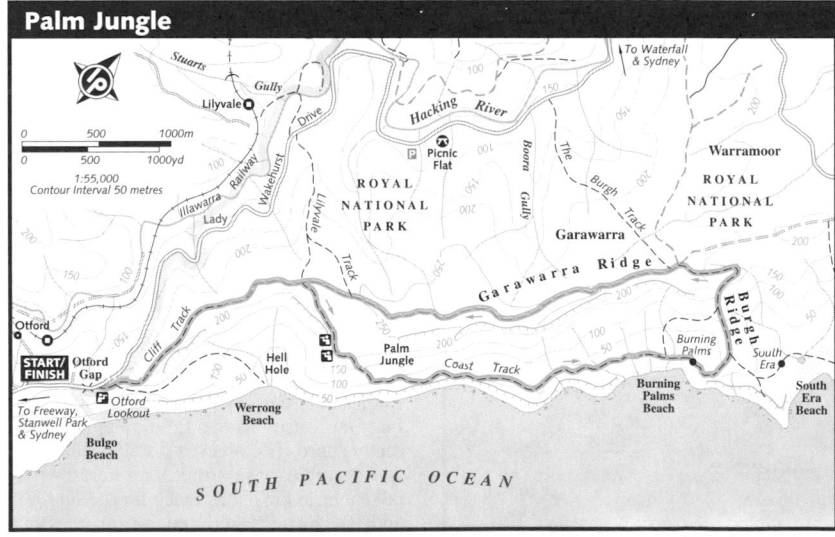

walk up the steps from the platform and keep right along a sealed path to the end of Station Rd; follow it to a T-junction with Domville Rd and walk on up to Lady Wakehurst Drive. Otford Lookout is 500m to the left.

THE WALK

The trail to Burning Palms Beach begins at the Otford Lookout. After a short stretch in the open, the cliff-top track soon enters tall forest and generally climbs, in places near the edge, for 1.4km to meet the Cliff Track fire trail. Continuing on, you reach a signposted junction for the **Coast Track** (about 45 minutes from the start). Turn right here and soon you'll come to two informal lookouts a few metres to the right, with spectacular views down to Werrong Beach and the south coast.

Then you plunge into the fantastic **Palm Jungle**. After nearly an hour, you emerge blinking into the sunlight and open grassland. The rather eroded track leads down to a hut (used by park rangers) then through patches of scrub and bracken above **Burning Palms Beach**. The easiest course is to go down to the beach as soon as possible and walk along the sand to a large green building at the northern end (30 minutes from the jungle).

To continue, walk up to the building (the surf life-saving club) and follow a track north-eastwards past various shacks and up to the spur rising from the northern end of the beach. Walk up the crest of this, **Burgh Ridge**, into eucalyptus and palm forest. The track climbs through a band of rock to a junction at Garawarra (the site of a farm, about 50 minutes from the beach). Follow the fire trail signposted to Lilyvale and Otford; after 40 minutes pass the turn-off to Lilyvale, then the track to Burning Palms. Then, it's just another hour back to Otford Lookout.

Other Walks

BOUDDI NATIONAL PARK
Maitland Bay Circuit

Although Mt Bouddi (152m) is the highest point in Bouddi National Park, tall forest largely obscures the views. Instead, there's Bouddi Lookout, a few hundred metres south, on the edge of the forest. This can feature on a circular walk of about 6km (two hours) from Maitland Bay car park. Go down the track to Maitland Bay (detouring on the way to Bullimah Lookout for superb views of Maitland Bay) and follow the route described for the main walk to the signposted junction with the track to Mt Bouddi. Follow this track up to a car park and picnic area, continue along the sealed access road for 600m and turn left along a fire trail, near the Scenic Rd. This trail leads south-west for 2km to a gate; walk up to the right and the Maitland Bay car park is a short distance farther on.

KU-RING-GAI CHASE NATIONAL PARK
Euroka & Beyond

This very varied walk includes Euroka Clearing and fine views of the Nepean River and Glenbrook Creek Gorges. Euroka Clearing, settled in 1826 and now home to large numbers of tame kangaroos, is one of the designated camping areas in the national park. The walk starts 200m up the road beyond Glenbrook Causeway. Allow at least 4½ hours for this 15km walk, including 360m ascent.

Follow the signposted Euroka Walking Track to the clearing. For Nepean River Gorge, bear left as you reach the clearing, cross a bridge and skirt the clearing to a track into the forest. After about 10 minutes, descend many steps to the Nepean River. Climb back up the steps and follow Bennetts Ridge Track to Euroka. Cross the clearing to rejoin the track by which you reached here earlier. Climb to the signposted junction and turn right towards Portal Waterhole; go left at a T-junction and on to the waterhole. Bear right following the track into forest; turn right at a gravel road. Just past a steep climb, a track leads to Tunnel View Lookout for excellent views of the railway tunnel and Glenbrook Gorge. Go on along the road to Portal Lookout at the edge of the escarpment. Return along the road for 2.6km to a T-junction; turn right and right again and continue down to the starting point.

ROYAL NATIONAL PARK
The Coast Walk

This 26km walk crosses Royal National Park from Bundeena on the shore of Port Hacking to Otford Lookout, keeping close to the coast almost all the way. Camping is permitted at four sites and there's also a youth hostel at Garie Beach (see the Royal National Park section earlier for camping and accommodation details). The walk is described in Volume 1 of *Bushwalks in the Sydney Region* (see Books in the introduction to this chapter). Access to the start is by train to Cronulla and ferry from there to Bundeena (phone ☎ 02-9523 2990 for timetable details).

Waterfall to Heathcote

This station-to-station walk in the Royal National Park takes in a high sandstone plateau and a creek with fine swimming pools. Follow the route described for the Forest Path from Waterfall (see the Royal National Park section earlier) and continue past the turn-off to Couranga Track along Uloola Track (a fire trail). At the apparent end of the track, descend to Uloola Falls and continue towards Heathcote via Uloola Turrets (sandstone boulders) then Karloo Pools. From here follow the track up to Heathcote, turning left near the fire station and right at the next two junctions to the train station. Allow about 4½ hours for this 11km walk. It's covered by the CMA 1:25,000 *Appin*, *Otford* and *Port Hacking* maps; however, neither these nor the 1:30,000 *Royal National Park* map show the tracks accurately.

New South Wales

It might be Australia's most populous state, but New South Wales (NSW), with the vast majority of its six million-plus residents living by the coast, has a partially forested and mountainous hinterland that's a bushwalker's delight. The state has over 80 national parks to explore, covering about four million hectares and protecting environments as diverse as the peaks of the Snowy Mountains, the subtropical rainforest of the Border Ranges and the vast arid plains of the Outback. Many parks are World Heritage Areas of exceptional beauty and significance; some include protected wilderness zones, which offer outstanding remote-area walking.

HISTORY

Aboriginal tribes wandered south-eastern Australia many millennia before James Cook landed in 1770 and, perplexingly, named the land New South Wales. The seafarer had never been to Wales, and the countryside, covered in gum trees and scrubby bush and dominated by a seemingly impenetrable low mountain range, hardly looked Welsh, either. No matter, since fate would soon cast NSW as the British Empire's first antipodean penal colony, when the First Fleet arrived with some 800 convicts in 1787.

NSW really began to develop a distinct identity under the stewardship of Governor Macquarie in 1810; his enlightened policies helped both former convicts and those Aborigines lucky enough to have survived European diseases and extermination by settlers. By 1819 NSW was top of the list for voluntary immigration from the UK, and by 1823 it had become an official colony.

Exploration of the state was also under way. A path through the Blue Mountains to the western plains was forged in 1813 by Blaxland, Wentworth and Lawson. Soon after, George Evans led two expeditions across the mountains and found the Macquarie and Lachlan Rivers. Other notable explorers of the period included John Oxley,

Highlights

SIMON RICHMOND

Historic Jenolan Caves House offers accommodation at the end of the Six Foot Track

- Experiencing the full range of Blue Mountains natural environments along the Six Foot Track
- Trekking down into the Grose Valley to discover the serene Blue Gum Forest
- Climbing Australia's highest peaks in Kosciuszko National Park
- Exploring the pitted limestone gorges of the Blue Waterholes area
- Discovering the untracked plains of the upper Thredbo River
- Descending through spectacular Bungonia Gorge for a lazy swim in the Shoalhaven
- Navigating the sandstone maze of Monolith Valley to breathtaking views from the Castle summit

who found a way across the Great Divide and followed the fertile Hastings Valley to Port Macquarie, and Hume and Hovell, who made the first overland journey southwards to Port Phillip Bay, discovering the Murray River en route (see the boxed text 'Hume & Hovell Track' later in this chapter).

By the mid-1830s the general layout of present-day NSW was fixed, and settlers with their herds and flocks eagerly followed the explorers' routes. The 1850s gold rush saw another rapid influx of immigrants to the state, so much so that the British government stopped transportation in 1853.

Come the turn of the century, Sydney was a vigorous city of nearly 500,000 people and a great port. Federation of the country loomed, and after much bickering between Sydney and Melbourne, the Australian Capital Territory (ACT) was created in 1911. Around the same period, the recreational sport of bushwalking was developing a head of steam. The 21-year-old Myles Dunphy, considered the father of Australian bushwalking, started the first such club in Sydney in 1914 and declared his vision for what is now the Blue Mountains National Park.

NSW was not saved from the effects of the global cycle of boom and bust that characterised the interwar years. Through it all, however, Sydney continued to grow, a process which culminated in the multiple developments for the Olympic Games in 2000.

NATURAL HISTORY

The Great Dividing Range dominates NSW, running the length of the state. The range and its surrounds contain a mixture of rocks, some 500 million years old. At the Three Sisters in the Blue Mountains, for example, you can see layers of sandstone, alternating with strips of red and grey shale. The nearby Megalong Valley and along Cox's River are predominantly granite.

Most of the Great Dividing Range's ancient peaks have been worn down to a series of plateaus or tablelands – most notably the New England tableland, the Blue Mountains, the Southern Highlands and the Monaro Tableland. In the Snowy Mountains, in the south of the state, by contrast, the highlands rise above 2000m, culminating in Australia's highest peak, Mt Kosciuszko at 2228m. There's evidence here of the last ice age in the moraines and lakes left by retreating glaciers.

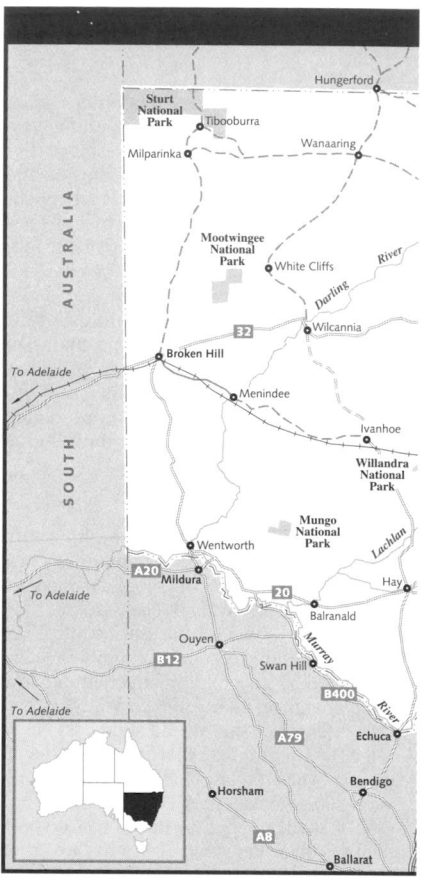

Pockets of limestone have provided the raw material for notable cave systems at Jenolan in the Blue Mountains, the Bungonia State Recreation Area, and at Cooleman and Yarrangobilly in Kosciuszko National Park. In the north of the state, tough volcanic trachyte rocks form the basis for the Grand High Tops ridge of Warrumbungle National Park.

INFORMATION
Maps

If you're planning to do a lot of driving, take along the series of regional road maps by the National Roads & Motorist's Association

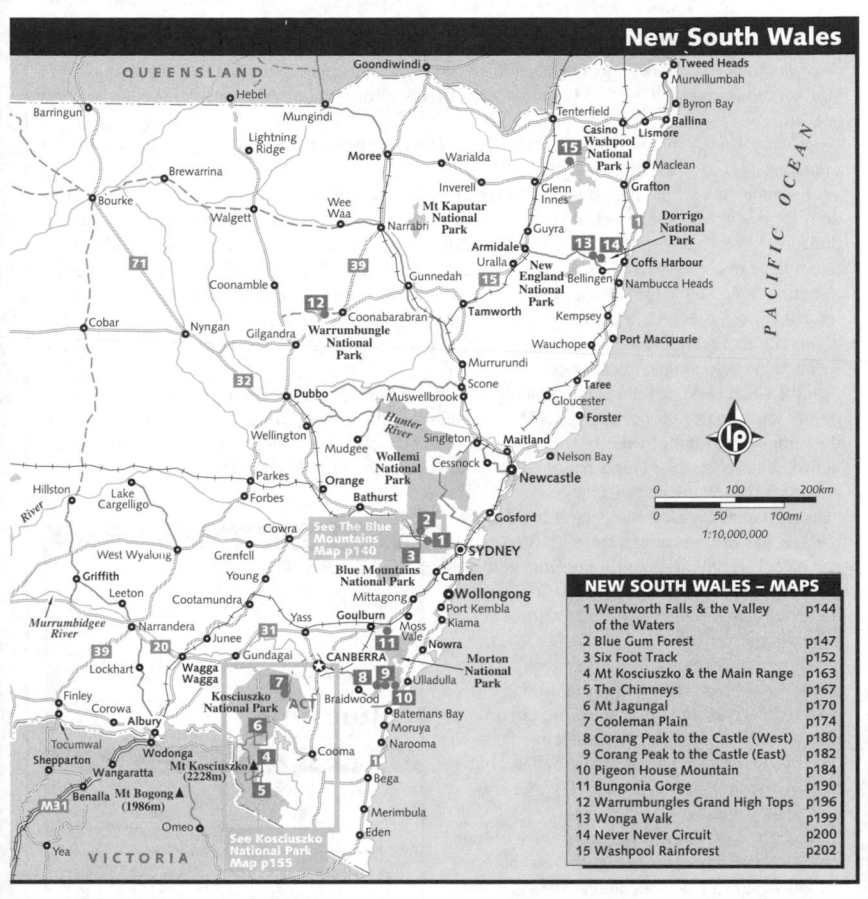

New South Wales

NEW SOUTH WALES

(NRMA), which shows almost every road and track in the state, although not the topography. The descriptions of road conditions are accurate and up to date.

Take a general road map of the whole state, such as UBD's *New South Wales* state map, because the detailed maps show so many alternative routes that it can be difficult to work out which is the most direct. All NRMA offices (and some associated garages) will have the maps to their area, and probably the whole set. They're free to members, and to the members of motoring organisations in other states.

As of January 2000, Land & Property Information New South Wales (LPINSW) produces the most up-to-date series of 1:25,000 topographical maps. The LPINSW used to be called the Central Mapping Authority (CMA), and will continue producing new editions of the old CMA maps.

For maps covering individual walks, see Planning in the introduction to each walk.

Books

For the most extensive coverage of the state's national parks, use the National Parks Association (NPA) guide in two volumes:

The Climate of New South Wales

The climate of NSW varies depending on the location, but the rule of thumb is that the farther north you go, the warmer it'll be. Geographical factors tend to make it hotter (and drier) the farther west you are.

Although there's more likelihood of cloudy weather in midwinter, rainfall is generally sparse and unpredictable.

In summer, the whole state is hot, with temperatures rising above 40°C in the north-west corner, and not much less on the rest of the baking plains. The air quivers and shakes above the boiling horizon, and mirages are common. Bourke holds the record for the state's highest recorded temperature, a blistering 51.7°C in the shade (that's 125°F), and shares an old record of 37 consecutive days over 100°F (38°C). Tibooburra, in the north-western corner, is regarded as the state's hottest town. Of course, there are a lot of empty spaces in the far west, and who knows how hot it gets out there. Luckily, the places with extreme temperatures are also very dry, and the heat can be bearable if you drink lots of water.

In the Great Dividing Range, the days can be hot, but the nights are often pleasantly cool. Summer on the south coast is as hot as you could want for a seaside holiday, but when a cool change arrives, the temperature drops lower than it would on the north coast. Sydney and the north coast can be humid, with spectacular thunderstorms. Although you get the odd very hot day, coastal temperatures are usually below the mid-30s.

In the Great Dividing Range and the southern parts of the western slopes, the autumn days become cool, deciduous trees turn red and gold, and the clear nights often bring frosts. On the coast the water temperature stays quite warm until the beginning of winter.

Winter temperatures in the far west drop to a comfortable level and the skies are often blue and clear. There can be frosts at night out on the plains. Up on the Great Dividing Range it's chilly, with heavy frosts and occasional snowfalls, but it's only in the high Snowy Mountains that snow is able to accumulate.

You don't have to look hard to be aware of spring in NSW. After the warm spring rains on the plains, carpets of flowers emerge among the tall grasses, and on the north coast the frangipani blooms. Animals, birds and insects burst into frenetic activity and snakes sun themselves after their winter hibernation. The wattle blooms, and in the old towns of the Great Dividing Range and the Central West, deciduous trees put forth their new leaves.

In the north, spring is well under way by September, and by the end of October the far west is becoming uncomfortably hot. On the ranges the cool nights linger and pockets of snow remain.

For more detailed climate information, see the regional climate sections later in this chapter.

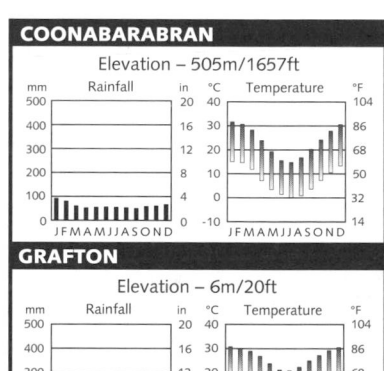

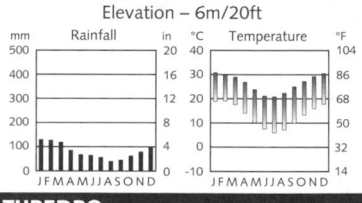

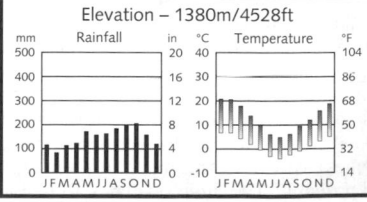

NEW SOUTH WALES

The NPA Guide to National Parks of Northern NSW and *The NPA Guide to National Parks of Southern NSW*.

For walkers wanting to explore the state in greater depth, Tyrone Thomas has written two books crammed with suggestions for walks, *100 Walks in New South Wales* and *50 Walks in New South Wales and the ACT*.

Information Sources

Tourism NSW is the state government's tourist promotion body and it runs the Sydney Visitor Centre. For the cost of a local call, you can phone ☎ 13 2077 for recorded information and to have brochures sent out to you. It also maintains a good Web site at 💻 www.tourism.nsw.gov.au.

Almost every major town (and many minor ones) has a tourist office with local information not readily available from the larger state organisation (see individual walks later in this chapter for details).

For information on NSW park offices and bushwalking organisations, all based in Sydney, see Information Sources in the introduction to the Sydney Region chapter.

The *Sydney Morning Herald* and the *Australian* daily newspapers carry detailed weather reports and forecasts.

Permits & Regulations

National park regulations vary across the state. Some parks require permits and some place restrictions on camp sites and campfires. For more detail, see the Permits & Regulations section for each park or area within this chapter. During days of Total Fire Ban, all fires are forbidden, even fuel stoves. If you are caught with an open fire on these days, you are not only endangering yourself and the environment, but you can also cop a hefty fine and/or prison sentence.

There's a $50 annual pass that gives free entry (but not free camping) to all national parks except Kosciuszko. It probably isn't worth buying unless you plan a systematic coverage, but the $60 pass that includes Kosciuszko is definitely worthwhile if you plan to visit Kosciuszko plus a few other parks. For information on park fees, see the Permits & Regulations section for each park.

For information on how to minimise your impact on the environment, see the section on Responsible Walking in the Facts for the Walker chapter.

GATEWAY

See the introduction to the Sydney Region chapter for information on accommodation and other services available in Sydney.

The Blue Mountains

The Blue Mountains, part of the Great Dividing Range, have some truly fantastic scenery, excellent bushwalks and all the gorges, gum trees and cliffs you could ask for. The foothills begin 65km inland from Sydney and rise to 1100m, but the mountains are really a sandstone plateau riddled with spectacular gorges formed over millennia by erosion.

The blue haze that gave the mountains their name is a result of the fine mist of volatile oil given off by eucalyptus trees – which is also why eucalyptus forests can explode into firestorms.

For more than a century, the area has been a popular getaway for people seeking to escape the summer heat of Sydney. Despite the intensive tourist development, much of the area is so precipitous that it's still only open to bushwalkers.

As well as the three walks described here, the Sydney Region chapter includes a description of the Red Hands Cave walk around Glenbrook, at the base of the Blue Mountains. The four-hour circuit features a cooling swim in a rock pool and a visit to the Aboriginal rock art site at Red Hands Cave.

HISTORY

The first Europeans in the area found evidence of extensive Aboriginal occupation but few Aborigines. It seems quite likely that catastrophic diseases had travelled up from Sydney long before the explorers arrived.

The colonists at Port Jackson attempted to cross the mountains within a year or so of their arrival, driven not just by the usual lust for exploration but also by an urgent need to

The Blue Mountains

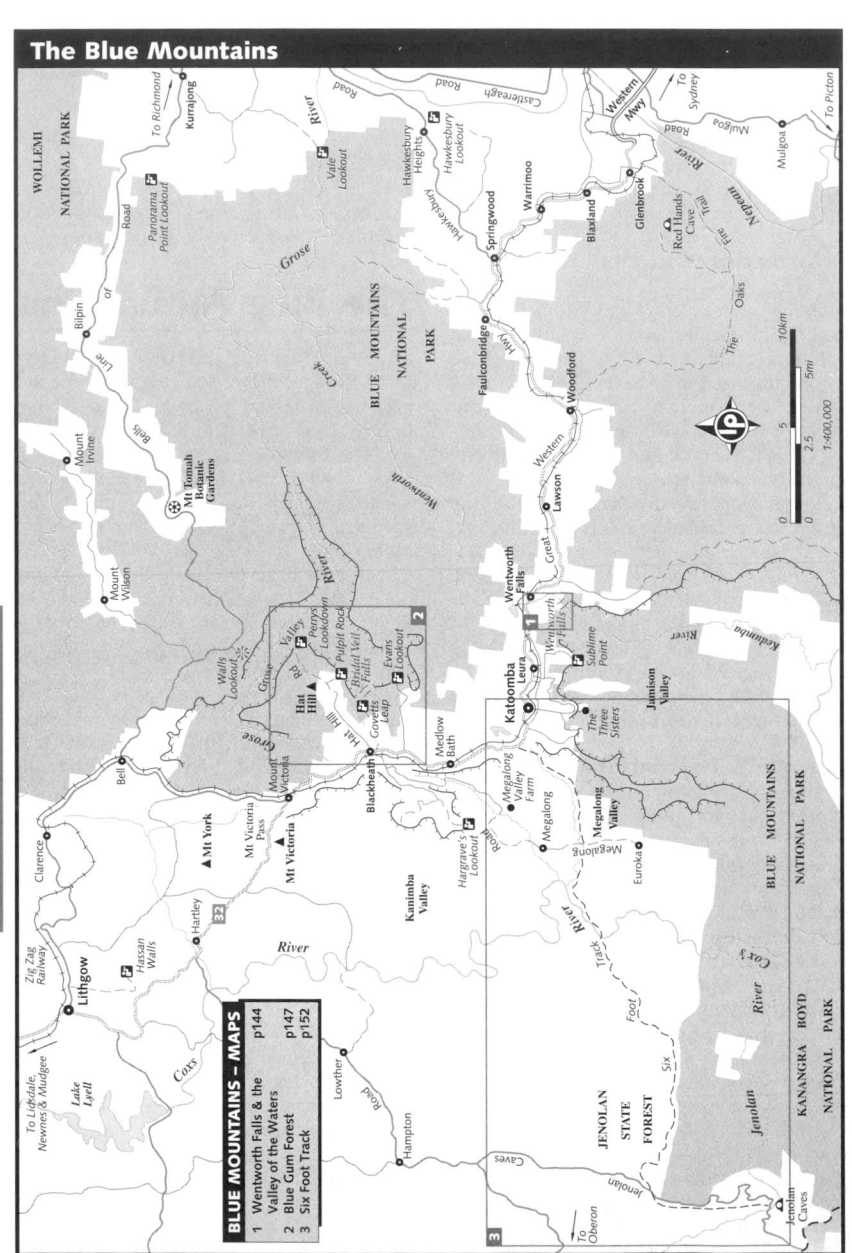

NEW SOUTH WALES

BLUE MOUNTAINS – MAPS

1	Wentworth Falls & the Valley of the Waters	p144
2	Blue Gum Forest	p147
3	Six Foot Track	p152

find land suitable for growing food for the new colony. However, the sheer cliffs, blind valleys and tough terrain combined to defeat their attempts for nearly 25 years.

The first crossing was made in 1813 by Blaxland, Wentworth and Lawson. They followed the ridge tops and their route is pretty much the same route of today's Great Western Hwy. The first road across the mountains was built in just six months, and the great expansion into the western plains had begun.

After the railway across the mountains was completed in the 1860s, wealthy Sydney residents began to build mansions here, as summer retreats from the heat and stench of Sydney town. By the turn of the century, grand hotels and guesthouses had opened to cater for the increasing demand. This early tourist boom tapered off by the 1940s, but today there is a resurgence of interest. Some old guesthouses have made a comeback and new resorts have been built.

In 1959 the Blue Mountains National Park was created, covering over 200,000 hectares. The vision for this park is said to have come from one of the most famous figures in Australian bushwalking, Myles Dunphy.

PLANNING
When to Walk

With none of the summer haze or problems with water scarcity and bushfires, winter can be the best time for bushwalks – days are often clear and down in the valleys it can be comparatively warm. But beware of sudden changes in weather and come prepared for freezing conditions; snow is possible between June and August. Autumn's mists and drizzle can make bushwalking less attractive, but the mountains in a thick mist are an atmospheric place. Summer days can be very hot (in the high 20s).

Books

Neil Paton's *Walks in the Blue Mountains* is a detailed guide to scores of walks in the area, mainly of a day in length, but several stretching over longer periods.

National Park Explorer, Around Sydney by Alan Fairley is a readable guide to the Blue Mountains as well as Ku-ring-gai Chase and Royal National Parks; it includes information on geology, flora and fauna as well as suggested walks.

Information Sources

The excellent NPWS Blue Mountains Heritage Centre (☎ 02-4787 8877, fax 4787 8514) is on Govetts Leap Rd near Blackheath, about 3km north of the highway. It has all the information, maps and books you could need for walking in the area, plus a small selection of snacks and drinks. It's open daily from 9 am to 4.30 pm.

Closer to Sydney on the Great Western Hwy, the Glenbrook Visitor Information Centre (☎ 1300 653 408, @ bmta@lisp .com.au) carries a good range of maps and guides on the national park.

GETTING AROUND

Pearce Mountainlink (☎ 02-4782 3333, 1800 801 577) bus services operate between Leura, Katoomba, Medlow Bath, Blackheath and Mt Victoria, with some services running down Hat Hill Rd and Govetts Leap Rd, which lead respectively to Perrys Lookdown and Govetts Leap. Services are sparse, with only two buses running on Saturday to Hat Hill Rd and Govetts Leap, and none on Sunday. In Katoomba the bus leaves from the top of Katoomba St, just outside the Carrington Hotel (timetables are posted there).

The Blue Mountains Bus Company (☎ 02-4782 4213) runs between Katoomba, Leura, Wentworth Falls and east as far as Woodford. There's roughly one service an hour from Katoomba train station.

On weekends and public holidays the Blue Mountains Explorer Bus offers all-day travel for $18 ($9 children). It departs regularly from Katoomba train station and visits the Scenic Railway, Skyway, Echo Point, Leura village and other places. Contact Fantastic Aussie Tours (☎ 02-4782 1866), 283 Main St, Katoomba.

There are train stations in most Blue Mountains towns along the Great Western Hwy. Trains run roughly hourly between stations east of Katoomba and roughly two hourly between stations to the west.

GATEWAY
Katoomba

The best all-round base is Katoomba, although there are accommodation options throughout the Blue Mountains; there's a free Blue Mountains accommodation booking service (☎ 02-4782 2857, ℮ info@bmbookings.com.au) at 157 Lurline St, open daily.

If you need gear, tents, sleeping bags and stoves can be hired from Mountain Designs (☎ 02-4782 5999), 190 Katoomba St.

Places to Stay & Eat The centrally located *Katoomba YHA Hostel (☎ 02-4782 1416)* was, at the time of research, at 66 Waratah St, but is set to move to an ex-Bible, Art Deco college on the corner of Edward and Katoomba Sts. Dorm beds cost from $16 to $20 and doubles with en suites are $30 per person.

The VIP *Blue Mountains Backpackers (☎ 02-4782 4226, 190 Bathurst Rd)* receives consistently good reviews from travellers. Beds in large dorms are $18 ($20 for nonmembers) and good twins/doubles cost $46 ($50 for nonmembers).

No 14 (☎ 02-4782 7104, 14 Lovel St) is a peaceful and homely guesthouse run by ex-travellers. Beds costs $20 per person in double or twin rooms.

In the style of the grand guesthouses, but with a lower tariff than many, the *Cecil Guesthouse (☎ 02-4782 1411, 108 Katoomba St)* charges from $40/75 for singles/doubles with breakfast.

Katoomba St has plenty of good places to eat. The pleasant and reasonably priced Art Deco *Savoy (12 Katoomba St)* has an interesting menu of the focaccia, pasta and Asian-inspired variety. Also part of the old Savoy Theatre is *Avalon (☎ 02-4782 5532, 18 Katoomba St)*, one of the town's best restaurants with a quirky style and plenty of tempting meals. The eternally popular *Blues Cafe (57 Katoomba St)* serves mostly vegetarian (and vegan) food, but also has some meat dishes.

There's a *Coles* supermarket on the corner of Parke and Waratah Sts.

Getting There & Away Katoomba, 109km from Sydney's city centre, is almost a satellite suburb. CityRail trains run more or less hourly from Central ($11.80 off-peak return, $10 one way, two hours).

By car, exit the city via Parramatta Rd and detour onto the Western Motorway tollway ($1.50), known as the M4, at Strathfield. The motorway becomes the Great Western Hwy west of Penrith.

Wentworth Falls & the Valley of the Waters

Duration	5½–7 hours
Distance	7km
Standard	easy-medium
Start/Finish	Conservation Hut, Wentworth Falls
Nearest Towns	Wentworth Falls, Katoomba
Public Transport	yes

Summary A classic Blue Mountains day walk, combining glorious cliff-top panoramas, numerous pools and waterfalls and a challenging side trip into the secluded, sylvan Valley of the Waters.

Adding to the pleasure of walking at Wentworth Falls is the convenience of its location (a day trip from Sydney is easily accomplished) and the wide range of trail variations on offer. The most popular route is the circuit from Conservation Hut following the Overcliff-Undercliff Track to Wentworth Falls and then back along the National Pass. This covers 5km and takes from three to four hours. It's a spectacular route, coupling amazing views with refreshing waterfalls, but it can also get busy – especially at weekends.

The route we describe (in reverse) adds on a couple of challenging side trips to extend the walk to a full day (seven hours maximum), with several options for picnics and swims in secluded pools. Although most of the route is very clear, the trail down to Vera Falls is more tricky; that's why we've graded this walk easy-medium. The reward of making the trip to Vera Falls, especially if you walk during the week, is that most likely, beyond the odd snake and kangaroo, you'll have the Valley of the Waters to yourself.

The route can be tackled in either direction; it's best to go to Vera Falls first, though, so as not to be faced with the 450m vertical slog back up to the Conservation Hut at the end of the day.

HISTORY

There have been walking tracks at Wentworth Falls since the 1830s; Charles Darwin came in 1837 and one route is still named after him. The falls had been noted as far back as 1815 when they were called Campbell's Cataract. So popular did the area become that the National Pass – a remarkable route cut into the side of the cliff over 100m above the valley floor – was started in the 1890s and finished by 1908. The track was last upgraded in 1988.

Wentworth Pass, which runs below the National Pass, was constructed between 1901 and 1902, and was extended to join with Vera Falls in 1913. The Slacks Stairs, down to the base of Wentworth Falls, were added in 1932.

PLANNING

For information on when to walk, what to bring and on the NPWS Blue Mountains Heritage Centre, near the trailhead, see Planning in the introduction to the Blue Mountains.

Maps & Books

The Blue Mountains National Park Walking Track Guide, *Bushwalking in the Wentworth Falls Area*, contains brief walking notes and a map (not to scale) showing all the main walking routes in the area. Estimated times are very generous. The LIC 1:25,000 topographic map *Katoomba* covers the Wentworth Falls area (note the old CMA version does not show Wentworth Pass or the route to Vera Falls).

NEAREST TOWN

Although Wentworth Falls is the nearest Blue Mountains town to the walk, most visitors will find Katoomba (see Gateway earlier) a more convenient base.

GETTING TO/FROM THE WALK

Regular buses leave from outside the Carrington Hotel on Katoomba St, Katoomba, to Fletcher St, Wentworth Falls (15 minutes, $3.10); get off where the road turns into Mitchell St and walk less than 100m to the Conservation Hut. The last bus back to Katoomba is at 5.05 pm Monday to Friday, 3.44 pm on Saturday and 3.35 pm on Sunday. For further information, call the Blue Mountains Bus Company (☎ 02-4782 4213).

From Wentworth Falls train station, Conservation Hut is around 20 minutes' walk away. Turn left after crossing the bridge out of the station and pass the short parade of shops to reach the Great Western Hwy. Cross this road and walk to the right, until you reach Falls Rd (you can take a short cut through Wilson Park). Keep heading down Falls Rd until you reach Fletcher St, where you'll turn right; the Conservation Hut is at the end of this road.

If driving you can park either at the Wentworth Falls Picnic Area, within 30 minutes' walk of the falls, or at the Conservation Hut – the Short Cut Track links the two.

THE WALK

From Conservation Hut take the right-hand track due west, heading downhill towards the Valley of the Waters. You'll reach Queen Victoria Lookout – the first of many view points along the walk – within 10 minutes. From here you can see the Valley of the Waters way below, sandwiched between sheer ruddy cliffs, a creek winding its way through the dense temperate rainforest of coachwood, sassafras and lilly pilly. A minute later, the Empress Lookout provides a balcony view above the Empress Falls.

Two flights of steep metal stairs take you down into the valley towards the base of the falls, where the atmosphere becomes damp, lush and dark. In wet weather you'll need to watch your footing. At the next junction take the left-hand **National Pass** route, following the stone steps down to the crossing at the base of Empress Falls. The route shadows the creek as it twists and drops in tiny cataracts over the rocks.

Just after the point where you cross the creek again, the track to Vera Falls turns off to the right. This is a narrower, less well-defined track, with some junctions where

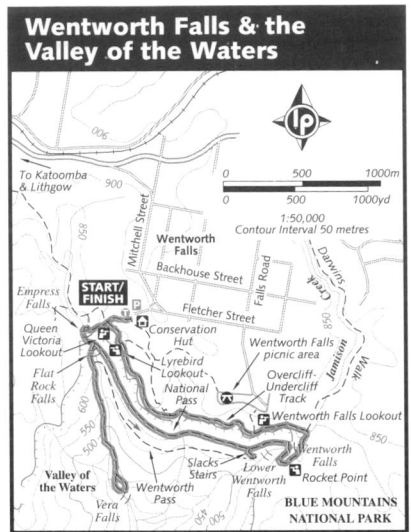

Wentworth Falls & the Valley of the Waters

you need to take care you're going the right way. A return journey to the top of the falls takes around two hours. Initially, there's a steep zigzag down to Flat Rock Falls. Negotiate your way across rocks in the creek to the west side (true right). The route then heads steeply downhill.

After 15 minutes, you'll reach the junction for the **Wentworth Pass** track, which crosses the creek again at Red Rock Falls and runs through the forest along the base of the cliffs towards the Lower Wentworth Falls. Our route sticks to the west bank of the creek. You'll need to be careful here; there are two turn-offs to the right that you should ignore. The second is clearly marked as the Roberts Pass track – don't take this but look for the tree marked with a red arrow and continue to head downstream. Here the trees twist into fantastic shapes to reach the light above, and stealthy creepers wait to trip up walkers.

The track crosses the creek one last time – there are pools to soak in, if you're getting warm – and then continues for around 15 minutes sharply downhill to the top of the 380m-tall **Vera Falls**. There are actually two tracks, both ends of a loop to the falls – you can take either. There's a lovely vista of the

valley and cliffs from Vera Falls and some more pools that are perfect for bathing in. You're likely to see flocks of white cockatoos and need to keep alert for snakes. To return the way you came to the junction with the National Pass takes around one hour.

From this junction, the views along the next couple of kilometres of the **National Pass** are some of the most remarkable of the whole walk. The track is cut into the sandstone cliffs, with multicoloured rock faces soaring above and the vast expanse of the Kedumba Valley spread out below towards the distant Kanangra Boyd wilderness. Runoff from the cliff tops provides the occasional cool shower.

After 30 to 45 minutes you'll arrive at the turn-off on the right to **Slacks Stairs** and the Wentworth Pass. These nine flights of steep metal stairs (named after an early trustee of the park) and the rocks you have to scramble over at the bottom, make this a diversion for the fit and confident bushwalker only. The reward at the base, though, of a sandy beach before the 48m drop of the **Lower Wentworth Falls**, makes the effort of getting there well worthwhile. It's one of the best spots on the walk for a swim or picnic lunch.

Returning to the National Pass, it's a short walk to the glittering 110m **Upper Wentworth Falls**. You'll have to hopscotch across the ledge of the falls to rejoin the track. It's a very stiff but relatively short climb of around 15 minutes to the top of the falls, where you can also make a five-minute side trip to **Rocket Point**, another photographic vantage point.

From the falls follow the **Overcliff-Undercliff Track** back to Conservation Hut, around one hour's walk. The track's name becomes obvious as soon as you have to squat to negotiate the undercliff, a Lilliputian world of ferns, flowering heaths and stunted eucalyptuses clinging to the rocks.

There are several more view points, none far from the main track and all worthwhile side trips. Along the more exposed overcliff section of the track you're likely to scatter mountain dragons and skinks basking in the afternoon sun. **Lyrebird Lookout** provides a final panorama of the valley before the last

10-minute steady climb back to **Conservation Hut** (*☎ 02-4757 3827*). Open daily from 9 am to 5 pm, it is a fine place to stop for breakfast, lunch or an afternoon tea of fresh scones, especially out on the deck with views over the Jamison Valley.

Blue Gum Forest

Duration	2 days
Distance	19km
Standard	medium
Start	Neates Glen car park
Finish	Evans Lookout
Nearest Town	Katoomba
Public Transport	yes

Summary A series of beautiful secluded worlds are revealed on this circuit walk through the Upper Grose Valley, starting with the dramatic Grand Canyon and culminating in the serene Blue Gum Forest.

The panorama at the end of Govetts Leap Rd, overlooking the yawning expanse of the Grose Valley, is one of the most breathtaking in the Blue Mountains – a sea of greenery stretching to the horizon, constrained by sheer cliffs of rippling sandstone. The first day takes you into the depths of this valley to the atmospheric Blue Gum Forest. Day 2 starts with the heart-busting 2km climb up Docker Buttress to Perrys Lookout. The effort is rewarded by the rest of the day's route along the cliff ledge past many excellent vantage points over the valley, including Pulpit Rock and Govetts Leap Falls, to end at Evans Lookout.

Although the route is generally easy to follow and reasonably well signed, we've graded it medium because of the difficulty of climbing into and out of the Grose Valley, especially if you're carrying a heavy overnight pack. Water is available along the route, but you'll need to boil it before drinking. There are plenty of alternative day walks or longer walks in the area.

If you wish to extend the walk to three days, start at Victoria Falls Lookout, 10km north of Blackheath, and follow the undulating track for five to seven hours to reach the Blue Gum Forest and Acacia Flat. Take care around the junction of Victoria Creek and the Grose River – don't cross either and stay on the track on the true left of the Grose. On Day 2, if you're fit, a round trip of 17km from Acacia Flat is possible, via the Rodriguez Pass to Govetts Leap and Pulpit Rock, before returning via Perrys Lookdown and Docker Buttress. This should take seven to nine hours. The final day retraces the route to Junction Rock and up past Beauchamp Falls to the Grand Canyon.

HISTORY

Govetts Leap takes its name from William Govett, assistant surveyor, who came across the cascades dropping 170m into the Grose Valley in June 1831. Leap is a Gaelic word for waterfall. From the end of the 19th century the area began to be managed and developed for sightseeing and walkers, with the local railway master, Tomas Rodriguez, achieving the seemingly impossible task of building a track down the cliff face into the valley in 1899. The route along the Grand Canyon was opened in 1907.

It was the fight to save the Blue Gum Forest, though, that helped secure national park status for this and other parts of the Blue Mountains. In 1932 a group from the Sydney Bushwalkers Club discovered that the forest was about to be cut down. The club managed to raise the cash to buy out the lease for the land and thus preserve the Blue Gum Forest for the enjoyment of future generations. Their fight raised awareness about protecting the natural environment, but it wasn't until 1959 that the Blue Mountains National Park was created, centred around the Grose Valley.

Bushfires in 1994 damaged large areas of the Grose Valley, but the Blue Gum Forest escaped intact, and much of the rest of the bush has now regenerated.

PLANNING

For information on when to walk, what to bring and on the NPWS Blue Mountains Heritage Centre, which is near the start of the walk, see Planning in the introduction to the Blue Mountains.

Maps & Books

The LPINSW 1:25,000 *Katoomba* map and the CMA 1:25,000 *Mount Wilson* map cover the Grose Valley area.

The Blue Mountains National Park Walking Track Guides, *Walking in the Grose Valley*, *Blackheath Walking Tracks* and *The Grand Canyon, Blackheath*, contain brief walking notes and maps (not to scale) showing all the main walking routes in the area. Estimated walking times are very generous.

NEAREST TOWN
Blackheath

Blackheath, 10km west of Katoomba on the Great Western Hwy, has several quintessential but pricey Blue Mountains B&Bs, a small **grocery store** and plenty of cafes. For budget accommodation, Katoomba is a better option (see Gateway earlier).

If you have your own tent, camping at the **Blackheath Caravan Park** (☎ *02-4787 8101)*, on Prince Edward St, just off Govetts Leap Rd, costs $7 per person. The historic **Gardners Inn** (☎ *02-4787 8347, fax 4787 7725, 255 Great Western Hwy)* is opposite the train station and charges $35 per person per night including continental breakfast.

GETTING TO/FROM THE WALK

From Katoomba, you can get to Blackheath either by train or bus. From the Blackheath train station on the Great Western Hwy to the Neates Glen car park, it's around a 4km walk, or a short taxi ride.

Pearce Mountainlink (☎ 02-4782 3333) operates a none-too-frequent bus service from Katoomba and other destinations (see Getting Around in the introduction to the Blue Mountains) that stops on the Great Western Hwy by Evans Lookout Rd, and at the Blue Mountains Heritage Centre on Govetts Leap Rd. The bus doesn't always pull into the centre's car park; it's better to stand on the road by the roundabout.

A taxi from Katoomba to Neates Glen car park will cost around $17. If you're driving and plan to leave your car overnight, the NPWS recommends you use the Grand Canyon Loop car park (which has toilets and water), farther down Evans

Lookout Rd, rather than the Neates Glen car park. Walking tracks link the Loop car park with both the start of the walk at Neates Glen and the finish point at Evans Lookout.

THE WALK
Day 1: Neates Glen to Acacia Flat
6–7 hours, 8km

From Neates Glen car park, a clear, moderately steep track winds its way down into a narrow gully, a shrouded, dripping world of mosses and ferns, many towering like verdant parasols. Take care, since it can be slippy here. To reach the bottom of the canyon takes around half an hour; have a rest and soak up the otherworldly atmosphere of this rocky enclosure before continuing through a short tunnel and along the track shadowing Greaves Creek, way below. Amazing views of the **Grand Canyon**, in places 30m deep and a few metres wide, open up from this point and the route makes some thrilling passes under waterfalls and cliff overhangs before dropping to the creek. This is a truly magical spot, with the reflected light from the water dappling the umber cliffs and lush vegetation. With time spent dallying, you'll probably spend around two hours in the canyon.

The track hopscotches across the creek several times before reaching a junction; a track up to Evans Lookout heads across the creek to the left, taking around one hour to climb out of the canyon. Our route sticks to the right bank of the creek following the sign to the Rodriguez Pass and **Beauchamp Falls**, which you'll come across in around half an hour.

There are several spots from which to admire the falls, but take care since this is the trickiest part of the track to follow, with the route across boulders being far from clear. Keep an eye out for steps in the rocks and for a collapsed metal railing to know you're heading in the right direction. Eventually, this steep route will bring you to a broad plateau in the cascades, a good spot for lunch and to bathe in one of the pools. Cross the creek at this point and go left, the *opposite* direction from the white arrow on the rock, which points to a dead end farther up.

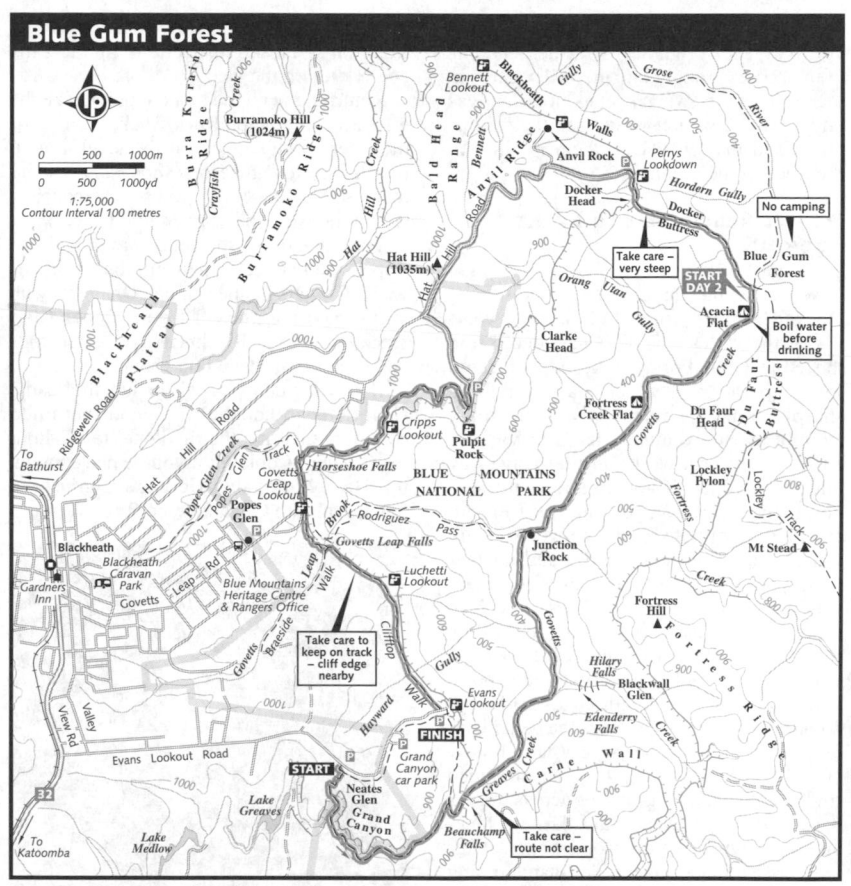

Blue Gum Forest

After an hour's walking you'll have reached the valley floor and will be following the **Rodriguez Pass** to **Junction Rock**, at the confluence of Greaves and Govetts Creeks. This is another fine spot for a cooling dip and you're likely to encounter many cat-sized eastern water dragons guarding the rocks. If you're doing a day walk, the Rodriguez Pass runs uphill from here to Govetts Leap Lookout, the last section being a tough haul up metal ladders.

The track to **Acacia Flat**, around one hour's walk, continues across Govetts Creek and along the stream's left bank, initially passing through an unofficial camp site. The going can get a bit jungly, and at one point you'll wade through a sea of knee-high ferns. It's generally flat, but there's one short climb just after the Fortress Creek Flat *camp site*, now regenerating after the 1994 bushfires. At the crest of the hill, take the track to the right heading back down to the creek; Acacia Flat is less than a half-hour's walk from here.

The extensive *camp site* has two toilets and several paths leading down to the creek where you can get water (which must be boiled). After downing your pack, take time to enjoy the calm, cool atmosphere of the nearby Blue Gum Forest. If you're lucky, you may spot brumbies, wild descendants of the horses brought into the valley early in the 20th century when coal exploration was under way. You'll certainly see their droppings and may well hear them rustling in the trees in the night.

Day 2: Acacia Flat to Evans Lookout
6–7 hours, 11km

In warm weather, an early start to climb the Docker Buttress – one of the steepest ways out of the valley – is recommended. From the Blue Gum Forest, take the left-hand route up the hill, which starts climbing sharply almost immediately. (The track straight ahead eventually leads to Victoria Falls, 12km north-west – an alternative way out of the valley, if you've arranged transport to meet you at Victoria Falls Rd.) There are a few short fact sections between the uphill slogs, which get steeper and steeper until you're virtually rock climbing. Depending on your level of fitness, the 2km route, which rises 600m from the valley floor, takes between 1½ and three hours.

Docker's Head is the first view point you'll come to on the cliff edge, but **Perrys Lookdown**, a bit farther on, is the better vantage point. From the nearby car park, follow Hat Hill Rd for around 4km, an unshaded trudge enlivened by glimpses across the expanse of the valley and the flashing blue-and-red plumage of crimson rosellas. After around 45 minutes take the left-hand turning down Pulpit Rock Rd to the lookout, 10 minutes away. There are toilets and shelter here, but no water, so make sure you've brought plenty with you from the valley.

Pulpit Rock provides a magnificent view of the Grose Valley and an opportunity to study the layer-cake effect of the different types of vegetation from the open forest of black ash and peppermint gums on the cliff tops via patches of swamp and woodland to the coachwood and sassafras in the valley below. On the north-east horizon is 944m Mt Hay, while south-west there's a view of Govetts Leap Falls, a slender ribbon of white water looking like a length of billowing

muslin, hence the alternative name of Bridal Veil Falls; closer inspections of the falls come later on the walk.

Returning from the lookout point, take the left turn along Pulpit Rock Track, a route that meanders pretty much on the level around the cliff top towards **Horseshoe Falls**, a name that's self-evident once you see the concave recess the water has carved into the rock.

The track drops shortly before the falls to Popes Glen Creek, then climbs again towards Govetts Leap Lookout. On the way up you'll pass the turn-off for the **Popes Glen Track**, leading to Blackheath via woodlands and swamp, in around one hour.

If you haven't paused for lunch already, **Govetts Leap Lookout** is a good spot to do so before tackling the final one- to 1½-hour leg to Evans Lookout; if you've had enough, the Blue Mountains Heritage Centre is a 500m walk up Govetts Leap Rd.

ROSS BARNETT

Govetts Leap Falls, also known as Bridal Veil Falls, is a spectacular sight from Pulpit Rock

The route drops down to and crosses Govetts Leap Brook (there's a short track to the right here along the brook, called the Braeside Walk) and then climbs again to the cliff edge, affording eye-catching vistas of the Grose Valley most of the way. The track then shadows the Griffith Taylor Wall of rock shooting down some 600m to the valley floor and crosses a minor depression at Hayward Gully, before rising to the car park at **Evans Lookout**, which has toilets, water and a *barbecue area*. The actual lookout is a brief walk from here, but worth making the effort for one last look across Govetts Gorge towards the imposing bluff of Fortress Hill.

Six Foot Track

Duration	3 days
Distance	42km
Standard	medium
Start	Explorers Tree, Great Western Hwy
Finish	Jenolan Caves
Nearest Towns	Katoomba, Jenolan
Public Transport	yes

Summary Traversing the full range of Blue Mountains landscapes, from lush rainforest glens to open woodland, this heritage track follows the original route taken by late 19th-century walkers from Katoomba to the spectacular Jenolan Caves.

The appeal of the Six Foot Track (claimed to be the most popular overnight bushwalk in Australia, after Tasmania's Overland Track) derives from a combination of historical associations and gorgeous, constantly changing scenery. It's far from the most ambitious walk you can take in the Blue Mountains, although its difficulty shouldn't be underestimated. It's certainly among one of the prettiest trails, particularly in spring, when wild flowers bloom in profusion.

Starting from the Explorers Tree just outside Katoomba, the track drops down through the rainforest of Nellies Glen, crosses the rolling meadows of the Megalong Valley and fords Cox's River. It then climbs over both the Mini Mini Saddle and Black Range

to reach the Gothic splendour of Jenolan Caves, as awe-inspiring a climax today as it was a century ago.

Although it's possible to cover the route in less time (the record is an incredible three hours, 12 minutes set during the annual marathon run), the best way to fully appreciate the landscape is to take three days, camping at Cox's River and on the Black Range. If you're a fast, strong walker and have arranged transport back from Jenolan (or an overnight stay there), a two-day itinerary is possible, camping at Alum Creek, roughly halfway.

We've graded the walk medium; while the route is clear and well signposted, its length and the two sustained climbs on Day 2 make it a challenge, especially with a heavy pack. On weekends and during holidays you're sure to encounter several walking parties along the track; if you want a quieter experience, plan a midweek trip. The track can be walked in either direction, but it's considered slightly easier to go from Katoomba to Jenolan, so as to not finish with the climb up Nellies Glen.

HISTORY

It was the lure of Jenolan Caves as a tourism hot spot that caused a government survey party to forge a route across the Megalong Valley in 1884. The first recorded trip along the whole track was by the NSW governor, Lord Carrington, and his wife in 1887. Although built as a bridle trail, the route quickly became popular with walkers, who romanced the idea of striking out through nature to reach the caves. Accommodation was offered at various homesteads along the way, such as at Kyangatha, where fenced yards can still be seen today. Other notable historic spots along the route include the Oakburn homestead, which was the early Megalong Post Office, and Megalong Cemetery, in use since 1892. By contrast, the Explorers Tree, a rotten stump said to bear the carvings of Blaxland, Lawson and Wentworth, is of more dubious heritage.

The Six Foot Track gained its present name in 1937 – by this stage the 6ft-wide bridle trail was already close to impassable.

Limestone Landscapes

Limestone, made from calcite (calcium carbonate), is responsible for some of the most dramatic features of the landscape. The scenery is often characterised by barren, rocky ground in otherwise fertile country, dramatic gorges, sinkholes and extensive cave systems with underground rivers – in short, a speleologist's dream. Along with Jenolan Caves, two other walks in this chapter traverse limestone country: Cooleman Plain, and Bungonia & the Shoalhaven River (see the boxed text 'Caves of Bungonia State Recreation Area' later in this chapter).

Limestone landscapes occur in areas where there are dense, well-jointed pockets of limestone near the surface, fed by rainfall and circulating groundwater. In a process called carbonation, the limestone reacts with the acid from rainwater as it seeps through the soil, then dissolves and is carried away. The water flows through existing joints in the limestone, often along bedding planes, and enlarges them to form passages, caves and other calcite features. Caves can be extremely varied, ranging from soaring gothic caverns to vertical shafts or narrow passages. If a series of caverns collapses, it can create a steep-walled limestone gorge. Below are some of the features you may find in a limestone landscape:

❶ **limestone pavement** – an area where ground water has enlarged joints in the limestone to form a roughly geometric pattern of blocks
❷ **clint/grike** – a ridge/cleft in a limestone pavement
❸ **sinkhole** – a depression in the limestone through which surface streams disappear
❹ **doline** – depression caused by a roof collapse
❺ **resurgence** – the point where an underground stream re-emerges
❻ **gour** – a series of calcite ridges deposited by running water (eg, an underground stream)
❼ **stalactite** – a limestone pendant hanging from a cave ceiling, formed by deposits of calcite in dripping water
❽ **stalagmite** – a calcite pinnacle formed as water drips from the stalactite
❾ **cave**

Caring for Caves

The cave environment is sensitive to human presence. Touching features or trekking mud over the limestone can do irreparable damage, so always treat caves with care, and if in doubt, check with local authorities. Entry to many caves is restricted, either by regulations or by difficulty.

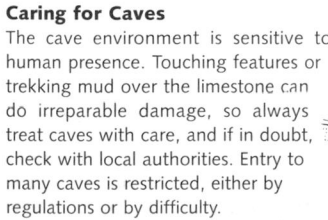
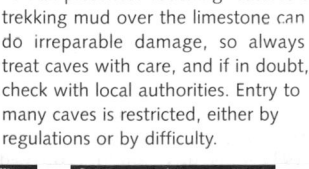

The rise of motor transport caused the track to decline even more after WWII, reaching a nadir in the 1960s when an ill-conceived and later abandoned scheme to build a road down Nellies Glen scarred the landscape almost irreparably. However, two decades later, a bushwalking revival and interest in local heritage sparked a reconstruction of the track by local authorities. Although fire trails now cover large sections of the original route, the route retains much of the fascination of its earlier years.

PLANNING

If you're walking in winter, spring or autumn, it can get pretty chilly up on the Black Range; snow is not unheard of. Thermal underwear, a warm sleeping bag and woolly hat and gloves are all recommended. In summer, an adequate supply of water, a fuel stove to boil up extra supplies and purification tablets for emergencies are all essential – reliable water sources are one of the main difficulties of walking the track.

Maps

The LIC 1:25,0000 topographical maps for *Katoomba*, *Hampton* and *Jenolan* cover the route in the most detail. An adequate alternative is the NSW Department of Land and Water Conservation map and pamphlet entitled *Six Foot Track*, although you won't get as clear a picture of the gradients involved in the walk.

Guided Walks

The attraction of taking an organised tour along the Six Foot Track is that your luggage will be transported between camp sites by 4WD and you won't need to worry about food and water for the three days.

Several operators run supported walks, including Sydney-based Great Australian Walks (☎ 1300 360 499, fax 02-9810 6429, @ walkaus@nswbigpond.net.au, 💻 www.walkaustralia.com). Its three-day programs, all including accommodation at a private lodge by Cox's River, cost $450. The downside is that trips generally run on weekends and during holidays when the track is at its busiest.

Departure dates are more flexible and group sizes tend to be smaller with Cox's River Escapes (☎ 02-474 1621, fax 4784 2450, @ coxrivesc@autralis.net.au). Three-day trips cost around $440 and generally start from Jenolan Caves.

NEAREST TOWNS

For a description of Katoomba, which is the closest town to the start of the track, see the Gateway section in the introduction to the Blue Mountains.

Jenolan

At the other end of the track, there are several accommodation options at Jenolan Caves. The *Jenolan Caves Resort (☎ 02-6359 3322, fax 6359 3388, @ bookings @jenolancaves.com)* includes the upmarket *Jenolan Caves House*, with rooms from $50 a night, and a bed in a dorm room costs from $15 per night at the Gatehouse. These rates increase significantly on weekends and during all holiday periods. *Camping* is also an option; it costs $10 for a tent at a site around 45 minutes' walk from the caves downstream beside the Jenolan River – just follow the path.

Getting There & Away Jenolan is 72km from Katoomba. If you have not arranged a pick-up from Jenolan, Fantastic Aussie Tours (☎ 02-4782 1866, fax 4782 1860), 283 Main St, Katoomba, runs a daily transfer service to or from the caves for $36, departing from the caves at 3.45 pm.

NSW Wilderness Transit Service (☎ 02-4683 2344, fax 4681 9094, 💻 www.wildernesstransit.com.au) also runs services from Monday to Friday, departing from both Sydney Central Station and Katoomba and running to the caves and back. The charge is $36 per person from Sydney to Jenolan, with half-price stand-by tickets available 24 hours before departure.

GETTING TO/FROM THE WALK

The start of the Six Foot Track, at the Explorers Tree, is 2km west of Katoomba, just off the Great Western Hwy; a taxi to here costs $5.

THE WALK
Day 1: Katoomba to Cox's River
6–7 hours, 15km

From the Explorers Tree head down the badly weathered track to the start of the route into **Nellies Glen**. After 10 minutes, the track turns sharply right and descends into the glen along a series of uneven steps. To reach the bottom takes around 45 minutes, by which time your knees are likely to be rather wobbly.

The old track snaked in a more leisurely fashion through this beautiful enclave of warm temperate rainforest; at one place you can still see an original stone culvert. Through the trees you'll hear, if not clearly see, **Bonnie Doon Falls**; this is one of the very few unpolluted creeks along the track and the water here is safe to drink in an emergency. The glen is named after a 19th-century mine operator's daughter – looking ahead you can see Narrow Neck Plateau, a knobbly finger of rock soaring out of the Megalong Valley, under which the coal and shale mines were once located.

At the bottom of the glen, the vegetation abruptly changes to drier woodland dominated by scribbly gum and smooth-barked apple, which is neither smooth barked nor an apple tree. The narrow route widens into an access road for the water board, which you follow as it shadows Narrow Neck on the left-hand side. Where you pass a paddock is the site of the long-abandoned **Megalong Village**, an early 20th-century community for workers at the nearby shale mine.

A short way ahead, the track splits – you can take either fork, but the right-hand one is the easier to follow. There are several locked gates to go through, some with stiles over them. Just after the Oakburn homestead, the track continues through woods brimming with blackberry bushes; indulge in some berry picking in time for lunch beside the **Megalong Cemetery**, just across Megalong Valley Rd. At the entrance to the overgrown cemetery, a cairn lists those who are known to be buried here; only two marked graves remain, one fenced in by ornate ironwork.

Descending the track as it follows Megalong Creek, keep an eye out for sharp-edged

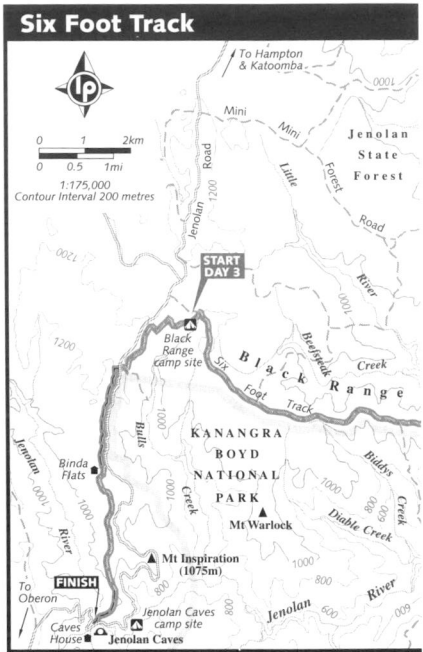

Six Foot Track

bits of pale stone on the ground. This is chert, brought by Aboriginals to this area for use as cutting tools. The track undulates gently across open meadows, very English in feel until you look back towards the towering sandstone cliffs and take in the gum trees. One particularly fine old river gum marks the spot where you'll cross a small creek before climbing a hill that affords a beautiful panorama of the valley.

Approaching the **Cox's River valley**, the track drops back into woodland, punctuated by huge lichen-splashed granite boulders. Keep an eye out for one particularly large one known as Toad Rock, and for an enchanting glen of giant split boulders. This is one of the prettiest sections of the walk, sticking to the track's original route and dimensions. Below, the Cox's River can be heard and eventually the track will reach its side.

As long as the river isn't in full flood, there's a choice of crossings. The most thrilling is by the 90m-long **Bowtells Swing**

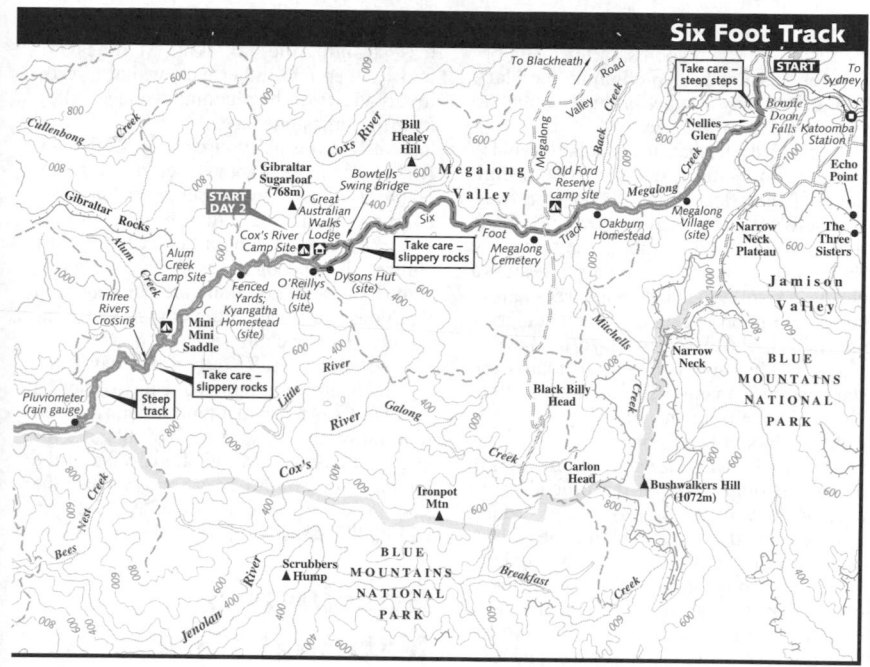

Six Foot Track

Bridge. Only one person at a time is allowed to cross this metal suspension bridge, swaying alarmingly 30m above the rocky river bed. The best way to negotiate the bridge, if you take fright, is to look straight ahead and sing/whistle a tune.

If the water is low, it's usually possible to cross by the rocks below the bridge, or follow the track down the true left bank of the river for 1km to a narrow, shallow section at the confluence with Murdering Creek. Take care when crossing the river bed as the granite rocks are very slippery.

The official *Cox's River camp site* (with toilets) is around 15 minutes' walk from the bridge, although you'll pass an unofficial *camp site* closer to the river. Any water gathered from the creek and river must be boiled.

Day 2: Cox's River to Black Range
7–8 hours, 19.5km

This is the toughest, longest day of the walk so an early start and a steady pace are recommended. Also make sure you have sufficient water, especially as there are no sources at all once you start the long climb up and along the Black Range.

As a warm-up for the day ahead there's a one-hour climb of around 300 vertical metres along the fire trail beside Murdering Creek. At the top, the land opens up beside the **fenced yards** of the old Kyangatha homestead. A pear tree stands in the paddock and you're likely to encounter several ponies and horses, plus some cattle farther along.

Enjoy the view before climbing another 200m over undulating fields across the **Mini Mini Saddle**. At the top, a forest of smooth-barked apple begins again as you drop down sharply towards Alum Creek, an official *camp site*, with no facilities and no guarantee of water in the creek either. *Camping* a little farther along beside the Little River is a better prospect as far as water's concerned. Here you may want to remove your boots as the route crosses the river three times, but take care not to slip in the water. This is a good spot for lunch before the sustained steep climb up the **Black Range**. You may also be fortunate enough to spot grey kangaroos here.

At a steady trudge, it takes between 1½ and 2½ hours to reach the 1000m-high ridge of the Black Range. About halfway up, there's a track heading downhill to the right that you should ignore. The best view back is just before the summit, beside a cluster of spiky-headed grass trees. From here, with good eyesight – or binoculars – you'll be able to see the Hydro Majestic Hotel at Medlow Bath. A sign marks the start of the Kanangra Boyd National Park on the left side of the track, while to the right is Jenolan State Forest.

The track twists for a leisurely 8.5km along the ridge towards the official camp site. On the way, you'll pass several striking termite mounds. It's also high enough here for subalpine snow gums. After a couple of hours you should reach the junction with another fire trail, where the forest has been cleared; turn left and walk for 500m to the next left turn-off to the *Black Range camp site*, which has a toilet and shelter.

Day 3: Black Range to Jenolan Caves

3–4 hours, 9.5km

The Black Range camp site is on a recently cut deviation from the original Six Foot Track, which for a large part of this day's walk has long since been covered by Jenolan Rd. From the camp to the road via the deviation is 3km, around a one-hour walk through shaded woods of brown barrel eucalyptus and radiata pine (spreading from a nearby pine plantation). There's one short steep section to negotiate before reaching Jenolan Rd. Cross this and follow the adjacent track for another hour to **Binda Flats**, where you'll find *cabins* for rent.

The cleared grassy area of Binda Flats was once used to grow vegetables to feed residents at Jenolan Caves. Now, particularly in the late afternoon, it's possible to see grey kangaroos and wallabies grazing here. The route continues behind the cabins

and down towards the caves in a more or less straight line for 4km. At times it's rocky, steep and rather narrow, but affords lovely views of the plunging wooded valley near the limestone caves.

You'll eventually arrive at **Carlotta's Arch**, a gap in the rock that acts as a window on the Blue Lake not far below, its luminous colour caused by the dissolved limestone. From here you can either reach **Caves House**, the end of the walk, by the direct right-hand route, or along the left-hand trail that goes via the looming cavern known as the Devil's Coachhouse.

Since this is really only a half-day walk, you'll have plenty of time to enjoy exploring **Jenolan Caves**. Regular tours are run through nine show caves, and if you've still got some energy, there are several short walks in the vicinity. For details of cave tours contact the Jenolan Caves Trust (☎ 02-6359 3311, fax 6359 3307, @ jencaves@jenolan.org.au).

Kosciuszko National Park

In south-east NSW, about 150km inland from the coast, is an area of high peaks, deep valleys, plateaus and plains collectively known as the Snowy Mountains (or 'Snowies'). Within this area are Australia's highest summits and the only direct evidence on the Australian mainland of glaciation dating from the last ice age. When viewed from the Victorian (west) side, the Snowy Mountains present a most imposing sight. The large Kosciuszko National Park is over 150km long and between 20km and 50km wide, encompassing an area of 660,000 hectares. It contains a rich variety of flora and fauna, all of NSW's ski resorts, and is the backbone of the Snowy Mountain Hydroelectric Scheme, arguably Australia's greatest engineering feat.

Kosciuszko National Park is ideal for bushwalking. The most popular areas are the Main Range (containing Australia's highest peaks) and, a little farther north, the region of snow plains and low hills surrounding

Kosciuszko National Park

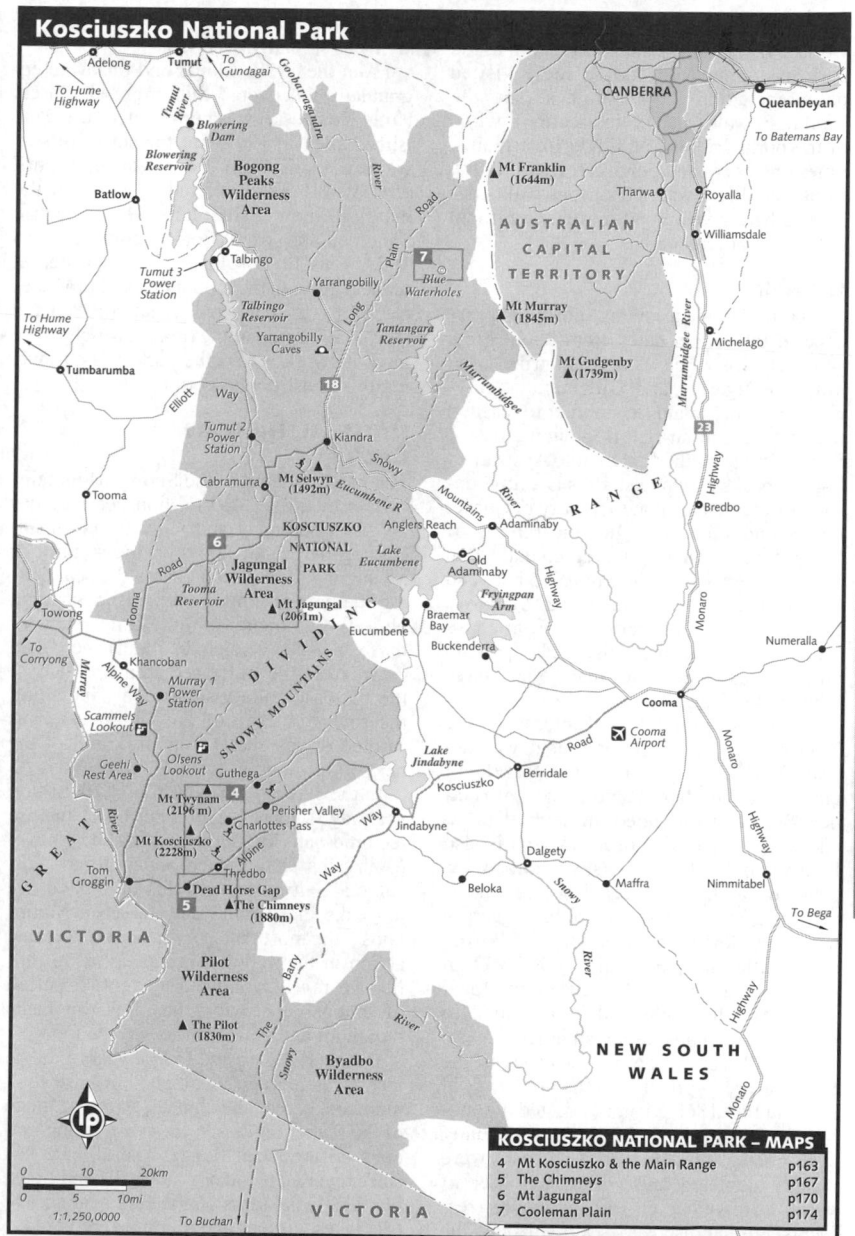

NEW SOUTH WALES

Mt Jagungal. But other areas are certainly worth a visit, too. The southern region of the park has some wild and scarcely visited parts, including the Chimneys (see the Chimneys walk later in this section), while in the north are lower-altitude frost plains, limestone caves and gorges (featured in the Cooleman Plain walk). The four walks described here give a good introduction to all these very different areas.

HISTORY

The earliest evidence of an Aboriginal presence in the region dates from about 5000 years ago, as three Aboriginal tribes, the Walgalu, Ngarigo and Djilamatang, travelled to the mountains in summer to feast on the protein- and fat-rich Bogong moths.

The timing of the first visit to Australia's highest peaks by white settlers is a little unsure. In 1824 the exploratory party of Currie, Ovens and Wild gave glowing reports of the pastures in the Cooma region and, soon after, graziers moved into the area between Cooma and the mountains – the 'Monaro'. It is probable that stockmen from these properties visited the Kosciuszko plateau around this time, and may even have climbed the highest peak.

Many explorers passed close to the Monaro area in the 1830s, but it was not until 1840 that Paul Edmund Strzelecki climbed to the Main Range by way of Hannels Spur and summited the highest peak, which he named Mt Kosciuszko. (It is also likely that Dr John Lhotsky climbed the peak in 1834, but direct proof of this is missing after a vital section of his scientific notes was lost.) Other explorers followed swiftly after Strzelecki, and the NSW High Country was gradually settled by local stockmen who brought their livestock to graze on the plains during summer.

In 1859 word of gold discoveries in the Kiandra area spread and inspired a gold rush, and by 1860 Kiandra boasted a population of more than 15,000. As with many such booms, however, gold deposits were rapidly depleted and within a matter of years the town had only a few hundred residents. Further discoveries were made in the 1870s and 1880s, but by about 1905 the area was virtually deserted.

From the 1920s, skiers and bushwalkers gradually discovered this impressive area. Hotel Kosciusko was constructed near Perisher Valley in 1909, but the ski resorts as we now know them did not develop until after WWII. Work started in 1949 on the massive Snowy Mountains Hydroelectric Scheme, and were finally completed in 1972. This huge scheme diverts water in tunnels through the mountains and produces electricity at many power stations on the steeper west side of the ranges. Much of the track network across the park was cut during this construction period.

NATURAL HISTORY
Geology

The basic material of the Snowy Mountains was formed over 430 million years ago as layers of sediment and volcanic lavas (including the basalt found on the summit of Mt Jagungal) built up beneath the sea. During the next 50 million years (the Sylurian period), sediments of limestone (such as those beneath Cooleman Plain) were laid down over the older sediments. Much of the park's granite visible today, including the rocky outcrop of the Chimneys, was formed during the Devonian period of the next 30 million years.

In the Tertiary period (around 70 million years ago), there began a period of intense tectonic activity, during which the Snowy Mountains were folded and uplifted. Volcanic activity at around this time gave rise to peaks like Round and Tabletop Mountains – the most recent evidence of volcanic action in the region. Further uplift 30 million years ago, followed by another period of extensive erosion, has left the basic mountain and valley forms we see today.

Between 25,000 and 15,000 years ago, the last great ice age to affect the Australian mainland cooled the climate, covering much of the higher regions in ice and forming glaciers on the Main Range. The climate has since reverted to today's 'normal' conditions, but the glacial scars on the park's landscape (the lakes, cirques and moraines) remain.

Flora

It is not surprising in an area with terrain as mountainous and varied as Kosciuszko National Park that there is such a diverse range of flora and fauna. The flora of the park is dependant on many factors, but two of the main ones are elevation (and hence, temperature) and precipitation.

There are five main zones of mountain flora. On and around the valley floors are savanna woodland, with forests of white and yellow box, black sallees and white manna gums, often with an understorey of low grasses. Heading uphill you come to dry sclerophyl forests of scribbly gums, peppermints, stringybarks and messmates.

Between about 900m and 1450m is wet sclerophyl forest of tall and slender mountain ashes, mountain gums and alpine ashes (often called woollybutt because of the wool-like appearance of the bark near the base of the tree); the understorey consists of species such as ferns, grasses and native cherry bush.

Higher again, from 1450m to 1800m, is the subalpine zone, made up predominantly of snow gums – tall and straight at lower elevations and short and gnarled near the tree line. In some cases there is a thick understorey of tussock grass and shrubs, purple hoveas, royal grevilleas, yellow kunzeas and pink grass trigger plants.

Above 1800m is the alpine zone, where the climate is generally too cold and severe for any tree growth at all, except in isolated locations. This region consists mainly of heaths, grasses, herbs and snowpatch vegetation, not to mention the rare feldmark, a low, ground-hugging migratory plant, which grows on the most exposed (and often damaged) sites. Sphagnum bogs develop on wet sites, absorbing water and releasing it slowly throughout the year. Alpine plants are generally fragile and are slow to recover when damaged.

Sometimes an area of alpine vegetation can exist in a subalpine zone, as is the case with a snow plain or frost hollow, where the valley floor is devoid of forest. The trees in these locations are unable to survive the cold air that drains down the hillsides and pools in low areas during the night.

Fauna

In Kosciuszko National Park there are about 200 species of birds, 30 species of reptiles, 30 species of mammals and 200 species of insects. Some of the more commonly sighted animals include eastern grey kangaroos, wombats, echidnas, ringtail and brushtail possums, native bush rats and marsupial mice. In rivers and streams you might see (apart from fish) platypus (be very quiet!) and water rats. Birds that frequent the region include gang gang and yellow-tailed black-cockatoos, wedge-tailed eagles, pied currawongs and ravens, Japanese snipes, colourful flame robins and, in alpine ash forest, elusive lyrebirds. In some areas you may even espy an emu or two!

Lizards and skinks are common reptiles, but there are also some undesirables which you do not want to see, such as black, brown and tiger snakes.

Apart from various types of annoying flies, look out for insects such as large mountain grasshoppers, earthworms, Bogong moths (hidden in rock crevices during summer), and wolf spiders. You're unlikely to come across any funnel web spiders (found in tussock-type grass), but be aware that these have a potentially deadly bite (for information on how to treat snake and spider bites, see Bites & Stings in the Health & Safety chapter).

Unfortunately, many feral animals now inhabit the park, including the ugly and frightening feral pig, brumbies (wild horses), rabbits, hares, foxes and even cats.

CLIMATE

As you'd expect of a mountainous region, there is a wide range of weather phenomena influencing the park's climate.

Temperature is significantly affected by altitude, dropping about 1°C for every 150m of altitude gained, making the mountain tops over 10°C cooler than the lowlands. Average daily maximums at about 2000m range from 15°C in summer to 0°C in winter, but strong variations are common. Summer can still get quite hot at times and temperatures in autumn and spring can be anything from comfortably mild to cold (frosts are common during these times). Winter is cold everywhere in the park.

Precipitation is heavy all year, but in summer tends to be more erratic; torrential thunderstorms are a feature of summer bushwalking. Autumn and spring, where wet weather can set in for days, are interspersed with lengthy fine spells. Snowfalls are frequent in winter and snow covers most of the terrain above 1400m during this time. In the most elevated areas and on the western slopes of the ranges, rainfall can exceed 2000mm a year, tapering to less than 1000mm in the far north-eastern sector of the park.

Wind is a common companion in the mountains, especially on the higher summits and plains. It can be a blessing on a hot day, but combined with cold can become uncomfortable and even dangerous. In the cooler months, wind-chill is a factor worthy of consideration.

Mountains can generate their own weather, and a sunny day in the lowlands doesn't always mean sunshine in the mountains. Cloud and showers (or other precipitation) can develop rapidly.

PLANNING
When to Walk

Winter is really the only season when walking is out of the question, either because of the deep snow that covers the walking areas described here, or because of road closures affecting access. In most areas of the park you can walk any time between October and April, although in the higher areas, such as the Main Range, snowdrifts may linger up until December. The most popular bushwalking months are January to March, when weather is warm and generally stable and frosts are least likely.

What to Bring

You need to be prepared for mountain weather in all parts of the park, although some areas (eg, around Cooleman Plain) are less severe. Even during prime walking times, carry wet-weather gear and warm clothing. You can wear runners (training shoes), but proper walking boots offer better foot support and protection against the

Emergency Beacons

For the very safety-conscious, emergency beacons can be hired for a flat fee of $10 ($20 deposit) from visitor centres in Tumut, Khancoban and Jindabyne. Call ☎ 02-6450 5600 for details.

weather. Lightweight gloves also come in handy in cool, damp conditions, and a warm hat is a must.

For the overnight walks described, a good waterproof tent (one strong enough to withstand powerful winds) is essential. Don't rely on sleeping in huts; while there are many of them in the Australian High Country, they are often dirty and provide less comfort and protection than a good tent. They may also be full.

A warm, high-quality sleeping bag is also a good idea, especially in the highest areas, or during winter and spring when the nights are frosty.

Fuel stoves are another essential item on overnight walks. Campfires are not permitted above the tree line (1800m) and firewood can be scarce in some areas. Stoves are also quicker to light in bad weather.

Water points are described in the text but do dry up occasionally, so it is imperative that you carry at least one large (1L) water bottle per person and have it full when you commence your walk.

There is an increased risk of sunburn at altitude, so apply sunscreen liberally and frequently; lip balm can be used to prevent dry and cracked lips.

Maps & Books

There are many good general maps of the park, most of which are available at the larger visitor centres (see Information Sources), some local newsagents and bookshops. *Snowy Mountains – Australia's High Country*, a free 1:400,000 map published by Cartoscope's, provides a good overview of the park and features some town maps as well. Other maps include the CMA's *Snowy-Kosciuszko – The Snowy Mountains* at 1:250,000, and the *Australian Alps Tourist Map* by Ausmap at 1:500,000.

Some handy walking guides to the region are *Snowy Mountain Walks* by the Geehi Bushwalking Club and *Bushwalking in Kosciuszko National Park* by Charles Warner (primarily a guide for experienced walkers). *Australian Alps Walking Track* by John Siseman has detailed track notes on this long-distance track as it meanders through the park; Tyrone Thomas' *100 Walks in New South Wales* also has a good selection of walks. *Australian Alps – Kosciuszko, Alpine & Namadgi National Parks* by Deirdre Slattery has some track notes, but also contains loads of other information on the environment, history and development of the Snowy Mountains region.

For the history of the Snowy Mountains and the Snowy Mountains Hydroelectric Scheme, have a look at *Huts of the High Country* by Klaus Hueneke, *Kosciusko – The Mountain in History* by Alan EJ Andrews, *Snowy* by Brad Collis and *Mud, Sweat & Snow* by Noel Gough.

Flora and fauna of the region are also well covered. Three guides worth considering are *Wildlife of the Australian Snow-Country* by Ken Green & William Osborne, *The Plant Life of Kosciusko* by Peter Codd, Bill Payne & Colin Woodcock and *Wildflowers of the Snow Country – A Field Guide to the Australian Alps* by Ian Fraser & Margaret McJannett.

Information Sources

The best sources of park information (including accommodation, transport, maps and books) are probably the visitor centres at Jindabyne and Tumut (see Gateways earlier for details). To the north, the Cooma Visitor Centre (☎ 1800 636 525, 02-6450 1742), in Sharp St, Cooma, has a large selection of maps and brochures, and a helpful inquiries desk.

If approaching the park from Victoria, the Khancoban Visitor Centre (☎ 02-6076 9393), in Scott St, sells a range of maps, books and park visitor permits. When the office is closed, you can purchase permits at the nearby Khancoban Roadhouse.

Petrol stations, outdoor gear shops and newsagents may also be worth approaching for local and regional information.

On the Internet, the Australian Alps National Parks Web site (🖳 www.australianalps .environment.gov.au) is an excellent source of general background information on the High Country.

Permits & Regulations

While there are no camping fees, there is a fee required for every car entering the park. The permit costs $15 per day or $65 for a year. If staying more than a few nights, the annual pass is definitely the way to go as it also gives you unlimited entry to every national park in NSW. Permits can be obtained at the visitor centres listed under Information Sources or at the toll booth on the Alpine Way just east of Thredbo.

There are also some restrictions applying to bushwalkers (and skiers). No camping is permitted within the water catchments of the five glacial lakes (on the Main Range) and no campfires are permitted above the tree line (1800m).

GETTING AROUND

Several private transport companies operate to locations around the park. The Adaminaby Bus Service (☎/fax 02-6454 2318) specialises in bushwalker transport and can provide a charter service to most areas of the park. The Jindabyne-based Snowy Mountains Taxi Service (☎ 02-6457 2444) and Snowy Mountains Bus & Shuttle Services (☎ 02-6456 2957) are also worth contacting for local transport needs.

On the Victorian side of the park, if you require transport from either Corryong or Khancoban, try contacting Bob Wilkinson (☎ 02-6076 1418); he operates taxis and minibuses into the national park from his base in Corryong.

GATEWAYS
Jindabyne

For walks in the southern part of Kosciuszko National Park, Jindabyne makes an excellent base. The Snowy Region Visitor Centre (☎ 02-6450 5600), beside the main road in town, can provide plenty of information on Kosciuszko National Park; the Internet can be accessed at Jindabyne NETcafe (☎ 02-6457 1722), in the Town Centre Plaza at the eastern end of town.

At Nuggets Crossing Shopping Centre, you'll find a chemist and a large number of shops, including Wilderness Sports (☎ 02-6456 2966), which sells a wide range of outdoor gear. Camping equipment can also be purchased at Paddy Pallin (☎ 02-6456 2922), on Kosciuszko Rd, a few kilometres west of town at the Thredbo turn-off. There is a post office on Snowy River Ave, behind the Nuggets Crossing complex.

Places to Stay Just west of town, at the Thredbo turn-off, is the *Snowline Caravan Park* (☎ 02-6456 2099), which has tent sites from $15, backpacker accommodation from $10 and various cabins starting from $36 a night. Right in town is *Jindabyne Holiday Park* (☎ 02- 6456 2249); tent sites here cost $13, on-site vans start at $35 and five-bed units cost around $60. The *Jindy Inn* guesthouse (☎ 02-6456 1957, 18 Clyde St) has en suite double rooms from $45 and share rooms for $25 per person. You could also try the *Lake Jindabyne Hotel* (☎ 1800 646 818), on Kosciuszko Rd; it has a spa and hotel pool and offers single/double B&B accommodation from $55/56 in summer.

Further accommodation options can be gleaned from the Snowy Mountains Reservation Centre (☎ 1800 020 622), Kosciuszko Accommodation Centre (☎ 1800 026 354) or Alpine Resorts & Travel Centre (☎ 1800 802 315). Note that prices increase in winter.

Places to Eat While many restaurants in Jindabyne are closed during summer, there are still a few cafes and takeaway outlets open all year at the two shopping precincts. One restaurant that does remain open is *Il Lago* (☎ 02-6456 1171), in the Nuggets Crossing complex, an Italian restaurant serving pizza and pasta. There's also a good bistro in the *Lake Jindabyne Hotel* (☎ 1800 646 818), while a good place for a coffee, breakfast or just a snack is *Wilfred's Cafe*, in the Snowy Region Visitor Centre.

Food supplies can be bought from the *supermarket* in the Town Centre Plaza or from Nuggets Crossing Shopping Centre.

Getting There & Away Oz Experience (☎ 1300 300 028) runs shuttles from Canberra to Jindabyne via Cooma for $25. It operates three times a week in each direction.

By road, Jindabyne is about 468km from Sydney by way of Goulburn, Canberra and Cooma. From Cooma, follow the Snowy Mountains Hwy, then the Kosciuszko Rd west for 65km to Jindabyne.

There are two routes (both long trips) from Melbourne to Jindabyne: the first (560km) is via Wodonga, Corryong and Khancoban and the second (535km) through Gippsland and the towns of Traralgon, Bairnsdale, Bruthen and Buchan. Much of Barry Way between Buchan and Jindabyne is unsealed.

Corryong

While only a small town, Corryong (west of the Snowies) is the nearest substantial settlement to Kosciuszko National Park in Victoria with basic camping supplies (don't expect to find specialist outdoor equipment, however). The Corryong Visitor Information Centre (☎ 02-6076 2277), in the town's main street, has a reasonable range of brochures, books and maps.

Places to Stay & Eat Seven kilometres west of town on the Murray Valley Hwy is *Colac Colac Caravan Park* (☎ 02-6076 1520), which has tent sites for $10, vans from $22 and cabins from $32. Just 1km west of the town centre is *Mt Mittamatite Caravan Park* (☎ 02-6076 1152); tent sites cost $10, vans cost from $20 and cabins start at $40 a night.

The *Corryong Hotel* (☎ 02-6076 1004, 54 Towong Rd) has singles/doubles from $30/40 and also serves meals. Just off the main road in Jardine St is *Jardine Cottage* (☎ 02-6076 1318), a cafe/teahouse, which serves light lunches and dinner, and has accommodation from $75 (double).

Other places to eat can be found in the main street, which has a *bakery* and a number of *takeaway outlets*. You can stock up on last-minute food items at Corryong's small *supermarket*.

Getting There & Away As there is no public transport to Corryong, you'll need to arrive by private vehicle or hire car. The town is 432km from Melbourne. From Wodonga (302km), head 130km east along the Murray Valley Hwy (B400); allow five hours for the journey.

Tumut

North-west of Kosciuszko National Park, Tumut is the nearest sizable town to the northern and central regions of the park. The Tumut Region Visitor Centre (☎ 02-6947 1849), in the Old Butter Factory on Adelong Rd, is open daily and has plenty of information; you can access the Internet from the library (☎ 02-6947 1969), at 169 Wynyard St. Also on Wynyard St is the post office.

For last-minute camping equipment, try the High Country shop (☎ 02-6947 1744), on the corner of Wynyard and Capper Sts.

Places to Stay The *Riverglade Caravan Park* (☎ 02-6947 2528), a few blocks north of the town centre, and *Blowering Holiday Park* (☎ 02-6947 1383), 5km south of town, charge similar rates, with tent sites from $12 and cabins from $33. Both are on the Snowy Mountains Hwy. Hotel-style accommodation can be found at the *Oriental Hotel* (☎ 02-6947 1174), on the corner of Wynyard and Fitzroy Sts, with rooms at $20 per person. *Royal Hotel* (☎ 02-6947 1129, 88 Wynyard St) has rooms from $28 and motel-style units from $50 a double.

Places to Eat As is the case in most country towns, you can get a reliable meal (lunch and dinner) at any of the hotels. *Terrace Cafe*, in the Connection Arcade across from the Royal Hotel, sells light lunches and coffee, while for breakfast you could try the *Heritage Coffee Lounge*. A more upmarket restaurant for dinner is *Brooklyn on Fitzroy* (☎ 02-6947 4022, 10 Fitzroy St), but it's not open on Sunday. There's also a selection of *bakeries* and *fast-food outlets*, as well as a *supermarket* on Russell St.

Getting There & Away Tumut, on the Snowy Mountains Hwy, is about 445km south-west of Sydney via Gundagai and the Hume Hwy.

Countrylink buses run between the towns of Cootamundra, Gundagai, Tumut, Adelong, Batlow and Tumbarumba every day except Saturday, stopping in Tumut outside the National Bank on the corner of Russell and Wynyard Sts. This bus connects with the Sydney to Melbourne XPT train at Cootamundra. Call Countrylink (☎ 13 2232) for reservation details. Harvey World Travel, on Wynyard St, also sells bus tickets.

Mt Kosciuszko & the Main Range

Duration	3 days
Distance	38km
Standard	medium
Start/Finish	Thredbo
Nearest Towns	Jindabyne, Corryong, Khancoban
Public Transport	yes

Summary An exposed walk across Australia's highest countryside on mostly good tracks. Views of distant peaks, crags, five glacial lakes and an ascent of the country's two highest peaks are the main highlights.

The mountainous region north-east of the Rams Head Range for about 20km to the Rolling Ground is known as the Main Range. Within this area you'll find Australia's largest area of truly alpine country – terrain that is largely above the limit of tree growth – incorporating Australia's highest peaks and five glacial lakes. While snow gums can survive in a few isolated localities, the vegetation is predominantly snow grass, herb fields, shrubs and sphagnum bogs. Numerous granite outcrops, some forming spectacular and gravity-defying tors, are scattered across the barren (and often inhospitable) landscape. The growing season for flora in this area is short and plants, when damaged (whether by human feet or some other force), take many years to recover.

NEW SOUTH WALES

In the past, grazing, particularly of sheep, had such a severe effect on the ground cover protecting the fragile soil that whole mountain slopes were literally washed away. In the 1950s grazing was gradually banned from the highest areas and erosion control programs were instigated. Drainage works can be seen in many areas of the Main Range, particularly in the vicinity of Carruthers Peak and Mt Twynam, where the Soil Conservation Service has erected low rock retaining walls to slow the runoff and encourage plant regrowth.

The large number of walkers heading to Mt Kosciuszko only adds to the erosion problem; so heavily trampled and damaged was this popular route from Thredbo that there is now a paved path and raised metal walkway from the top of the chairlift. Other sections of walking track on the Main Range have also been paved, camping has been banned within the watersheds of all the glacial lakes (to protect water quality) and maintenance works are ongoing.

The route for this walk takes you to the highlights of the Main Range. Three days allows plenty of time to take in all the sights and complete a few side trips along the way.

PLANNING

For a detailed description on when to walk, what to bring and permits and regulations, see Planning in the introduction to the Kosciuszko National Park. It must be emphasised that as this is a very exposed walk you must have a strong weather-proof tent, wet-weather gear, good sleeping bag, warm clothes and a fuel stove.

Maps

The best topographic map, one which covers the whole walk, is the CMA's 1:50,000 *Mt Kosciusko* map. It is excellent for general features and topographic information, but some of the 4WD tracks marked are so overgrown that they are no longer passable. Also, the southern section of walking track from the top of the Thredbo chairlifts to Rawsons Pass is incorrectly marked (a bit too far east of its actual position); it is shown correctly in this guide.

NEAREST TOWN
Thredbo

The pretty ski resort village of Thredbo (33km west of Jindabyne on the Alpine Way) is certainly a lovely place to stay. While the resort has a number of choices for accommodation and places to eat (as well as a small general store), prices are generally cheaper – and the convenience for visiting other areas of the park greater – in Jindabyne.

You can get information on Thredbo from the local visitor centres (mentioned under Information Sources earlier in this section), but you can also contact the Thredbo Resort Centre (☎ 02-6459 4294, 1800 020 589), or visit the information section of the Valley Terminal in Thredbo (at the base of the Crackenback chairlift). Further information can be found on the Internet at ⌨ www.thredbo.com.au, or from the park ranger station (☎ 02-6457 6255) in the village centre.

Getting There & Away For public transport options to Thredbo, contact one of the operators listed under Getting Around in the introduction to the Kosciuszko National Park.

Thredbo is an easy 33km drive west of Jindabyne (along Kosciuszko Rd for a few kilometres, then along the Alpine Way). If coming from Victoria, Thredbo is 28km from Corryong to Khancoban, then another 71km to Thredbo along the Alpine Way. You can leave your vehicle in one of the designated overnight car parks east of the chairlift terminal.

THE WALK
Day 1: Thredbo to Mt Townsend
3 hours, 11km

The start of the walk is at the top of the Crackenback chairlift. The fare is $18 and you'll need to keep your ticket for the return ride. If the Crackenback lift is closed for maintenance, the adjacent Snowgums chairlift will operate. The ride takes 10 minutes (or 20 minutes on the slower Snowgums lift) and it operates between 9 am and 4 pm daily.

The paved track begins right at the top of the Crackenback lift and heads north, soon crossing a creek which is a good place to

Mt Kosciuszko & the Main Range

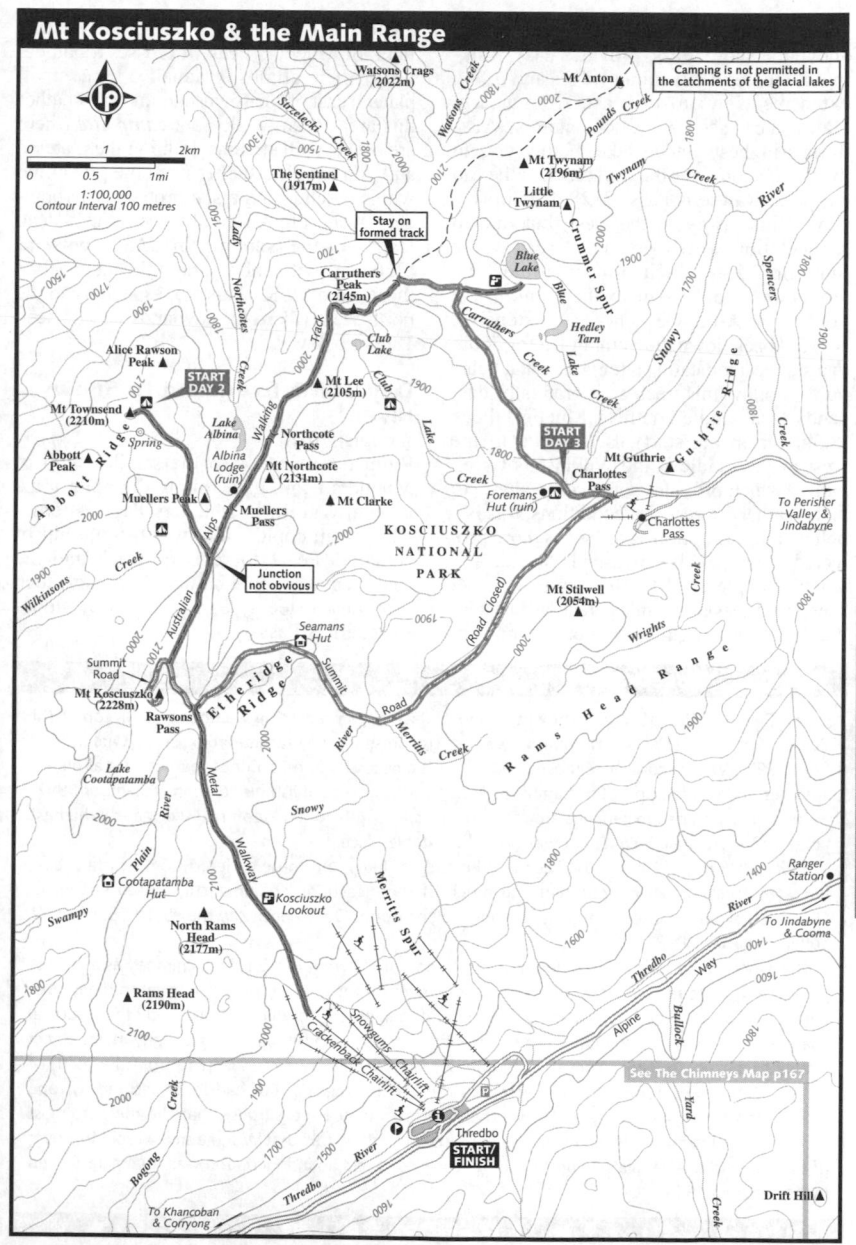

Camping is not permitted in the catchments of the glacial lakes

Watsons Crags (2022m)

Mt Anton

The Sentinel (1917m)

Mt Twynam (2196m)

Little Twynam

Stay on formed track

Carruthers Peak (2145m)

Blue Lake

Club Lake

Hedley Tarn

Alice Rawson Peak

START DAY 2

Mt Lee (2105m)

Mt Townsend (2210m)

Lake Albina

Northcote Pass

Abbott Peak

Albina Lodge (ruin)

Mt Northcote (2131m)

START DAY 3

Mt Guthrie

Charlottes Pass

Muellers Peak

Muellers Pass

Mt Clarke

KOSCIUSZKO NATIONAL PARK

Foremans Hut (ruin)

Charlottes Pass

To Perisher Valley & Jindabyne

Junction not obvious

Mt Stilwell (2054m)

Seamans Hut

Summit Road

Mt Kosciuszko (2228m)

Rawsons Pass

Etheridge Ridge

Rams Head Range

Lake Cootapatamba

Cootapatamba Hut

Snowy

Kosciuszko Lookout

North Rams Head (2177m)

Merritts Spur

Ranger Station

To Jindabyne & Cooma

Rams Head (2190m)

See The Chimneys Map p167

Crackenback Chairlift

Snowgums Chairlift

Thredbo

START/FINISH

Drift Hill

To Khancoban & Corryong

NEW SOUTH WALES

collect water. The metal walkway, raised above the snow grass, provides easy walking. It crosses a few minor ridges and offers extensive views to the east. After nearly 4km you can see Lake Cootapatamba, Australia's highest glacial lake, below you to the west; soon after the trail reaches the old car park, Rawsons Pass (2228m) is only a short climb away to the west, but due to revegetation works you must follow the Summit Rd – which almost circles the mountain – for 1.5km to the summit. As you'd expect, the views here are extensive.

Head back down the Summit Rd for 750m to a signpost indicating a foot track that bears north. Follow this track as it gradually descends to a saddle south of Muellers Peak (8.5km from the start). Below you to the west of the saddle is the Wilkinsons Creek valley, which provides some *camp sites*. (In bad weather, or very dry conditions, this is a better camping option as the site is more protected than the Mt Townsend Plateau and water is plentiful.) The route to Mt Townsend leaves the main track at this saddle and heads north-west (not obvious for

about the first 50m), skirting the western flank of Muellers Peak. It crosses a boulder field, then climbs gradually to a small plateau east of Mt Townsend. In fine weather this area makes a pleasant *camp site* (there are often small streams draining the plateau) and you can find shelter from the prevailing winds by choosing a site protected by boulders. A short rock scramble from the plateau leads to the summit of **Mt Townsend** (2209m), with more dramatic views than those from Mt Kosciuszko, especially to the north-west where the lowlands can be seen 1800m below.

Day 2: Mt Townsend to Snowy River
4 hours, 14km

Retrace your steps to the saddle south of Muellers Peak, then follow the main track generally north to Muellers Pass. Alternatively, you could walk over the summit of Muellers Peak (there is no track and the route requires some boulder hopping), then drop down steeply east over grassy slopes to Muellers Pass.

Wragge's Observatory

When Clement Wragge, a government meteorologist, began recording weather data on top of Mt Kosciuszko, little did he know what he was letting himself in for. A meteorologist for Queensland from 1887, Wragge convinced those in power of the necessity of measuring weather data at higher altitudes and headed up to the summit of Mt Kosciuszko to establish his camp in December 1897. He had earlier gained experience around Ben Nevis, in Scotland, but soon realised that the highest point on the Australian continent was not a hospitable place.

Initially 'Wragge's Observatory' consisted mainly of tents, but these suffered from constant buffeting by incessant winds; one tent and much of the measuring equipment it housed ended up 1600m below in the Geehi Gorge during one violent storm. Out of necessity they built a permanent building in May 1898.

This wooden hut measured 12 feet x 24 feet and utilised what looked like a chimney as a way of gaining entry into the building – one of the allowances for the deep snow which covered the mountain during winter. The hut was also equipped with a lightning conductor; apparently the electrical charges in the air were sometimes so powerful that sparks could be seen flying off any metal object waved in the air. The story goes that on one occasion flames were seen leaping from the teeth of a saw! Many times, too, the winds were so strong that Wragge's staff had to be secured by rope when heading outside to check the weather instruments. It is no surprise that the meteorologist earned the nickname 'Inclement Wragge'; it's also understandable that Wragge saw a rapid turnover of staff. By 1900 Australia's highest building was closed and abandoned, and was finally destroyed by lightning in 1914.

BY PERMISSION OF THE NATIONAL LIBRARY OF AUSTRALIA

For many years the title of Eugene von Guérard's 19th-century painting, 'North-east view from the top of Mt Kosciusko, New South Wales', caused confusion to those who climbed Mt Kosciuszko. The surrounding terrain simply did not match the view in the painting. It was later discovered that von Guérard had in fact painted his scene from Mt Townsend's summit, 4km to the north.

At the pass you'll see Lake Albina to the north, the headwaters of Lady Northcotes Canyon. As you continue along the track you can see the ruins of Albina Lodge just below you. It was originally constructed for use by skiers, but the environmental problems the hut caused led to it being dismantled. The track skirts the western fall of Mt Northcote (2131m), joins the main divide again at Northcote Pass and continues just to the west of Mt Lee (2105m). Along this section information boards highlight areas of **feldmark**, which grows on damaged points along the exposed crest.

From the saddle beyond Mt Lee you get your first good look at Club Lake. The track then climbs north, zigzagging steeply to the summit of **Carruthers Peak** (2145m). There are great views from here, particularly south-west to Mt Townsend and north-east to the distant Mt Jagungal (2061m) over the pyramid-like Sentinel (1917m) and Watsons Crags (2022m).

As the track descends from the summit, you will notice the preventative measures (stone walls and drains) taken against soil erosion and vegetation loss on the eastern slopes of Carruthers Peak. Soon you reach a saddle where the main route swings east, while an old, faint 4WD track climbs northeast to Mt Twynam. The saddle is covered with fragile feldmark and walkers are encouraged not to stray off the tracks. Follow the main route east for 1km as it gradually descends to a paved area in a shallow saddle. Leave your backpacks here and follow the track for 1km to the glacial **Blue Lake**, which is tucked in at the base of cliffs on Mt Twynam's southern slopes.

Return to the saddle, gather your packs and follow the heavily used path down to cross **Carruthers Creek**. The track climbs a little to the crest of a spur (where you can catch the occasional glimpse of Hedley Tarn to the east), then descends for about 2.5km to the valley. Here there are two large watercourses to cross – **Club Lake Creek** and the **Snowy River**; both can be waded or crossed on stepping stones (unless the water levels are high, in which case it is best to walk upstream to find a suitable crossing, or wait). An often cold *camp site* exists between the two rivers a short distance upstream, near a lonely chimney stack, the last vestige of Foremans Hut.

Day 3: Snowy River to Thredbo
3½–4 hours, 13km
After you've negotiated the river crossing, take the path steeply east to rejoin the Summit Rd at Charlottes Pass. The Summit Rd provides easy walking as it skirts the north-western slopes of Mt Stilwell and the Rams Head Range. A little over 4km from Charlottes Pass the trail crosses a bridge over Merritts Creek; soon after you cross the Snowy River before climbing to **Seamans Hut**. This solid stone hut was constructed in 1929 in memory of Laurie Seaman and Evan Hayes who perished on the slopes of Mt Kosciuszko in the winter of 1928.

Summit Rd continues for 1.7km to Rawsons Pass, from where you retrace your steps of the first day to the top of the Thredbo chairlifts.

The Chimneys

Duration	5–6 hours
Distance	17km
Standard	easy-medium
Start/Finish	Dead Horse Gap
Nearest Towns	Jindabyne, Corryong
Public Transport	yes

Summary A generally easy walk across the attractive Boggy Plain culminates in a scramble to the rocky summit of the Chimneys. Some route finding is required in this mostly trackless terrain.

While most of the popular walks in Kosciuszko National Park lie in the area between Thredbo and the ghost town of Kiandra, some particularly interesting country can be found south of the Alpine Way in the southern section of the park. The Chimneys are a high, rocky outcrop dominating the Chimneys Ridge a few kilometres south of Thredbo. Other than Cascade Trail, the only tracks in the area are those formed by wildlife, including emus and brumbies.

Although most of this route is off formed trails, the open snow plains of Boggy Plain – also known as the 'Big Boggy' – provide easy walking, and the upper reaches of the Thredbo River provide reliable guidance in a trackless landscape.

Starting near Dead Horse Gap the walk follows the north bank of the Thredbo River, then climbs gradually to the base of the Chimneys (the last section a bit scrubby). The final ascent is a rock scramble – not too difficult – to the twin rocky prominences of the Chimneys. The described route is a moderate day walk, but two days could easily be filled in this wild and scenic region.

PLANNING
For details of when to walk, what to bring and permits and regulations, see Planning in the introduction to the Kosciuszko National Park.

Maps
The 1:50,000 *Thredbo* map produced by the CMA is all you'll need.

GETTING TO/FROM THE WALK
The walk begins a few hundred metres east of Dead Horse Gap itself, where the Alpine Way crosses the Thredbo River; there is a car park on the south side of the road. The trailhead is 4km west of Thredbo and 37km west of Jindabyne (along Kosciuszko Rd, then the Alpine Way). If coming from Victoria, access is via Corryong and Khancoban (Dead Horse Gap is 67km from Khancoban along the Alpine Way).

For information on shuttle services to and from the trailhead, see Getting Around in the introduction to Kosciuszko National Park.

THE WALK
Cascade Trail climbs south-east away from the Alpine Way and above the **Thredbo River**. After 2km the trail fords the river – there's also a footbridge – and heads south, but the route to take follows the north (true right) bank generally east. A brumby pad (trail) begins here and heads upstream into pretty **Boggy Plain**. About 2.5km from the ford, the river veers to the south; cross the river on some rocks as it begins to turn back

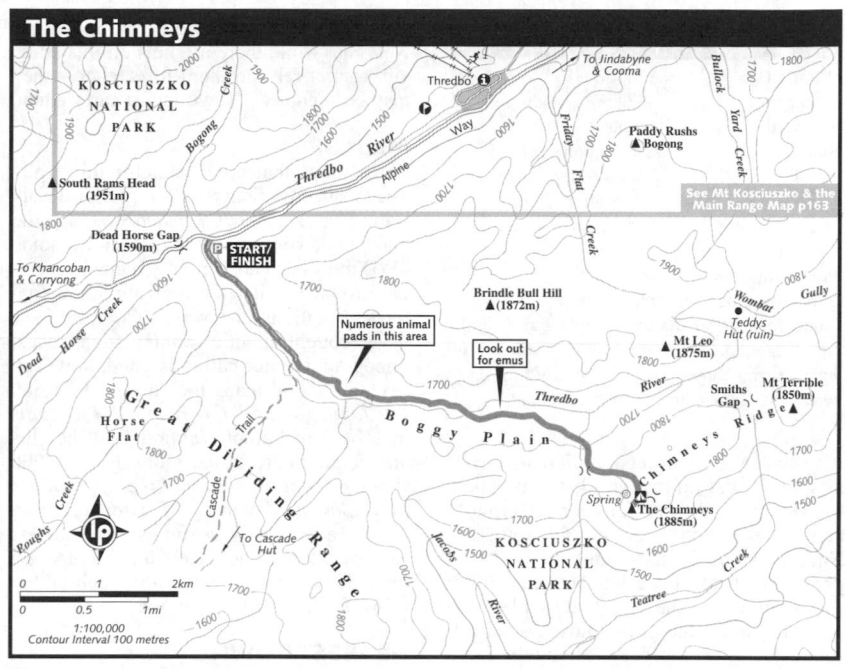

The Chimneys

See Mt Kosciuszko & the Main Range Map p163

eastwards and walk a little way uphill to lo-cate some more brumby pads. Follow these east across the plain – or walk cross-country if you don't find them – but after about 1km from the river crossing you will need to bear south-east and ascend away from the river. There are faint pads in places, but it may be more convenient to make your own way. There are often **emus** grazing in the upper reaches of Boggy Plain and you will no doubt have noticed the huge piles of brumby droppings along the route.

You will soon be able to see the rocky outcrop of the Chimneys in the distance through a gap in the Chimneys Ridge – walk towards this prominent saddle. As you get closer to the saddle and gain height you reach a small stream, which runs north from the saddle. Cross the stream at any suitable point and climb south up the valley; the best route is about 50m east of the stream on an animal pad. Once on the saddle, climb east (there is no pad) and ascend the Chimneys

Ridge. There is some scrub at first but it's not unduly thick and the best route seems to be slightly on the north side of the ridge. Avoid the temptation to head directly for the Chimneys – the scrub is thicker on the south side and there are some boulders that make walking difficult.

At a point directly north of the Chim-neys, walk south and head downhill onto a snow plain 200m west of a saddle. There are some *camp sites* in the trees at the base of the Chimneys; water can usually be found in the gully west of the snow plain. From the plain, a rock scramble through stunted, gnarled snow gums is required to reach the top – there is no marked route, so pick the best way you can. The highest point of the **Chimneys** (1885m) is marked by a cairn and ruined trigonometric point. There are excellent views of the Main Range to the north and the Jacobs River valley far below you to the south. Return to the start via the outward route.

Mt Jagungal

Duration	3 or 4 days
Distance	46.5km or 54km
Standard	medium
Start	Out Station Creek
Finish	Round Mountain or
	Out Station Creek
Nearest Towns	Tumut, Adaminaby,
	Corryong
Public Transport	yes

Summary Open snow plains, snow gum woodlands, four historic mountain huts and a climb up Mt Jagungal for grandstand views are highlights of this three-day, or optionally four-day, walk. Only a few steep climbs are required.

It's been called a 'crouching lion' and even a 'sphinx', but no matter what you call it, Mt Jagungal's distinct form stands proudly aloof in the central region of Kosciuszko National Park. From all directions it is a prominent peak, towering between 300m and 400m above the surrounding plains. It also provides some of the most distant all-round views in the park. Strangely for a peak as dominant and impressive as Mt Jagungal, there is no major path to its summit; fortunately, however, there are a few faint tracks to guide you to the top. The plains and valleys in the Jagungal wilderness area are so vast that you could 'lose' yourself here for days – but you will only require three or four days for this walk.

Starting at Out Station Creek on the Tooma Rd, the route follows mainly good tracks to the base of the mountain, passing a few huts along the way. Then you climb a route on the north side of the mountain as a side trip before returning to Tooma Rd along the scenic Farm Ridge. The walk finishes at Round Mountain and requires a shuttle to return to any vehicles left at Out Station Creek. As a difficult alternative, a fourth day can be spent walking along a very faint and heavily overgrown trail to return to Out Station Creek.

PLANNING

For details of when to walk, what to bring and permits and regulations, see Planning in the introduction to Kosciuszko National Park. Note that while there are huts on this walk, you cannot rely on them for shelter – they may be occupied – so you must carry a tent.

Maps

Three maps that are useful for this walk. The most convenient map for the entire walk is the CMA's 1:50,000 *Khancoban* map. The main fault with this is that it shows some 4WD tracks that are virtually nonexistent on the ground, while not showing some foot tracks at all; in the walk description we have brought attention to any such tracks. Topographic information is good, however.

Other useful maps include the 1:31,680 *Mt Jagungal and the Brassy Mountains* map by Tim Lamble (although all heights and contours are in feet) and the 1:50,000 *Round Mountain Area and the Approaches to Mt Jagungal* map by SR Brookes. Both maps are extremely useful as they indicate foot tracks not shown on the *Khancoban* map, as well as other features such as hut ruins, fences and water points.

NEAREST TOWN

Although Cabramurra is the nearest town to the trailhead, it has only very basic amenities (including a general store and petrol station).

GETTING TO/FROM THE WALK
To the Start

It is quite a distance from any of the nearest towns to the start of the walk on Tooma Rd at Out Station Creek. The road crosses Out Station Creek on a sharp bend where a 4WD track joins the road on the south side; there is enough room here to park a few vehicles off the road. Access is easiest by private vehicle or hire car.

Corryong, in Victoria, is the closest main town to the walk (56km). It is 23km from Corryong to the Tooma Rd junction (Khancoban is 5km south from this junction), then another 33km to the start of the walk.

If coming from Adaminaby, follow the Snowy Mountains Hwy west for 34km to a road junction just north of the ghost town of Kiandra. Turn left here (west) and drive towards Cabramurra; just before you enter the town, turn left (south) onto Tooma Rd and continue 29km to the start. From Tumut, follow the Snowy Mountains Hwy south for 93km to the road junction north of Kiandra.

For shuttle services to and from the trailheads, see Getting Around in the introduction to Kosciuszko National Park.

From the Finish
The finish of the walk is on Tooma Rd, 9km east of the start, where the Round Mountain Fire Trail joins the road. If you intend to complete your walk here, you will need to organise a pick-up or leave one of your own vehicles here – there is room off the road.

THE WALK
Day 1: Out Station Creek to Hell Hole Creek Fire Trail
5–6 hours, 16km
At the start, an overgrown track (quite easy to follow, but not shown on the *Khancoban* map) heads west and after 1km joins the Dargals Fire Trail east of Tooma Reservoir. This good trail takes you south and skirts the edge of **Toolong Plain**, soon passing **Patons Hut**. Continue past the Theiss Village Fire Trail junction (signposted, but the trail is not obvious); for the next 5km the trail undulates and meanders south providing pleasant walking. You eventually reach a track junction 7.5km from the start. Take the left branch here, which is the continuation of Dargals Fire Trail; the track to the right leads to Broadway Plain and Wheelers Hut.

In 2km the trail drops down to a treeless valley and a ford over the **Tooma River**. After crossing the river, the trail heads along the west (true left) bank for a few hundred metres, passing an area that would make a pleasant *camp site* during warm weather (night-time temperatures here can, however, fall very low), before climbing onto a spur. Turn left at a track junction (1km from the ford) onto Hell Hole Creek Fire Trail and follow this for 2.5km to another ford of the Tooma River. Here, too, is a small *camp site*.

Across the river the track climbs steeply away from the valley and soon enters the forest. After a stiff 45-minute ascent from the river you reach a high point, before dropping

rather steeply for a short distance to the edge of a large snow plain. The track swings to the south-east here and climbs a little to a saddle with a lovely *camping area* – water can be obtained in the open valley to the north in one of the heads of Hell Hole Creek.

Day 2: Hell Hole Creek Fire Trail to O'Keefes Hut
5–6 hours, 12km
The fire trail continues its climb south-east, soon crossing a small stream before reaching the open plains of the **Toolong Range**. From here you'll get your first tantalising glimpses of Mt Jagungal. The track swings to the north-east and joins Round Mountain Fire Trail 2.5km from the camp site. Turn south here onto Round Mountain Fire Trail, which soon crosses over a ridge and descends gently to cross **Pugilistic Creek** via a bridge. Not far beyond the creek a walking track leads off to the right to **Derschkos Hut**, which you can see ahead. The hut comfortably sleeps four to six people; water can be obtained from the tiny stream just out the front. There are also *camp sites* nearby.

A walking track heads uphill behind the hut, crosses the ridge and drops down to rejoin Round Mountain Fire Trail. This old 4WD track snakes its way south-east across the broad snow plain that forms the upper reaches of the Tooma River before reaching the Grey Mare Fire Trail at a junction 1.5km from Derschkos Hut. The Grey Mare Fire Trail leads you uphill and into the forest briefly, then crosses the upper reaches of the **Tumut River** (here just a stream). There are some *camp sites* beside the creek, as well as a short way upstream. The main route continues in a north-east direction to eventually reach a **weather station** 5km from Derschkos Hut. Here begins a faint track to Mt Jagungal (see the Mt Jagungal side trip). Another 2km leads to *O'Keefes Hut*, with a number of good *camp sites*.

Side Trip: Mt Jagungal
2–3 hours, 3.5km return, 400m ascent, 400m descent
A faint track leads south from behind the weather station and away from the Grey

Mare Fire Trail. This can be difficult to follow in places, but ascends steadily towards Mt Jagungal. As you gain height and pass the tree line the route becomes steeper and sidles to the east of some large, rocky bluffs. The route swings to the south-west as you approach the exposed mountain top. A short scramble brings you to the summit of **Mt Jagungal** (2061m), where views are extensive. Return to Grey Mare Fire Trail by the same route.

Day 3: O'Keefes Hut to Tooma Rd
5–6 hours, 15km
Grey Mare Fire Trail heads north away from the hut, then descends to cross **Bogong Creek**. A short, steep climb greets you on the east side, leading to the site of the now-ruined Farm Ridge huts. There is an indistinct track junction here; the route to follow is the faint and partly overgrown Farm Ridge Fire Trail, which heads north. This track offers easy walking in attractive forest – some sections ghostly white after bushfires some years ago. The conical-shaped Round Mountain can be seen occasionally in the distance to the north. About 7km from the Farm Ridge huts site, the track begins to drop steadily towards the **Tumut River**. Once on the valley floor, a short stroll brings you to a river ford (which may be difficult in flood conditions). Wade the river and immediately the track climbs very steeply, easing off just before reaching *Round Mountain Hut*. There are some rough beds inside the hut, but *camping* is much nicer outside; water is available just north of the hut.

Follow the track uphill from the hut until you reach a T-junction 500m away. Turn right (north) here and 1.5km away is the end of the walk at Tooma Rd.

Alternative Finish
3–4 hours, 9.5km
This route from Round Mountain Hut to Out Station Creek is for experienced walkers only. If you have good navigation skills and don't mind a bit of scrub-bashing, then this extra day of walking conveniently brings you back to the start of the walk.

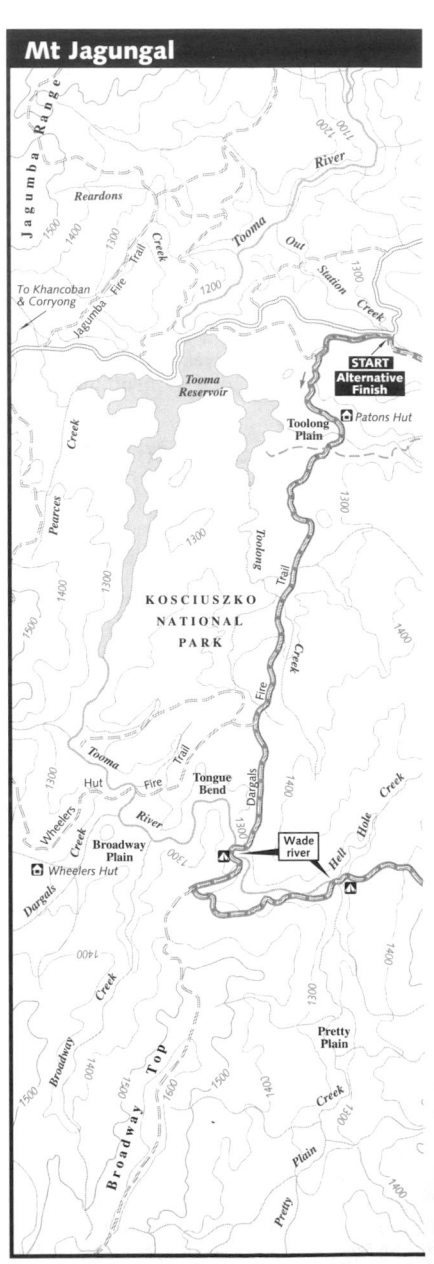

Mt Jagungal

NEW SOUTH WALES

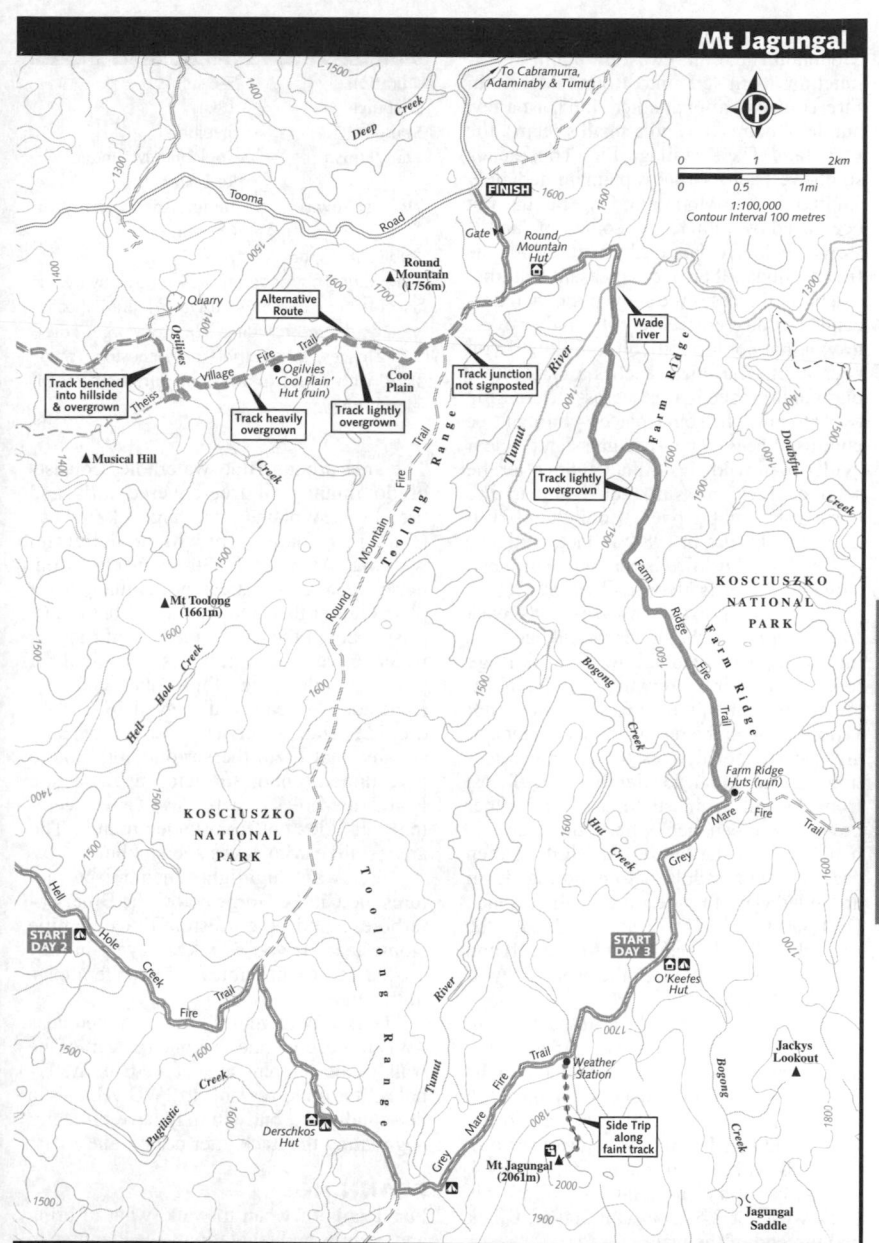

Mt Jagungal

To Cabramurra,
Adaminaby & Tumut

0   1   2km
0   0.5   1mi
1:100,000
Contour Interval 100 metres

Deep Creek

Tooma Road

FINISH

Gate

Round Mountain Hut

Round Mountain (1756m)

Quarry

Ogilvies

Village

Fire Trail

Ogilvies 'Cool Plain' Hut (ruin)

Cool Plain

Wade river

Alternative Route

Track benched into hillside & overgrown

Theiss

Track heavily overgrown

Track lightly overgrown

Track junction not signposted

Tumut River

Farm Ridge

Track lightly overgrown

▲ Musical Hill

Creek

Round Mountain Fire Trail

Toolong Range

▲ Mt Toolong (1661m)

KOSCIUSZKO NATIONAL PARK

Farm Ridge Fire Trail

Bogong Creek

Hell Hole Creek

Farm Ridge Huts (ruin)

Mare Fire Trail

START DAY 2

Hell Hole Creek Fire Trail

KOSCIUSZKO NATIONAL PARK

Toolong Range

Tumut River

Hut Creek

START DAY 3

O'Keefes Hut

Jackys Lookout ▲

Bogong Creek

Puglistic Creek

Derschkos Hut

Grey Mare Fire Trail

Weather Station

Side Trip along faint track

Mt Jagungal (2061m)

Jagungal Saddle

After camping overnight at Round Mountain Hut, climb west for 500m to a T-junction. Turn left onto Round Mountain Fire Trail and, after another 1km (just a few hundred metres beyond a small stream), the very faint Theiss Village Fire Trail heads south-west across a snow plain immediately south of Round Mountain. This trail has not been used by vehicles for some time and is slowly being reclaimed by nature, but the first section still provides pleasant walking.

The trail crosses the snow plain then descends beside a creek. Here it is rather overgrown, but not too difficult to follow if you keep alert. The track reaches a large snow plain and proceeds west across it, crossing two streams. In some places you can see clumps of heavily churned grassland – clear evidence of wild pigs. About 400m after the second creek crossing you come to the burnt ruins of Ogilvies 'Cool Plain' Hut, destroyed by fire in 1988; in fact, evidence of this large bushfire is obvious with dead snow gum forests all around you.

The very faint trail now ascends west from the ruins to the ridge top and becomes increasingly hard to follow. On the ridge top, vigorous fire regrowth has all but obliterated any sign of the track. The route is not visible through the regrowth, but the lack of grass underfoot defines the general direction; you need to head slightly south of west from the hill behind the hut ruins. Farther down, you can see where the track is benched into the side of the hill; it then passes over a saddle before sidling down around the north side of a knoll to reach Ogilvies Creek. If you cannot locate the track then simply head west (downhill) and you will eventually reach the open valley of Ogilvies Creek.

Cross the creek and scrub-bash north down its west (true left) side. If you stay about 40m above the creek, heading into the forest, you will find evidence of an old track heading north – this too is heavily overgrown and benched into the side of the hill, but leads within 1km to a good 4WD track south-west of a disused quarry. Follow this track west for 2.5km to Out Station Creek and the end of the walk.

Cooleman Plain

Duration	5–6 hours
Distance	18km
Standard	medium
Start/Finish	Cooleman Mountain Rest Area
Nearest Towns	Tumut, Adaminaby, Corryong
Public Transport	yes

Summary This moderate walk, with only minor ascents and descents, traverses dramatically varied terrain, including a pretty gorge, limestone caves, a waterhole and limestone sinkhole, with a visit to a historic farm homestead along the way.

The area around Blue Waterholes consists predominantly of tree-covered hills and broad grassy plains – the largest known as Cooleman Plain – providing delightful walking. At around 1300m in elevation, these open grassy areas are actually frost plains rather than snow plains. What is surprising about the area is the lack of running water above Blue Waterholes; a result of the plain's underlying limestone geology. Limestone is readily dissolved by carbon dioxide and water (rainwater) causing streams that drain the surrounding hills to dive underground, surfacing again at the Blue Waterholes (where Cave Creek seemingly bubbles out from underground). The area is alive with caves and sinkholes.

Other walk highlights include the picturesque Clarke Gorge below the Blue Waterholes and the restored Coolamine Homestead. If you've a keen eye you may see kangaroos, brumbies and even feral pigs in the area.

The Blue Waterholes Fire Trail, a popular 4WD route, continues beyond the start of the walk to the camping area at the Blue Waterholes. It is quite passable to 2WD vehicles in dry conditions, but you may have difficulty negotiating the track after heavy rain.

PLANNING

For details of when to walk, what to bring and permits and regulations, see Planning in

Coolamine Homestead

When Sir Terence Murray, a Canberra pioneer, was looking for new farmlands in January 1839, he stumbled upon the lush grasslands of the isolated Cooleman Plain and wasted no time in staking his claim. By February he had established Coolalamine Station, with a small slab hut on the site. The station was later renamed Coolamine.

The first of seven major buildings – another larger dwelling – was built in 1873, and in 1881 the lease was sold to Frederick Campbell. In 1882 a manager by the name of George Southwell was employed and he constructed a more hospitable house. Local building practices included using horse hair for insulation under the roof and lining internal walls with newspaper. Corrugated iron was becoming increasingly popular as a roofing material – a more effective rain deterrent than bark and wood shingles.

As the station prospered, the house was extended many times to accommodate the growing number of employees; in 1889 a cheese hut (a structure made out of grass thatch and clay to store cheeses while they matured) was built.

There is some conjecture as to the construction date of the other Coolamine homestead on the site – the building with the high-pitched roof – although sometime between 1890 and 1907 is likely. This large building may have been transported there from another site near Peppercorn Hill, although other evidence suggests it was built on site.

Around 1900 Campbell acquired more land on the plain in the homestead's vicinity, and with more employees on the station he added a bedroom and storage room. One particular room was used as a Sunday post office when mail was being delivered from Berridale. Other buildings were constructed over time, but have not survived.

The Taylor family took over from the Southwells as managers in 1907, and they remained there for 20 years. As Coolamine later passed through a succession of owners (sold in 1927 to the Litchfield brothers, then sold again in 1933 to the Naughton brothers), the complex of buildings gradually succumbed to neglect. In 1944 Kosciuszko National Park was declared, but Coolamine remained freehold land until 1975. The homestead deteriorated further over the years to a state of virtual ruin; in the late 1960s only four buildings remained. Fortunately, the Kosciuszko Huts Association saw the historical value and importance of the homestead and began its restoration in 1977. The result of their handiwork, persistence and vision can clearly be seen today.

GLENN VAN DER KNIFF

NEW SOUTH WALES

the introduction to the Kosciuszko National Park. Note that this walk cannot be accessed in winter and spring (between June and October) as the Long Plain Rd is closed to all traffic during this time. If you wish to have a peep inside any of the caves, you need to carry a torch (flashlight). Also, make sure you carry drinking water from the start.

Maps

You need two maps for this walk. The 1:25,000 *Peppercorn* and *Rules Point* maps, both by the CMA, show excellent detail and have a useful 10m contour interval.

GETTING TO/FROM THE WALK

Cooleman Mountain Rest Area is a long way from any of the nearest towns. This is a good camping area – equipped with toilets and tables – with plenty of space for cars.

From Adaminaby, continue for 55km along the Snowy Mountains Hwy to the Long Plain Rd turn-off to the right (on a sweeping bend). Take this dirt road north for 17km to the Blue Waterholes Fire Trail turn-off to the right (east); another 2.5km brings you to the rest area.

If leaving from Tumut, drive south along the Snowy Mountains Hwy for about 74km to the Long Plain Rd turn-off.

The closest main in town in Victoria is Corryong (141km). It is 23km from Corryong to the Tooma Rd junction (Khancoban is 5km south of this junction), then another 81km to the Snowy Mountains Hwy (via Cabramurra). The highway heads north for 19km to the Long Plain Rd turn-off (right).

For shuttle bus transport to and from the trailhead, see Getting Around in the introduction to the Kosciuszko National Park.

THE WALK

From Cooleman Mountain Rest Area the trail heads east and begins to drop immediately. After a little more than 1km the trail reaches the open meadows of **Cooleman Plain** and continues east for 2km to **Coolamine Homestead**, off the trail to your left. It is definitely worth having a look at the homestead; the information boards in the area give further insight into the history of this mountain outpost.

The trail crosses a low hill then descends steadily to the Blue Waterholes *camping area*. There are often kangaroos grazing here. At the **Blue Waterholes**, which form the beginning of **Cave Creek**, a trail heads downstream on the left bank. This soon crosses a broad stream, then immediately crosses over Cave Creek itself on stepping stones, before continuing downstream on the right bank. It is worth following this track downstream for about 1km from the Blue Waterholes (or more if you wish) to gain access into the scenic **Clarke Gorge**. It is possible to venture a long way downstream, eventually reaching some waterfalls and cascades about 2.5km from the Blue Waterholes.

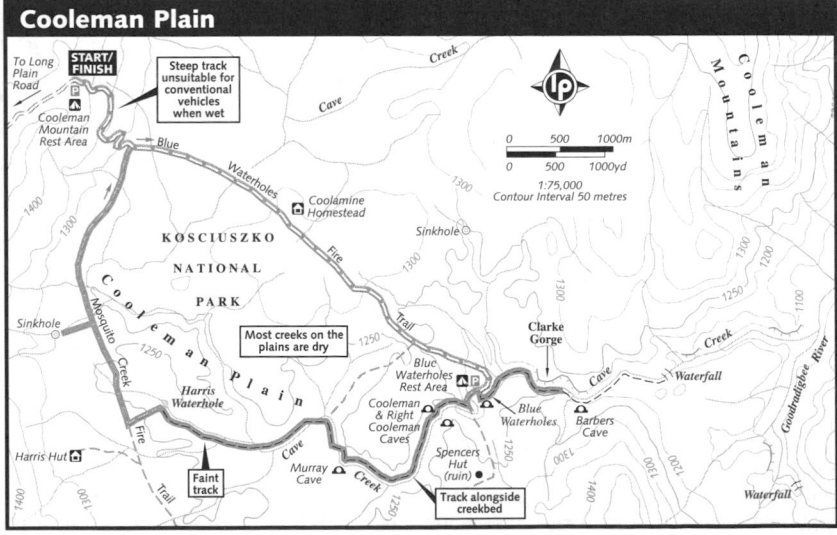

After inspecting the gorge, return to the waterhole – fill your drink bottles – and locate Blue Waterholes Fire Trail where it crosses the usually dry creek bed just above the waterhole. Follow the trail for a few hundred metres before leaving it to follow a walking track alongside the dry Cave Creek, or walk up the bed of the creek itself. This part of the walk is named Jennings Walk and is very easy to follow. Heading upstream, you soon pass **Cooleman Cave** (worth a cursory look) and, about 1.5km farther on, **Murray Cave**, one of the more impressive of all the caves in the Cooleman Plain area. It has a narrow opening but a rather large chamber inside.

Not far beyond Murray Cave the valley broadens, but the walking track soon turns away and heads north to join the Blue Waterholes Fire Trail. Leave the walking track, cross Cave Creek to the north (true left) bank about 1km past Murray Cave – there was water running at this point at the time of research – and locate a faint foot track heading west. This stays north of the creek for 750m then crosses the creek again before heading gently up a side valley to **Harris Waterhole**.

This waterhole, appearing more like a small dam, is an anomaly on these plains, being one of the few places where surface water exists naturally. Climb up the grassy slope south-west from the waterhole and you'll locate a grassy 4WD track. This soon meets another faint 4WD track, the Mosquito Creek Fire Trail, which you follow north. It descends into a shallow valley and climbs a low spur before dropping to another shallow valley, 1.5km from Harris Waterhole. Leave the track here (there are no signs to point the way) and walk southwest up this valley for 300m to an interesting phenomenon. Here, two small creeks flow down the hillside only to plummet underground into a **sinkhole** – evidence of the presence of limestone under the plains.

Return to the faint track and continue north to rejoin the Blue Waterholes Fire Trail 1km east of Cooleman Mountain Rest Area. It's a 25-minute climb back up the trail to the end of the walk.

The Budawangs

The Budawangs provide some of the most spectacular bushwalking in the state. They form a complex maze of deep valleys and heavily forested canyons, stretching over the Morton and Budawang National Parks, and are presided over by towering cliffs. All walks described here, including the peaks around Pigeon House Mountain and the Castle, lie within the borders of the 162,000-hectare Morton National Park. The wild, densely timbered escarpment of Budawang National Park continues south of here, with Yadboro Creek forming the boundary between the two regions.

The landscape of the Budawangs consists of a complex maze of flat-topped sandstone peaks, rugged gorges and towering cliffs. The spectacular Monolith Valley presents a vision of a Lost World of hidden valleys surrounded by towering cliffs and adds to the amazing diversity of landscapes found within the park.

Despite the encroachment of farmers, prospectors and timber-getters into the valleys, and continuing conflict between conservationists and logging interests, the Budawangs still have a primordial, rugged feel, and give us an inkling of what untouched Australian wilderness might have been like before European settlement.

HISTORY
Aborigines from the Wodi-Wodi and Wandandian tribes were the first inhabitants of this area, and recognised the suitability of the local sandstone for sharpening tools. Deep grooves worn into sandstone throughout the region are evidence of this. Harder rocks (usually of volcanic origin) were used for making stone implements, which were then traded with neighbouring tribes. With their mythical appearance, the Budawangs were the source of many Aboriginal Dreamtime legends, although there is little evidence of occupation of the deeper valleys beyond 3500 years ago.

Captain Cook gave the first European name to a feature of the area (Pigeon House

Mountain) during a voyage up the east coast in 1770; the first European explorer, George Evans, entered the bush farther north in 1812. The subsequent arrival of European settlers brought a wave of gold prospectors, pioneer settlers and loggers searching out valuable red cedar trees, who succeeded in all but wiping out the local Aboriginal population. The indigenous people who remained, decimated by smallpox and other introduced diseases, were relocated to reserves.

Visits by walkers to the area in the early years of the 20th century led to significant conservation efforts. In 1934 Australia's first wilderness area – the 3100-hectare Tallowa Primitive Reserve – was gazetted, primarily as a result of the work of Myles Dunphy and his National Parks and Primitive Areas Council. (See the boxed text 'Myles Dunphy, Wilderness Advocate' in Facts about Australia for an account of Dunphy's much-valued contribution to the environment.) Mr Mark Morton, a local member of the NSW parliament at the time, provided significant support and vision, and the national park today bears his name.

NATURAL HISTORY

Due to a combination of high rainfall and significant altitude variation, the Budawangs are able to support a rich and varied flora and fauna. Rainforest thrives in the valleys and canyons where moist sheltered conditions prevail (trees present include the highly prized red cedar, used in making furniture, and brown beech). Coachwood forest exists farther south towards Yadboro Creek, while eucalyptus forest, on the dry slopes, and mallee species eke out an existence on high rocky plateaus and exposed sandstone platforms. Heath and some alpine species dominate the higher altitude areas and windswept mountain tops.

Wildlife includes the usual Australian species (kangaroos, wallabies, koalas and dingos), with platypuses and native water rats common. Black-cockatoos are often seen, and the superb lyrebird can frequently be heard mimicking the calls of other birds as it scratches around the leaf litter on the forest floor.

PLANNING
When to Walk

It is possible to walk here year-round. The eastern sections of the park tend to receive more rain and fog than the drier western section, due to their coastal location. Weather changes can occur rapidly (within hours) throughout the year, producing rain and low cloud, which can make navigation difficult and quickly cause flooding of rivers and creeks.

Generally, the summers are dry and hot and the winters cold and moist. Exposed walks along high ridges and plateaus can be very hot and dry from November to March. Windy, cold conditions (occasionally accompanied by snow on the higher peaks) are not uncommon from June to September. Overnight temperatures in the valleys in winter are often well below freezing, and heavy frosts (especially on the western slopes towards Corang Peak) are usual at this time. Despite this, beautiful sunny days are common in all seasons.

What to Bring

Take a tent, although camping caves are numerous and at times comfortable enough to accommodate large parties. A sleeping bag capable of keeping you warm in temperatures down to at least -5°C is advisable for frosty winter nights.

Although many bushwalkers have done the walks described in light runners (training shoes), high-ankle boots are recommended for the steep, rocky terrain to help avoid ankle injuries.

To assist in scaling some of the more exposed cliffs and hauling packs – for example on the route to the summit of the Castle – a 25m length of 9mm rope is useful. Make sure someone in the party knows how to tie appropriate knots and set up a safety belay.

While water tanks and creeks exist in many of the camping and picnic areas, they may be dry in summer, so it's best to carry sufficient water to the start of your walk.

Maps

Produced by the Budawang Committee (Coast and Mountain Walkers Club), the

1:50,000, *The Northern Budawang Range and the Upper Clyde River Valley Sketch Map* is an excellent publication. It includes much detail that is not shown on standard 1:25,000 topographic maps. Locations of camping caves and other useful features are also indicated. On the back of this map, some historical notes and handy walk summaries have been printed.

The CMA 1:25,000 *Corang* and *Milton* maps provide topographical coverage of all walks listed here.

Books

Pigeon House and Beyond produced by the Budawang Committee is the definitive reference to the history, geography, wildlife and bushwalks in this area. It is available throughout Australia from outdoor gear suppliers and bookshops. Extensive walk descriptions are included, and much information is given explaining the development and gazetting of Australia's national parks.

70 Walks in Southern New South Wales and ACT and *120 Walks in New South Wales* by Tyrone Thomas give good walk descriptions for Pigeon House Mountain and the Castle, and can be useful for walk planning.

Information Sources

The NPWS (☎ 02-4423 2170) has a district office at 55 Graham St, Nowra; a subdistrict park office at Ulladulla (☎ 02-4455 3826); and a visitor centre at Fitzroy Falls (☎ 02-4887 7270), on the park's northern boundary.

Permits & Regulations

No permits for camping or bushwalking are currently required, and no park fees are charged. Walkers are advised, however, to submit their itinerary by phone to the subdistrict park office in Ulladulla before setting off on an overnight walk (see Information Sources). Bush camping is permitted everywhere except Monolith Valley, where overuse has damaged this fragile area.

NEAREST TOWNS & FACILITIES
Ulladulla

Ulladulla, a holiday town on the NSW south coast, about 225km from Sydney, is the only

---

Warnings

- Severe bushfires have ravaged the Budawangs in past years. Due to the difficult nature of the terrain and the lack of surface water in summer, when streams and creeks often dry up, there is little protection for walkers if caught out in a fire. Prevention is better than cure, so keep a look out for signs of trouble, such as smoke, and plan on changing your route early to avoid being swallowed by a fire front. It's best to avoid the region in very hot, dry weather, especially if a north or westerly wind is blowing. Check with the Nowra district NPWS office (see Information Sources) for current fire risk status before entering the park in danger periods.

- Topographic maps and a compass are mandatory for walks in this area. Since the NPWS made a decision recently to let this area regenerate back into wilderness, some areas, such as the track to Corang Peak, are becoming increasingly overgrown, and route finding can be tricky. To further complicate matters, the high ridges and plateaus attract morning fog and low cloud which may obscure all visible landmarks.

---

sizable settlement relatively close to the park that provides accommodation and walk supplies. Ulladulla's visitor centre (☎ 02-4455 1269) is in the Civic Centre opposite the harbour.

Places to Stay & Eat The *South Coast Backpackers* (☎ 02-4454 0500, 63 Princess Hwy) provides dorm beds at $20 and doubles or twins for $42 per night. Management also operates a shuttle service to the Budawangs (details are covered in Getting To/From the Walk for both walks).

There are several *motels* in Ulladulla, although vacancies can be scarce in summer and school holiday periods. *Top View Motel* (☎ 02-4455 1514, 72 South St) has a good location overlooking the town and is possibly one of the friendliest motels on the south coast.

Various restaurants, cafes and small eateries can be found in Ulladulla's main street. Down at the harbour, *Fisherman's Wharf Seafood* is the place to buy fresh fish, and across the road on Wason St, *Tory's Seafood Restaurant* is a licensed restaurant with good views.

Getting There & Away If driving from Sydney, take the Princes Hwy straight down the south coast – the highway runs directly through Ulladulla (225km).

A number of bus services from Sydney and Melbourne pass through Ulladulla, including Premier Motor Service (☎ 13 3410).

Braidwood

Braidwood is on the road route to the Budawangs area from Canberra (89km), and has basic supplies, a *supermarket* for food, and several accommodation and eating options. It's about 40km from here to the start of the walks, however, and it is not a convenient staging post if you have time to drive all the way to the camping areas at Yadboro Flat or Blue Gum Flat within the park, or the Wog Wog park entrance at the start of the walk.

Nerriga

Only basic supplies from the *general store* and petrol are available here. Nerriga also has a basic *caravan park*.

Morton National Park

Bush camping with car access but no facilities is possible at *Blue Gum Flat* and *Yadboro Flat*, both off the dirt Yadboro Rd within Morton National Park. These sites are marked on *The Northern Budawang Range and the Upper Clyde River Valley Sketch Map* (see Maps earlier). Walkers travelling by car may opt to drive to these sites directly and camp prior to starting the walks mentioned.

Camp sites also exist at the Wog Wog entrance to the park, which is at the start of the Corang Peak to the Castle walk. It has pit toilets, however, no other facilities or water are available.

Corang Peak to the Castle

Duration	3 days
Distance	52km
Standard	medium-hard
Start/Finish	Wog Wog park entrance
Nearest Towns	Nerriga, Braidwood
Public Transport	yes

Summary An extremely varied walk among some of the most spectacular sandstone escarpment country Australia has to offer. Monolith Valley, the Castle and Mt Owen are all highlights.

This is spectacular country. The views across the heavily forest-clad valleys and ridges are breathtaking, and the walker is regularly presented with something new to look at. The craggy rock walls of the lower sandstone plateaus are capped by dark, brooding sandstone peaks such as the Castle. Monolith Valley is a highlight, with an 'other worldly' feel to it, dissected as it is by a maze of clefts and canyons scoured into its rocky battlements.

If you do not have time for the three-day Corang Peak to the Castle stretch, the Castle and Monolith Valley can also be accessed from Yadboro Flat (off the Yadboro Rd) via the Kalianna Ridge in a two-day hard overnight circuit walk.

Supplies of stove fuel and food are best obtained before you approach the national park, as Nerriga has little to offer in the way of shops and facilities.

GETTING TO/FROM THE WALK

From Sydney, take the Princes Hwy down to Nowra on the NSW south coast (about 165km). Take the right turn to HMAS Albatross Naval Base (signposted just south of town) and turn right again at the first road intersection encountered. Pick up the gravel-surfaced Braidwood–Nowra road, and follow it past Tianjara Falls (worth a look) and through Sassafras to Nerriga (about 21km from Sassafras). Continue down this road for 17km, before turning left onto the Mongarlowe Rd. A creek ford is crossed before the signposted Wog Wog park entrance is reached, 22km from Nerriga. Leave cars at the Wog Wog parking area.

From Canberra or Melbourne, drive to Braidwood. Take a left turn onto the Nerriga–Nowra road, immediately before the town centre. Continue along this to the Mongarlowe Rd turn-off on the right, and cross the creek ford to reach the Wog Wog park entrance.

Trips to the Wog Wog park entrance and the trailhead can be arranged through South Coast Backpackers in Ulladulla (see Nearest Towns earlier) on special request. You need to be a guest to take advantage of this service.

An organisation called New South Wales Wilderness Transit (☎ 02-4683 2344) provides a service to the Wog Wog park entrance from Campbelltown train station in Sydney for $55 one way.

THE WALK
Day 1: Wog Wog Park Entrance to Bibbenluke Mountain Camp Site
6 hours, 18km

The walk starts from the area just behind the national park information board. Take the walking track to Wog Wog Creek, a short distance down the hill. Head upstream and along the track, crossing Wog Wog Creek and continuing up the hill for about half an hour. The track is well marked up to this point.

After passing a sandstone overhang, continue along the top of the next rise and descend to cross a saddle, before climbing again, heading in a southerly direction. Continue to follow the track through a gully, and crest the ridge ahead.

The track continues south-east, crossing an exposed rocky area for a few hundred metres, then passes a vague track junction about 6.5km from the start. Take a left turn here and continue along the track, traversing the northern side of Korra Hill and reaching another track junction at the flat saddle. From here, an indistinct track can be taken south along the ridge to **Admiration Point** (1.8km return), which has excellent views across the Yadboro River to Currockbilly Mountain and east to the ramparts of the Castle and Mt Owen.

To continue from the Korra Hill track junction, take the left fork to the summit of **Corang Peak** (a 70m altitude gain to the 864m summit), from where great views of all the surrounding peaks and the heavily forested valleys unfold (about three hours from the Wog Wog car park).

Continue off the summit of Corang Peak to the north-east, passing **Corang Arch** along the way – a sandstone formation that is a remnant of a collapsed rock overhang. It lies about 50m to the left of the main track. From here the route descends indistinctly down a sloping conglomerate ramp to Canowie Brook. Some *camp sites* are on the grassy border of the cleared area near the brook, with water available 400m to the east up the obvious small creek.

Continue across the Canowie Brook swamp and on to the next track junction over the rise, continuing up Burrumbeet Brook valley. Some good *camping caves* are just south of here, and numerous small tracks lead to these and some other *camp sites*.

Continue north-east and follow the route along a scenic ridge crest on the way to Bibbenluke Mountain. The track swings north and crosses a creek before reaching a *camp site* a few hundred metres farther on, near the banks of another arm of the creek.

Day 2: Bibbenluke Mountain Camp Site to Monolith Valley & the Castle Return
8½ hours, 16km

This section is strenuous and involves significant height gains and descents, so an early start is necessary to ensure you won't be finishing in the dark, especially on short winter days. Cross the creek, following the track east from the camp site, and climb towards the forested area where the track becomes a bit obscure. At the next track junction, turn right (the left branch goes to Mt Tarn) and continue for about 500m to another track junction.

From here follow the more clearly defined path up through some trees and then down again to a saddle. From here it's a 90m climb to the base of Mt Cole. Head towards the cliffs and take the left fork when the track divides, climbing until you reach the bottom escarpment of Mt Cole. The

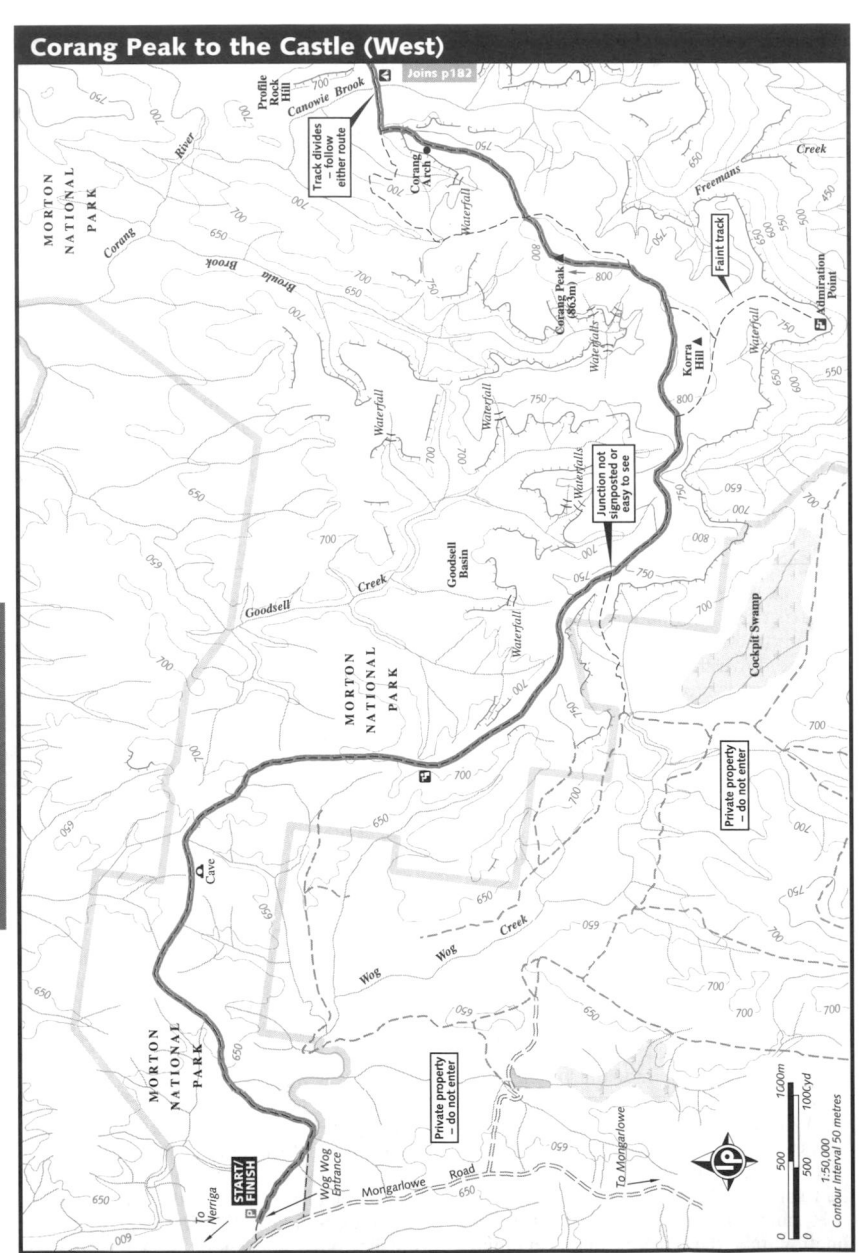

Corang Peak to the Castle (West)

route then continues around Mt Cole's base to the north, passing three camping caves before surmounting the saddle between Mt Cole and Donjon Mountain. Signs here indicate the protected region surrounding Monolith Valley. Within this area, camping and fires are not permitted.

From here, it is necessary to descend slightly, then follow the track south to the saddle between Mt Cole and Seven Gods Pinnacle and continue down the small ravine along the course of the creek into **Monolith Valley**. As the gully widens, an **arch of rock** appears on the right, and is worth exploring. Deeper into the valley still, just off the main track, a disused flat camp site and many tree ferns appear. The trip from Bibbenluke Mountain camp site to here should take two hours, and allow another three to four hours return to the Castle and back to this point.

To climb the Castle, continue on the main walking track, veer right to cross the small bridge and head up and east, following the track round to Nibelung Pass, between Mt Mooryan and Mt Nibelung. The track drops into a tight, narrow defile down right, but it is possible to avoid this by traversing along the rock and heading for the base of the gully via a fixed chain. Continue round south-east and east, until the sign indicating the end of the protected area is reached.

The Castle track continues south, skirting the base of the cliffs of Mt Nibelung, dropping south-east into a saddle. A signpost indicates the way to the Castle as the trail climbs slightly before heading farther along the cliffs past some *camping caves* to the tunnel. This feature is a constricted slot, marked by an arrow and yellow writing on the rock wall. Clamber over the boulders and crawl through for about 12m, before negotiating a deep drop at the other side.

Continue along the track to the right, keeping an eye out for arrows scratched on the rock and a log as you surmount the rocky spur of the Castle. Follow the arrows up, while angling to the right, and watch for some more arrows pointing left 25m farther on. Follow them over the rock overhang, then follow a ledge for about 40m to the last major obstacle, a chimney. Here you may

want to use the rope (mentioned in What to Bring earlier), to assist less confident members of your group. There is sometimes a section of rope hanging from the final pitch, left by previous parties.

Traverse out and round the bulge to the right, before bridging the final two short chimneys. This brings you out on the **summit plateau**, where the views are spectacular, particularly to the south and south-east. A logbook is kept in a container about 15 minutes' walk from where you finished climbing, to record your ascent.

To return to Monolith Valley, reverse your route exactly, using the same track back over the small bridge. From here, retrace your steps to the old disused camp site at the start of Monolith Valley, and climb a steep, rocky track through a small slot and down into a little valley. Follow the cairns across the base of this and up the very steep track along the system of ledges to the eastern side of Mt Owen Plateau via a gully. Continue following cairns towards the west for about 1km to the saddle between Mt Owen and Mt Cole (marked by large cairns).

A strenuous return detour (1½ hours) to the summit of Mt Owen from here is worthwhile. Follow the vague but cairned route south-west then south to **Mt Owen's southern pinnacle**, where magnificent views across to the Castle are apparent. Reverse this route back to the large cairns.

From the cairns, head north to the rim of the plateau (following cairns) and drop down the saddle between Mt Owen and Mt Cole. Continue following the cairns to the west down the obvious steep gully, and carefully descend the tricky rock slab on the gully's left side, to the protected area signpost.

From the base of the gully, head to the right past two camping caves, and follow the track down away from the cliffs towards the north-west, to a junction with the track used earlier in the day; continue down onto the saddle. From here, pick your way along the track through the trees for 1.5km to the obvious track junction 500m south-east of the Bibbenluke Mountain camp site, returning from here via the same route used earlier in the day.

Corang Peak to the Castle (East)

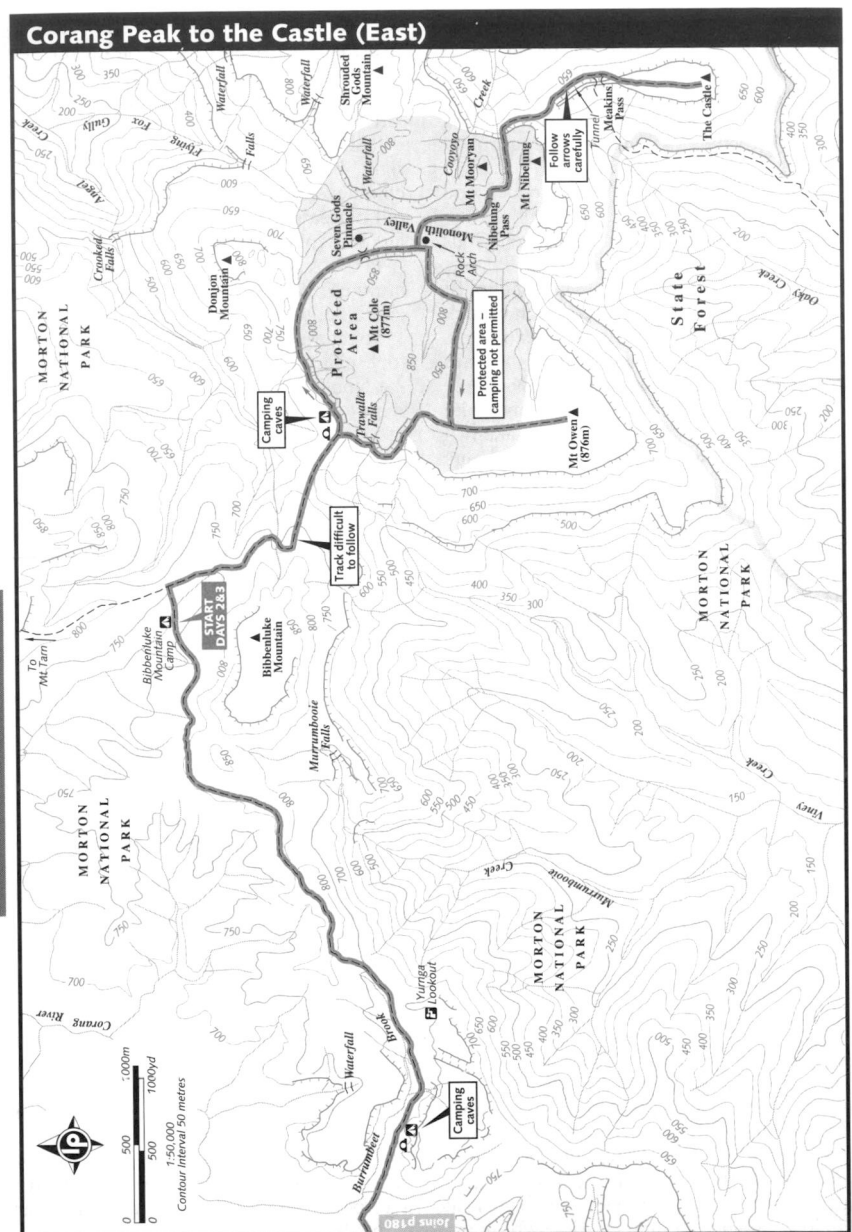

Day 3: Bibbenluke Mountain Camp Site to Wog Wog Park Entrance

6 hours, 18km

Continue back along the track used on the walk in, heading south from the camp site to pick up the track once again. Head west towards Corang Peak and, about 2.5km past Corang Peak, take the right fork at a vague track junction, heading uphill to the top of a rocky ridge. Continue along the clearly defined track from here to the Wog Wog park entrance.

Pigeon House Mountain

Duration	3 hours
Distance	5km
Standard	medium
Start/Finish	Pigeon House Mountain car park
Nearest Towns	Ulladulla, Braidwood
Public Transport	yes

Summary A short but exhilarating walk via a series of ladders to the summit of Pigeon House Mountain, with sweeping views of the ocean and coastal plains.

This day walk provides magnificent 360-degree views of the Castle, Byangee Walls and the rugged escarpments to the north and south of the park. The ocean is also clearly visible, giving an interesting contrast between the dissected valleys of the Clyde River and its tributaries, and the distant coastal plains, from Mt Dromedary in the south to Point Perpendicular in the north.

A series of metal ladders need to be negotiated near the summit. These are very safe but quite exposed, and the metal rungs may be slippery after rain.

While the walk is short, it is fairly steep and quite hot and dry in summer – remember to take plenty of water. A water tank is available at the car park but is rain-fed and may be dry in summer.

HISTORY

Pigeon House Mountain was named by James Cook in 1770 as he sailed past on his way up the east coast of Australia. To the local Murrumarang Aborigines, it was Dithol or Did-Dell, meaning 'Woman's Breast', and it was a women's Dreaming area. Archaeological evidence dates the Aboriginal presence near Pigeon House Mountain to as far back as 3500 years ago.

The first visit to Pigeon House Mountain by Europeans was made by Alexander Berry, Thomas Davison and the explorer Hamilton Hume, who arrived in 1822.

GETTING TO/FROM THE WALK

Take the Princes Hwy from Sydney down to Ulladulla (approximately 225km) and continue past Burill Lake for 3km to the Pigeon House Mountain turn-off (Wheelbarrow Rd) on the right. Turn left into Woodburn Rd and then right up Clyde Ridge Rd for 7.8km to reach the picnic area at the start of the walk.

Alternatively, turn right off the Princes Hwy at Milton, before Ulladulla, and 70km south of Nowra. Turn right down Croobyar Rd and follow the signs, turning right into Clyde Ridge Rd. The car park and picnic area are 30km from Milton.

From Canberra and Melbourne, it is easiest to turn left onto Monkey Mountain Rd from the Princes Hwy (heading from south to north), following this to the junction with Clyde Ridge Rd, where a left turn takes you 7.8km to the walk start.

Without a car, it is possible to travel by bus to Ulladulla from Sydney, Melbourne or Canberra, and arrange transport from there through South Coast Backpackers, provided you are a guest (see Nearest Towns & Facilities in the introduction to The Budawangs for contact details). Two 4WD vehicles are available for shuttles to Pigeon House Mountain car park at $28 per person, with a minimum of two people required. The cars will return to pick up walkers at a prearranged time the same day.

THE WALK

From the picnic area and car park, head straight up the hill on the obvious track past the interpretive NPWS sign. Continue for 800m until a small band of low cliffs and rocky outcrops is reached. Follow the track

NEW SOUTH WALES

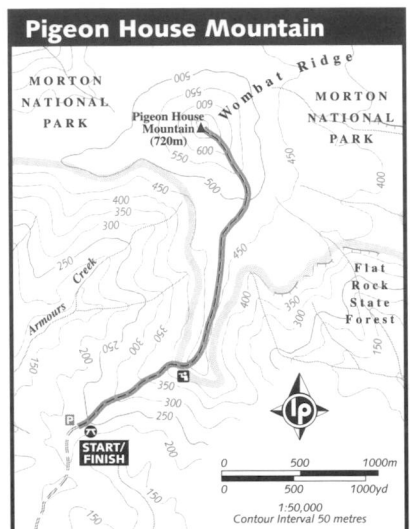

Pigeon House Mountain

MORTON NATIONAL PARK

Pigeon House Mountain ▲ (720m)

Wombat Ridge

MORTON NATIONAL PARK

Flat Rock State Forest

Armours Creek

START/ FINISH

0   500   1000m
0   500   1000yd

1:50,000
Contour Interval 50 metres

and wooden steps round to the left, up to the top of the bluffs, and across the national park boundary proper (the car park is actually in state forest). A small **lookout** here on the right, slightly off the track, gives great views to the south.

The track flattens out from here on a lightly forested plateau, and the walking is easy and pleasant for 1km. After this, the track steepens considerably, and remains steep right up to the rocky base of Pigeon House Mountain. Take the track round to the left from here, up the wooden steps, as it snakes round to the eastern and southern sides of the mountain below the cliff. On the southern side, a handrail leads to the base of four metal ladders, which lead up through some chimneys to the **summit massif** on the top. The ladders are very exposed but solid and safe. Take care of slippery rails in the wet.

The views are fantastic from the top, although it is necessary to walk around to get the best vantage points. Byangee Walls, the Castle and the craggy cliffs of the central Budawangs are all revealed in sharp relief. A logbook is in a metal stand at the summit. Return to the start along the same route.

Bungonia State Recreation Area

The Bungonia Gorge and Shoalhaven River valley area is a rugged, beautiful place. The limestone landscape defines it as a unique Australian region, formed by the action of rainwater on what was once an ancient coral reef (for a discussion of limestone features, see the boxed text 'Limestone Landscapes' earlier). The towering cliffs of the 500m-deep Bungonia Gorge make this the deepest limestone gorge in Australia. The area is significant as it provides some of the most difficult long rock climbs in the country. It is also a major caving area, and speleology clubs flock here to explore the maze of caverns and tunnels, most of which can only be entered using fixed ropes and caving ladders.

The two-day walk described lies within the Bungonia State Recreation Area, which at 3893 hectares is the largest of its kind in NSW. The reserve protects an area of the Southern Tablelands running from Bungonia Gorge, to the south and up the steep west bank of the Shoalhaven River, where it borders nearby Morton National Park.

The reserve has been protected since 1872; however, a reminder of the ugly march of progress – a gaping limestone quarry that produces ingredients used for making concrete, among other things – is visible from the start of the described route.

HISTORY
The name 'Bungonia' is a bit of a mystery, but it is thought to have originated from the Aboriginal term for 'camp on a creek' or 'good camp site'. Stone tools made of quartz have been found in the park, and an Aboriginal child's skull was discovered in a cave in 1892; little else is known, however, of the area's pre-European history.

Europeans explored the area shortly after the arrival of the First Fleet, and in 1822 the first grazing rights were issued to William Bradbury, who is thought to have given the Bungonia area its name.

Early explorations of the caves were conducted by botanist Alan Cunningham in

Hume & Hovell Walking Track

This long-distance track traces part of the route taken by two of the first explorers to traverse a substantial section of the Australian continent. Hamilton Hume, one of the first children born in the new colony, was involved in the discovery of the Goulburn Plains and Lake George. William Hovell was an English sea captain who settled in the colony in 1813, but spent most of his time seeking adventure on the Southern Ocean.

Hume and Hovell set off from Hume's property near Lake George in October 1824 to strike a land route between the settled districts of New South Wales (NSW) and the poorly known country on the continent's southern coast, 1000km away. After two weeks the explorers, toting the usual cavalcade of carts, cattle and convicts, struck the broad Murrumbidgee River. By early November they were entering the foothills of the Australian Alps, and on the brilliant spring morning of 6 November became the first Europeans to sight the snow-clad peaks. Wisely, they turned south-west to skirt the range and 10 days later encountered the youthful upper reaches of Australia's mightiest river, the Murray, just upstream of the present site of Albury.

The party continued south-west, broaching the beautiful Ovens Valley on 21 November and naming the imposing Mt Buffalo (see the Victoria chapter). From here the going was increasingly scrubby and heat, flies and the dry and difficult terrain blighted the explorers and their animals. Turned back at Mt Disappointment, not 100km from their objective, a final desperate foray south in the teeth of a bushfire at last brought them on 16 December to a vantage point in the Yarra Ranges north-west of Melbourne that afforded them their long-hoped-for view of the sea.

While both Western Port and the adjacent Port Phillip had been roughly charted more than 20 years before (there had even been an ill-starred settlement in the latter in 1803–04), the area was so poorly known that Hume and Hovell thought they had struck Western Port; the explorers actually surveyed the country near the site of modern-day Geelong before high-tailing it back to Sydney by the more direct route now followed by the Hume Fwy.

Not long after the successful expedition Hovell was sent to Western Port to help in another attempt to settle the southern coast. Not surprisingly, he found its mangrove swamps and languid waters far less appealing than the grassy plains flanking Corio Bay and this attempt, too, failed. It was not until 1834 that a Tasmanian grazier was inspired by an account of Hume's and Hovell's expedition to found an unauthorised settlement on the Yarra River at Port Phillip – Melbourne.

First proposed in 1925 on the centenary of the journey, the Hume and Hovell Walking Track was researched during the 1970s. About 300km of track had been marked and prepared by 1988 (with the aid of funding for that year's Australian Bicentennial), with a further 150km completed over the next decade. It now takes about a month to walk.

The track runs from Yass, 200km south-west of Sydney, to Albury on the NSW–Victoria border; the southern state is yet to take up the baton and extend the route to its logical conclusion at Geelong. Skirting the Australian Alps, much of the track is along forestry roads or through farmland. Camp sites, pit toilets and other facilities are provided along most of the track. The definitive guidebook is *The Hume and Hovell Walking Track Guidebook* by Harry Hill (1993), and dedicated strip maps are available from the Department of Land & Water Conservation's Information Centres.

1824, and explorer Major Thomas Mitchell in 1828. Their reports brought many recreational visitors from the colony of Sydney, leading to the creation of Australia's first public recreation reserve in 1872. The NSW Government Tourist Bureau published the first Bungonia Caves guidebook in 1902. Recreational caving surged in popularity after WWII, through the activities of the Sydney Speleological Society (formed in 1949). The area became the Bungonia Caves Reserve in 1974; subsequent additions increased its size to the present 3893 hectares and brought its administration under the umbrella of the NPWS.

NATURAL HISTORY

The low nutrient content of limestone soils here leads to scrubby, stunted vegetation on the upper slopes and plateaus, with stringybark, yellow box, grey box and broad-leaved peppermint trees common. Many huge grass trees grow in the area; some fine examples are passed at the start of the walk as you descend into the gorge from a side tributary of Bungonia Creek.

The lower reaches of the gorge provide suitable conditions for the growth of rainforest trees, including red cedars, giant stinging trees and sandpaper figs. At camp sites along the Shoalhaven River and the borders of Bungonia Creek, casuarinas or she-oaks provide a pretty canopy and ground cover of soft, pine-like leaves. Casuarinas make great windbreaks, and it's quite calming to lie back after a hard day's walking and listen to the gentle swish of breezes rustling through their foliage.

Bats (including the eastern horseshoe bat and the common bent-wing bat) are permanent dwellers in the extensive cave systems, and their droppings support a rich invertebrate community within the gloom, which includes spiders, flies, millipedes and slaters that are uniquely adapted to living in total darkness.

Bungonia's gorge started out as an ancient coral reef, laid down by tiny organisms that constructed shells around themselves, which were later crushed and compressed to form limestone about 400 million years ago.

Bungonia's limestone belt is one of the largest in NSW, and was once divided by a layer of less resistant shale. Water has carved a swathe through this shale, exposing the two limestone deposits and creating the deep, narrow canyon. The limestone deposits also provide a rich source of raw material for the limestone quarry on the northern side of the gorge, visible from the Bungonia State Recreation Area. The scar of the quarry is due to be relocated north and out of sight of the lookouts by the year 2010.

PLANNING
When to Walk

Walking is possible year-round. Take care when entering Bungonia Gorge to check the weather first, as summer thunderstorms and heavy winter rains can raise the water level of Bungonia Creek drastically. Current conditions are available from the Bungonia State Recreation Area information centre (see Information Sources).

While summer can be very hot and dry, the Shoalhaven River and Bungonia Creek provide great swimming holes to reduce the effects of walk-induced heat.

What to Bring

This can be a cold place in winter, so take adequate warm and wet-weather clothing. Summer is very hot, and on the steep climbs at least 1L of water per person should be carried (eg, when ascending the spur along the White Track on the return from the Shoalhaven River valley).

Portable water filters or purification tablets are useful, as the Shoalhaven River and Bungonia Gorge are fed by some runoff from farmland and are not generally safe to drink without chemical treatment, filtration or vigorous boiling (see Staying Healthy in the Health & Safety chapter for a discussion of water treatment).

Maps & Books

The CMA 1:25,000 *Caoura* map fully covers the region in the walk description. A useful NPWS visitor's leaflet, *Bungonia State Recreation Area*, is available from the information centre within the park. The leaflet

Warnings

Falling Debris

Due to the gorge being very narrow and high, debris falling from above, including rocks and tree branches, can be a significant hazard along the boulder-choked bed of Bungonia Creek. This can be especially risky during storms and strong winds, when it may not be entirely obvious that stuff is getting blown around up top until it starts raining down on you. There is really nowhere to run if you're caught, so keep an eye out for windy weather before heading into the constricted area of the gorge.

Water Levels in the Gorge

Water levels can rise very quickly and without warning. Check at the Bungonia State Recreation Area information centre at the park entrance for current conditions, and be cautious about weather patterns that may bring rain to the catchment area upstream of Bungonia Creek. The boulder choke at the eastern end of the gorge is particularly difficult to negotiate when water levels are high.

Quarry Blasting

A 700m-long restricted area is indicated by signs along the banks of Bungonia Creek, on the Red Track route used on Day 1. This zone, on the north side of Bungonia Creek just after you leave the boulder-choked exit of Bungonia Gorge, lies below a limestone quarry perched on the ridge high above. It is occasionally affected by rock falls triggered by blasting at the quarry.

Blasting occurs at 3.10 pm on weekdays. Listen for several warning sirens preceding the blast. A continuous siren will sound for one minute before blasting until all is clear. A full explanation is given on the signs at each end of the affected area, so read these carefully. Remain outside the indicated area when blasting is taking place.

indicates the location of all major tracks down to the junction of Bungonia Creek and the Shoalhaven River.

Useful books include *Fitzroy Falls and Beyond* published by the Budawang Committee, and *70 Walks in Southern New South Wales and ACT* by Tyrone Thomas.

Information Sources

There is a Bungonia State Recreation Area information centre (☎ 02-4844 4277, fax 4844 4331) within the reserve at Lookdown Rd, Bungonia, right near the park gate.

Permits & Regulations

Walkers should register their intended route and times of departure and return at the information centre on entering the park. A book is provided for this purpose.

No permits or fees are required for bush camping while walking in the gorges of Bungonia Creek and the Shoalhaven River. However, a $5.50 car entry fee is payable per vehicle on entering the recreation area.

The park may be periodically closed for the control of feral animals. At this time, high-powered rifles are used within the confines of the gorge. Check with the Lookdown Rd park information centre for dates.

NEAREST TOWNS & FACILITIES
Goulburn

This is the nearest sizable town to the walk, and is the best place to stock up on supplies, irrespective of the direction from which you approach. Several petrol stations sell fuel, and stove fuels (Shellite, or white spirits, and methylated spirits) are available from hardware shops in the main street.

The new Goulburn Visitor Centre (☎ 02-4823 4492), at 221 Sloane St opposite Belmore Park, has regional information.

Places to Stay & Eat On the old highway north of town, ***Governor's Hill Carapark (☎ 02-4821 7373, 77–83 Sydney Rd)*** has tent/powered sites for $12/16 and on-site vans/cabins for $30/37.

Sloane St (running parallel to the railway line) has a number of pubs offering basic accommodation, including the **Coolavin** (☎ 02-4821 2498), with rooms for $20 to $30, and the **Carlton** (☎ 02-4821 3820), with rooms from $30.

The **Exchange Hotel** (☎ 02-4821 1566, 9 Bradley St) has singles/doubles for $28/46 with breakfast. Several **motels** are located around town, with singles from $35 and doubles from $45.

Getting There & Away Goulburn is 201km from Sydney, 659km from Melbourne and 89km from Canberra. Greyhound Pioneer, Murrays and Fearnes stop in Goulburn. The visitor centre makes bookings. Trains between Sydney and Melbourne also stop here daily. The one-way fare to Canberra is $12 and to Sydney $31; ring Countrylink (☎ 13 2232) for information.

Bungonia

There's not much here except a small **general store** and a **teahouse**, 1km from the town centre on the road out to Bungonia Gorge.

Marulan

The small town of Marulan, near the turn-off to the gorge on the Hume Hwy, offers little other than a small **general store** and a **pub** (which was not offering accommodation at the time of writing).

Bungonia State Recreation Area

There is a convenient and well-equipped **camping area** just behind the information centre near the park entrance gate. Hot showers, toilet facilities and a community kitchen are provided. Charges for campers are $11 per night for the first two people, and $2.20 per person per night for the following four. It is recommended that walking parties stay at this camp site on the night prior to the walk.

Bungonia Gorge

Duration	2 days
Distance	22km
Standard	medium-hard
Start/Finish	David Reid car park
Nearest Towns	Goulburn, Marulan, Bungonia
Public Transport	no

Summary A fascinating walk through spectacular limestone gorge country, with some pretty camp sites along the banks of the Shoalhaven River. There are numerous opportunities for swimming in the heat of summer, in Bungonia Creek and the Shoalhaven River.

Despite the relatively short length of this walk, the variety of geographical features encountered and the rugged nature of the limestone gorge country make it an interesting ramble. A lot of clambering over boulders and ascents and descents of steep gullies and ridges is involved, so the walk receives a medium-hard rating despite its short length. It's possible to extend the walk significantly by adding in more of the country bordering the Shoalhaven River, both north and south of its junction with Bungonia Creek. However, the route as described presents a nice balance of the area's most characteristic features.

GREG CAIRE

Ascending the steep White Track, with the Shoalhaven River in the background

NEW SOUTH WALES

GETTING TO/FROM THE WALK

Driving from Sydney on the Hume Hwy, look for the signposted turn-off to Bungonia Gorge on the left, about 2km south of the Marulan exit (soon after passing the BP petrol stations).

Driving from Canberra or Melbourne, take the same signposted exit as above to the right off the Hume Hwy. The turn-off can be a little difficult to spot from this side of the highway, so watch carefully for the sign.

The Bungonia State Recreation Area is 35km west of Goulburn and 13km from the turn-off. Follow the signs through the small township of Bungonia, turning left where indicated; the park gate is another 8km along a good sealed road. The gorge area and the trailhead are a little farther along this road after the gate (the route to David Reid car park is well signposted).

Without a car, the only way to reach Bungonia Gorge is to arrange for a taxi from Goulburn. This would have to be ordered twice, once for the trip out and again from the park information centre (which has public phones) for the trip back. It is possible, but would be quite expensive (about $60 to $70 each way).

THE WALK
Day 1: David Reid Car Park to Shoalhaven River Camp Site
5–6 hours, 12km

Water is available from a tank near the car park, and it is advisable to stock up here if you are unsure of water availability in the gorge, particularly in summer. Leave the car here and pick up the start of the Red Track, heading west. All the walks in the recreation area are colour coded and well marked, with appropriately coloured arrows and squares appearing on geographical features and signposts along the trails.

After 300m the track divides: follow the Red Track markers to the right and northwest. From here the track descends very steeply past some enormous old grass trees, through very dry, scrubby vegetation and over loose, broken shale. The track steepens still further as it funnels down into the little gorge carved by Bretons Creek.

Caves of Bungonia State Recreation Area

Bungonia is an area containing predominantly vertical caves, where water and dissolved carbonic acid from the atmosphere have carved their way through the limestone bedrock to form deep underground ravines. Because of their vertical nature, descent into the chambers requires rope techniques and caving ladders, making exploration possible only by experienced cavers. The Limestone Belt here is about 4km long, 670m wide and 300m deep. Over 170 caves are recorded within the recreation area, and the region contains some of the deepest caves on mainland Australia, including Blowfly Cave (152m), Odyssey Cave (142m) and Fossil Cave (131m).

The first cave was recorded as being found in Bungonia around 1824; in 1872, a reserve titled Water Reserve No 27 was set up to both protect the caves and provide an area for public recreation. This was very likely the first reserve established for the purpose of public recreation in Australia, and perhaps the world. In 1892 the Skull Cave was discovered, which contained the skull of an Aboriginal child.

As limestone is very porous, water tends to permeate it quickly, draining through the soil and leaving little surface moisture. This is the reason for the rugged, stunted appearance of most of the vegetation in the area.

Continue descending, following the red marker arrows and squares, which can be hard to find, carefully climbing down the steeper rocky sections where appropriate. Use caution if the limestone underfoot is wet as it can get very slippery, especially with a full pack. The creek disappears periodically underground, but after 1km reappears and empties itself into the entrance of **Bungonia Gorge** proper. The going gets a little easier from here.

Continue right and east into the gorge, along the boulder-strewn bed of Bungonia Creek. Towering above you, on either side of this deep, narrow defile, are limestone cliffs hundreds of metres high. The gorge is

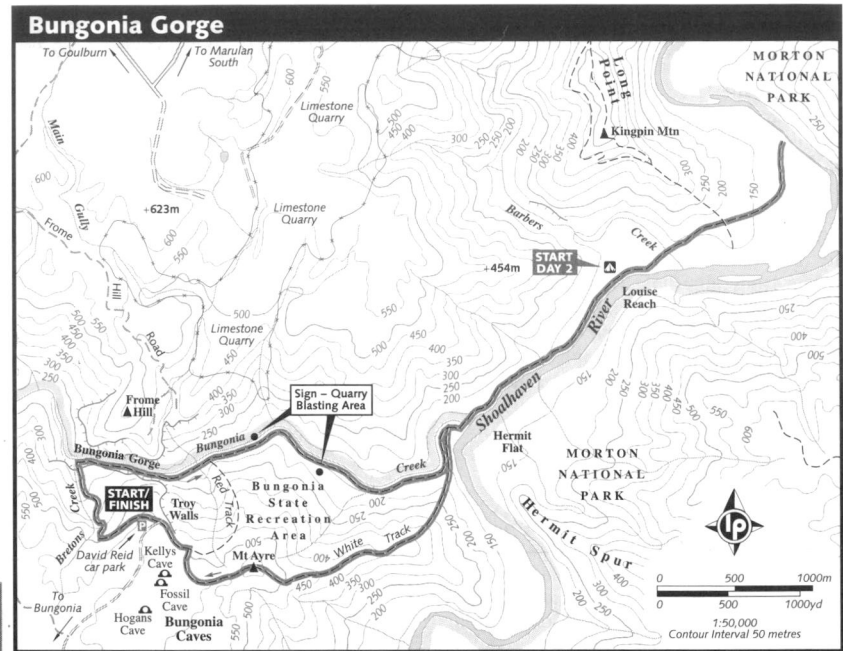

Bungonia Gorge

so constricted, however, that it feels as if you can touch both walls with outstretched hands. Follow the gorge down along the course of Bungonia Creek. There is a risk of rock fall from the high walls here, so proceed with caution (see the 'Warnings' boxed text earlier). The boulders gradually increase in size, and near the end of the gorge they are several metres high, making progress difficult. Climb over and under the boulders, removing packs and passing them down by hand as required. In times of high water in the creek, it may be necessary to wade across short sections.

After the boulder choke and a short walk along the true right (south) bank of the creek, it is necessary to cross to the true left (north bank), where the first of two signs is encountered that mark the start of the rock fall danger area below the limestone quarry (again, see the warnings earlier). Only proceed down the creek if the time and absence of warning sirens indicates it is safe. After

700m, the creek needs to be crossed to the right (southern) bank (the track is indistinct here), and a second warning sign is reached. This indicates the end of the danger zone below the quarry.

The Red Track continues uphill from here to the south-east, heading back to the car park; however, keep following the vague track that continues along Bungonia Creek downstream on it's true right bank. Walk past several deep-green waterholes and on to a rocky section of creek bed, crossing and recrossing the stream where necessary, before reaching a tight left-hand bend in the creek, 2km from the quarry sign. Follow the creek left, passing a large flat *camping area* and another deep-green waterhole. This is a beautiful, shady swimming spot in summer.

Cross the creek to the south bank at the end of the pool, and a few hundred metres downstream, the intersection of Bungonia Creek and the Shoalhaven River is reached. From the car park to this point is about 5km.

Cross Bungonia Creek to the north and continue up the west bank of the Shoalhaven River, following the well-worn but unmarked track. Numerous camp sites are sited along here. Continue up to the crossing of Barbers Creek, and then follow the cairned track up and north-east over the low hill to a large flat area looking across to the saddle of Rainbow Ridge, just before a big horseshoe bend in the Shoalhaven River. A quick excursion down to the **rapids** of the Shoalhaven River (a 30-minute return trip) is well worthwhile.

It is possible to camp here, but there's a nicer *camp site* underneath shady casuarinas about 2km back along the outward route, near Louise Reach on the Shoalhaven River (about 500m south-west of Barbers Creek).

Alternative Camp Sites

There are some excellent *camp sites* around the junction of Bungonia Creek and the Shoalhaven River. Be sure to camp well above river level to ensure you stay dry if water levels rise overnight after rain.

Day 2: Shoalhaven River Camp Site to David Reid Car Park

4–5 hours, 10km

Leaving the casuarinas, continue south-west along the Shoalhaven River, reversing your route of the previous day back to the junction of Bungonia Creek and the Shoalhaven. From here, pick up the White Track, indicated by a signpost on the south bank of Bungonia Creek, slightly up the hill.

This track continues gently up and across a flat plateau for 500m, before climbing suddenly at a much greater angle. This track is steep! However, going up is easier than going down. Watch out for the slippery, loose shale that lies underfoot, as the path is so steep that falling is easy. On a hot day make sure you have plenty of water for the climb.

The track climbs steadily, with great views back across the Shoalhaven River valley from the previous day's walk. You pass Mt Ayre 4.5km from Bungonia Creek. A few hundred metres on, there's a junction with the Red Tack: ignore it and continue along the White Track for 500m to the David Reid car park and the end of the walk.

Warrumbungle National Park

The volcanic spires that define the skyline of the 21,000-hectare Warrumbungle National Park rise abruptly from the surrounding flat plains of western NSW like clusters of jagged, rocky teeth. The spires, domes and craggy shapes are visible for many kilometres before the approaching traveller reaches the park boundary. About 490km north-west of Sydney, this is an ancient landscape of imposing rocky buttresses, deep wooded valleys and primordial beauty, and is justifiably one of the state's most popular national parks, receiving up to 80,000 visitors per year.

The walk takes in some of the best features of the area, including spectacular circuits of the Grand High Tops, Dows High Tops and the more remote Mt Exmouth, at 1206m the highest point in the park.

Prior to 1939 the area's significance was known only to a core of hardy bushwalkers, climbers and local landowners. The region came to national prominence when the renowned adventurer and photographer Frank Hurley made the Grand High Tops region the subject of an illustrated magazine article, turning the Breadknife into a widely recognised Australian icon.

HISTORY

Aborigines are thought to have lived in the area bordered by the park boundary for at least 5000 years, and from archaeological evidence are known to have lived in the surrounding plains for at least 25,000 years. Signs of their early camp sites and fragments of stone implements, including quartz flakes used to fashion axes and cutting tools, are to be found all over the park. The Gamilaroi (or Kamilaroi) Aboriginal people in the Coonabarabran region were closely linked with the land around the Warrumbungles, and the unique geographical features were part of their creation or Dreamtime stories. These stories are transmitted by word of mouth, and unfortunately, with the arrival of Europeans and active attempts to 'civilise'

Rock Climbing in the Bungles

The volcanic spires and imposing bluffs of the Warrumbungles offer some of the most atmospheric and challenging long rock climbs Australia has to offer. The area has been a mecca for climbers for many years, and enjoys a deserved reputation as being a serious and scary place to touch rock. The history of climbing in the 'Bungles (as it's known to climbers) is a fascinating tale in itself, and starts in the early 1930s. A wild (and some would say completely crazy) bunch of hard-core bushwalkers started pursuing rock climbing as an activity in itself at about this time, and formed a club known as the Blue Mountaineers. Their weekends were filled with horror ascents of iconic rock formations in the Blue Mountains, including the Three Sisters at Katoomba. With virtually no equipment, very poor quality ropes and incredible bravado, they achieved feats that would leave modern rock climbers, with their camming devices and strong harnesses, quaking in their sticky rubber boots. Two of the main crazies were the legendary Eric (Dr) Dark and Dot Butler, known as the 'Barefoot Bushwalker' – a name earned from the many wilderness walks she completed without shoes.

In 1932 Eric Dark and Osmar White made the first ascent of Belougery Spire after drinkers at the local pub proclaimed the ascent 'impossible'. In 1936 a party of three including Eric Dark and Dot Butler made the first ascent of Crater Bluff, an incredible achievement considering the technical nature of the climb, and the wildly exposed route they took. Take a moment to have a good look at Crater Bluff from the Grand High Tops track and you'll see what I mean. Dot Butler, of course, completed the entire first ascent in bare feet.

Today, the 'Bungles have lost none of their seriousness and awe-inspiring grandeur. As the rock routes are very long (up to 500m), climbing should only be attempted by very experienced parties who are familiar with long, multipitch climbs. Climbing permits can be obtained from the visitor centre before heading out; climbing is now banned on the Breadknife and Chalkers Mountain.

and relocate the Gamilaoi to other areas, many of these creation stories were lost.

Explorer John Oxley first entered the region in 1818 while tracing the course of the Macquarie River, and found many huts and evidence of long-term Aboriginal occupation. Twenty years after Oxley's visit, the first white settlers arrived, establishing sheep stations focused on wool production. Conflicts between squatters and the local Aborigines were violent and frequent.

Calls for the preservation of the Warrumbungles first started in 1936, when Myles Dunphy's National Parks and Primitive Areas Council recommended that the 'Warrumbungle National Monument' be declared. A parcel of 3360 hectares was set aside in 1952 as a national park, and further additions over the last few decades have increased the park's size to its present-day extent.

NATURAL HISTORY

About 17 million years ago, a group of active volcanoes let fly to produce a thick layer of volcanic debris and molten lava on top of the area's sandstone base. Due to eons of erosion and the action of water, the surrounding softer clays were removed, leaving the harder volcanic plugs and dikes exposed and forming the jagged peaks and rugged buttresses we see today. Some of the park's well-known features, including the Breadknife, Belougery Spire and Crater Bluff, are the remnant cores of volcanoes long since eroded away.

The Warrumbungles form a boundary between the dry Western Plains and the more humid regions of coastal NSW. As a result, it is a meeting place for moist coastal species and plants from the dry inland regions. Remnant rainforest plants such as Port Jackson fig trees and maidenhair ferns exist side by side with white Cyprus pines and red gums.

Due to the wide variety of habitats formed by the park's diverse geography, many different types of fauna inhabit the area. Over 90 species of birds are known in the park, and goannas, king brown snakes, koalas, grey kangaroos, emus, wallaroos, and red-necked and swamp wallabies exist in large numbers. Sunset at the various grassy picnic and camping areas can be an interesting time to view wildlife.

PLANNING
When to Walk

Walking is possible here at any time of year, with autumn and spring providing the most pleasant conditions. In summer, temperatures in the high 30s and 40s are common.

Despite the park's reputation for being hot and dry, winter can occasionally bring with it some cold and rapidly changing weather. Thick fog, strong winds and driving rain are not uncommon at this time of year. About 900mm of rain falls per annum, most of it during the winter months. This wet weather is often associated with the southerly cold fronts that bring snow to the higher mountains of NSW. Cold overnight temperatures (down to -5°C and associated with heavy frosts) are common, and the ranges have very different weather patterns from the sheltered valleys. The park's high peaks may be enveloped in fog and lashed by driving rain and high winds while conditions in the valleys and camp sites are fine and pleasant.

Easter, Christmas holidays and long weekends can be very crowded, with up to 10,000 people visiting the area. The quietest time to visit is in winter and mid-week, when it's quite likely you will have the trails to yourself.

What to Bring

A standard kit of bushwalking gear will see you through this walk. Take a fuel stove, as all wood fires are banned within the national park. Sunscreen and a broad-brimmed hat are essential in summer, while thermals, warm clothing and a sleeping bag capable of keeping you warm down to overnight temperatures of around -5°C are advisable in winter.

A minimum quantity of 4L of water per person per day should be carried in the heat of summer – bring adequate supplies with you from the valley. Creeks marked on the topographic maps rarely flow, and aside from a small rainwater tank next to Balor Hut (which is often empty), there is no tap water on the higher walking trails. It is also wise to boil any tap water taken from within the park, or treat it with iodine to make it safe to drink.

Maps & Books

The CMA 1:30,000 *Warrumbungle National Park Tourist Map and Guide*, while a little dated, still covers the entire area of the park in good detail. Note that Canyon Camp no longer exists and is now Canyon Picnic Area, and that all roads within the park are now sealed.

The park is also covered by four of the maps in the CMA 1:50,000 series: *Tenandra*, *Tooraweenah*, *Bugaldie* and *Coonabarabran*.

The NPWS guidebook *Warrumbungle National Park* by Peter Fox is an excellent resource and is small enough to take on the walk with you. It includes a useful *Walks Guide* booklet with some sketch maps and descriptions of major features in the park.

Information Sources:

There is a visitor centre (☎ 02-6825 4364) inside the national park, about 300m off the John Renshaw Parkway (signposted on the right when driving from Coonabarabran). It stocks information booklets and topographic maps and staff can organise hut bookings and payment of camping fees. Some information can also be obtained at the Coonabarabran visitor centre (see Nearest Towns).

Permits & Regulations

It costs $2.20 per person per night for bush camping within the park. Car entry is $5.50 per vehicle, or $3.30 for motorcycles. All fees should be paid at the visitor centre. Bookings for overnight stays at Balor Hut ($4.40 per person per night) can also be made here. After payment of hut fees a key will be handed over and must be returned on completion of your walk.

Permits are required for anybody wishing to go rock climbing in the area (see the boxed text 'Rock Climbing in the Bungles' earlier).

GETTING THERE & AWAY

The park lies 35km west of the town of Coonabarabran, and 490km north-west of Sydney. Driving from Sydney, it takes six hours to reach the park via Mudgee and about seven hours through the town of Dubbo (via the Oxley and Newell Hwys). It is also possible to reach the park via Gulargambone and Coonamble from the Castlereagh Hwy to the west.

All access roads within the park have been sealed in recent times, making wet-weather access easy.

NEAREST TOWNS & FACILITIES
Coonabarabran

Coonabarabran is 35km east of the park entrance and the logical place to stock up on any last-minute requirements. If driving from Sydney, it may be wise to stop in Mudgee or Dubbo for a major resupply of food and stove fuel as you will probably hit Coonabarabran late in the evening when the shops are shut.

The Coonabarabran Visitor Centre (☎ 02-6842 1441), on John Street, has some park information and walking books.

Petrol and kerosene are available from the service station at the end of the main street. Shellite for fuel stoves may be available from the hardware store in town, but it is generally a better idea to bring it with you; methylated spirits for stoves is available from the supermarkets.

Places to Stay & Eat The *Coonabarabran Hotel* (☎ 02-6842 3164) has basic single/double rooms for $20 per night, while the *Imperial Hotel* (☎ 02-6842 1023), opposite the clock tower, has rooms from $20 ($26 including breakfast). Other pubs in town, including the *Royal Hotel* ($15 per person for a basic twin), have accommodation and cheap pub meals, and the road in to the town's centre is lined with several motels.

The *Jolli Cauli Cafe*, opposite the Royal Hotel in John St (the main street), is a pleasant cafe with a good selection of light food, cakes and coffee, and also provides Internet access for email.

For self-caterers, the *IGA* and *Tuckerbag* supermarkets are centrally located in Dalgarno St, near the intersection with John St.

Gilgandra

This is the next-closest large town to the Warrumbungles (slightly smaller than Coonabarabran and 94km farther south on the Newell Hwy). It can be used as an alternative supply and accommodation point to the park. It has a *caravan park*, *hotel* and *motel* accommodation, and a small *supermarket*.

Warrumbungle National Park

Vehicle camping is available at Camp Elongery, a few hundred metres north of the visitor centre; Camp Wambelong, west of Canyon Picnic Area on the John Renshaw Parkway; and Camp Blackman (with hot showers), east of Canyon Picnic Area. Ask at the visitor centre for booking and payment details. Camping costs $11 for two people per night on an unpowered site, and $3.20 for each extra person.

Warrumbungles Grand High Tops

Duration	2–3 days
Distance	35km
Standard	medium
Start/Finish	Canyon Picnic Area
Nearest Towns	Coonabarabran, Gilgandra
Public Transport	no

Summary A unique foray into one of Australia's most spectacular volcanic landscapes. The walk is extremely steep in places, but the extensive views across rocky peaks and enormous bluffs make the climbs well worth the effort. The trail network within the park is quite extensive and well maintained.

The three-day walk described here takes in all of the major sights and formations visible in the central region of the national park. This includes the Grand High Tops, a walk across Dows High Tops with fantastic views of Bluff Mountain's massive west face, and a visit to Mount Exmouth, the park's highest peak. The walk could be done in two days; however, due to the steep nature of the terrain and the numerous possible detours, allowing three days provides a more relaxed pace.

GETTING TO/FROM THE WALK

Drive into the park on the John Renshaw Parkway, and after organising camping and walking fees at the visitor centre, continue along a sealed road to the trailhead at Canyon Picnic Area. Leave your vehicle here.

THE WALK
Day 1: Canyon Picnic Area to Balor Hut via Bress Peak
5–6 hours, 13km

From the picnic area, follow the road back past the visitor centre, cross John Renshaw Parkway and take the sealed road almost opposite signposted to *Camp Pincham* (2.5km from the picnic area). Continue along the well-defined and clearly signposted walking track from Camp Pincham for another 2km over several wooden bridges to the Bress Peak track junction on the right (do not take the right-hand turn to Ogma Saddle or the left-hand turn to Goulds Circuit passed on the way).

Drop packs at the track junction and take the steep side trip up to **Bress Peak**, a 1.1km return walk via **Bridget Peak**. The track is amazingly steep, and walkers often pass it by, but the view from the summit across to the Grand High Tops from an unusual angle is well worth the effort. If climbing up in warmer weather, take plenty of water.

Returning to the packs, continue south along the track towards the Grand High Tops for 500m to a junction with the end of the Goulds Circuit track on the left. Drop packs again and complete the circuit (about 3.5km of steep ups and downs) as it heads back north over the rocky outcrops of **Macha Tor** and **Febar Rock**. When you meet the Grand High Tops track once again, follow it back up to the packs. Although this involves some doubling back, the views in all directions are worth the effort. If doing this walk in two days rather than three, you can eliminate the Goulds Circuit from your itinerary, but make sure you still head up to Bress Peak.

From the intersection of Goulds Circuit and Grand High Tops tracks, continue south towards the High Tops. The track begins to climb up toward the base of the Breadknife, and a bizarre section of paved track, looking like a back-yard barbecue area, continues steeply up for several hundred metres (this is known affectionately by track workers as the 'Yellow Brick Road'). Just below the towering wall of the **Breadknife** is a track junction; turn right to reach *Balor Hut*. From the Canyon Picnic Area to here is about 13km.

Balor Hut was built in 1967 by Colin Dow to house workers doing early track construction. Coonabarabran Bushwalking Club maintains the hut, and it can sleep six people in reasonable comfort. It's often used as a base by climbers operating in the park. Beware the resident hut rat! He or she is a particularly voracious eater, and the little wire hooks dangling from the roof are for hanging food out of harm's way. Bookings for the hut are essential.

Alternative Camp Sites

If you do all the detours recommended, you'll probably want to stay in Balor Hut. If, however, you're feeling fit and have plenty of daylight, continue for 5km to the *camp sites* at Nuada Saddle (at the Bluff Mountain turn-off) or Ogma Saddle (at the junction of the Western High Tops and West Spirey Creek tracks).

Day 2: Balor Hut to Danu Saddle
7–8 hours, 15km

Leaving Balor Hut you have two options. You can return to the track junction, continuing along the Grand High Tops track on the eastern side of the Breadknife (marked by giant yellow reflectors glued to the rock, and painted emu tracks!). The track heads south then turns right (west) at Lughs Shield before passing a **lookout** and continuing to Dagda Saddle. Alternatively, continue south-west down the track behind the hut and along the western side of the Breadknife. The tracks join at Dagda Saddle after about 1km. Doing a complete circuit of both tracks is worthwhile for the views if you have good weather.

Warrumbungles Grand High Tops

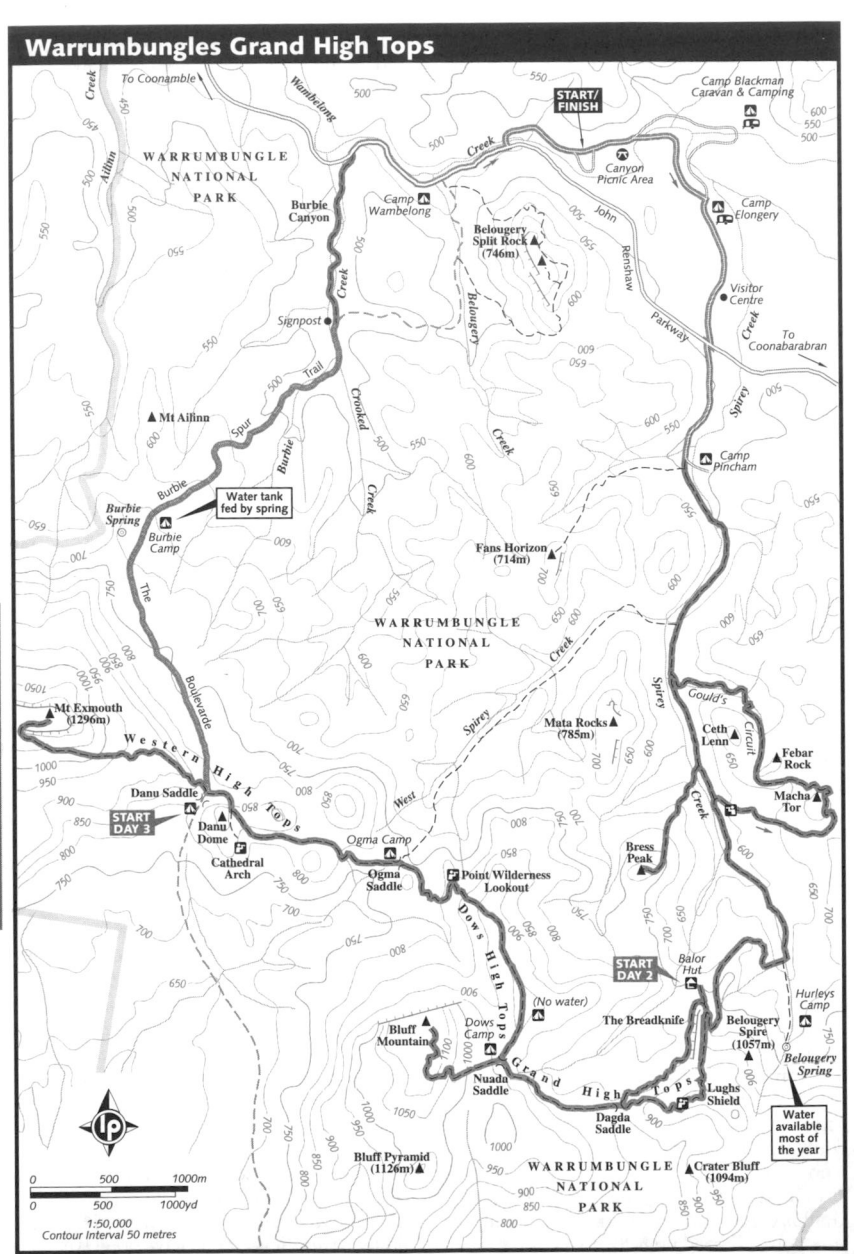

From Dagda Saddle, continue west along the Grand High Tops track to Nuada Saddle. Dump packs at the track junction and take the 2.6km return detour to **Bluff Mountain**. This trip is not to be missed; the 360-degree views from the 1200m summit are breathtaking. Further views are to be had by following an indistinct track north a few hundred metres from the summit cairn. Take warm clothes in winter as the summit may be cold and windy. Returning to the packs, head to Ogma Saddle via the Dows High Tops track. The saddle is reached after about 2km. The tracks from here to below Danu Saddle are not as well defined and maintained as those in the rest of the park.

From Ogma Saddle, continue along the Western High Tops track to Danu Saddle; (do not take the right-hand turn from Ogma, which heads north-west back to Camp Pincham). On the way to Danu Saddle a long section of loose scree and boulders is crossed, as well as a track to Cathedral Arch – a worthwhile side trip giving good views of Bluff Mountain.

At Danu Saddle, several tracks meet. Drop packs here and take the signposted walk to **Mt Exmouth**, about two hours return. The track passes over rocky scree slopes on the north side of the peak, before doubling back to meet the summit and spectacular views across the park and over to the plains in the west. Return to the *camp site* at Danu Saddle. If doing the walk in two days, it is about 2½ to three hours back to Canyon Picnic Area and the car.

Day 3: Danu Saddle to Canyon Picnic Area via Burbie Canyon
2½–3 hours, 7km

Pick up the old 4WD track from Danu Saddle and head north for 2km to *Burbie Camp*, where spring water is available from a tank. Head north-east along the sandy 4WD track until the signposted walking track to **Burbie Canyon** is met. After walking through the pleasant narrow canyon, where kangaroos and emus are commonly seen, the sealed road near Camp Wambelong is reached. Turn right and head on to the Canyon Picnic Area (about 2km farther).

Dorrigo National Park

This beautiful region of 11,732 hectares of true rainforest is 600km north of Sydney in the Great Dividing Range near Dorrigo, on the edge of an escarpment overlooking the Bellingen River valley. The area is of worldwide significance, and as such has been given a World Heritage listing. Having one of the highest rainfalls of any area in NSW, there are many small waterfalls dotted around the park, cascading through glades of rainforest trees with buttressed roots and thick hanging vines.

HISTORY
The coastal Gumbainggirr Aboriginal people lived in a territory that extended from the present-day national park area to Coffs Harbour on the coast. In summer, visits to the higher plateau regions were made to exploit seasonal food sources.

European timber-getters entered this region in about 1830, looking for the high-value red cedar trees that characteristically thrive in rainforests. Pastoralists soon followed them into the area and, after extensive grazing and logging, much of the rainforest was cleared. The local Aborigines were also driven from their lands. Fauna and flora reserves declared in 1902 saved the remaining pockets of rainforest from destruction, and these have been progressively added to, forming the present-day Dorrigo National Park.

NATURAL HISTORY
Strangler figs, red cedar trees and giant stinging trees tower over the forest floor, forming a dense canopy that blocks out most of the light. Hanging gardens of orchids and epiphytes – ferns that use larger trees for support – dangle from high branches in the canopy. Vines are draped across the trees, and ground orchids thrive in rocky fissures. Below this subtropical forest, poor yellow clay soils lead to a more open forest of mosses, orchids, fungi and ground ferns, beneath a canopy of coachwood, sassafras and

NEW SOUTH WALES

corkwood trees. Cool temperate rainforest, with moss-covered Antarctic beech trees growing among coachwoods, is found on the higher areas on the Never Never Circuit, described later.

Over 120 species of birds, including currawongs, king parrots, honeyeaters, lyrebirds, satin bowerbirds and brush turkeys are common here. They have little fear of visitors. Mammals include pademelons (tiny kangaroo-like animals), which can be seen feeding in the grassy picnic areas in late afternoon. Ringtail and brushtail possums, sugar gliders, bandicoots, echidnas, bats, koalas and spotted quolls are all common inhabitants. The rare parma wallaby has also been seen in wet forest areas.

PLANNING

Any time of year is suitable for walking in the Dorrigo area. The park has a very high rainfall (2500mm in summer), and winters can be a little cold, due to the altitude, around dusk. The driest time is usually August, September and October.

Carry a light waterproof jacket at all times. Insect repellent is useful in the warmer months, as mosquitoes are common.

Maps & Books

The CMA 1:25,000 *Darkwood* and *Dorrigo* maps cover the full Wonga Walk. Alternatively, the interpretive leaflet *Dorrigo National Park* by the NPWS, available at the Rainforest Centre near the Wonga Walk, is a brief but adequate reference for the walk.

Tyrone Thomas' *50 Walks: Coffs Harbour and Gold Coast Hinterland* has route descriptions of day walks in the park.

Information Sources

The Rainforest Centre (☎ 02-6657 2309) and district NPWS office is on Dome Rd in Dorrigo, at the start of the Wonga Walk. It has a shop and information about the park's many walks.

Permits & Regulations

No permits or fee payment are required. Stay on the wide and well-marked tracks to prevent damage to the rainforest understorey.

NEAREST TOWNS & FACILITIES
Coffs Harbour

Coffs Harbour is the biggest town between Newcastle and the Gold Coast, and an important regional centre. It is the best access point to the Dorrigo National Park from the coast, with a good range of shops, supermarkets, and plenty of accommodation. The Visitor Information Centre (☎ 02-6652 1522, 1300 369 070), on the corner of Rose Ave and Marcia St, should be able to advise you.

The town has excellent bus and train transport links, and an airport with several flights daily from Brisbane and Sydney.

Dorrigo

About 4km north of the Rainforest Centre lies Dorrigo. It is a quiet country town and the closest to the national park.

Food, film and fuel can be purchased here, but it's best to bring your requirements with you from Coffs Harbour.

Places to Stay & Eat The *Commercial Hotel/Motel* (☎ 02-6657 2003) has singles/doubles at $15/20. The *Dorrigo Hotel/Motel* (☎ 02-6657 2017) has $45 motel units and $35 pub rooms for weary bushwalkers.

Mistys is a small restaurant with great food. Mains from a small but innovative blackboard menu cost $14 to $19. Cheaper pub fare can be obtained at the *Dorrigo Hotel/Motel*, with lunchtime meals for $5.

GREG CAIRE

A stream cascades through tropical rainforest in Dorrigo National Park

Getting There & Away Dorrigo is 600km north of Sydney, and is best reached by driving north from Coffs Harbour along the coast. The national park entrance is passed 4km before the township, and is 60km from Coffs Harbour and 4km east of Dorrigo via the Dorrigo–Bellingen road.

Kean's bus company uses Dorrigo as a meal stop on its Port Macquarie–Tamworth run. It also has short trips such as Bellingen to Dorrigo ($10).

Wonga Walk

Duration	3 hours
Distance	7km
Standard	easy
Start/Finish	Dorrigo Rainforest Centre
Nearest Town	Dorrigo
Public Transport	no

Summary A short circuit walk through one of Australia's most accessible World Heritage List rainforests. Platforms along the route give an 'up with the birds' view of the rainforest canopy.

Dorrigo's Wonga Walk takes you through the understorey of a dark, tropical rainforest. The area is a tribute to the efforts of conservationists to save this area from extensive logging. The walk can be done in reverse, but this involves more uphill work than the route described.

Before leaving for the walk, be sure to visit the high wooden platform called the Skywalk, behind the Rainforest Centre. It affords superb views over to the Bellingen Valley, and offers a rare eye-level look into the dense rainforest canopy.

PLANNING
For details of when to walk, what to bring and permits and regulations, see Planning in the introduction to the Dorrigo National Park.

Maps
CMA 1:25,000 sheets *Dorrigo* and *Darkwood* cover the Wonga Walk in more detail, but are difficult to use because only a small section of the circuit appears on each map.

GETTING TO/FROM THE WALK
From Coffs Harbour and Bellingen, drive towards Dorrigo on the Dorrigo–Bellingen road, and turn right onto Dome Rd and the Dorrigo Rainforest Centre (signposted) 60km from Coffs Harbour. The walk starts near the treetop walkway (Skywalk) behind the visitor centre.

THE WALK
From the Rainforest Centre, a track called the Lyrebird Link (400m) connects with the main Wonga Walk, a 7km circuit. Walk down the wooden ramp and head south for about 1km. Visit the **Walk with the Birds platforms** and viewing area for a further look at the forest canopy.

Stay on the lower tracks, descending on the Wonga Walk. Passing a small waterfall (Tristania Falls), continue another 250m to pass behind the **Crystal Shower Falls**. Continue on (east) and up, reaching **Hardwood Lookout** on a bend in the track where it switches back (west) to start descending. Head north and along down to a third small waterfall. From here the track gradually climbs back up onto the north ridge. The forest here is very tall. The track then heads

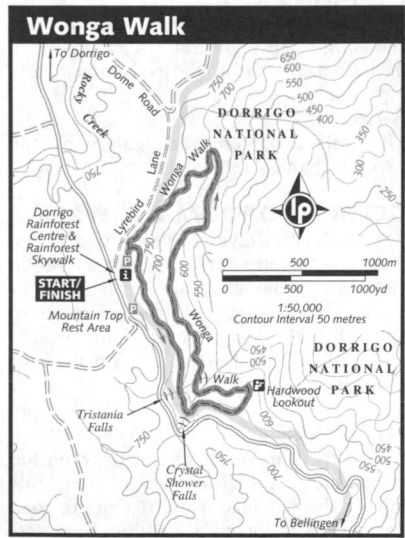

Wonga Walk [map]

south to complete the circuit. Another 400m up the Lyrebird Link takes you back to the Rainforest Centre.

Never Never Circuit

Duration	4 hours
Distance	8.5km
Standard	medium
Start/Finish	Never Never Picnic Area
Nearest Town	Dorrigo
Public Transport	no

Summary A relatively easy circuit walk through a section of the World Heritage List Dorrigo National Park, with forest lookouts to Cedar and Coachwood Falls.

The walk follows a well-maintained circuit known as the Rosewood Track through the subtropical rainforest. The forest here is of a different character to that around the Wonga Walk, being more open and dominated by coachwood trees. It is a relatively easy walk, but has a steep section near the pretty Cedar and Coachwood Falls, which gives it a medium grading.

PLANNING
For details on when to walk, what to bring and permits and regulations, see Planning in the introduction to the Dorrigo National Park.

Maps
The walk is covered adequately by the CMA 1:25,000 *Brooklana* map.

GETTING TO/FROM THE WALK
For the Never Never Circuit, drive to the Rainforest Centre (the route is described in Getting to/From the Walk for the Wonga Walk), then continue past the centre along Dome Rd. The Never Never Picnic Area is about 10km from the centre; this is the start of the walk.

THE WALK
Locate the start of the circuit track on the south side of the cleared picnic area, following the remains of a dirt logging road downhill for 1km to a junction. Turn left

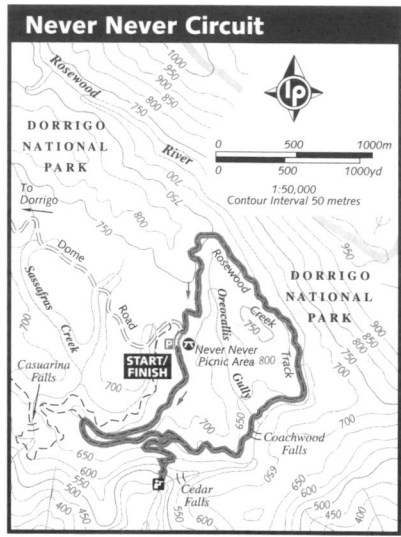

and continue for about 800m to the intersection with the track to Cedar Falls. This descends the hill in a series of switchbacks for 1.5km to a **view point** near Cedar Falls. Reverse the last section after viewing the falls, and regain the main track. Follow it for another 1km to **Coachwood Falls**.

The track from the falls then surmounts a ridge, heading up the valley of the Rosewood River. After 2.7km of pleasant walking through rainforest, the trail returns to the Never Never Picnic Area and the start of the walk.

Washpool National Park

Washpool was declared a national park in 1983, and today consists of 27,700 hectares of unique forests and valleys. Saved from extensive logging after a protracted conservation battle, it is the largest area of old-growth, warm temperate rainforest in NSW, and of sufficient value to have been added to the World Heritage List. It is one of a few precious places in Australia where human impact is invisible away from the peripheral access roads and tracks that penetrate only a small area of the park.

Occupying a place on a raised plateau reaching 1200m in places, this area of wilderness protects the world's largest remaining stand of coachwood trees. The forest stretches out from the lookouts at the entrance to the park like a carpet of tangled green. On the forest floor, delicate ferns and mosses secrete themselves in dark, moist pockets under boulders and beside creeks, and fungi and rotting vegetation give the landscape a surreal quality, like Tolkien's Middle Earth. Huge staghorn, bird's nest and elkhorn ferns are common.

Washpool is also one of the richest fauna areas in NSW, populated, among a host of other species, by lyrebirds, honeyeaters, king parrots, satin bowerbirds, possums and sugar gliders. In most areas of NSW, feral cats, foxes, rats and other introduced species have irreparably altered native habitats. Washpool has thankfully been spared much of this destruction and as a result spotted-tailed quolls, long-nosed potoroos, native Australian water rats and parma wallabies are all found in the park. The parma wallaby was thought to be extinct in Australia up until about 1967.

PLANNING

Walking is possible year-round. Washpool is a region of very high rainfall, and showers and storms can be expected at any time of year. Midsummer temperatures can make walking a hot proposition.

Maps & Books

The CMA's 1:25,000 *Coombadjha* map covers the walk. Tyrone Thomas' book *50 Walks: Coffs Harbour and Gold Coast Hinterland* describes the route of this day walk with sketch maps.

Information Sources

While there are no park visitor centres, information can be obtained from the NPWS office at Glen Innes (☎ 02-6732 5133), or from interpretive signs at the park entrance on Coombadjha Rd, and at the Bellbird and Coombadjha camping areas.

Permits & Regulations

No permit or fees are required to do this walk. However, if attempting multi-day wilderness walks in this area, it is necessary to register your intentions at the registration board on Coombadjha Rd as you enter the park. Forms are available next to a deposit box for this purpose.

NEAREST TOWNS & FACILITIES
Grafton

On the Pacific Hwy 88km from Washpool, Grafton is the largest town between the park and the coast. The town's facilities include supermarkets, much accommodation, petrol stations and camping stores. The Clarence River Tourist Centre (☎ 02-6642 4677) is on the highway south of the town near the turn-off to the bridge. There's an NPWS office (☎ 02-6642 0613) at 50 Victoria St.

Grafton is connected by air, bus and train transport links. Countrylink buses (☎ 13 2232) run up the Gwydir Hwy to Glen Innes ($24) on Tuesday, Thursday and Saturday and can drop you near Washpool and Gibraltar Range National Parks.

Glen Innes

Glen Innes is 75km from Washpool National Park on the New England Hwy, and this is the nearest town in which to buy fuel, food and other necessities if approaching from the south-west (ie, inland).

The visitor centre (☎ 02-6732 2397) is on Church St, near the town centre, and there's an NPWS office (☎ 02-6732 5133) on the New England Hwy at the junction with Oliver St.

A number of bus services connect Glen Innes with other destinations in NSW and Queensland. Impulse Airlines (☎ 13 1381) flies to Sydney at least twice daily for $199.

Washpool National Park

National park camping areas include the *Bellbird* and *Coombadjha Camping Areas*, with firewood, fireplaces and toilets. A fee is charged for camping at both these areas: $5 per person per night for two people, and $2 per person thereafter. Use the envelopes and deposit boxes provided for payment.

Washpool Rainforest

Duration	3 hours
Distance	8.5km
Standard	easy
Start/Finish	Coombadjha Picnic Area
Nearest Towns	Grafton, Glen Innes
Public Transport	no

Summary An easy half-day walk in national park rainforest around the Coombadjha Creek catchment area, with a side trip to Summit Falls.

This walk covers the southern valleys and slopes of the upper section of Coombadjha Creek. The predominantly coachwood-based rainforests of Washpool provide a different walking experience from the dark recesses of Dorrigo National Park. In Washpool the canopy is a little more open and the understorey of ferns and creeping vines is somewhat thicker. In world terms, Washpool represents the largest area of coachwood rainforest to be found undisturbed anywhere. Despite the provision of walking tracks and picnic facilities in the area around Coombadjha Creek (described in this walk), most of the park is relatively inaccessible, existing in a true wilderness state.

GETTING TO/FROM THE WALK

Washpool National Park is on the Gwydir Hwy, between Glen Innes and Grafton. Turn off the highway onto Coombadjha Rd, 85km from Grafton and 75km from Glen Innes; the Coombadjha Picnic Area is reached after 4km. The park is relatively remote, but is accessible to 2WD vehicles.

THE WALK

The track begins from the Coombadjha Picnic Area, north-east of the car parking area, and heads down to Coombadjha Creek. From here, cross to the northern bank over the wooden boardwalk and continue for 500m on this side of the creek. Cross another wooden boardwalk and climb steadily to another small stream, Cedar Creek, which needs to be crossed. Continue for nearly 1km, where a short side track to **Summit Falls** can be seen. This is worth a quick look.

From here the track climbs steadily to the south, passing many small, slender-trunked trees. These are known as 'walking stick' trees, as their dimensions and extreme straightness at one time made them very suited to this purpose. Continuing upwards, the forest opens out into eucalyptus woodland, and **Washpool Lookout** is passed. At a total of nearly 2km from Summit Falls, the track divides: take the left fork. Back under the rainforest canopy now, continue for 500m to cross Cedar Creek; another 500m on, a track junction on the right is reached. Follow it down to two magnificent **red cedar trees**, both enormous and both hung with massive gardens of epiphyte ferns high up on the trunks and branches. Some interpretive signs and a platform and walkway are located here. Stay on these to prevent destruction of the understorey vegetation below. Return to the track junction.

Back on the main track, continue northwest until, just before the track descends into the valley, a track appears on the left; this is Acacia Walk, which extends for 5km to meet the Coombadjha Rd you drove in on. Ignore this, and continue on the main track back to Coombadjha Creek and the rest area.

Other Walks

BLUE MOUNTAINS

Federal Pass

This classic Blue Mountains track (6km to 8km, depending on where you start the walk) through the Jamison Valley can be joined at Leura Falls Lookout, the Jamison Lookout or the Giant Stairway beside the Three Sisters, all near Katoomba. It's a relatively easy, but long day walk, with a haul up the Golden Stairs at the end to get to the top of Narrow Neck. The drop into the valley is around 300m.

Grose River

The Blue Gum Forest walk can be extended for another three to four days (65km) with this medium-hard bushbash following the Grose River downstream to the Nepean River, finishing near Richmond. Hard going because there's no track, but navigation is easy because you follow the river. Once in the Grose Valley, the walk beside the river to Richmond is more or less on the flat.

Katoomba to Kanangra Walls

A scenic four-day (45km) trek starting at the Narrow Neck Plateau and crossing over the Wild Dogs to end at the spectacular Kanangra Walls in Kanangra Boyd National Park. Advanced bushwalking and navigational skills are necessary. The distance and elevation involved make this a hard route. The climb up from Cox's River to Mt Cloudmaker is around 700 vertical metres.

Katoomba to Mittagong

A challenging four- to six-day (120km) walk for experienced bushwalkers. Start at Narrow Neck and continue to the Cox's River. Follow the Scotts Main Range Fire Trail to Yerranderie and then continue via the Wollondilly and Nattai Rivers to Mittagong. Check with the NPWS on conditions before starting.

Katoomba to Wentworth Falls via Mt Solitary

A medium two-day (30km) trek, requiring some navigational skills. Starts at Narrow Neck, dropping down to the Jamison Valley and camping on Mt Solitary (919m). The tricky bit comes next – the track is becoming clearer, but take advice from the NPWS before setting out on the walk to Wentworth Falls.

The Three Peaks

A classic three- or four-day (80km) circuit starting at Katoomba, proceeding via Narrow Neck and the Cox's River, then traversing Mt Cloudmaker (the highest point), Mt Guouogang and Mt Paralyser to finish at Kanangra Walls. It's difficult and you'll need to be fit and have bushwalking/navigational skills. An extended trek could be undertaken if you connect this circuit with the walk from Katoomba via Narrow Neck and the Cox's River.

KOSCIUSZKO NATIONAL PARK

Australian Alps Walking Track

This long-distance route (680km) actually begins in the tiny town of Walhalla (Victoria) and ends at Namadgi Visitor Centre (near the outskirts of Canberra) in the ACT, traversing the highest peaks and ranges in the country. It takes about eight weeks to walk the entire track and requires food caches to be stored along the way, but few people attempt the whole walk in one trip. For more information, see the boxed text 'Australian Alps Walking Track' in the Victoria chapter.

Guthega to Mt Jagungal Circuit

A popular southern route to Mt Jagungal starts at Guthega Power Station (about 37km from Jindabyne along Kosciuszko and Island Bend Rds). The walk takes five to six days. A good track heads north up Munyang River valley and passes Whites River Hut, Schlink Pass and the Schlink Hilton (a large hut) to Valentines Hut. Valentines Falls, near the hut, are worth a look. From here, the route follows the Valentine and Grey Mare Fire Trails north to Mt Jagungal (2061m). The return route to Guthega Power Station crosses the heads of the Geehi and Valentine Rivers to Mawsons Hut, then traverses the Kerries – some of the most scenic walking in Australia – before climbing Gungartan (2061m). The route then descends west to Schlink Pass and finishes via the outward path.

Cascade Hut

This 20km day walk passes through some very scenic Kosciuszko country along the relatively untrodden Cascade Trail. The walk begins at a point 300m east of Dead Horse Gap on the Alpine Way. Follow the Cascade Trail south as it heads up the valley of the Thredbo River into the lower reaches of Boggy Plain. The trail crosses the river via a footbridge and climbs steadily to cross the Great Dividing Range, 4km from the start. The Cascade Trail then drops over 300 vertical metres in forest to emerge at the western end of a long snow plain. From here, it crosses Cascade Creek and continues about 1km upstream to Cascade Hut. Return via the outward route.

Northern Territory

The Northern Territory (NT) has an undeniable aura. Many visitors to Alice Springs still expect to find a dusty, Wild West town full of outlaws settling scores, and while this is far from the case, the NT is still a place of extremes. Droughts are followed by floods, and 35°C daytime temperatures by freezing nights. The NT is a land of rainforest and desert, and stark mountains and sweeping plains. The various walks described here involve all these extremes.

Having a vehicle is a great advantage, especially for Kakadu. There is huge potential for exploration – the Larapinta Trail (a three-day section of which is covered in this chapter) offers weeks of walking.

HISTORY

Aboriginal people have been in the region for at least 50,000 years (see the boxed text 'Aboriginal Culture & the Top End' later in this chapter). An Asian naval fleet arrived in the 15th century, and 16th-century Portuguese sailors where probably the first Europeans to arrive in the NT. Dutch sailors followed in the 17th century and finally the British in 1801, when Matthew Flinders sailed hastily along the coastline.

Considerable exploration of the interior took place in the mid-1800s (most successfully by John McDouall Stuart), but settlement never really got off the ground until after South Australia (SA) gained control of the NT and the construction of the Overland Telegraph Line began in 1870. Once a permanent route between Adelaide and the fledgling settlement at Darwin was established, mining and cattle raising began. Pastoralism has since given way to mining and tourism as the major income earners – almost one million people travel around the NT each year.

NATURAL HISTORY

Although the majority of the NT is in the tropics, the northern quarter (the Top End) is really the only part to experience anything

PAUL SINCLAIR

Highlights

Walking the Larapinta Trail is a superb way to experience Australia's arid Centre

- Walking the ridges in West MacDonnell National Park
- Hiking over Nourlangie Rock and between important Aboriginal art sites in Kakadu National Park
- Swimming in cool, clear pools beneath the waterfalls of Litchfield National Park
- Walking out into Ormiston Pound at first light
- Tackling the 'Creekbed Challenge' at Standley Chasm, in the West MacDonnell Ranges
- Camping above the thundering 17 Mile Falls, Nitmiluk National Park

like a tropical climate. Tropical woodland, monsoon rainforest, extensive low-lying wetlands and billabongs (often seasonal) are all common. Typically the coastline is flat and backed by swamps, mangroves and wide estuaries.

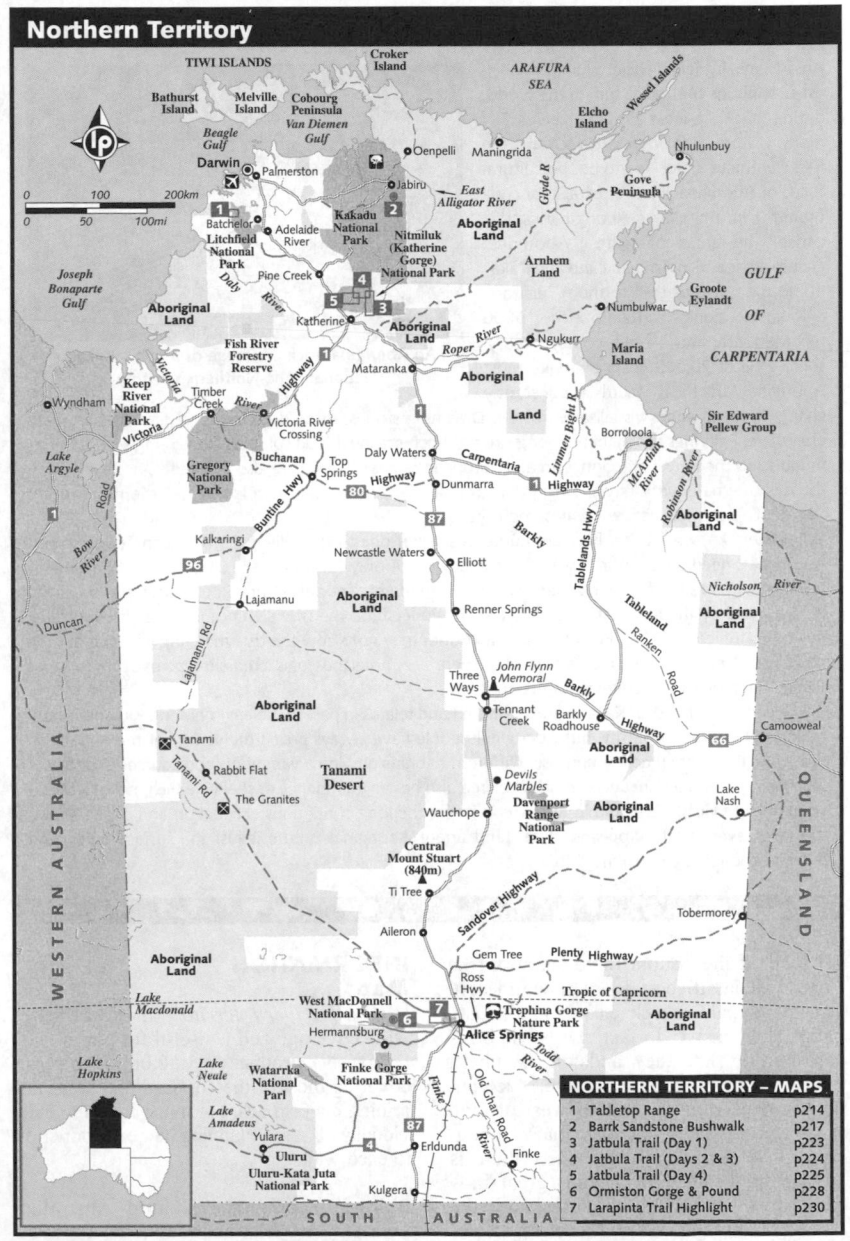

Northern Territory

TIWI ISLANDS

Bathurst Island
Melville Island
Cobourg Peninsula
Van Diemen Gulf
Croker Island

ARAFURA SEA

Wessel Islands

Elcho Island

Nhulunbuy

Beagle Gulf

Darwin
Palmerston

Oenpelli
Maningrida

Jabiru

East Alligator River

Glyde R

Gove Peninsula

Batchelor
Adelaide River

Kakadu National Park

Nitmiluk (Katherine Gorge) National Park

Aboriginal Land

Groote Eylandt

GULF

Litchfield National Park

Pine Creek

Daly River

Katherine

Aboriginal Land

Roper River

Numbulwar

Arnhem Land

Maria Island

OF CARPENTARIA

Joseph Bonaparte Gulf

Fish River Forestry Reserve

Highway

Mataranka

Aboriginal

Land

Ngukurr

Sir Edward Pellew Group

Keep River National Park
Victoria

Wyndham

Timber Creek

Victoria River

Victoria River Crossing

Daly Waters

Carpentaria

Borroloola

Limmen Bight R

McArthur River

Robinson River

Lake Argyle

Gregory National Park

Buchanan

Top Springs

Buntine Hwy

Highway

Dunmarra

Highway

Aboriginal Land

Bow River

Kalkaringi

Newcastle Waters

Elliott

Barkly

Tablelands Hwy

Duncan

Lajamanu

Lajamanu Rd

Renner Springs

Tableland

Ranken Road

Nicholson River

Aboriginal Land

WESTERN AUSTRALIA

Aboriginal Land

Three Ways

John Flynn Memorial

Barkly

Camooweal

Tanami

Tennant Creek

Barkly Roadhouse

Highway

Aboriginal Land

Lake Nash

QUEENSLAND

Rabbit Flat

The Granites

Tanami Rd

Tanami Desert

Wauchope

Devils Marbles

Davenport Range National Park

Aboriginal Land

Tobermorey

Central Mount Stuart (840m)

Ti Tree

Sandover Highway

Aileron

Gem Tree

Plenty Highway

Lake Macdonald

Ross Hwy

Tropic of Capricorn

Aboriginal Land

Lake Hopkins

West MacDonnell National Park

Hermannsburg

Trephina Gorge Nature Park

Alice Springs

Todd River

Old Ghan Road

Lake Neale

Watarrka National Park

Finke Gorge National Park

Finke River

Lake Amadeus

Yulara

Uluru

Erldunda

Finke

Uluru-Kata Juta National Park

Kulgera

SOUTH AUSTRALIA

NORTHERN TERRITORY

0   100   200km
0   50   100mi

Aboriginal Culture & the Top End

Australian Aboriginal society has the longest continuous cultural history in the world, dating back at least 50,000 years. For many visitors Uluru (Ayers Rock) and the Red Centre are perceived to be the cultural focus of Aboriginal life in Australia, and although Uluru has deep Aboriginal significance, the areas of richest Aboriginal culture are found in Arnhem Land and Kakadu, in the north of the Northern Territory.

Kakadu alone contains over 5000 recorded art sites, some contemporary, some at least 20,000 years old. Like most Aboriginal art they record a constantly

An Aboriginal rock art image of a fish – Kakadu National Park, Northern Territory

changing world and a visualisation of the Dreaming stories, often depicted more literally here than elsewhere. Paintings show animals long since extinct, seasonal food sources, the varying size of barramundi, and the arrival of Indonesian and European sailors. Styles have also evolved. One of the earliest was the 'naturalistic' style, which depicted people and animals in colour, while the more recent 'X-ray' style shows creatures' bones and organs.

For every known art site there are numerous secret ones, especially in Arnhem Land (which non-Aboriginals need a permit to visit). This secrecy is not only to protect the sites from vandalism, although sadly this is a factor, but because some are of very special cultural importance and must not be disturbed by the ignorant or uninitiated. To understand the true significance of a site you must belong to the correct clan. Even the clan next door may not know the true meaning of some of their neighbours' paintings. As well as art sites there are thousands of sacred sites across the Top End where ceremonies and cultural events are held.

The cultural richness of Kakadu and Arnhem Land relates in part to the environment. Kakadu is now celebrated for its biodiversity, but Aboriginal people have always prized the variety of the region, although with a more practical purpose. Different habitats provide a variety of food sources in different seasons, so shortages are uncommon. The area also has an abundance of shelter, which makes Kakadu an excellent place to live, and in turn accounts for the long continuous occupation and depth of culture. However, what Europeans understand about Aboriginal culture is just the surface layer, and there's undoubtedly much more to it.

Much of the bottom three-quarters (the Centre) is classified as desert or semidesert. The archetypal Outback terrain of red, dusty plains is extensive. In fact, the NT is basically quite flat, the sandstone Arnhem Plateau in the north-east and the MacDonnell Ranges running east to west around Alice Springs being the only major topographical features. However, where there is such relief, it's magnificent and a great draw for bushwalkers. Wildlife is abundant in the NT, especially in parks and other reserves.

INFORMATION

Maps

UBD's *Northern Territory* map has statewide coverage and is useful for planning.

MapsNT produces a 1:50,000 map series covering most of the Top End and areas adjoining major roads. For maps covering individual walks, see Planning in the introduction to each walk.

Buying Maps The Central Australian Tourism Association (Catia; ☎ 08-8952

5199, fax 8953 0295, @ visinfo@catia
.ash.au), 60 Gregory Terrace, Alice Springs,
sells maps of the MacDonnell Ranges and
trail notes for the Larapinta Trail. MapsNT
(☎ 08-8951 5344, 💻 www.lpe.nt.gov.au) is
in Gregory Terrace, Alice Springs, and in the
Department of Lands, Planning and Environment (1st floor), on the corner of Bennett
and Cavenagh Sts, Darwin.

Books

Lonely Planet's *Northern Territory* and *Outback Australia* are highly recommended for
more detailed information about the NT.
Outback on a Budget by Brian Sheedy is
useful for those travelling with their own vehicle. For more walking information, try Neil
Paton's *Walks in the Northern Territory*.

The Parks & Wildlife Commission of the
Northern Territory (PWC) pocket guides to
the Top End and Centre, *Plant Identikit* and
Wildlife Identikit, are certainly worth carrying, while *A Field Guide to Central Australia* by Penny van Ooosterzee is a more
comprehensive wildlife guide.

See also Books in the Facts for the
Walker chapter for a list of recommended
reading on contemporary Aboriginal history
and issues.

Information Sources

The Northern Territory Tourist Commission
(NTTC; ☎ 1800 621 336, 💻 www.nttc.com
.au) has offices in the NT's major towns,
state capitals around the country and several
overseas cities.

The PWC (☎ 08-8999 5511, 💻 www.nt
.gov.au/paw) has a main office in Palmerston, 18km south of Darwin (see Gateways
later), and regional offices in Alice Springs
(also under Gateways) and Katherine.

There are two main bushwalking clubs in
the NT: Darwin Bushwalking Club (☎ 08-
8985 1484), 19 Ostermann St, Coconut
Grove, and the Central Australian Bushwalking Club (☎ 08-8952 7558, @ long
walk@topend.com.au), PO Box 1818, Alice
Springs NT 0871.

The *Northern Territory News* is a state-
wide daily paper that provides up-to-date
weather information.

The Climate of the Northern Territory

Strictly speaking the climate is divided into
two sections. The Top End has two distinct
seasons, Wet and Dry, with a build-up period
of occasional storms, rising temperatures and
great humidity two months before the Wet.
Roughly 1600mm of rainfall occurs during the
Wet and temperatures rise to the high 30s. It's
no time to be out walking, although wildlife
watching in this season of plenty is ample reward for getting out into the bush.

The Centre has more extreme variations of
temperature, both daily and seasonally. In
winter, daytime temperatures can fall as low
as 15°C, plunging to below freezing at night.
Even in summer, when it's often over 35°C
during the day, low night-time temperatures
justify carrying a fleece jacket and good
sleeping bag.

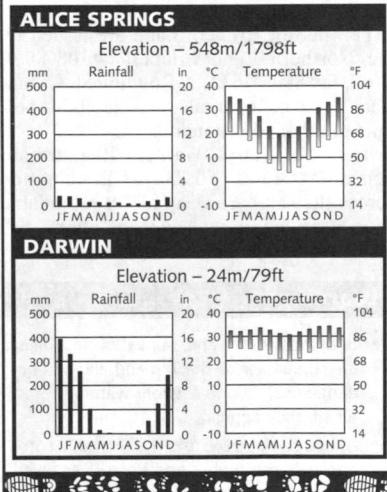

Permits & Regulations

Permits are required for most overnight
walks in the NT. For Kakadu National Park
the process can take considerable time. Permits for Nitmiluk and Litchfield National
Parks must also be organised in advance.
For the Larapinta Trail, they're relatively
easy to obtain.

Bushwalking & Aboriginal Land

When the British arrived in Australia they colonised the continent on the basis of *terra nullius*, a British legal doctrine which claimed unoccupied, or 'empty', land – belonging to no one – for the British Crown. It wasn't until 1976, and the Aboriginal Land Rights (NT) Act, that Aboriginal people could stake a claim on their traditional lands. At present almost half of the NT has been claimed or is being claimed on behalf of the traditional owners; this affects many areas used by bushwalkers.

It's important to realise that this is not about land ownership in a Western European sense. It's about having access to, and protection over, land you've a spiritual and physical connection with – there are no comparisons in western culture that adequately describe the land's importance to Aboriginal people. If a walker wanders into an art site meant only for clan elders to see, or swims at a sacred site, there can be great and far-reaching repercussions. What's more, Aboriginal elders feel personally responsible for the people on their land, including white folks wandering about in it. If a stranger out walking were to die, some elders would take the view, 'I let the white fella onto our land, it's therefore my fault he died, I won't let it happen again'. Hence the reluctance to encourage walkers.

So when walking on Aboriginal land it's important to obey the rules. If you're asked not to go a certain way or visit a certain site, then don't. If you have to wait months for a permit to be approved it's to stop you making a cultural gaffe that may not affect you very much, but could have deep repercussions for others.

Permits for Arnhem Land are issued by the Northern Land Council (☎ 08-8920 5100, fax 8945 2633), 9 Rowling St, Casuarina, Darwin. It can also advise about permits to other Aboriginal lands.

The Voluntary Walker Registration Scheme (☎ 1300 650 730) is in operation across the state. You pay a $50 refundable deposit by credit card over the phone, tell them your walk details, and if you don't check they organise a search party. Some walks in this chapter have Emergency Call Devices (ECDs) en route; these can be used if you require emergency assistance from the park rangers.

During days of Total Fire Ban, all fires are forbidden, even fuel stoves. If you are caught with an open fire on these days, you are not only endangering yourself and the environment, but you can also cop a hefty fine and/or prison sentence. See Responsible Walking in the Facts for the Walker chapter for suggestions on how to further minimise your impact on the environment.

Guided Walks

Willis's Walkabouts (☎ 08-8985 2134, ℮ walkabout@ais.net.au, 🖳 www.bushwalkingholidays.com.au) has a worldwide reputation and is probably one of the best organised and most original walking outfits in Australia. Walks are tailored to ability and degrees of luxury/adventure. They roughly cost between $500 and $1200 for seven days, depending on logistics.

From April to October, Trek Larapinta (☎ 08-8953 2933, fax 8953 2913, ℮ charlie @treklarapinta.com.au, 🖳 www.treklarapinta.com.au) offers tailor-made guided walks

Warnings

- Both freshwater and saltwater crocodiles are spread across the Top End and can be dangerous, so don't ignore warning signs where they appear.

- Although not a big risk, walkers have contracted scrub typhus and Ross River fever when walking in Litchfield and Kakadu National Parks, so cover up and wear insect repellent. Scrub typhus is a rare disease found in tropical Australia which is transmitted via bites from infected mites. At the time of writing, nine cases have been reported in Litchfield National Park since 1990. See the Health & Safety chapter for further details on Ross River Fever.

along the Larapinta Trail for around $175 per day and night. These expeditions are heartily recommended.

GETTING AROUND

The Blue Banana bus (☎ 08-8945 6800, fax 8927 5808, ✆ banana@octa4.net.au, 🖳 www.octa4.net.au/banana) offers a regular jump-on, jump-off circuit from Darwin to Katherine and back to Darwin via Kakadu, Nitmiluk and Litchfield National Parks. This is very handy for getting to and from trailheads in the Top End (special rates apply – see specific sections for details), although the bus only runs from April to October. A round-trip ticket, valid for three months, costs $170.

GATEWAYS
Darwin

Darwin's proximity to Asia (it's closer to Jakarta than to Canberra) gives it a surprisingly cosmopolitan, upbeat feel. There are plenty of good restaurants and it's worth spending a few days there before heading to Litchfield or Kakadu.

Information The handy Darwin Region Tourism Association (☎ 08-8981 4300, ✆ drtainfo@ozemail.com.au), on the corner of Knuckey and Mitchell Sts, is open daily, and the NTTC (☎ 08-8999 3900, fax 8999 3888) has an office at 43 Mitchell St.

The head office (and comprehensive information centre) of the PWC (☎ 08-8999 5511) is at 25 Chung Wha Terrace in Palmerston, 18km south of Darwin. More convenient, but with less information, is the park's desk in the tourism association in Darwin.

Darwin Bushwalking (see Information Sources earlier) can be a good source of information, although you'll need to join ($25) before taking part in any club walks.

The Rock Climbing Gym (☎ 08-8941 0747), on Doctors Gully Rd, is open seven days a week ($10 a session, no time limit).

Supplies & Equipment Snowgum (☎ 08-8941 7370), 32 Cavenagh St, and Adventure Equipment (☎ 08-8941 0019), 41 Cavenagh St, stock the latest fashionable lightweight gear. NT General Store (☎ 08-8981 8242), 42 Cavenagh St, is a vast treasure trove of army surplus kit, camping equipment and off-roading essentials. It also stocks some topographic maps.

Places to Stay & Eat The *Shady Glen Caravan Park (☎ 08-8984 3330)*, on the corner of Stuart Hwy and Farrell Crescent, Winellie, provides the closest and best camping to town. Sites cost from $8, and air-con vans from $50. There's a shop, pool and laundry.

Darwin City Lodge (☎ 08-8941 1295, 1800 808 151, 144 Mitchell St) is a 20-minute walk from town, but it's small and relaxed and the owners know Kakadu well. Dorm/twin beds are $14/38.

The *YHA (☎ 08-8981 3995, ✆ darwinyha@yhant.org.au, 69 Mitchell St)* is part of the Transit Centre and a friendly, clean institution with great facilities. Dorms cost from $15 per person, and doubles/twins from $19 per person, YHA discounts included. Book in advance.

For a splurge, *Yot's Café (☎ 08-8981 4433, 54 Marina Blvd, Cullen Bay)*, set on the water's edge, is open seven days a week until late. Mains cost from $9.90.

The *Mental Lentil*, in the Transit Centre on Mitchell St, serves up generous portions of delicious vegetarian food (from $4) and fresh juices.

Woolworths supermarket on Smith St is open daily.

Getting There & Away Darwin is at the very northern end of the Stuart Hwy, 1476km north of Alice Springs and 947km north of Three Ways, where the Mt Isa road meets the Stuart Hwy.

Air Darwin International Airport receives a fair number of international flights and is well worth considering as a first port of entry (especially if your ticket allows you to exit elsewhere). Ansett (☎ 13 1300) and Qantas (☎ 13 1313) fly to destinations all over Australia, while AirNorth (☎ 08-8945 2866, 1800 627 474) services destinations within the NT.

Bus Greyhound Pioneer (☎ 13 2030), run out of the Transit Centre at 69 Mitchell St, services south to Alice Springs, west to Western Australia (WA) and east to Queensland. McCafferty's (☎ 13 1499), 71 Smith St, plies the same southern and eastern routes, but does not go into WA.

Car Rental Car hire companies offering daily rates of $50 or under (with 100km free) include Delta Car Rentals (☎ 08-8941 0300, ✉ deltant@octa4.net.au), 77 Cavenagh St; Cheapa-Rent-a-Car (☎ 08-8981 8400), 89 Smith St; and Nifty Rent-a-Car (☎ 08-8981 2999), 86 Mitchell St.

Getting Around A taxi to the airport costs around $15; the door-to-door airport shuttle (☎ 1800 358 945) is $6. To get around town, use Darwin City Shuttle (☎ 08-8985 3666) or Darwin Mini Bus (☎ 08-8947 0416), which go anywhere within a 4km radius of the city centre ($2).

Alice Springs

From a lonely telegraph station in the desert Alice Springs, or 'Alice' as it's affectionately called, has grown into a thriving city and the launching point of many an Outback adventure. Uluru (Ayers Rock) is five hours away, but it's the MacDonnell Ranges close by that are the attraction for walkers. The Outback tourist industry and US 'space base' in the hills nearby ensure that the infrastructure here is as good as anywhere in Australia.

Information The NTTC has an office in Alice (☎ 08-8951 8555, fax 8951 8550), 67 Stuart Hwy North. Catia (☎ 08-8952 5199, fax 8953 0295, ✉ visinfo@catia.ash.au), 60 Gregory Terrace, is open from 8.30 am to 5.30 pm weekdays and from 9 am to 4 pm at weekends.

The PWC (☎ 08-8951 8211) is at the Arid Zone Research Institute, South Stuart Hwy. The Central Australian Bushwalking Club (see Information Sources earlier) holds walks open to nonmembers nearly every week. Contributions towards costs are required.

Supplies & Equipment Basic camping kit (no three-layer Gore-Tex here) can be found at Alice Disposals (☎ 08-8953 2933), on Reg Harris Lane off Todd Mall.

Places to Stay & Eat The *MacDonnell Range Holiday Park* (☎ 08-8952 6111, 1800 808 373, ⌨ www.macrange.com.au), with excellent facilities, is at Palm Place, 4.5km south of town (a pick-up service is provided). Camp sites cost between $18 and $28, with accommodation from $17 per person.

Melanka Motel & Backpackers (☎ 08-8952 2233, 1800 896 110, ✉ melanka @ozemail.com.au, 94 Todd St) is a huge, friendly place with a lively bar and nightclub. Air-con dorms start at $14, doubles/ twins at $34, and there's three-star motel accommodation next door. Facilities are excellent.

The small and well-equipped *YHA Pioneer* (☎ 08-8952 8855, ✉ pioneer1@dove .net.au), on the corner of Parsons St and Leichhardt Terrace, is built around a pool and courtyard. Dorm beds are $18 ($15 YHA members). Book in advance. It has air-con and secure left-luggage facilities.

The Mediterranean-style BYO (Bring Your Own) restaurant *Bar Doppio*, on Fan Lane off Todd Mall, is worth a try (mains start from $9). *Sultan's Kebab's* (☎ 08-8953 3322), on the corner of Hartley St and Gregory Terrace, serves up traditional Turkish cuisine (mains start at $14), and has belly-dancing on Friday nights.

The pubs and backpackers do the cheapest meals in town. Self-caterers have the choice of the *Bi-Lo*, *Woolworths* and *Coles* (open 24 hours) supermarkets.

Getting There & Away The basic thing to remember about Alice Springs is that it's a long way from anywhere: 1180km from Mt Isa, 529km from Three Ways and 1476km from Darwin. Even Uluru is more than 400km away.

Air Both Ansett (☎ 13 1300) and Qantas (☎ 13 1313) connect Alice with Yulara (for Uluru) and major cities. The airport is 15km south of town, a $20 taxi ride or $10 with the airport shuttle (☎ 08-8953 0310).

Bus Greyhound Pioneer (☎ 13 2030), on the corner of Gregory and Railway Terraces, has daily services to Adelaide, Darwin and Uluru. Northbound services connect with WA services at Katherine and with Queensland services at Tennant Creek. McCafferty's (☎ 13 1499), 91 Gregory Terrace, runs similar services, although without connections to WA.

Train The *Ghan* (☎ 13 2232) train runs twice weekly, in either direction, between Alice and Adelaide. Book well in advance.

Car Rental There's no public transport to the trailheads around Alice, but hiring a car is an option, as walks are all accessible by 2WD. There are numerous companies, including all the major players. Companies with daily rates of $50 or under (with 100km free) include Boomerang Rentals (☎ 08-8955 5171), 1–3 Fogarty St, and Outback Auto Rentals (☎ 08-8953 5333, 1800 652 133, fax 8953 5344), 78 Todd St. Thrifty Car Rental (☎ 08-8952 9999, ☻ thrifty@rentacar.com.au) rents expensive new cars and cheap old ones.

Litchfield National Park

From Darwin, access to Litchfield National Park's main attractions, mostly waterfalls and swimming holes, is quick and easy. Consequently Litchfield is very popular with locals and tour groups, particularly at weekends. However, once off the beaten track you're unlikely to meet another soul.

HISTORY
Litchfield National Park is named after Frederick Litchfield, a member of the 1864 Finniss Expedition that explored the Northern Territory of South Australia (as it was then called). However, the park is of great significance to the Wagait Aboriginal people and it's likely that in the future the park will be managed jointly by the PWC and the traditional owners.

Abandoned 19th-century tin mines can be seen at Bamboo Creek in the north-west of the park and at Blyth Homestead, which served as the base for Stapleton Pastoral and Development Company. The lease owners were the first to raise the possibility of a national park, finally established in 1986.

NATURAL HISTORY
Generally speaking the ecosystems found here are similar to those in Kakadu. Vegetation is mostly open woodland of Darwin woollybutt and stringybark eucalyptus. Wetland and swamp areas are also common (and prone to flooding during the Wet) and pockets of monsoon rainforest are found close to waterfalls and sheltered springs.

The sandstone Tabletop Range plateau rises to just over 200m and dominates the north end of the park. It is covered in low tropical woodland with pockets of grassland and low banksia woodland. There's also one large swathe of tall eucalyptuses running south-east across the whole plateau. The spectacular Tolmer, Wangi and Florence Falls are fed by creeks that run off the plateau. Despite large visitor numbers the endangered orange leafnosed-bat breeds near Tolmer Falls (swimming here is prohibited). The park's large pools contain harmless filesnakes and archer fish, which knock insects into the water with jets of water. At Wangi look out for ferocious (well, relatively) northern quolls at night. Also, you're bound to see great bowerbirds, blue-winged kookaburras and magpie-larks around the main camp sites. The antilopine wallaroo is the largest mammal in the park.

Magnetic termite mounds are the park's most amazing wildlife phenomena. Standing like huge tombstones in low-lying grassland, their narrow, flat shape and precise orientation (10° east of true north) reduces exposure to the midday sun. Cathedral termite mounds prefer well-drained soil and can reach over 6m in height.

PLANNING
When to Walk
The park is open all year but some unsealed tracks are normally closed during the Wet.

Generally speaking the dry season from May to September is the best time for walking. June and July are the coolest months (top temperatures only around 30°C), with lows of 10°C at night. The build-up to the Wet starts in October – humidity and temperatures are high and dramatic storms common. The Wet begins at the end of December and can last until April – expect heavy rainstorms, high humidity and temperatures of up to 35°C. During the Wet many walking trails are flooded.

Walking is best between May and July when temperatures are lower and water abundant. Mosquitoes and flies can be intolerable during the build-up. Numbers don't really diminish until the Dry.

What to Bring

Sleeping under fly nets is ideal in the Dry, when you'll also need a sleeping bag. Insect repellent is standard issue at all times, and after September a tent and waterproof gear are required. All overnight walks are fuel stove only.

Skinny dipping in the waterholes is forbidden so be sure to take along a swimming costume if you want to swim.

Maps

MapsNT's 1:50,000 *Mount Tolmer* and *Rum Jungle* maps cover the walk. They're topographically accurate, but new sealed roads are not shown. The sketch map produced by rangers (available in Batchelor) shows the route accurately, and MapsNT's 1:100,000

Litchfield National Park is good for planning and orientation. All maps are available in Darwin.

Information Sources

The park headquarters (☎ 08-8976 0282, fax 8976 0292) is 14km west of the Stuart Hwy in Batchelor and is signposted from the main road. Rangers give free guided walks, talks and slide shows between May and September.

There are also information bays located inside the park's eastern and northern boundaries, explaining the park's geology, flora and fauna, as well as Aboriginal activity in the area.

Permits & Regulations

There is no charge to enter the park or for bush camping permits, although these must be obtained from rangers in Batchelor. There are ECDs at Wangi, Florence and Tolmer Falls.

NEAREST TOWN & FACILITIES
Batchelor

Once a service town for the Rum Jungle uranium mine, Batchelor, 43km from the park boundary, is the nearest town to Litchfield. Batchelor General Store (☎ 08-8976 0454) is open seven days a week, sells fuel and has Eftpos. There's a post office (with a Commonwealth bank agency) next door.

Batchelor Caravillage (☎ 08-8976 0166, fax 8976 0118), on Rum Jungle Rd, is the McCafferty's agent and very prim and tidy. It has camp sites from $9, cabins for $80 and dorm beds for $13 per person.

Litchfield National Park

The PWC maintains a number of camping grounds with facilities within Litchfield National Park for which no permit is required. *Camp sites* at Wangi and Florence Falls both have hot showers and barbecues ($5 per person; pay at the honesty box). Camping at Buley Rockhole also costs $5 per person. *Wangi Kiosk* sells drinks, snacks, barbecue packs and enormous steak sandwiches ($8), and is open year-round. There's a public phone here.

Warnings

- Both saltwater and freshwater crocodiles inhabit the park. Never ignore the warning signs. There are permanent croc traps downstream of Wangi and Florence Falls, but crocs occasionally get around them in the Wet.

- There's a very small risk of contracting scrub typhus and Ross River Fever when walking in Litchfield (for information on Ross River fever, see the Health & Safety chapter).

Tabletop Range

Duration	2 days
Distance	20.5km
Standard	medium
Start	Wangi Falls
Finish	Florence Falls
Nearest Town	Batchelor
Public Transport	yes

Summary Part of a new 66km circular trail around the Tabletop Range, this walk follows a number of creeks from one set of stunning waterfalls, across the plateau, to another.

At the time of writing, a 66km circuit around the Tabletop Range, linking some of the park's main attractions, had been surveyed and was being walked. The two-day section described here leads from Wangi Falls, in the west, up the escarpment and over the Tabletop Range to Florence Falls in the east, although you won't regret attempting the whole five-day circuit. Creeks are followed for much of the trail's length, while swamps and a band of tall eucalyptus woodland are just two of the environments encountered.

At present the route is marked with fluorescent tape, but further trail development is likely. Getting up-to-date information from the rangers at Batchelor is essential.

GETTING TO/FROM THE WALK

Access to the park is possible by two routes off the Stuart Hwy. The first enters the park from the north by going via the Berry Springs Rd (and Territory Wildlife Park) and 42km of dirt road (check road conditions during the Wet), but the simpler, sealed route is via Batchelor, the turn-off to which is 90km south of Darwin.

In the Dry season the Blue Banana (☎ 08-8945 6800) bus enters the park on Saturday, Sunday, Tuesday and Wednesday. Batchelor to the park costs $20 and Darwin to the park is $36. However, the bus will have come up from Katherine, so if you're coming from Darwin you'll need to get to Batchelor (or the Batchelor turn-off) first in order to hook up with it. McCafferty's runs into Batchelor, and Greyhound stops at the turn-off.

THE WALK
Day 1: Wangi Falls to Tabletop Range Plateau
4 hours, 8.5km

Turn right below the falls onto **Wangi Falls Trail**, which leads through river pandanus and past a colony of black flying foxes into monsoon rainforest. Climb past an excellent forest canopy viewing platform to a **lookout**, continuing to a boardwalk and a bridge that crosses the creek just above the falls. Once across, turn right off the path and walk due east to a small stream and, after spotting the orange fluorescent markers, cross it and walk into a pocket of banksia woodland. Keeping the creek to your right, climb north-east to the foot of a hill.

Below the hill is a junction, a path to Cascades leading off to the north. Bear right (east) for a few metres then cut down south to the river. Cross and turn left (east) following the route to higher ground and then back to the river, a pattern of ascent and descent that is set for the next 1½ hours as the route follows the creek (on the southern bank) north-east, east then south-east. Clear pools, waterfalls and spinifex-covered, boulder-strewn hills are passed in this section before the river turns north-east past a small set of falls to a larger set with a wonderful broad **pool**. It's a great place to stop.

Bear right above the pool, where the river forks, and head south-east then east into flatter country. After 25 minutes, with the river little more than a stream, the route crosses to the north bank then peels away north-east into tall grassland. Five minutes later, in open woodland, is a good **camp site**. The ground is flat and not littered with rocks, as it becomes a few minutes later.

Day 2: Tabletop Range Plateau to Florence Falls
4–4½ hrs, 12km

Continue north-east for 20 minutes, following the trail as it makes evasive turns north, east then north again round the large Tabletop Swamp. Magnetic termite mounds can be seen in the banksia woodland.

Once around the swamp the route continues north-east into tall eucalyptus woodland,

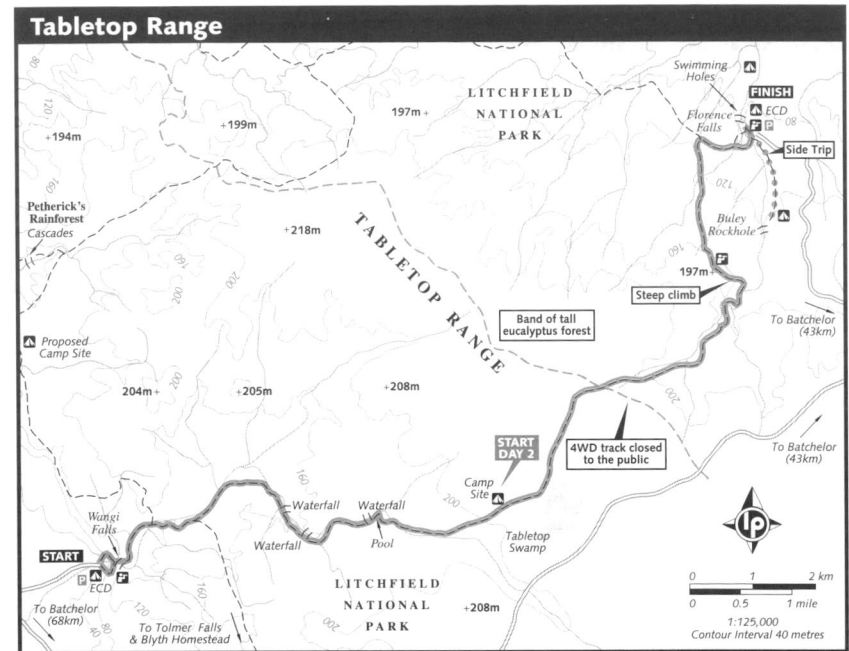

Tabletop Range

reaching a 4WD track (closed to the public) in 20 minutes before descending east into a flat-bottomed gully, then north-east following the diminutive tributary of Florence Creek. Stick to the east bank, climbing up the hillside then down into a narrow, rocky gully. As the river starts to meander, there's a dramatic balancing rock to the east; the route crosses boulder-strewn cliffs and then the creek (to the true left bank) as it turns east. Head east through a pocket of lush forest, Carpentaria palms and cycads, then cut the corner by recrossing the river (to the true right bank) then follow it downstream as it bends north into an area of grassland.

A couple of minutes later cross to the west bank (you'll get wet) and head north for 200m onto a rocky hillside popular with euros and black-footed rock-wallabies. The trail now swings left (north-west), climbing steeply uphill. After 20 minutes' climbing you're on a large flat hilltop with views east, south and north. It's an excellent **lookout**.

At the northern edge of the hilltop the route descends diagonally (north-west) into dry eucalyptus woodland, then continues north between two large piles of rocks through an undulating, less wooded landscape, crossing a stream after 20 minutes. Ten minutes later a junction beside a jumble of rocks is reached. The main trail heads off north-west, but turn right for Florence Falls.

Head south-east for 100m then east over boggy ground into denser vegetation as the route zigzags down a rocky slope back to Florence Creek. Follow the river downstream to a junction with a circular tourist trail where a left or right turn leads to the *camp site*. However, turn right to go via the plunge pool at the base of **Florence Falls**. A separate 4WD *camp site* is 400m north of the **viewing platform** above the falls.

From the main car park a simple 1.6km trail leads to **Buley Rockhole**, a popular bathing spot where Mertons' water monitors are often seen. There's also a *camp site*.

Kakadu National Park

Kakadu is a very special park. Contained within its boundaries is a variety of habitats, an entire river system and one of the highest concentration of rock art sites in the world. No wonder that in 1992 the entire park attained World Heritage listing for cultural and ecological importance.

Throughout the park short, marked trails (many around 5km long) lead through different habitats to a variety of attractions. There are also endless possibilities for extended walks. However, no fixed long-distance routes or marked trails exist and a strict permit system regulates all overnight walks. What's more, publicity about possible routes is minimised, so the excellent 12km Barrk Sandstone Bushwalk described in the special section is just a taste of what the park has to offer. The rest is up to you.

HISTORY

Kakadu protects a rich Aboriginal heritage and is jointly managed by the traditional owners and Parks Australia, a Federal government department. Kakadu is home to a number of different Aboriginal clans who have lived here for at least 23,000 years (possibly 50,000).

In the early 1970s major uranium deposits were discovered in the Kakadu area. The Ranger Uranium Environment Enquiry was set up and in 1977 the government endorsed three uranium mining leases. One of these, the Ranger Mine, is currently operational. The first area of Aboriginal land title was granted in 1978 and the first stage of Kakadu National Park was declared in 1979. In 1991 Kakadu was enlarged to 22,000 sq km, becoming Australia's largest national park.

Uranium is still a hot issue with environmentalists and Aboriginal title holders opposed to future mining. The government's support of the development of the proposed mining site at Jabiluka has increased tensions and periodically returned uranium mining to the centre of national political debate.

NATURAL HISTORY

Very few extinctions have occurred in Kakadu in the last 200 years (unlike much of Australia) and numerous endemic species remain unknown to science. Four major rivers flow through the park, including the entire South Alligator River and catchment.

The spectacular sandstone Arnhem Land Escarpment and Plateau were sea cliffs about 140 million years ago. Sandstone outcrops like Nourlangie Rock and Ubirr would have been islands in a vast shallow sea. Today 80% of the park is lowland plains covered in a patchwork of eucalyptus woodland (mostly Darwin woollybutt) and grassland that supports a great variety of wildlife, including kangaroos and wallabies. Beautiful salmon gums and several endemic plants grow on the southern hills and basins, providing habitat for rare Gouldian finches and red goshawks. The nutrient-rich flood plains are of international importance as waterfowl breeding grounds and as a stopover for about 30 species of migratory birds. These wetlands are a stronghold for magpie geese, which once occurred throughout eastern and southern Australia. In the dry it's worth staking out a billabong for a few hours. Often the last remaining water sources, they draw in a huge range of wildlife, not least the occasional saltwater crocodile, of which Kakadu has many.

The tidal flats and estuaries are important breeding and feeding grounds for many of the park's animal and fish species. Pockets of monsoon rainforest are found on the coast and along the sheltered gorges of the Arnhem Land Escarpment.

PLANNING

The same walking season and equipment needs that apply to Litchfield National Park apply here (see Planning in the introduction to Litchfield National Park earlier).

Maps & Books

Kakadu National Park Visitor Guide is included in your entrance fee. Also free is *Bushwalking in Kakadu*, available from

continued on page 219

NORTHERN TERRITORY

Barrk Sandstone Bushwalk

Duration	4½–5 hours
Distance	12km
Standard	medium
Start/Finish	Nourlangie Rock car park
Nearest Town	Jabiru
Public Transport	no

Summary An excellent introduction to walking in Kakadu National Park, this route links two very important Aboriginal rock art sites via a challenging hike up and over Nourlangie Rock.

This spectacular walk links Anbangbang and Nanguluwur, two of the most important Aboriginal rock art sites in Kakadu. These sites offer a visual record of a constantly changing world and Dreaming stories, often depicted more literally here than elsewhere. Paintings show extinct animals (like thylacines, the Tasmanian tiger), seasonal food sources and the arrival of Indonesian and European sailors. Some paintings are contemporary, others 30,000 years old. Interestingly, marine animals are missing from the earlier art, a reflection of the fact that Kakadu was once inland. The identity of some of the animals depicted has still not been finally determined.

The trail is well marked with orange triangle markers. This is just as well as the route across the top of the rock is full of small gullies and rocky hillocks, descents, climbs and geological mazes that are impossible to

View east of the sandstone Nourlangie Rock (Burrunggui) from Nawurlandja Lookout, Kakadu National Park

RICHARD I'ANSON

show on the map. Start walking early in the morning and carry at least 3L of water per person. Ranger-led guided walks take place at Anbangbang (which has some wheelchair access) during the Dry.

When walking in the Nourlangie area, keep an eye out for black wallaroos (males are called barrks), which occur only in Kakadu and Arnhem Land. Also endemic to this region is the chestnut-quilled rock-pigeon. Frilled lizards are often seen during the build-up and the Wet parading on the access road.

GETTING TO/FROM THE WALK

The turning for Nourlangie Rock is 19km south of Bowali Visitor Centre off Kakadu Hwy. The 12km sealed access road (open from 7 am until sunset) begins 19km south of Jabiru. There's a car park and toilet close to the Anbangbang Galleries, at the start of the trail.

THE WALK

From the car park at the base of **Nourlangie Rock** (Burrunggui) follow the main trail past the Anbangbang Shelter to the **Anbangbang Main Gallery**. Two of Anbangbang's highlights are the depictions of Namarrgon, the 'Lightning Man', and Nabulwinjbulwinj, a dangerous spirit who eats females after striking them with a yam. Namarrgon wears his lightning as a band connecting his arms, legs and head, while the stone axes on his knees and elbows make the thunder.

Just past the Anbangbang Main Gallery the trail forks. Go right following orange triangle markers steeply north-east up to **Gunwarddehwarde Lookout**. Bear right off the pleasant little peak, before turning north-west down to a junction. Turn right (south-west), climb north-east up a gully then cut right between two large rocks to a cliff wall – a waterfall in the Wet. Turn right (south-west) and begin the steep rocky climb to a stunning lookout, reached about 45 minutes from the start.

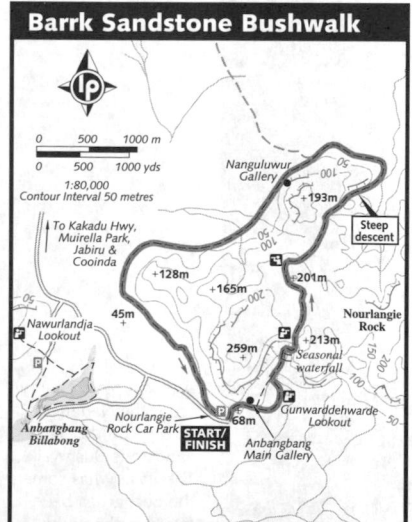

Head north across a flat wooded area encircled by huge boulders and cliffs. The path bends left, leading across a boulder-strewn saddle before heading west through a maze of sandstone pillars and boulders south of the highest point of the rock – keep your eye on the triangular markers. After passing a **lookout** with great views north across the huge expanse of forest, the trail continues north-east, descending then climbing before passing between two huge boulders and descending to a narrow gully. Turn left and head north to a flat wooded area hemmed in by rocky hillocks. The trail continues north of the hillside, bearing right across the eastern flank before passing between a large rock outcrop and a (seemingly) precariously balanced boulder onto a saddle.

Barrk Sandstone Bushwalk

0   500   1000 m
0   500   1000 yds
1:80,000
Contour Interval 50 metres

Nanguluwur Gallery

+193m

Steep descent

To Kakadu Hwy, Muirella Park, Jabiru & Cooinda

+128m   +165m   +201m

45m   Nourlangie Rock

Nawurlandja Lookout

259m   +213m

Seasonal waterfall

Anbangbang Billabong

Nourlangie Rock Car Park   68m   Gunwarddehwarde Lookout

START/FINISH

Anbangbang Main Gallery

The trail then cuts back north before traversing north-east below the summit cliffs to a long slab of rock. Descend east then turn left (north-east) and head through a flat wooded area to a large cliff face with caves at its base. Turn right (east) along the cliff face and follow the dry creek east then north-east down to the valley floor.

The trail heads north across flat land into open eucalyptus woodland, then slowly swings south-west past the end of a dirt track to a path T-junction. Take the left turn, leading to **Nanguluwur Gallery**, a long overhanging cliff which displays 30,000 years of Aboriginal rock art. Huge barramundi, once often caught in the East Alligator River, are displayed in X-ray style along with paintings of European ships. Stencilled hand prints (a form of artist signature) are also found here.

Continue south-west along the trail, which slowly curves west and after 30 minutes leads through a maze of boulders. Shortly afterwards the trail bears left (due south) then cuts up a spur of boulders. After a short climb descend into a rocky sort of valley with great views of the Nourlangie's cliffs.

Head south-east, crossing a stream 100m from the base of the cliffs, and after 10 minutes' walking through woodland the road becomes visible. Weave through big rocks close to the road to return to Nourlangie Rock car park.

RICHARD I'ANSON

An example of 'X-ray' art in the Nanguluwur Gallery, on the Barrk Sandstone Bushwalk. The gallery has some of the best art to be found in the park.

continued from page 215

Bowali Visitor Centre (see Information Sources). *Kakadu by Foot*, a useful guide to marked walking trails, is also available there and in Darwin. HEMA's up-to-date 1:390,000 *Kakadu National Park* map and Auslig's 1:250,000 *Kakadu* map are good for planning and are widely available.

The whole park is covered by MapsNT's 1:50,000 series. The *Nourlangie Creek* map covers the Barrk Sandstone Bushwalk, but the park notes are of more practical use. MapsNT sheets are available from the Bowali Visitor Centre.

Kakadu by Ian Morris gives an excellent background to the park, its wildlife, culture and people.

Information Sources

The excellent Bowali Visitor Centre (☎ 08-8938 1120), on the Kakadu Hwy, 2.5km south of the Arnhem Hwy, is open daily and has a cafe, gift shop, library and film screenings. There are park notes for all the marked trails plus information on permits for overnight treks. A walking track connects the visitor centre with Jabiru, 2km (30 minutes) away.

Warradjan Aboriginal Cultural Centre, also open daily, is a 15-minute walk from Cooinda resort, just off the Kakadu Hwy. It has good information on the area's traditional owners and a crafts shop.

Permits & Regulations

Park entrance, valid for 14 days, costs $15 per person. Pay at the park gate or purchase a permit from the Darwin Region Tourism Association (see Gateways earlier).

Permits are not required for day walks, although park notes and a chat with a ranger are often useful.

Overnight Walks When applying for a permit it's important to remember that Kakadu is Aboriginal land. The permit procedure takes account of the concerns of traditional owners (see the boxed text 'Bushwalking & Aboriginal Land' earlier in this chapter) by limiting numbers, banning solo walkers and the use of GPS receivers (to safeguard the location of the most important sites), and vetting every route and walker.

Contact the Permits Officer (☎ 08-8938 1100, fax 8938 1115), Kakadu National Park, PO Box 71, Jabiru, NT 0886, at Bowali Visitor Centre for a permit form, which should be returned with a copy of a topographical map showing your proposed route and camp sites. No clues as to routes will be given by parks staff, but a number of recognised, unmarked routes lie along dry gorges and creeks in the sandstone plateau country south-east of Jabiru.

It takes between one week and several months (for obscure routes) to process permits. June and July are the busiest times. Alternative routes are often worked out if there's a problem. Permits and bush camping are free.

Within 24 hours of finishing your walk, notify rangers on ☎ 08-8938 1179 (a dedicated line) and leave your name, date and permit number.

GETTING THERE & AWAY

Greyhound runs a bus service into the park, heading up to Ubirr (39km north of the Arnhem Hwy) in the Dry. Also in the Dry, Blue Banana services Jabiru, Ubirr, Nourlangie Rock, Cooinda and Gunlum.

GETTING AROUND

Access to marked walking trails is possible with a 2WD, but some overnight routes are not. Large cars are available from Thrifty Car Rentals (☎ 08-8979 2552, 0418 858 601 mobile) at Gagudju Crocodile Hotel in Jabiru (book in advance, around $100 per day), although it's cheaper to get a deal in Darwin (see Gateways earlier). All hire companies ban their 4WDs from the road to Jim Jim Falls.

> **Warning**
>
> Saltwater and freshwater crocodiles inhabit the park so be extremely cautious around water, especially in lowland areas. 'Salties' have killed a number of people in the Northern Territory.

NEAREST TOWN & FACILITIES
Jabiru
Jabiru, 260km from Darwin and 36km from Nourlangie Rock, on the Arnhem Hwy, is the service centre of Kakadu National Park. It has a post office and bank.

Places to Stay & Eat The *Kakadu Lodge & Caravan Park (☎ 08-8979 2422)* has good facilities and a bar serving meals from around $12. Camping costs $20 to $25 (two people). A dorm bed costs $30 and a six-bed cabin $190.

The *Gagudju Crocodile Hotel (☎ 1800 808 123)* was built in the shape of a 250m crocodile. It's a comfortable enough hotel, with a small swimming pool, bars and a good restaurant. Room prices start from $210 (plus tax) during the Dry and from $170 during the Wet.

There's a cracking *bakery* behind the Mobil service station in Leichhardt St. The *supermarket* (with Eftpos) is open seven days a week (no alcohol is sold).

Camping Grounds
Muirella Park Camp Site is 25km from Nourlangie Rock (head south down Kakadu Hwy) beside a large billabong. It has hot showers and costs $5 per person per night, payable on site (check Wet season access).

About 15.5km and 17.5km respectively south of Jabiru on the Kakadu Hwy are the *Burdulba* and *Malabanjbanjdju* free camp sites. They are basic, but have toilets.

Nitmiluk (Katherine Gorge) National Park

Originally called Katherine Gorge National Park, the area was renamed Nitmiluk. (meaning 'Cicada Place') in 1989 when the Jawoyn Aboriginal people gained title to the land. They now jointly manage the area with the PWC.

Nitmiluk is a popular and accessible park, with the 13 sandstone sections of Katherine Gorge and Leliyn (Edith Falls) the area's main attractions. A series of walks, some overnight, lead to various points along Katherine Gorge, which can also be explored by hiring a canoe, and there are a series of walking tracks around Leliyn. However, there's much more to this 2920 sq km park than these small corners. Still culturally active in the park, numerous Jawoyn art sites remain, some over 7000 years old.

In August 1999 a bushfire that started in the north of the park burned for over two months, sweeping across the park and resisting all measures to control it.

NATURAL HISTORY
A variety of habitats are represented in the park. You'll see noisy flocks of spectacular red-tailed black-cockatoos and little corellas in the dry open woodland. This dominant vegetation is also home to agile wallabies and euros. Gould's goannas and tiny fire-tailed skinks are the most commonly seen reptiles. Groups of red-backed fairy-wrens and red-winged parrots are found in lusher woodland close to the escarpment. Great bowerbirds and blue-winged kookaburras are common around the main camp sites.

The high sandstone ridges are covered in spinifex and drought-resistant shrubs such as grevilleas and various acacias. Remnant pockets of lush monsoon rainforest grow in sheltered gorges, providing habitats for fruit-eating flying foxes.

Paper-barks and river pandanus fringe the rivers and areas prone to flooding, while beautiful large mauve and tiny yellow water lilies grow in sheltered water. You may see timid freshwater crocodiles and Mertens' water monitors sunning themselves beside the larger pools.

Feral donkeys, cattle and water buffalo are sometimes seen grazing in the meadows, but keep your distance – they may charge if startled.

PLANNING
When to Walk
May (when there's plenty of water around) through to early September is the best time

for walking. It's dry, with temperatures between around 10°C overnight and 27°C during the day. The peak visitor months are June and July. From October to December it gets steadily hotter (up to 45°C) and more humid, with torrential storms a constant threat; the flies at this time can be maddening. The Wet starts in December and lasts until April. The trail may close for periods between October and April due to flooding.

What to Bring
Lightweight boots will do here and a swimming costume is essential. Sleeping under a mosquito net is ideal in the Dry, when you'll need a sleeping bag. Insect repellent is standard issue at all times, and after October a tent and waterproofs are required.

Maps & Books
PWC's pocket-sized *Jawoyn Plant Identikit* gives a fascinating insight into common plant use and is well worth carrying.

MapsNT's 1:50,000 *Nitmiluk National Park* map (widely available locally) displays the whole trail and it's all you should need. However, also carry MapsNT's 1:50,000 *Katherine*, *Seventeen Mile* and *Edith River* maps as a precaution.

Information Sources
The Nitmiluk Visitor Centre (☎ 08-8972 1886, fax 8971 0702), the park headquarters 30km north-east of Katherine, has excellent displays on Jawoyn culture and the park's natural history. It's open daily. From May to September rangers hold evening talks and slide shows. You can organise overnight canoeing trips and gorge cruises here.

Permits & Regulations
The Jatbula Trail can only be walked one way, from Katherine Gorge to Leliyn. However, overnight walks from Leliyn up to Sweetwater Pool are permitted. Camping permits are $3 per person per night, and are only available at Nitmiluk Visitor Centre and are subject to availability, so apply well in advance. A $50 cash deposit (per party) is required, which is redeemable at Edith Falls Kiosk at the trail's end.

Checkpoints are dotted along the trail. Write your permit number, time of arrival and destination in each one. Use ECDs in an emergency only. Rangers actively discourage lone walkers and will not permit you to start the Jatbula Trail after about 1 pm.

Permits aren't required for day walks, but are required for two-day walks, along with a $20 deposit. Edith Falls Kiosk (☎ 08-8975 4869) issues camping permits for overnight walks to Sweetwater Pool.

NEAREST TOWN & FACILITIES
Katherine
Katherine is not the most stimulating of towns, but it is good for a quick resupply, a function it has been fulfilling successfully since a station of the Overland Telegraph Line was built here in the late 1800s.

The Katherine Region Tourist Association (☎ 08-8972 2650, ❻ krta@nt-teck.com.au) is on the corner of Stuart Hwy and Lindsay St, diagonally opposite the 24-hour BP petrol station and Transit Centre. The regional PWC office (☎ 08-8973 8888) is at 1920 Giles St.

Outback Disposals, on the corner of Katherine Terrace and Murphy St, has a good range of camping and backpacking gear.

If you're stuck in Katherine for a day, venture south along the river to the hot springs (a 30-minute walk).

Places to Stay & Eat The best choice is the family-run *Kookaburra Backpackers* (☎ 08-8971 0257, 1800 808 211, ❻ *kooka burra@nt-tech.com.au*), on the corner of Lindsay and Third Sts. Air-con twins are $45 and dorm beds $17. There is a laundry, swimming pool and parking.

The low-key *Victoria Lodge (☎ 1800 808 875, 21 Victoria Hwy)* is a good alternative. Dorm beds cost $14 per person, singles $35 and doubles $45.

For a cheap feed, venture into *Bucking Bills Burger Bar*, on Katherine Terrace (generous portions for $5).

Mekhong Thai Café & Takeaway, on the corner of Katherine Terrace and Murphy St, is a taste oasis in a swathe of greasy takeaways. For self-caterers, the *Woolworths* supermarket is open daily.

Getting There & Away From Katherine, Greyhound and McCafferty's have daily bus services to/from Alice Springs and Darwin. Greyhound also has direct daily services to WA, and the Blue Banana runs down from Kakadu and up to Litchfield (see Getting Around in the introduction to the chapter).

Nitmiluk National Park

At Katherine Gorge the well-appointed *Nitmiluk Tours Caravan Park* (☎ 08-8972 3150, 1800 089 103, @ info@travelnorth .com.au) has shady pitches from $7 per person. Food is available at the Nitmiluk Visitor Centre's *Nitmiluk Restaurant and Café* (excellent steak sandwiches cost $6.90).

A site at *Edith Falls Camp Site* costs $5 per person (pay at the kiosk). There are barbecues, a phone, a washing machine and showers. Snacks and basic food supplies can be bought at the *Edith Falls Kiosk*.

Jatbula Trail

Duration	4 days
Distance	66km
Standard	medium
Start	Nitmiluk Visitor Centre, Katherine Gorge
Finish	Leliyn (Edith Falls)
Nearest Town	Katherine
Public Transport	yes

Summary A well-marked trail leading through woodland along the Arnhem Land Escarpment in the heart of Jalowyn country. Attractions include rock art, tremendous waterfalls and perfectly positioned camp sites.

The Jatbula Trail links Katherine Gorge and Leliyn via a 66km trail along the edge of the Arnhem Land Escarpment, far from the madding crowd, passing spectacular scenery, waterfalls, clear isolated swimming holes, Aboriginal art sites and all manner of habitats. The walk can be completed comfortably in four days, but extra days are worth budgeting for – the camp sites en route have tremendous locations.

GETTING TO/FROM THE WALK

Travel North (☎ 08-8972 1044, @ info @travelnorth.com.au) runs five buses a day, in either direction, over the 30km between the Katherine Transit Centre and Nitmiluk Visitor Centre ($9 one way, $16 return).

Things are more difficult from Leliyn, which is 20km from the Stuart Hwy and 60km north of Katherine. However, the Blue Banana bus will transfer walkers between Leliyn and Katherine Gorge via Katherine for $20. During the Dry it leaves Leliyn at 3.30 pm Friday, Saturday, Monday and Tuesday. Book in advance.

THE WALK
Day 1: Nitmiluk Visitor Centre to Crystal Falls

5½–6½ hours, 23.5km

From the petrol station follow the sealed road east past the Youth Group Area then turn right onto **Jatbula Trail**, following the blue triangle markers down to **Katherine River**. Head upstream to a footbridge. Follow the 4WD track up the bank and then bear right onto a footpath leading north-east a short distance before turning north and arriving back on the 4WD track beside a river crossing in 30 minutes.

Cross to the east bank and follow the 4WD track through the open woodland of Seventeen Mile Valley to the right turn for Northern Rockhole, a spectacular seasonal waterfall 10 minutes away. Keep on the track as it climbs steadily up towards the escarpment, cutting east round a hill strewn with boulders and north over a pronounced gully. About 2¼ hours after setting out, and after passing the camp toilets, **Biddlecombe Cascades** is reached. Just 100m before the falls is the ECD and *camp site* (with barbecues), a good first-night stop if you've left in the late morning.

Crystal Falls, the next definite water stop, is 12km away. From Biddlecombe Cascades move north-west along a trail leading upstream across some boggy ground to a boardwalk that leads across the creek – if there's been any rain you will probably have to wade.

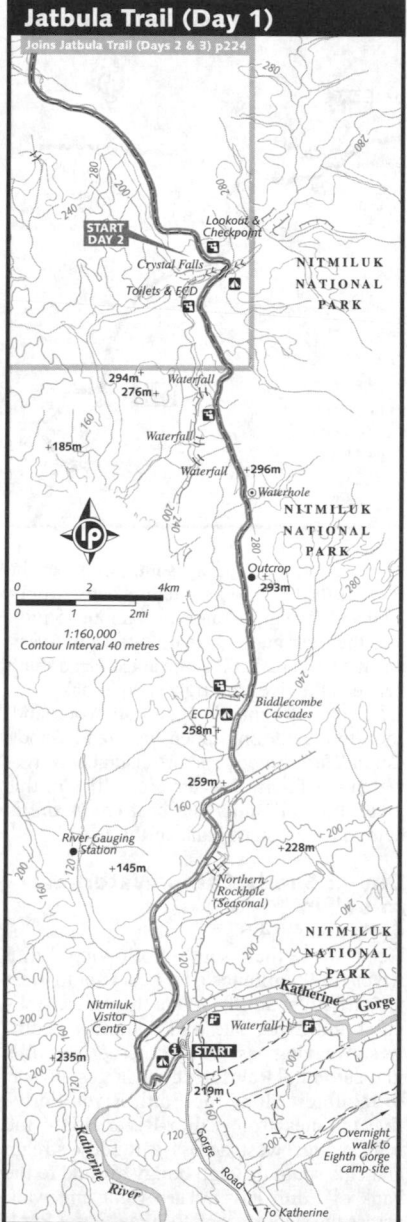

Jatbula Trail (Day 1)

Joins Jatbula Trail (Days 2 & 3) p224

START DAY 2

Crystal Falls
Toilets & ECD

NITMILUK NATIONAL PARK

Lookout & Checkpoint

294m
276m+
Waterfall

+185m
Waterfall

Waterfall
Waterhole
+296m

NITMILUK NATIONAL PARK

Outcrop
293m

0   2   4km
0   1   2mi
1:160,000
Contour Interval 40 metres

Biddlecombe Cascades
ECD
258m+

259m+

River Gauging Station
+145m

+228m

Northern Rockhole (Seasonal)

NITMILUK NATIONAL PARK

Katherine Gorge

Nitmiluk Visitor Centre

Waterfall

START

+235m

219m

Overnight walk to Eighth Gorge camp site

Katherine River

Gorge Road

To Katherine

The trail now moves north climbing gradually across open, flat ground punctuated by piles of round boulders. After 45 minutes a corridor of rock is reached, and there are a few rocky sections to climb over as the trail follows a series of small creeks north, past a number of seasonal waterholes to an impressive rock outcrop.

Twisting and turning, the trail works its way over a series of gullies and hillocks and then drops down to cross a stream. Before the crossing, a sign points right to a beautiful waterhole 100m away. Ford the stream and continue heading north-west. In 30 minutes a faint path leads (left) to a **lookout**, after which the trail cuts north-east across a couple of small, dry creeks until it descends north-west to a permanent stream. Follow it downstream for a short while before crossing and heading north-west uphill to a lookout, toilet and ECD. Fifteen minutes farther on is **Crystal Falls** and a shady *camp site* (with barbecue) beside an excellent swimming hole.

Day 2: Crystal Falls to Seventeen Mile Falls
2½–3 hours, 11.5km

Cross the river downstream from the camp site and follow the trail up to a lookout and checkpoint above the 30m Crystal Falls. The trail climbs north then north-west to the summit plateau, before gradually bending west for the next hour through a series a shallow valleys, meadows and tall woodland. A sign eventually points left down to the **Amphitheatre**. This wonderful curving rock art site is perched above a reliable stream and a remnant of monsoon rainforest sheltering huge numbers of birds and the occasional euro.

Seventeen Mile Falls is 3.5km away. From the Amphitheatre, the Jatbula Trail joins a rough 4WD track that heads west along, and then across, a creek. Five minutes later the trail bears off left to a fantastic view point overlooking **Seventeen Mile Falls**. Continue north to Seventeen Mile Creek then head downstream to the falls. Cross to the true right bank and climb up to the *camp site* (with an ECD but no other facilities).

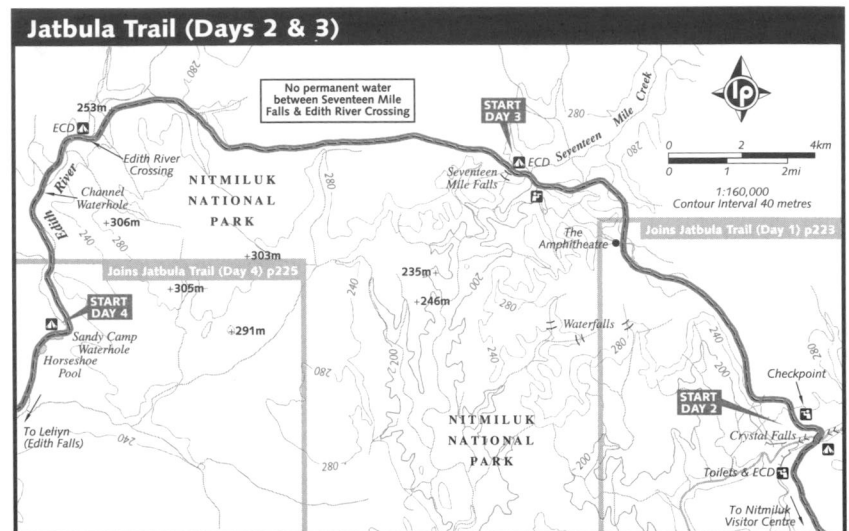

Jatbula Trail (Days 2 & 3)

Day 3: Seventeen Mile Falls to Sandy Camp Pool

5½–6 hours, 16.5km

The next 11km section to Edith River Crossing has no permanent water sources, so stock up at Seventeen Mile Falls.

After initial bursts of heading west then north, the trail heads west across gently sloping valleys and through patches of dense woodland. After about 90 minutes the top of the climb is reached and a descent into more rocky country begins, the trail making a sharp right turn (north-west) down among the tributaries of **Edith River**. With the presence of water the vegetation becomes lush and spear grass and spiral pandanus become common, while bird life is more evident. Upon reaching a sandy seasonal creek, head south (downstream) to the rocky open area that's **Edith River Crossing**. Stepping stones lead across Edith River to a checkpoint and ECD. The *camp site* is nothing special, so it's better to continue to Sandy Camp, 5.5km to the south.

Follow the trusty blue triangles along the river bank for 200m and then up and over a series of rocky slopes to **Channel Waterhole**, a deep narrow pool cut through the sand-stone. Continue roughly south, close to the river, as the trail moves into low dense woodland and then grassland. After about 45 minutes the river makes a sharp turn right (west) and the trail crosses it at the apex. Head south between the river (on right) and a rocky outcrop (on left) into lush, dense woodland, soon to emerge into open grassland. **Sandy Camp Waterhole** is a short distance away – watch out for freshwater crocodiles in this great, tranquil spot. The best *camp site* is behind the western bank of the pool.

Day 4: Sandy Camp Waterhole to Leliyn

4–4½ hours, 14.5km

Head west, then south, following Edith River for 90 minutes as it bears south-west to **Edith River South**, where there's a checkpoint and ECD. The trail continues south-west, weaving past rocky outcrops and hills into **Lerombol Rainforest**, the largest pocket of rainforest along the Edith River. Forty-five minutes from Edith River South the trail swings west across a muddy stream and cuts south through boggy ground to the bank of Edith River. Turn right and walk across the slabs of rock to **Sweetwater Pool**.

Top Left: The Shoalhaven River near Louise Reach, Shoalhaven River Valley, NSW. **Top Right:** The narrow entrance to Bungonia Gorge, Bungonia State Recreation Area, NSW. **Middle:** View across Dorrigo NP towards the Bellingen River Valley, NSW. **Bottom Left:** Belougery Spire, Warrumbungle NP, NSW. **Bottom Right:** Afternoon sun lights up the Dows High Tops, Warrumbungle NP, NSW.

MATTHEW FLETCHER

MATTHEW FLETCHER

MATTHEW FLETCHER

RICHARD I'ANSON

Top: The rugged expanse of Gastrolobium Saddle on the Larapinta Trail, West MacDonnell National Park, NT. **Middle Left:** Walking through woodland regenerating after bushfire, Nitmiluk National Park, NT. **Middle Right:** Light and shade above Ormiston Creek in West MacDonnell National Park. **Bottom:** Nourlangie and the lush habitat of Anbangbang Billabong, Kakadu National Park, NT.

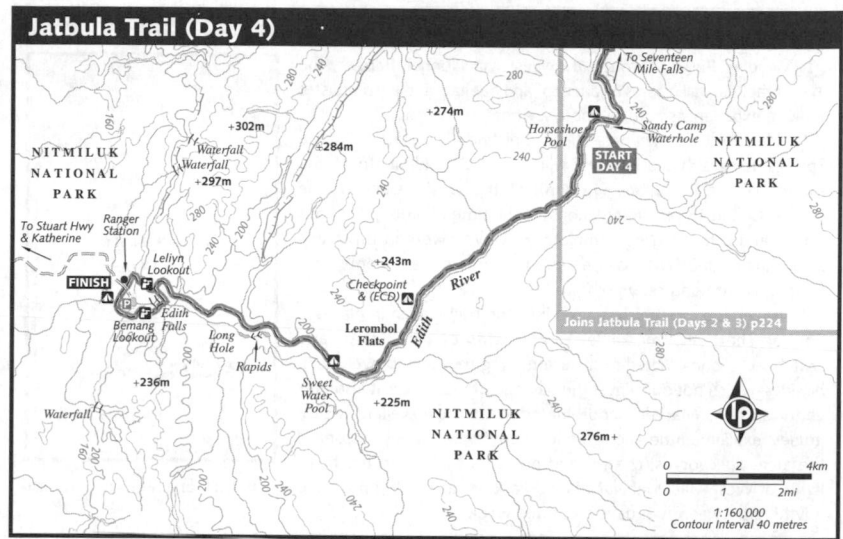

Jatbula Trail (Day 4)

If you're lucky you may see the resident freshies in the beautiful, wide pool. The water channels through the top end are quite spectacular and at the southern end is a great *camp site*. There are barbecues and a toilet. Although Leliyn is only 4.3km away, it's well worth spending an extra night here.

The well-defined trail leads along the river reaching **Long Hole**, another good swimming spot, in 30 minutes. It then continues downstream for another 15 minutes (avoid the service trail on the right) before turning right to begin a short, sharp climb away from the river. Turn sharply left (west) at the top and ride out the now zigzagging trail to a rocky saddle and T-junction with a wide, easy tourist trail. Turn right for an unexceptional 630m descent to the car park or left onto the Leliyn Trail leading to **Leliyn Lookout** (down a little 20m side track), down through **Upper Pool** (you can swim here) and up to **Bemang Lookout**, which gives great views of the whole, dramatic Leliyn area – the *camp site* is 1km from here.

The large pool at the base of Leliyn (Edith Falls) is great for swimming, but closed between 7 pm and 7 am, so you can't enjoy late-night skinny dipping.

West MacDonnell National Park

This wonderful park stretches west from Alice Springs for more than 160km along the MacDonnell Ranges, enclosing 1333 sq km of varied, arid habitats. The mountains, with their jagged cliffs and high, sparsely covered ridges, provide a rugged and dramatic backdrop, and the ecosystems of the arid valley floor, sheltered gorges and permanent waterholes contain all manner of fascinating wildlife. Although tourism is concentrated at 10 small areas, the Larapinta Trail (see the boxed text later) takes you into the heart of the West MacDonnell Ranges.

NATURAL HISTORY

The colourful landscape of the West MacDonnell Ranges was formed 350 million years ago when massive earth movements created a mountain range of quartzite several kilometres high. Mt Zeil (1531m), in the far north-west of the park, remains the highest point in the NT. Extensive erosion has since exposed ancient metamorphic rock two billion years old.

Larapinta Trail

Winding 220km through the West MacDonnell Ranges, the Larapinta Trail crosses a variety of arid habitats and encompasses walking experiences hard to find elsewhere in Australia.

Divided into 13 sections, the unfinished trail starts at Alice Springs Telegraph Station and will eventually culminate at the summit of Mt Razorback (1254m), at the western end of the ranges. Of the 13 planned sections, at the time of writing Sections 1 to 4 and 8 to 12 were complete. However, work in this harsh environment, mostly by conservation volunteers (and some prisoners!), is hard and slow going.

Considerable thought has gone into the trail, which in places is nothing short of remarkable. Huge flights of rocky steps and switchbacks, constructed from surrounding rock, climb over steep hillsides, which not only eases the passage of walkers, but also prevents erosion. Markers, coordinated with the excellent visitor guides, explain a little about the local environment and history of the area. The gorges, chasms and pools that make up the highlights of West MacDonnell National Park act as staging posts along the trail, enabling treks to last anything between two days and three weeks.

NORTHERN TERRITORY

Darwin

Mt Zeil (1510m) Alice Springs

With permanent water and diverse flora and fauna, the area has supported the Western Arrernte Aboriginal people for thousands of years. The tribe maintains a strong link with the park (rituals and ceremonies are still performed here) and the waterhole at Ormiston Gorge (or Kwartetwenne) is just one of many sacred sites. These permanent water sources support a rich diversity of life, including birds such as darters and Australasian grebes, as well as up to nine species of fish, stranded until the river floods maybe once a year.

Damp gorges dotted throughout the range shelter moisture-loving plants such as the MacDonnell Ranges cycad, a relic of wetter days 22 million years ago. Along the creeks, lined with river red gums, you may see rainbow bee-eaters and colourful ringneck parrots.

Spinifex covers much of the park's flatter areas (as well as many of the ridges), of which Ormiston Pound is of particular interest. Through this habitat flows Ormiston Creek, a tributary to the 100 million-year-old Finke River, which flows south into the Simpson Desert and is one of the oldest rivers in the world. The hardy spinifex grass in this marvellous natural enclosure provides food and shelter for numerous insects and animals, including euros (more properly called common wallaroos), tiny stripe-faced dunnarts and spinifex hopping-mice. Budgerigars, zebra finches and spinifex pigeons feast on the abundant seeds, and rufous-crowned emu-wrens shelter in the pointed grass. Lizards thrive here; you are likely to see military and bearded dragons and possibly perenties, which can grow up to 3m long.

Whistling kites and little woodswallows soar above the red quartzite ridges, which are covered with various eucalyptuses, white cypress pines and spinifex. On lower slopes, in dry, open woodland you may see the bower, often littered with bright objects, where the male western bowerbird dances about to impress the ladies.

The park has 23 species of native mammals; many are nocturnal and several are rare or endangered. You'll probably see black-footed rock-wallabies on the rocky slopes at Simpsons Gap, Standley Chasm, Ormiston Gorge and Redbank.

PLANNING
When to Walk
The ideal time to walk is between April and September when maximum daily temperatures hover around 20°C, although you should walk before 11 am and after 3.30 pm at either end of this period. It get incredibly hot (40°C-plus) between October and March. June and July are the coldest months (-10°C has been recorded), although nights are cold even in summer. Statistics will tell you that most rainfall occurs in the summer, but in reality rainfall is low, nonseasonal and unreliable. The ecosystem is rain-driven: it doesn't matter if it's spring, if it hasn't rained there won't be water in the creeks.

What to Bring
Definitely bring walking companions – solo walking isn't recommended. The terrain is rocky, so sturdy boots will save your feet. The quartzite rock is reflective, so slap on sunscreen, even under your chin. In winter bring warm clothes and a sleeping bag comfortable below 0°C – you'll need a fleece jacket year-round. A swimming costume for a dip in the opaque swimming hole near the visitor centre is a great idea (remember, don't pollute the water with sunscreen or soap).

Maps & Books
The PWC has produced an excellent set of trail guides for the Larapinta Trail. Leaflets 2 and 3 cover Simpsons Gap to Standley Chasm, and leaflets 9 and 10 cover Ormiston Gorge. They are available from Catia in Alice Springs (see Buying Maps under Information in the introduction to the chapter), some bookshops and all PWC offices.

The ranges from Alice Springs to Standley Chasm are covered by MapsNT's 1:50,000 *Alice Springs*, *Simpsons Gap* and *Brinkley* topographic maps (laid over aerial photographs). The 1:50,000 coverage does not stretch to Ormiston Gorge, although Ormiston Pound and Mt Giles are covered by an accurate sketch map produced (along with some notes) by park rangers.

MapsNT's 1:250,000 *West MacDonnell National Park* map covers the park and includes blow-ups of the main tourist areas.

Information Sources
There are visitor centres at Ormiston Gorge (☎ 08-8956 7799) and Simpsons Gap (☎ 08-8955 0310), both open daily. Walks can be registered here. The rangers give evening talks and slide shows between May and October. A number of water tanks have been installed in the park, but check with the rangers on their levels, plus the levels of the numerous waterholes and springs.

Permits & Regulations
No permits are required, but fuel stoves are encouraged and fires may be banned between October and April. There are free, basic camp sites throughout the park, but camping is not permitted at Fish Hole, Spring Gap and Bond Gap.

NEAREST TOWN & FACILITIES
For information on accommodation, eateries and other services in Alice Springs, see Gateways in the introduction to this chapter.

Ormiston Gorge
Close to Ormiston Gorge, *Glen Helen Resort* (☎ 08-8956 7489, ☻ glenhelen@melanka .com.au) has a mix of budget ($16 per person or $8 camping) and motel accommodation ($58 per person). There's a bar and restaurant, and fuel is available.

Camping at Ormiston Gorge costs $5 per person (there's an honesty box). The site has free barbecues and hot showers.

Standley Chasm
At Standley Chasm (☎ 08-8956 7440, fax 8956 7325, ☻ standleychasm@bigpond.com .au) there's a *restaurant*, shop and phone, and *camping* is possible but strictly by prior arrangement ($4 per person).

> ### Warnings
> - Heat stroke can be fatal so avoid walking between 10 am and 4 pm in hot weather.
> - Keep all clothing (including boots) and food secure at night, so as not to attract dingoes.
> - Don't camp in creek beds if it's raining, as they can flood suddenly.

GETTING TO/FROM THE WALKS

Vehicle access is from Larapinta Drive, which starts just outside Alice Springs. However, Simpsons Gap (22km from Alice) is only open between 5 am and 8 pm daily, and the gates to Standley Chasm (53km from Alice) are only open from 8 am to 6 pm. Ormiston Gorge (144km from Alice) is always accessible.

A car is very useful for day walks, but the Larapinta Trail is linear, which makes logistics tricky. Numerous companies run tours along the range, visiting some of the trailheads.

Trek Larapinta (see Guided Tours earlier in the chapter) runs transfers when not busy and is the best option: Simpsons Gap $55, Standley Chasm $80, Ormiston Gorge $170. Prices are per vehicle (with a maximum of seven people).

The Alice Wanderer (☎ 1800 669 111, ✉ alicwand@ozemail.com.au) is among the cheapest, but you'll have to pay for a full tour in each direction.

Hitching is an option (easier heading back to Alice), while an Alice Springs Taxi (☎ 13 1008) to Simpsons Gap costs $35.

The walk described is easily completed in one day, but you can overnight at Bowmans Gap, a short detour off the marked Pound Walk. Set off early and carry a full day's supply of water.

THE WALK

From the visitor centre walk south-east down the road, crossing Ormiston Creek after five minutes, following signs for the Pound Walk (marked by blue triangles). Head 20m downstream before turning left, off the Larapinta Trail, and heading uphill thorough a network of gullies and over small hillocks to a saddle, the gateway to Ormiston Pound, reached in 45 minutes. There's a fantastic **view point** on the ridge to the north.

Descend east, bearing right (south) behind and round the pronounced hill east of the saddle and then turn north down into the Pound. After 20 minutes walking through spinifex and scrub **Ormiston Creek** is reached. It's usually dry, but semipermanent waterholes can occur after heavy rains. Turn right off the Pound Walk and head upstream (north-east) along the river bed, avoiding the tributary on the right. The river soon swings

Ormiston Gorge & Pound

Duration	4½–5 hours
Distance	18km
Standard	easy-medium
Start/Finish	Ormiston Gorge Visitor Centre
Nearest Town	Alice Springs
Public Transport	no

Summary A beautiful walk through the spinifex-covered Ormiston Pound to a series of gorges and waterholes, returning via Ormiston Gorge. Overnight camping among stunning scenery.

Ormiston Gorge is one of the main attractions in West MacDonnell National Park. There's a large waterhole suitable for swimming, it's a dramatic (short) walk into the gorge and facilities are good. However, day visitors rarely wander into the arid Ormiston Pound east of the gorge, where a fascinating landscape awaits.

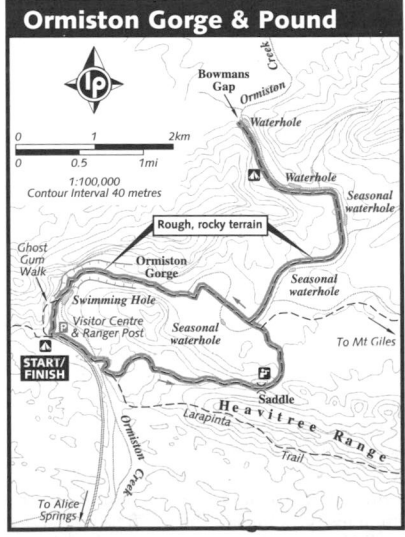

Ormiston Gorge & Pound

Bowmans Gap
Ormiston Creek
Waterhole
Waterhole
Seasonal waterhole
Rough, rocky terrain
Ghost Gum Walk
Ormiston Gorge
Seasonal waterhole
Swimming Hole
Visitor Centre & Ranger Post
Seasonal waterhole
To Mt Giles
START/FINISH
Saddle
Larapinta
Heavitree Range
Trail
Ormiston Creek
To Alice Springs
0 1 2km
0 0.5 1mi
1:100,000
Contour Interval 40 metres

Driven to Extinction

Central Australia has lost 40% of its indigenous mammals in the last 200 years. There are many reasons for this, but mostly it boils down to changes in land use brought about by European colonisation. Small, furry mammals weighing around 1.5kg are the most vulnerable, their larger and smaller cousins being more adaptable to environmental change. Rearing livestock has had a tremendous effect on the arid red Centre, especially in times of drought when grazing is intensely focused around remaining waterholes. Small mammals are thus forced out of these crucial habitats of last resort and into early graves.

In addition, insatiable European rabbits are capable of reproducing far faster than native mammals such as the rare bilby or rabbit-bandicoot, and out-compete native mammals by sheer numbers. Rabbit populations may crash during a good long drought, but instead of being good news for our more adaptable furry friends, this means increased predation by (introduced) foxes and feral cats. In addition, before European colonisation Aboriginal people had long used fire to manage the land. Once Aboriginal people were forced off their land, the burning regime ended, the diversity of habitat reduced and small mammals suffered.

However, it is not all doom and gloom. At Ormiston Gorge in the NT a population of central rock rats, previously thought extinct in Central Australia, was found during a pest control program, while the insectivorous long-tailed dunnart, also thought to be extinct in the area, was rediscovered in 1993 during the construction of the Larapinta Trail. Within a month another was trapped, and although none have been found since, conservationists remain hopeful that it and other populations of lost species survive in remote areas.

east, then north and then west, shortly after which the most extensive and most populated (by wildlife) of the **waterholes** is reached; if you plan on camping, make sure you pitch your tent at least 100m away.

Cross to the river's eastern bank and continue upstream as the gorge walls, like red-brown Lego blocks, rise up on either side. Pines, river red gums and Sturt's desert roses all grow here. In 30 minutes you'll reach a fence and a waterhole; time to turn back.

Retrace your steps to the Pound Walk track (reached in 90 minutes), turn right and follow the path over a large meander and then along the creek's northern bank into **Ormiston Gorge**. After 40 minutes the river swings left to the swimming hole. The visitor centre is five minutes south. Alternatively, go via the **Ghost Gum Walk** (on the right, west) which leads up to a view point on the cliffs.

Larapinta Trail Highlight

Duration	3 days
Distance	37.4km
Standard	medium
Start	Simpsons Gap
Finish	Standley Chasm
Nearest Town	Alice Springs
Public Transport	no

Summary In the heart of the West MacDonnell Ranges this excellent section of the Larapinta Trail crosses a variety of arid habitats; it includes high ridge walking and an adventurous gorge descent.

Sections 2 and 3 of the Larapinta Trail, from Simpsons Gap to Standley Chasm, contain some of the best walking in the West MacDonnell Ranges. Waterholes, springs, gorges, high ridges and chasms are all covered on this three- to four-day walk. It's magical country.

Half the logistical problems relating to transport for the walk can be overcome simply by starting from Alice Springs Telegraph Station (2km north of town), the trail's very beginning. This adds an easy 29km (camp at Wallaby Gap), with Day 2 from Wallaby Gap to Mulga Camp, thus reducing the overall total to four days.

The tricky climb up to the high ridge on the second day can be bypassed, as can the 'Creek Bed Challenge' in Standley Chasm, which requires a few climbing moves and some pack hauling.

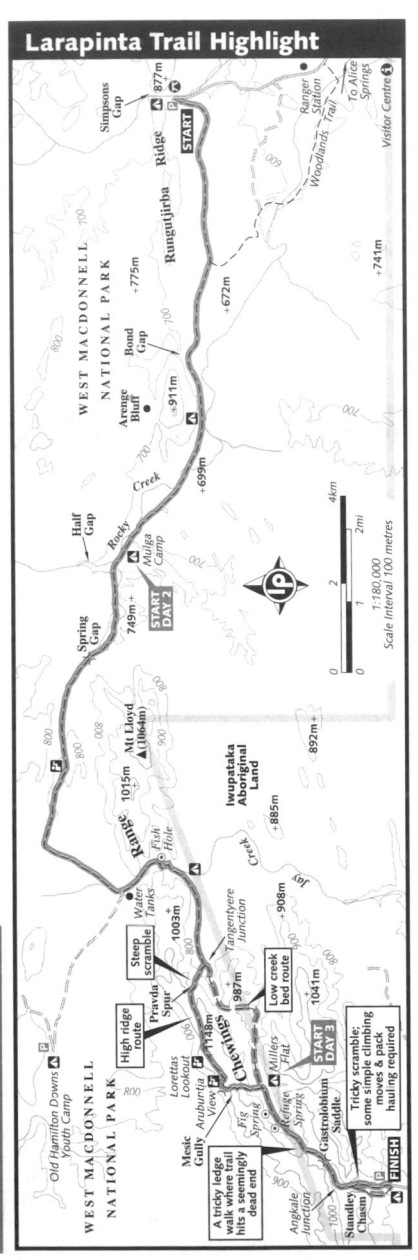

Larapinta Trail Highlight

THE WALK
Day 1: Simpsons Gap to Mulga Camp

3½–4 hours, 13.3km

From just south of the toilet block (with cold showers) at Simpsons Gap, head east past an information display, gas barbecues and the *walkers' camp site* (free), following the trail, marked by blue triangles, as it heads south then west parallel to an impressive bluff and ridgeline. After 90 minutes' walking through scrub and grassland you reach the junction with the Woodland Trail, which originates close to the Ranger Station 7.5km away (handy if you've walked from the road).

The trail now climbs a rocky hillock before continuing west past **Bond Gap** (whose tall walls shield a dependable waterhole) and below the mighty **Arenge Bluff** – look out for brushtail possums – to Arenge View, where the trail drops down to the wide Rocky Creek. Red river gums and tea-trees provide a shady *camp site*.

Heading into mulga woodland the trail follows Rocky Creek upstream (south-west) for another hour or so until a fine stand of mulga trees on an alluvial flat marks *Mulga Camp*. There's a toilet, barbecue (wood supplied), picnic bench and water tank. Shortly after heavy rains water may be available at **Half Gap**, 1km north-west.

Day 2: Mulga Camp to Millers Flat

6–6½ hours, 19.1km

From the camp the trail quickly climbs north-west into a range of small hills, with a large bluff to the right and Mt Lloyd (1064m) away to the west, reaching **Spring Gap** about an hour out of camp. There is semipermanent water here, but you'll need to purify it.

Stay on the right through Spring Gap and keep an eye out (to your right) for the blue triangles that lead over some low cliffs and up a ridge that forms a fork in the creek. After 10 minutes of climbing north-west the trail reaches the top of the ridge and swings west, running parallel to the main MacDonnell Range, but now on the northern side. About an hour from Spring Gap there are excellent views west of the ragged Chewings Range.

The path soon leaves the ridge, descending steeply across several seasonal streams and out onto the valley floor. Jay Creek is reached after another 30 minutes of westwards travel. There are water tanks here, but check the levels with rangers in advance.

Turn left (south) at the water tanks and walk down the creek bed to **Fish Hole**, which completely blocks the gorge. A path up a gully on the right just before the waterhole leads round to a sandy beach on the southern side.

The gorge and Fish Hole are of special spiritual significance to the Western Arrernte people, who believe that ancestors from the Dreamtime found passage through the ridge here. The waterhole and gorge are thus sacred and the custodians ask that you respect their law by only walking on the creek bed. Bird life is abundant. You can *camp* here, but do so at least 100m downstream.

Walk downstream on the true right bank for 300m then turn right walking up the hillside on a winding path through mulga woodland, interspersed with ghost gums and bloodwood thickets, to Tangentyere Junction. Here you have two choices: right along the High Route (a steep 300m scramble north-west to the ridgeline) or left (west) along the Low Route (a gentler route that rises to a saddle before following a creek bed upstream to Millers Flat). The views are worth the climb, first from the top of Pravda Spur (reached after 40 minutes) and then from **Lorettas Lookout** (among callitris, or cypress pine) at the very top (1148m).

Soon after, the trail descends south-west to **Arubuntja View** where it swings south behind the lookout before dropping to a narrow col, the start of Mesic Gully. From this wonderful vantage point Millers Flat, a fantastic *camp site* cradled by the surrounding hills, is 45 minutes away at the bottom of the gully, but the route is very steep and treacherous when water is flowing over the waterfalls. MacDonnell Ranges cycads thrive in the moisture of the gully and it's well worth exploring. From Millers Flat the reliable Fig and Refuge Springs are 40 minutes south-west.

Day 3: Millers Flat to Standley Chasm
2½ hours, 5km

Head south-west following the creek bed as it winds up the valley past the rocky outcrops seen from the camp site. After 25 minutes the trail emerges from the narrow creek bed into a wide shallow area encircled by dramatic cliffs. A track on the right (easily missed) leads south-west, cutting a corner, before dropping back to the overgrown, rocky creek bed and up past **Fig and Refuge Springs** to what seems like a dead end. With low, eroded cliffs ahead of you walk up to the end wall, turn right and climb a short distance, then cut left along a 3m-long ledge to a gap in the wall. Emerging into a wide valley continue west following the trail as it bears up right between two small pointy hills to **Gastrolobium Saddle** – growing here is *Gastrolobium brevipes*, an attractive but poisonous member of the poison pea family with pretty red-and-yellow flowers. The saddle marks the watershed between Cycad (east) and Angkale (west) Creeks.

Descend south-west on a series of steep rocky staircases, then head west to Angkale Junction. Turn left (south) down Angkale Creek and bear right where the trail climbs above the creekbed for a steep 1.5km (40-minute) detour around **Standley Chasm**.

Alternatively, for the Creekbed Challenge continue scrambling down through Standley Chasm until reaching a jumble of boulders and a 3.5m drop where the chasm is at its narrowest. This is where basic climbing skills are required. Squeeze through the hole on the right (without a pack) then work your way across to a narrow, smooth ledge on the left of the chasm. The creek bed is a gentle slide away, but packs must be ferried through the gap first. Five minutes later there is a 2m drop. The climb is simple and there's a dead tree to scoot down. The rest is easy walking down through the twisting, turning chasm. Look out for river red gums, cycads and black-footed rock-wallabies. Camping at Standley Chasm is by prior arrangement (see Nearest Town & Facilities earlier).

Other Walks

LITCHFIELD NATIONAL PARK
To The Lost City

From Tolmer Falls in Litchfield National Park an informal route leads upstream along a meandering creek to a 4WD track and then on south to the Lost City, a collection of eroded sandstone blocks that looks (slightly) like a ruined city. From here the route follows a 4WD track east past Mt Tolmer to the ruins of Blyth Homestead, before heading north to Greenant Creek and the Litchfield Park Rd. Alternatively, head due north-west from the Lost City back to Tolmer Falls. The walk takes a day, although bush camping permits are available from the rangers in Batchelor (☎ 08-8976 0282), who can also provide up-to-date information and directions. MapsNT's 1:50,000 *Mt Tolmer* map covers the area.

KAKADU NATIONAL PARK
The East Alligator River

Although slightly contrived, and a combination of some very short walking tracks, if you have a day (or half a day) to spare in Kakadu consider the trails beside the East Alligator River. Many of them start within a 2km walk of the (cheap) *Kakadu Hostel* (☎ 08-8979 2232) at Ubirr and lead through monsoon rainforest, jagged sandstone and wetland environments. Together these routes roughly add up to 15km. Park notes and the booklet *Kakadu on Foot*, available at Bowali Visitor Centre, cover these parks well. In the Dry, Greyhound and Blue Banana bus services run north from Jabiru to Ubirr.

WEST MACDONNELL NATIONAL PARK
Mt Giles

This two- to three-day walk from Ormiston Gorge Visitor Centre is roughly 18km each way, with the last 3km a difficult climb to the peak of Mt Giles (1389m). Graded as difficult, and suited to experienced walkers only, once you're off the marked Pound Walk track that leads into Ormiston Pound it's up to you. There's one source of water at the base of the mountain close to the best camp site. It's possible (and rewarding) to camp on the summit of Mt Giles, but you'll need to hump all your water up there.

A detailed map showing the suggested route west through the Pound, camp sites, water sources and recommended routes up the eastern gullies is available from rangers (see Information Sources in the introduction to West MacDonnell National Park).

Redbank Gorge to Mt Sonder

This route, 8km in each direction, is essentially for peak baggers. Following Section 12 of the Larapinta Trail up from Redbank Creek can be a little monotonous, but the views from Mt Sonder (1380m), in the west of West MacDonnell National Park, are magical. To make all the hard work worthwhile, camp at the summit to catch the sunset and sunrise. Experienced bushwalkers can then descend south-east on to the Larapinta Trail.

Down by the gorge the *Woodland Camping Area* is the best of two sites, while Sections 11 and 13 (proposed at present) of the Larapinta Trail lead off from the Ormiston Gorge entrance (two to three days east).

TREPHINA GORGE NATURE PARK
Trephina Gorge

About 70km east of Alice off the (sealed) Ross Hwy is Trephina Gorge Nature Park. From the gorge a trail traverses the ridges south-west to John Hay's Rockhole. This takes a day, with the return walk either back the way you came or north along an unsealed road. There are basic camp sites at the gorge and rockhole. Rangers (☎ 08-8956 9765) at the park sell the useful *Walks of Trephina Gorge Nature Park* and give fireside talks during the winter months.

WATARRKA NATIONAL PARK
Kings Canyon

Despite being something of a tourist magnet, there's an excellent one-way overnight walk in this park, about 300km south-west of Alice Springs. From Kathleen Spring the Giles Track traverses 22km north-west below the George Gill Range before descending into the 'Garden of Eden' in Kings Canyon itself. Camping is above Lilla (Reedy Creek) and there are a number of semipermanent springs en route. Contact the rangers (☎ 08-8956 7488) for park notes and a sketch map. *Kings Canyon Resort* (☎ 1800 089 622) is expensive, but camping is available. You will need your own transport to reach the park.

Queensland

The self-styled 'Sunshine State' has an abundance of natural riches. The Great Barrier Reef, Fraser Island and the Wet Tropics rainforests in the Far North have all been classified as World Heritage List sites and it is rainforest that plays the biggest part in Queensland's walking scene. Lamington National Park, Mt Bartle Frere and the Thorsborne Trail on Hinchinbrook Island all provide excellent rainforest experiences, while the sandy trails of Fraser Island are just about as special a walking experience as you'll get anywhere.

Southern Queensland has more marked long-distance walking tracks than the Wet Tropics, where the climate is less suited to walkers and trail infrastructure.

HISTORY & NATURAL HISTORY

Aboriginal peoples populated Queensland around 40,000 years before Europeans arrived. Before colonisation, the state had up to 120,000 people divided among 200 or so clans. Some were coastal dwellers, others were inlanders, many of whom subsequently lost their land. Today more than two-thirds of Queensland's 3.5 million people are crowded along the southern coastline.

Queensland featured in two of Australia's most famous expeditions of discovery. In 1768 James Cook found anchorage in Botany Bay and then sailed up the Queensland coast to claim the continent for George III. In 1860 Robert O'Hara Burke and William John Wills set out on the now infamous expedition to walk from Melbourne to the Gulf of Carpentaria. Theirs is a classic story of sheer guts triumphing over incompetence. Both men made it to the Gulf, but perished on the return journey. Ironically, it was the numerous search parties sent out to look for them that really began to open up the formidable interior.

Queensland's first settlements were established as penal colonies at Moreton Bay and Brisbane between 1824 and 1825. Hugely rich in mineral reserves and land of

Highlights

A rich forest ecosystem on Fraser Island has managed to grow out of an island of sand

- Walking through pristine wilderness on Hinchinbrook Island
- Exploring the cliff-top paths and view points on the western edge of Lamington National Park
- Trekking across Hammerstone Sandblow for a swim in the cool, clear waters of Lake Wabby on Fraser Island
- Arriving at the summit of Mt Bartle Frere after climbing through 1500m of constantly changing rainforest
- Testing your nerve on the rainforest canopy walk at Green Mountains in Lamington National Park

agricultural potential, the gusto to develop Queensland continues today, with the environment often taking second place to mining, logging and tourism. Around 580,000 hectares of marginal land and rainforest are cleared each year, mostly for sugar cane.

Queensland

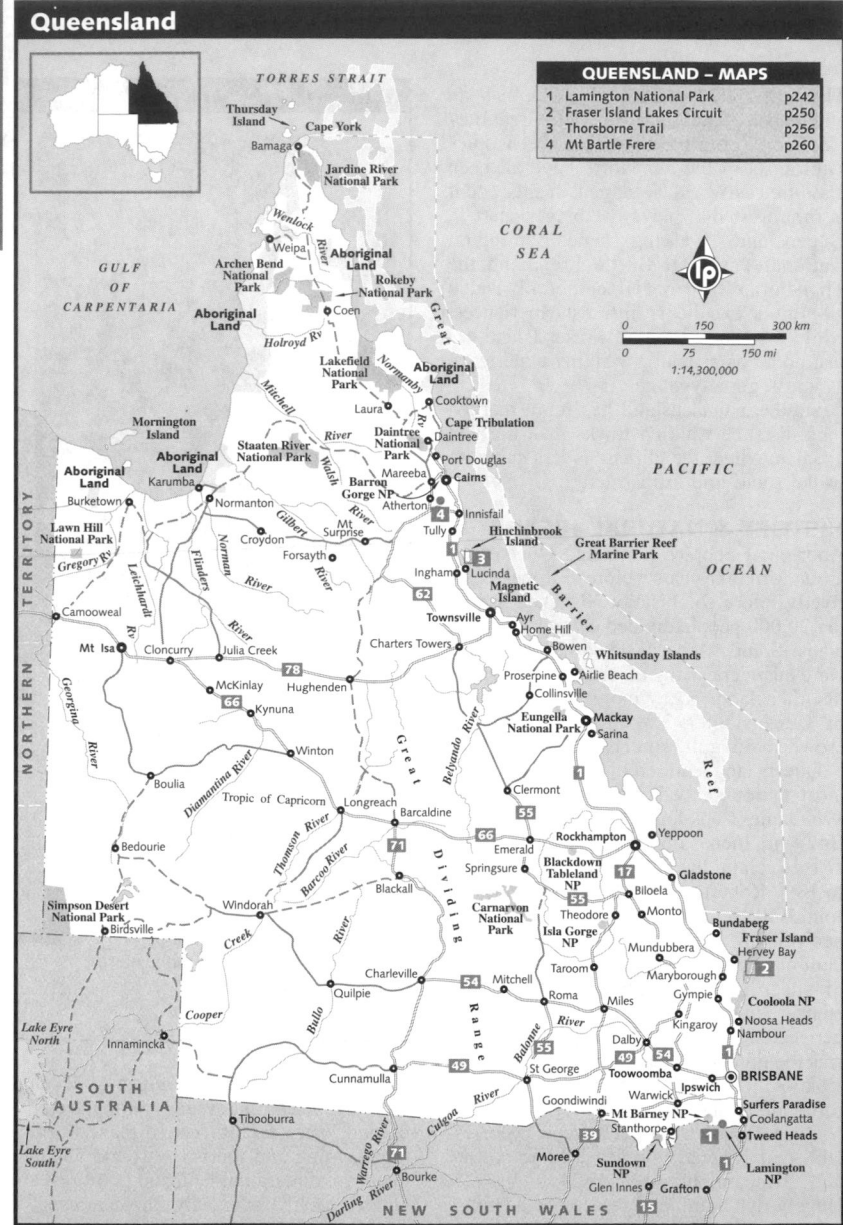

QUEENSLAND – MAPS	
1 Lamington National Park	p242
2 Fraser Island Lakes Circuit	p250
3 Thorsborne Trail	p256
4 Mt Bartle Frere	p260

While about 75% of Queensland's rainforest has been cleared, the Great Dividing Range, which runs parallel to the coast down from northern Queensland, protects some of the oldest rainforest in the world. The highest point in the range is Mt Bartle Frere (1622m), just south of Cairns where the mountains run close to the sea.

Between the mountains and the deep, blue sea is a fertile coastal strip of rainforest pockets and huge agricultural plains. Mangrove swamps are found along Queensland's 5208km coastline and support a staggering number of wildlife species.

Flat agricultural areas of rich volcanic soil, the tablelands, lie to the west of the range; farther west again the arid Outback begins. Pockets of eucalyptus woodland can be found almost anywhere and native pine forest grows on the more exposed mountain ridges.

INFORMATION
Maps
Auslig publishes a 1:100,000 series of the whole state. UBD's 1:2,500,000 *Queensland* map is an excellent alternative.

Sunmap (part of Queensland's Department of Natural Resources) publishes a series of 1:25,000 (limited at present) and 1:50,000 maps covering the coastal strip and most popular walking areas. For maps covering individual walks, see Planning in the introduction to each walk.

Buying Maps In central Brisbane, World Wide Maps and Guides (☎ 07-3221 4330, ✉ wwmaps@powerup.com.au), 187 George St, has an excellent selection of topographical maps and books. It's open daily (although only from 11 am to 3 pm on Sunday).

Further north in Cairns, Absells Chart and Map Centre (☎ 07-4041 2699), in Andrejic's Arcade, 55 Lake St, or the Department of Natural Resources (☎ 07-4052 3431), at 15 Lake St, stock topographical maps.

Books
Lonely Planet's *Queensland* is an excellent guide to the state. Also useful is *Camping in Queensland: National Parks, State Forests and Water Reservoirs*, both comprehensive

and widely available. *The Travellers' Guide to North Queensland, Cairns and Surrounds* by Paul Curtis is also readily obtainable and details numerous day escapes from Cairns.

Bushwalking in South-East Queensland by Ross Buchanan is a dry collection of long and short walks; *Secrets of Scenic Rim* by Robert Rankin is a much better read. *50 Walks in North Queensland* by Tyrone Thomas is a good collection of short day walks.

Eucalyptus Forest Guide edited by the Brisbane Forest Park Authority is an excellent, clear guide to southern Queensland's flora and fauna. *North Queensland Wet Tropics – A Guide for Travellers* by Rod Ritchie and others contains good practical and wildlife information.

Information Sources
The vast majority of tourist information centres in Queensland exist to sell tours. However, most will try to provide relevant information. Offices of the 14 regional tourist associations are the most useful.

The Queensland Tourist & Travel Corporation (☎ 13 1801, ✉ qldtravl@ozemail .com.au, ⌨ www.qttc.com.au) has offices across Australia and in numerous overseas cities. Don't expect information on obscure walking areas.

Queensland's national parks are managed by the Queensland Parks & Wildlife Service (QPWS), under the auspices of the Environmental Protection Agency (☎ 07-3227 8185, ✉ nqic@env.qld.gov.au, ⌨ www.env.qld .gov.au), 160 Ann St, Brisbane (PO Box 155, Albert St, Brisbane, Queensland 4002). New walking trails in the Wet Tropics are planned, so inquire at state-wide information centres.

The Queensland Federation of Bushwalking Clubs (PO Box 1573, Brisbane 4001, ⌨ www.qldwalking.org.au) has a Web site packed with useful information and links to local clubs.

The Brisbane Bushwalkers Club, PO Box 1949, Brisbane 4001, meets at 7.30 pm on the second and fourth Wednesday of the month at Newmarket Memorial Hall, on the corner of Enoggera Rd and Ashgrove Ave.

Weather charts and forecasts appear in the daily *Courier-Mail* and on the evening news.

QUEENSLAND

The Climate of Queensland

The northern two-thirds of Queensland is within the Tropic of Capricorn, although only the extreme north, the Wet Tropics (including Cairns), lies within the monsoon and cyclone belt. Between December and April, Cairns receives around 1300mm of rain; Tully, 100km south, can receive 4400mm! During the Wet, temperatures and humidity are very high – 35°C and 90% is not uncommon – and it's doubly unpleasant when carrying a pack through rainforest. Walking from May to September is best, when 25°C is normal, it's not cold at night and rainfall is minimal.

Down in Brisbane the same seasons of Wet and Dry apply, although rainfall is not as extreme and doesn't come all at once. After September, which is the driest month, the next eight months have rainfall of around 100mm (February is wettest). However, temperatures have a greater variation between summer (25°C to 28°C during the day) and winter (20°C to 10°C or lower at night). Walking in southern Queensland is feasible in summer, but not ideal.

Little of the Outback receives more than 400mm of rain annually and temperatures are extreme (45°C at the height of summer and around 20°C in winter when night-time temperatures can be below 0°C).

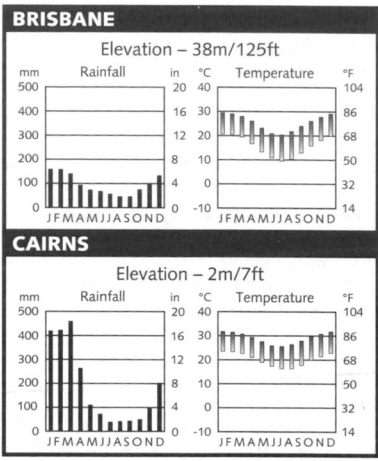

Permits & Regulations

Permits are required for all overnight walks. For the Thorsborne Trail and Lamington National Park permits should be arranged many months in advance. Demand is generally highest during school holidays and from June to August.

During days of Total Fire Ban, all fires are forbidden, even fuel stoves. If you are caught with an open fire on these days, you are not only endangering yourself and the environment, but you can also cop a hefty fine and/or prison sentence. See Responsible Walking in the Facts for the Walker chapter for some suggestions on how to minimise your impact on the environment you are walking through.

Guided Walks

Jungle Tours (☎ 1800 817 234, ✆ reservations @jungletours.com.au) runs two- to three-day rainforest walks, with hammocks provided for sleeping in.

Wooroonooran Safaris (☎ 07-4031 0800, ✆ info@wooroonooran-safaris.com.au) runs walks up and over Mt Bartle Frere from the western side ($119 per person).

To the north, Barron Gorge Wilderness Walks (☎/fax 07-4093 9490, PO Box 492, Kuranda Queensland 4872, ✆ nature@walks .com.au) offers leisurely and informative six-hour walks in Barron Gorge National Park for $75, including lunch.

GATEWAYS
Brisbane

Brisbane has some interesting districts, lots of old buildings and is a pleasant place to spend a few days. The city centre is enclosed within a U-shaped loop of the Brisbane River and tourists (and walkers) are well catered for.

Information There is a city-specific information kiosk (☎ 07-3229 5918) on the corner of Queen and Albert Sts in the city centre. Also in the centre, the Queensland Travel and Tourism Corporation (☎ 07-3874 2800) is on the corner of Adelaide and Edward Sts.

Open weekdays, the Naturally Queensland Information Centre (☎ 07-3227 8187, @ nqic @env.qld.gov.au), 160 Ann St, provides information on parks and wildlife. It also sells a wide range of wildlife and environmental books. You can organise park permits here.

Angus and Robertson Bookworld and the Mary Rhyan Bookshop, both on Queen St, have good selections of Australiana.

Climbing at Rocksports Indoor Climbing Centre (☎ 07-3216 0492), 224 Barry Parade, Fortitude Valley, costs $11 all day. Gear can be hired.

Supplies & Equipment For quality outdoor gear head to Wickham St, Fortitude Valley, where there's a cluster of camping shops, including Mountain Designs (☎ 07-3216 1866) and Paddy Pallin (☎ 07-3252 4408). Sherry's Camping and Disposals (☎ 07-3229 3422), 33 Adelaide St, in central Brisbane, sells cheaper equipment.

Places to Stay & Eat Out of the centre in Fortitude Valley, *Balmoral House (☎ 07-3252 1397, 33 Amelia St)* has good facilities. You can park out the front and it's quiet. Dorm beds cost $13 and a standard twin/double $32. There's free pick-up from the airport and Transit Centre. YHA and VIP discounts apply.

Globe Trekkers Hostel (☎ 07-3358 1251), on Balfour St in New Farm, is a small and friendly place with a pool. Dorms cost $14 and twins/doubles $32. Camper vans can park here and use the facilities ($7).

The enormous *Palace Backpackers (☎ 07-3211 2433, 1800 676 340)*, on the corner of Ann and Edward Sts, can be noisy but it's a fine place. Dorm beds cost from $15 and doubles are $40. Facilities are very good and there's the popular Down Under Bar and Grill serving cheap food and drink.

For low-cost food with minimal interaction, try *Winter Garden Foodcourt*, between Albert and Elizabeth Sts, or *Myer Centre Foodcourt*, on Queen St.

Fortitude Valley is the place for budget restaurants. Try *Asian House Chinese Restaurant (☎ 07-3852 1291, 165 Wickham St)* or *Luckys (683 Ann St)*, an excellent Italian place. Both have good vegetarian selections and are open seven nights a week. Mains start at $9.50.

Getting There & Away Brisbane is located on the Brisbane River, between the Gold and Sunshine Coasts, on the Pacific Hwy. The M1 passes through Brisbane north-south, and the Ipswich Motorway (M2) services the city from the west.

Air Qantas (☎ 13 1313) and Ansett (☎ 13 1300) have frequent flights between Brisbane and Australia's major cities. Their regional partners/subsidiaries, Sunstate (Qantas) and Flight West (☎ 13 2392), pick up the state's regional traffic.

A large number of international airlines fly into Brisbane, so there's no need to go to Sydney first.

Bus The Transit Centre on Roma St combines the coach, train and bus stations. The Brisbane Visitors Accommodation Service Desk (☎ 07-3236 2020), on the 3rd floor, can help find you a bed.

Greyhound Pioneer (☎ 13 2030) and Mc-Cafferty's (☎ 13 1499) have daily services to Adelaide, Cairns, Darwin (via Townsville), Melbourne and Sydney.

Coachtrans (☎ 07-3236 1000) runs Skytrans buses every 45 minutes from the Transit Centre to the airport ($9.50 to be dropped at your hotel). This company also runs services down to the Gold Coast, while Suncoast Pacific (☎ 07-3236 1901) runs services up to the Sunshine Coast.

Train A variety of rail services run between Brisbane and Cairns and Sydney and into the Outback. The speedy Tilt Train service from Brisbane to Rockhampton had just begun at the time of research. Contact Queensland Rail on ☎ 13 2232 or look up its Web site at ⌨ qroti.bit.net.au.

The Citytrain network, which operates through Central Station, on the corner of

Ann and Edward Sts, links Brisbane to the Gold and Sunshine Coasts.

Car Rental All the major companies are represented both in town and at the airport. For better deals try Integra Car Hire (☎ 1800 067 414), or Network Car and Truck Hire (☎ 07-3252 1599, 🖳 www.networkrentals.com.au), 398 St Pauls Terrace, which both have cars from around $29 per day.

Cairns

Surrounded by forested hills on three sides, Cairns is a major launching point for trips to the Great Barrier Reef, and the town is geared to tourist activities – bungee jumping, kayaking and skydiving are all possible.

Information The Regional Tourist Association Visitor Information Centre (☎ 07-4051 3588, 🅴 information@tnq.org.au), 51 The Esplanade, is OK for general information, while the Department of Environment and Heritage (☎ 07-4052 3096), 10–12 McLeod St, is the place to go for books, information and bushwalking permits. It's open weekdays.

Supplies & Equipment City Place Disposals (☎ 07-4051 6040), 50 Shields St, is ideal for basic kit. For flasher equipment visit Extreme (☎ 07-4051 0344, 4051 0488, 🅴 sales@itsextreme.com), 32 Spence St, or Adventure Equipment (☎ 07-4031 2669, 🅴 service@adventurequip.com.au), 133 Grafton St. The former organises cheap walking and rock climbing trips, and the latter hires outdoor equipment.

Places to Stay & Eat The excellent and bright *Travellers Oasis* (☎ 07-4052 1377, 1800 621 353, 🅴 travoasis@iig.com.au, 8 Scott St) has dorms for $16 and twins/doubles for $36. It's well equipped and there's a good pool. Book in advance.

Gone Walkabout (☎ 07-4051 6160, 274 Draper St) is a quiet, cheap, family-run place with air-con. Dorms cost $14 and twins/doubles $32.

The Bellview (☎ 07-4031 4377, 85–87 The Esplanade) is a little shabby but a good-value

place in the thick of the action, with $17 dorms, $36 doubles and motel rooms for $50.

Havanas (☎ 07-4041 3673, 183 Bunda St) is a relaxed place good for breakfast (excellent coffee) and delicious Cuban-style meals.

Enjoy soya-based ice cream, juices and vegetarian/vegan meals from $7 at the friendly *Honeyflow Café* (☎ 07-4031 0411), next to the market on Grafton St.

The Wool Shed (☎ 07-4031 6304, 24 Shields St) is a good drinking parlour and backpacker mainstay, thanks to very cheap food and long happy hours.

Getting There & Away
For train services see the Brisbane Getting There & Away section earlier.

Air Cairns is served by the same internal flight arrangements as Brisbane and an increasing number of international flights make it a useful entry and exit point. The Airporter airport bus (☎ 07-4031 3555) costs $5. A taxi to the airport (☎ 13 1008) is $13.

Bus All bus companies operate from the Transit Centre at Trinity Wharf. Combined, Greyhound and McCafferty's have at least five buses to and from Brisbane. Both also have daily Darwin services via Townsville. Coral Coaches (☎ 07-4031 7577) runs daily services to north Queensland.

Car Rental All the major car hire players are in town. For cheaper rates, try Delta (☎ 07-4032 2000), Billabong Car Rentals (☎ 07-4051 4299) or All Day Car Rentals (☎ 07-4031 3348), which all offer cars from around $29 per day. The latter has 4WDs from $59 a day. Most of the car hire companies are on Sheridan and Lake Sts.

Lamington National Park

In the 1840s Europeans started to settle here and logging began. Although the idea of a park was floated as early as 1878, it wasn't until 1915 that Lamington National Park was declared. In 1994 the Central Eastern Rainforest World Heritage Area was established. It includes Lamington, Main Range, Mt Barney and Springbrook National Parks. This protects the most extensive area of subtropical rainforest in the world, most of the world's warm temperate rainforest and nearly all of the Antarctic beech rainforest.

With extensive marked trails through varying types of subtropical rainforest, along pretty forest creeks and past beautiful waterfalls, this park is not to be missed.

The trails are divided into two main areas: those accessed from Binna Burra and those accessed from Green Mountains. The two trailheads are linked by the 21.4km Border Track (an easy walk). Walks from both trailheads are described here.

NATURAL HISTORY

Now called Mt Warning, the area south of Lamington was 24 million years ago the centre of a giant volcano 80km across and 2km high. Lamington National Park sits on the crest of the McPherson Range, the northern part of a huge horseshoe of ridges on the New South Wales (NSW)–Queensland border, which is all that remains of the giant volcano long since eroded by the Tweed River system.

Lamington contains more than 170 rare and threatened plant species and 38 rare or endangered wildlife species. Dry eucalyptus or native pine forest (the habitat of whiptail, or prettyface, kangaroos) is found on the park's fringes and more exposed ridges and outcrops, where areas of heathland also occur. Dry deciduous rainforest rings the subtropical rainforest, which prefers higher, wetter altitudes. Unfortunately, extensive logging has left few mature hook pine, onionwood or red cedar trees. Strangler figs, slowly adopting the shape of a doomed host tree, are common, as are crow's nest and stag's horn ferns. Small golden leaves carpet the ground under stands of rare Antarctic beech in high, often cloud-covered areas. In September the knobbly, moss-covered trunks are brightened with the pale yellow flowers of beech orchids.

Pademelons are common at Green Mountains, while nocturnal mammals include spotted-tailed quolls, mountain brushtail possums and yellow-bellied gliders; bring a torch (flashlight). On sunny days keep an eye out for big reptiles – land mullets (a species of large, black skink) and brightly marked carpet and diamond pythons are often found basking in sunny spots beside the trail.

The creeks contain large eels, Lamington spiny crayfish (a distinctive blue colour) and hip-pocket frogs (the male raises tadpoles in skin pouches on his hips).

Brush-turkeys, crimson rosellas, king parrots, and regent and satin bowerbirds are common around the main camp sites, where at night you may hear the macabre call of the sooty owl. Rufous fantails flit about in the undergrowth, while the rare rufous scrubbird is confined to the highlands of the park. Albert's lyrebird is close to extinction.

A visit to one of the park's visitor centres should convince you of the detrimental effects of feeding the wildlife, unfortunately a common practice at O'Reilly's Rainforest Guesthouse nonetheless.

PLANNING
When to Walk

All bush camp sites are closed in summer between 1 December and 31 January, when it's hot and wet – conditions that bring out millions of leeches. May to October are the best walking months, when rainfall and temperatures are both low. However, in the depths of winter (also the fire danger season when the park may be closed) temperatures can be as low as 12°C during the day and close to freezing at night. The heathland communities flower in August.

What to Bring

Always walk with a torch, as the forest becomes dark early. Insect repellent is advised, although these complex chemicals have detrimental effects on aquatic ecosystems. No chemical methods work against leeches (see the boxed text 'Beat the Leech' for the best methods of leech deterrence). All camp sites are fuel stove only. The weather can change quickly so bring wet-weather gear and warm clothing.

Warning

Giant stinging trees colonise open areas in the canopy created by tree falls. Reaching up to 35m high, these trees have very large heart-shaped leaves covered in tiny glass-like hairs that lodge in the skin and can cause irritation and pain for many weeks – they're almost impossible to remove.

Maps & Books

HEMA's 1:35,000 *Lamington National Park* map is useful, but detailed park leaflets displaying trails emanating from Green Mountains or Binna Burra are free and more up to date. Sunmap's 1:25,000 *Beechmont* and *Tyalgum* maps should also be carried. Get your maps in Brisbane.

Green Mountains is an autobiographical account of how Bernard O'Reilly went looking for a Stinson plane that had crashed in Lamington rainforest and successfully rescued the survivors.

Information Sources

There are ranger stations at both Binna Burra (☎ 07-5533 3584) and Green Mountains (☎ 07-5544 0634, fax 5544 0633), PO Box 4, Via Canungra 4275. Both are open weekdays only, from 1 to 3.30 pm. Green Mountains deals with all camping permits.

Permits & Regulations

Park camp sites are used in rotation, so those listed here may be closed. Coomera Circuit is closed indefinitely due to landslides.

Bush camping ($3.50 per person per night) is by permit only. Apply at least one month in advance. Numbers are limited to one group per site (six people maximum) and stays are possible for one night only. Leave a detailed schedule of your walk with someone responsible.

NEAREST FACILITIES
Green Mountains

The Green Mountains *camp site* (with hot showers) is 500m north of the ranger station (book and pay your $3.50 here), where there are gas barbecues.

O'Reilly's Rainforest Guesthouse (☎ 07-5544 0644, 1800 688 722, @ reservations @oreillys.com.au), at the start of the walk, has rooms from $120 per person. *O'Reilly's Rainforest Bar* is a great place to watch the sunset and does evening bar meals (steak sandwich $12.50). There's also an expensive restaurant, cheaper cafe and a shop selling basic supplies plus self-sealing gas canisters, methylated spirits and a good range of books. There's a public phone.

Binna Burra

At the Binna Burra trailhead, north-east from Green Mountain over the Darlington Range, you've the choice between *Binna Burra Camp Site* or *Mountain Lodge* (☎ 07-5533 3622, 1800 074 260, @ binnabur @fan.net.au). Camp sites start at $9 and there are beds in comfortable, permanent tents ($36 for two, $54 for four), while the lodge costs from $125 a night with full board. If

Beat the Leech

Leeches are an occupational hazard for walkers in the rainforests of Queensland. These aren't the huge slug-like creatures of horror movies, but small maggot-sized beasts that burrow through your socks in order to suck on your ankles or other more intimate parts. During summer you're unlikely to have many problems, but after periods of sustained rainfall the leeches come out to play. Commonly they're found in leaf litter, but you'll often find them on foliage overhanging the trail.

No repellent seems particularly efficient, and these nasty chemicals accumulate in the ecosystem, damaging wildlife (particularly aquatic). A couple of things may help. Gaiters provide some protection, especially when worn with two pairs of tightly woven socks (definitely not the fluffy walking variety leeches delight in burrowing through). Secondly, soak the top sock layer in very salty water, dry it, then apply a 'comfort layer'. This is your best shot at an effective leech barrier, but it's amazing where you'll find them.

you're camping bring your own linen and 20c pieces for the coin-operated barbecues.

The camp site *Craft Shop* is open daily and sells groceries, stove fuel and packed lunches (order the night before).

With great views of the Numinbah Valley, *Lamington Tea House* (open daily) serves a truly world-class cooked breakfast ($8.50), fine teas and other culinary wonders.

Green Mountains

Duration	2 days
Distance	27.4km
Standard	medium-hard
Start/Finish	Green Mountains Visitor Centre
Nearest Town	Canungra
Public Transport	yes

Summary A challenging rainforest walk that frequently follows beautiful, clear creeks and is an excellent introduction to rainforest walking. There are some (potentially) stunning views, but heavy rain brings out the leeches.

This two-day walk takes in some of the best features of the north-west of the park, including wide bubbling creeks, waterfalls, ancient rainforest and stunning views down into NSW. The walk through varying strata of rainforest is taxing. If you are feeling super fit you could add the West Canungra Creek Circuit to the first day's walk. However, it's recommended that this beautiful section is tackled as a warm-up day walk.

Be sure to leave enough time to complete the tree-top canopy walk a short distance from O'Reilly's Rainforest Guesthouse – a head for heights is recommended.

GETTING TO/FROM THE WALK

It's sealed road for the 115km from Brisbane via Canungra or 70km from the Gold Coast via Nerang and Canungra. Allstate Scenic Tours (☎ 07-3003 0700) has services to Green Mountains from the Brisbane Transit Centre from Sunday to Friday ($35 for an open-ended return). The Mountain Coach Company (☎ 07-5524 4249) runs a similar service from Surfers Paradise Transit Centre.

THE WALK
Day 1: Green Mountains to Bithongabel Camp
4–4½ hours, 11.5km

Opposite O'Reilly's Rainforest Guesthouse fork left onto the Border Track and walk 2.5km through the forest to a junction. Bear left onto the Box Forest Circuit, descending past a huge hollow box tree to another junction. Turn right – after 10 minutes the ground to the left falls away, giving views down into a deep valley. After five more minutes you're at **Picnic Rock** on top of **Elabana Falls**. Descend (steeply) along the trail to the base of the falls, continue north-east to a junction and then bear right onto Toolona Creek Circuit. Follow the path east, crossing Toolona Creek to the north bank and following the trail as it climbs round a series of falls to **Burraboomba Falls**.

The route then continues south-east following the beautiful narrowing creek to the moss-covered boulders of **Yilgahn Falls**. Climb steadily through a series of switchbacks to a position above Toolona Falls (there are some great canopy views), arriving at **Eerigingbooa Falls** 15 minutes later. This is a good spot to collect water.

The gradient now slackens as the trail heads south-east through a pocket of Antarctic beech, reaching the Border Track 25 minutes later. Turn right towards Green Mountains (7.6km away, excluding the Day 2 circuit), walking past a series of **lookouts** to **Bithongabel Camp**, nestled among the Antarctic beech. It's a beautiful spot, but quite exposed. There are no facilities.

If you have not carried water up from Toolona Creek it must be fetched from the spring that lies 20 minutes north-west along the Border Track.

Day 2: Bithongabel Camp to Green Mountains via Albert River Circuit
6 hours, 15.9km

Turn left onto the Border Track and walk for about 40 minutes to a junction with the Albert River Circuit. Continue straight ahead for 100m then fork left, climbing to a third junction. Turn left onto the Albert River Circuit,

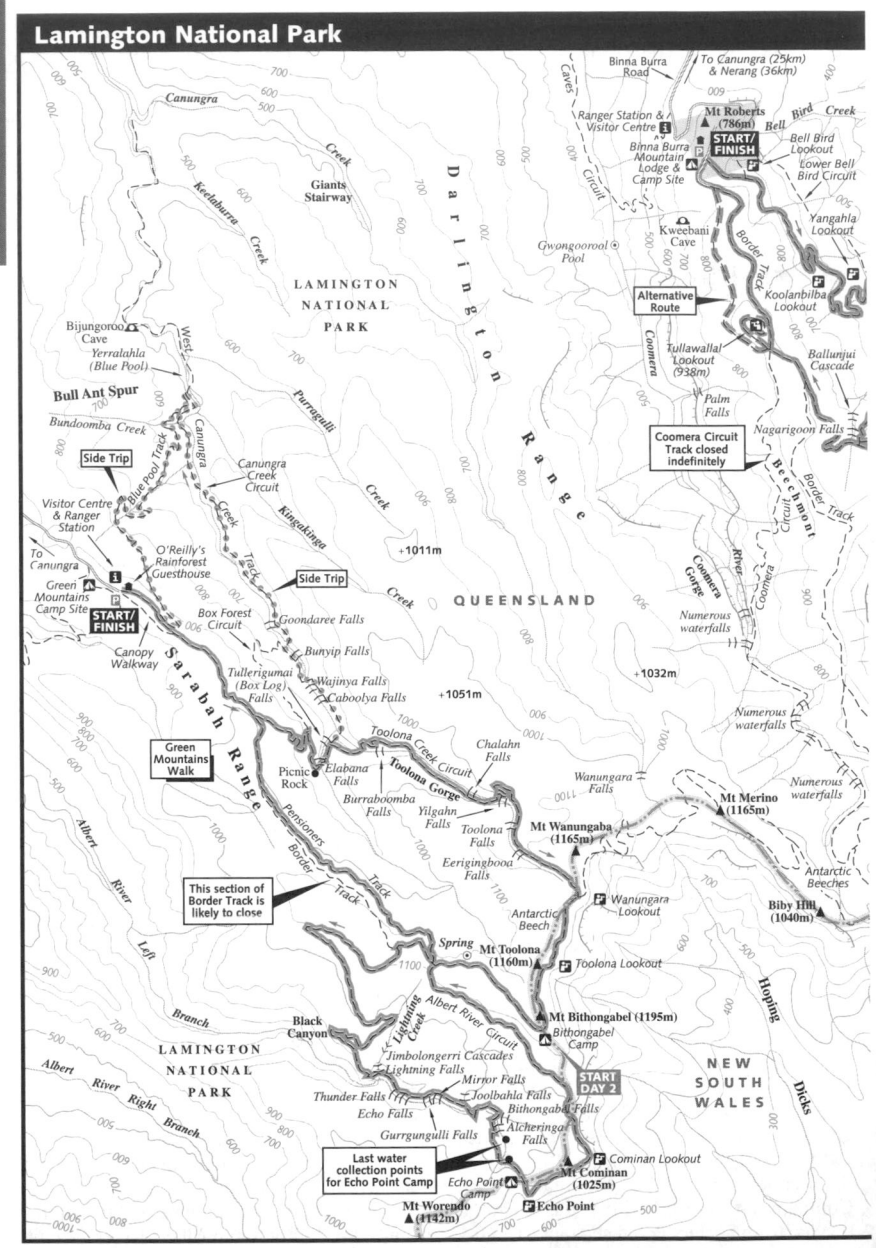

Lamington National Park

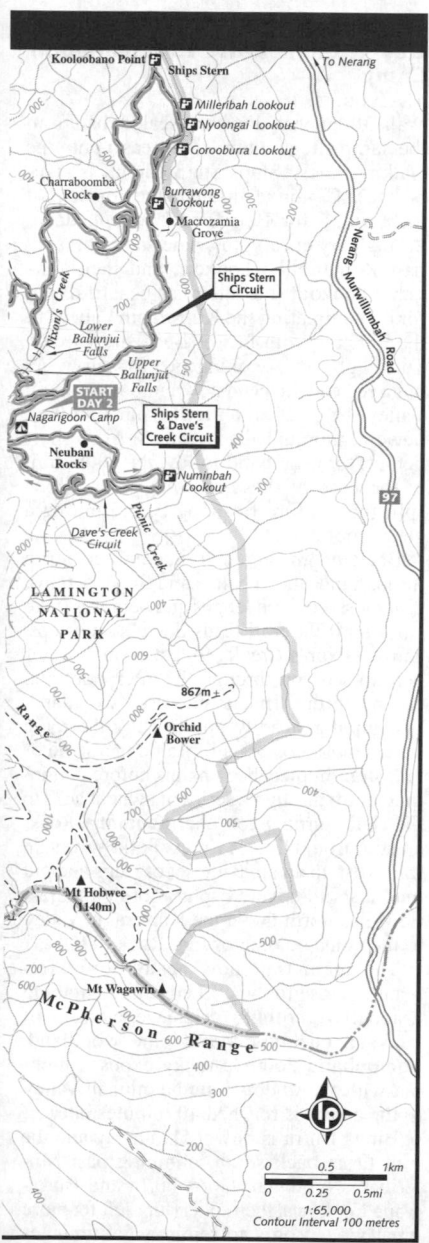

Kooloobano Point · Ships Stern · To Nerang
Milleribah Lookout
Nyoongai Lookout
Gorooburra Lookout
Charraboomba Rock
Burrawong Lookout
Macrozamia Grove
Ships Stern Circuit
Nerang Murwillumbah Road
Lower Ballunjui Falls
Nixons Creek
Upper Ballunjui Falls
START DAY 2 · Ships Stern & Dave's Creek Circuit
Nagarigoon Camp
Neubani Rocks
Numinbah Lookout
97
Dave's Creek Circuit
Picnic Creek
LAMINGTON NATIONAL PARK
867m
Orchid Bower
Range
Mt Hobwee (1140m)
Mt Wagawin
McPherson Range

0   0.5   1km
0   0.25   0.5mi
1:65,000
Contour Interval 100 metres

which traverses round a series of gullies on the southern slopes of a 1100m hill, before descending south-east through low scrub and palms. After about 45 minutes **Jimbolongerri Cascades** is reached. For the next 15 minutes, the trail meanders erratically until reaching a switchback and turning left (east) along the edge of an escarpment. After cutting north-east into a large river valley with views of Lightning Falls, the trail zigzags down to cross **Lightning Creek**. Once across, bear right over a ledge and continue east past **Echo Falls** upstream (good for a rather cold dip). Apart from a short interlude on the south bank after Joolbahla Falls, the trail continues east on the north bank to the small, but perfectly formed **Bithongabel Falls**. Cross to the south bank and bear right (north-west) up a series of switchbacks through Antarctic beech, continuing upstream to the stunningly beautiful **Alcheringa Creek** and **Falls**. Ten minutes later two small creeks are crossed, offering the last chance of water before reaching *Echo Point Camp*, five minutes later. **Echo Point lookout**, a mass of huge boulders, is 160m farther south, although clouds can obscure the stunning views.

Past the view point the trail hugs the very edge of the cliff, leaving little between you and the cattle down in the valley. Once away from the cliff edge the trail climbs steadily to reach the Border Track in 25 minutes. Turn left, then fork right onto **Pensioners Track**, which leads the 4.9km back to Green Mountains.

Side Trip: West Canungra Creek Circuit
3½–4 hours, 9.8km

About 250m along the Border Track from Green Mountains, Blue Pool Track bears off to the left, descending north-west then north-east to **Yerralahla** (Blue Pool) and West Canungra Creek, which is hemmed in by overhanging rainforest. A rough trail (the West Canungra Creek Track) leads upstream (south), crossing the creek frequently, for an hour to **Goondaree Falls**. At the top of these large falls cross to the western bank and climb up to the junction with the Box Forest Circuit. Turn left down to the creek, cross to the eastern bank at Wajinya Falls, and continue upstream past the beautiful boulder field of Caboolya Falls. Where the main creek splits, cross **Toolona Creek** (the east fork) and head up to the junction with Toolona Creek Circuit and Box River Circuit. A signpost here points back to Green Mountains (3.7km and very straightforward) via Box Log Falls, Elabana Falls and Picnic Rock, which are all worth investigating if you have the time.

Ships Stern & Dave's Creek Circuit

Duration	2 days
Distance	26.4km
Standard	easy-medium
Start/Finish	Binna Burra car park
Nearest Town	Canungra
Public Transport	yes

Summary Concentrates on the more exposed side of the park and hence covers more temperate habitats. However, there are plenty of attractions: stunning lookouts, majestic waterfalls and excellent cliff-top paths.

This very popular walk offers fantastic views over rocky cliff edges and dramatic terrain and passes through pockets of eucalyptus and native pine well-suited to these exposed conditions. All tracks are marked and easy to follow.

Book all camp sites through the rangers at Green Mountains (see Permits & Regulations earlier in this section).

GETTING TO/FROM THE WALK

If you're driving to Binna Burra from Brisbane, Surfers Paradise or the Pacific Hwy head to Nerang and then Beechmont.

Public transport is provided by Binna Burra Mountain Lodge, which runs a daily afternoon bus service from Surfers Paradise Transit Centre via Nerang station ($40 return, but book 24 hours in advance). From Brisbane, catch a train to Nerang or a Coachtrans (☎ 07-5588 8777) service to Surfers Paradise.

THE WALK
Day 1: Binna Burra to Nagarigoon Camp

4½–5 hours, 16.7km

Walk 300m back down the sealed road from the camp site and turn right (east) onto the walking track (Ships Stern Circuit is signposted). Continue through the forest past the turning for Bell Bird Lookout, down through dry eucalyptus, pine and rainforest, past **Koolanbilba Lookout** and then **Yangahla Lookout** (the latter is a beautiful spot for contemplating the Kurraragin Valley) to the junction with Lower Bell Bird Circuit. Turn right and, looking out for surviving huge red cedars, head down into Kurraragin Valley. After 25 minutes the junction with **Lower Ballunjui Falls** is reached. For a short detour, turn right and follow the 600m trail to the base of these stunning falls, which split the rainforest canopy before hitting a clear, cool pool.

Back on the main trail continue north through piccabeen palms and flooded gums, past moss-covered ledges and boulders (take care) until the trail leads down some steps, across **Nixon's Creek** (collect enough water here to see you through the afternoon) and climbs north then east into drier woodland.

Climbing steadily up the gully the route passes moss-covered cliffs among a stand of tall, straight piccabeen palms before continuing north through a series of switchbacks to the (left) turning for **Charraboomba Rock**, an hour from Nixon's Creek. Follow the side trail west up an amazing set of steps and out onto a scrub-covered spur affording majestic views north down the Kurraragin Valley to the volcanic plug of Egg Rock (425m).

The main trail now heads north, frequently close to the cliff edge and climbing gradually through drier vegetation of banksia, eucalyptus and pine woodland. **Kooloobano Point** (a rocky exposed lookout with views down the Numinbah Valley to the coast) is reached 40 minutes later.

Binna Burra is now 9.5km away and the trail turns back south, climbing past Milleribah, Nyoongai, Gorooburra and Burrawong Lookouts, then splits (fork left for more great views) only to rejoin a few minutes later before descending (steeply) to a saddle. Head south-west through a small pocket of rainforest before climbing steadily for the next 30 minutes to the junction for **Upper Ballunjui Falls** (2.4km, 60 minutes return). The falls are as dramatic as they are beautiful and hours can disappear here, so they are probably best visited on the second day. One look at the surrounding cliffs explains why there's no connector track between the upper and lower falls.

Continue south-west along the main trail for 20 minutes to **Nagarigoon Falls** and then up a series of switchbacks to *Nagarigoon Camp*, a pleasant, grassy oasis surrounded by temperate trees. There are no facilities.

Day 2: Nagarigoon Camp to Binna Burra via Dave's Creek Circuit

3½–6 hours, 9.7km

Leave your kit at Nagarigoon Camp and climb south up the track above Nagarigoon Falls to a T-junction. Turn left onto Dave's Creek Circuit. The trail winds east uphill through temperate vegetation to **Neubani Rocks** (worth a stop for morning tea) before switching back left (descending steeply) twisting and turning east, south, then east along the escarpment, through patches of banksia woodland, to **Numinbah Lookout**.

Turn right at the lookout, heading south-west along the cliff edge before bending right into **Picnic Creek**. The trail continues to climb past a series of **lookouts** (the eroded cliffs are stunning) as the vegetation turns to scrub and heathland (popular with wallabies), before turning north and climbing for 10 minutes north-west into pine and eucalyptus, and then rainforest. After a short descent a T-junction is reached. Turn right and walk 50m back to the junction of Dave's Creek and Ships Stern Circuits, then head back down to Nagarigoon Camp and your packs.

Binna Burra is only 3.9km from Nagarigoon Camp. Retrace your steps south to the end of Dave's Creek Circuit and continue (north-west) to join the **Border Track**. You can stay on this track all the way back to Binna Burra.

Alternatively, for the more energetic there's an alternative route back to Binna Burra via the pocket of Antarctic beech at the summit of **Tullawallal** (a 15-minute climb). Turn left from the Border Track onto the Tullawallal Circuit, 35 minutes from the junction with Dave's Creek Circuit (from this junction Binna Burra is only 1.9km north along the Border Track). The right turning for the summit itself is reached after 30m (1.4km return). The trail to the north-west joins The Border Track 30m short of Binna Burra.

Fraser Island

The thing to keep in mind about Fraser Island is that it's all sand. There's no soil, no clay and only a few small rocky outcrops. It's one gigantic 120km by 15km vegetated sand bar – the world's largest. It was inscribed as such on the World Heritage List in 1993 and the northern half of the island is protected as the Great Sandy National Park.

Despite its popularity with tour groups, relatively few bushwalkers visit the island. This means camping permits are usually not a problem to obtain; the trails are mostly well shaded and maintained, often running along old logging tracks.

HISTORY

Aborigines lived on Fraser Island for at least 5000 years, but European settlement in the 1860s forced the Butchulla people off their land, destroyed their traditional lifestyle and decimated the population. For seven years from 1897 'troublesome' mainland Aborigines were relocated to a station on Fraser Island, where many died as a result of malnutrition and disease.

James Cook wrote the first record of the island in 1770, but evidence of Portuguese navigation charts and Dutch clay pipes suggests an earlier European discovery. The island is named after the ill-fated Captain James Fraser and his wife Eliza, who landed here after having been shipwrecked in 1836. Aborigines took care of the pair, but only Eliza survived and was later rescued.

The Lakes of Fraser Island

With an average 1600mm of rainfall a year, it's not surprising that Fraser Island has so many creeks and lakes. 'Perched lakes' sit high above the water table cradled in a saucer of compact organic debris, accumulated over centuries. Many of the lakes to the north are 'window lakes', which form when the water table is higher than the ground surface level. Sand can hold 30% of its volume in water, so swampy ground is also common in low-lying areas. Lake Wabby is a barrage lake, formed when Hammerstone Sandblow (a large drifting dune) dammed a stream or swamp. It is unusual not only for this, but because it supports 11 fish species.

Some lakes, like Lake McKenzie, are crystal clear, their waters having percolated through sand coated in minute quantities of aluminium and iron, minerals that remove tannin. Golden-brown lakes such as Lake Boomanjin, the largest perched lake in the world, are rich in tannins and organic acids as

Beautiful perched lakes are just some of the natural wonders found on Fraser Island

their catchment water remains unfiltered by the pure white sand. Both types of freshwater lakes are low in nutrients and usually support only two or three fish species, freshwater turtles and the rare Cooloolah tree frog. Musk ducks are among the few water birds you'll see, while insectivorous sundew and pale blue-flowered bladderwort grow in waterlogged sand.

Most of the lakes are contained systems with no water outlets and are extremely vulnerable to contamination. Do not wash in them and wear a T-shirt rather than using sunscreen.

Areas in the south of Fraser Island were sand mined until 1976 and logging, once a major industry, only ceased completely in 1991. The whole island was declared a World Heritage List site in 1992.

NATURAL HISTORY

Fraser Island is the world's largest sand island, measuring 123km long and 15km wide. Over the past two million years, sand eroded from the tablelands of NSW has been carried by ocean currents and deposited on the island, which originally formed around three rocky headlands.

An amazing variety of vegetation and wildlife is present. Mangrove swamps line the western shores, while offshore beds of seagrass feed dugongs and green turtles. The wild exposed eastern shore is characterised by huge sandblows and foredunes colonised

by salt-tolerant plants like goatsfoot vine and beach spinifex. Small trees like beach she-oak, coastal banksia and pandanus form a buffer zone useful for campers.

Inland, wallum banksia, black she-oaks and pink bloodwoods grow in stunted forests. Paperbarks fringe the swamps and lakes. Distinctive scribbly gums, smooth-barked forest gums and blackbutt trees grow in tall woodland. Sheltered in gullies, lush rainforest, or vine forest, grows up to 50m high. The canopy is dominated by satinay and brush box (species once logged extensively); their trunks are often covered in lianas, bird's-nest ferns and elkhorns.

More than 200 freshwater lakes and creeks are found on the island, giving vital sanctuary to numerous birds and animals (see the boxed text 'The Lakes of Fraser Island'). On either shore look out for the brahminy kites and white-bellied sea-eagles above the shores and pied oystercatchers and red-capped plovers feeding at low tide. In the woodlands, look out for noisy yellow-tailed black-cockatoos and king-parrots.

At night sugar gliders, brushtail possums and flying-foxes become active. Dingos are omnipresent (see the boxed text 'Dingo').

PLANNING
When to Walk
The subtropical climate is moderated by sea breezes. December is the hottest with temperatures ranging from 22°C to 28°C. July is the coolest, with temperatures from 14°C to 21°C. There are often severe tropical storms from January to March. August to September is best for wild flowers, and migratory bird numbers peak between October and March.

What to Bring
Bring plenty of 20c coins for the barbecues and hot showers at Central Station, a fuel stove (fires are only permitted in fireplaces), lightweight walking boots and a swimming costume.

Maps & Books
Based on aerial photographs, Sunmap's 1:25,000 *Lake McKenzie*, *Boomanjin* and *Lake Wabby* maps cover terrain well, but trails are incorrectly marked. QPWS's *Forest Lakes Hiking Trail* shows the trails and is available from all permit-issuing and ranger information centres. HEMA's 1:130,000 *Fraser Island* map has walking trails marked and includes enlarged maps of key areas. Sunmap produces a similar map.

Bushpeople's Visitor Guide to Fraser Island & Cooloola is a good guide to the island.

Information Sources
On the island, Eurong Ranger Station (☎ 07-4127 9128) is open daily, while the post at Central Station (☎ 07-4127 9191) is open weekdays. The Eurong station has plenty of leaflets detailing walking trails and flora and fauna, while at Central Station there's a small display on the history of exploration and logging on the island.

Warnings

- Fraser's dingos are a particularly pure breed and of special conservation importance. No domestic dogs are allowed on the island. Do not feed or pet the dingos. This reduces their natural wariness of humans and gives them the bravado to steal food at any opportunity, a real problem around Central Station and Lake McKenzie.

  Never leave food inside tents (even when you're sleeping next to it), use the food cages provided and put all rubbish in the bin. When away from camp, leave your tent open to prevent it being ripped open by inquisitive dingos.

  Fearless animals (subsequently destroyed) have bitten solo walkers and children. All 'dingo incidents' must be reported.

- Don't swim off the east coast. If the fierce rip currents don't get you then sharks, stingers or box jellyfish probably will.

Permits & Regulations
You must get camping ($3.50 per person) and vehicle permits ($30 for one month) before going to Fraser Island. These are available from Hervey Bay City Council (☎ 07-4125 0222), 77 Tavistock St; River Heads General Store (☎ 07-4125 7133), 9 Ariadne St; or the Whale Watch Tourist Centre (☎ 07-4128 9800, ❷ buccaneers @coastnet.net.au) at Urangan Harbour.

Open fires are only permitted in the park's established fireplaces.

GETTING AROUND
Fraser Island's sandy tracks are 4WD only. You need good clearance and a tide timetable is useful. Hiring a 4WD in Hervey Bay costs about $130 a day, but Aussie Trax (☎ 1800 062 275), 56 Boat Harbour Drive, has ex-army Land Rovers for less.

For a 4WD taxi on the island call ☎ 07-4127 9188 – Kingfisher Bay to Eurong costs $45 for one to two people.

Fraser Venture Day Tours (☎ 07-4125 4444) cost $70, and when booking you can arrange to be dropped at Eurong Beach Resort and collected after a few days' walking.

NEAREST TOWN & FACILITIES
Hervey Bay

Hervey Bay is 10km of disjointed, low-rise, coastal sprawl, but it's easy to organise supplies and transport to Fraser Island. Bus No 5 runs from the Bay Central Coach Terminal to Urangan Harbour via Charlton Esplanade. All the town's hostels will pick you up. For a taxi (expensive) call ☎ 13 1008. Look out for the playful humpback whales that visit Hervey Bay between July and October.

The Village Pottery (☎ 07-4124 4987, ✉ villagepottery@bigpond.com.au), 65 Old Maryborough Rd, dispenses good tourist information. The town also has a Web site (🖳 www.herveybaytourism.com.au).

Torquay Disposals & Camping on Charlton Esplanade is the most convenient place for basic camping gear.

Places to Stay & Eat The *Koala Backpackers (☎ 07-4125 3601, 1800 354 535, 408 Charlton Esplanade)* is a VIP hostel with a party atmosphere. Dorms start at $13 and doubles/twins at $34.

Set in 1.8 hectares of bushland, *Colonial Backpacker Resort (☎ 07-4125 1844, 1800 818 280, ✉ herveybay@bigpond.com.au)*, on Pulgul St, is similarly priced. Camping is $5 per person.

Much of the (good) accommodation at *Fraser Escape Backpackers (☎ 1800 646 711, 21 Denman Camp Rd, 🖳 www.fraserescape.com.au)* is in converted caravans and starts from $10 for a dorm bed. Facilities are quite reasonable, as are its 4WD tours of Fraser Island.

All the hostels do cheap eats, but the *Black Dog Café*, on the corner of Dewnan Camp Rd and Charlton Esplanade, is worth a go – sushi costs about $4 and sweet chilli chicken $9.50.

The *Buy-Rite Express* supermarket, close to Koala Backpackers, is open daily until midnight. *Franklins* is close to Bay Central Coach Terminal.

Getting There & Away Hervey Bay is about 25km east of the Bruce Hwy, some 300km north of Brisbane. Sunstate and Flight West both fly to the town and there's a coach service linking trains passing through Maryborough (call ☎ 13 2232 for details).

Greyhound, McCafferty's and Suncoast Pacific all stop at Bay Central Coach Terminal (☎ 07-4124 4000), which is 7km from Urangan Harbour.

Fraser Island

On Fraser Island, if you've got the cash ($109 a night) it's worth staying at *Kingfisher Bay Resort and Village (☎ 07-4125 5511, 🖳 www.kingfisherbay.com)*, on the west side of the island (the starting point for the walk). The resort's Sand Bar is open to the public and serves decent food. There's also a bakery, a petrol station and a general store for supplies.

See the walk description for details of the Eurong Beach Resort.

Fraser Island Lakes Circuit

Duration	4 days
Distance	76.1km
Standard	medium
Start/Finish	Kingfisher Bay Resort
Nearest Town	Hervey Bay
Public Transport	yes

Summary A walk along sandy trails that link an important series of perched lakes on the world's biggest sand island, a World Heritage site. Walking infrastructure is good.

Walking between the lakes of Fraser Island is a unique experience mixing rainforest, drier woodland, scrub and coastal environments. However, a sand island doesn't mean a flat island, and Fraser Island is surprisingly hilly – this is a drain when combined with pockets of soft sand.

Kingfisher Bay Resort makes a good trailhead (although this adds 2.3km to the walk), but if you have your own vehicle you'll miss little by starting the circuit at Lake McKenzie or Eurong.

GETTING TO/FROM THE WALK

If you're on foot you can take the passenger-only Kingfisher Bay Resort Fastcat ($30

Dingo

Dingos are thought to have been introduced (perhaps accidentally) to Australia around 4000 years ago by seafaring people from South-East Asia. Their range once extended throughout Australia and it it believed that their adaptability and general cunning may have led to the extinction of the thylacine (Tasmanian tiger) and the Tasmanian devil on the mainland.

Speaking crudely, dingos are dogs, easily distinguished by their pointed ears and ginger fur, although they can be pure white or black. They usually have white-tipped feet and tail and a white chest, although due to interbreeding with domestic dogs pure strains are increasingly rare. However, dingos are in fact different from domestic dogs. They breed only once a year, usually producing a litter of up to six pups between April and June, and they cannot bark but howl instead, often in chorus.

Dingos live in groups of between three and 12 and mainly hunt alone for rodents, small mammals, birds and reptiles. Occasionally they form packs and hunt cooperatively to catch larger prey (some Aboriginal clans domesticated dingos and used them to hunt kangaroos and wallabies). However, if there's a free meal going they become adept scavengers and have become pests in some areas (eg, Fraser Island).

Livestock farming has brought dingos, partial to a bit of lamb, into direct conflict with humans and they have been systematically exterminated from many agricultural areas. The Dog Fence, which runs for some 5500km across South Australia and southern Queensland, with some sections 100 years old, does protect livestock to some extent. However, in some arid areas permanent water sources established for livestock have helped dingo numbers increase. On the plus side, research has shown that dingos may help control feral animal populations of rabbits, goats and even foxes.

return; 45 minutes) from Urangan Harbour, Hervey Bay, to Kingfisher Bay. Departures start at 8.30 am and finish at 10.30 am, while return services start at 7.40 am and finish at 11.30 pm. The resort also runs vehicular services ($65 per vehicle and driver plus $5 per passenger; 45 minutes) which depart from River Heads (20 minutes south of Urangan Harbour).

Fraser Island Vehicular Ferry Services (☎ 07-4125 4444, fax 4125 4000) runs similarly-priced vehicle ferries from River Heads to Wanggoolba Creek (south of Kingfisher Bay) and Moon Point (north of Kingfisher Bay), and from Inskip Point (north of Cooloola National Park) to Hook Point (the southern tip of Fraser Island).

THE WALK
Day 1: Kingfisher Bay to Central Station

4–4½ hours, 17.3km

Fill your water bottles at Kingfisher Bay Resort then climb south 20m past the general store, before turning left onto a 4WD track marked as 'Lake McKenzie Route One' and 'Beerillbee Trail'. Follow triangle markers and signs to Lake McKenzie as the trail twists and turns through soft sand for 25 minutes to a ridge behind the resort. With a toilet block to the north-east, turn right (east) and continue along the ridge and down through tall eucalyptus woodland until forking right off the 4WD track into the Great Sandy National Park.

QUEENSLAND

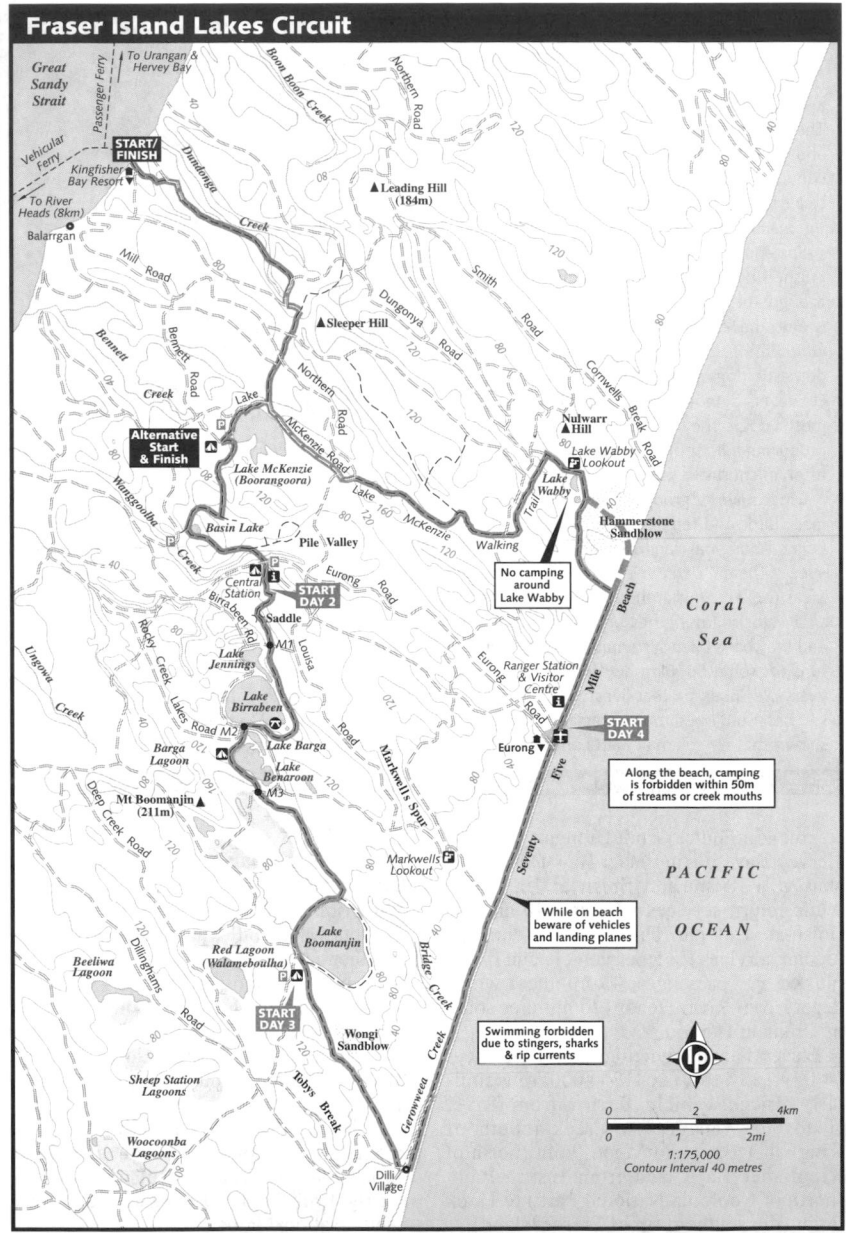

Fraser Island Lakes Circuit

Great Sandy Strait

To Urangan & Hervey Bay

Passenger Ferry

Vehicular Ferry

START/ FINISH

Kingfisher Bay Resort

To River Heads (8km)

Balarrgan

Boon Boon Creek

Northern Road

▲ Leading Hill (184m)

Dundonga Creek

Mill Road

Bennett Creek

Bennett Road

Lake

▲ Sleeper Hill

Dungonya Road

Smith Road

Cornwells Break Road

Northern Road

Alternative Start & Finish

Lake McKenzie (Boorangoora)

McKenzie Road

Lake McKenzie Walking Trail

Nulwarr ▲ Hill

Lake Wabby Lookout

Lake Wabby

Hammerstone Sandblow

Wanggoolba Creek

Basin Lake

Pile Valley

Central Station

Birrabeen Rd

START DAY 2

Saddle

Lake Jennings

M1

Lake Birrabeen

Lake Barga

Eurong Road

McKenzie Walking

No camping around Lake Wabby

Coral Sea

Ranger Station & Visitor Centre

Eurong Road

Louisa Road

START DAY 4

Rocky Creek

Lakes Road M2

Barga Lagoon

Lake Benaroon

M3

Mt Boomanjin ▲ (211m)

Eurong

Markwells Spur

Along the beach, camping is forbidden within 50m of streams or creek mouths

Deep Creek Road

Markwells Lookout

While on beach beware of vehicles and landing planes

PACIFIC OCEAN

Beeliwa Lagoon

Red Lagoon (Walameboulha)

Lake Boomanjin

Dillinghams Road

START DAY 3

Wongi Sandblow

Sheep Station Lagoons

Tobbs Break

Bridge Creek

Garrawonga Creek

Swimming forbidden due to stingers, sharks & rip currents

Woocoonba Lagoons

Dilli Village

0   2   4km
0   1   2mi

1:175,000
Contour Interval 40 metres

The route continues along this walking trail, high above **Dundonga Creek**, for an hour before finally emerging at a road. Turn right (south) then after 10 minutes left (east) onto a walking track leading after 100m to another T-junction. Cut back right along a sandy trail that climbs and descends southwards over **Sleeper Hill** and across two roads to a third road. With Lake McKenzie straight ahead, visible through the trees, turn right then bear left down a 4WD track closed by a barrier. Follow the walking track that soon peels off left to run along the beaches bordering **Lake McKenzie**. A signpost signals the way to the 'Walkers Camp Site', but continue along the lake's shore to the start of the (signposted) track to Central Station (6.3km).

After moving through paperbarks and swamp banksias the route climbs south for a short while before descending steeply to the south-west, passing a swamp (on the left) and bending south-east to climb to the top of the hill. Ignore the blocked track straight ahead and turn right (west), entering an area of dense tree cover after 25 minutes. At a T-junction on the crest of the ridge, turn left (east) and head down to **Basin Lake**, one of the most beautiful places on the island. Set against tall, dense forest it contains small, inquisitive turtles. Camping is not permitted.

Head east away from the lake climbing to a saddle, then descending south-east, before bending round to the north-east as a steep-sided creek appears to the right. A tall stand of plantation eucalyptuses is passed before drawing near **Wanggoolba Creek**, where a well-made path and elevated boardwalk lead through vine forest and piccabeen palms to **Central Station**.

A great *camp site* sits below tall kauri pines. There's a food cage, hot showers (got those 20c pieces?), barbecues, a covered cooking/eating area and an excellent information display. A great short walk leads through the vine forest of **Pile Valley**.

Day 2: Central Station to Lake Boomanjin
3½–4 hours, 14.6km
Walk past the litter bins, diagonally left across the road and up a set of zigzagging steps that climb south into vine forest, reaching a T-junction after 15 minutes. Here, turn left. The trail climbs steadily south-east to a ridge of tall blackbutt forest and after 10 minutes a saddle is reached. The trail turns west then south, descending steadily and crossing a road at meeting place M1. The trail quickly gains altitude, eventually blending with an old 4WD trail that appears on the left just as **Lake Birrabeen** becomes visible through the trees on the right. The trail then heads through melaleuca heathland to the lake's shore and round to a picnic site.

Walk up to meeting point M2 above the picnic site, cross the road and follow the trail past **Lake Barga**, choked with reeds and small paperbarks, then through wet and dry heathland around **Lake Benaroon** (the basic *Hikers Camping Area* is signposted halfway round). Cross the road at meeting point M3 and climb steeply to a wooded spur, in which satinay, blackbutt and scribbly gum are common, and traverse south-east towards the sea (glimpsed occasionally). After descending gradually for about an hour from M3, a T-junction with an old forest track is reached. Turn right (south) off the ridge down a wide track that arrives suddenly at **Lake Boomanjin**.

Turn right and walk for about 30 minutes round the lake to a 4WD track leading to the *camp site*, with water, fireplaces and cold showers, beside a road.

Day 3: Lake Boomanjin to Eurong
4–4½ hours, 16.8km
South of the camp site is the signposted trail to Dilli Village. After a quick climb and ridge walk, **Wongi Sandblow** is reached – the short walk onto the blow itself offers great views north to Lake Boomanjin and south-east to the sea. The trail skirts the blow to the head of a small gully, where it bears right up a small slope. For the next hour the path hops between parallel ridges (some with view points) and gullies of beautiful mixed woodland, moving south-east towards the sea.

Finally, after a steep climb, the trail crosses a wide gully of banksia woodland

and drops down to a swamp. Turn right (south-west) then left and follow the boardwalk across coastal heath swamp to a road. Turn left and walk past **Dilli Village** resort (☎ 07-4127 9130) to the sea. Behind the dunes, Dilli Village is a fine establishment with *camp sites* for $3 per night (no permit required) and cabin beds from $10. There are barbecues, hot showers, laundry facilities and a small freshwater swimming hole.

Once you hit the beach turn left and keep going. A few small creeks are worth a look (and a dip), but you may be able to hitch the 10.5km to *Eurong Beach Resort (☎ 07-4127 9122, ✪ eurong@fraser-is.com, ⊒ www .fraser-is.com)*. Accommodation starts at $15 for dorm beds, and there's the Beach Bar, a restaurant (rather average; book in advance), petrol station and shop (open daily).

Just 500m farther on is Eurong Visitor Information Centre. There's a good information display, fresh water, toilets and firewood. Another 15 minutes' walk will take you to the first of the basic beach *camp sites* – avoid these during storms.

Day 4: Eurong to Lake McKenzie
4½–5 hours, 19.5km

On the eastern beach 3.5km north of Eurong is a clear trail leading west to Lake Wabby. For an alternative, Lawrence of Arabia-style route, continue 800m farther north to where a second trail heads west across the mighty **Hammerstone Sandblow** to the lake. Spotting the trail's beginning is tricky – look for 4WD tracks cutting into the foredune. A clearing and stile mark the head of the trail, which leads for 15 minutes through dense, beautifully scented coastal rainforest to the sandblow. Ready the camels, then set off north-west. **Lake Wabby** (which is great for swimming) is reached in 15 minutes.

From the lake, head north-west to a path through the woodland and up to **Lake Wabby Lookout**, the best vantage point on the walk. Head west from the lookout, then turn left onto Lake McKenzie Walking Trail. Turn left (roughly south) at the next T-junction descending south into a cycad-filled gully. Continue south for the next 30 minutes, climbing then descending, before finally climbing

south-west to a junction. Here, turn right (west). After 10 minutes the vegetation changes from dry woodland to palms, bracken and tall, straight brushwoods, and for the next 20 minutes the route leads through magnificent forest in deep shade.

After a brief stint of north then south, the route steams north-west, climbing onto a pass between two ridge lines before descending to Lake McKenzie Rd. Turn left, then right following the road back to Lake McKenzie. The *Walkers Camp Site* above the stunning lake has firewood, food cages and cold showers, but it can get crowded.

All that is left is to retrace your steps to Kingfisher Bay Resort (2½ hours).

Hinchinbrook Island

This spectacular island is a patchwork of different ecosystems and a pristine wilderness. Huge granite mountains tower over the island, which is lined by extensive mangrove swamps on the west coast and beautiful bays and beaches on the east.

The Thorsborne Trail stretches for 32km along the east coast. It's possible to walk north to south or south to north (the way described here) in three days, but by taking four or five days and spending each night at a different camp site, you'll better enjoy the island's beautiful waterfalls, swimming pools and beaches.

HISTORY
Hinchinbrook Island is the country of Bandyin Aborigines, who lived here for thousands of years. Today shell middens are the only evidence of their occupation.

The Thorsborne Trail commemorates the life of Arthur Thorsborne who, with his wife Margaret, worked to ensure that Torresian imperial pigeons migrating from New Guinea were protected on this and other local islands – you may see pigeons feeding on forest fruit from August to March.

NATURAL HISTORY
The island was formed during great periods of upheaval when the earth's crust folded

and lifted to form a huge mountain range that ran down the Queensland coast. After the retreat of the last ice age most of this range was submerged, some of it becoming the foundation of the Great Barrier Reef, while the remaining peaks formed the Great Dividing Range and islands such as Hinchinbrook. The island was declared a national park in 1932.

Surrounded by the Great Barrier Reef Marine Park, beds of seagrass grow in the shallow, warm waters off Hinchinbrook's northern, eastern and western shores and support dugongs and green turtles. On the eastern coast shovel-nosed sharks feed in the bays, beach stone-curlews strut around and nest on the foreshore, and white-bellied sea-eagles soar above. Hundreds of tiny soldier crabs are often seen scuttling around the beaches.

The rugged volcanic peaks are covered in fragile heath vegetation and are often shrouded in cloud – Mt Bowen (1121m) is the highest. In the cold streams that run off the mountains are endangered jungle perch, and eastern water dragons are often seen basking on rocks.

The extensive mangrove forests on the west and north of the island are important breeding grounds for fish, and red mangrove flowers are the favourite food of black flying-foxes. Look out for striped skinks and large orange-and-black Christmas beetles in the dry open woodlands of wattle, she-oak and grass trees. Yellow-breasted sunbirds, forest kingfishers and emerald doves may be seen in the extensive eucalyptus forests.

The tropical rainforest is mainly confined to the southern and western foothills on the island. The broad, dark green leaves form a dense canopy, and the trunks are often covered in lichen, vines and bird's-nest ferns. Look out for a colourful variety of fungi, iridescent blue Ulysses butterflies and ground-dwelling orange-footed scrubfowls and brush-turkeys.

Unfortunately, Hinchinbrook has aliens. Keep clear of feral pigs and brain all cane toads – these are seriously damaging to the native environment.

Warnings

- Swimming in the sea during the box jelly-fish season (October to May) is not advisable. They are considered some of the most deadly jellyfish in the world, their poison affecting the heart and breathing mechanism, as well as causing scarring and ulceration of the skin.
- Saltwater crocodiles inhabit mangrove forests so take care around all tidal lagoons and estuaries. There have been croc sightings at North Zoe and South Zoe Creeks.
- Heavy rain and high tides can make creek crossings dangerous; if in doubt, wait or turn back.
- Keep away from lawyer vine, an innocent-looking palm vine that has spikes on the stems and tendrils and hooked thorns on the leaves.
- Remember that medical assistance can be two days away.

PLANNING
When to Walk

The best walking months are from May to September, when the climate is drier and cooler. There are usually heavy rains from December to March, but always be prepared for rain. The trail is closed when there's not enough water to support walkers, when it is too wet, during a cyclone threat or when prescribed burning is taking place.

What to Bring

A long-sleeved shirt, trousers and insect repellent are essential to keep mosquitoes and sandflies at bay. A tent, waterproofs, light walking boots and a change of shoes – your feet will get wet – are advisable. Food and rubbish should always be stored in metal boxes. Where these are not available, suspend food bags 1m from the ground on a cord tied between two trees. Attach two spinning plastic bottles on either side of the bags. This should prevent great white-tailed rats (sometimes called mosaic-tailed rats) from taking your dinner, although they are extremely cunning.

Excess luggage can be left with either of the ferry services operating to the island, and will be stored and transported to the other end.

Maps & Books

The *Thorsborne Trail* park notes given out with your permit are essential. Sunmap's 1:50,000 *Hillock Point* map covers the area, but doesn't mark the trail. The Lucinda tide timetable is available from ferry operators.

Hinchinbrook Island – the Land Time Forgot by Margaret & Arthur Thorsborne is a widely available and fascinating coffee-table book. Warren McDonald's *One Step Beyond* is a harrowing account of Warren's accident on Hinchinbrook, as a result of which he lost both his legs, and of his inspiring recovery.

Permits & Regulations

A permit is essential and must be booked through the Rainforest & Reef Information Centre in Cardwell (see Nearest Towns for details), which can take credit card payments. Book at least three months in advance.

There is a strict limit of 40 people on the trail and group sizes are restricted to six. All walkers must watch *Without a Trace*, a 15-minute minimal impact bushwalking video, before permits are issued. Permits can be collected from other QPWS offices – phone Cardwell for details.

Only camp in designated camp sites. Climbing the mountains (other then Nina Peak) is by prior permission only. The trail is fuel stove only.

NEAREST TOWNS
Cardwell

A pleasant, if somewhat sprawling town, Cardwell is the northern jumping-off point for the trail. The Rainforest & Reef Information Centre (☎ 07-4066 8601, fax 4066 8116), 142 Victoria St, PO Box 74, Cardwell 4849, sits in the middle.

Cardwell Agencies, at 71 Victoria St, sells everything from sealant to tent repair kits.

Places to Stay & Eat The YHA-affiliated *Kookaburra Holiday Park* (☎ 07-4066 8648, @ kookaburra@znet.net.au, 175 Bruce Hwy) has good facilities and is the best place to stay. You can hire camping gear here. Dorm beds cost $15, doubles/twins start at $32 and camping is $7.50 per person.

For a post-walk pig-out try *Muddies Café & Bar* (☎ 07-4066 8907, 221 Victoria St). It's open daily until late. Seafood is the speciality (from $15.90), but vegetarians can be catered for. Movies are screened in the beer garden.

The excellent and cheap *Annie's Kitchen (107 Victoria St)* does good T-bone steaks for $8.50.

For food supplies, there's *DA's Supermart (113 Victoria St),* open daily.

Getting There & Away Cardwell is 58km north of Ingham on the Bruce Hwy, opposite the northern tip of Hinchinbrook. Greyhound and McCafferty's stop at the bus stop beside the BP petrol station.

Cardwell also has a train station (☎ 13 2232), and is on the Brisbane to Cairns line.

Lucinda

The ferry leaves for George Point, on Hinchinbrook Island, from Lucinda, at the southern entrance to the Hinchinbrook Channel. If you have transport the *Wanderer's Holiday Village* (☎ 07-4777 8213), in Lucinda, has camp sites at $13 for two people; cabins sleeping four cost $50.

Ingham

Twenty-five kilometres south-west of Lucinda, Ingham is the last place for supplies for those starting from the south. The QPWS (☎ 07-4776 1700) has an office on Cassidy St. Mitre 10 (☎ 07-4776 1622), 72 Townsville Rd, stocks some camping gear.

Places to Stay & Eat The *Royal Hotel (☎ 07-4776 2024, 46 Lannercost St)* has dorm beds for $10. *Hotel Hinchinbrook (☎ 07-4776 2227, 83 Lannercost St)* is somewhat better and has beds from $15.

There's a range of *cafes*, or try *La Trattoria Della Pasta (☎ 07-4776 5166, 45 Lannercost St),* with mains from $12.50. There's also a *Coles* supermarket on Main St and a *Woolworths* on the Bruce Hwy.

Getting There & Away Ingham is on the Bruce Hwy, 110km north-west of Townsville. Greyhound and McCafferty's stop in the town centre. Ingham is also on the main east coast railway line.

Thorsborne Trail

Duration	4 days
Distance	32km
Standard	easy-medium
Start/Finish	George Point
Nearest Towns	Cardwell, Ingham
Public Transport	yes

Summary One of Australia's classic walks, the Thorsborne Trail heads through pristine wilderness to link a remarkable string of amazingly beautiful places, from deserted tropical beaches to powerful waterfalls.

There's little difference between walking the trail south to north or north to south. However, those who choose to walk south to north will enjoy a pleasant half-day trip to Macushla and Cape Richards after being picked up.

Yellow triangles point north along the trail and orange ones point south.

GETTING TO/FROM THE WALK
To the Start
Hinchinbrook Wilderness Safaris (☎ 07-4777 8307, fax 4777 8436) provides ferry services from Lucinda to George Point ($40 one way), plus bus transfers to/from Ingham ($45 including ferry) and Cardwell ($50 including ferry). The arrival time at George Point is 2.30 pm. Ferries run daily in the peak season (May to October) and every other day at off-peak times.

From the Finish
Running cruises from Port Hinchinbrook Marina in Cardwell, Hinchinbrook Island Ferries (☎ 07-4066 8270, fax 4066 8271, @ hinchinbrook@4kz.com.au) sets down walkers at Ramsay Bay ($55), before returning to Cardwell (via Cape Richards) at 11.30 am. Walkers can order packed lunches for $9.

THE WALK
Day 1: George Point to Mulligan Falls
1¾–2¼ hours, 7.5km
Fill your water bottles at Lucinda as George Point (*camp site* and drop-off point) has no water. Once on the island head north along the coconut-fringed beach for 50 minutes, crossing **Mulligan Creek** (best done at low tide) and then, 300m before the end of the beach and Diamantina Creek inlet, turning left along a signposted trail. Head west inland, then north through lush tropical forest. After 40 minutes, and after crossing five semipermanent creeks, turn right at the fork and walk into Mulligan Falls *camp site*. **Mulligan Falls** are 150m farther on. You can camp here for one night only. There's a toilet, a rat box and good swimming below the falls, but don't try climbing them!

Day 2: Mulligan Falls to Zoe Bay
2¾–3¼ hours, 6.5km
Walk out of the camp site and turn right, zigzagging north-east up and round a large hill and into dry woodland – there are great views of the island and mainland at the top of this 20-minute climb. The trail then drops to Diamantina Creek. Cross the creek (the boulders are treacherous when wet) and climb north-east to a T-junction.

To the right a trail leads down over steep, rocky ground to **Sunken Reef Bay**, a 2.2km round trip (one hour). You can *camp* here behind the foredune, but be aware that green sea turtles and beach stone-curlews sometimes nest here. There is a small freshwater creek at the north end of the beach.

Back at the junction it's a 10-minute climb to the top of the hill and fantastic views north and over Sunken Reef Bay. The undulating trail then traverses north through she-oak woodland and tiny patches of lush forest for an hour to **Sweetwater Creek**, where water can usually be collected.

Cross and head upstream, before turning north-west and climbing through tall heathland and she-oak woodland to a broad saddle. At 260m this is the highest point of the trail.

Head north down past a large slab of granite and across a number of rocky tributaries

Thorsborne Trail

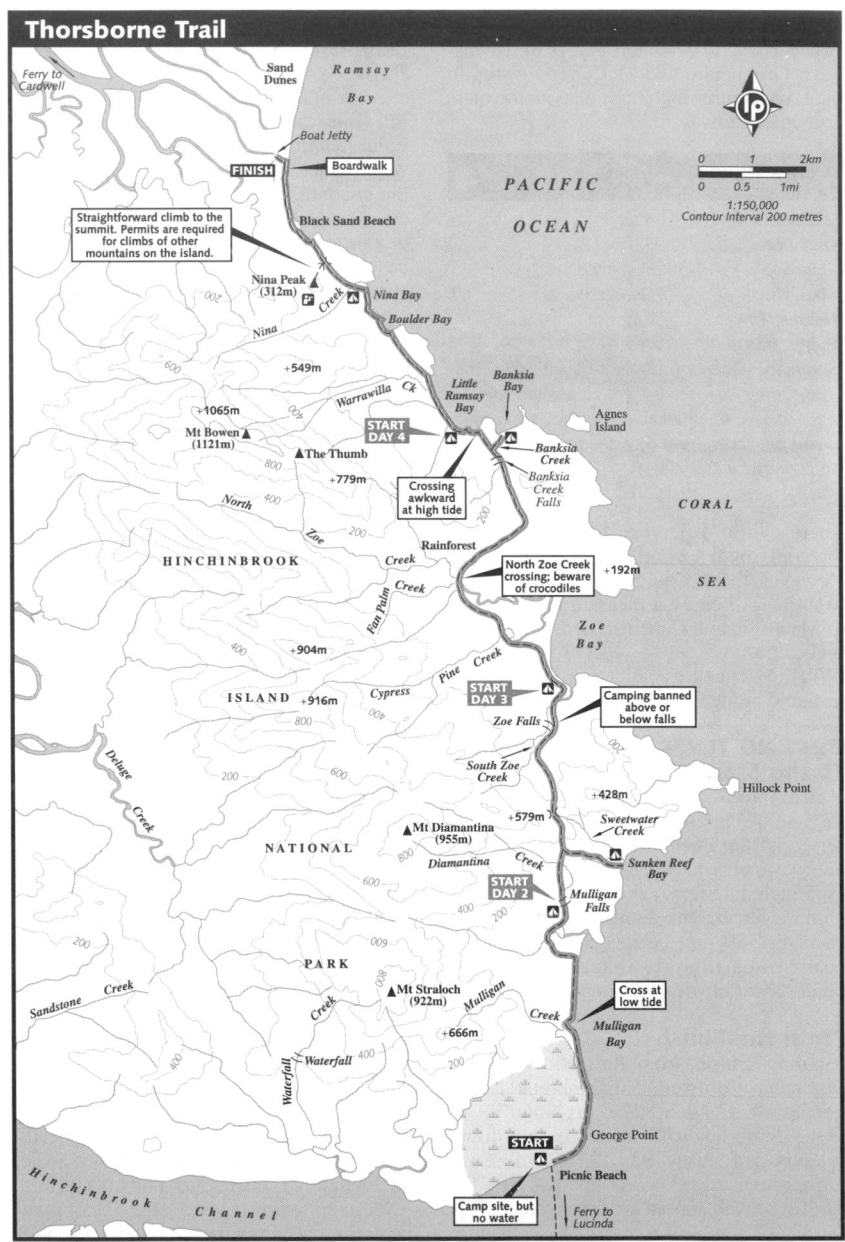

Ferry to Cardwell

Sand Dunes

Ramsay Bay

Boat Jetty

FINISH — Boardwalk

PACIFIC

Black Sand Beach

OCEAN

Straightforward climb to the summit. Permits are required for climbs of other mountains on the island.

Nina Peak (312m)

Nina Bay

Nina *Creek*

Boulder Bay

+549m

Warrawilla Ck

Little Ramsay Bay

Banksia Bay

Agnes Island

+1065m

START DAY 4

Banksia Creek

Mt Bowen (1121m)

▲The Thumb

Banksia Creek Falls

North *Zoe*

+779m

Crossing awkward at high tide

CORAL

HINCHINBROOK

Rainforest *Creek*

Fan Palm *Creek*

North Zoe Creek crossing; beware of crocodiles

+192m

SEA

Zoe Bay

+904m

ISLAND +916m

Cypress

Pine Creek

START DAY 3

Camping banned above or below falls

Zoe Falls

South Zoe Creek

+579m

+428m

Sweetwater Creek

Hillock Point

Deluge *Creek*

Mt Diamantina (955m)

Diamantina Creek

NATIONAL

START DAY 2

Mulligan Falls

Sunken Reef Bay

+200m

PARK

Sandstone *Creek*

Mt Straloch (922m)

Mulligan Creek

Cross at low tide

Mulligan Bay

+666m

Waterfall

Waterfall

Hinchinbrook

Channel

START

George Point

Picnic Beach

Camp site, but no water

Ferry to Lucinda

0   1   2km
0   0.5   1mi
1:150,000
Contour Interval 200 metres

RICHARD I'ANSON

PAUL SINCLAIR

MATTHEW FLETCHER

MATTHEW FLETCHER

MARK KIRBY

Top Left: Egg Rock in a sea of rainforest viewed from Bellbird Lookout, Lamington NP, Queensland. **Top Right:** Elabana Falls, Lamington NP. **Middle:** The clear, sand-filtered waters of Lake McKenzie, Fraser Island, Queensland. **Bottom Left:** Following 4WD tracks along 75 Mile Beach, Fraser Island. **Bottom Right:** Lake Wabby, Fraser Island's deepest perch lake, dammed by Hammerstone Sandblow.

Top: Mud flats, the preferred habitat of soldier crabs, Zoe Bay, Hinchinbrook Island, Queensland.
Middle: Clouds gathering over the peaks behind Zoe Bay, Hinchinbrook Island, Queensland.
Bottom: A walking party in dappled rainforest light on Mt Bartle Frere, Queensland.

of South Zoe Creek before finally settling on its western bank as it broadens before reaching the top of Zoe Falls (40 minutes from the saddle). Cross to the east bank and climb down (there's a fixed rope in one place) to a wonderful swimming hole (with rope swing) at the base of the falls.

Camping is not permitted at or above the falls so head downstream, cross South Zoe Creek (collect water here) and in 10 minutes you're at the *forest camp site*. However, the *beach camp site* a little farther on is better and has its own rat box and a toilet. Shoals of soldier crabs (responsible for the tiny balls of sand) can occasionally been seen scuttling around on the beach.

Day 3: Zoe Bay to Little Ramsay Bay
3¾–4¼ hours, 10.5km
Turn left out of the camp site and walk 400m down the beach (lined with yellow-flowering hibiscus in spring) and turn left onto a signposted trail that soon crosses a slow-moving, tannin-stained creek and passes some giant boulders. Twenty minutes after entering rainforest the trail turns left (west) and you skirt west of a large mangrove swamp before crossing the clear waters of **Cypress Pine Creek**.

For the next 40 minutes (to **Fan Palm Creek**) the route is characterised by creek crossings and boggy waterlogged palm swamp (you'll have to wade). The trail, which twists and turns north-west, can be unclear so keep your eye on the markers.

After crossing Fan Palm Creek (usually flowing), the trail heads downstream a short way before bearing left (north-west), reaching the wide **North Zoe Creek** after 15 minutes. Cross and head north-east into drier forest – saltwater crocodiles have been seen here so don't dawdle! The route then crosses several creek beds and drops to the western edge of a swampy plain before heading back into the forest. Twenty minutes later the trail starts following a small creek gully north uphill, eventually joining a well-made track that leads through tall grass and casuarina to a saddle with views of Zoe Bay.

The trail then winds down to **Banksia Creek Falls** (there's a small pool). Cross to the west bank and follow the well-constructed path to a T-junction. Turn right for Banksia Bay or continue straight for Little Ramsay Bay. Banksia Bay is a great place to *camp*, but there are no facilities – you will need to collect water from Banksia Creek. (However, the walk east to the headland opposite Agnes Island is sufficient compensation.)

Continuing on, the trail soon follows a gully north-west down to the edge of a small bay. Turn left, cross a tiny creek, walk to the end of the beach and scramble over a rocky headland to another small bay. Repeat this procedure across the second bay, then wade the tidal creek (difficult at high tide) at the south of **Little Ramsay Bay**. The *camp site*, 200m along the beach, has a rat box, but the toilet had been burnt down and not rebuilt at the time of research. Collect fresh running water where it enters the brackish lagoon behind the camp site. The beach offers fantastic views of the surrounding mountains.

Day 4: Little Ramsay Bay to Ramsay Bay
2½–4 hours, 6.5km
Cross the creek at the top of the beach and follow the trail inland (north-west). After climbing to a saddle the trail descends north to **Boulder Bay** 30 minutes after leaving the camp. Bear left along the shore, hopping over the beautifully rounded boulders, to a large balancing rock at the headland. The trail stays high on the rocks as it bends into **Nina Bay**, which is reached after climbing down a small cliff and crossing a tidal creek (at high tide a detour over the headland may be necessary). You may see green sea turtles on this section.

Nina Bay camp site is five minutes up the beautiful beach, which is lined with she-oaks, coconuts and mangroves. There's a toilet and rat box. Collect water from the creek at the southern end of the beach.

The trail moves through the camp site and heads west round an impressive mangrove forest, crossing wide sections of Nina Creek a couple of times (crossing may be difficult at high tide, and there's lots of rock hopping) before reaching higher ground and dry woodland. The trail then heads north following a small seasonal watercourse up to a saddle.

Here a worn trail (stick to it to prevent further erosion and damage to fragile heathland) leads west (sometimes a scramble) to **Nina Peak** (312m), reached in about 30 minutes. There are fantastic views of the island's rugged cliffs and mountains as well as the mangrove forests of Missionary Bay. Return by the same route.

Descend north-west from the saddle down to **Black Sand Beach** (water is usually available behind the small lagoon between January and August). Turn left and follow the trail as it turns away from the ocean, climbing to a ridge and arriving at **Ramsay Bay** 20 minutes later. Turn right and walk up the beach for about 15 minutes until spotting a path over the foreshore (it's halfway between the headland behind you and the dunes). Markers then lead past an Aboriginal shell midden and along a boardwalk to the boat jetty.

Wooroonooran National Park

Wooroonooran National Park not only provides a chance to tackle Queensland's highest peak (not something to be undertaken lightly), but also to climb through the varying strata of forest, from tall lowland rainforest to cloud forest. The national park's upland rainforest is part of a forest tract that's been growing here for 140 million years, since Australia was part of the great continent of Gondwanaland. It's of fantastic importance, so much so that Wooroonooran National Park was added to the World Heritage List in 1988.

NATURAL HISTORY

At lower altitudes evidence of cyclone damage can be seen – pockets of broken canopy have encouraged prolific growth, often of vine species. Look out for lawyer vines and stinging gympie trees.

With increasing altitude the forest reduces in size (both of leaf and trunk). On the peaks above 1500m the cloud forest has a low, dense canopy as a result of frequent high winds. Up on exposed high ridges (such as Top Eastern Camp) pockets of low scrub, grassland and heathland occur.

The park is home to several endemic plants and animals, including the Bartle Frere coolskink (restricted to exposed granite boulders at high altitudes). Other rare mammals include the green ringtail possum and tree-kangaroo, but most animals are nocturnal.

Birds are difficult to spot in the dense forest, but you'll certainly hear them. One speciality is the golden bowerbird, which only occurs above 900m and builds its bower around tree trunks. It collects shiny, often white, objects to display next to its bower. In spring these can be rare orchid petals!

PLANNING
When to Walk

For much of the year onshore winds blow up the Bellenden Ker Range, so be prepared for low cloud and rain – rainfall of 10m per annum has been recorded. The Wet lasts from December to April. At this time it's very wet and humid and leeches are a real problem. When Majuba Creek rises too high the trail is closed. Temperatures remain between 25°C and 32°C year-round, but July to September, when the views are best, is less humid. Temperatures can fall to zero at Top Eastern Camp.

What to Bring

Wet-weather gear, warm clothing, a fuel stove, compass and topographical map are essential. Stout boots are also recommended. You'll need a good strong tent for the exposed and windy Top Eastern Camp.

Maps

Sunmap's 1:50,000 *Bartle Frere* and *Malanda* maps cover the trail east to west. The *Bartle Frere* map is sufficient for the eastern route. The QPWS produces some good trail notes and these should be carried (they're available from the trailhead and park offices).

Information Sources
The QPWS office (☎ 07-4061 4291), Rising Sun Arcade, Owen St, Innisfail, is the best source of information. Rangers are also based at Josephine Falls (☎ 07-4067 6304, fax 4067 6443).

Permits & Regulations
Camping permits ($3.50) are acquired by self-registering at Josephine Falls car park. Take your rubbish out and do not walk alone. This is a fuel-stove-only walk.

NEAREST TOWNS
For a description of accommodation and other services in Cairns, see Gateways in the introduction to the chapter.

Innisfail
Innisfail, on the North and South Johnstone Rivers, is the nearest town to the trailhead. Basic camping supplies are available at Northern Stock Supplies (☎ 07-4061 1674), 131 Edith St, which is open from Monday to Saturday.

Places to Stay & Eat The pleasant *River-drive Caravan Park* (☎ 07-4061 2515, @ www.riverdrive@comnorth.com.au), 1km south of town on the Bruce Hwy, has good facilities – camp sites from $12 and cabins from $35 (for two). In town stay at *Codge Lodge*, with dorms from $17 and doubles from $35.

Close to Josephine Falls is *Bartle Frere Homestay* (☎ 07-4067 6309, @ bfhouse @fastinternet.net.au), which has a camp site and B&B accommodation.

The *Cane Cutter Pub* does a $6 buffet at lunch and dinner, while *Menamkhong Lao-Thai Restaurant* (☎ 07-4061 2822) is the sophisticated choice (mains start at $8.50). For self-caterers, there is also a *Coles* supermarket in the centre of town.

Getting There & Away Innisfail is 88km south-east of Cairns on the Bruce Hwy. Greyhound and McCafferty's stop opposite King George V Park on Edith St. Innisfail is serviced by the main east coast railway line (☎ 13 2232).

Mt Bartle Frere

Duration	2 days
Distance	15km
Standard	hard
Start/Finish	Josephine Falls car park
Nearest Town	Innisfail
Public Transport	yes (plus 8km road walk)

Summary A sustained climb of 1500m to the summit of Queensland's highest mountain, through varying strata of rainforest, and with camping beside the trail. Rain and low cloud are possible year-round.

The eastern approach (described in the main walk description) follows a clear, well-marked route to the summit, but it's not possible in one day. The western approach (described as an alternative route at the end of the walk description), where the trail starts at around 600m, offers the possibility of a complete traverse in one day and is arguably the most beautiful route up the mountain. However, there are considerable logistical problems and the trail, although marked, is sometimes unclear (seek ranger advice before setting out).

It's a 7.5km walk to the summit from both sides, but the trail is very steep in places and some scrambling is required. If you're fit and able, then the summit (a two- to three-hour round trip) can be reached late in the afternoon of the first day, which leaves more time on the second day for Broken Nose.

Due to the nature of the terrain and lush vegetation, view points are hard to find. The best ones are not from the summit, but from the ridge and boulder field close to Top Eastern Camp, and from Broken Nose. It's also worth remembering that only about 30% of the time (mostly during winter) will you get any really clear views from the top.

GETTING TO/FROM THE WALK
Both Greyhound and McCafferty's will drop you at the Josephine Falls turn-off on the Bruce Hwy, 43km south of Cairns. You may need to speak to their local offices in Cairns. The car park below Josephine Falls is another 8km from the highway along a sealed road.

QUEENSLAND

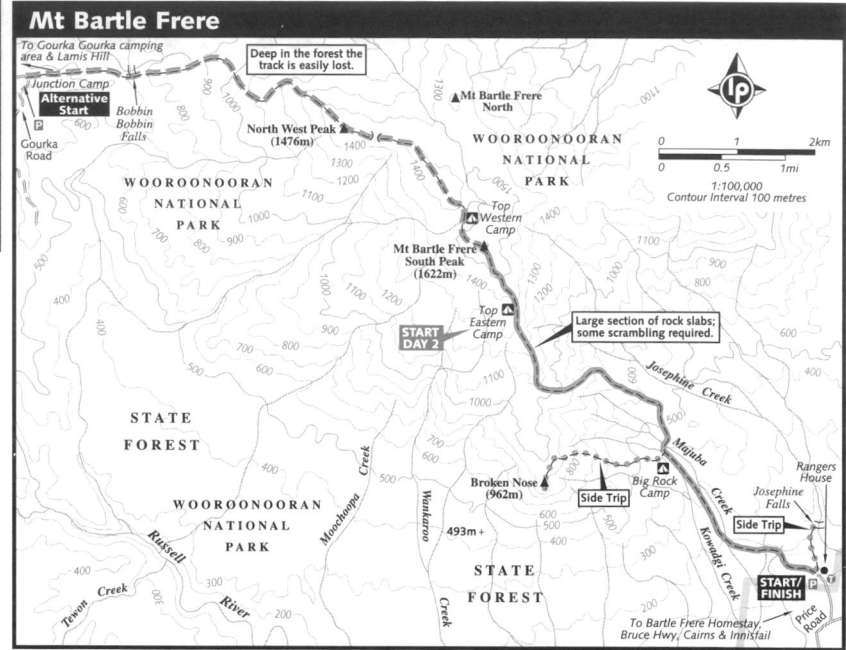

Mt Bartle Frere

The western trailhead (for the alternative route) is off Topaz Rd (south of the Gillies Hwy) in the Atherton Tablelands. Once past Butchers Creek turn left onto unsealed Gourka Rd and follow the signs past Gourka Gourka camping area (2WD vehicles may have to be left here) to Junction Camp (7km from Topaz Rd), where the trail begins. Wooroonooran Safaris (see Guided Walks under Information in the introduction to the chapter) starts its one-day traverse from here.

THE WALK
Day 1: Josephine Falls Car Park to Top Eastern Camp
5–6 hours, 6.5km, 1300m ascent
Follow the well-marked trail from Josephine Falls car park (where there are toilets and a shelter), which leads into dense rainforest, climbing steadily north-west across a series of low spurs and small, rocky creeks. After about an hour a creek is reached, followed shortly by the crossing of **Majuba Creek**.

The trail then climbs steeply to a narrow ridge; keeping the creek to your right, advance to ***Big Rock Camp*** beside Majuba Creek (a little over two hours' climb from the car park). It's a great spot (there are no facilities and watch the creek level in the Wet). A signpost points out the trail (south-west) to Broken Nose (962m) – see the side trip at the end of the Day 2 walk description.

Turn right for the summit, cross the creek (the last water before Top Eastern Camp) and begin the steep climb north then north-west along a spur. The route passes over a huge boulder in 10 minutes. For the next hour of the climb you'll have to make do with the occasional half-view through the trees as the trail climbs, increasingly steeply, past another enormous boulder and towards the main southern ridge of the mountain – some sections are a scramble.

Once on the main ridge, very narrow in places, the gradient eases off a little and after 1½ hours you emerge onto a pleasant grassy saddle. A sign points west to water in 300m. Follow this sign to a spring and *Top Eastern Camp*. On a good day the views from this exposed camp site at sunrise and sunset more than compensate for the arduous climb.

Day 2: Top Eastern Camp to Summit to Josephine Falls Car Park
7–8 hours, 8.5km, 220m ascent, 1520m descent

From Top Eastern Camp, walk back to the main ridge, dump your packs and turn left (north). Follow the trail up the ridge to the start of an impressive boulder field. Arrows and markers lead up through the mass of rock, from the top of which there are 180-degree views. Thirty minutes later the trail enters a patch of stunted cloud forest, then moves across a ridge of open heathland before climbing to the summit. The only view point is from a broad rock to the west.

From the summit the trail continues north down the western route, so turn around and retrace your steps to the car park or on to Broken Nose. If you've the energy for a cool swim, Josephine Falls are reached via an 800m trail from the car park.

Side Trip: Big Rock Camp to Broken Nose
1–5 hours, 4km return, 560m ascent, 560m descent

From the camp follow the sign south-west along a marked trail. Head south then west for over an hour, climbing steeply up the side of the main ridge emanating south from Mt Bartle Frere. The trail then swings south, crossing a number of rocky knolls before finally reaching Broken Nose (962m) after 40 minutes. The peak itself is more like the top of a cliff (and treacherous when wet), but the views out across the rainforest of the Russell River catchment are excellent.

Alternative Route: Gourka Rd to Summit
4½–5½ hours, 7.5km

Orange markers show the western approach to the summit of Mt Bartle Frere, but seek ranger advice before setting out.

From Gourka Rd, a 2km track leads east into the rainforest to a T-junction. Turn left descending along a narrow trail before climbing steeply and steadily past Bobbin Bobbin Falls (only 50m from the trail). The trail continues to climb east then south-east for the next three hours, often cutting across, round or under giant boulders, when track markers become obscured.

From North West Peak (1476m) the route continues down onto a ridge, reaching another view point in 15 minutes. From here there are great views north to Bellenden Ker (1582m) and the Mulgrave River valley. Descend south and continue along the ridge for 20 minutes, crossing one creek and reaching *Top Western Camp* before crossing a second creek. There's always water in the creek, but it can flood the camp site.

The trail then crosses an exposed ridge, passes the emergency helipad and scrambles through a patch of cloud forest to the summit.

Other Walks

Goldfield Trail
The 19km Goldfield Trail (once used by Aborigines, loggers and gold prospectors) cuts between Mt Bartle Frere and Mt Bellenden Ker in Wooroonooran National Park. There are camp sites at the western trailhead (15km from the Gillies Hwy into the Atherton Tablelands) and on the East Mulgrave River, about halfway, but not in the east, which does have access to the Bruce Hwy. Further information and park notes are available from rangers at Josephine Falls (☎ 07-4067 6304) or Innisfail (☎ 07-4061 4291).

Cooloola Wilderness Trail
Just south of Fraser Island is Cooloola National Park. A 43km walking trail, starting at Elanda Point on Lake Cootharaba, leads through wetland areas, forests and open plains on a three-day walk north to Rainbow Beach. Logistics can be a problem, but bus companies can get you near both trailheads. There's a good selection of bush camp sites in the park, but a quota system limits numbers so organise your permit well in advance. If you've had enough of walking, hire a boat from Tewantin, Booreen Point or Elanda Point and paddle up the Noosa River.

For more information contact the rangers at Elanda Point (☎ 07-5449 7364) or Rainbow Beach (☎ 07-5486 3160).

Carnarvon Gorge

About 21km of graded trails explore Carnarvon National Park in Queensland's Central Highlands. The gorge is the main attraction, with spectacular white cliffs, lush vegetation and Aboriginal rock art. A three-day walk follows the gorge upstream, climbs Battleship Spur and continues north-west to Mt Percy before descending Delay Ridge to Carnarvon Creek Camp and following the gorge back to the start. Basic supplies are available from the *Oasis Tourist Lodge* (☎ *07-4984 4503, 1800 644 150*), which also has cabins, 3km from the main camping area. Fuel stoves are essential for overnight walks. The creek water is not suitable for drinking. All proposed bushwalking routes must first be discussed with the rangers (☎ 07-4984 4505, fax 4984 4519).

Brisbane Forest Park

Brisbane Forest Park (☎ 07-3300 4855, **✉** Brisbane ForestPark@dnr.qld.gov.au) comprises 28,500 hectares of bushland, rainforest and eucalyptus woodland in the D'Aguilar Range, 11km north-west of Brisbane. Bushwalking areas include Walk-About Creek, Mt Nebo, Mt Glorious and Mt Samson. The park is also developing a long-range trail system. Information is available at the Naturally Queensland Information Centre (see Gateways earlier), which sells the good *Brisbane Forest Park* map, and from rangers at the park, with whom you'll need to book bush camping ($3.50 per person per night). Mountain biking and horse riding are also permitted.

Frequent No 385 buses run up to the park headquarters on Mt Nebo Rd.

The Glass House Mountains

For peak baggers and rock climbers these 13 abrupt volcanic crags close to the Sunshine Coast are a must. Col Smithies' *A Guidebook to Rockclimbing on the Glass House Mountains* is the best guide. Mt Ngungun is an easy climb, while the trails up Mts Beerwah and Tibrogargan are steep and tricky. More information can be gained from the rangers at Beerwah (☎ 07-5494 6630). There's also a series of walking trails around the bases of these mountains, which are enclosed within various small national parks.

Mt Barney National Park

Many of the mountains along the Queensland–NSW border offer good bushwalking and there are a number of tough routes around Mt Barney, many of which require route finding and serious scrambling. One challenging 20km-plus circuit leads from Cranes Creek up along the south-east ridge to the East Peak of Mt Barney. Descend along the south-west ridge and head on to Mt Ernest. The terrain is tough, with scrub woodland and rainforest encountered. Sunmap's 1:25,000 *Mt Barney* and *Mt Lindesay* maps cover the area. Bush camping permits and advice should be sought from the ranger at Boonah (☎ 07-5463 1579).

Baron Gorge

In the mountains about 15km north-west of Cairns lies Baron Gorge National Park, 284,000 hectares of World Heritage List rainforest. At the time of writing a camp site and several walking tracks were under construction, being upgraded or awaiting signage. The existing Smith and Douglas Tracks (old Aboriginal tracks, used by early gold diggers) were being connected and a camp site at Speewah is planned. When complete this should allow two- to three-day walks in the area. For further information contact the Department of Environment and Heritage in Cairns (☎ 07-4052 3096).

South Australia

A network of accessible, well-maintained parks and reserves in South Australia (SA) offers numerous walking possibilities. With 21% of SA's land under some form of conservation control and considerable official enthusiasm for walking, marked trails run across many of the state's parks. Much of the protected land is in the vast, arid, low-lying (rarely above 300m) region of plains, salt pans and desert to the north and east. This is the true Outback, forming 80% of SA and with a population of only about 15,000 people.

The Flinders Ranges rise to the east of this region. Running 800km north-east from the Adelaide Hills to the Gammon Ranges, they offer gorge walking par excellence (Morialta Conservation Park and Mt Remarkable National Park), peak bagging (at 1170m St Mary Peak at Wilpena Pound in Flinders Ranges National Park is the highest point in the range) and long-distance walks (the Heysen Trail follows the range for its entire length) in beautiful, arid and dramatic country. And some of it, eg, Morialta Conservation Park, is only a short bus ride from Adelaide. Farther south, Kangaroo Island is brimming with wildlife and offers a complete change of landscape.

HISTORY

There has been considerable human influence on SA's landscape. At the time of colonial settlement in the 1830s, 43 Aboriginal tribes totalling between 10,000 and 15,000 people populated the state. Those living in the temperate area between Gulf St Vincent and the Victorian border had done so for tens of thousands of years.

In 1836 Kingscote, established by the British on Kangaroo Island, became the first official European settlement in SA. Shortly after Adelaide was settled, there was a rush to cultivate all available land; wheat was the major crop and millions of sheep were raised in the arid lands farther north. Copper discoveries in the mid-1800s

Highlights

JASON EDWARDS

The dramatic ridgelines of the Flinders Ranges, seen from near Wilpena Pound

- Walking the wild west coast of Kangaroo Island through Ravine des Casoars Wilderness Protection Area

- Climbing St Mary Peak in Wilpena Pound to get some spectacular views across the Flinders Ranges

- Strolling between the stunning red cliffs of Alligator Gorge in Mt Remarkable National Park

- Traversing along the cliffs and deep gorges of Morialta Conservation Park

made many people rich, while oil, gas, gold, silver and uranium reserves still sustain an economy prone to a pattern of boom and bust. In recent years tourism has become a major industry and is worth around $1.9 billion annually.

NATURAL HISTORY

About 800 million years ago the earth's crust thinned and formed a long trough

South Australia

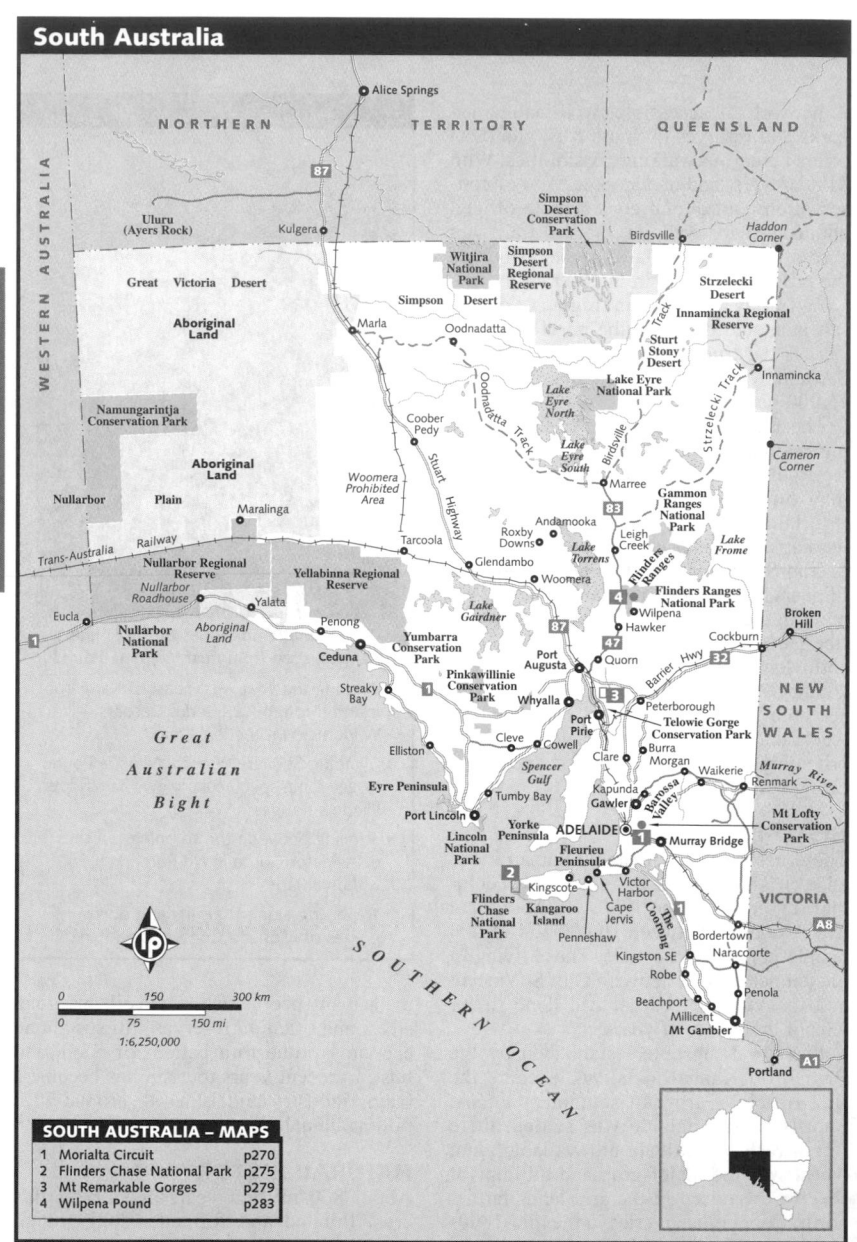

	SOUTH AUSTRALIA – MAPS	
1	Morialta Circuit	p270
2	Flinders Chase National Park	p275
3	Mt Remarkable Gorges	p279
4	Wilpena Pound	p283

called the Adelaide Geosyncline. Submerged under the ocean, it reached from Kangaroo Island in the south to Mt Hopeless in the north and filled with sediment over the next 300 million years. Subsequent geological upheavals folded and buckled the sedimentary rock into the mountain ranges that run north from Cape Jervis to the Strzelecki Desert. The prominent ridges are comprised of quartzite, a rock resistant to weathering, while less resistant mudstone, shale and siltstone have formed plains and valleys. There's a distinct difference between the vegetation types to the north and south of this range, with eucalyptus woodland and scrub to the south and acacia and saltbrush to the north – Mt Remarkable National Park is a good place to spot this crossover.

The rest of SA is made up of several ancient, stable blocks (or cratons) of igneous and metamorphic rocks separated by younger sedimentary basins. Some of these blocks are over 2.7 billion years old and probably formed part of the earth's first continental crust.

INFORMATION
Maps
UBD produces the very good 1:1,750,000 *South Australia* map, which covers the entire state and is widely available overseas. The state is covered by Auslig's 1:250,000 and 1:100,000 map series, which are useful for trip planning.

Landsmap (part of the Department of Lands and Planning) publishes a 1:50,000 series covering settled areas and national parks. Useful small-scale walking maps are available for popular walking areas close to Adelaide, where you should buy all your maps. For maps covering individual walks, see the Planning section in the introduction to each walk.

Buying Maps The Map Shop (☎ 08-8231 2033, @ mercator@mapshop.net.au, 🖳 map shop.net.au), 16a Peel St, just off Hindley St, Adelaide, is a one-stop shop for topographical maps and regional guides. You can mail order through its Web site.

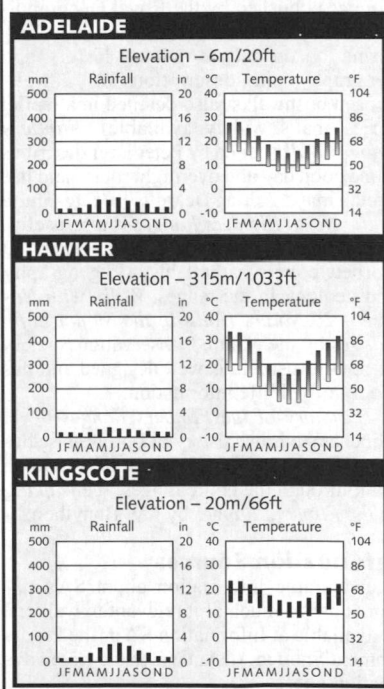

The Climate of South Australia

South Australia has hot, dry summers and cool winters, and the farther north you go the hotter and drier it becomes. Most rain falls between May and August, with June usually the wettest month. Winters are mild, but snow occasionally falls high in the Mt Lofty and Flinders Ranges. The state is fiercely hot between October and April, with temperatures over 35°C not uncommon in Adelaide and normal in the Outback (where 50.7°C is the highest recorded temperature).

South Australia is the country's driest state, with 80% of the land receiving less than 250mm of rainfall per year. Kangaroo Island and the Mt Lofty Ranges, east of Adelaide, fare better than many areas, receiving over 750mm of rainfall annually. Mt Lofty, east of Adelaide, receives an annual average of 1200mm.

SOUTH AUSTRALIA

Heysen Trail

Named after Sir Hans Heysen (1877–1968), a renowned painter of the Flinders Ranges and Mt Lofty areas, the Heysen Trail stretches for a whopping 1200km from Cape Jervis on the south coast to Parachilna Gorge in the Northern Flinders Ranges. In between it crosses large tracts of farmland and numerous national parks, including Mt Remarkable and the Flinders Ranges.

Guides and maps to the different sections of the trail are available in Adelaide. For up-to-date information, contact The Friends of the Heysen Trail (☎ 08-8212 6299, fax 8211 8041, ❻ heysentrail@newave.net.au, 🖳 www.newave.net.au/~heysentrail), at 10 Pitt St, Adelaide. The group maintains the trail and organises transport and food and water drops for long-distance walkers.

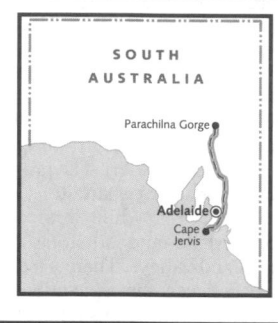

Books
Lonely Planet's *South Australia* is an excellent guide to the state. *Explore the Flinders Ranges* published by the Royal Geographical Society of Australia contains heaps of information on culture, natural history and geography, plus descriptions of 12 well-chosen bushwalks (also detailed in a leaflet series that's widely available). *Flinders Ranges Walks* edited by Peter Beer describes some good day and overnight routes and has sketch maps. Adrian Heard's *Walking Guide to the North Flinders Ranges* is also useful. *A Field Guide to the Flinders Ranges* by D Corbett covers natural history, geography and geology in the ranges. *Walks with Nature – 20 Nature Walks in the Mount Lofty Ranges* by the Nature Conservation Society of South Australia is well designed and has plenty of wildlife information.

The Story of the Flinders Ranges by H Mincham tells the history of European settlement. For an inspiring account of a 1000km walk through the entire ranges, see *Walking in the Flinders Ranges* by CW Bonython.

Information Sources
Considerable information about SA's national parks, much of it relevant to walkers, is available at Information SA or the Environment Shop in Adelaide (see the Gateways section later).

The state-wide Walking Federation of SA (☎ 08-8363 6955, ❻ walksa@senet.com.au, 🖳 users.senet.com.au/~walksa/walksa), PO Box 509, Stepney, SA 5069, publishes the excellent (free) *Walking SA Resource Book*, widely available in Adelaide.

Weather charts and forecasts are published in the daily Adelaide *Advertiser*, as well as appearing on the evening television news bulletins.

Permits & Regulations
During days of Total Fire Ban, all fires are forbidden, even fuel stoves. If you are caught with an open fire on these days, you are not only endangering yourself and the environment, but you can also cop a hefty fine and/or prison sentence. See Responsible Walking in the Facts for the Walker chapter for suggestions on how to minimise your impact on the environment.

Guided Walks
Ecotrek/Bogong Jack Adventures (☎ 08-8383 7198, ❻ ecotrek@ozemail.com.au, 🖳 www.ecotrek.com.au) and Nature Trek South Australia (☎ 08-8387 3588, ❻ naturetrek@dove.net.au, 🖳 naturetrek.mtx.net) are two reputable companies that organise day and overnight walks throughout SA.

GATEWAYS
Adelaide
Adelaide is a superbly situated city with much to commend it. The cool, tranquil Adelaide Hills lie a few kilometres to the

east of the city centre, while 10km to the west are the sandy beaches of Gulf St Vincent. Art galleries and fine historic buildings abound and there are more restaurants here per capita than in any other city in Australia. It's also relatively easy to replace gear and pick up walking information here.

Information Information SA (☎ 08-8204 1900) and The Environment Shop (☎ 08-8204 1910, @ environmentshop@dehaa .sa.gov.au) are at 77 Grenfell St (PO Box 1047, Adelaide, SA 5001). Both are open on weekdays, offer good regional information and sell books and topographical maps.

Adelaide Bushwalkers, PO Box 178, Unley, SA 5061, meets at 8 pm on the first and third Wednesday of the month at the Girl Guides Hall, 278 South Terrace.

Tourist and general information is available from the South Australian Travel Centre (☎ 1300 65 5276, @ info .visit-southaustralia@saugov.sa.gov.au, 🖳 www.visit-southaustralia.com.au), 1 King William St. The travel centre is open daily and can provide some bushwalking information.

Supplies & Equipment Take your pick from a cluster of well-stocked camping shops at the eastern end of Rundle St. These include Flinders Camping (☎ 08-8223 1913), Snowgum (☎ 08-8223 5544) and Paddy Pallin (☎ 08-8232 3155).

Places to Stay & Eat The friendly *Backpack Australia* (☎ 08-8231 0639, 1800 804 133, 128 Grote St) is a well-run hostel close to the main bus station on Franklin St. Dorm beds cost $14 and twins/doubles $32. It's linked to the *Hampshire Hotel*, a lively pub with cheap food.

Opposite the main bus station is the huge *Cannon St Backpackers* (☎ 08-8231 0639, 1800 069 731, @ cannonst@senet.com.au, 110 Franklin St), a brightly painted place with secure parking and good facilities. Dorm beds cost $15 and doubles/twins $36.

The *Central Market*, between Gouger and Grote Sts, is great for all types of cheap food. *Chinatown* lies at the western end of Central Market.

If you want to spend up big ($20 to $30 per head) try *Gouger Fish Café* (☎ 08-8231 2320, 100 Gouger St), which serves excellent seafood and grills.

Two supermarkets, *Woolworths* on Rundle Mall and *Coles* on Grote St, are open daily.

Getting There & Away Adelaide is located in the Gulf St Vincent on Australia's south coast. From Melbourne, take the Western and Dukes Hwys, or the Princes Hwy for a longer but more scenic coastal route. From Sydney, take the Hume and Sturt Hwys. The Great Eastern and Eyre Hwys span the Nullarbor to Perth in the west.

Air Adelaide's airport caters for domestic and international flights (a bus to the city centre costs $6). Adelaide is a long way from other major cities and Qantas (☎ 13 1313) and Ansett (☎ 13 1300) fares are high. Kendell Airlines (book through Ansett) operates regional services, but also is not cheap. International fares to Adelaide compare well with those into Sydney.

Bus Greyhound (☎ 08-8231 1701, 13 2030, @ express@greyhound.com.au) and McCafferty's (☎ 08-8212 5066, 13 1499, @ in fomcc@mccaffertys.com.au) for interstate buses and Premier Stateliner (☎ 08-8415 5500, @ premstat@premierstateliner.com .au) for regional services all use the bus station at 101–111 Franklin St. McCafferty's passes are valid for the *Indian-Pacific* train between Perth and Port Augusta. Firefly (☎ 08-8231 1488, 1800 631 164) operates between Melbourne and Adelaide and leaves from outside its office at 110 Franklin St.

Train Interstate trains arrive at the station on Railway Terrace, Keswick, south-west of the city centre (the city bus to the station costs $3). Great Southern Railway (☎ 13 2147) runs services between Adelaide and Melbourne, Alice Springs, Perth and Sydney. Inquire about budget stand-by tickets; $30 for Melbourne–Adelaide is common.

Getting Around Adelaide's city centre is laid out on a grid so it's easy to get around.

TransAdelaide (TA; ☎ 08-8210 1000), on the corner of King William and Currie Sts, runs a comprehensive, integrated and relatively cheap public transport system covering buses, trains and trams. One-way tickets cost $2.80 before 9 am, after 3 pm and on weekends, and $1.60 between 9 am and 3 pm weekdays. Tickets are valid for two hours from the start of your journey. An all-day ticket is $5.40.

There are dozens of car hire agencies in Adelaide, including all the majors. Try Hertz (☎ 08-8231 2856), 233 Morphett St, Delta (☎ 13 1390) or Access Rent-a-Car (☎ 08-8212 5900; 1800 812 580, fax 8212 4499). Access is the cheapest, with small cars from $54 per day with 100km free. Daily rates decrease for longer hiring periods.

Port Augusta

If you're walking in the Flinders Ranges you're likely to end up at Port Augusta at some point. For walking information try The Wadlata Outback Centre (☎ 1800 633 060, fax 8642 4288, @ wadlata@wadarid .mtx.net), on the corner of Flinders Terrace and Marryatt St. Open daily, it has plenty of information about the Ranges. Home Hardware (☎ 08-8641 0011), on the corner of Commercial Rd and Flinders Terrace, also open daily, has limited camping supplies.

Places to Stay & Eat The *Shoreline Caravan Park (☎ 08-8642 2965)*, on Gardiner Ave, has camping from $8 per person and caravan-style accommodation for $30 to $50 for two people. The facilities at the park are good.

Hotel Flinders (☎ 08-8642 2544, 39 Commercial Rd) is central and offers 1970s-style rooms for $45/60 per single/double. Dorm beds (not available Sunday) are $15. Reasonable meals cost from $4.50.

Sandwich boards outside pubs and hotels display the best meal deals (around $6 for a buffet). *Peppers Café (☎ 08-8642 2549, 34 Commercial Rd)* is the flashest cafe in town.

For general supplies, *Woolworths* supermarket, on Tassie St, is better stocked than *Coles*, on the corner of Jervois and Marryatt Sts. Both are open daily until late.

Getting There & Away Port Augusta is 308km from Adelaide on the Stuart Hwy.

Air Several regional airlines fly into the airport, on Caroona Rd West. Qantas (☎ 13 1313) flies from Adelaide, and the full economy off-peak fare is $286.

Bus The bus terminal (☎ 08-8642 5055) used by Premier Stateliner and Greyhound is on Mackay St in the town centre. The McCafferty's stop is at the Shell Meteor Roadhouse on Hwy 1.

Train The train station lies south-east of the town centre on Stirling Rd. Book trains to Adelaide, Alice Springs and Perth through Harvey World Travel (☎ 08-8642 6699).

Car Rental Budget Rent-a-Car (☎ 08-8642 6040) is at 16 Young St. Port Augusta Rent-a-Car (☎ 08-8642 6827, 0408 387 545), 2 Caroona Rd, offers cars from $64 per day including 200km free. 4WD vehicles are in short supply and expensive.

Mt Lofty Ranges

These ranges on the edge of Adelaide have some excellent day walking in Morialta Conservation Park on purpose-built trails, through a forested landscape cut by tremendous gorges and stunning waterfalls. On the crest of the Mt Lofty Ranges you could be 100km from the nearest drive-in burger joint or crowded supermarket, yet Adelaide is just a 30-minute bus ride from the park gate.

The Kaurna (pronounced gowna) Aboriginal people named the area Morialta, meaning 'Overflowing', a reference to Fourth Creek, which in the past flowed year-round. On its banks you're likely to see white-faced herons. The native yellow-footed antechinus is also a speciality of this 536-hectare park.

PLANNING
When to Walk
The best time to walk is between May and October when the park is cooler and the creek

is flowing well. In high summer (when the park occasionally closes due to the high risk of fire) you'll have to carry a full day's water. Wild flowers bloom in late winter and spring. Rock climbing is also possible in the park.

Maps

The Friends of Black Hill and Morialta produces the useful 1:20,000 *Black Hill and Morialta Conservation Parks* map showing all the major trails. Landsmap's 1:50,000 *Adelaide* map covers this and other parks in the Adelaide Hills.

Morialta Circuit

Duration	4½–5 hours
Distance	13.5km
Standard	easy-medium
Start/Finish	Corner of Stradbroke and Morialta Rds
Nearest Town	Adelaide
Public Transport	yes

Summary Well-made marked walking trails with some cliff-side traverses wind through a forested landscape cut by deep gorges and waterfalls. The Heysen Trail lies at the western-most point, on the Adelaide Hills summit ridge.

NEAREST TOWN & FACILITIES

For a description of accommodation and other services in Adelaide, see Gateways in the introduction to the chapter.

There's a basic *youth hostel* on Moores Rd in Norton Summit. Dorm beds cost $15, payable in advance at the Adelaide YHA office (☎ 08-8231 5583, @ yhasa@ozemail.com.au), 38 Sturt St, where you can pick up the keys.

GETTING TO/FROM THE WALK

Take the regular bus No 105 (Monday to Saturday) from stop E3 on Currie St in Adelaide to stop 26 on the corner of Stradbroke and Morialta Rds (35 minutes). Bus Nos 105, 116 or 112 will get you back to town.

THE WALK

From the bus stop walk up the drive into the park, past the ranger post (on the left) and turn right (before crossing Fourth Creek) onto a 4WD track. Fork left immediately onto the very steep Hogan Hill Track, leading to a **lookout** in 10 minutes. On a good day Gulf St Vincent is visible beyond Adelaide's skyscrapers. Head south-east over the summit to a crossroads. Turn left then bear right following a broad trail east (uphill) to **Pretty Corner**. Just before the **lookout** (which has great views of First Falls) turn left (north) down a steep trail. Turn left at the first T-junction and then bear left after passing a collection of boulders on your right, zigzagging down to a T-junction below another collection of rocks. Turn right then fork right along the She-Oak Trail, which hugs the side of the gorge down to Fourth Creek. Cross and then turn left up to the excellent lower **viewing platform** above First Falls.

Return to Fourth Creek and continue upstream along the north bank until a series of steps leads up to a higher parallel path before **Second Falls**. Continue upstream, below the impressive cliffs and past **Third Falls**, before zigzagging high above the creek to a hut, water tank and 4WD track. Turn left and begin to climb as the route leads up Twin Creek Track to Centre Track, then through eucalyptus and banksia woodland to a T-junction on the very crest of the range. Straight ahead the land drops away to a beautiful valley, while to the right is Moores Rd leading to the youth hostel. Turn left then after 10 minutes turn left again beneath some power lines onto Rocky Hill Track.

Keep to this well-made track as it descends (there are two excellent **lookouts** on the left) over a saddle and down a very steep slope. Halfway down this slope, turn left down a small, easily missed narrow track leading to **Deep View Lookout**.

Turn left (east) and walk along Banksia Trail around a steep gully and south to Lovers Creek, where a 4WD track is met. Bear right, climbing steeply up the 4WD track until reaching a switchback where a gentle trail (the Stringybark Trail) bears off left down to Fourth Creek. Cut back west (right) to Second Falls, staying on the higher path to the higher **viewing platform** above First Falls.

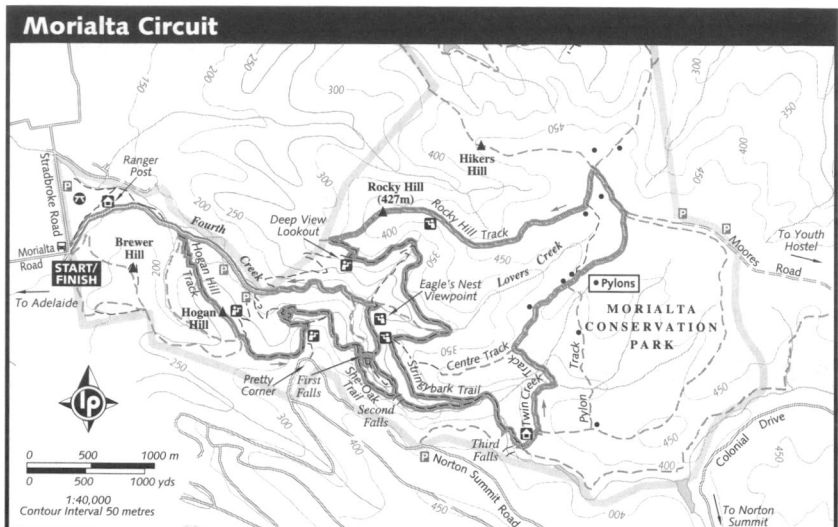

Morialta Circuit

SOUTH AUSTRALIA

From there a path leads past the shaded **Eagle's Nest Viewpoint** back to Lovers Creek, from where Centre Track leads to the main car park and back to Stradbroke Rd.

Flinders Chase National Park

The only Wilderness Protection Areas in SA are on Kangaroo Island, and the largest of these is Flinders Chase National Park, on the wild west coast. Wildlife abounds on the island and challenging walking trails give access to this wonderful area of dense mallee scrub, narrow creeks, isolated bays and towering cliffs eroded by the powerful Southern Ocean.

HISTORY

Aboriginal people once inhabited Kangaroo Island, but abandoned it around 2250 years ago. Matthew Flinders noted the first European sighting of the island in 1802 and gave it its name (after collecting many of the island's bouncing inhabitants for his larder). The first European settlers were escaped convicts, deserting sailors and sealers and whalers, although the island didn't officially become a settlement until 1836.

Generally, the land is agriculturally poor – and was particularly so before the introduction of chemical fertilisers in around 1900. Consequently, the western end of the island was never developed and is now protected by Flinders Chase National Park.

NATURAL HISTORY

The oldest section may be 750 million years old, but most of Kangaroo Island is sedimentary sandstone, shale and schist formed around 550 million years ago. Kangaroo Island was separated from the mainland about 9500 years ago by a rise in the sea level after the last ice age.

Ten thousand years of isolation has led to some species variation between the island's fauna and that of the mainland. Much of the fauna still thrives as foxes, rabbits and feral cats were never introduced. The Kangaroo Island kangaroo is a smaller sub-species of the western grey kangaroo, while the fangs of the island's black tiger snakes are smaller than their mainland cousins. Here the tammar wallaby is common to the point of being a pest, although only tiny numbers exist on the mainland. Also look out for the short-beaked echidna and Rosenberg's sand goanna, which grows up to 1m long and is the island's largest predator.

Along the coast are large colonies of Australian sea-lions and New Zealand fur-seals, and little penguin (sometimes called fairy penguin) rookeries dot the western coastline. Southern right and humpback whales annually migrate down the west coast between May and October.

The island has 251 recorded bird species and you may see white-bellied sea-eagles and ospreys soaring above the rocky cliffs. Rarities include bush stone-curlews, beautiful firetails and glossy black-cockatoos (around 250 exist in the wild). In creek beds, purple-crowned and rainbow lorikeets feed on the nectar of tall sugar and river red gums.

There are over 400 species of plants in the park, including 40 endemic to Flinders Island. Scarlet bottlebrush, pig face (a succulent with large daisy-like pink flowers), coastal heath, daisies and rosemary are all common along the cliff tops. Dense thickets of mallee dominate much of the park. Patches of banksia, yaccas, she-oaks and various species of eucalyptus are also found.

In the 1920s and 1930s, nonendemic animals and birds were introduced when it was feared mainland populations would disappear. Species that survived and thrive include the koala (see the boxed text 'Don't Shoot the Koalas'), Cape Barren goose, platypus and ringtail possum.

PLANNING
When to Walk
The island's climate is milder than the mainland, being cooler in summer and warmer in winter. March to May and August to October are probably the best times to walk. Numerous wild flowers bloom from late July to November. In January and February average temperatures range between 20°C and 25°C, and prevailing winds mean coastal temperatures rarely exceed 35°C. In the depths of winter (when night-time temperatures of 1°C can occur) biting winds blowing off the Southern Ocean make the exposed west and

Don't Shoot the Koalas

Koalas are not indigenous to Kangaroo Island but were introduced in 1923 when numbers on the mainland had declined so severely it was feared they'd become extinct. Since then the cuddly-looking creatures have reproduced so successfully that they're now fast eating themselves out of habitat – due to sustained browsing, trees in some areas have lost 50% of their canopy. So numbers must be reduced, although rest assured, no koala will bite the bullet on Kangaroo Island. Koalas are captured, sterilised, tagged and either returned to the same tree or relocated to a suitable habitat elsewhere in SA.

For more information, you can contact Koala Rescue (fax 08-8204 9383), PO Box 1047, Adelaide, SA 5001.

southern coasts unpleasant. In fact, be prepared for driving rain and strong winds at any time of year. River crossings can remain difficult until September.

At peak periods camp site water tanks are filled, but they're often empty late in the Dry. Check with the rangers.

What to Bring
The weather is unpredictable so be prepared with waterproofs, warm clothes, hats and sunscreen. Fractured rock is common terrain along the cliff tops so stout boots are recommended. During the Dry season you will probably need to carry an entire day's water between camps. Park regulations require that you use a fuel stove for cooking.

Maps
Landsmap 1:50,000 *Borda* and *Vennachar* maps cover the area, but trails are not marked. Landsmap also publishes the useful *A Tourist's Map of Kangaroo Island* (available locally), which shows some trails. The park notes are very useful.

Information Sources
The visitor centre is at Rocky River (☎ 08-8559 7235). The useful Kangaroo Island

SOUTH AUSTRALIA

Gateway Information Centre (☎ 08-8553 1322, fax 8553 1355, ✆ tourki@ozemail .com.au, 🖳 www.tourkangarooisland.com .au) is on Howard Drive in Penneshaw, not far from the ferry terminal. Both are open daily (weekends 10 am to 4 pm). There's also a park office in Kingscote (see Nearest Town & Facilities later in this chapter).

Rainbow Walkabout (☎/fax 08-8553 5350, ✆ kiecology@kin.on.net) runs group bushwalks with overnight camping and 4WD wildlife tours. Kangaroo Island Walking Club (☎ 08-8559 2222), PO Box 251, Kingscote, Kangaroo Island, SA 5223, welcomes nonmembers (it's $1 per walk plus a share of costs).

Permits & Regulations

At the time of writing a major assessment of all safety and conservation issues related to walking in the park was being undertaken. A Minimum Impact Code is currently in place, but it's likely that even tighter controls on bush camping and long-distance walking will be imposed, especially along the popular coastal Harvey's Return to Hanson Bay route. It's essential to contact the rangers to discuss routes, arrange permits and book camp sites.

Entry to the park is $8 per car (maximum five people) or $3.50 per person per day. However, you need pay this only once if you're staying within the park.

If you wish to walk away from the marked trails or camp in nondesignated camp sites you must complete a Trip Intentions Form and discuss your proposal with the Ranger-In-Charge (☎ 08-8559 7235, fax 8559 7268), Flinders Chase National Park, PO Box 246, Kingscote, SA 5223. You *must* inform park staff on completion of your walk.

Camping is $3 per person per night, either in bush camps or established sites. Arrange all camp sites and bush camping permits at least one month in advance, and far earlier if you're intending to visit during public or school holidays. Bookings can be made by phone, but you'll need to pay and collect your permits at the Rocky River visitor centre.

Fuel stoves only must be used on all walking routes.

GETTING AROUND

Without a vehicle, getting around the island is a nightmare. Hitching is possible if you have the time and patience, but hiring a car is a good idea. At the time of writing Hertz (☎ 08-8553 2390, 1800 088 296, ✆ hertzki @kin.on.net) in Kingscote was offering small vehicles for $50 per day including 200km free. Budget (☎ 08-8553 3133, ✆ budgetki@kin.on.net) and Penneshaw Car Rentals (☎ 08-8598 0023) are slightly more expensive. Kangaroo Island Kombi Campers (☎ 08-8553 7195, ✆ kicamp@kin.on.net) rents campervans from $100 per day and sometimes runs walkers to the trailheads ($1 per kilometre, with a maximum of five people). Petrol is unavailable in the park and roads are unsealed.

The major coach tour operators on the island, such as Sea Link (see Getting There & Away for Kingscote), may have a cheap spare seat into the park, but availability is only clear on the day of departure and it cannot guarantee getting you back out of the park.

PAUL SINCLAIR

Strangely eroded rock formations at Remarkable Rocks, Flinders Chase National Park

Phytophthora

Phytophthora cinnamomi, also called dieback, is a serious threat to native plants on the island. It's spread by the movement of soil and plant material so you must clean all shoes, tents, trowels etc before leaving a camp site: use the special cleaning boxes provided.

NEAREST TOWN & FACILITIES
Kingscote

With more facilities than Penneshaw (where the ferry comes in), this small town makes a better base. There's a park office (☎ 08-8553 2381), 37 Dauncey St, and branches of the Bank of SA (with an ATM) and ANZ on Dauncey St. Eftpos is available at many shops.

Places to Stay & Eat On the Esplanade *Kangaroo Island Caravan Park (☎ 08-8553 2325)* has sites from $12, self-contained cabins for $45 and flats for $55.

Kangaroo Island Central Backpackers Hostel (☎ 08-8553 2787, 19 Murray St) is spartan but clean and friendly. Dorm beds cost $14 and doubles $37 (linen $3).

The *Caltex garage*, open daily, is good for basics. The *Foodland* supermarket, on Commercial St, is open Monday to Saturday.

Getting There & Away Kendell Airlines (☎ 08-8231 9567, ✉ pfurseman@hotmail .com) has flights to the island for between $49 and $90 one way. Emu Airways (☎ 08-8234 3711, 1800 182 353, ✉ emuair@dove .net.au) has a standard return for $160, although there are discounts for advance purchase. The Airport Shuttle (☎ 08-8553 2390) into Kingscote is $10.

The Sea Link Kangaroo Island (☎ 08-8553 1122, 13 1301, ✉ kiexpert@sealink .com.au) ferry leaves Cape Jervis on the mainland at 9 am and 6 pm, departing from Penneshaw at 8.30 and 10.30 am, and 7.30 pm. It has offices at the Adelaide bus station, Penneshaw and Kingscote. The 40-minute journey costs $32/64 single/return for foot passengers and $48/96 with a coach transfer from Adelaide. Cars cost $69/138 including

the driver, but all other passengers pay. Coach transfer between Penneshaw and Kingscote costs $11.

Flinders Chase National Park

The *camp site* at Harvey's Return, 3km east of the lightstation, has toilets, a water tank, possums and superb fairy wrens. It costs $3 per person.

The *camp site* at Rocky River has the best facilities (hot showers, a kiosk selling ice cream and hot snacks, plus a phone). You can rent *Mays Homestead* ($27.50 per person) or the *Postman's Cottage* ($15 per person).

There's a variety of self-catering heritage accommodation near the trailheads. At the lightstation *Woodward Hut*, *Hartley Hut* and *Flinders Light Lodge* cost $10/20/30 per person respectively and sleep two, four and six. Bring your own linen.

West Coast Circuit

Duration	2 days
Distance	33km
Standard	medium
Start/Finish	Ravine des Casoars car park
Nearest Town	Kingscote
Public Transport	no

Summary This walk takes in a superb slice of the exposed wild, west coast of Kangaroo Island, including the picturesque West Bay and Ravine des Casoars (a haven for wildlife).

Covering part of the west coast of Kangaroo Island, this walk heads south across high limestone cliffs, passing shipwreck sites and isolated rocky coves to West Bay. At the very beginning the route leads down into Ravine des Casoars, with abundant wildlife, while on the return leg you may see a koala or glossy black-cockatoo.

Due to the terrain (fractured rock), Day 1 is hard going, but fitter walkers can make it more challenging by starting from the Cape Borda Lightstation (featured in the boxed text 'Cape Borda Lightstation') – a highly recommended detour whichever route you take. From the lightkeeper's kiosk (which sells hot snacks, sweets etc) head north to the wooden barrier then turn south-west and south, heading across the windswept, rocky cliff tops. It's slow going.

Alternatively, the Cape Borda section could also be done as a circular day walk linking the lightstation with Ravine des Casoars and Harvey's Return. From the Ravine des Casoars, walk north along the road for 9.5km back to Cape Borda (taking in some fine sugar gum stands).

Cape Borda Lightstation

Cape Borda Lightstation became operational on 5 July 1858 and lightstation keepers tended the light continuously until March 1989 when the station was automated. The lightstation has also been a weather observation station since 1865 and rangers still pop outside several times a day to take a look at the clouds and check the thermometer and barometer. In the days before radio a small cannon was fired to alert ships to danger. Until 1923 lightstation keepers used to haul stores up the steep slope from Harvey's Return (3km away) with the help of a horse-drawn winch. Unloading stores in high seas cost several men their lives.

Today a tour of the lightstation costs $6 ($4.50 for children/concessions).

MATTHEW FLETCHER

GETTING TO/FROM THE WALK

Flinders Chase National Park is at the western end of the island, 150km from Penneshaw. From Kingscote, follow the Playford Hwy in the direction of the Cape Borda Lightstation. A left turn before the car park takes you down to the Ravine des Casoars car park, roughly 6km away.

THE WALK
Day 1: Ravine des Casoars to West Bay
7–7½ hours, 19km

South of the car park a sign marks the start of the Ravine des Casoars Wilderness Walk. Follow the path into the bush and fork left. Walk south through young eucalyptus and casuarina scrub for 30 minutes until, with the river visible through the sugar gums, the trail swings west to run beside a fine section of boulder-strewn river. After 20 minutes the trail arrives at a set of caves close to the river mouth. Wildlife is abundant within the valley – look out for Rosenberg's goannas digging up the track – and little penguins roost in sea caves overlooking the river mouth.

In the Dry season the trail continues downstream, reaching the beach after a short wade. However, when the river is high the driest option is to scramble up the steep rocky slope just before the first cave, traverse the caves and then cut down to the beach close to the sea. From the beach a clear, steep trail zigzags south up to the cliff tops. West Bay is 15km away to the south and the route simply follows the cliff edge all the way, across numerous patches of fractured limestone (feral goats and kangaroos are common here). There's no set trail, but the best policy is to maintain a constant height and keep within 15m of the cliff edge where the mallee scrub is thinnest.

After 2½ hours the cliffs swing southwest, forming a huge headland. Continue close to the cliff edge, west then south through thicker vegetation. The coastal scenery of high cliffs, dramatic rocky bays and coastal caves is magnificent. There's also a patch of pure limestone eroded into a weird landscape. Twenty minutes after this

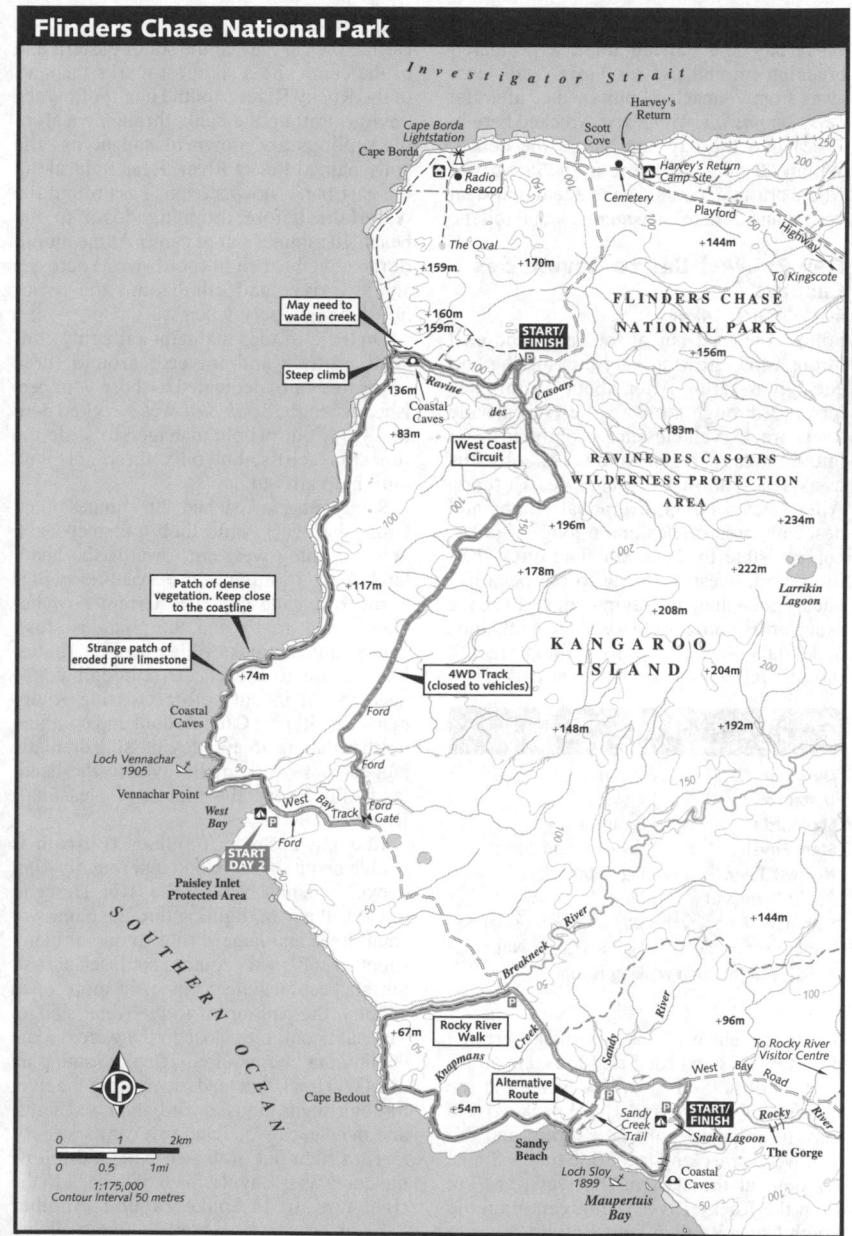

Flinders Chase National Park

SOUTH AUSTRALIA

geological anomaly are the first views of **West Bay** and **Paisley Inlet**, a protected breeding ground for sea birds. Walk east away from **Vennachar Point** (named after the *Loch Vennachar*, which was wrecked here in 1905) into the bay and across the beach. Within 40 minutes you're at the *camp site* where brushtail possums will attempt to steal your dinner. There's a water tank and toilets.

Day 2: West Bay to Ravine des Casoars
4–4½ hours, 14km

Follow the road out of the camp and east through low-growing yacca, casuarina and eucalyptus scrub. After about 35 minutes turn left through a metal gate onto a wide 4WD track (vehicles are prohibited) and into an area of regeneration. This obvious track leads north to Ravine des Casoars. After several hours of gradual climbs and descents, green fields and a long ridge become visible to the north. The track then turns north-west dropping to the beautiful eucalyptus-shaded **Ravine des Casoars** (keep an eye out for glossy black-cockatoos and koalas here) before climbing steeply through tall woodland to the car park.

Rocky River

Duration	6 hours
Distance	21.6km
Standard	medium
Start/Finish	Snake Lagoon camp site
Nearest Town	Kingscote
Public Transport	no

Summary An enjoyable day walk encapsulating some great elements of Flinders Chase National Park. Even the road walking is fun.

This excellent walk takes in rocky creeks, deserted bays, exposed cliff tops and abundant wildlife. Some shallow wading at the mouths of Rocky and Breakneck Rivers may be required until late spring and it's also worth checking local tide times. Snake Lagoon, at the start of the walk, is 7km from the Rocky River visitor centre on the South Coast Rd then West Bay Rd.

THE WALK
Beside the car park at the south-eastern end of the camp site a signpost marks the start of the Rocky River Mouth Hike. Follow the obvious trail up the bank, through eucalyptus saplings and down to and across the aptly named **Rocky River**. Bear right along the east bank, downstream. Pass round the **waterfalls** before dropping down to the beach 40 minutes out of camp. At the mouth of the cove bear right (north-west) across a shallow river and climb onto the rocky headland (slippery when wet).

On the cliff tops maintain a roughly constant altitude and traverse around three coves to a cairn dedicated to those who perished when the *Loch Sloy* was wrecked here in 1899. Four people managed to scale the limestone cliffs, but only three survived until help arrived.

Sandy Bay is reached 20 minutes later. Cross the beach and climb the steep bank before turning west out towards the headland. After 15 minutes the coastline swings north to a wide bay. The terrain now becomes very rocky and the going is slow; vague animal tracks offer the best routes. Keep close to the coast (although you'll need to cut inland before crossing Knapmans Creek) past **Cape Bedout** and continue north for about 45 minutes, passing dramatic jagged rocks and small coves to the headland high above the mouth of (seasonal) Breakneck River.

Looking upstream (north-east) a path is visible about 150m inland and roughly 10m above the south bank of the river. Descend towards the path, fighting through a mass of small trees and large shrubs to one of many tributary trails – the route is confused at first, but all becomes clear when, in more open country, the path drops to the water's edge. The path continues close to the water (some wading may be required), finally joining an old 4WD track that leads away from the river through sugar gums, sword and coral ferns, and melaleuca woodland to a car park.

Turn right out of the car park and follow the quiet West Bay Rd the 6.5km back to the right turn-off to **Snake Lagoon**. Another 4km or so can be added to this walk by detouring right down the Sandy Creek Trail past towering sand dunes to the coast, from where it's about 2.5km south-east back to the mouth of Rocky River. Return from here to Snake Lagoon upstream along the Rocky River path.

Mt Remarkable National Park

This national park, about 250km north of Adelaide, includes some of the most stunning scenery in the southern Flinders Ranges. Understandably popular with walkers and day-trippers, access is good, wildlife varied and prolific, and the trails extensive and well maintained. Despite the park's small size, walking here is challenging with the spectacular red quartzite gorges providing a lengthy and fascinating distraction. Many of the trails follow dry river beds and creeks, but if you have the time the high ridges provide stunning views across the semiarid landscape to Spencer Gulf.

HISTORY & NATURAL HISTORY
Small parcels of land have steadily been added to the park since it was gazetted in 1972 and the grassy woodland areas are still regenerating after agricultural and forestry usage. The area was regarded highly by the Aboriginal people due to the permanent water at Pine Flat, where the ruined huts of the early settlers lie.

The park is the meeting point of semiarid northern and temperate southern ecosystems, so the wildlife here is as diverse as it gets in the Flinders Ranges. There are large areas of blue gum, but sugar gums, long-leafed box woodland and rare white box eucalyptuses are also present. Gorges are lined with river red gums and native Murray pines, and the rare Krefft's tiger snake is found close to watercourses. The south-western ridges are covered with mallee and scrub. Wild flowers are prolific in spring, while those in Alligator Gorge have the longest season of all – look out for the large mauve flowers of Sturt's desert rose.

At Mambray Creek Australian magpies and galahs provide a noisy dawn chorus. Laughing kookaburras are common, as are the emus that stalk about like huge walking wigs looking for a free lunch. Wedge-tailed eagles and peregrine falcons soar high above the escarpments.

If you have a torch (flashlight) look out for the narrow-nosed planigale, a mouse-sized nocturnal marsupial. The really special animal here is the yellow-footed rock-wallaby, which is doing well due to reductions in fox, feral goat and rabbit populations.

PLANNING
Many creeks are dry by late spring. Although water tanks are found along the park's main trails, all water sources should be discussed with the rangers at Mambray Creek Information Centre (☎ 08-8634 7068, fax 8634 7085, ✉ mambray@dove .net.au), PO Box 7, Mambray Creek, Port Pirie, 5540 SA. Excess luggage can be left here by prior arrangement. The Mambray Creek, Blue Gum Flat and Alligator Gorge picnic areas have permanent water supplies.

The park is closed on high fire risk days. Temperatures can soar to over 35°C in summer, while between June and August there are occasional frosts – snow covers the high peaks every few years. Most rain falls between April and October.

Maps & Books
Landsmap's 1:50,000 *Melrose* and *Wilmington* maps cover the park. Buy them in Adelaide. The national park's informative leaflet shows all its trails and facilities. The excellent pocket-sized *Wildflowers of the Southern Flinders Ranges* is a small, widely available guide to local flora.

Permits & Regulations
Entry to the park is $5 per car for day visitors or $2 per person. There are self-registration stations at Mambray Creek and Alligator Gorge. Bush camping is permitted at eight designated sites ($3 per person). No fires are permitted at bush camps and no overnight camping is permitted during the fire danger season (1 November to 30 April).

NEAREST TOWN & FACILITIES

Port Augusta is the most convenient nearest town (see Gateways earlier in this chapter).

Mt Remarkable National Park

In the national park itself, a four-bed cabin ($25 per night) is available at *Mambray Creek camp site*, at the trailhead. Camping here costs $12 a night per vehicle or $3 per person. The site has flush toilets, cold showers and free gas barbecues. Book in advance during the peak season.

Mt Remarkable Gorges

Duration	2 days
Distance	39km
Standard	medium
Start/Finish	Mambray Creek camp site
Nearest Town	Port Augusta
Public Transport	yes

Summary A great circular walk at the meeting of temperate and semiarid ecosystems. Walking through Alligator and Hidden Gorges is amazing, but the Battery awaits. Water tanks are found throughout this well-run park.

This circular route can comfortably be completed in two days (the second day is longer than the first), although spending the second night at Hidden Camp or Fricks Dam and extending the walk to three days allows more time in the gorges.

GETTING TO/FROM THE WALK

Mt Remarkable National Park is 5km east of the Stuart Hwy. The turn-off is 45km south of Port Augusta and 245km north of Adelaide.

Premier Stateliner (☎ 08-8415 5500) will drop you at the Mambray Creek turn-off (you'll have to walk 5km to Mambray Creek). Greyhound (☎ 08-8231 1701, 13 2030) and McCafferty's (☎ 08-8212 5066) can only transport you to the Mambray Creek turn-off if you have a coach pass or are using part of another interstate ticket. You'll need to sort this out with their offices in Adelaide or Port Augusta at least 48 hours in advance.

THE WALK
Day 1: Mambray Creek Camp Site to Longhill Camp
4 hours, 13km

From the visitor car park cross **Mambray Creek** at the ford, ignore the left turn up to the Bluff and follow the 4WD track (taking a couple of 'walkers only' diversions if desired) north-east through wooded flood plain. River red gums line the creek and euros bound around. After 45 minutes a water tank and junction of creek and trail is reached.

Turn left off the 4WD track, cross **Mambray** and **Alligator Creeks**, then follow the meandering path northwards. In places the red and ochre cliffs close in and there are numerous crossings of the boulder-strewn creek. After 40 minutes' walking the trail turns north-east through an open landscape of grass trees, bottlebrush shrubs and native pines. The trail is confused in places, so stay with Alligator Creek through **Pine Flat** to the junction with Hidden Gorge Trail. Continue straight ahead through *Hidden Camp* (which sits below beautiful ochre cliffs, but has no facilities), then climb to a rocky 4WD track. Follow the track north through dense vegetation.

You'll get good views of the valley from various points along the way, passing the junction with Fricks Trail (and water tank) and then *Kingfisher Flat camp site* (which has a toilet) before climbing gradually to **Teal Dam** 90 minutes later. Continue to **Blue Gum Flat**, 400m farther north (where there's permanent water, a toilet and gas barbecues), then turn left and left again, heading back south about 400m to *Longhill Camp* (no facilities). Arrive early as it's well worth exploring the **Narrows** and **Alligator Gorge** in the evening.

Day 2: Longhill Camp to Mambray Creek Camp Site
6–6½ hours, 26km,

Walk back up to Blue Gum Flat then turn left onto a narrow (signposted) trail that winds down into the gully. Once down among the river red gums the path follows the river upstream (you'll be wading out of the Dry season) into a narrow gorge; the

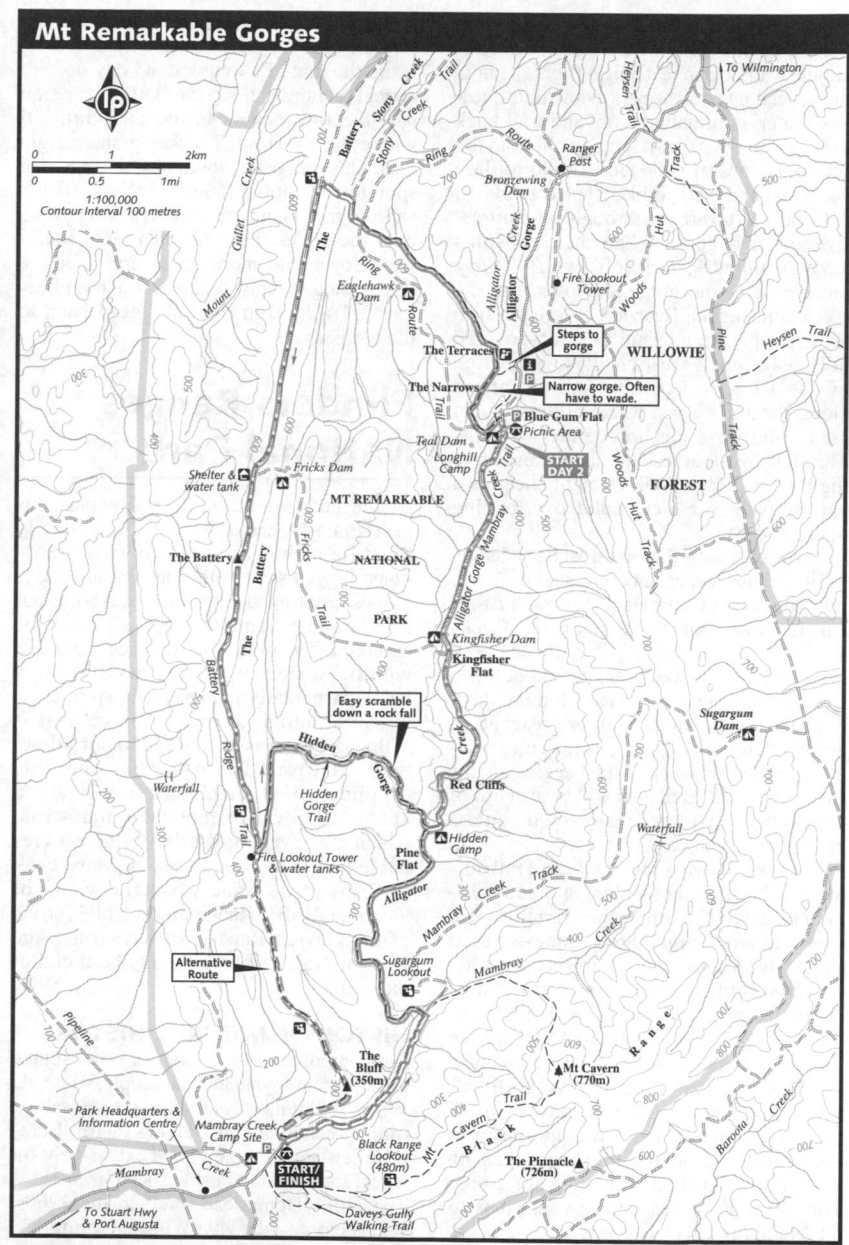

steep, red quartzite cliffs enclose pine trees, ferns and other flora. It's a stunning 30-minute walk. Upon reaching a flight of stairs (these lead up to a car park, view point, toilets, water, information point and trail back to Blue Gum Flat), turn left and climb to the **Terraces**, slabs of rock formed 600 million years ago and marked like rippled sand.

Continue upstream through an impressive section of gorge. Where the creek splits after 20 minutes, fork left (west). Thirty minutes later the gorge shallows and the creek splits again. Bear left before the trail leads steeply up a beautiful scrub-covered hillside (offering great views) to a junction of 4WD tracks. Continue straight ahead along the track (past a magnificent sugar gum stand) to a junction before a saddle. Turn left (west) across the saddle and up to the Battery Ridge Trail. Straight ahead is a narrow path to a **view point** overlooking Spencer Gulf.

Turn left along the broad Battery Ridge Trail. A large water tank and shelter at the junction above **Fricks Dam** (the basic *camp site* is under 1km away along the Fricks Trail and preferable to the more exposed one at Eaglehawk Dam) are passed before a fire lookout tower, water tank and the turning for Hidden Gorge Trail are reached in around two hours. Look out for emus, elegant parrots and wedge-tailed eagles on this fine ridge walk. Bull ants will swarm out of their (numerous) nests ready to do battle a second after you pass.

Turn left down Hidden Gorge Trail following the silver posts along a gradual 15-minute descent north before turning right into **Hidden Gorge**. Steep pine-covered slopes soon give way to towering cliffs, which steadily become more impressive. Where the creek cuts back west after 30 minutes there's a beauty – coloured light purple and lilac where a watercourse has stained its jagged face. Keep to the right as shortly afterwards there's a scramble down a rock fall. Ten minutes later the gorge narrows dramatically before opening out as the path leads to the junction with Alligator Gorge Trail. Turn right and retrace your steps to the Mambray Creek car park.

Alternative Route: Over the Bluff
1 hour, 4km

If the thought of a long second day doesn't appeal, continue along the Battery for 1km past the fire lookout tower, then turn left where the 4WD track makes a sharp right turn. This trail heads south-east down a long spur to the **Bluff** (350m), reached after a short climb. There are some cracking views over the plains. The trail then turns south-west down into more open terrain before descending steeply to the main Mambray Creek Track. Turn right and head back to the car park.

Flinders Ranges National Park

At the heart of the Flinders Ranges, this vast (94,500 hectares) and dramatically beautiful park is filled with diverse attractions: jagged saw-tooth ridges, tremendous gorges, gum-lined river valleys, Aboriginal sites and some fantastic walking trails to be explored. The park is easily accessible and wildlife abundant, native wild flowers being particularly impressive in spring.

The beautiful geological marvel that is Wilpena Pound is one of the major attractions in the park. The rugged hills and cliffs of this natural amphitheatre contain a 16km-long oval of grassland and scrub, which is a haven for wildlife as there's a reliable spring at Pound Gap. St Mary Peak (1171m) offers some wonderful views of the jagged ABC Range and the high peaks of the Heysen Range, between which the Heysen Trail runs into the northern end of the park.

HISTORY & NATURAL HISTORY

Long important as a permanent water source to the local Adnyamathanha people, who hold Wilpena Pound's south-east corner sacred (thus precluding any walking there), European settlers used the Pound extensively for wheat farming and raising sheep from 1851. The Hill's Homestead, built in the 1900s, stands close to the vital Wilpena Spring.

Wilpena Pound was formed by huge earth movements around 550 million years ago, when the whole area was elevated. Where the Pound now lies a patch of soft rock surrounded by hard red quartzite was created. The soft rock eroded and left a depression, but the quartzite remained to form the rugged Pound walls. Earth movements elsewhere in the park folded sandstone, limestone and quartzite rocks to create parallel ranges made up of successive different rock types.

The Pound remains a haven for wildlife in this semiarid region. River red gums line the creeks and native pines and spinifex cover the hillsides, creating a rich habitat for reptiles. Around St Mary Peak you may see red-barred crevice-dragons sunning themselves, while down in the Pound Gould's monitors are sometimes seen.

Yellow-footed rock-wallabies inhabit rocky outcrops, and stocky euros are seen in hilly areas. Gregarious red and western grey kangaroos live on the open plains that are also the habitat of the Australian kestrel and peregrine falcon. The small, and nocturnal, fat-tailed dunnart is difficult to see, as is another rarity, the little mastiff-bat, which roosts in river red gums. The noise from miner birds, Australian ravens, ringneck parrots and galahs is bound to wake you early.

PLANNING
When to Walk
Walking is best between May and October, when temperatures average between 13°C and 25°C and there is usually water in the creeks. Nights are generally cold year-round, but some winters it drops below freezing. Average annual rainfall is around 380mm, most of it occurring between May and August, but it varies greatly. In the height of summer temperatures frequently rise to 45°C.

What to Bring
A fuel stove is required and nights are cold, so bring warm clothes and a good sleeping bag. Light walking boots or running shoes (trainers) are suitable. If the Rockhole at Cooinda is dry, you'll have to carry two days' supply of water.

Maps & Books
Landsmap's 1:50,000 *Wilpena* map covers the whole Pound. The visitor centre often has these. *Bushwalking in the Flinders Ranges National Park* published by National Parks & Wildlife South Australia (NPWSA) is a useful leaflet.

Information Sources
The visitor centre (☎ 08-8648 0048, 🖳 www .wilpenapound.on.net) at Wilpena Pound Resort is open daily and is an excellent source of information. There are daily guided walks into the Pound. Walks elsewhere in the park should be discussed with a ranger as up-to-date information about water supplies, which are scarce by late spring, is essential. Solo walking is discouraged.

Flinders Ranges Adnamatna Yarta Cultural Tours. (☎ 08-8648 4122, 🖳 www .hawker.mtx.net) offers 4WD and walking

Fire
Aboriginal people have used fire as a land management tool for thousands of years. By burning areas systematically, a mosaic of burned and unburned areas is created, encouraging both fire-loving and fire-sensitive plants. This ensures maximum food production from the land and the creation of a range of habitats, particularly beneficial to small mammals. Patch burning also reduces the risk of large, destructive wildfires.

European settlers didn't understand this and traditional burning was discouraged by pastoralists on the grounds that it reduced grassland around cattle stations. As Aboriginal land management decreased, the countryside became vulnerable to uncontrolled wildfires (particularly at the end of summer), which can even cause local species extinction.

Many national parks now run a controlled burning program mimicking Aboriginal land management methods. Most burning is done early in the Dry season when there are still areas of damp vegetation to provide safe refuge for wildlife and break up and limit fires.

SOUTH AUSTRALIA

tours exploring the culture of the Adnya-mathanha people, the custodians of the Flinders Ranges.

Permits & Regulations

The national park entrance fee is $5 per car (or $2 per person), although if you're bush camping ($3 per night per person) there's no entry fee. Cooinda is the only permitted bush camp within the Pound. Park fees and bush camping permits are paid for at the visitor centre along with fees for camping at the resort (use the self-registration bays out of office hours).

Walks of more than three hours must be written into the Bushwalkers' Register outside the visitor centre. Let a responsible person know your planned route and expected return time, as the lack of a sign-out time in the register will not instigate a search. Fires are banned in the park.

NEAREST TOWN & FACILITIES

Hawker, 52km south of Wilpena Pound, is a pleasant historical town with petrol stations and basic supplies. However, it's better to get organised in Port Augusta, which has more facilities (see Gateways earlier).

Wilpena Pound Resort

The shop at *Wilpena Pound Resort* (☎ 08-8648 0004, ✉ wilpena@adelaide.on.net,

RICHARD I'ANSON

Crater-shaped Wilpena Pound is a haven for wildlife and a playground for peak baggers

🖳 *www.wilpenapound.on.net)* is open daily, is well stocked (with some camping supplies) and has a petrol station attached. Camping at the resort starts at $11 for two people. Hot showers, gas barbecues and laundry facilities are available and you can leave surplus kit at the visitor centre. Basic motel accommodation is $85/95 per single/double. Restaurant meals start at $12.50 ($5 at the bar).

Wilpena Pound

Duration	2 days
Distance	17.5km
Standard	easy-medium
Start/Finish	Wilpena Pound Resort
Nearest Town	Hawker
Public Transport	yes

Summary A simple circuit illustrating the best of this natural amphitheatre. The optional peak bagging and gorge exploration is well worth the effort.

The walk described here is an easy two-dayer (blue triangles mark the way). At the time of writing a connector trail was being planned from Rawnsley Park Station (☎ 08-8648 0008) to the Heysen Trail, south of the Pound. The Heysen Trail leads through the Pound, so once the trail is completed starting from Rawnsley Park Station may be an interesting option. Premier Stateliner trains (☎ 08-8415 5500) will stop at Rawnsley Park Station on request. Also likely is a change of the route to St Mary Peak.

GETTING TO/FROM THE WALK

From the Stuart Hwy turn-off 8km south of Port Augusta, the roads are sealed all the way through Quorn and Hawker to Wilpena Pound (a 2¼-hour journey). Premier Stateliner (☎ 08-8642 5055 Port Augusta, 8415 5555 Adelaide) runs services from Adelaide ($57) to Wilpena Pound via Port Augusta on Wednesday and Friday, and from Port Augusta ($28) on Sunday. Returning services (to Adelaide) are on Thursday, Sunday and Friday. Greyhound pass holders are entitled to a 50% discount.

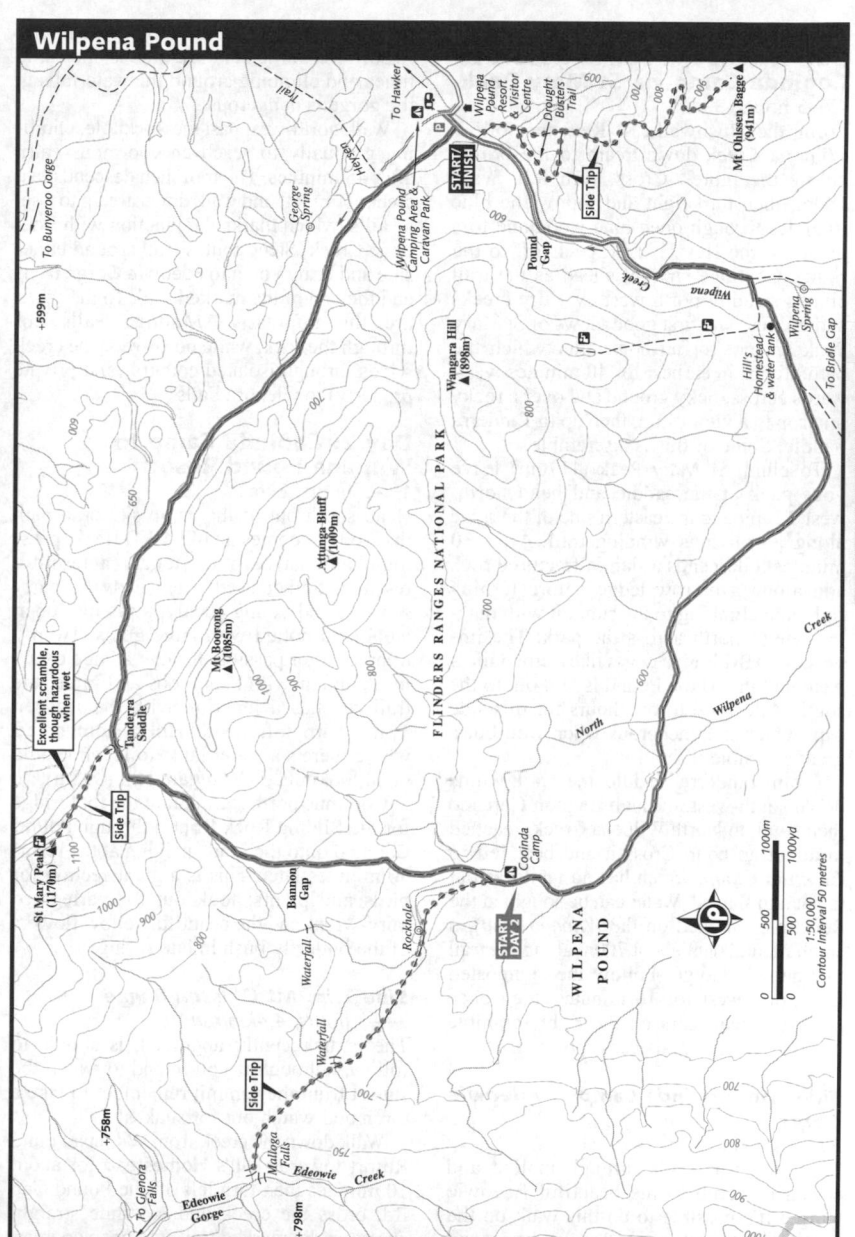

Wilpena Pound

THE WALK
Day 1: Wilpena Pound Resort to Cooinda Camp via St Mary Peak
4½–5 hours, 9.5km

From the Bushwalkers' Register follow **Wilpena Creek** downstream to the bridge below the motel. Cross, turn left, walk 100m, then turn right and follow the blue triangles through open pine woodland to a junction (the Heysen Trail peels off to the right). Continue straight ahead as the trail climbs steadily north-west over dry creeks and gullies. The first good views of St Mary Peak are not for an hour, after which the path climbs in earnest for 40 minutes westwards across rocky ground and over a rocky outcrop to a view point, then up to Tanderra Saddle. Some of this is a scramble.

To climb **St Mary Peak** (1170m) leave your pack at the saddle and head northwest, keeping to the eastern side of the ridge along an obvious winding trail. After 30 minutes it descends a slab of fractured rock and along a narrow ledge before turning right and climbing to the summit with magical views north across the park. The impressive ABC Range twists like a crocodile's back and the whole Pound is laid out to the south. Allow 1¾ to two hours for this side trip, which is treacherous when wet, but a great scramble if dry.

From Tanderra Saddle the trail winds down south-west, through Bannon Gap and then south to North Wilpena Creek, reached in about an hour. Cross it and bear left to *Cooinda Camp*, which has no facilities but is flat and shaded. Water can be sought at the **Rockhole** (marked on the *Wilpena* map), a small natural dam about 700m along the trail to Edeowie Gorge. Follow the signposted trail north-west for 10 minutes, then once the creek reappears on the right scramble down at the first real access point.

Side Trip: Cooinda Camp to Edeowie Gorge
2 hours, 6km return

This side trip leads through mallee and casuarina scrub to the beautiful Edeowie Gorge. It's possible to do this walk on the first day, but most people do it on the second

before the easy walk back to Wilpena Pound Resort. Be warned that the path is unclear at times and climbing around the waterfalls in the gorge is dangerous.

Walk north-west past the **Rockhole**, climbing gradually to reach an enormous cairn after 45 minutes. The trail then descends to a creek. Turn left and walk downstream to a set of falls, which marks the junction with Edeowie Creek. Steep routes lead around either side and bring you into **Edeowie Gorge** itself and the end of the marked trail. To the south are the impressive **Malloga Falls** cut through the rock, while north-west the creek winds through isolated country (and private property) to Glenora Falls.

Day 2: Cooinda Camp to Wilpena Pound Resort
1¾–2 hours, 8km

Head south out of the camp site on a path that soon becomes an old 4WD track, passing from native pine stands (a termite-resistant timber used extensively by early settlers) and young eucalyptuses into open woodland dotted with large gums. Twenty minutes after passing through a large clearing, popular with kangaroos and birds, the trail reaches a junction with the Heysen Trail. Turn left up to **Hill's Homestead** where there's a water tank, toilet and some good lookouts on **Wangara Hill** (898m).

Continue north (turn left at the footbridge for the Sliding Rock Route) through **Pound Gap** and onto the road, arriving at the resort 30 minutes later. This is a great section for birds and plants; look out for variegated fairy-wrens and the beautiful yellow flowers of the butterfly bush in late spring.

Side Trip: Mt Ohlssen Bagge
2½–3 hours, 4.4km return

The path, recently upgraded, is simple to follow, although if you intend to watch the sunset from the summit remember to take a torch and watch out for snakes!

Walk down the creek from Wilpena Pound Resort towards **Hill's Homestead** for about 10 minutes then turn left off the Pound Gap Rd, cross the creek and continue straight ahead up the marked trail into open country.

Avoid the right turn leading down the Drought Busters Trail and continue up the steps through an arid landscape of spinifex and red rock. The trail zigzags round a series of outcrops, working its way south-east up a spur, then cuts east before making one final push south for the summit of **Mt Ohlssen Bagge** (941m). From this fine vantage point the southern end of the Pound can be fully appreciated, the huge enclosing peaks like the walls of a fortress. Return the way you came – a diversion along the **Drought Busters Trail**, which explains how local plants survive in this arid region, is worthwhile.

Other Walks

Mt Remarkable

There's a new trail to the summit of Mt Remarkable, in the national park of the same name. From Melrose the Showgrounds Track sets off at a gentle gradient for 3.8km before climbing steeply for 600m along the top of the main ridge. It's then an easy 600m to the summit. You'll need Landsmap's 1:50,000 *Melrose* map. This walk could be linked with numerous tracks emanating from Mambray Creek, although getting out of Melrose could be a problem. Phone Mambray Creek Ranger Station (☎ 08-8634 7068) for more information.

Up the ABC Range

From Wilpena Pound the Heysen Trail winds north beside the ABC Range to Bunyeroo, Brachina and Parachilna Gorges. This is great walking country and a number of camp sites and simple huts (at Yanyanna and Elatina) with rainwater tanks or springs line the route. Landsmap's 1:50,000 *Orraparinna* and *The Bunkers* maps cover the area.

Wilpena Pound Resort can run transfers into the area (see Nearest Town & Facilities under Flinders Ranges National Park earlier). Costs start at around $85 per vehicle for Bunyeroo (taking five people). More information is available from the Friends of the Heysen Trail (see the boxed text 'The Heysen Trail').

Fleurieu Peninsula

This coastal area has numerous walking trails (including the Heysen Trail) through 21 conservation parks. Deep Creek Conservation Park

(☎ 08-8598 0263) in the Southern Mt Lofty Ranges has 18km of spectacular coastline, camp sites and cottages, but no public transport access. Landsmap's 1:50,000 *Cape Jervis* and *Torrens Vale* maps cover the area.

Gammon Ranges

In the remote, arid Gammon Ranges, 750km north of Adelaide (4WD-only within the park), a hard five-day circular walk from Loch Ness Well crosses a rugged landscape to Mt John Roberts, Wildflower Creek and Rover Rockhole. This is serious stuff; you must be totally self-sufficient and carry a lot of water.

For more information and permits contact the rangers at Balcanoona Homestead (☎ 08-8648 4829) or Hawker (☎ 08-8648 4244). Arkaroola provides various visitor facilities, but there's only bush camping within the park. Landsmap's 1:50,000 *Illinawortina* map is required.

Telowie Gorge Conservation Park

A two-day bushwalk, 20km south of Mt Remarkable, follows the Barbecue Track (great views of the Spencer Gulf) then Telowie Creek through the spectacular gorge back to the starting point. The Heysen Trail can be joined here and offers the possibility of walks into Wirrabara Forest (no camping between 1 November and 30 April). Further information (and permits) should be obtained from the rangers at Mt Remarkable National Park (☎ 08-8634 7068). Landsmap's 1:50,000 *Pirie* map covers the area.

Mt Lofty Conservation Park

A slightly contrived, although nevertheless rewarding, day walk loops through Cleland Conservation Park in the Adelaide Hills, linking Mt Lofty Botanical Gardens, Cleland Wildlife Park, Waterfall Gully and Mt Lofty (take bus No 820 or 822 from Currie St to stop 30F on Piccadilly Rd). The route is best covered by Outdoor Information's 1:15,000 *Mt Lofty Special* map, which is widely available. Much of the Adelaide Hills are covered by Landsmap's 1:50,000 *Adelaide* map. Prebooking is essential for a place at the convenient *Mt Lofty Youth Hostel* (☎ 08-8231 5583, ✉ yhasa@ozemail.com.au), a timber bunkhouse near the Mt Lofty summit, to allow for overnight walks in the hills.

For further information contact Mt Lofty Summit Information Centre (☎ 08-8370 1054, 🖥 www.denr.sa.gov.au/nrg/mlofty).

Tasmania

The Southern Ocean island state of Tasmania is home to some of the most adventurous and challenging walking in Australia. With a total area roughly the size of Ireland, it is compact by Australian terms. Lying 240km south of Victoria across tempestuous Bass Strait, Tasmania feels remote. New Zealand lies over 2000km to the east across the Tasman Sea, while the next landfall is Argentina, over 10,000km away. Antarctica is 3000km south across the Southern Ocean. With frequent gales and storms blowing in from the Southern Ocean and Antarctica, 1.38 million hectares (20% of the total landmass) listed as a World Heritage Area (WHA) and swathes of the most valuable temperate wilderness in the world, Tasmania has every right to proclaim itself a world-class walking destination.

Because of its relative remoteness, Tasmania does not attract the same numbers of walkers as that other great southern hemisphere walking destination, New Zealand. However, walkers from the Australian mainland flock to 'Tassie' (as it is affectionately known) each summer to walk tracks such as the Overland and South Coast, escaping from the heat that can make walking in the other states a real chore.

The walks in this chapter are divided into three sections: West & World Heritage Area, East Coast & Islands and Hobart & Mt Wellington. Each region is characterised by the style and difficulty of walking, exposure to bad weather and marked differences in vegetation and geography.

The West & World Heritage Area features the most difficult and strenuous walks, covering high and potentially dangerous terrain on rough tracks exposed to the worst weather. But they are also what most walkers come to Tasmania to experience: wild and remote. The Overland Track in Cradle Mountain–Lake St Clair National Park follows a pioneer route across the highest country in the state and is probably the most famous and popular track in Tasmania. To

Highlights

RICHARD I'ANSON

The picturesque Hazards in Freycinet National Park, near Coles Bay

- Exploring rugged peaks, waterfalls and temperate rainforests on the classic Overland Track

- Looking out across the Tasmanian World Heritage Area from the high summit of Mt Anne

- Cooling off after a hot morning's walk in the turquoise waters of Wineglass Bay, Freycinet Peninsula

- Trying not to get dizzy peering over Australia's highest sea cliffs on Cape Pillar

the east in the Walls of Jerusalem National Park, shorter, high-quality walks can be found with relatively smaller numbers of walkers. To the south, Mt Field National Park, lying just outside the WHA, offers easy access, good facilities and high-level walking with superlative views of the western wilderness. Visible from Mt Field National Park is the stunning peak of Mt Anne,

Tasmania

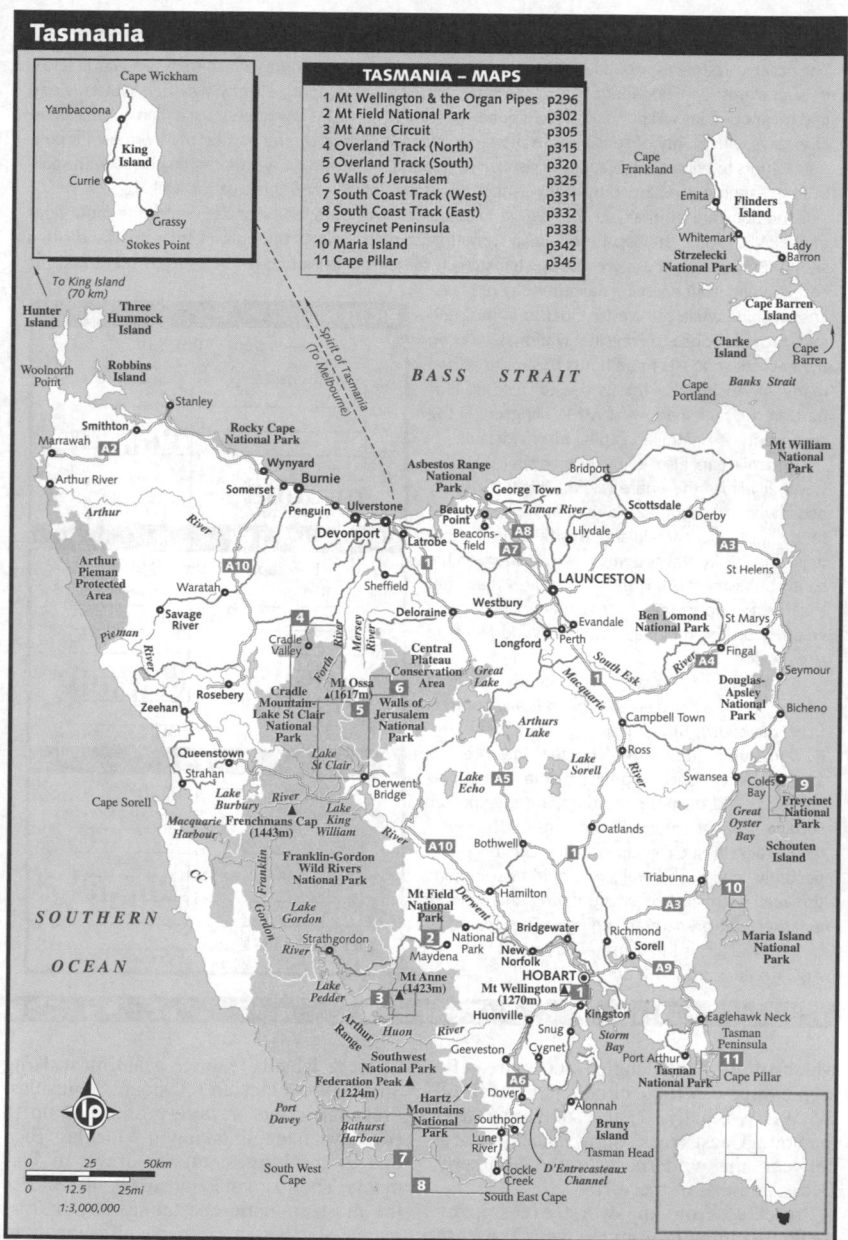

TASMANIA

The Climate of Tasmania

The oceanic vastness surrounding Tasmania, including the Roaring Forties which track eastwards across it, is an almost constant influence on Tasmania's fickle and frequently stormy weather. Winter is cold and the mountains will normally have a good covering of snow. At lower altitudes and in coastal areas, crisp days with plenty of sunshine are often experienced. Spring can be particularly stormy with periodic returns to winter, while summer sees more settled periods of fine weather interspersed with spells of rain. Autumn is regarded by many as the most stable season and the best for walking.

Conditions are normally at their worst in the west and south of the state, where the mountains of the WHA force the Southern Ocean frontal systems to unload the bulk of their rain (and often snow). By the time these weather systems reach the east coast much of their fury is spent and the east can find itself enjoying day after day of pleasant sunshine while the west is cloaked in mist and rain. Bicheno (close to Freycinet National Park) on the east coast boasts more hours of sunshine than many of Australia's famous coastal resorts. Hobart, in the rain shadow of Mt Wellington, is the second-driest Australian capital after Adelaide.

Tasmania can also enjoy longer spells of fine weather across the entire island. This will usually occur when a substantial ridge of high pressure extends south from mainland Australia and either weakens the frontal systems or drives them to the south of Tasmania. It is these interludes that offer the best opportunity for experiencing good weather on the multiday West & World Heritage Area walks.

In contrast to this are the southerly blasts of wind and wintry squalls that periodically come in from the south, bringing air right out of Antarctica. In spring, around the equinox, these can be a weekly occurrence, producing drops in temperature of 10°C or more and dumping unexpected snow on the mountains. Conditions on the Overland Track in such circumstances can be unexpectedly severe, and walkers should bear in mind the real possibility of encountering this kind of weather and prepare accordingly. The best forecast for walkers is the nightly TV forecast from the ABC news at around 7 pm.

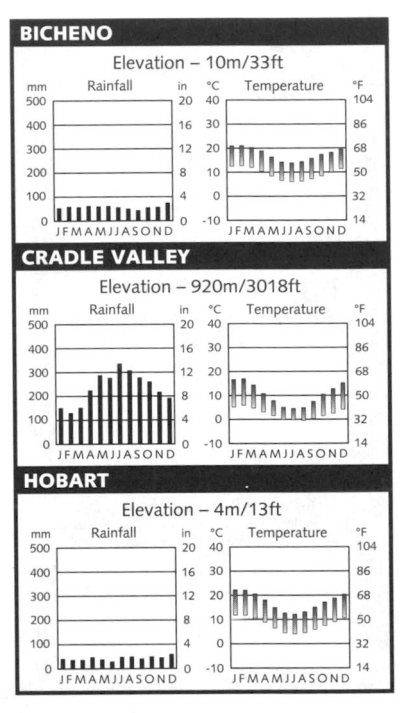

which offers a challenging and extremely scenic three-day ridge circuit in the heart of the WHA. Finally, on the southern coast, the South Coast Track follows the boundary between the wilderness of the Southern Ocean and that of the WHA.

Protected from the worst excesses of weather coming in from the west, The East Coast & Islands features beautiful walking on the Freycinet and Tasman Peninsulas. Freycinet offers a variety of walks up to two days in length taking in Wineglass Bay, one of the biggest tourist draws in Tasmania. The Tasman Peninsula Walk features the most dramatic coastal scenery in Tasmania, skirting an extensive cliff line up to

Top Left: The rugged coast of Kangaroo Island, SA. **Top Right:** Sunset over West Bay, Flinders Chase NP, Kangaroo Island. **Middle:** The long, rocky ridgeline seen from the summit of Mt Ohlssen Bagge, Flinders Ranges NP, SA. **Bottom Left:** Cairn inside Wilpena Pound, Flinders Ranges NP. **Bottom Right:** An oasis for wildlife: the green and fertile Wilpena Pound, Wangara Hill, Flinders Ranges NP.

PAUL SINCLAIR

KRZYSZTOF DYDYNSKI

GRANT DIXON

KRZYSZTOF DYDYNSKI

ROB BLAKERS

ROB BLAKERS

The rugged grandeur of Tasmania's World Heritage Area. **Top Left:** Mt Oakleigh, Cradle Mountain–Lake St Clair NP. **Top Right:** Mt Ossa (1617m), Tasmania's highest peak. **Middle Left:** Dawn on the cliffs of Mt Geryon, Du Cane Range. **Middle Right:** Mt Ida and Lake St Clair, Australia's deepest natural freshwater lake. **Bottom Left:** Cradle Mountain and autumn forest. **Bottom Right:** Walls of Jerusalem.

300m in height. If all of this seems too strenuous, a short hop on a ferry provides access to a pleasant day walk on historic Maria Island.

Finally, Hobart & Mt Wellington features two walks on Mt Wellington that can be completed in a day and are accessible by public transport from Hobart, the state capital.

INFORMATION
Maps

The Royal Automobile Club of Tasmania (RACT) 1:500,000 *Tasmania* Touring Map is the perfect reference for planning your trip around the island, as it features road maps of major towns on the reverse.

The smaller-scale maps needed for the walks described in this chapter are all published by Land Information Services (previously known as Tasmap). For maps covering individual walks, see Planning in the introduction to each walk.

Buying Maps Maps can be purchased directly from Tasmap (☎ 03-6233 3382, fax 6233 2158, ✆ LIB.sales@delm.tas.gov.au), 134 Macquarie St, Hobart 7000, or at good bookshops and information centres.

In Hobart's centre, the Tasmanian Map Centre (☎ 03-6231 9043), 96 Elizabeth St, stocks a good range of walking maps and books, as does the Backpackers Barn (☎ 03-6424 3628), 10–12 Edward St, Devonport.

Books

Lonely Planet's *Tasmania* guide is an excellent in-depth supplement to the general travel information given in this chapter. It also has a special section on flora and fauna.

For walking Tasmania-wide, Tyrone Thomas' *100 Walks in Tasmania* is a useful reference. The Tasmanian Parks & Wildlife Service (PWS) produces a book called *Walking the Wilderness: Minimal Impact Bushwalking Techniques for Tasmania's National Parks*. For walking in specific areas, see Maps and Books in each section.

The photogenic qualities of the Tasmanian wilderness and its unique flora and fauna have given rise to a plethora of pictorial and natural history books, the most impressive of

which are those by wilderness photographer Peter Dombrovskis. *Alpine Tasmania* by Jamie Kirkpatrick is an illustrated guide to the flora and vegetation of the mountainous regions of the island. *Tasmanian Mammals* by wildlife photographer Dave Watts is an excellent field guide. You might also want to look at *The Fauna of Tasmania – Birds* and *The Fauna of Tasmania – Mammals*, both by RH Green.

Information Sources

The privately run Tasmanian Travel & Information Centres (TTICs) are a good first port of call for general tourist information. There are centres in Hobart, Launceston, Devonport and Burnie. As well as supplying brochures, price lists, general maps and other information, they will often book transport, tours and accommodation for you.

In addition to the main centres mentioned above, there are visitor centres in smaller towns that are members of the Tasmanian Visitor Information Network.

With such a huge area of its total landmass contained within national parks, it is no surprise that Tasmania has a large government body set up to manage them. The Parks & Wildlife Service (PWS; ☎ 03-6233 6191, fax 6233 2158, 🖳 www.parks.tas.gov.au), 134 Macquarie St, Hobart (PO Box 44A, Hobart 7001), has an excellent Web site providing good information on particular parks and on flora and fauna. It should also list the current park fees.

Some national parks have their own visitor centre and staff are generally helpful and enthusiastic and will be able to give good first-hand advice on issues such as current track conditions.

Major Tasmanian walking clubs are included in the Federation of Tasmanian Bushwalking Clubs (☎ 03-319 336) PO Box 1190, Launceston 7250, which is involved in areas of interest to walkers, especially political campaigns.

Tasmanian Travelways is an invaluable free publication available from all visitor centres. It has bus, ferry and plane timetables and is crammed with accommodation listings for all towns and villages in Tasmania.

TASMANIA

Phytophthora

Phytophthora cinammoni (cinammon fungus) is a root rot, a fungal pathogen that is thought to have been introduced to Australia by Europeans. Affecting a variety of woody sedgeland species below 650m, including banksias, it has killed many plants in affected areas.

The Parks & Wildlife Service (PWS) places a strong onus on walkers to help prevent the spread of the disease carried in microscopic quantities on dirty boots, gaiters or tent pegs. You should make sure that your gear is thoroughly washed after leaving a root rot area; in some walking areas the PWS has installed boot-cleaning stations.

Park Fees & Regulations

While Tasmania has so far avoided introducing a permit system (see the boxed text 'A Permit System for the World Heritage Area?'), entry fees do apply to all national parks in Tasmania.

There is one fee for vehicles and another for pedestrians. For vehicles with up to eight people the charge for 24 hours is $9; a two-month holiday pass costs $30 and an annual pass is $42. For visitors who enter a national park on foot or by bus, bicycle, motorbike or boat, the entry fees are $3 for 24 hours, $12 for two months and $15 for a year. Make sure when you buy a pass that it will cover your needs. For example, if you plan to visit the Walls of Jerusalem National Park by car you'll only need a pedestrian pass as the car park is just outside the boundary of the park.

Application forms can be downloaded from the PWS Web site (see Information Sources earlier) and sent to the Park Entry Clerk, GPO Box 44A, Hobart 7001. Passes can also be obtained from major park visitor centres, from Service Tasmania's state-wide offices, and from on board the *Spirit of Tasmania* and *DevilCat* (during the summer). Tasmanian Travel Centres on the mainland (Australian Capital Territory, New South Wales, Queensland, South Australia and Victoria) all sell passes.

Most popular tracks have a registration book at the start and finish, which walkers are encouraged to fill in to give the PWS more information about track usage. The books are not used for safety purposes, and walkers are advised to register their trip with a local police station.

During days of Total Fire Ban, all fires are forbidden, even fuel stoves. If you are caught with an open fire on these days, you are not only endangering yourself and the environment, but you can also cop a hefty fine and/or prison sentence.

For more information on how to minimise your impact on the environment, see the section on Responsible Walking in the Facts for the Walker chapter.

Leaving Luggage

Most hostels will let you leave gear for a few days while you are out on a walk. The Backpackers Barn in Devonport (see that section) has luggage storage in secure lockers for $5 for a week, a good option if you plan to return to Devonport after the Overland Track. All of the track transport bus services operated by TWT's Tassielink feature an option to have your luggage forwarded to your next destination and stored for a $5 charge.

GETTING AROUND

Most track transport in Tasmania is operated by TWT's Tassielink (☎ 1300 300 520, fax 03-6344 5895, @ info@taswildtravel .com.au) and is entirely restricted to the summer months (1 December to 3 April). Most track services will only run with a certain number of full-fare passengers, so the onus is on the walker to book in advance, although this doesn't leave much scope to choose the best weather. TWT's Tassielink also has discount passes for people planning to do a lot of bus travel, with passes available for a range of travel within restricted time frames. The shortest pass gives seven days' travel in 10 days ($129.90) and the longest gives 30 days' travel in 40 days ($230). Used correctly they can save you money, but they do not qualify you as a full-fare passenger on a track service.

A Permit System for the World Heritage Area?

For the best part of the last decade the Parks & Wildlife Service (PWS) has been wrestling with the thorny issue of permits as a means of restricting walker numbers and erosion on delicate environments in the World Heritage Area (WHA). In 1999 the Tasmanian government deferred the introduction of a regulatory system for the WHA, due both to financial considerations and the strong objections expressed by many Tasmanian walkers, who were fearful of bureaucratic interference in their wilderness experience.

The need for action is evident on many tracks in the WHA, especially in the south-west where tracks in the Arthur Ranges and on Mt Anne have become severely eroded. Muddy pits develop, and in an effort to avoid them walkers inadvertently create new tracks and more erosion. With walking becoming ever more popular and with increasing numbers of overseas visitors, it was envisaged that some action was needed to protect the environment.

Two possibilities were proposed: that tracks would be constructed to take the pressure of thousands of walker visits annually; and that walker numbers would be restricted by a permit system to a level the environment could sustain. Opposition to the latter system was obvious, but so also was opposition to the artificial manipulation of the environment and the resultant loss of wilderness required by the first option.

In late 1999 a Track Assessment Group (TAG) was set up and discussion on the issue continues at the time of writing. While walkers may be discouraged from visiting certain areas, it seems unlikely that any regulatory or permit system will be introduced in the near future.

For up-to-date information on the issue, check the PWS Web site at ⬛ www.parks.tas.gov.au.

GATEWAYS
Hobart

Hobart is the second-oldest, second-driest, smallest and most southerly of Australia's major cities. It is a pleasant and compact place, built at the mouth of the Derwent River and dominated by the presence of Mt Wellington (1270m). With a beautiful and lively seafront area and good access to the WHA and the east coast, it makes an excellent base with all the facilities the walker would expect, including cafes, restaurants, bookshops and equipment shops.

Information For general tourist information and national park passes, the TTIC (☎ 03-6230 8233) is on the corner of Davey and Elizabeth Sts.

Drifters Internet Cafe (☎ 03-6224 3244), in Salamanca Place, is a pleasant spot for emailing, but will seem a little on the expensive side if you are used to prices in Melbourne or Sydney.

Photoforce E6 Lab, 178–180 Campbell St, is a convenient and reliable photo lab for same-day slide processing.

Supplies & Equipment You can buy stove fuel and lightweight freeze-dried meals, as well as outdoor equipment, at Mountain Designs (☎ 03-6234 3900), 74 Elizabeth St; Paddy Pallin (☎ 03-6231 0777), 76 Elizabeth St; and Snowgum (☎ 03-6234 7877), 104 Elizabeth St. Kathmandu (mainly an outdoor clothing shop) is around the corner on Liverpool St.

Places to Stay & Eat Hobart has a good range of accommodation options, but during the busy summer months (November to March) it is always advisable to book ahead if you want to be sure of a bed in a place of your choice. The main areas for budget accommodation are the city centre and the older suburbs to the north and west. Middle and upper-end accommodation is spread all over town.

Sandy Bay Caravan Park (☎ 03-6225 1264, 1 Peel St, Sandy Bay) is less than 3km from the city centre and has a good range of accommodation options. Powered sites are $16, while on-site vans are $35 for a double and $55 cabins. Metro bus Nos 54, 55 or 56

TASMANIA

from Franklin Square will take you to the junction of Sandy Bay Rd and Peel St. There are a couple of large *supermarkets* within walking distance.

Central City Backpackers (☎ 03-6224 2404, 138 Collins St) is conveniently placed in the city centre, and is surprisingly quiet for a city hostel. The staff are helpful and there is a large and clean kitchen and communal area. There are also laundry and Internet facilities and rates start at $14 for a dorm bed and rise to $19 per person in a twin and $30/38 for a single/double. There is no parking, although it is possible to park on the street outside meter hours.

Travellers with a car might prefer to stay at *Adelphi Court YHA (☎ 03-6228 4829, 17 Stoke St, New Town)*. It has excellent facilities including a laundry and Internet access and charges $14 for a dorm bed, $38 for a twin room with shared facilities, and $42/48 for ensuite rooms. Tasmanian Redline Coaches (TRC; see Getting There & Away) provides a drop-off and pick-up service to and from the airport. The hostel is also within walking distance of a couple of large *supermarkets*. The office shuts at 9 pm.

For carbohydrate loading before or after a big walk, *Little Italy (152 Collins St)* does good pasta and pizza prepared by the exuberant Italian owner. On Elizabeth Pier, *Fish Frenzy* does fresh takeaway or eat-in fish and chips.

Getting There & Away Hobart is within easy driving distance of most of the national parks and major towns in Tasmania (200km from Launceston).

Air The airport is 16km from the city centre and is serviced by a TRC shuttle bus, which will drop you off at several accommodation spots on request. The fare is $7. Both Ansett (☎ 13 1300) and Qantas (☎ 13 1313) and their respective subsidiaries, Kendell (☎ 1800 338 894) and Southern Australian Airlines (☎ 13 1313), fly into Hobart from Melbourne and some other towns in Victoria. A standard one-way economy fare from Melbourne is around $260, although you may well be able to get a significant discount if you have a backpackers card. However, if you want to get to Tasmania by air, flying into Devonport is probably a cheaper option (see Getting There & Away under Devonport for details).

Bus Most bus services to other towns in Tasmania operate from the Transit Centre at 199 Collins St. The two main companies are TRC (☎ 1300 360 000), which services the east coast and Launceston, and TWT's Tassielink, servicing the east and west coasts, Devonport and some of the national parks. Hobart Coaches (☎ 03-6234 4077), 4 Liverpool St, services the Tasman Peninsula.

Car Rental Hobart has several car rental companies. The cheaper ones include Rent-a-Bug (☎ 03-6231 0300), 105 Murray St, and Selective Car Rentals (☎ 03-6234 3311), 132 Argyle St.

Devonport

The town of Devonport is a popular arrival point for travellers entering Tasmania. The local airport has daily connections to Melbourne, and the *Spirit of Tasmania* car-ferry operates between Devonport and Melbourne. It is a convenient base for walkers heading for the Overland Track and the Walls of Jerusalem National Park.

Information The waterfront Devonport Visitors Centre (☎ 03-6424 8176, fax 6424 8476), 92 Fromby Rd (near the post office), is open seven days and can make most travel and accommodation bookings. It also sells national parks permits.

The library on Oldaker St has rather slow Internet access – free for Australians and $5 per hour for overseas visitors. It's open from 9.30 am to 6 pm weekdays. A better bet is probably Red Hot CDs on William St, where the connection is faster for a similar charge for all users.

Supplies & Equipment The Backpackers Barn (☎ 03-6424 3628), 10–12 Edward St, stocks a good range of walking equipment, including tents, stoves, stove fuel and freeze-dried meals. Most essential walking and camping items are also available for hire, including tents, sleeping bags and mats, 70L to 80L backpacks and cooking sets. The owners, Carl and Cathy, have extensive experience on Tasmanian tracks and are a mine of information on the Overland Track and the Walls of Jerusalem. They can also arrange charter transport to Cradle Mountain and the start of the Overland Track for those days when there is no TWT's Tassielink service. A one-way trip for four people works out at around $120.

Places to Stay & Eat The *Mersey Bluff Caravan Park (☎ 03-6424 8655)* is 2.5km north of town on the western side of the river. It is right next to some good beaches and has tent sites for $7 per person, cabins for $50.

Abel Tasman Caravan Park (☎ 03-6427 8794) is on the eastern side of the river and has sites for $7 for one person and $10 for two. On-site vans are $35 and cabins are $56 for a double.

Tasman House Backpackers (☎ 03-6423 2335, 169 Steele St) is conveniently on the waterfront just east of the town centre. Dorm beds are $10 and en suite private rooms are $28. *Mid-City Backpackers*, above Molly Malones pub on Best St, has dorms for $13, but is a fairly basic place to stay.

Devonport has a wide selection of eateries. Takeaway food after 5 pm in the town centre is limited to *McDonald's (1 Best St)* and *KFC*, on the corner of William and Steele Sts. *Klaas's Bakehouse (11 Oldaker St)* has a good reputation for cakes and pastries (closed weekends). Next door, *Mallee Grill* serves grilled steaks, gourmet sausages, kebabs and chicken from $14 to $17. It's a good spot for a post-walk eating splurge, but vegetarians will be limited to the salad bar.

Getting There & Away Devonport is 100km from Launceston along the Bass Hwy; Hobart is another 200km farther south along the Midlands Hwy.

Air Devonport airport is 4km east of town. Kendell and Southern Australian Airlines fly several times daily to Melbourne. The flight takes just over an hour and one-way economy

fares cost around $200. At the time of writing Kendell had a special fare for overseas travellers; a one-way, stand-by fare of $90 was available on production of a passport and overseas air ticket. The fare is only available at the airport on the day of the flight but last-minute seats are often available. Tasair Regional Airlines (☎ 1800 062 900) flies between Devonport and Hobart ($99 one way).

Sea The *Spirit of Tasmania* (☎ 13 2010, @ reservations@tt-line.com.au) operates between Melbourne and Devonport, taking 14½ hours to make the crossing. The ferry departs from the terminal on the east bank of the Mersey River on Tuesday and Thursday at 6 pm and Saturday at 4.30 pm. It leaves Melbourne Monday, Wednesday and Friday from Station Pier at 6 pm. The cheapest fares include a bed in hostel-style accommodation, evening buffet and a continental breakfast. During off-peak times (late April to late September) this costs $119 one way. During peak times (December and January) it's $152. A 'shoulder' fare, which is basically any other time of the year, is $126. There are no discounts for backpackers unless you are booking a cabin ($156 to $232 in the off season). The fare with a vehicle is $30 during off-peak and shoulder periods and $40 during peak times.

The faster *DevilCat* catamaran operates between Melbourne and George Town, east of Devonport. Departures are on Monday, Tuesday, Thursday and Saturday from Melbourne, and Monday, Wednesday, Friday and Sunday from George Town. The crossing takes six hours and one-way fares are $125 in the off season (24 January to 24 April) and $130 in the peak season. Bookings can be made through TT-Line (details as for the *Spirit of Tasmania*). From George Town there are good bus connections with Devonport, Launceston and Hobart.

Bus TRC (☎ 1300 360 000) runs the main bus services from Devonport through to Burnie, Launceston and Hobart. Buses depart from the TRC terminal in Edward St and stop at the ferry terminal when the *Spirit of Tasmania* is in town. TWT's Tassielink (☎ 1300 300 520) and Maxwells (☎ 03-6492 1431) run services to Cradle Mountain (see Getting There & Away for the Overland Track later in this chapter).

Car Rental There are plenty of cheap car-rental firms such as Range/Rent-a-bug (☎ 03-6427 9034), 5 Murray St, East Devonport, where high-season rates for a VW Beetle start from $45. Major companies like Avis, Thrifty and Budget deliver to the ferry terminal.

Mt Wellington Area

For many Tasmanian walkers, Mt Wellington is perhaps the first track they ever walk and the first peak they ever climb. Rising west of the state capital, Hobart, to a height of 1270m, the summit is not more than 10km from the wharfs, marinas and office blocks of the city. On a clear day the views from the top are stunning. Crossing the boulder-strewn summit plateau evokes a sense of wildness that contrasts well with the proximity of the city centre. Between Hobart and the top of Mt Wellington, a network of tracks and paths worm their way through the bush picking out points of interest like O'Gradys Falls and the tremendous soaring dolerite columns of the Organ Pipes. A trip up Mt Wellington is a good way to get out and stretch for walkers who have just arrived in Tasmania. It's also a great vantage point from which to appreciate the city and surrounding bays.

Two walks are described here: a reasonably tough outing to Mt Wellington's summit, and a more sedate exploration of O'Gradys Falls and the Organ Pipes. The tracks on both routes are generally well signposted, in excellent condition, and can be pieced together into a seven- to eight-hour trip.

NATURAL HISTORY

Mt Wellington has been described as a 'suburban summary' of Tasmanian bush. Although bushfires have encouraged eastern eucalyptus species, tea-trees and banksias, damp gullies like Fern Glade still provide refuge for pockets of rainforest species such as myrtles and sassafras. On the summit plateau, alpine species common to areas in the west thrive in the harsh conditions.

PLANNING
When to Walk

In the winter months (May to September) Mt Wellington will normally have snow on the top. As long as the visibility is fine this should not deter well-prepared walkers. The route across the summit plateau is well marked by snow poles. Bear in mind though that whiteouts can occur at any time and there is a good deal of dangerous ground to come to grief on should you become disoriented. The only other winter danger might be from ice on the lower tracks. Other times of the year should present no problems, but because of its height Mt Wellington can experience atrocious weather at any time of the year.

What to Bring

Leaving Hobart on a fine summer's day, it can be a bit of a shock to feel the need for gloves and fleece jackets on the summit of Mt Wellington. Bring everything you would normally bring on a day trip to an alpine area if you are going to the summit, and wear strong boots for the trip across the summit plateau. If you are just visiting the Organ Pipes you'll be much more sheltered and you can get away with running shoes (trainers) on the good tracks.

Maps & Books

The Land Information Services 1:20,000 *Mt Wellington Walk Map* covers both walks and has some good background information on the history and natural history of the mountain. If you plan to spend more time exploring the other tracks on the mountain, then *Mt Wellington Walks* by Jan Hardy & Bert Elson might be worth checking out.

NEAREST TOWN

For a description of accommodation and other services in Hobart, see Gateways in the introduction to the chapter.

Although you won't find accommodation in the small suburb of Fern Tree, you will find a *general store* and small *cafe* just opposite the start of these walks.

GETTING TO/FROM THE WALKS

Bus Nos 48 and 49 from Franklin Square in Hobart will drop you at Fern Tree, where the tracks to Mt Wellington and the Organ Pipes begin. If you don't fancy walking to the top, you can take a bus to the summit from Franklin Square (running from the start of December until mid-February). A taxi to Fern Tree will cost about $12 and a taxi to the top will cost about $23 (for up to five people).

Mt Wellington

Duration	6–7 hours
Distance	12km
Standard	medium
Start/Finish	Fern Tree
Nearest Town	Hobart
Public Transport	yes

Summary Pleasant forest tracks and a steep climb lead to the summit of Mt Wellington and panoramic views across Hobart. The return leg crosses an alpine plateau before descending via some ice house ruins.

This is a reasonably strenuous walk to the summit of Mt Wellington, returning via the Devils Gulch and some ice house ruins. The route follows good tracks and markers for most of the distance, except for the short section across Mt Wellington's summit plateau. Although this stretch is marked with poles, snow and low cloud could make it a tricky navigational exercise, with potentially serious consequences if you make a mistake. Both the ascent and descent are quite steep, but the switchbacks help to lessen the strain.

THE WALK

From the shop and cafe at Fern Tree cross the Huon Rd to a small car park and picnic area. At the bottom of this, a track disappears into the trees. Follow this and almost immediately turn right onto the Fern Glade Track, keeping left at a second junction

100m farther along. Climb to the top of Fern Glade Track to reach **Radfords Monument** at a network of track junctions. The monument is dedicated to GH Radford who died, along with JM Richards, descending from the Pinnacle during a 1903 race from the city to the summit and back. Turn left at the top of the Fern Glade Track onto Radfords Track, and follow this uphill, crossing Pinnacle Rd three times before reaching a track junction. Turn right and continue to climb ever more steeply on the Pinnacle Track. Where a series of switchbacks begins, the track becomes the Zig Zag Track, climbing steeply to emerge on the summit plateau just south of the huge communications tower, which is visible from Hobart. The **summit** itself, marked by a trig point, is just beyond the tower in the middle of a parking area. Below the car park is a **viewing platform** from where you can take in the expansive views of Hobart and the bays and islands beyond. To the north, the bush-clad hills and green pastures of the Derwent Valley spread out of sight beyond the shoulder of the mountain.

Return along the summit plateau to the south, ignoring the Zig Zag Track to follow

GARETH McCORMACK

These shapely dolerite boulders on the summit are a highlight of the Mt Wellington walk

Mt Wellington & the Organ Pipes

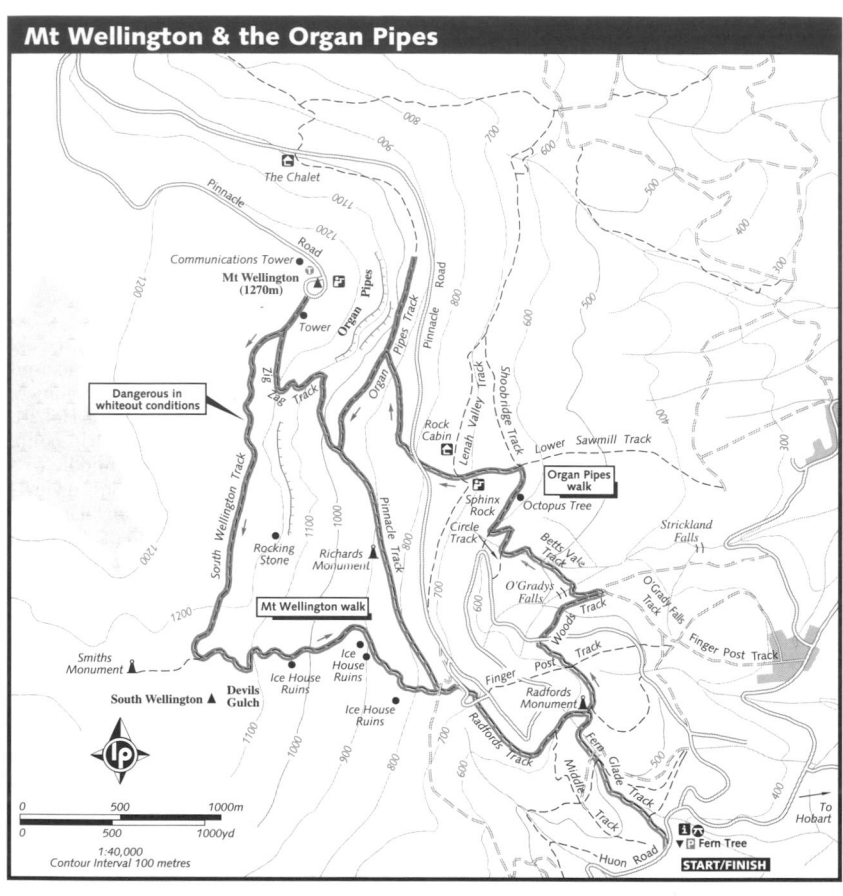

the South Wellington Track, a rough, marked route along the edge of the cliffs. The alpine landscape on this section is wonderful, with odd jumbles of frost-weathered, egg-shaped dolerite boulders littering the plateau. In the gaps, hardy alpine plants find shelter to grow. Continue along this route, which after 1km begins to descend gently, opening up new views to the south across Bruny Island and the Huon Valley. After a few hundred metres you reach a junction where a marked route heads west a short distance to **Smiths Monument**, dedicated to Dr John Smith, a surgeon who died after becoming separated

from his group while descending from Mt Wellington. To the east, the route becomes a proper track and begins to descend steeply through bush. The next kilometre is all steep descent, but on the way you'll pass several old **ice house ruins**, built to make ice in the days before refrigeration. When in operation, convict labour was used to pack the structures with snow, which over the rest of the winter would become ice. The ice was then carved into blocks and carried down the mountain on ponies.

Once you reach the Pinnacle Track, retrace your route of ascent back to Fern Tree.

The Organ Pipes

Duration	3–4 hours
Distance	9km
Standard	easy
Start/Finish	Fern Tree
Nearest Town	Hobart
Public Transport	yes

Summary Pleasant tracks take the walker through rainforest, eucalyptuses and past a waterfall on the way to the impressive dolerite columns known as the Organ Pipes.

This is a much more sedate walk than the trip to the summit of Mt Wellington. It is an exploration of the most interesting features of the mountain's lower slopes. O'Gradys Falls and the Organ Pipes are the two main points of interest, the latter being particularly impressive and visible from the streets of Hobart. The tracks are generally in excellent condition and well signposted.

THE WALK

From the shop and cafe at Fern Tree cross the Huon Road to a small car park and picnic area. At the bottom of this, a track disappears into the trees. Follow this and almost immediately turn right onto the Fern Glade Track, keeping left at a second junction 100m farther along. Climb to the top of the Fern Glade Track to reach **Radfords Monument** (see the Mt Wellington walk for a description) at a network of track junctions. Continue out to the right of Radfords Monument on Woods Track, descending across Finger Post Track and Pinnacle Rd to reach O'Gradys Falls Track. Climb up to the left (west) to view **O'Gradys Falls** and continue on, now on the Betts Vale Track, up a small gully to reach the Circle Track. Turn right and then right again, passing Octopus Tree to arrive at the junction with the Lower Sawmill Track. Turn left (uphill) onto this track and follow it across Pinnacle Rd to reach the bottom of the **Organ Pipes**.

According to geologists, the vertical columns of the Organ Pipes represent a fracture line of sorts in the break up of the ancient supercontinent of Gondwanaland.

The other half of this fracture is now in Antarctica. By walking along the Organ Pipes Track for 500m you can take in the full extent of the cliffs and perhaps get a stiff neck watching the climbers who frequent these crags in summer.

Return along the Organ Pipes Track and continue on this track rather than turning off back down the Lower Sawmill Track. After 500m it joins the Pinnacle Track; descend along this for over 1km, passing **Richards Monument** to reach a track junction at a small road. Cross over the road and descend steeply, crossing the Pinnacle Rd three times to join Radfords Track. From the Radfords Track a descent can be made to Radfords Monument and from there back to Fern Tree down Fern Glade Track. Alternatively, you can turn right before the monument to follow the Middle Track back to Fern Tree.

West & World Heritage Area

The Tasmanian WHA was given official recognition in 1982 and legal status in 1983, following a failed attempt by the Tasmanian government to dam the Franklin River (see the boxed text 'The Tasmanian World Heritage Area – the Fight for Protection' later). When Unesco was asked to consider the nomination of the area for listing, it was accepted on the basis of satisfying a record seven out of a possible 10 criteria. After a number of significant additions, 1.38 million hectares are now incorporated. In 1999 a new management plan was launched to control, among other things, the problem of track erosion and walker pressure on delicate areas (see the boxed text 'A Permit System for the World Heritage Area?' earlier in this chapter).

The walking within the WHA is at significant altitudes, which brings with it the difficulties of low temperatures, high winds and heavy rain or snow. Snow is a possibility in the alpine areas of Tasmania at any time of the year. Although the Overland Track is now quite well constructed, many of the other tracks can be rough, muddy and difficult to follow in places. Walkers considering walking in the WHA should be well equipped for mountain weather.

NATURAL HISTORY

In a very general sense the forests of Tasmania are divided into two types: rainforest, which thrives in the mountainous west, and sclerophyll forest, dominated by eucalyptuses, which occurs predominantly in the east. However, true rainforest is considered to have 5% eucalyptus cover or less, and in reality the great forests of the west have significant intrusions of eucalyptus species wherever soil type, rainfall, aspect and altitude suit best. Thus a good deal of Tasmania's western forest is really mixed. True rainforest is found in its highest concentrations in the north-west. Within the WHA region, Cradle Mountain–Lake St Clair and Franklin–Gordon Wild Rivers National Parks have the best rainforest.

Tasmanian rainforest is dominated by the myrtle beech; species such as sassafras, leatherwood, pencil pine and King Billy pine are also common. The rainforests are dated to ancestor species that lived on the supercontinent of Gondwanaland some 60 million years ago, roots shared with the rainforests of New Zealand, South America and the fossilised remains of rainforests in Antarctica. Mammals common in the rainforests include the long-tailed mouse, ringtail possum, pademelon (a tiny wallaby now extinct elsewhere) and the spotted-tailed quoll. Logging and fire (mostly started by people) remain the most significant threats to the rainforest.

The alpine plant species of Tasmania are also relics of Gondwanaland, and many of them have evolved in isolation on the island and are found nowhere else in the world. One example is the pandani, the world's tallest heath plant and one of the more conspicuous of the alpine species. Another species that is hard to miss is the cushion plant, which grows in giant, brilliant-green mounds. Unfortunately its springy nature has encouraged walkers to favour it instead of walking on muddy sections of alpine tracks. Bear in mind that these remarkable colonies can take up to 30 years to recover from the damage caused by one boot. A more robust alpine species is the snow gum, surviving in shelter at altitudes of 1300m.

The Tasmanian World Heritage Area – the Fight for Protection

Few World Heritage Areas (WHAs) have been as contentious or involved so much environmental change as the Tasmanian Wilderness WHA. The flooding of Lake Pedder, then part of Southwest National Park, by the HEC (Hydro Electric Commission) in 1972 prompted concern over the levels of protection afforded by national park status. The Tasmanian Wilderness Society (now the Wilderness Society) was founded to provide organised opposition to the HEC's planned damming of the Gordon and Franklin Rivers.

It succeeded in having the area listed for World Heritage status but that, and a change in state government, did not prevent the beginning of construction on the Franklin. In the summer of 1982–83 the issue burst into the national arena with the 'Franklin River Blockade' and the arrest of 1400 protesters. In the 1983 Federal election, the Australian Labor Party was elected on a promise to enforce the WHA's protection. Despite a legal challenge by the Tasmanian government, it followed through and the Franklin River scheme was abandoned.

GARETH McCORMACK

Lake Pedder, as seen today, holds 27 times the volume of water in Sydney Harbour

Minimal Impact Walking in the World Heritage Area

In order to preserve Tasmania's wilderness areas, care must be taken to ensure a minimal impact presence. The Parks & Wildlife Service (PWS) produces a booklet on minimal impact walking, available from ranger stations, and has information on its Web site. The following are some minimal impact practices you may want to consider when walking in the World Heritage Area (WHA).

In some areas (especially the delicate alpine areas), you should consider carrying out toilet waste: bring some strong, sealable plastic bags for this purpose. At the very least, bring a trowel for burying it, and use the toilets provided wherever possible.

It is also very important to be aware of the impact of soap and detergents on the fragile environment. These should never be used in or near water sources, and it is preferable not to use detergents at all. For cleaning hands, a disinfectant gel is very effective, and will not harm the environment.

The WHA is a fuel-stove-only area, so you will need a stove and fuel for any walks within its established boundaries.

For more information on minimal impact walking, see Responsible Walking in the Facts for the Walker chapter.

Mt Field National Park

Duration	5–6 hours
Distance	18km
Standard	medium
Start/Finish	Lake Dobson car park
Nearest Town	National Park
Public Transport	summer only
Summary	A pleasant outing to an exposed alpine area, with a beautiful return along Tarn Shelf. A side trip to Mt Field West can extend the walk by three to four hours, and increases the grade to medium-hard.

Located 75km north-west of Hobart, Mt Field National Park lies on the eastern fringes of the WHA. From the towering swamp gums and tree ferns around Russell Falls and the park entrance, a dirt road winds up to Lake Dobson and the start of several fine walking tracks exploring the alpine forests, moors and boulder fields in the upper reaches of the park.

The one-day walk described here makes a beautiful alpine circuit across the Rodway Range, returning along Tarn Shelf. While there are no tough ascents or large gains in altitude, the going on parts of the track can still be quite arduous. Scrambling and hopping across jumbles of boulders is the order of the day on the ascent to K Col. Fit walkers will be able to make the worthwhile side trip to Mt Field West. Given clear weather, the views from the high sections of this walk are absolutely tremendous.

A two- to three-day circuit taking in Mt Field West and Mt Field East is possible. Moderately fit walkers would do best taking three days to complete this circuit. Huts in the park are small and rough, and carrying a tent is recommended. Also, before going up to Lake Dobson, it's worth taking the 10-minute stroll around the Russell Falls walk, not just to view the waterfall, but also to see the huge swamp gums and tree ferns along the way.

HISTORY

Mt Field National Park was created in 1916 after being a reserve for more than 30 years, making it one of Tasmania's oldest parks. At this time the park area was a mere 2000 hectares and it has subsequently increased to 16,756 hectares. However, in 1949 timber interests managed to excise 1472 hectares for logging, much of which was swamp gum, with 1500 hectares of mixed forest added in return. Logging continues in the Florentine Valley, in uncomfortable proximity to both Mt Field and the eastern fringes of the WHA. The operations in the Florentine Valley are readily viewed from the summit of Mt Field West.

NATURAL HISTORY

The upper reaches of the park show plenty of evidence of glaciation during the last ice age. The valleys now holding Lake Seal and Lake Newdegate were once accumulation zones for small glaciers and snow spilling down from the upper reaches of Mt Mawson and the Rodway Range. The resulting glacier carved through where Lake Webster is today and down into the Broad River Valley. The Tarn Shelf area is thought to have been the final refuge for these glaciers as they retreated under a warming climate. They have left evidence of their presence everywhere – U-shaped valleys, cirques, tarns and jumbles of moraine debris.

With trees like the swamp gums shading the forest floor at lower elevations, a park sign points out that species diversity is in fact higher in the alpine areas of the park.

PLANNING
When to Walk

Mt Field is described on the PWS brochure as 'a park for all seasons' because skiing is sometimes possible in the winter months. For most walkers the ski season is not a time for walking at Mt Field. While the short nature trails close to the park entrance might be open and free of snow, the high-level walks such as the one described in this book will be difficult and treacherous. Walking in the alpine regions of Mt Field is normally feasible from October to April. Bear in mind though that the ridges are very exposed to bad weather and high winds and the track is not always easy to follow. With a good deal of steep and dangerous ground around the ridges, inexperienced walkers should always err on the side of caution when deciding on suitable weather for this walk.

What to Bring

You'll need to bring gear suitable for a one-day alpine walk. Waterproof and windproof clothing should be carried as a precaution, even on fine days. Boots with good ankle support are recommended for the rough, bouldery sections, while gaiters will be useful in the wetter areas. You should also carry navigational and emergency gear.

Maps

Use Tasmap's 1:50,000 *Mt Field National Park*. This can be purchased from the park offices.

Information Sources

Information brochures are available from the PWS office near the Russell Falls car park, while passes can be bought from the toll booth (☎ 03-6288 1311) at the entrance to the park. At the time of writing, a park visitor centre was also under construction.

Permits & Regulations

Mt Field National Park is subject to the normal park fees (see Park Fees & Regulations in the introduction to this chapter). If you arrive by car you'll need a vehicle pass to get to the top car park.

NEAREST TOWN & FACILITIES
National Park

Outside the Mt Field National Park entrance on the Gordon River Rd, National Park consists only of a few places to stay and the park offices. It is, however, an extremely convenient base for both Mt Field and the Mt Anne Circuit (described later in this chapter). Russell Falls is only a short stroll away, and if viewing marsupials is your thing, then a visit to the open lawns at the park entrance at dusk will reward you with plenty of possums and pademelons.

Places to Stay & Eat The *National Park YHA Hostel* (☎ 03-6288 1369) is on the left, 200m past the entrance to the park. Dorm beds are $13 for members and $16 for nonmembers. The hostel has a cosy feel but when we visited at the end of the off season, it was in need of a spring-clean.

If you are travelling in a group, *Russell Falls Holiday Cottages* (☎ 03-6288 1198) is excellent value. The cottages have one or two bedrooms and are fully equipped. They are just at the entrance to the park in a peaceful setting. Rates are $50 for a double and $10 for each additional adult.

National Park Hotel (☎ 03-6288 1103), just opposite the YHA, has single rooms with shared facilities for $30 and doubles for $50.

This is the only place to eat out in National Park, with counter meals served nightly.

Groceries are available from small stores at Westerway (8km east on the B61) and Maydena (13km west on the B61). However, it is best to bring fuel and freeze-dried foods from Hobart.

Mt Field National Park

Just inside the park, **Mt Field Camping Ground** (☎ *03-6288 1149)* has tent sites for $5 per person. Powered sites are $7 per person. You will need a park entry permit to stay and all food should be well secured against marsupials.

GETTING TO/FROM THE WALK

Mt Field National Park is 75km north-west of Hobart along the Brooker Hwy, B62 and then the Gordon River Rd.

TWT's Tassielink (☎ 1300 300 520) runs a daily summer (1 December to 3 April) service between Hobart and Mt Field National Park. Fares are $25 one way and $50 return. It also runs a one-day tour that includes a return bus ticket and park entry for $49. Unfortunately the service does not run to the top car park.

Bottom Bits Bus (☎ 1800 777 103) runs a Mt Field day trip out of Hobart for $40, including hostel/hotel pick-up, park entry permit and an optional guided walk of one to two hours. The trips run Monday, Wednesday and Friday during October and November and daily from December to April. The bus will drop you at the start of your chosen walk.

THE WALK

Leave the Lake Dobson car park and follow the boardwalk around the southern shores of the lake. Ignore the junctions on the left and keep following the track to the Pandani Nature Trail, which takes you through a dense stand of pandani before emerging onto a 4WD road at the western end of Lake Dobson (about 10 minutes). Turn left onto the road and climb through several hairpin bends to reach a little cluster of ski lodges. Follow the signposts for the 'Alpine Tracks' along the front of the buildings, where the road quickly deteriorates into a simple walking track.

Views across the eastern section of the park are fairly unobstructed as you begin to climb through stands of beautifully twisted snow gums. The alpine feel is well established and the track is rough and rocky in places before it emerges onto a broad shoulder 15 minutes from the ski lodges. Well-constructed duckboards carry you across flat ground towards Rodway Hut. Along the way there is a lookout across the impressive glacial bowl containing Lake Seal. Ten minutes of easy walking on the duckboards brings you to a track junction just above Rodway Hut (day shelter and overnight emergency use only). The Tarn Shelf Track descends to the north past the hut while a track climbs in the opposite direction onto the Mawson Plateau. Continue to the west on a third track signposted for the Rodway Range. The track quickly deteriorates into a route marked with poles and splashes of red paint. The going is arduous, hopping between boulders, but the dolerite provides excellent friction.

After a short climb the route travels to the north-west along the crest of the Rodway Range. In clear conditions views extend right across Southwest National Park, and north across the Central Plateau towards the distant peaks of Cradle Mountain–Lake St Clair National Park. More immediately, Mt Field West (1434m) is the highest point on the impressive ridge stretching 3km to the north-west from K Col.

Descend to **K Col** (45 minutes from the Rodway Hut), where the boulders give way to wet ground carpeted with alpine flora, and in particular many cushion plants. Fitter walkers with time and good conditions on their side can now make the side trip to Mt Field West (see the Mt Field West side trip at the end of this walk description). Otherwise follow the muddy, marked track almost due north towards Newdegate Pass. The track climbs gently, reaching the pass in around 30 minutes. The track disappears in the area of the pass and is very easy to lose – it's best to look carefully for markers as the route swings sharply to the east. If you

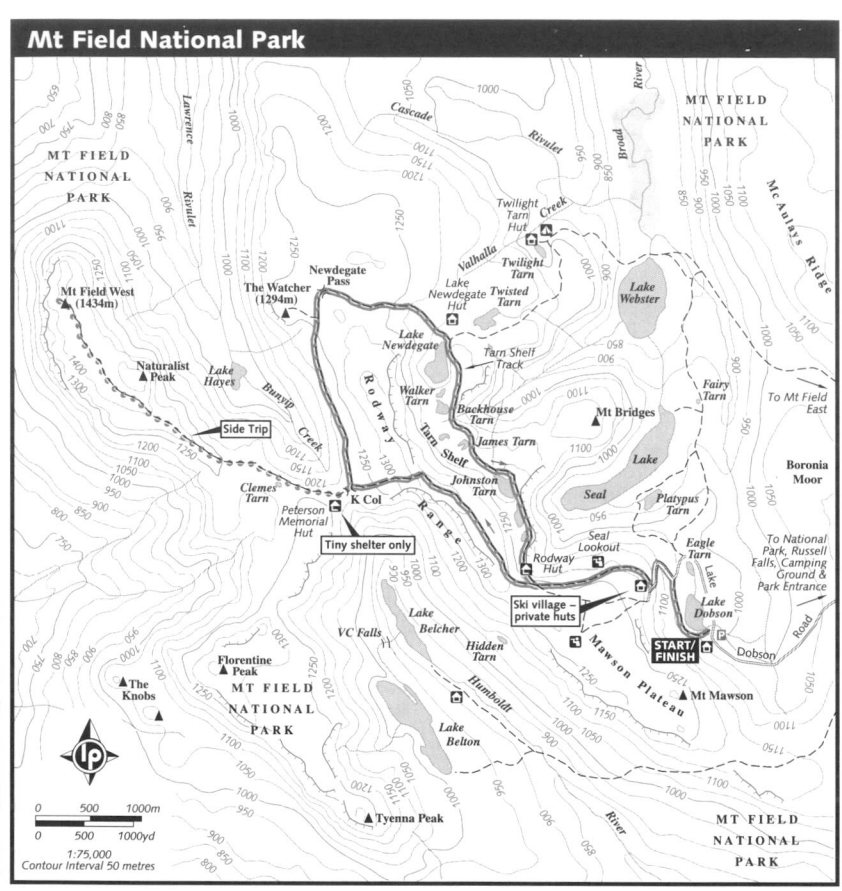

Mt Field National Park

do lose the route climb onto one of the higher bits of ground and look for a section of duckboard. Continuing now on a definable track, a steep descent is made to reach Lake Newdegate Hut at the northern end of Lake Newdegate.

Turn right at a junction onto the Tarn Shelf Track. This well-constructed track skirts the eastern shores of Lake Newdegate and climbs a series of old moraine ridges on the way to the Rodway Hut. In between the ridges are lakes and small tarns grouped together in small glacial cirques. Some people liken the **Tarn Shelf** to a miniature version

of the Labyrinth on the Overland Track. About an hour of walking will bring you back to the track junction just above the Rodway Hut. Turn right and retrace your steps to the car park (45 minutes).

Side Trip: Mt Field West

3–4 hours, 240m ascent, 240m descent
Cross the boggy flats of K Col and climb steadily past Clemes Tarn and round the western slope of Naturalist Peak. From here a generally flat walk of 1km takes you past many beautiful small tarns to the summit of Mt Field West. The views across the heavily

logged Florentine Valley into the WHA present a stark juxtaposition of wilderness lost and wilderness protected. Return to K Col by the route of ascent.

Mt Anne Circuit

Duration	3 days
Distance	27km
Standard	hard
Start	Condominium Creek
Finish	Red Tape Creek
Nearest Towns	Maydena, National Park
Public Transport	summer only

Summary A difficult, challenging and exposed alpine ridge walk for fit and experienced walkers only. A good head for heights and confidence on steep ground is required. The mountain scenery is stunning.

From most angles, Mt Anne (1423m) looks like improbable terrain for walkers. It rises to the east of Lake Pedder, a towering fang of dolerite with sheer faces on all sides. Connected to the more rounded peaks of Mt Eliza, Mt Lot and Mt Sarah Jane by sometimes razor-edged ridges, the circuit of this mountain group provides an exciting three-day walk with incredible views across much of the south-west wilderness.

Walkers attempting the Mt Anne Circuit should be fit, well equipped and comfortable on steep, exposed ground, as well as with scrambling over boulders. The final section of the ascent to Mt Anne is the most difficult part of the route, but as it is a side trip you can choose to avoid the final scramble and still complete the circuit.

Many walkers will also find a there-and-back visit to Mt Anne less strenuous, starting and finishing at Condominium Creek car park. A fairly long one-day effort or a more leisurely two days will be needed for this. Even if you do not get to the summit, the views of both Mt Anne and the WHA from Mt Eliza are well worth the effort. Similarly, a one-day or overnight trip to Lake Judd from the Red Tape Creek car park provides wonderful views of the large cliffs and ridges of the Mt Anne Range.

Mt Anne, like all Tasmanian mountain areas, regularly experiences awful weather. Walkers should be wary of being caught in a cold snap on this circuit as many of the exposed sections could be very dangerous if covered in snow or ice.

NATURAL HISTORY

One of the most interesting aspects of the Mt Anne massif is the mixture of quartzite and dolerite rock, which serves as a small-scale model of the interplay of these two rock types within the rest of the WHA. In areas where the marbly white quartzite is on the surface, producing nutrient-poor soils (most notably on the ridge to High Camp Hut), the vegetation is limited to hardy ground scrub. However, where the rough dolerite surfaces, weathering to relatively rich soil, pandani and snow gums grow at high elevations. Mt Eliza Plateau has some beautiful colonies of cushion plant, often fringed by stunted pandani. The cushion plants may seem like a wonderfully flat and soft camping surface, but these fragile plant communities can take up to 30 years to recover from damage, so avoid walking on them.

PLANNING
When to Walk

Due to the complexity of the terrain and the remote nature of this walk the Mt Anne Circuit should only be attempted in reasonably stable weather, when the tops are free of ice and snow. This will normally mean late spring, summer and early autumn (mid-October to April). In winter conditions the route will require mountaineering skills.

What to Bring

You'll need to carry a good three- or four-season tent and a fuel stove on the circuit. Although High Camp Hut can provide shelter for the first night, it can only sleep about six people comfortably and may be full when you arrive. (At the time of writing it had a particularly noisy and bold resident rodent.) You'll also need full protective clothing for wind, rain and snow, plus strong boots and gaiters. Some groups might also consider carrying 20m of walking rope for

TASMANIA

pack hauling and to safeguard members of the group on exposed ground.

Maps
The most suitable are Tasmap's 1:25,000 *Anne* and *Scotts* maps.

Permits & Regulations
You will need a national parks pass to set out on the Mt Anne Circuit (see Park Fees & Regulations in the introduction to Tasmania).

NEAREST TOWN
Maydena
Maydena is a tiny settlement just outside the entrance to Southwest National Park on the Gordon River Rd. It has a couple of small grocery stores but very little else, so you should plan to bring your own provisions with you from Hobart. As it does not have a scheduled bus service Maydena will only be of interest to those with their own transport. About 13km to the east of Maydena is National Park (for details see the Mt Field National Park section earlier).

Accommodation in Maydena is limited to *Tyenna Valley Lodge* (☎ 03-6288 2293), signposted off the main highway, where B&B costs $55 for a double with shared facilities, while accommodation in a private cottage is $80 for a double. The host can provide transport to the start of the Mt Anne Circuit for around $20 for two people.

On Junee Rd, *Cockatoo Cafe* (☎ 03-6288 2166) serves lunch and evening meals from Wednesday to Sunday.

GETTING TO/FROM THE WALK
To the Start
For those with their own transport, simply follow the B61 highway (Gordon River Rd) towards Strathgordon and turn left onto the unsealed C607 (Scotts Peak Rd), signposted for Mt Anne and Scotts Peak. The trailhead at Condominium Creek is signposted on the left about 20km to the south.

TWT's Tassielink (☎ 1300 300 520) runs a summer service from Hobart to Scotts Peak via the start and finish of the walk. It operates on Monday, Wednesday and Friday. The return fare is $79 and the bus arrives at the start of the Mt Anne Circuit (Condominium Creek) at 11.35 am, with the return service picking up from the end of the circuit (Red Tape Creek) at 1.30 pm. Like all of the TWT's Tassielink track transport services it will only run with sufficient numbers.

From the Finish
The finish of the walk is 8km to the south of Condominium Creek on the same road. Walking back to Condominium Creek from the finish will take around two hours if you cannot organise a car shuffle (leaving a car at either end of the walk).

THE WALK
Day 1: Condominium Creek to High Camp Hut
1½–2½ hours, 5km, 720m ascent
A well-constructed track leaves the car park at Condominium Creek and crosses buttongrass plain for a few hundred metres to reach the foot of Mt Eliza's west ridge. There are several flat and sheltered *camp sites* at Condominium Creek. The track, which is constructed into large wooden steps, climbs onto the ridge, and magnificent views of Lake Pedder begin to open out behind. The steps can seem very strenuous with a heavy pack, but some relief is gained after 30 minutes of steep climbing. A flat section of track, muddy in places, leads into a dip from where the track climbs steeply for 10 minutes to gain the crest of Mt Eliza's west ridge. From here a steady ascent of one to two hours leads to *High Camp Hut*, tucked into a small swathe of stunted gums. The hut has a water tank at the back and a toilet just below. There are a few small *tent sites* nearby.

Day 2: High Camp Hut to Judds Charm
6–7 hours, 9km
From High Camp Hut the track becomes much rougher and is marked with cairns. It swings to the north-east and climbs steeply over boulders and rock steps, then comes back to the east following a ridge line to the summit of **Mt Eliza** (1289m). The strenuous climb from High Camp Hut takes 45 minutes to one hour and is rewarded (in clear

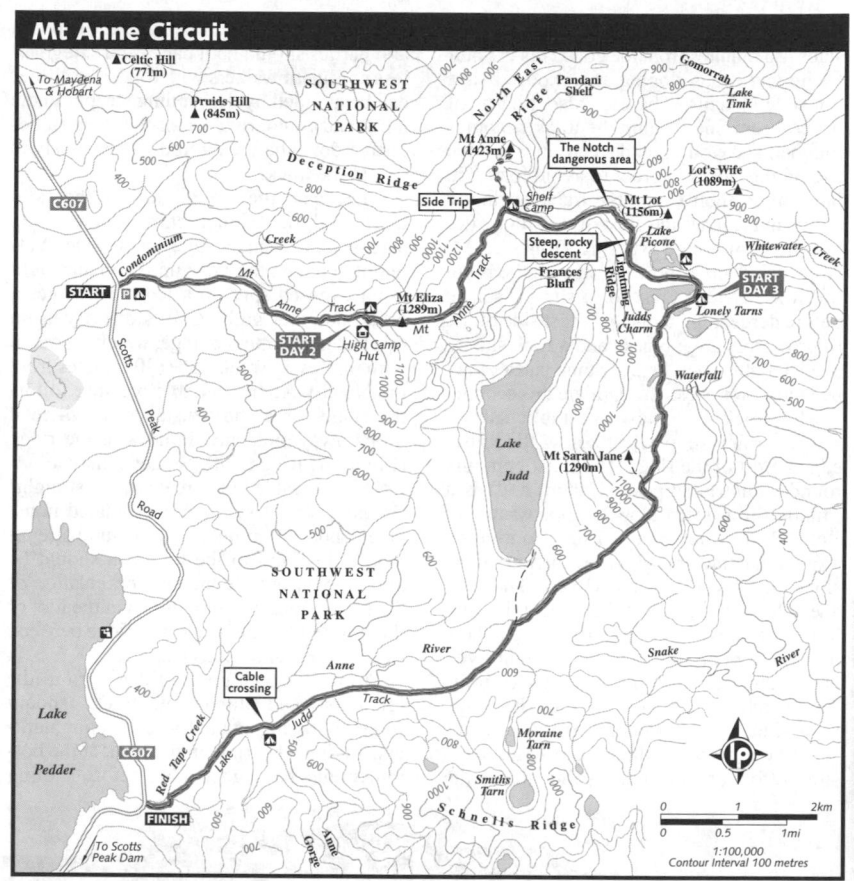

Mt Anne Circuit

weather) by spectacular views of the Frank-land Range across Lake Pedder. Descend slightly and then climb gently over a crest. It is well worth detouring 100m or so to the east to view the airy drop to Lake Judd. Another gentle descent and ascent leads to a broad col dotted with an assortment of tarns. Cushion plant communities abound on this col and are complemented by clusters of stunted pandani. There are some very flat areas for camping on the col, but the delicate flora and absence of shelter from strong winds should convince most walkers to forgo the option of overnighting here.

From the col, a short climb leads round the western shoulder of an unnamed summit (1357m). Descend awkwardly across large boulders to reach the col beneath Mt Anne (two to 2½ hours from High Camp Hut). For a detailed walk description, see the Mt Anne Summit side trip later. From the col there is a good if somewhat intimidating view of the ridge you must negotiate to reach Judds Charm and Lake Picone. Fortunately the route is not as difficult as it looks, although it is still exposed and quite strenuous.

Descend from the col following a rough but well-defined track to a large and fairly flat area of small pools held between rock slabs (20 minutes from the col). This is Shelf Camp and it has sloping and exposed sites for several tents. There is also plenty of water. From Shelf Camp the track becomes rougher and you should keep an attentive eye on the cairns in order to avoid losing it. Soon after Shelf Camp the track begins to climb and reaches the crest of the ridge after one hour of rough walking from the Mt Anne col. Cairns show the way as the route follows the ridge crest for a short distance before descending to the left (east side of the ridge) across large blocks and a rock slab to reach a flatter shelf below. Some parties may need to lower packs to negotiate this section.

The track becomes re-established on steep, scrubby slopes just below the knife-edged crest of the ridge. The track contours round an unnamed peak (1200m) and, as it rounds the eastern slopes, good views of Lot's Wife (1089m) open up. Continuing around, the track reaches a steepening in the slope just level with the **Notch**. The way ahead looks extremely difficult. At this point look just above for the cairns which show the way around this impasse, bringing you down into the Notch through a loose gully. The Notch is the crux section of the ridge, involving a 5m scramble up the obvious square-cut corner. Although the scramble is straightforward on large, solid holds, the exit moves from the corner are very exposed and parties should haul packs and safeguard less confident walkers with rope. The corner can be avoided by descending steeply to the north and contouring across the steep slopes farther down before climbing strenuously to regain the track.

Once past the Notch, follow the faint track and occasional cairns, contouring across the extremely steep slopes. Don't attempt to regain the ridge until you turn right at an exposed spur on a ledge and enter a broad and wet gully. Cairns direct you up this and back onto the ridge, which is strewn with impressive rock slabs (30 minutes from the Notch). After a suitable breather follow the ridge for a short distance to where it drops away suddenly. Following the ridge (Lightning Ridge) directly down may look a little improbable but is really quite straightforward. The descent to a vegetated notch takes about 30 minutes and is quite strenuous. Below and to the left, you should be able to pick out the muddy continuation of the track, emerging from forest at the foot of the ridge and heading across a ridge between Lake Picone and Judds Charm.

From the notch on the ridge, turn to the left (east) and plunge into thick pandani forest following a faint track and poor markers. Taking a bearing on the track at the bottom might be a good idea before starting

The barren and craggy summit of Mt Anne at sunset

out. The forest is at times a real struggle to walk through and it is very easy to lose the track. Once at the bottom follow the obvious track to the outlet of **Judds Charm**. You can camp near here or just north at the outlet of **Lake Picone**. Continuing on a rough track from Lake Picone, you can reach the summit of Lot's Wife (1089m) in a little over an hour. The route to the summit runs round the north face of the mountain before a scramble up the eastern side deposits you on top. Return along the same route.

Side Trip: Mt Anne Summit

1½–2 hours, 200m ascent, 200m descent
The route to the summit of Mt Anne described here is the marked route and is also the most direct. The most difficult section requires confidence on steep ground. By scrambling to the north side of the mountain it may be possible to find a slightly less exposed route to the top.

Follow the marked track across the col and climb around to the left of an outcrop. The track drops down to an extensive boulder field beneath the cliff-ringed south face of Mt Anne. The route is cairned diagonally left across the boulder fields to a square-cut corner close to the eastern extent of the cliffs. Once at the foot of the corner you'll need to use your hands and exercise great care. If in doubt, or if the rock is wet or icy, do not attempt this section. Climb directly up for 2m or 3m to reach a ramp, which can be followed to the left (as you face the cliff) and upwards to a sloping platform on a blunt and very exposed arete (narrow ridge). Make a slightly awkward move off this to another ledge (this may need to be safeguarded) and then walk carefully back to the right on a wide and sloping ledge. Now climb through a small notch onto the eastern side of the mountain and walk along a wide ledge to where cairns show the way across the last scramble to the **summit**. A small visitors' book resides in a metal case. Not surprisingly, the views and sense of achievement are considerable, and you get a particularly good view of the ridge that has to be negotiated to reach Judds Charm and Lake Picone. Return to the col along the same route.

Day 3: Judds Charm to Red Tape Creek

6 hours, 13km
The walking becomes much easier between Judds Charm and the beginning of the descent into the Anne River Valley. The track climbs steadily from the lake outlet across boggy ground and then crosses broad shoulder with great views back into the heart of the Mt Anne massif. A short descent is made to an unnamed lake set beneath steep rock walls; another steady ascent brings you round the eastern shoulder of Mt Sarah Jane (1290m) to a junction where the marked route to the summit of **Mt Sarah Jane** begins (1½ hours from Judds Charm). A return trip to the summit without packs should take no more than an hour.

Continuing on the main track, a steep descent begins across open slopes. However, After 10 to 15 minutes the tree line is reached and the track begins to fight its way through dense and tangled scrub. You'll need to be careful to stay on the track, which at times becomes little more than a dim tunnel in which to scrape through the bush. Towards the bottom of the descent the situation becomes worse, with deep pools of mud and water filling the depressions in the track. Although the vegetation opens out as you approach the south end of Lake Judd, the going underfoot becomes even wetter and muddier.

From the junction with the Lake Judd Track, conditions don't improve for a considerable distance. The valley floor is crossed to reach drier ground on the south side, and about 3km from the finish (45 minutes from Lake Judd junction) a well-constructed track begins. However, a cable crossing over the Anne River provides a final challenge. The two-wire crossing is too much of a balancing act for most and at normal water levels the river can be safely waded. If it is in flood it will probably be wiser to camp on the flat, sheltered ground nearby until the waters recede. From the crossing, the end of the track is 30 to 40 minutes away.

continued on page 323

TASMANIA

Overland Track

Duration	7 days
Distance	81km
Standard	medium
Start	Cradle Valley
Finish	Lake St Clair
Nearest Towns	Cradle Valley, Derwent Bridge
Public Transport	yes

Summary The most famous multi-day walk in Australia. A good track crosses the highest ground in Tasmania, taking in wild alpine moors, craggy peaks and swathes of luxuriant rainforest.

The Overland Track covers 81km of some of the highest and most spectacular terrain in Tasmania. Monolithic ranges of shattered peaks rise above flat alpine moorland. Towards its southern end at Lake St Clair, the track descends into valleys cloaked in wet eucalyptus and haunting myrtle rainforest. It is arguably the best multi-day walk in Australia and is justifiably popular, so much so that it has a reputation for being crowded. The volume of walkers crossing the delicate alpine terrain has created a problem with track erosion emblematic of the difficulties on other popular tracks in the WHA. Over recent years a good deal of the track has been built up, replacing the once infamous mires of knee-deep mud with long sections of duckboard, parallel planks and log paths.

Depending on how much time and energy you have, how fit you are and how much you want to see, the Overland Track can be walked in as little as four days, or in up to eight or even 10 days. A straight-through walk skipping side trips will take five days for an average group (four if the ferry at Lake St Clair is used). Taking in most of the side trips will require about eight days, including ascents of Cradle Mountain and Mt Ossa. There are also several side trips to view some impressive waterfalls, and the chance to wander through the tarns and snow gums of The Labyrinth. Even if you don't have the time to walk the whole track, both the Cradle Mountain and Lake St Clair ends of the walk provide numerous options for half-day, full-day and overnight trips.

Times given for the individual stages may in many instances seem particularly short, but remember to add on the time given in the track notes for side trips. Starting out with a pack laden with food for several days, these half-day stages may well seem a blessing, giving you time to explore the surrounds of huts and camping areas. Finally, the walk can be done in the other direction, although it is more commonly walked from north to south.

HISTORY

Tasmanian Aboriginal people made seasonal visits to the Cradle Mountain area and evidence of their temporary camps have been found at altitudes above 1000m. After the arrival of Europeans, the Van Diemen's Land Company employed Joseph Fossey and Henry Hellyer in the 1920s to assess the area for its potential for sheep grazing and stock routes. But the difficult terrain and harsh weather were considered unsuitable. That left the area to the fur trappers like Paddy Hartnett who worked the forests in the Mersey River Valley during the early 1900s. In 1930 a fur trapper named Bert Nicholls blazed the Overland Track, providing access for ponies and men from the north to the developing transport route between Hobart and the west coast (now the Lyell Hwy). It was a surprisingly short time before walkers followed his trail. In January 1931 eight members of the Hobart Walking Club walked the entire track.

Gustav and Kate Weindorfer were instrumental in the process of recognition that led to the area becoming a national park. Gustav built the Waldheim Chalet in 1912 and cut tracks onto Cradle Plateau for guests to use. After his wife's death in 1916, Gustav continued to publicise the Cradle Mountain–Lake St Clair area through newspaper articles and lecture tours, and finally put a proposal to the Tasmanian government in 1921, suggesting the area receive legal protection. In 1922 the area became a Scenic Reserve and Wildlife Sanctuary, finally becoming a national park in 1971, almost 40 years after Gustav's death.

NATURAL HISTORY

Much of the rock beneath the Overland Track is quartzite as much as a billion years old. Sandstones and conglomerates have been laid down on top of this. The conglomerate looks like boulders and pebbles cemented together and is particularly evident around Waterfall Valley. Around 175 million years ago a volcanic period forced dolerite into the sandstone. The dolerite is now evident in distinctive columnar structures around the tops of the major mountains. The columnar formations are thought to have been caused by the patterns of cooling in the rock.

The main topographical features of Cradle Mountain–Lake St Clair National Park are also very much a result of glacial action. Deep lakes

View of Cradle Mountain from above Lake Dove

SARA-JANE CLELAND

and cirques such as Lake Dove, Crater Lake and Lake St Clair were gouged out during the last ice age. The lake-scattered alpine plateau between Cradle Mountain and Pelion Gap is also a glacial feature, with the many lake-filled depressions created by the weight of the ice sheet.

You stand a good chance of seeing several of Tasmania's native marsupials. Bennett's wallabies (a sub-species of the red-necked wallaby) are common around Waterfall Valley and New Pelion Hut, while the tiny pademelon is happier in the thick bush around Windy Ridge Hut. Dusk strolls by torchlight (flashlight) should reveal sightings of ringtail or brushtail possums and possibly a wombat or Tasmanian devil. During heavy rain you may be rewarded by the remarkable sight of what would appear to be a small lobster in a muddy puddle on the track. This is a burrowing freshwater crayfish (often referred to as a 'yabbie'), growing to between 15cm and 20cm in length. It can be found anywhere there is moisture or where it can burrow to the water table, even on the summits of some Tasmanian mountains. Details of birds and flora of interest along particular stretches of the Overland Track are given in the track notes.

PLANNING
When to Walk

With as many as 8000 walkers covering the track between December and March, it can become very crowded. During this time huts will often be full (first come, first served) and a veritable city of tents will appear around them in the evening. The presence of so many other walkers will, for some, spoil the wilderness experience. For less experienced walkers, the company will provide reassurance and security. The winter months of June through to the start of September see the track snowbound and exposed to some violent storms and blizzards. Only very experienced and well-prepared walkers tackle the Overland in winter conditions.

Balanced between these seasonal extremes, the spring months of October and November can be a good time to visit. The track is quiet and generally free of snow. Warm weather is not unusual, but gales and sudden returns to winter conditions can also be expected on a weekly basis. Moving into autumn, March and April feature the colours of the deciduous beech and some of the most settled weather of the year. Local walkers tend to come out for these prime moments, and crowding can still be a problem.

What to Bring

Although the track is well constructed, it is still necessary to wear boots with good ankle support. Even in summer you'll need a waterproof coat and plenty of warm clothing. Necessary peripherals run the full gamut from warm hat and gloves, to sunhat, sunglasses and sunscreen. You'll survive without gaiters, but they are an advantage on muddy sections and when walking through ground scrub. For the evening you'll need a warm (three-season) sleeping bag and a sleeping mat for the wooden bunks in the huts. As with all of the WHA you'll need a fuel stove for cooking. At any time of the year it is recommended that you carry a tent in the event of a hut being full. However, if you are not expecting the huts to be crowded and are determined not to carry the extra weight, carry a good emergency bivvy bag in case of injury or stranding by poor weather between huts.

Maps & Books

The Land Information Services 1:100,000 *Cradle Mountain–Lake St Clair* map is published specifically for the Overland. On the reverse it has notes on history, ecology and walking times. These notes have been extended in *The Overland Track – A Walkers Notebook*, published by the PWS, a compact and light reference that can be carried on the walk. It is a particularly useful guide to the flora and fauna of the track. *A Walk in the Wilderness* by Nic Haygarth is a personal account of a crossing of the track. Walkers contemplating shorter excursions at either end of the Overland should use the Land Information Services 1:20,000 *Cradle Mountain – Day Walk Map* and 1:50,000 *Lake St Clair – Day Walk Map*.

Information Sources

The Cradle Mountain visitor centre (☎ 03-6492 1133), at the park entrance about 7km from the junction with the main highway, is open all year. The ranger station is in the same building. The centre has an Overland Track Information Kit, which it will send anywhere in the world for $25.

Permits & Regulations

You'll need a national parks pass to walk the Overland Track (see Park Fees & Regulations in the introduction to this chapter). All of the national parks within the WHA are fuel-stove-only areas. Camping is forbidden between Cradle Valley and Waterfall Valley Huts. Elsewhere, camping is permitted throughout, except where signs indicate otherwise.

Guided Walks

Several companies offer guided walks on the Overland Track. Both Craclair Tours (☎ 03-6424 7833) and Tasmanian Expeditions (☎ 1800 030 230) run eight-day trips including supply of all equipment and protective clothing. The cost is around $1000. Tasman Bush Tours (☎ 03-6423 4965) offers cheaper seven-day tours, but you'll need to supply your own backpack and clothing.

Perhaps the most luxurious guided trip is operated out of Launceston by Cradle Huts (☎ 03-6331 2006). The walk takes six days and the price of $1450 includes accommodation in pleasant and unobtrusive private huts. Best of all, the huts are stocked with food and wine so you can travel with a light pack.

NEAREST TOWNS & FACILITIES
Cradle Valley

Cradle Valley, near the north end of the track, isn't so much a town or village as a collection of tourist facilities strung along the length of the Cradle Mountain access road. You can buy petrol and diesel at Cradle

View Restaurant, 2.5km north of the park entrance, from 8 am to 8 pm daily. You should plan to bring all your supplies for the walk with you from Devonport.

Places to Stay & Eat The *Cradle Mountain Tourist Park and Campground* (☎ 03-6492 1395) is about 2km north of the visitor centre and is the cheapest accommodation option in the valley. Camping costs $8 per person, but the facilities and surroundings are excellent. Bunkhouse accommodation costs $20 per person and cabins with en suite bathroom and TV are $80 per double.

Just opposite the visitors centre, *Cradle Mountain Lodge* (☎ 03-6492 1303) is a good option if you have walked the Overland in the opposite direction and really want to splash out. It has attractive cabins for $174 to $225 for a double. Inside, the *Highland Restaurant* serves excellent meals ($20 for a main course) beside an open fire and a huge, inspirational topographic wall map of Tasmania. Nearby, the *Tavern Bar* serves cheaper counter meals from 10 am. Opposite the visitor centre is a very limited *general store*, which is open until 6 pm.

Getting There & Away TWT's Tassielink (☎ 1300 300 520) operates scheduled bus services between Devonport, Launceston and the west coast towns of Strahan and Queenstown via the Cradle Mountain visitor centre. From 1 December to 3 April the service runs daily in each direction, but during the rest of the year it only runs on Tuesday, Thursday and Saturday. The one-way fare from Devonport is $30 and the driver makes stops at the various accommodation areas on the Cradle Mountain access road.

There are a number of operators who will arrange charter services direct to the track start. Maxwells (☎ 03-6492 1431) runs services on demand to both ends of the Overland Track, while in Devonport the

CHRIS KLEP

Cradle Mountain seen from the southern end of Lake Dove

Backpackers Barn (☎ 03-6424 3628) can arrange charters to the Cradle Mountain end for around $120 for four people.

Cynthia Bay

At the southern end of Lake St Clair, *Lakeside St Clair (☎ 03-6289 1137)* has tent sites ($12 for two people), powered sites ($15 for two), a backpackers lodge ($25 per person), double cabins ($132/$184 off-peak/peak) and a cafe/restaurant, which also sells basic food supplies and takeaway food.

If you wish to camp free of charge, *Fergy's Paddock*, about 10 minutes down the Overland Track, has tent sites and toilets.

Derwent Bridge

Only 5km south of Lake St Clair, and for most walkers the end of the Overland, Derwent Bridge is especially popular for its pub.

Places to Stay & Eat At the southern end of the track, David and Carol Fitzgibbon run the excellent *Derwent Bridge Hotel (☎ 03-6289 1144)*, where a post-Overland steak ($16.50) is a real treat. Small, single-bed cabins cost $20 per night and hotel rooms are $75 for a double or $85 for a double with en suite. There is a huge open fire in the lounge and continental breakfasts ($9.50) are served from 8 to 9.30 am. Lunches ($4 to $6) are served between noon and 2 pm. Nearby, *Derwent Bridge Chalets (☎ 03-6289 1126)* charges $128 per double with continental breakfast.

Getting There & Away TWT's Tassielink operates scheduled bus services between Hobart and Strahan and Queenstown via Derwent Bridge and the Lake St Clair visitor centre. From 1 December to 3 April the service runs daily in each direction, and another service operates from Launceston on Monday, Wednesday and Friday. Another scheduled service operates from Hobart all year on Tuesday, Thursday and Saturday but only stops in Derwent Bridge. The one-way fare from Hobart to Lake St Clair costs $28.70. For details of charter services see Getting There & Away under Cradle Valley earlier.

GETTING TO/FROM THE WALK
To the Start

Maxwells (☎ 03-6492 1431) runs a daily shuttle service from the park entrance to Lake Dove and Waldheim ($7 for the 7km journey). Outside busy times the service will go when there are a reasonable number of people, often around lunchtime when a tour bus pulls in. In the summer months, the bus runs more regularly.

From the Finish

The MV *IdaClair* (☎ 03-6289 1137) operates the length of Lake St Clair between the visitor centre and Narcissus Hut. From December through to the beginning of March the service leaves the visitor centre at 9 and 11 am, and 12.30, 2 and 3 pm, arriving at the hut 30 minutes later.

Outside the busiest times the service only runs on demand unless you book in advance. There is a radio at Narcissus Hut for contacting the ferry. If there are less than four people the minimum charge is $60; otherwise the normal fare is $15 one way. Maxwells (☎ 03-6492 1431) runs an on-demand shuttle bus between Lake St Clair and Derwent Bridge. The one-way fare is $5.

THE WALK
Day 1: Lake Dove to Waterfall Valley Huts
3½–5 hours, 13km

There are three tracks that can be used to access the Overland from Cradle Valley. The most popular start is probably from Waldheim Chalet. This track passes through lush rainforest of pandani and King Billy pine before ascending past Crater Falls to Marions Lookout. It offers a good deal of shelter if the weather is poor.

A second track leaving from Waldheim is known as the Horse Track and takes in Crater Peak and the western rim of Crater Lake before joining the Overland Track at the Kitchen Hut emergency shelter. It is a more gradual ascent but offers little protection against poor weather.

Finally, a third option (shown on the map) is to take the track from the north end of Lake Dove, passing the Wombat Pools to reach the Waldheim Chalet track below Marions Lookout. This option provides the opportunity to see the reflection of Cradle Mountain (1545m) in Lake Dove.

From Lake Dove take the track headed west from the car park and turn right at a junction. After a brief descent through forest the trail rounds the northern shores of Lake Lilla and then begins to climb, mostly on wooden steps past Wombat Pools and up to a broad shoulder where the track from Waldheim Chalet joins from the right. Climb steeply now to reach **Marions Lookout** after an hour of walking from Lake Dove.

The views across to the shattered crest of Cradle Mountain are spectacular, as are those back down into the cirque of Crater Lake. From Marions Lookout the track climbs gently onto a high and exposed plateau of buttongrass and alpine cushion plants. The imposing summit of Barn Bluff (1559m) comes into view as you cross a creek. (This is the last opportunity for water until Waterfall Valley Huts.) Twenty minutes of walking from Marions Lookout brings you to Kitchen Hut, an emergency shelter set at a track junction. There is a very eroded trail, signposted for **Cradle Mountain** (see the Cradle Mountain side trip at the end of the day's walk description).

From this junction the Overland Track heads south (left) and almost immediately the going becomes more arduous. Small sections of duckboard are interspersed with sections across large angular boulders. Ten or 15 minutes of walking takes you into a swathe of snow gums; many of the trees are bleached skeletons from an old bushfire. Thirty minutes from Kitchen Hut you'll reach a junction with a track coming up from Lake Rodway and the Scott Kilvert Memorial Hut. The Overland continues south-west from this junction across a broad, exposed shoulder forming the western bounds of Cradle Cirque. The going across planks is easy and on a clear day you should have excellent views of the Pelion peaks to the south.

Overland Track (North)

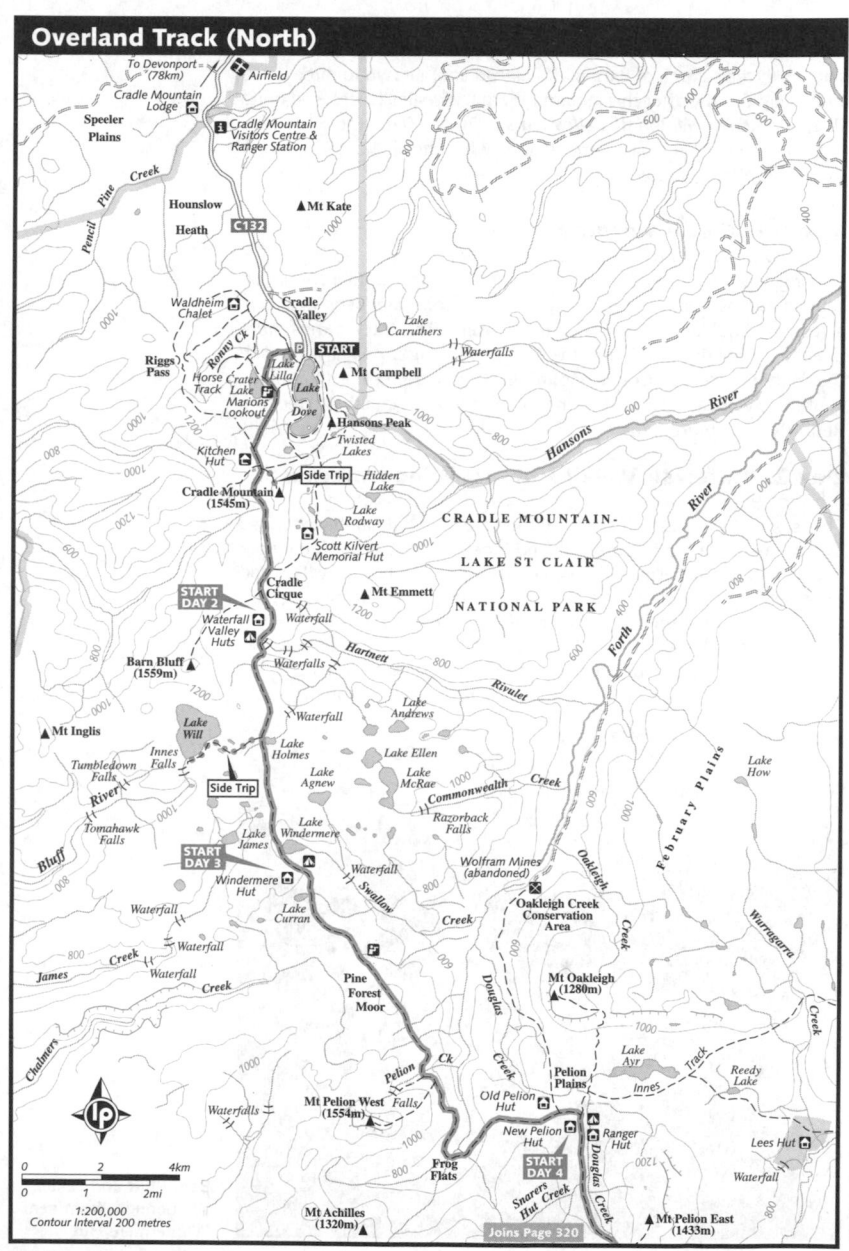

To Devonport (78km)

Airfield

Cradle Mountain Lodge

Speeler Plains

Cradle Mountain Visitors Centre & Ranger Station

Hounslow Heath

C132

▲ Mt Kate

Pencil pine Creek

Waldheim Chalet

Cradle Valley

START

Lake Carruthers

Waterfalls

Riggs Pass

Ronny Ck

Horse Track

Crater Lake

Lake Lilla

Lake Dove

▲ Mt Campbell

Marions Lookout

Kitchen Hut

▲ Hansons Peak

Twisted Lakes

Hansons River

Side Trip

Hidden Lake

Cradle Mountain (1545m) ▲

Lake Rodway

Scott Kilvert Memorial Hut

CRADLE MOUNTAIN-

LAKE ST CLAIR

NATIONAL PARK

Forth River

START DAY 2

Cradle Cirque

▲ Mt Emmett

Waterfall Valley Huts

Waterfall

Barn Bluff (1559m) ▲

Hartnett

Waterfalls

Rivulet

▲ Mt Inglis

Waterfall

Lake Andrews

Lake Will

Innes Falls

Lake Holmes

Lake Ellen

February Plains

Lake How

Tumbledown Falls

River

Side Trip

Lake Agnew

Lake McRae

Commonwealth Creek

Tomahawk Falls

Lake James

Lake Windermere

Razorback Falls

START DAY 3

Windermere Hut

Wolfram Mines (abandoned)

Waterfall

Swallow

Oakleigh Creek Conservation Area

Bluff

Lake Curran

Creek

Oakleigh Creek

Wurragarra

Waterfall

James Creek

Waterfall

Creek

Pine Forest Moor

Mt Oakleigh (1280m)

Lake Ayr

Inness Track

Reedy Lake

Creek

Chalmers

Waterfalls

Pelion Ck

Falls

Douglas Creek

Pelion Plains

Lees Hut

Mt Pelion West (1554m) ▲

Old Pelion Hut

New Pelion Hut

Ranger Hut

Waterfall

Frog Flats

Snarers Hut Creek

START DAY 4

Douglas Creek

▲ Mt Pelion East (1433m)

0   2   4km
0   1   2mi

1:200,000
Contour Interval 200 metres

Mt Achilles (1320m) ▲

Joins Page 320

Continue round Cradle Cirque to a junction where a track leaves the Overland and continues along the shoulder to Barn Bluff (1559m). A side trip to the summit of Barn Bluff will add another two to three hours to the day. Shortly after this junction the track begins to descend quite steeply, reaching *Waterfall Valley Huts* in 30 to 40 minutes. The new hut here sleeps 20 and has a large heater, while the old hut farther back towards the trees sleeps eight.

Side Trip: Cradle Mountain
1–1½ hours, 340m ascent, 340m descent
Leaving the Kitchen Hut junction the track to the Cradle Mountain summit climbs relatively gently at first but soon steepens and cuts across the boulder-strewn slopes to the right. The track climbs more directly for the final section to the top, zigzagging up a gully to reach the shattered crest of **Cradle Mountain**. If you are feeling fit and adventurous you can scramble farther along the crest in either direction. Return via the route of ascent.

Day 2: Waterfall Valley Huts to Windermere Hut
3 hours, 9km
This is one of the shortest stages on the Overland but can be extended by making a side trip to Lake Will and Innes Falls. Much of the terrain between Waterfall Valley and Windermere Hut is at a high elevation and extremely exposed to wind and poor weather. Be very wary of setting out on this stage if there is a chance of snow covering the track.

From Waterfall Valley Hut a short descent brings you to a bridge over the Hartnett Rivulet. Climb gently away from the rivulet, turning to the west along a small spur coming down from Barn Bluff. Turning south

Barn Bluff and Lake
Windermere from near
Windermere Hut

again, the track continues to climb gently, often on duckboards. An hour from Waterfall Valley Hut the track reaches open alpine moor looking down on **Lake Holmes**. From here you can see the track drop down past the western shores of Lake Holmes before climbing again to another treeless crest. Just beside Lake Holmes, a track runs off to the west signposted for Lake Will (see the Lake Will & Innes Falls side trip at the end of the day's walk description).

Back on the main track, Lake Holmes is left behind and the track climbs across a very exposed plateau with views across the myriad lakes and tarns to the west. At a rocky crest, Lake Windermere comes into view nestled among patches of eucalyptus. Behind it, to the south, Mount Pelion West rises starkly above Pine Forest Moor. Descend steeply on a rocky track for 20 minutes to reach the shores of **Lake Windermere**, where camping has been restricted in marked areas. Another five minutes of walking will bring you to *Windermere Hut* set in the shelter of some myrtle. The hut has a heater and will sleep 40 people. There are several flat camping areas not far from the hut.

Side Trip: Lake Will & Innes Falls
2 hours, 6km return
The trip down to **Lake Will** takes around an hour return and is quite muddy in places. Views across the lake to Barn Bluff can be very beautiful. The trip can be extended by following the shore of Lake Will west for 1km and then descending for a short distance along the outlet river to view **Innes Falls**. Add another hour for this longer trip.

Day 3: Windermere Hut to New Pelion Hut
5 hours, 14km
From Windermere Hut a pleasant 15-minute walk through scattered eucalyptus forest leads past the eastern end of **Lake Curran**. There is a short, steep ascent onto an open top and then two more small rises are crossed to reach the northern edge of **Pine Forest Moor**. This difficult, waterlogged terrain is crossed dry-shod and fairly effortlessly on duckboard and parallel planks, bringing you in 15 or 20 minutes to a track junction. Here a stretch of duckboard nips off to the east to a **lookout** across the forests of the Forth Valley (one minute return to the lookout). Meanwhile the Overland Track reaches the northern slopes of a hill forested with the pencil pines that give their name to the moor, mixed with snow gums and myrtle. The track leads into the forest and climbs steadily on a boulder-strewn path. Along the top of the hill the forest becomes much thicker, consisting predominantly of small myrtle. Descending the southern slopes, towering pandani are frequent at the side of the track.

Some two hours from Windermere Hut, the Overland emerges from the trees and crosses a small creek. Another 30 minutes of relatively flat walking through broken forest brings you to Pelion Creek, a good spot for a break before the section to Frog Flats. At the time of writing, the camping area just above the bridge at Pelion Creek was closed for rehabilitation. Leaving Pelion Creek the track enters thick myrtle forest and the track becomes quite rough, with tree roots and arduous log walkways prevalent. The track climbs for about 30 minutes and then descends gradually for another 30 minutes to the open button-grass plains of Frog Flats. Duckboards lead across Frog Flats to a bridge across the Forth River and then the track heads back into the forest across what is the roughest section of terrain on the entire walk.

Climb gently for 1km before swinging sharply to the east into light forest on the fringe of **Pelion Plains**. A signposted track leads down to **Old Pelion Hut** (five minutes), which was built back in 1895 following the discovery of copper in Douglas Creek. It sleeps around eight people and there is a good swimming hole close to the hut. **New Pelion Hut** is sited on the main track 10 minutes past this junction. This rather battered hut sleeps 16 people and has a single potbelly stove for heating. There is a good deal of flat ground around the hut for tent sites and water is available from Douglas Creek nearby. Evenings at New Pelion Hut see Bennett's wallabies, pademelons and possums visiting the clearing, so food should be well secured.

There are excellent views across the buttongrass of Pelion Plains to Mt Oakleigh (1280m), which can be climbed by following the rough track north from New Pelion Hut and turning left onto a track leading to the summit. The ascent takes about four to five hours return. The Innes Track itself is a possible escape route, leading in about four hours to Arm Rd. You won't find much traffic on this road but it does lead to an Outdoor Education Centre, 10km to the north.

Day 4: New Pelion Hut to Kia Ora Hut
3 hours, 8km

The track climbs gently away from New Pelion Hut, heading south towards Pelion Gap through mixed forest. After 20 minutes the track crosses Snarers Hut Creek and in another 20 minutes climbs past a small waterfall on Douglas Creek. The track begins to climb in small, steep sections, interspersed by flatter stretches through dense myrtle forest. Finally the gradient steepens consistently and the trees begin to thin as you reach **Pelion Gap** (1126m) and a world of new views (1½ to two hours from Pelion Hut).

To the north-east, open slopes climb to the summit tor of Mt Pelion East (1433m). Without packs, it should take around 1½ hours return to make an ascent. The actual summit is gained via a short rock scramble; from the top there are unfettered views out across the Mersey River Valley and into the Walls of Jerusalem National Park. To the south a signposted track leads away from Pelion Gap towards Mt Ossa (1617m), the highest summit in Tasmania (see the Mt Ossa side trip at the end of the day's walk description).

From Pelion Gap head south-east on duckboards and wooden struts. The slopes here are scattered with small snow gums among the bleached, dead trunks of pencil pines, burnt in a past bushfire (see the boxed text 'Dead Stags on the Overland Track').

Descend gently into light forest before dropping more steeply into Pinestone Valley. Drop steeply again to the mixture of forest and open flats that surround *Kia Ora Hut* (one hour from Pelion Gap). The hut is a fairly new construction, sleeping 24 people, with water tanks at

Dead Stags on the Overland Track

Native conifers are badly affected by fire. Unlike eucalyptuses they do not regenerate quickly and you'll see large stands of dead 'stags' in several upland areas (eg, Pelion Gap on the Overland Track). Over 30% of Tasmania's King Billy pines have been lost to bushfires. Many of these over the past two centuries are thought to have been caused by campfires and it is largely because of this that the WHA is a fuel-stove-only area.

the back. The surroundings are very pleasant, with good views of Mt Ossa and a pretty stretch of small waterfalls on the nearby **Kia Ora Creek**. Camping, however is very limited.

If you look around the back of the hut you may well see the nests of welcome swallows under the eaves. These small blue-and-orange birds flit tirelessly around the hut in spring and summer. Look out also for the yellow wattlebird with its curious neck flaps. This bird is the largest of Australia's honeyeaters.

Side Trip: Mt Ossa
2–3 hours, 307m ascent, 307m descent
The track to Mt Ossa contours round the southern slopes of Mt Doris to reach a col beneath the tremendously steep north-east ridge of Mt Ossa. A rough trail leads up into a gully, from where you can scramble up to the summit plateau. The **summit** itself is a short walk to the south-west from where there are particularly impressive views to the south across the Du Cane range. Return to Pelion Gap via the route of ascent. This trip is probably best left out if the weather looks threatening.

Day 5: Kia Ora Hut to Windy Ridge Hut
3–4 hours, 11km
The track crosses Kia Ora Creek on a wooden bridge and continues south-east through thick eucalyptus and myrtle scrub. It climbs gently for 30 minutes and then descends very slightly before making a final short climb to *Du Cane Hut*, set in a small clearing backed by a couple of mature wattle trees. The sign at Du Cane Hut indicates Windy Ridge Hut to be 2½ hours away. In between are some of the most beautiful swathes of rainforest on the Overland. The track immediately descends into dark myrtle forest, becoming muddy in places, and after 30 to 40 minutes of gentle undulations brings you to a junction with a track signposted to the left (east) for Fergusson and D'Alton Falls (see the Mersey River Waterfalls side trip at the end of the day's walk description).

The Overland Track climbs steadily to the Hartnett Falls turn-off (see the Mersey River Waterfalls side trip) and the myrtle gives way to fairly open eucalyptus forest. Glimpses of Falling Mountain (1482m) to the west and the Traveller Range to the south can be had through the trees as you climb over a rough, stony trail to **Du Cane Gap** (45 minutes from the Hartnett Falls turn-off). From Du Cane Gap the track descends steeply into a beautiful stand of Tasmanian alpine yellow gums, spread

Overland Track (South)

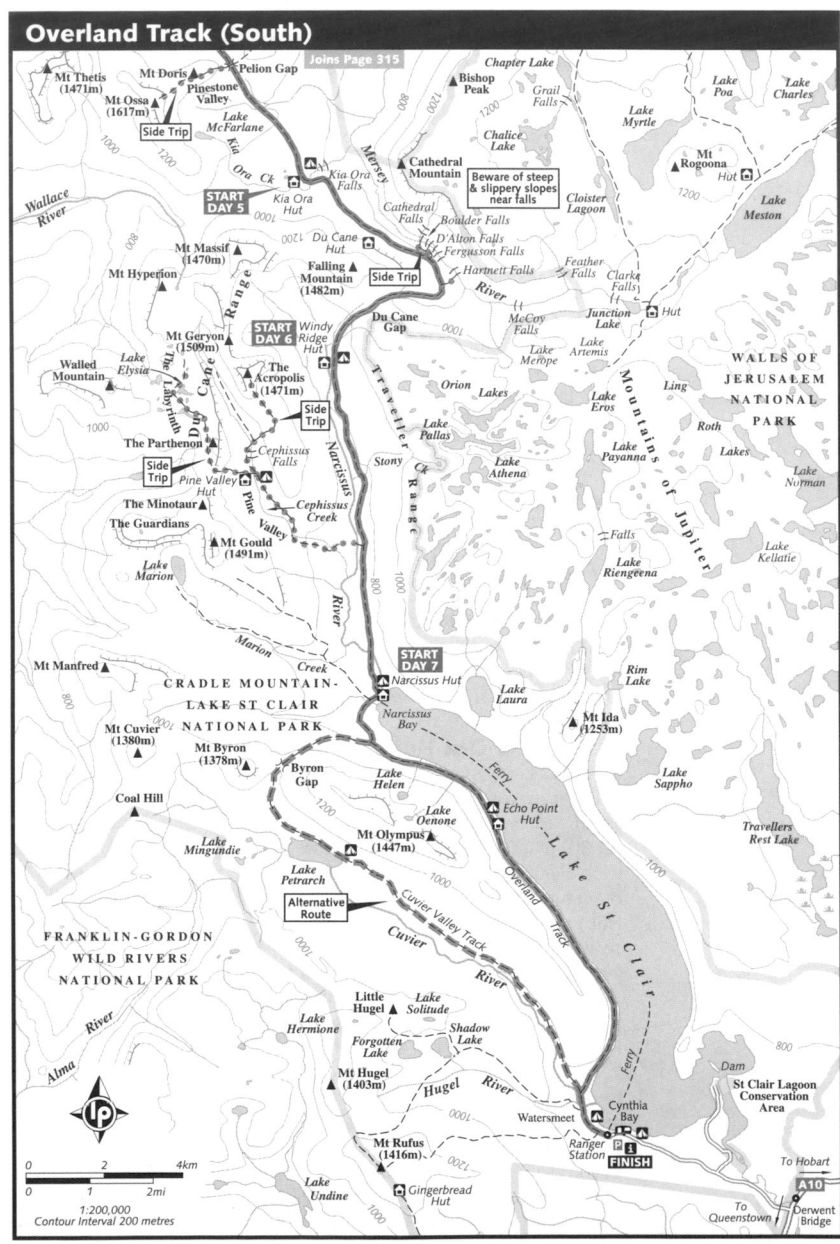

Top Left: Tarn above a glacial valley, Walls of Jerusalem NP, Tasmania. **Top Right:** Walking the Mt Anne Circuit, Southwest NP, Tasmania. **Middle:** On the summit of Mt Anne, before a cloud-capped vista of mountain ranges. **Bottom Left:** View of the Hazards across the inviting waters of Honeymoon Bay, Freycinet NP, Tasmania. **Bottom Right:** Pandani with Mt Anne in the distance.

CHRIS MELLOR

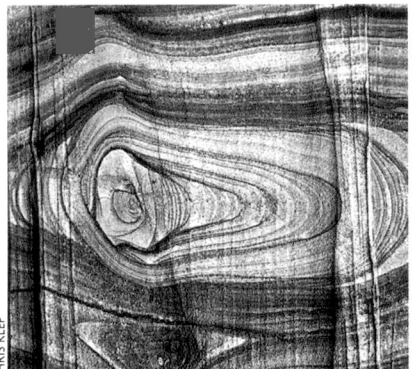

CHRIS KLEP

GARETH McCORMACK

GARETH McCORMACK

Top Left: The perfect white crescent of Wineglass Bay, Freycinet National Park, Tasmania. **Top Right:** The imposing 65m Totem Pole off Cape Hauy, Tasman NP. **Middle Left:** Fossil-studded sandstone and limestone cliffs, Maria Island NP, Tasmania. **Bottom:** The setting sun's light hits dolerite boulders on top of Mt Wellington, high above Hobart and the Tasman Sea.

among moss-cloaked myrtle. In heavy rain the mustard colour of the gum bark has to be seen to be believed, contrasting wonderfully with the deep greens of the myrtle and the luminous greens of mosses.

As the yellow gums are left behind, the trail descends steeply again, reaching *Windy Ridge Hut* in 30 to 45 minutes from Du Cane Gap. This is a pleasant hut set into a thickly wooded hillside. The hut sleeps 24, and despite what it says on the Land Information Services map notes, there is some reasonable camping for a couple of tents just above the hut.

Side Trip: Mersey River Waterfalls
2–2½ hours, 4km return
Fergusson and D'Alton Falls are about 1km down a side track and the return trip will take about one to 1½ hours. The track begins with a steep descent north-east and a right turn at an unmarked junction. Follow the main track downstream to reach the falls after another few hundred metres. The falls are at their best after a good deal of heavy rain. If you are a bit short on time and energy, the side trip to Hartnett Falls is probably a bit more spectacular. The track leading down to these falls is found off the Overland Track about 10 minutes' walk towards Windy Ridge Hut from the Fergusson and D'Alton Falls turn-off. This side trip takes about one hour return. On both of these side trips be careful around the viewing areas as there have been several accidents on the slippery ground.

Day 6: Windy Ridge Hut to Narcissus Hut
3 hours, 9km
The track descends very gently for the first 30 minutes from Windy Ridge Hut. Dense thickets of myrtle give way to very open eucalyptus forest (mostly alpine ash) as the track flattens out. Here and there the track skirts the fringes of buttongrass plains. Almost two hours from Windy Ridge Hut, a junction is reached. The right-hand track is signposted for Pine Valley. Pine Valley Hut can be found 1½ hours farther along this track (see the Pine Valley Hut, the Labyrinth & Acropolis side trip at the end of the day's walk description).

The Overland continues along the flat bottom of the valley as the gums gradually thin out to be replaced by stretches of buttongrass spanned on duckboard. The view of the valley holding Lake St Clair opens out and within another few minutes you arrive at *Narcissus Hut* (one hour from the Pine Valley junction). The lake is visible just a little way to the south-east and a track leads down to the jetty where the MV *IdaClair* docks.

Side Trip: Pine Valley Hut, the Labyrinth & Acropolis
8–10 hours, 15km return
The modern **Pine Valley Hut** is 1½ hours up Pine Valley from the junction with the Overland Track. Sleeping 24, it is a base for two of the most popular side trips on the Overland Track. Because of its popularity and the delicate nature of the alpine environments on the Labyrinth plateau and on The Acropolis, the PWS is urging walkers either to seek

out different areas to explore or else make sure that their impact is absolutely minimal. This should mean no camping in the Labyrinth and the complete removal of all toilet waste.

To reach the **Labyrinth** from Pine Valley Hut follow the Acropolis Track for a short distance and turn left following a reasonably good track into forest. After a few minutes the track begins to climb steeply and continues to climb for the next hour. A short descent then leads to the south-eastern end of **Lake Ophion** (1½ hours from Pine Valley Hut). The track can be followed 1km farther to **Lake Elysia**, from where there are good views of Mt Geryon (1509m), often reflected in the lake waters. Return to Pine Valley via the route of ascent.

You should allow a similar amount of time (three to five hours from Pine Valley Hut) for the trip to the summit of the **Acropolis** (1471m). Follow the signposted track from the hut, climbing north past **Cephissus Falls** and onto a broad, open shoulder. A final scramble (difficult in places) leads through the upper bluffs onto the flat summit plateau. After enjoying the considerable views, the return to Pine Valley is made via the route of ascent.

Day 7: Narcissus Hut to Cynthia Bay
5 hours, 17km

Many walkers find this final leg of the Overland Track round the western shores of Lake St Clair to be a little dull in comparison to the rest of the walk, and recommend dropping it in favour of taking the ferry, especially if you are tired or the weather is poor. An alternative is to take the longer and more strenuous **Cuvier Valley Track**, which has better views. For brief notes, see the Cuvier Valley Track alternative route described at the end of the walk description.

From Narcissus Hut the Overland heads south-west and crosses buttongrass swamp on duckboards. Apparently before the track was constructed, this section was a mud quagmire more than 50m wide and up to 1m deep! Once across the plains the track goes into the forest and follows the western shores of Lake St Clair reaching *Echo Point Hut* in two hours. The hut sleeps eight and the camping area around it is poor. The track continues for another three hours to the finish at the visitor centre at Cynthia Bay, with plenty of tree roots and an interesting mix of trees and ground ferns.

Alternative Route: Cuvier Valley Track
7 hours, 19km

This seven-hour track linking Narcissus Hut and Cynthia Bay is a favoured final leg for the Overland Track, giving better views than the lakeshore track. From a junction on the Overland Track, just 1km south-west of Narcissus Hut, climb gently to the west and then more steeply to the south to pass through Byron Gap. Drop down to Lake Petrarch (camping potential at either end) and follow the northern shore before winding down the Cuvier Valley, with good views of Mt Olympus (1447m). Rejoin the Overland Track just 15 minutes from Cynthia Bay.

continued from page 307

Walls of Jerusalem

Duration	2–3 days
Distance	23km
Standard	easy-medium
Start/Finish	Walls of Jerusalem car park
Nearest Town	Mole Creek
Public Transport	summer only

Summary A beautiful trip to a compact alpine area. Extensive cliffs, glacial tarns and quiet pencil pine forests are easily explored on the well-constructed track.

Bordered to the west by Cradle Mountain –Lake St Clair National Park, and to the east by the flat moors and lakes of the Central Plateau Conservation Area, the Walls of Jerusalem National Park brings together a mixture of these features in a compact and intimate area. The 'walls' are a group of cliff-ringed summits sheltering several small and very beautiful valleys dotted with lakes and groves of pencil pines. The valleys are linked by low cols, and once you've walked in, the whole area can be explored in a day, providing a generous variety of walking and views. It takes around three to four hours to reach the centre of the Walls from the car park, and another few hours to explore properly. The route described here combines this with a return along a less-frequented track that runs down to Lake Ball and Lake Adelaide before returning to the car park across wild and windswept moorland. The walk can be done in two days but the area is worth a leisurely three days.

Even though the first stage of this route is described as finishing at Dixon's Kingdom Hut, this may not be where you actually camp overnight. The hut itself is in poor condition and is intended only as an emergency shelter. The camping is good, although the possums are reputed to be a real nuisance. At busy times of the year camping may be restricted at Dixon's Kingdom. There are, however, several other excellent camping areas (see Permits & Regulations under Planning later).

HISTORY

The surveyor James Scott applied the name 'Walls of Jerusalem' to the area in 1848. He noted some good grazing for stock and it was used for this purpose to some degree, and also for trapping. In the 1920s Reg Hall and other members of the Launceston Walking Club began to visit the area, and Hall devised most of the biblical names that appear on the map today. Reg Dixon began to visit the Walls in the 1930s and built Dixon's Kingdom Hut as a base for trapping.

NATURAL HISTORY

The topography of the Walls of Jerusalem has been heavily influenced by glaciation and most of the walls were glacially carved. Gouging by the ice along natural fault lines created the many depressions and drainage channels along a south-east/north-west orientation. The depressions have filled with water, resulting in a scattering of lakes and tarns of all sizes throughout the area. On the route into the Walls you'll notice several glacial erratics, ie, large boulders deposited by the retreating ice sheets.

One of the best features of the Walls of Jerusalem is the pencil pines, especially the large swathe growing south of the Temple fire. These conifers, which are unique to Tasmania, grow at altitudes in excess of 800m and can live for more than 1200 years. They are complemented by stunted snow gums and large bolster plants growing on the exposed hillsides.

Wallabies are very common in the area, and you may well see an eastern quoll scampering around your camp site at dusk.

PLANNING
When to Walk

The summer months (December to April) offer the warmest and most settled weather, although the Walls of Jerusalem can be very beautiful in snow, so if you are suitably prepared and the access road is open, it is certainly worth a visit in winter. However, the trail between Lake Adelaide and the Trappers Hut is not well marked and could be difficult to follow in snow. Also note that public transport to the walk only operates between 1 December and 3 April (see Getting To/From the Walk later in this section for details).

What to Bring

Waterproof boots with ankle support are recommended for the rough sections of the trail. Gaiters will also prove beneficial on the boggy sections returning from Lake Adelaide. While there are huts in the Walls of Jerusalem area, these are maintained as a reminder of the trapping heritage of the park and are really only suitable as emergency shelters, being too dirty and uncomfortable for normal use. You'll therefore need a three-season tent and a fuel stove. Warm waterproof and windproof clothing is also essential at any time of the year.

Permits & Regulations

You'll need a national parks pass for this walk (see Park Fees & Regulations in the Information section in the introduction to this chapter), although as the car park is just outside the park boundary you won't need a permit for your car. Camping is currently forbidden within 200m of the Pool of Siloam to allow plant regeneration. In the busier months other sections in the park are restricted and you should check with the ranger at Mole Creek (☎ 03-6363 5133) for the current status of areas.

Maps & Books

The excellent Land Information Services 1:25,000 *Walls of Jerusalem Walk Map* is very useful. There are some detailed notes on the back of the map on the history and natural history of the area. *Cradle Mountain –Lake St Clair and Walls of Jerusalem National Parks* by John Chapman & John Siseman is worth a look if you'd like to explore the more remote tracks in the park.

NEAREST TOWN
Mole Creek

Mole Creek is only a small village, so you should plan to take groceries with you from a larger town. There are, however, quite a few places to stay and eat in Mole Creek, although the accommodation in the village is

not cheap. The Mole Creek Guesthouse (see Places to Stay & Eat) doubles as the town's visitor centre.

Places to Stay & Eat The *Mole Creek Camping Ground (☎ 03-6363 1150)* is 3km west of Mole Creek en route to the Walls of Jerusalem. Tent sites are $5 for one person ($8 for two people) and powered sites are $10 for two people. The camping ground has coin-operated showers.

Mole Creek Hotel (☎ 03-6363 1102) has been recently refurbished and provides comfortable B&B for $30/55 for a single/double with shared facilities and $60 for a double with en suite. It serves counter meals daily at the bar.

Just a little more upmarket, *Mole Creek Guesthouse (☎ 03-6363 1399)* has doubles for $70 with a private bathroom across the hall, and $92 for a double with en suite. The price includes a cooked breakfast in the cafe downstairs, which also serves reasonably priced meals and snacks daily.

Getting There & Away Mole Creek is 23km west of Deloraine. Because of the limited public transport access to Mole Creek and the fact that public track transport originates in Launceston or Deloraine, only walkers with their own transport will find Mole Creek a good base.

GETTING TO/FROM THE WALK

From Mole Creek, take the B12, then the C138 and finally the C171 (Mersey Forest Rd) to Lake Rowallan; remain on this road, following 'Walls of Jerusalem' signs to the car park at the trailhead.

Transport to and from the start and finish of the Walls of Jerusalem is operated by TWT's Tassielink (☎ 1300 300 520) from 1 December to 3 April. The service leaves Launceston at 9.30 am on Tuesday, Thursday and Saturday, passing through Deloraine and Mole Creek before arriving at the Walls car park at 1.30 pm to pick up walkers. The bus returns to Launceston at 5 pm. The return fare is $80 from Launceston and $75 from Deloraine. Taswalks (☎ 03-6363 6112) runs guided trips to the Walls.

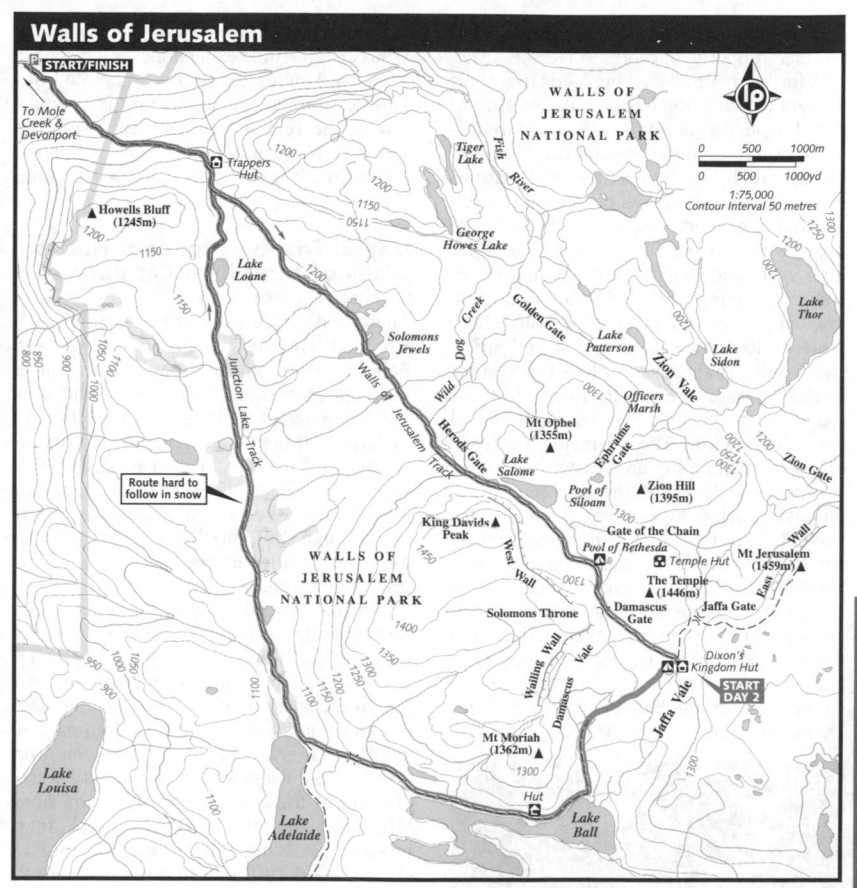

Walls of Jerusalem

P START/FINISH

To Mole
Creek &
Devonport

Trappers Hut

Howells Bluff
(1245m)

Lake
Loane

Lake
Louisa

WALLS OF
JERUSALEM
NATIONAL PARK

Tiger
Lake

Fish River

George
Howes Lake

Solomons
Jewels

Golden Gate

Lake
Patterson

Zion Vale

Lake
Sidon

Lake
Thor

Officers
Marsh

Mt Ophel
(1355m)

Lake
Salome

Pool of
Siloam

Zion Hill
(1395m)

Zion Gate

King Davids
Peak

Gate of the Chain

Pool of Bethesda

Temple Hut

Mt Jerusalem
(1459m)

WALLS OF
JERUSALEM
NATIONAL PARK

West Wall

Wailing Wall

Solomons Throne

The Temple
(1446m)

Damascus
Gate

Jaffa Gate

East Wall

Dixon's
Kingdom Hut

START
DAY 2

Mt Moriah
(1362m)

Jaffa Vale

Hut

Lake
Adelaide

Lake
Ball

Route hard to
follow in snow

Junction Lake Track

Herods Gate

Wild Dog Creek

Walls of Jerusalem Track

Ephraims Gate

Damascus Vale

0   500   1000m
0   500   1000yd
1:75,000
Contour Interval 50 metres

TASMANIA

THE WALK
Day 1: Walls of Jerusalem Car Park to Dixon's Kingdom Hut

4 hours, 14km

From the right-hand side of the car park rough steps lead onto a good track that climbs up past a registration booth. Current restrictions will probably be posted here. The track continues to climb quite steeply, emerging after 10 or 15 minutes onto flatter ground amid towering gums. The rest of the climb to **Trappers Hut** is in stages, steep sections interspersed by flat sections, which allow you to grab a breather. The final haul

to the hut is steep and bouldery and most walkers will need about an hour to reach the hut from the car park.

Beyond the hut the track continues to climb, passing a junction with a right-hand fork signposted for Lake Adelaide (the return route). Continue to the left on the Walls track, climbing less steeply as the trees become thinner and stunted. About 20 to 30 minutes past the Trappers Hut the track flattens out and continues to undulate across a wonderful landscape of rocky outcrops, small lakes and stunted growths of snow gum and pencil pine. In the distance King

Davids Peak is visible, its precipitous eastern face dropping abruptly to Herods Gate.

A further hour of walking leads to a short descent to Wild Dog Creek and a section of parallel planks. A short, steep climb follows, bringing you to **Herods Gate** and the entrance to the Walls of Jerusalem. Continuing south a small lake is passed on the left and the track contours along slopes to the south-west of **Lake Salome**. On your right, high cliffs and boulder slopes come down from the summit of King Davids Peak. The track climbs across a low ridge from where you can look back to the west and spy a steep gully giving access to King Davids Peak. Continuing from the ridge the track passes some pencil pines on the left and reaches a junction. The left-hand track leads off to a flat camping area just 100m away, set above the **Pool of Bethesda**. Meanwhile, the main track climbs on parallel planks towards the prominent pass known as **Damascus Gate**. From this pass another side track leads off to the right, giving access via a steep climb) to the top of Solomons Throne (1½ hours return). From Damascus Gate the track descends into a wonderful growth of pencil pines that extends all the way to **Dixon's Kingdom Hut** (15 minutes from Damascus Gate).

Dixon's Kingdom Hut borders a fine pencil pine forest below the Temple

From your choice of camp sites in the Walls area possible excursions include: a trip up King Davids Peak crossing Solomons Throne en route (three hours return); an ascent of the Temple (one hour return); or an ascent of **Mt Jerusalem** (1459m), following a good track north from Dixon's Kingdom Hut (two hours return).

Day 2: Dixon's Kingdom Hut to Walls of Jerusalem Car Park
5–6 hours, 19km

There is no track as such between Dixon's Kingdom Hut and the eastern end of **Lake Ball**. However, navigating your own course down through Jaffa Vale is easy and provides wonderful walking, albeit a little wet underfoot. It is probably best to bear off towards Mt Moriah and then drop down to meet the Lake Ball track directly, rather than crossing the swampy flat ground at the end of Lake Ball. A pole set on a prominent hummock indicates the beginning of the track round Lake Ball.

For the first 30 minutes the track winds through beautiful myrtle forest and crosses an awkward boulder slope before reaching an old trappers hut. Towards the western end of the lake, views across the water open out and stunted snow gums are dominant. A small creek is crossed just before you drop down to the water's edge at the very western end of the lake (1½ to two hours from Dixon's Kingdom Hut). The track then crosses low-lying flat ground and fords a sizable creek (difficult to cross in flood) to reach a small saddle. A short detour can be made from here across rough slopes to the south-west to gain views along the entire length of **Lake Adelaide**. Meanwhile, the main track descends steeply to meet the Junction Lake Track. There are some good flat camping areas at this junction.

Turn right onto the Junction Lake Track and climb gently to the north across open ground. Follow the rough track for the next 5km as it undulates across a series of broad treeless valleys. The going is muddy in places and the track can be a little bit difficult to follow around Lake Loane. Direction markers are pretty much absent on this track, so in snow conditions you'll be hard pushed to stay on the track and may need to navigate a general line. About 2½ hours of walking should see you at the track junction just above the Trappers Hut. Descend past the hut and back to the car park, remembering to sign out. The descent from the hut takes 30 to 45 minutes.

South Coast Track

Duration	7 days
Distance	86km
Standard	medium-hard
Start	Melaleuca
Finish	Cockle Creek
Nearest Towns	Dover, Lune River
Public Transport	summer only

Summary A diverse wilderness walk with remote beaches, buttongrass plains and rainforest, spectacular scenery and views to the inland mountains. While an ongoing works program has improved the track greatly, parts can be quite muddy in wet weather.

The South Coast Track is, after the Overland Track, the most popular long-distance walk in the WHA. But it has quite a different character to that of the Overland Track in terms of both landscape and a lesser level of development.

The walk traverses the remote southern fringe of the WHA, with access usually via light aircraft. The landscape of the south coast is diverse. The coast is deeply embayed with long, sandy beaches alternating with steep and rocky headlands. Hills, their slopes sometimes thickly forested, rise steeply from broad buttongrass plains. Scrub-fringed creeks meander across the plains. Offshore, the many islands are the last land before Antarctica.

The South Coast Track is a wilderness walk, lacking any huts, and is much less extensively hardened than walks such as the Overland Track. The PWS has undertaken significant works on the South Coast Track since the mid-1980s, with extensive sections boarded, re-routed and stabilised. These works are ongoing but sufficient muddy sections remain to give a taste of what the track was once like.

Depending on your level of fitness and the weather, the walk can be quite arduous with significant ascents and descents and several muddy and rooty sections. The track does, however, have a range of sheltered camp sites at beaches, so that if sufficient food is carried, pleasant rest days can be planned.

HISTORY

Shell middens in several places attest to the occupation of the south coast by Tasmanian Aborigines for several thousand years before the arrival of European settlers.

A party from one of James Cook's ships, *Adventure*, landed briefly at Rocky Boat Inlet in 1773, and another mariner, James Cox, went ashore at Cox Bight in 1789. The first European to walk the south coast was GA Robinson, who reached the Port Davey Aboriginal tribe in 1830 as part of his five-year Friendly Mission, a scheme that ultimately resulted in the incarceration of most of Tasmania's Aboriginal population on Flinders Island.

The south coast was traversed by prospectors during the late 1800s, but it was not until 1915 that a government track cutting party went in and cleared the first official route. The South Coast Track was cleared in 1946 and again in 1964–65. Legendary track cutter Milford Fletcher, who worked on many tracks in south-west Tasmania from the 1930s to 1960s, was involved on both occasions.

Tin was discovered at Cox Bight in 1891, and Charles King commenced tin mining at Melaleuca in the 1930s. His son Denny and his family lived there after WWII, becoming the sole residents of south-west Tasmania. Denny built the first walkers' hut at Melaleuca in 1955.

Light aircraft engaged in aerial survey work commonly landed on Cox Bight beach during the 1940s. A rough airstrip was cleared at Melaleuca in 1947 to allow a plane that had landed to take off. Denny King constructed the present airstrip in 1956, facilitating today's frequent scenic and walker flights into the area.

The Rarest Parrot

The orange-bellied parrot *(Neophema chrysogaster)* is among the rarest and most endangered of the world's wildlife. It is a colourful bird, slightly larger than a budgerigar, with a bright-green back and distinctive orange patch between its legs. There are no more than 200 individuals in the wild and most of these breed at Melaleuca in summer.

The bird migrates to spend winter in coastal south-west Australia and south-east South Australia, where habitat reduction since European settlement has been blamed for the bird's declining numbers. A captive breeding program, with periodic release of young birds, aims to improve the outlook of the species.

In summer, the parrots can be observed from a hide, named in memory of Denny King, 100m east of the airstrip.

NATURAL HISTORY

The many rocky headlands and shore platforms on the South Coast provide an opportunity to walk through some major parts of Tasmania's billion-year geological history, with generally progressively younger rocks exposed as you walk east. They include ancient folded metamorphic rocks at Cox Bight, 500 million-year-old sandstone and siltstone in the Ironbound Range–Deadmans Bay area, colourful conglomerate rocks at Osmiridium Beach, sharply eroded limestone strata at Surprise Bay, once-molten columnar dolerite at Granite Beach, and sandstone deposited in a flood plain at South Cape Rivulet.

After the last ice age, the sea level rose and then stabilised at its current level approximately 6000 years ago. Prior to that the many offshore islands were hills on a broad coastal plain.

The soils of the buttongrass plains are peats, composed of decayed plant remains, and can be two or more metres thick. The small yabbie is common on the plains and lives in burrows visible at the surface as small round holes or mud chimneys.

The rare orange-bellied parrot can be seen around Melaleuca (see the boxed text 'The Rarest Parrot'), and you may flush the secretive ground parrot as you walk through buttongrass areas. Sea birds likely to be seen along the coast include terns, fairy prions (whalebirds) and the short-tailed shearwaters (mutton birds). Offshore, you may sight the shy albatross or Australasian gannet.

Much of the fauna is nocturnal but you will certainly come across the wombat's characteristic square droppings. You may also disturb snakes sunning themselves on the track.

PLANNING
When to Walk

The South Coast Track can be walked at any time of the year, although the weather is likely to be better and flooded streams less of a potential problem in summer (December to March). Also, regular public transport to the walk's finish and more frequent flights to the start are only available from December to March.

The track can be walked in either direction. However, access to Melaleuca, the western end of the track, is generally by light plane and so subject to weather conditions. To avoid the possibility of being stranded at Melaleuca by poor weather, it is recommended that the track be walked west to east (from Melaleuca to Cockle Creek).

While seven days is the recommended duration of the walk, it is worthwhile taking longer to allow time to explore the beaches and as a precaution against flood delays.

If you decide to start at Cockle Creek and walk west, this gives you the option to re-stock with food at Melaleuca (which you must arrange to have flown in prior to your walk) and continue on with other walks in the area.

What to Bring

While this is a coastal walk, high and exposed ranges are crossed at two points and it can be cold and windy on the long beaches. Extra warm clothing is therefore recommended.

Given the unbridged river crossings and mud, you are certain to get wet feet, but a pair of gaiters can at least keep the mud out of boots and socks.

Campfires are generally not permitted (see Permits & Regulations) so a fuel stove is essential.

Maps & Books

The Department of Environment and Land Management (now Service Tasmania) 1:100,000 *South Coast Walks* topographic map covers the walk and includes natural history information and brief track notes. It is available from Service Tasmania, 134 Macquarie St, Hobart.

The South Coast Track and other walks in the south-west are described in John Chapman's *South West Tasmania* and Ken Collins' *South-west Tasmania – A Natural History and Visitors Guide*. The latter includes much information on flora, fauna and geology.

Information Sources

Up-to-date South Coast Track information can be obtained from the PWS Dover office (☎ 03-6298 1577).

Permits & Regulations

The South Coast Track lies within Southwest National Park, entry to which requires a pass (see Park Fees & Regulations in the introduction to the chapter).

The track also lies within the WHA, and as such is a fuel-stove-only area. Campfires are allowed, however, at two camp sites – Surprise Bay and Deadmans Bay – but only within the designated fire sites. Fires are also permitted within one of the walkers' huts at Melaleuca.

There are no restrictions on camping on the South Coast Track, but to avoid the continued expansion of impact by walkers, you are encouraged to use the major established camp sites at the various beaches and rivers along the route. All the major camp sites have pit toilets and these should be used wherever possible.

NEAREST TOWN & FACILITIES
Melaleuca

If you fly in late in the day, or choose to spend time at Melaleuca (the start of the walk), a short track heads north from the airstrip to two *walkers' huts*. Alternatively, you can *camp* in the open tea-tree forest nearby, on the shore of Melaleuca Lagoon. Drinking water is only available from tanks, so use it frugally.

When wandering around Melaleuca, be aware that an area (denoted with signs) around the home and garden of the late Denny King remains under private leasehold to his family. Please respect it as such.

Dover

If starting the South Coast Track from Cockle Creek, Dover (21km south of Geeveston on the Huon Hwy) has a *supermarket* and is the last chance to buy any food items you haven't brought from Hobart (for details on services available in Hobart, see Gateways earlier in this chapter). If passing through Dover at the end of your walk, the excellent *Gingerbread House* bakery, on the corner of Main and Station Rds, is worth a visit.

Lune River

If you don't feel like rushing back to Hobart after your walk, the *Lune River YHA Hostel* (☎ 03-6298 3163) is a pleasant place to relax. The cost is $15 per night for non-

The (Slowly) Disappearing Mud

Lengthy sections of planking snake across the buttongrass south of Melaleuca and at Louisa Plains. The planking at Louisa Plains was installed in the late 1980s and was the first such work on the South Coast Track. The Louisa Plains bogs had quite an infamous reputation in the 'old' days, so spare a thought for the walkers of not so long ago when you encounter the relatively few boggy sections that remain elsewhere on the track.

Track works to date have been undertaken mainly for environmental reasons and, despite considerable and ongoing expenditure over the past 15 years, the South Coast Track remains a basic track. Deep mud sections still exist, especially in wet weather.

TASMANIA

Warning

None of the rivers and streams crossed by the South Coast Track are bridged and most must be forded. Heavy rain can cause rivers to rise quickly and some can become difficult or impossible to cross safely, particularly Louisa River. South Cape Rivulet can also be difficult to cross in such circumstances, especially if the tide is high or a storm swell is running (for a discussion of safe river crossings, see Safety on the Walk in the Health & Safety chapter).

High tides combined with storm swells can also render coastal traverses at the base of cliffs at Cox Bight, Granite Beach and near Lion Rock hazardous, with a real risk of being washed away by a misjudged wave.

YHA members. The hostel warden will collect you from Cockle Creek (call from the public phone) for $25 per trip; the minibus takes eight to 10 people. Or you can be dropped off by the TWT's Tassielink minibus (☎ 1300 300 520) en route to Hobart (see Getting To/From the Walk later).

There are no shops at Lune River, but the hostel warden will take you to Southport (nearer than Dover, but not on the main road to Hobart) where there is a shop and tavern.

GETTING TO/FROM THE WALK
To the Start
There is no road access to the start of the South Coast Track at Melaleuca – the only options is to fly in or walk. Small (two- to five-passenger) single-engine planes fly on demand from Hobart to Melaleuca, subject to weather conditions, and are run by Tasair (☎ 03-6248 5288) and Par Avion (☎ 03-6248 5390), both based at Cambridge airport. The fare is $100 per person. A minimum of two is required, but the carriers generally try to fill planes by combining groups where possible. Bookings are essential. In the peak summer months there are generally several flights per day, so even solo walkers can usually make it to Melaleuca on their preferred day.

Melaleuca can also be reached by a four-day walk along the Port Davey Track from the Huon River camping ground at the end of Scotts Peak Road. A TWT's Tassielink minibus (☎ 1300 300 520) services this track during summer.

From the Finish
Cockle Creek is serviced by a TWT's Tassielink minibus three days per week from 1 December to 31 March. The bus departs Hobart Transit Centre, 199 Collins St, at 9 am Monday, Wednesday and Friday, and returns from Cockle Creek at 1.45 pm on the same day. The fare is $45 one way. Booking is recommended.

THE WALK
Day 1: Melaleuca to Cox Bight
3–4 hours, 13km

The South Coast Track starts on the western side of the Melaleuca airstrip and passes through old mine workings before crossing Moth Creek on a log bridge. Cox Bight is a 10km level walk on a well-defined track south down the broad valley from the Melaleuca airstrip.

Walk eastwards along the first of Cox Bight's broad beaches. There is a sheltered *camp site* at the outlet stream of freshwater **Freney Lagoon** (1km). Beyond the end of the beach, another 2km, Point Eric is crossed on a marked inland track. There is sheltered *camping* on the eastern side of **Point Eric**, with water from Goring Creek, just a few hundred metres east along the beach.

Light aircraft can actually land on the flat white sand at the western end of Cox Bight beach (subject to tides and weather) and this is an alternative access point for the start of the walk.

Day 2: Cox Bight to Louisa River
5–7 hours, 18km

Despite its name, the South Coast Track partly traverses country some distance inland. The most lengthy inland section commences at Buoy Creek, at the eastern end of Cox Bight. From here, a level section precedes the very sharp ascent of the **Red Point Hills**, the first of a number of high points on the track providing extensive views. A gradual descent to Faraway Creek follows, and

South Coast Track (West)

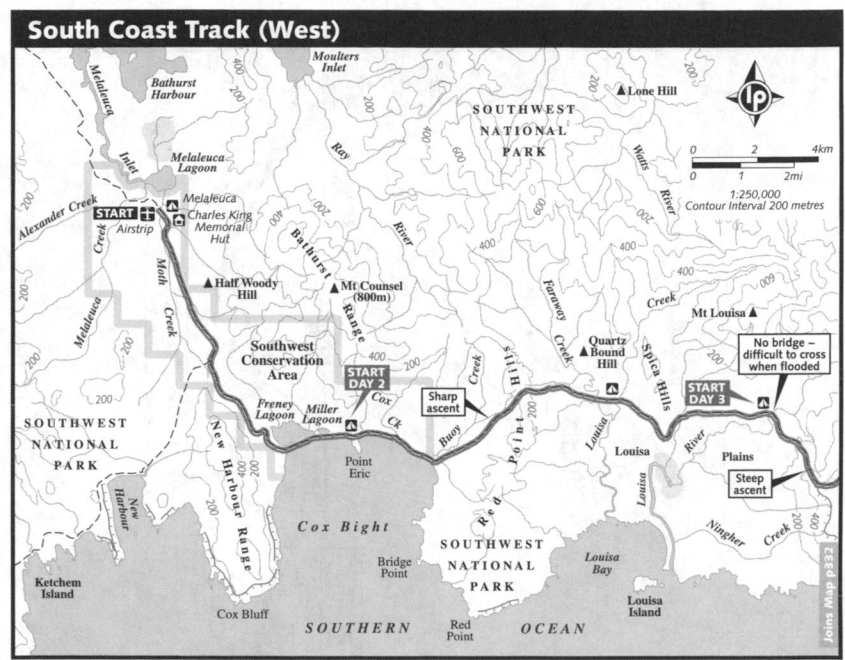

the sheltered *camp site* at Louisa Creek is only a short distance farther east (2½ to 3½ hours from Cox Bight).

The track then sidles round the Spica Hills before crossing the extensive buttongrass Louisa Plains on a lengthy section of planking. The easy mud-free walking afforded by the planking allows you to take your eyes off your feet and take in the surrounding landscape, including the broad expanse of the plains and the ominously steep slopes of the Ironbound Range ahead.

The Louisa Plains are bounded to the east by forest along the meandering Louisa River. The **Louisa River** is the largest stream crossed by the track and must be forded – there is a rope in situ to assist your balance. There are *camp sites* in the forest on both banks of Louisa River. If it is raining and the river appears crossable when you arrive, it may be prudent to camp on the far bank to avoid being held up by any overnight flooding.

Day 3: Louisa River to Deadmans Bay
6–10 hours, 12km

Most walkers consider the crossing of the **Ironbound Range** the most physically demanding part of the South Coast Track, and with good reason. The 900m climb up the western slope of the range is steep and largely without respite. Given the open nature of the country, if it looks like being a hot day an early start on the climb is recommended. This open terrain does allow you to stop almost anywhere to take in the extensive views while you catch your breath. On a more cautionary note, the range is also very exposed, and freezing wind-driven rain is possible at any time of the year. If the weather is poor and the range shrouded in cloud, it may be more pleasant passing a rest day exploring the rainforest along the banks of Louisa River.

The track traverses the only alpine country of the walk on the top of the Ironbound

TASMANIA

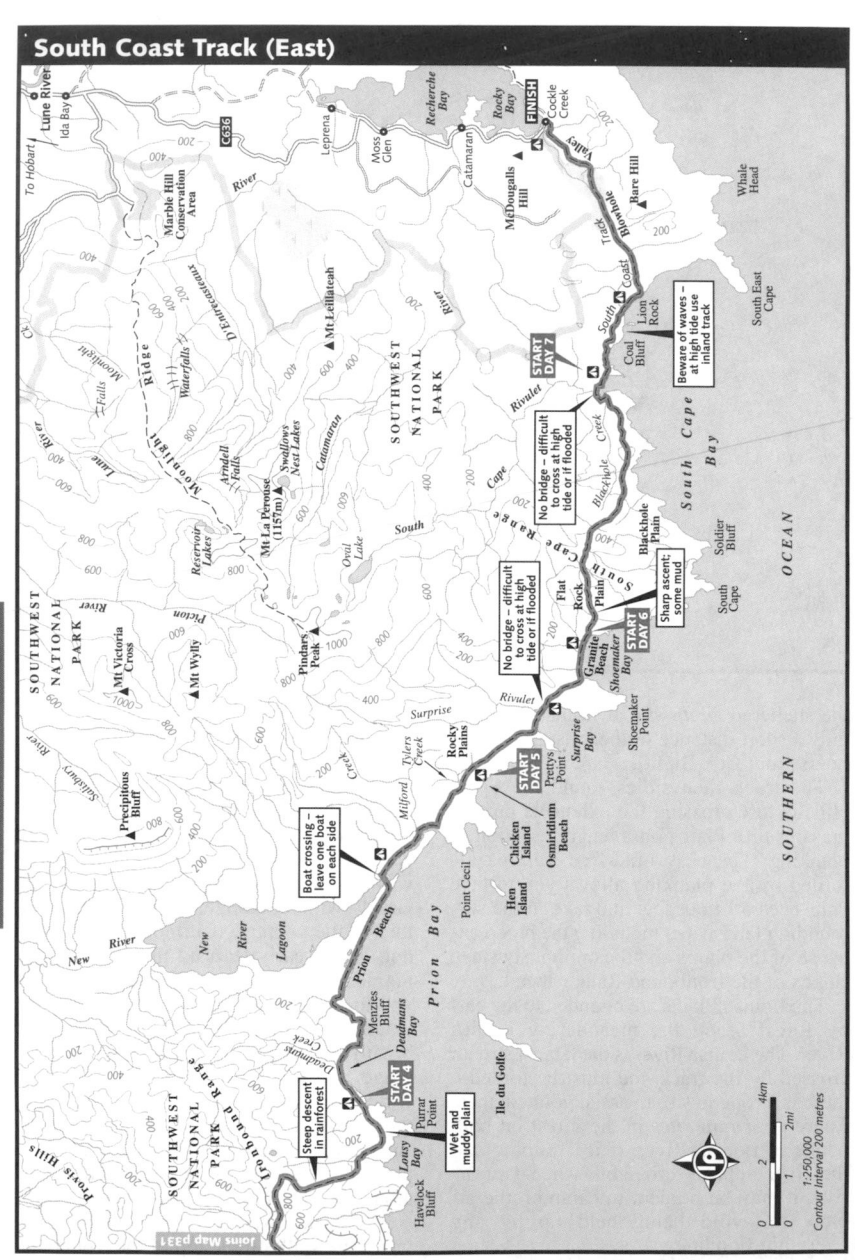

South Coast Track (East)

Joins Map p331

Range with, in clear weather, views along the entire south coast and out to various offshore islands. Water can be obtained from the small creek crossed several hundred metres east of the crest of the range.

After this creek, the track enters forest for the long descent of the south-eastern side of the range. Some sections are thick with tree roots and require care with foot placement, and you may have rather rubbery knees by the time you complete the long descent. However, it is not over yet and a wet and muddy plain must be traversed to **Deadmans Bay**. There is good camping here beside the large creek where the track reaches the coast.

Day 4: Deadmans Bay to Osmiridium Beach
4½–6 hours, 13km

Walk 100m east along the rocky foreshore to where the track again heads inland through buttongrass and then forest before emerging on **Turua Beach**. Walk east along the sand and round the small headland to the second beach. From the eastern end of Turua Beach the track follows the coast round Menzies Bluff towards Prion Beach with some fine views through openings in the coastal forest and scrub. Note that the small stream crossed at the far western end of Prion Beach may be the last good water before Osmiridium Beach.

The route now traverses **Prion Beach**, probably the most spectacular beach on the south coast, a long stretch of sand receding into the sea spray haze with the distinctive form of Precipitous Bluff rising inland beyond the dunes. Remove your boots and give your feet the pleasure of unconstrained walking along the 4km of sand, with the roar and foam of the Southern Ocean your constant companion.

The outlet of New River Lagoon, deep and wide, must be crossed from Prion Beach and two dinghies are provided for you to row across. Please ensure one boat (with its oars) is left upside down and tied up well out of reach of tides and floods on each bank for subsequent walkers after you have completed your crossing (follow the instructions posted at the boat crossing). If

Mobile Sands

The Prion Beach area provides a dramatic example of the dynamic nature of coastal environments. The long spit that impounds New River Lagoon, of which Prion Beach is the seaward side, has grown westwards and stabilised since the sea reached its present level 6000 years ago.

Rafts of slumped vegetation and root mats can be seen on the dune faces behind Prion Beach. These attest to periodic erosion during large storms, with the sand mined from the dunes probably distributed eastwards.

The position of the mouth of New River Lagoon moves periodically, sometimes quite rapidly. Storms during February 1999, and the resultant backing up of the lagoon waters, resulted in the break-out of the lagoon outlet near the boat crossing, 2km west of its previous position against the rocks of Point Cecil. One of the boats was washed away as a result (it has now been replaced and secured in a slightly different position). Since then the outlet has migrated several hundred metres eastwards again.

your party is large, several crossings will be required, as the boats will safely hold no more than three people and gear.

There is a sheltered *camp site* on the northern side of the Prion Beach boat crossing (2½ to 3½ hours from the Deadmans Bay camp site). Water can be obtained from a small creek five to 10 minutes' walk north-west of the camp site, but it can often be brackish.

From the camp site, the track traverses the crest of vegetated dunes east to Milford Creek. The waters of this creek are particularly dark, stained by buttongrass and other vegetation inland, and the ford of the creek can appear much deeper than it actually is. From Milford Creek the route follows the base of steep dunes (wading may be necessary if the lagoon level is high) to the eastern end of Prion Beach, where steps climb the steep scrub-covered dune face.

The track heads cross-country through low forest behind Point Cecil to the open Rocky Plains. **Tylers Creek** is reached after crossing a low hill. A spacious and sheltered *camp site* lies on its banks a short distance downstream, accessed by a side route from the main track. Osmiridium Beach is a short distance farther downstream.

Day 5: Osmiridium Beach to Granite Beach
3–4 hours, 8km
Return to the main track from the Tylers Creek camp site. The track leaves Rocky Plains soon afterwards and climbs into forest. From here eastwards the landscape through which the trail passes changes character from the open plains and beaches of the west to lengthy forest sections inland. However, the track does return to the coast at several large bays, the first being **Surprise Bay** (1½ to two hours from Tylers Creek). The spacious *camp site* here lies in coastal forest above the dark limestone strata at the eastern end of the beach. Surprise Rivulet must be forded to reach it, requiring care if it is in flood or the tide is high.

Soon after leaving Surprise Bay camp site, the track ascends steeply before descending rather more gently to **Granite Beach**. Traverse the dark sand and rounded dolerite boulders, with views of the spectacular **Fluted Cliffs**, to the waterfall at the eastern end of the beach. Scramble up beside the waterfall and follow the track 100m east to another spacious and sheltered *camp site*.

During storms with high tides, waves can break against the cliffs at the eastern end of Granite Beach, making access to the ascent next to the waterfall potentially hazardous. In these conditions spend time watching the waves to decide if it is safe to proceed, and then time your sprint with care.

Day 6: Granite Beach to South Cape Rivulet
5½–7 hours, 10km
You can take some of the sting out of the steep climb of the South Cape Range from Granite Beach camp site by telling yourself it is the last major ascent of the walk. **Flat Rock Plain**, an opening near the summit, is a great place to recline and take in the final view back along the coast and across the various islands.

There are some rather muddy areas to be traversed across the forested top of the South Cape Range before descending to a small creek, which is the only reliable water on the range (2½ to 3½ hours from Granite Beach). The track then climbs again, briefly, before beginning the long forested descent to the buttongrass opening of Blackhole Plain. The forest on this section is magnificent, with many of the trunks sheathed in climbing heath.

Beyond Blackhole Plain, another short climb and forested descent and you will suddenly emerge into the open on the bank of **South Cape Rivulet**. This must be crossed, which can be difficult at high tide or after heavy rain. The best *camp site* is on the east bank adjacent to the lagoon, but there is also a site on the west bank that can be used if the rivulet cannot be crossed.

Alternative Camp Site
If you still feel energetic you might walk still farther to the camp site near Lion Rock (another one to 1½ hours east). The sheltered *camp site* is atop the dune above the second creek east of **Lion Rock**, accessed by the obvious steps constructed to prevent erosion of the dune face. Water is obtained from the creek flowing out onto the beach.

Day 7: South Cape Rivulet to Cockle Creek
3–4½ hours, 12km
Continue eastwards along the beach, over a small headland and then along another beach. Here there are two options. A signposted track climbs high over Coal Bluff, with good views in places. Alternatively, you can scramble over the boulders strewn below the coastal cliffs to **Lion Rock**, a vaguely sphinx-like rocky island just offshore. If the tide is high or a storm swell is running, the inland route is definitely the better option to choose.

Just past Lion Rock the track reaches the last beach on the South Coast Track. This beach is a popular day-trip or overnight destination from Cockle Creek and the track from here on is well constructed and obvious. From the eastern end of the beach, climb the steps up and round the rocky headland, with its expansive view across South Cape Bay, then traverse the coastal scrub and heath of Blowhole Valley to the road head at Cockle Creek.

The East Coast & Islands

When you've had enough of western deluges, the east coast is a good spot for drying out your pack and soaking up some sunshine. The coastal walking along the brilliant white sands of Freycinet Peninsula and the 300m-high cliffs of Cape Pillar is some of the best in Australia and is considerably easier and on generally better and drier tracks than in the west.

NATURAL HISTORY

The rocks of the Freycinet Peninsula are part of a geological feature known as the Lachlan Fold Belt, which runs along much of the east coast of Australia. The area's distinctive reddish-pink granite (with white granite also present in the sea cliffs below the lighthouse) was injected into the crust during the Devonian period, approximately 400 million years ago, and is related to the granites of Flinders Island and Victoria's Wilsons Promontory.

With a greatly reduced rainfall and longer hours of sunshine, the eastern side of Tasmania is much drier than the west and this is reflected in the dominance of eucalyptus forests, with only small pockets of temperate rainforest existing. The fauna of the east has more in common with that of mainland Australia, with echidnas commonly observed on the tracks. Brushtail possums, skinks (a small lizard) and all three of the snake species to be found in Tasmania are also common, in particular black tiger snakes, which often curl up on tracks but usually slither away if disturbed.

Freycinet Peninsula

Duration	2 days
Distance	31km
Standard	easy-medium
Start/Finish	Parsons Cove car park
Nearest Town	Coles Bay
Public Transport	yes

Summary Beautiful coastal walking featuring one of the most scenic beaches in Australia. In dry summer periods water can be difficult to find, but the route can easily be shortened to a day walk.

For tourists and walkers alike, Freycinet National Park is probably the biggest draw on the east coast of Tasmania. The dramatic granite peaks of the Hazards and the turquoise waters and pristine white sand of Wineglass Bay have made it a postcard favourite. The bulk of the national park is comprised of the Freycinet Peninsula, and a network of well-maintained walking tracks allows access to the best bays, beaches and peaks. One-day walks to suit most time frames and fitness levels are available, and three or four hours is ample time to take in Wineglass Bay and return via Hazards Beach. The walk described here takes two days to make a fairly leisurely circuit of the whole peninsula. Short walking times on both days provide generous opportunities for exploration and swimming.

There is a hut at Cooks Beach with bunks to sleep about eight people, although it is fairly run-down and most walkers will find a tent more comfortable. Almost all of the camping areas have flat sites. See What to Bring under Planning for important details regarding drinking water.

PLANNING
When to Walk

You can walk around Freycinet Peninsula at any time of the year and it is an especially good option if the weather out west is poor. Towards the end of summer, or after a long dry spell, there may be no fresh water. Contact the ranger station (☎ 03-6257 0107) for the current drinking water situation and

TASMANIA

consider a day walk via Wineglass Bay and Hazards Beach. Springtime boasts the added attraction of wild flowers.

What to Bring

You should bring a tent and fuel stove for an overnight walk on the peninsula. During a large part of the year many of the creeks marked on the map are dry and water will only be available from certain spots, details of which are given in the track notes. Generally you should plan to carry 1L or more with you at the beginning of the day. If the water tanks at Cook's Beach Hut are empty, you will need to carry several litres of water with you on the first day.

Reasonably strong boots are advisable for the section of track between Mt Graham and Wineglass Bay, but you can get away with running shoes or light boots if necessary. The tracks on the rest of the peninsula are well constructed. As much of the walking is across unshaded beach, sunglasses, hat and sunscreen are a must.

Maps

The best map to use is Tasmap's 1:50,000 *Freycinet National Park*.

Information Sources

At the time of writing, it was intended that a Freycinet visitor centre would be constructed by 2001. Until then, the park entrance booth (☎ 03-6257 0107) has a brochure of the park's walking trails. The Coles Bay general store and post office also stock visitors' information.

Permits & Regulations

You'll need a national parks pass for this walk (see Park Fees & Regulations in the introduction to this chapter). A pedestrian pass will suffice if you are arriving by bus or on foot; otherwise you'll need a vehicle pass to get to the car park at the start. Only fuel stoves are permitted.

NEAREST TOWN &FACILITIES
Coles Bay

This small, pleasant coastal town has a relaxed atmosphere and wonderful views of

the Hazards. Until the proposed interpretation and visitor centre is built close to the ranger station, information is available from the post office and general store. The store itself has a reasonable selection of groceries, but you should aim to bring stove fuel with you from Hobart or Launceston.

Places to Stay & Eat The *Iluka Holiday Centre* (☎ 03-6257 0115) has tent sites at $12 for two people ($14 for powered sites). The facilities are good. It has a YHA hostel with dorms costing $13 for a night, and a range of cabins beginning at $50.

The *general store* does takeaway food and has a small snack and sandwich bar with seating overlooking Richardsons Bay and the Hazards. *Madge Molloy's* (☎ 03-6257 0102), next door, is a licensed, smoke-free, cafe-restaurant specialising in fresh seafood. It was under renovation when we visited, but should now be back in action, open Tuesday to Sunday from 6 pm. The *Iluka Tavern* has counter meals and dinners daily, with YHA members receiving a 10% discount.

Getting There & Away Bicheno Coach Services (☎ 03-6257 0293) operates scheduled and on-demand services between Bicheno (north of Freycinet Peninsula on the A3) and Coles Bay. The timetable can be a little confusing so it is wise to phone ahead as many of the services also need to be booked in advance. From June to October there are three services on weekdays, one on Saturday and one on Sunday. From November to May extra services will run if there are sufficient numbers. Many of the services are primarily for school children. The fare each way is $5 ($6 to the walking track car park). Some services also connect with TRC services (☎ 1300 360 000) from Hobart at the Coles Bay turn-off ($30.20 from Hobart to the turn-off).

Freycinet National Park

Freycinet Camping Ground (☎ 03-6257 0107) is just inside the national park boundary and a short walk from Coles Bay. It's in a pleasant location, in the shelter of trees at the back of Richardsons Beach. Tent sites are $10 for two people and powered sites are $12. There is no hot water and no showers and you'll need to be very careful with food as the local possums are quite aggressive.

GETTING TO/FROM THE WALK

It is 5km along a fairly uninteresting sealed road from Coles Bay to the beginning of the walking tracks. Bicheno Coach Services runs shuttle services to the walking track car park up to two or three times daily Monday to Saturday, depending on demand. A single fare costs $2 and a return $3.

THE WALK
Day 1: Parsons Cove Car Park to Cooks Beach via Hazards Beach
4–5 hours, 13km

The track begins just beyond the walker registration board in the car park. Follow the signposts for Wineglass Bay for a few minutes to reach a junction. The track to the left, which you'll return along, leads to Wineglass Bay. The track running straight ahead is signposted for Hazards Beach. Follow this as it contours round the base of Mt Mayson. The track is very well constructed, and the first 30 minutes are flat and easy with occasional views out of the scrubby bush across Great Oyster Bay. The track then climbs across rock slabs to negotiate a spur. Cairns and marker arrows indicate the route. Following the descent from the spur, the track is once again of a high standard, crossing several more small spurs and dry creeks. After an hour of walking from Coles Bay you enter a dense thicket of pines and another five minutes of flat walking brings you out of the pines and onto **Hazards Beach**, a 3km sweep of sand backed by Mt Freycinet (620m).

On the left, a track leads across the narrow isthmus of land that separates Hazards Beach from Wineglass Bay. Half an hour of walking will take you across to Wineglass Bay if you are doing a one-day circuit. On the peninsula circuit, continue along the length of the beach (45 minutes to one hour) to a creek and large camping area with toilets. The creek is brackish beside the *camping area* but a small trail leads upstream 100m or so to where better water is available.

A signpost directs you out of the camping area and south through open eucalyptus forest towards Cooks Beach. Don't expect to find water in the creeks along this section of the walk as they will often be dry. About two hours of pleasant, mainly flat walking brings you to the north end of **Cooks Beach**. The track swings off to the left here, headed for Mt Graham. To reach the *camping area* at Cooks Beach walk to the south end (20 to 30 minutes) where there are good sites for tents set in the shelter of trees at the back of the beach. The toilets, hut and water tanks are a little farther back inland.

Side Trip: Bryans Beach
2 hours, 6km

For views of Schouten Island, just off the tip of Freycinet Peninsula, a two-hour return trip to **Bryans Beach** is worthwhile. Follow the track from Cooks Beach Hut for 3km over flat ground. There are *camping areas* at the beach.

Day 2: Cooks Beach to Car Park via Wineglass Bay
6 hours, 18km

Leave the camping area and retrace your steps of the previous day across Cooks Beach. At the northern end of the beach at Regleeta Creek take the track to the right signposted for Wineglass Bay. It climbs gently to the south-east for a little more than 1km through light eucalyptus cover to reach Botanical Creek. At most times of the year

On the east coast of Freycinet Peninsula, Sleepy Bay is a pretty sight at dawn

TASMANIA

GRANT DIXON

Freycinet Peninsula

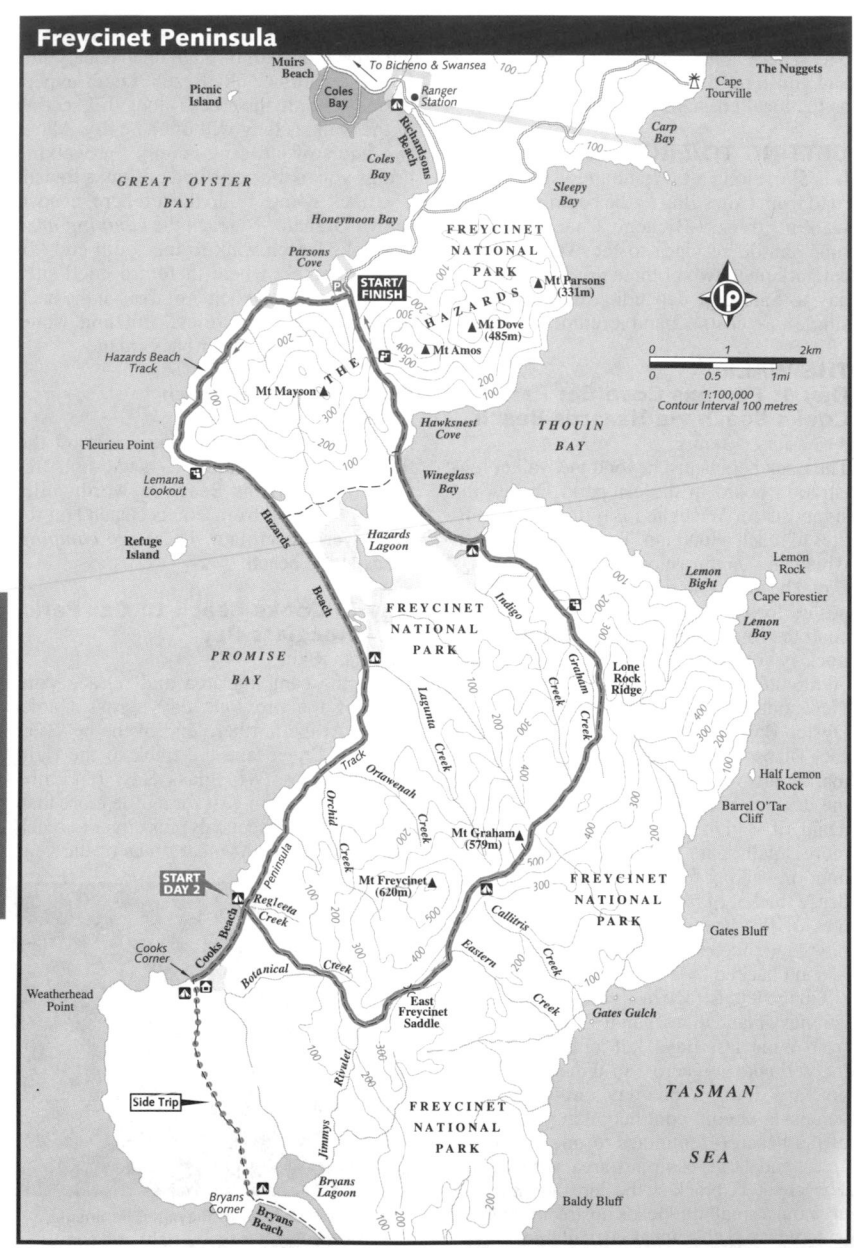

you can find water in this creek and there is also a *camp site* for a small tent close to the creek. The track continues in a south-easterly direction and steepens considerably for the next 500m to cross a ridge. Swinging to the north-east the track climbs on an easy gradient and the ground becomes increasingly boulder-strewn as you reach **East Freycinet Saddle** (just over 300m). A 500m detour to the south from the saddle provides some good views across Bryans Beach and the southern coastline of the peninsula.

Continue from the saddle for 20 minutes to reach a broad gully and camping area just below the col between Mt Freycinet and Mt Graham, the location of another *camp site*. The creek here is only semipermanent. The track steepens and becomes rougher during the ascent to the **Mt Graham** summit (579m; 30 minutes from the camping area). Dump packs at the track's high point and walk across rock slabs to get excellent views of the peninsula, including the northern reaches of Wineglass Bay and the rock walls of Mt Dove dropping almost sheer into the startling blue water. You should also be able to make out the line of the track that descends from Mt Graham and runs north-east across a flat and scrubby plateau before disappearing into a gully.

The far edge of this plateau is reached in about 30 minutes from the summit of Mt Graham and the track becomes rough and steep as it descends into the gully containing Graham Creek. This creek will sometimes have water in it. The track climbs onto the east wall of the gully and in one very short section skirts a vertical drop, which might give vertigo sufferers a hard time. Shortly after this point the track swings out of the gully and follows the lower extension of Lone Rock Ridge down to **Wineglass Bay** (45 minutes to one hour from Graham Creek).

At the southern end of Wineglass Bay is a well-shaded *camping area*. Any water found here is normally of poor quality. Wineglass Bay takes 30 minutes to skirt, and at the northern end there is a track junction. To the left, a track leads across the isthmus to Hazards Beach, while just inside the

shade of the trees a very well-constructed track begins the steady climb to the saddle between Mt Mayson and Mt Amos. A viewing platform 100m to the right of the saddle gives a final panorama of Wineglass Bay before the track descends steeply back to the car park (one hour from Wineglass Bay).

Maria Island

Duration	4 hours
Distance	12km
Standard	easy-medium
Start/Finish	Darlington
Nearest Towns	Triabunna, Orford
Public Transport	yes

Summary A pleasant half-day walk on an island steeped in convict history. Open cliff-top walking is complemented by eucalyptus forest and a rocky scramble to an airy viewing point on Bishop and Clerk.

Located 10km off the east coast of Tasmania, Maria Island has a significant place in the history of the European settlement of Tasmania (see History below). It now has no permanent residents and was declared a national park in 1972 with the later addition of a marine reserve incorporating all of the waters up to 1km off the north-west coast of the island. Just 19km long and about 10km across at its widest point, the island is primarily mountainous, dominated by the summits of Mt Maria (709m) and Bishop and Clerk.

This out-and-back walk (along the route of the Bishop & Clerk Mountain Walk) leaves from the old settlement of Darlington and climbs via the Fossil Cliffs to the summit of Bishop and Clerk, from where there are airy and wide-ranging views. The track is good and easy to follow, except in the final stages to the top where some easy scrambling is required. Those who don't like bouldery ground and some mild exposure will find the last 20m or so quite difficult. The walking time of around four hours means that you'll be back in Darlington in time to catch the ferry back to the mainland. There is no water on the walk so bottles should be filled in Darlington.

HISTORY

Maria Island has had a long and varied history of human occupation. Its first inhabitants were Aborigines of the Oyster Bay Clan who crossed Mercury Passage in canoe rafts and named the island Toarra Marra Monah. In 1642 Abel Tasman made the first European sighting of the island and named it Maria after the wife of Anthony Van Diemen. Europeans did not land there until 1789 when crew of the English brigantine *Mercury* went ashore for wood and water, and in doing so came into contact with the Aboriginal people of the island.

The Aborigines lived in relative peace until the first convicts arrived and founded Darlington in 1825, marking the beginning of permanent European occupation of the island and the decline of the Aboriginal population. Notable buildings like the commissariat store and penitentiary were built by the first convicts, and when the convicts were shifted in 1832, farmers, whalers and smugglers replaced them. From 1842 to 1850 the penal colony was re-established and expanded with more land opened to grazing and agriculture.

Agriculture continued as the main occupation on the island after the penal colony was closed for good, until 1884 when a Signor Bernacchi introduced wine making and silk industries to the island. These were followed by a succession of other enterprises (the most visible remains of which are the cement silos in Darlington), until by 1930 the island had reverted to its agrarian roots.

In the 1960s the government gradually bought up the island, reintroducing wildlife and declaring it a wildlife sanctuary in 1971. The following year it was declared a national park.

PLANNING

Walking at any time of the year is suitable. If the weather is fine and stable, you'll only need food and clothing for a day walk on modestly rough tracks. If there is any chance of the ferry not being able to pick you up in the afternoon, then you should bring a tent, food and stove to cope with the eventuality of having to overnight on the island. Those walkers planning to overnight at the penitentiary in Darlington will need a stove and sleeping bag.

Maps

The best map to use is the Tasmap 1:50,000 *Maria Island National Park*.

Permits & Regulations

You'll need a national parks permit, available from the commissariat store. Those who already have a permit will also need to register at the store. Open fires are not permitted in some areas, so check with the ranger if you are planning on lighting a fire.

NEAREST TOWNS & FACILITIES
Triabunna

Just 2km north of the Louisville Point turn-off (where the ferry to Maria Island departs), Triabunna is a quiet and convenient town to use as a base for a visit to Maria Island. The visitor centre (☎ 03-6257 4090) is on the corner of the Esplanade and Charles St, right on the water, and is a good spot to pick up maps and preliminary information about Maria Island. There are a couple of small general stores in town, but you should bring fuel stoves and camping needs from Hobart.

Places to Stay & Eat The budget find in Triabunna is the *Triabunna Caravan Park* (☎ 03-6257 3575), on the corner of Vicary and Melbourne Sts. A small area of flat grass at the back of the park provides tent sites for $10 for two people. Powered sites are $11. Even better are the on-site vans, which are a steal at $25 for a double. Alternatively, *Triabunna YHA Hostel* (☎ 03-6257 3439), across the bridge and a 10-minute walk from the main part of town, has dorm beds for $12.

Spring Bay Hotel (☎ 03-6257 3115) has rooms from $30 and serves meals. *Tandara Motor Inn* (☎ 03-6257 3333) has rooms for $50 and serves dinner on Friday and Saturday nights and lunch on Sunday.

If you're not on a tight budget and want to stay at Louisville Point, *Eastcoaster Resort* (☎ 03-6257 1172), with singles/doubles at $75/90, has a bar and restaurant. There is a *cafe* at the ferry terminal on Louisville Point.

Getting There & Away TWT's Tassielink (☎ 1300 300 520) and TRC (☎ 1300 360 000) run scheduled services through Triabunna from Hobart. Buses stop at the Shell service station; a one-way fare from Hobart costs $10.70.

Orford

The village of Orford, about 6km south of the turn-off to Louisville Point (the ferry departure point), has fewer services than Triabunna, but **Raspins Beach Camping Park** (☎ 03-6257 1771) has sandy tent sites at $9 for two people. The facilities aren't great but the views of Maria Island are. There is a host of *flats*, **cabins** and *motels* with rooms in the $40 to $100 price range. *East Coast Seafoods* does reasonable eat-in and takeaway fish and chips.

Orford is on the TWT's Tassielink and TRC east coast bus routes (see Getting There & Away for Triabunna).

Darlington

Darlington on Maria Island has no services except the ranger office, visitor centre and some basic accommodation. The *camping ground* (☎ 03-6257 1420) costs $6 and open fires are permitted when the fire risk is low. *The Penitentiary Units* (☎ 03-6257 1420), nearby, are basic bunkhouses without cooking facilities or electricity. The rooms have mattresses only, but despite this the units are very popular (as visitors attempt to get a little bit of that convict feeling). The cost is $8 and you'll also need your national park pass.

GETTING TO/FROM THE WALK

The *Eastcoaster Express* ferry (☎ 03-6257 1589) departs from Louisville Point (2km south of Triabunna) daily at 10.30 am and 1 and 3.30 pm, returning from Darlington 30 minutes later. In summer (December to April) there is an extra service at 9 am. The return ferry fare for a day trip costs $17. Overnighters will pay $20 for a return. TWT's Tassielink (☎ 1300 300 520) east coast bus services will make the short detour from the main highway to drop you at Louisville Point, provided you book ahead.

THE WALK

Follow the dirt track past the commissariat store, where park permits and maps may be purchased. Turn left after 100m and walk through the camping area, crossing a small footbridge to the right and climbing a grassy slope to pick up another dirt road. Follow this for a few hundred metres as it curves round to the north, fording a small creek. A track leads off to the left sign-posted for the Fossil Cliffs and Bishop and Clerk. Walk along this and onto grassy slopes, which are climbed in a couple of minutes to the edge of the **Fossil Cliffs**. Be wary of the cliff edge here as it is sloping and loose.

Looking along the cliffs, the eye is drawn to the pinnacles of Bishop and Clerk rising above Fossil Bay to the east. Climb easy grassy slopes along the cliff edge and enter open eucalyptus forest on a broad track. This climbs gently along Skipping Ridge with occasional glimpses of the ocean far below to the left. After 20 or 30 minutes the track becomes narrower and the forest more dense. Climb steeply for 15 or 20 minutes to the end of Skipping Ridge where the track flattens out for a short time, contouring to the north before climbing steeply again for a few minutes. From the top of this steep section, 15 to 20 minutes of easier walking through dense understorey brings you to the foot of a large scree slope, marking the beginning of the more difficult final stages of the climb.

Follow marker poles up the scree, which in places makes for quite strenuous walking. After 20 or 30 minutes the scree gives way to large boulders scattered among the small trees and shrubs close to the summit. Now yellow pointer arrows show the way, snaking round a difficult section before forcing you to scramble over rock for the final 20m. One haul over a rock ledge is a little awkward on the descent. From the **summit** you can look north across the Tasman Sea to the Freycinet Peninsula and the Hazards. To the west, a good portion of the rolling hills of Tasmania's east coast stretches along the horizon with Mt Wellington prominent to the south-west. Views of the island itself are

Maria Island

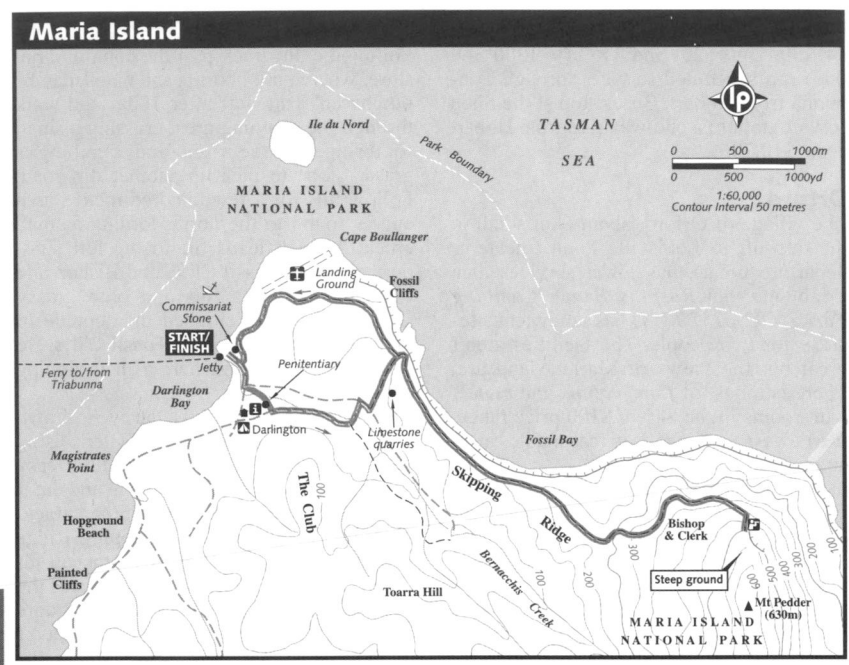

somewhat restricted. Mt Maria is visible to the south, and far below are the Fossil Cliffs.

Retrace your steps to Darlington, but on reaching the end of the Fossil Cliffs continue north-west to Cape Boullanger and then back to Darlington on grassy tracks.

Cape Pillar

Duration	3 days
Distance	35km
Standard	medium
Start	Fortescue Bay
Finish	Cape Pillar Track car park
Nearest Towns	Port Arthur, Eaglehawk Neck
Public Transport	no

Summary An exciting walk along the edge of the highest sea cliffs in Australia. The cliffs are complemented by a variety of vegetation. Dry eucalyptus forest, temperate rainforest and low coastal heath are all encountered.

Visitors to the Port Arthur Historic Site on the Tasman Peninsula rarely realise that just a few kilometres away, hidden by bush-clad hills, is the highest and most spectacular sea cliff line in Australia. Surprisingly, the cliffs are not very accessible. No roads have been constructed to take tourists to viewing areas, and the closest foot access to the beginning of the cliffs at Cape Hauy takes two hours across a bouldery track. With Cape Pillar and Cape Hauy incorporated into the recently proclaimed Tasman National Park, very little of the remoteness is likely to be lost.

This walk makes a two- to three-day circuit of the cliffs, beginning at Fortescue Bay and taking in Cape Hauy, before crossing Mt Fortescue and making a spectacular out-and-back trip to Cape Pillar itself. An easy walk along the Cape Pillar Track brings you to the finish just 2km west of Fortescue Bay. Those wishing to cut down the time could simply make an out-and-back walk on the Cape Pillar Track, which would be a long day walk or a more leisurely overnight trip. Shorter again would be a trip to Cape Hauy and back from Fortescue Bay (three to four hours).

The tracks are generally good, although some sections are quite rocky. There are no nasty ascents and your only concern could be finding fresh water – the creeks have very small catchment areas and are likely to dry up in summer after a few weeks without significant rainfall. Certainly you should take enough water for the whole day trip out to Cape Pillar from Lunchtime Creek. Also bear in mind that the cliffs are exposed to violent winds and if a gale is forecast, it may not be the best time to go.

PLANNING
When to Walk
You can walk this track at any time of the year. December to March may present difficulties with water, but at most other times of the year this should not be a problem.

What to Bring
Tents should be three-season or better, and able to cope with strong winds and rain. Boots should have ankle support and you'll need waterproofs and warm clothing. Bring water containers large enough for an entire day. Good weather can bring intense sunshine, and on the unshaded sections out to Cape Pillar you'll need sun protection.

Maps & Books
You'll need two maps: Tasmap's 1:25,000 *Tasman* and *Hippolyte* maps. *Peninsula Tracks* by Peter & Shirley Storey gives well-written coverage of 35 popular walks in the area and is worth checking out if you plan to spend more time there.

Permits & Regulations
As the area is a national park you'll need a pass (see Park Fees & Regulations near the start of this chapter). There is a voluntary registration box at Fortescue Bay.

NEAREST TOWNS & FACILITIES
Port Arthur
As one of the biggest mainstream tourist draws in Tasmania, it is a surprise to discover

that Port Arthur is not much more than the historic site plus a scattering of motels and guesthouses. Just before the turn-off to the historic site is a general store and petrol station on the left. Bring all your camping needs from Hobart.

Places to Stay & Eat The cheapest options in Port Arthur are the excellent *Port Arthur Caravan and Cabin Park* (☎ 03-6250 2340) and *Port Arthur YHA Hostel* (☎ 03-6250 2311). The caravan park is 2km north of Port Arthur above Stewarts Bay Beach and has bunkhouse accommodation for $13 a night. Tent sites are $12 and there is a cooking shelter and laundry facilities. A walking track will take you down to Port Arthur in 40 minutes. The hostel is right on the edge of the historic site and dorm beds are $13 a night. Both of these options, and indeed all of the more expensive motel accommodation in Port Arthur, can be heavily booked in summer.

Takeaway food is available from the *general store* and there is also a *restaurant-cafe* in the historic site. More upmarket meals are available from *Port Arthur Motel Inn*, next to the hostel.

Getting There & Away Hobart Coaches (☎ 03-6234 4077), 4 Liverpool St, Hobart, services the Tasman Peninsula from Monday to Friday, stopping at all of the towns on the main highway, including Port Arthur and Eaglehawk Neck.

To get there on the weekend you can try Tasmanian Tours and Travel/Tigerline (☎ 03-6231 2200), which operates day tours to Port Arthur. It will normally accommodate walkers but will probably charge the rate of two full-day tours as the price for an open return (around $70).

Bottom Bits Bus (☎ 1800 777 103) operates day trips to Port Arthur with the option of travelling back stand-by on a later trip. The cost is $45.

Eaglehawk Neck
The small settlement of Eaglehawk Neck is on the isthmus that joins the Tasman Peninsula to the mainland. It is about 15 minutes'

drive north (on the A9) of the turn-off for Fortescue Bay at the start of the walk. It has a general store in the visitor centre, but as with Port Arthur you'd be wise to bring all camping and walking needs from Hobart.

Places to Stay & Eat The *Eaglehawk Neck Backpackers* (☎ 03-6250 3248) is a small and friendly hostel charging $12 a night for dorm beds. There is also a small camping ground and the owners rent bicycles, which may be an option for reaching Fortescue Bay if you don't have a car.

On the road heading out to Port Arthur is *Eaglehawk Cafe*, which serves very good breakfasts, lunches and dinners.

Getting There & Away For information on public transport options to Eaglehawk Neck, see the Getting There & Away section for Port Arthur.

Fortescue Bay
Right at the start of the walk, *Fortescue Bay Camping Ground* (☎ 03-6250 2433) has sites for $6 per person in a pleasant shaded location overlooking the beach. You'll need a national parks pass to stay. There are cold showers, pit toilets and firewood. There are no powered sites.

GETTING TO/FROM THE WALK
With the start of the walk 12km off the main highway down a gravel road, the logistics of getting to and from the walk from Port Arthur or Eaglehawk Neck will not be easy for those relying on public transport. If you are driving, follow the Arthur Hwy through Eaglehawk Neck and Taranna. Turn left onto a gravel road about 5km north of Port Arthur. This should be signposted for Fortescue Bay. Follow the road to the car park and camping ground at the end. On the way you'll notice a small parking area on the right, 2km before you reach Fortescue Bay. This should be signposted 'Cape Pillar Track Car Park' and this is where the walk finishes.

Those relying on public transport can only hope to get to the turn-off from the main highway by bus, after which you'll be facing an unappealing two- to three-hour road bash

to reach Fortescue Bay. Alternatively, you could try to hitch or negotiate a lift from the owners of wherever you are staying.

THE WALK
Day 1: Fortescue Bay to Lunchtime Creek via Cape Hauy
7–8 hours, 16km
Cape Hauy and Mt Fortescue are signposted from the Fortescue Bay car park. The track initially follows the water's edge but then turns south-east and begins to climb inland. The track follows a different course from that shown on the Tasmap *Hippolyte* map. After an initial steep section, it climbs more gently and then undulates slightly to reach the Cape Hauy junction, one hour from Fortescue Bay. The trip down to **Cape Hauy** takes about 1½ hours return and is well worth the effort.

Turn left and follow the track steeply down across rock slabs. The trees fade away and views open out across the cliffs beneath Mt Fortescue and off into the hazy distance to Cape Pillar itself. Climb across a steep rise and descend towards Cape Hauy where the track gradually deteriorates. Continue to follow the crest of the headland until you reach a warning sign. Just beyond this you get dizzying views of the **Totem Pole**, a 65m-high rock stack slotted in a turbulent chasm between the end of Cape Hauy and the sheer-sided island that marks the continuation of the headland into the ocean. You can scramble down a little farther to get a more impressive view, but the descent becomes more dangerous as you continue. Return to the junction on the same track.

Back at the junction take the track signposted to Mt Fortescue and follow the orange markers gently uphill for 10 minutes to where it emerges on the cliff top at **Monument Lookout**. The principal view from here is back to the north-east to the Monument, a sea stack rising vertically 50m out of the Tasman Sea. Beyond the Monument, Cape Hauy and the Totem Pole forge towards the horizon. The track continues to climb close to the cliff top passing several other lookouts, drops into a small basin and then crosses a small spur before descending into

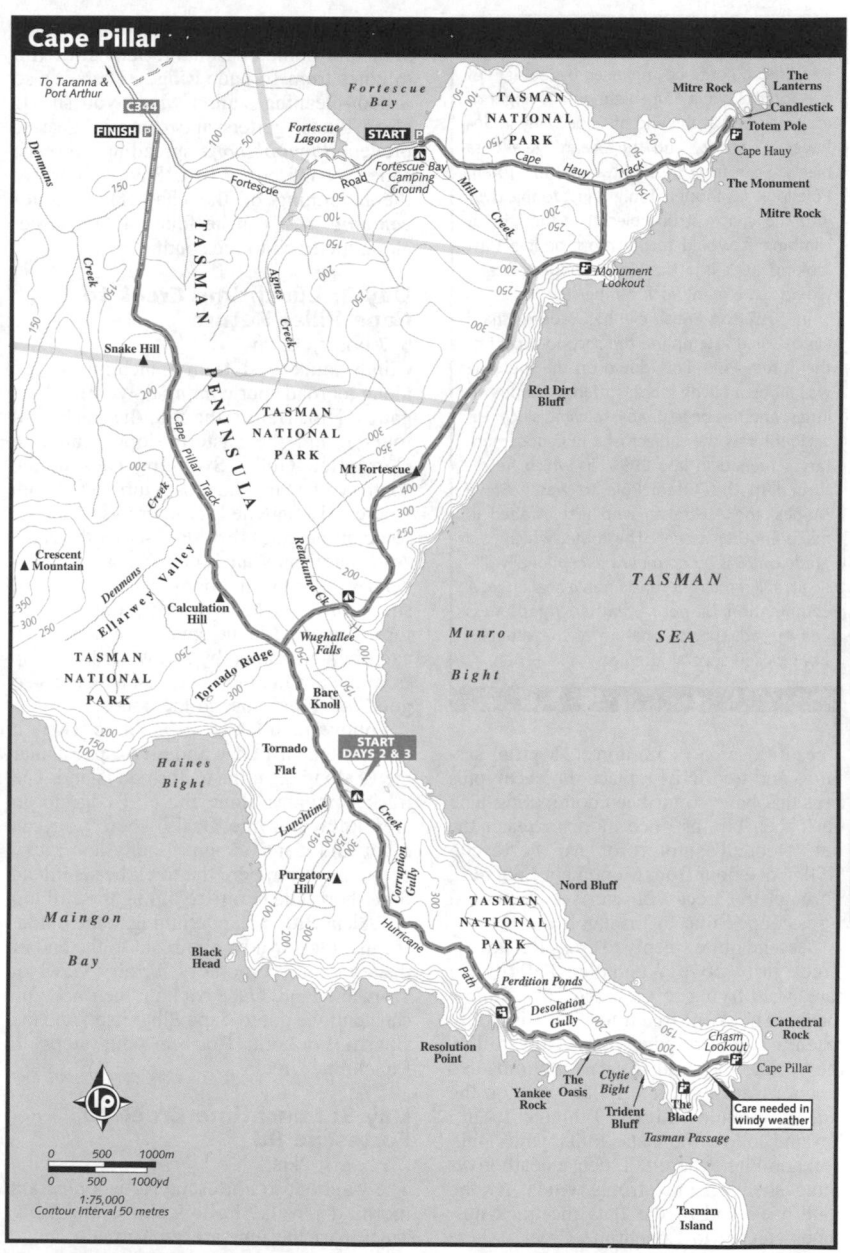

Cape Pillar

To Taranna & Port Arthur
C344
FINISH P

Denmans

Fortescue Bay

Fortescue Lagoon

START P

Fortescue Bay Camping Ground

Fortescue Road

TASMAN NATIONAL PARK

Cape Hauy Track

Mitre Rock
The Lanterns
Candlestick
Totem Pole
Cape Hauy

Mill Creek

The Monument
Mitre Rock

Agnes Creek

Creek

Snake Hill

TASMAN PENINSULA

Cape Pillar Track

Creek

Crescent Mountain

Denmans

Ellarwey Valley

Calculation Hill

Retakunna Ck

Wughalee Falls

Bare Knoll

Tornado Ridge

Tornado Flat

Lunchtime

Purgatory Hill

TASMAN NATIONAL PARK

Monument Lookout

Red Dirt Bluff

Mt Fortescue

TASMAN SEA

Munro Bight

Haines Bight

START DAYS 2 & 3

Creek

Corruption Gully

Hurricane Path

Nord Bluff

TASMAN NATIONAL PARK

Maingon Bay

Black Head

Perdition Ponds

Desolation Gully

Resolution Point

Yankee Rock

The Oasis

Clytie Bight

Trident Bluff

The Blade

Chasm Lookout

Cathedral Rock

Cape Pillar

Care needed in windy weather

Tasman Passage

Tasman Island

0   500   1000m
0   500   1000yd
1:75,000
Contour Interval 50 metres

TASMANIA

The Totem Pole

It is difficult not to be impressed by the sight of the Totem Pole, a 65m-high vertical finger of rock standing at the end of Cape Hauy in defiance of gravity and the ocean's relentless blasts. Seen from the right angle, the Totem Pole looks as though it might just topple over into the chasm it occupies. The thought of climbing it would terrify most people (just looking at it is a dizzying experience) and would scare many rock climbers.

In 1997 top British climber Paul Pritchard almost died attempting the second ascent of the Totem Pole. Low down on the route he was hit by a falling block, suffering serious injuries, and has been unable to climb since. His accident was the subject of a BBC documentary screened in late 1999, in which he returned to the Totem Pole to watch Steve Monks, the Australian who first climbed it, make another ascent. The route, which at a grade of 26 is by no means exceptionally difficult, still remains a considerable challenge. A combination of poor weather, remoteness and the adventurous nature of the situation has repelled several attempts.

a beautiful area of rainforest. Myrtle, sassafras and tree ferns replace the eucalyptus trees that have so far been dominating. The track then climbs once more to reach the flat, wooded summit of **Mt Fortescue** (490m; one hour from Monument Lookout). Through the trees you can see south-east across Cape Pillar to Tasman Island.

Descend quite steeply to cross Retakunna Creek just above Wughallee Falls. Take care when trying to view the falls. Follow the main track upstream for five minutes to reach a good *camping area*. Now follow the track to the south-west as it climbs to a junction with the Cape Pillar Track on the side of Tornado Ridge (30 minutes). Turn left and follow the Cape Pillar Track onto Tornado Flat, where tall, dense heath gives some shelter from strong winds. At the south-west end of the flats the track descends steeply to Lunchtime Creek, where

you'll find the most permanent water in the area and some reasonable *tent sites* (30 minutes from Tornado Ridge). There is also a boot-cleaning station where you should clean boots, gaiters and camping gear to prevent *Phytophthora* spreading onto the cape (see the boxed text 'Phytophthora' at the beginning of the chapter). A better *camping area* can be found 400m farther along the track to the south.

Day 2: Lunchtime Creek to Cape Pillar Return
5–7 hours, 12km

Climb south-west from Lunchtime Creek along a broad spur coming down from Purgatory Hill. Before the top, the track contours round the eastern slopes and into Corruption Gully. Swinging back to the south-west again you cross Hurricane Heath where only flattened scrub grows under the force of the gales that blast across the cape. An hour from Lunchtime Creek you descend to Perdition Ponds, a collection of small tarns set back a little from the cliff tops. The water in the ponds is drinkable but can often be tainted by salt water blown up from the ocean 300m below. There are also good *tent sites* close to the ponds.

Follow the track to the south to where it reaches the cliff edge and gives spectacular views along the cliffs to Tasman Island. The track continues along the cliff edge to an area known as the Oasis where you can often find water in some sandy and rocky openings. From here the track heads inland for a short time before rejoining the cliff top at Trident Bluff and continuing to the **Blade**. If it isn't too windy, climb out to the end of this exposed promontory for airy views of Tasman Island. Once back on the track you can continue out to **Cape Pillar** itself and the Chasm Lookout. Retrace your steps to Lunchtime Creek.

Day 3: Lunchtime Creek to Fortescue Rd
2½ hours, 7km

The walk out to Fortescue Rd is a pleasant morning's walk. Follow the Cape Pillar Track past the junction on Tornado Ridge and keep to the left at this and a second minor junction a little farther on. The track rounds Snake Hill to the east and joins an old road, which is followed for 2km to reach the car park at Fortescue Rd.

Other Walks

WEST & WORLD HERITAGE AREA
Western Arthurs Traverse
For many serious walkers, the traverse of the Western Arthurs is the finest walk in Tasmania. From Scotts Peak Dam, the route crosses the Western Arthur Range before returning along a valley running parallel to it. The walk normally takes nine to 12 days and would merit a grade of hard. Although the start and finish points are accessible by public transport, the walk is remote, strenuous and dangerous. The Western Arthurs are a rugged crest of steep quartzite ridges exposed to the full brunt of Southern Ocean weather. A high level of fitness, self-reliance and good route-finding skills are basic requirements for this walk, which repels most of walkers who attempt it.

Federation Peak & the Eastern Arthurs
The distinctive fang-like summit of Federation Peak (1224m) is an icon of the Tasmanian wilderness. Eight to 12 days are needed for the very hard return trip along the crest of the Eastern Arthur Range, which like the Western Arthur Range features spectacular, although very difficult terrain. However, the most difficult section of the entire walk is reaching the summit of Federation Peak itself, and at least one walker has been killed attempting the steep, exposed scramble.

The walk starts and finishes at Scotts Peak Dam and is served by public transport in the summer months. Only well-prepared, experienced and fit walkers should consider this route.

For more details on the route see *South West Tasmania* by John Chapman and consult Tasmap's 1:100,000 *Old River* map and the Hobart Walking Club's 1:25,000 *Eastern Arthur Range* map.

Frenchmans Cap
Along with Federation Peak and Cradle Mountain, Frenchmans Cap (1443m) must be one of the most inspiring mountains in Australia. Located in the Franklin–Gordon Wild Rivers National Park, its east face has been carved into extensive vertical cliffs up to 500m high, giving it a tremendous profile when viewed from the north or south. Three to five days are needed to walk to the summit and back from the Lyell Hwy (where public transport can be met) and the track has a reputation for deep mud. Expect a grade of medium to hard.

For more details see *South West Tasmania* by John Chapman and consult Tasmap's 1:50,000 *Frenchmans Cap* map.

Hartz Peak
Only 84km from Hobart, Hartz Mountains National Park is within the boundaries of the WHA. Following signposts from Geeveston, an access road climbs high up on the mountain, leaving a five-hour return walk across alpine terrain to reach Hartz Peak (1255m). You should expect a grade of medium for this ascent. Due to its proximity to Hobart the walk is popular on weekends, although it is not served by public transport.

EAST COAST & ISLANDS
Leeaberra Track
This two-day easy-to-medium walk traverses the fine eucalyptus bush of the Douglas–Apsley National Park. This is the largest dry forest in Tasmania, a significant remnant of the forests that once covered all of eastern Tasmania. From the start at Thompsons Marshes, dry and reasonably easy walking leads for 25km south to the Apsley Waterhole. The walk is designed to be done in this direction so as to prevent the spread of plant disease. Regular public transport services run within 7km of the start and finish. The walk is covered by Tasmap's 1:50,000 *Douglas-Apsley National Park* map.

Bruny Island
Quiet and rural Bruny Island is just one hour's drive and 20 minutes by ferry from Hobart. As well as having some beautiful white-sand beaches, penguin colonies and bush-clad hills, the southern coastline of the island has been incorporated into South Bruny National Park. The best walking in the park follows good tracks round the Labillardiere Peninsula, giving fine coastal views. This easy-to-medium circuit starts at the Jetty Beach camping ground and takes around six or seven hours. A *Walkers Guide to Bruny Island* is published locally and can be bought from the visitor centre at Kettering.

Melbourne Region

Bushwalking in the Melbourne region can be summed up in a word: variety. Many national parks and other reserves protect mountain forests in the Macedon and Dandenong Ranges, sparse box-ironbark woodlands in the Brisbane Ranges, the rugged Werribee Gorge and gently undulating country at Woodlands, and the rocky coast and beaches of Mornington Peninsula. Walkers are well looked after, with good networks of walking tracks in every park. A diverse collection of walks in these parks is described in this chapter, from an unusual stroll around a historic park overlooking Melbourne's international airport, to a two-day walk with an overnight bushland camp. These walks provide a very compressed introduction to the wealth of opportunities on offer, second to none among Australia's capital cities.

INFORMATION
Maps
For itinerary planning, Gregory's 1:400,000 *150km Around Melbourne* is the best among the several folded maps available. Melway's *Greater Melbourne* street directory has excellent street maps and adequately detailed maps of the hinterland; published annually, it's a worthwhile investment.

Details of topographical maps in the official Vicmap series (published by Geographic Data Victoria) are given under Planning for each area in the Melbourne Region.

Lonely Planet's *Melbourne City Map* is a portable and easy-to-use fold-out map of the city centre.

Buying Maps A good place to buy maps and guidebooks is Melbourne Map Centre (☎ 03-9569 5472, fax 9569 8000, ✆ info @melbmap.com.au), at 738 Waverley Rd, Chadstone. In the city, try Map Land (☎ 03-9670 4383, fax 9670 7779, ✆ mapland @lexicon.net), 372 Little Bourke St, and Information Victoria (☎ 1300 366 356), 356 Collins St, open weekdays. The latter is the state government's information centre.

Highlights

RICHARD I'ANSON

The rocky point of Cape Schanck, a scenic coastal walk close to Melbourne

- Walking among forests of grass trees and springtime wattles in the Brisbane Ranges
- Scrambling along sandy beaches and round rugged cliffs in Werribee Gorge
- Wandering among magnificent river red gums and past a historic homestead in Woodlands Historic Park
- Taking in panoramas, historic sites and mountain forest in the Macedon Ranges
- Paying homage to Sherbrooke Forest's towering mountain ash forests
- Enjoying precious unspoiled bushland and scenic coastline in Mornington Peninsula National Park

Books
Tyrone Thomas' long-established *120 Walks in Victoria* includes some near Melbourne. For the north-eastern fringes of the Melbourne region, John & Marion Siseman's *Melbourne's Mountains: Exploring the Great*

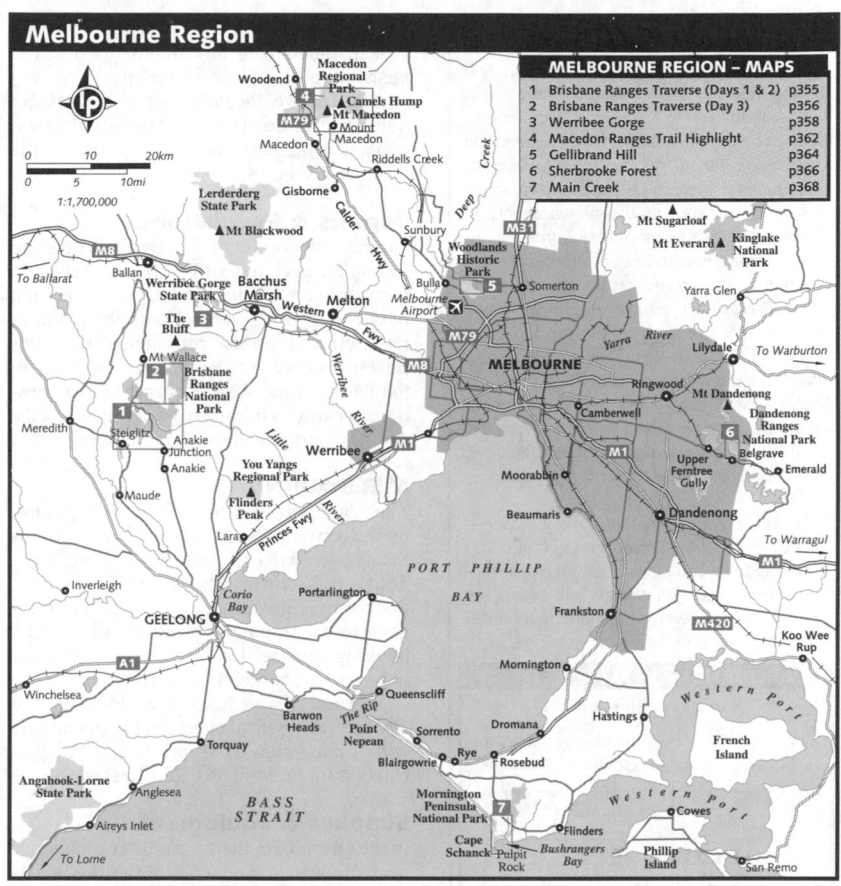

Melbourne Region

MELBOURNE REGION – MAPS

1	Brisbane Ranges Traverse (Days 1 & 2)	p355
2	Brisbane Ranges Traverse (Day 3)	p356
3	Werribee Gorge	p358
4	Macedon Ranges Trail Highlight	p362
5	Gellibrand Hill	p364
6	Sherbrooke Forest	p366
7	Main Creek	p368

Divide by Foot & by Car offers at least 50 walks of varying standards.

In addition to the natural history titles for Victoria (see that chapter), there's *Native Plants of Melbourne & Adjoining Areas* by David & Barbara Jones, which is well designed and easy to use. This and many other books about Melbourne are on sale at the excellent shop in the Royal Botanic Gardens, Birdwood Ave, South Yarra.

Some bushwalking clubs have published anniversary histories, including Melbourne Walking Club's remarkable *Footsteps from the Past 1894–1994*, with many priceless

historical photographs, and *The Melbourne Bushies: Fifty Years Along the Track.*

Lonely Planet's *Melbourne* guide is a useful practical guide to finding your way around Melbourne.

Information Sources

The excellent bookshop at the NRE (Department of Natural Resources & Environment) Information Centre (☎ 03-9637 8325, fax 9637 8150, @ publication.sales@nre.vic.gov.au), 8 Nicholson St, East Melbourne, sells maps and has information about national and other parks. It's open weekdays.

The Climate of Melbourne

The four seasons are quite distinct in and around Melbourne, with marked differences in temperatures within the region. Light snowfalls can be expected on Mt Macedon and the Dandenong Ranges, and frosts are quite common during winter. The average maximum for this season is 13°C and the minimum 6°C. In summer, the plains west of Melbourne experience warmer temperatures than elsewhere in the region; the coolest places are along the coast. The average summer high is 26°C and the low 13°C; quite often the top temperatures exceed 35°C. Rainfall is evenly distributed throughout the year, with the highest falls likely in April and May and from September to December. The prevailing winds are from the south-west; northerlies bring hot summer days, and southerlies bring cooler temperatures at any time.

However, typical weather for any season is difficult to describe. Locals will say that if you don't like the weather, just wait for a few minutes. The message for walkers is to expect the unexpected and, even if the morning promises a settled day, be prepared for a change.

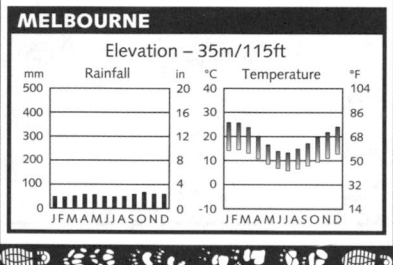

Parks Victoria (☎ 13 1963, 🖳 www.park web.vic.gov.au), which manages Victoria's national and other parks, has a telephone-only information centre for basic information, including the summer programs of activities and events in the parks; for detailed queries you'll be given the number of the individual park office. Its informative Web site includes a basic guide to a range of walking tracks in the parks.

The office of the Federation of Victorian Walking Clubs (☎ 03-9455 1876, fax 9457 5438, 🖳 vicwalk@vicnet.net.au) can put you in touch with any of the 25 or more bushwalking clubs in Melbourne.

Detailed weather charts and reports are published in the *Age* and *Australian* newspapers, with less detailed reports on the evening TV news.

Permits & Regulations

During days of Total Fire Ban, all fires are forbidden, even fuel stoves. If you are caught with an open fire on these days, you are not only endangering yourself and the environment, but you can also cop a hefty fine and/or prison sentence. See Responsible Walking in the Facts for the Walker chapter for suggestions on how to minimise your impact on the environment you are walking through.

MELBOURNE

The Victorian Visitor Information Centre, on the corner of Swanston and Little Collins Sts, is open daily (for walk-in visitors only). Tourism Victoria (☎ 13 2842, 🖳 www .tourism.vic.gov.au) can provide comprehensive accommodation information and a booking service. Its Web site is useful for links to accommodation state-wide.

Internet cafes are thick on the ground in the city centre. A typical charge is 15c per minute with a maximum of $6 per hour at Global-Chat (☎ 03-9654 3666), 22 Elizabeth St.

Supplies & Equipment

In the city centre, there's a cluster of outdoor gear shops in and near Little Bourke St, between Elizabeth and Queen Sts. Basic equipment can be hired at Paddy Pallin (☎ 03-9670 4845) and at Bogong Equipment (☎ 03-9600 0599), where the weekly rate for a tent is $40 and for a sleeping bag $30 . No deposit is required.

Places to Stay & Eat

Melbourne has a great range of accommodation, from budget hostels to five-star deluxe hotels. Stop by Tourism Victoria for a list of available options.

Regarded as the gourmet capital of Australia, Melbourne has a huge range of cosmopolitan restaurants and cafes right across the city and suburbs. Lonely Planet's *Victoria*, *Melbourne* and *Out to Eat – Melbourne* guides detail many of the best eating choices for all budgets.

Getting There & Away

Melbourne is reached by the Princes Hwy from destinations along the coast, the Great Western Hwy from Adelaide, and the Hume Hwy from Sydney and Canberra.

Air The state capital is well served by international and domestic flights, which land at Tullamarine airport, 22km north-west of the city centre. (For information on travel between Sydney and destinations outside Australia, see the Getting There & Away chapter.) Both Qantas Airways (☎ 13 1313) and Ansett Australia (☎ 13 1300) have frequent flights to other capital cities, while Impulse Airlines (☎ 13 1381) and Virgin Blue (☎ 13 6789) fly to Melbourne from several state capitals.

Bus Greyhound (☎ 13 2030) and McCafferty's (☎ 13 1499) buses link Melbourne with the other capitals and regional centres, and are much cheaper than air travel. The one-way adult fare from Sydney is $50 for the 12-hour journey.

Train Trains are more expensive, although slightly faster than buses. The Countrylink daily service from Sydney takes nearly 11 hours and costs $96 for an economy fare.

Getting Around

Melbourne's public transport system, the Met, incorporates buses, trains and trams; for timetables and fares call the Met Information Centre (☎ 13 1638), visit The Met Shop, at 103 Elizabeth St (open Monday to Saturday), or consult the excellent public transport Web site (🖳 www.victrip.com.au). The metropolitan area is divided into three zones and the price of tickets depends on which zones you travel in and across. Tickets are available from drivers on buses, machines on trams, at train stations and from newsagents and some other small businesses.

If you're using a car, it's difficult to avoid the City Link, a system of tolled freeways

Phytophthora

Phytophthora cinnamomi, cinnamon fungus, the microscopic scourge of peppermint and stringybark eucalyptuses, grass trees, banksias and bush peas, is doing its worst in Brisbane Ranges and Mornington Peninsula National Parks. It has caused the deaths of many plants in affected areas. Several tracks in both parks have been closed to try to limit the spread of the fungus, which can be dispersed in water and soil. Therefore, keep to the defined walking tracks and help to preserve the native flora.

linking the airport and other freeways west and south of the city. Motorists can buy and install in their vehicles an eTag, which is automatically 'read' each time they pass a checkpoint. Casual users can buy day passes in advance, most conveniently at post offices; for more information call ☎ 13 2629.

To/From the Airport If you're driving, the Tullamarine Fwy runs from the airport almost into the city centre, finishing in North Melbourne. A section of this is now run by City Link as a tollway and fees apply. The regular Skybus (☎ 03-9662 9275) links the airport and the city; the fare is $11.

Brisbane Ranges National Park

In Brisbane Ranges National Park and the adjacent Steiglitz Historic Park, you'll find one of the largest areas of bushland in the Melbourne region, and the opportunity to camp at peaceful bush sites. Rising steeply from the plains about 80km west of Melbourne, the park is particularly important for its native flora and presents brilliant displays of wattle during spring. A web of walking tracks and quiet 4WD trails crosses the 7718-hectare park, making it ideal for bushwalking. The walk described here is a varied and flexible traverse of the park, taking in many of its fine features.

Gold in the Ranges

It's a challenge to the imagination to picture Steiglitz as it was in the 1850s and 1860s when more than 1000 people lived there, lured by the prospect of wealth from gold. In the early years, miners scratched the surface seeking easily exposed reefs; in the 1860s machines enabled the exploitation of deep quartz leads. The town was laid out on a grid pattern and there were shops, a bank, bakery, a church and, of course, hotels. The courthouse (illustrated here) opened in 1875, after the first phase of excitement had died down.

The town revived briefly in the 1890s thanks to new mining techniques, but the resurgence was short-lived. Luckily, the solidly built courthouse survived and was taken over by the then National Parks Service in 1977. Now within Steiglitz Historic Park and superbly restored, it displays historic photographs of Steiglitz and is open on Sunday and public holidays. Two other survivors, the Church of England and Roman Catholic church buildings, are also within the park; the few other original buildings are on private land.

MARTIN HARRIS

In the 1860s gold mining boomed in the area, centred on the town of Steiglitz; although it is now just a handful of cottages, the surrounding creeks and hills bear witness to the feverish search for elusive wealth.

NATURAL HISTORY

The steep eastern escarpment of the Brisbane Ranges marks an ancient line of weakness in the earth's crust. About one million years ago land east of this line collapsed, leaving the country immediately to the west as a plateau. Several streams, notably Anakie and Little Rivers, cut steep-sided valleys through this undulating upland.

More than 600 species of native flora, including several that are rare, are found in the Brisbane Ranges, providing the principal reason for its establishment in 1973. Among the more prominent are golden and black wattles, blackwoods, purple-flowering mint bushes and spiky-leaved hakeas. During springtime these plants brighten the forests of relatively tall stringy barks, peppermints and grass trees, and the more open, drier box-ironbark community.

The park hosts around 170 species of birds, from the small honeyeaters, wrens and fantails of the dense bush, to the impressive peregrine falcon and wedge-tailed eagle among the valley cliffs. There's a good chance you'll see eastern grey kangaroos at dawn and dusk, while rather harsh, guttural grunting sounds from the branches of tall manna gums betray the presence of koalas, which are quite common in the park.

PLANNING

Easily the best time for the Brisbane Ranges is between August and November, when the wild flowers are out in their full glory. The park can become very dry during summer and water is usually scarce.

Firewood is provided for campers (as very large logs) but a stove is preferable. You'll also need enough cash to pay the camping fee (see Permits & Regulations later).

Maps & Books

Vicmap's 1:25,000 *Ingliston* and *Staughton Vale* maps cover the walk described in this section, but do not show the route or camping areas. SR Brookes' 1:50,000 *Brisbane Ranges National Park* topographical map, produced by and for walkers, includes both of the above.

Parks Victoria provides several useful park information sheets, including one for Brisbane Ranges National Park (with a planimetric map showing the walk), another about bush camping at Boar Gully, and others for Steiglitz Historic Park.

Information Sources

Parks Victoria (☎ 03-5284 1230) has an office at Anakie, 500m north of the town on the Geelong road, which is open weekdays. Camping permits can be organised here.

Permits & Regulations

You must obtain a permit to camp in the national park. This gives you permission to camp at all three camping areas along the Brisbane Ranges Traverse (described in this chapter): Old Mill, Little River and Boar Gully. Each has toilets, fireplaces and water. The fee, payable on site, is $8.30 per night for up to six people.

NEAREST TOWNS
Bacchus Marsh

This small, quiet town at the foot of the hills rising up to the Great Dividing Range is bypassed by the Western Fwy. Although it is now close to Melbourne's relentless westward sprawl, it still has the feel of a country town.

Places to Stay & Eat The *Cherry Inn Caravan Park (☎ 03-5367 2775)*, on Main St 1km west of the town centre, has tent sites at $12 for two and cabins for $45. About 1km east of town on Main St is *The Avenue Motel (☎ 03-5367 3766)*, where a double room costs $65.

Bacchus Marsh has its fair share of takeaway food places and pubs serving counter meals. *Penny's Mediterranean Restaurant (☎ 03-5367 5693)*, on Main St, serves simple lunches and Devonshire teas. Main St also has a *supermarket* and good *bakery*, as well as another *supermarket*, open 24 hours daily, in the nearby shopping centre. Don't miss the *fruit and vegetable stalls* along Memorial Drive, the eastern approach to Bacchus Marsh, for excellent and cheap local produce.

Getting There & Away Bacchus Marsh is 50km west of Melbourne via the Western Fwy and the Bacchus Marsh exit.

Anakie

This is the closest source of supplies to the park. The *One Stop Shop* is open daily for supplies (including stove fuel), car fuel and takeaway food; it has a phone. Anakie is on the Geelong–Ballan road (C141), 28km north of Geelong and 33km south of Ballan.

Steiglitz

Not quite a ghost town, Steiglitz is home to a handful of people and the *Peppercorn Place Cafe (☎ 03-5281 9229)*, open daily from 10 am to 6 pm for damper, toasted sandwiches, pumpkin soup, Devonshire teas and drinks. The proprietor has assembled a mass of information about the history of Steiglitz and environs for patrons to browse. For a picnic, stop at the Bert Boardman recreation reserve, about 500m south-east of Steiglitz, named for the prime mover behind the creation of Steiglitz Historic Park (see the boxed text 'What's in a Name?' later in this chapter).

Getting There & Away Steiglitz is on the Geelong–Meredith road (C142), which runs parallel to the Midland Hwy (A300); it is 8km north of Maude.

Brisbane Ranges Traverse

Distance	39km
Duration	3 days
Standard	medium
Start	Steiglitz
Finish	Boar Gully camping ground
Nearest Towns	Bacchus Marsh, Steiglitz, Anakie
Public Transport	no

Summary A unique opportunity for an extended walk close to Melbourne, starting at historic Steiglitz and passing through bushland brilliantly coloured with spring wild flowers.

Part of this three-day walk (the third day is very short) is along walking tracks specially

MELBOURNE REGION

developed to provide a long-distance trail through the park. Elsewhere, the walk follows park management tracks, many closed to public vehicles, and public roads for relatively short distances. Orange arrowheads are the markers to look for, usually in line of sight. There's quite a lot of climbing in and out of valleys but individual ascents, although typically steep, are never long.

The duration is governed by the location of camping grounds, the only places where you can be certain of finding water and fireplaces. Fit walkers should be able to complete this walk in two days; three days allows plenty of time for relaxation. If organising car transport at the start and finish is a problem, you could consider doing out-and-back walks from either Boar Gully or Little River camping grounds.

GETTING TO/FROM THE WALK

The walk finishes at the Boar Gully camping ground, in the north of the park. Turn off the Geelong–Ballan road at Mt Wallace, 22km north of Anakie, along a sealed road signposted 'Bacchus Marsh 25' and 'Brisbane Ranges'; make a right turn after 5km along the gravel Camp Track and the camping ground is 250m farther on.

THE WALK
Day 1: Steiglitz to Old Mill Camping Ground

3½–4 hours, 12km

From the front of the courthouse, head southwest along Stawell St, passing Maxwell, Barry and Pohlman Sts – now little more than names. Just past Wrixon St, continue ahead briefly, then follow Deadmans Track across **Sutherland Creek**. The track crosses a couple of low spurs, then you rock hop through a small gorge. Follow the track over another small spur on the southern side of the creek; cross it and climb diagonally up the side of the spur and generally northwards for about 1.6km to the road between Meredith and Steiglitz.

Cross directly and follow gravel Hut Rd down to the Crossing picnic area. From the car park, bear left along Box Track and almost immediately left again, steeply up the stony track. After about 12 minutes, turn right along a walking track that leads through to Grahams Creek Rd. Turn right for the short distance to Grahams Creek picnic area (1½ hours from Steiglitz).

Cross the causeway, go on about 75m to Hazel Track and turn left. The track takes you up a very pleasant, shallow valley. Pass a junction with Back Track then bear right along a walking track. This gains some height above the valley on the left, parallels an old fence for several hundred metres and then reaches a smallish clearing. Bear right here and go up and over to a shallow gully and a junction; continue on Banksia Track, passing Loggers Track on the right.

About 500m farther on, turn right along a foot track to shortly cross a gravel road (Lease Rd) and continue on a walking track. This soon takes you down to a boardwalk across swampy Yankee Gully, then up, across a fire trail and on, past Elise Reef Track on the right, to Bracken Track. Here, turn right. Not long afterwards you cross New Year Track and follow an old fire trail, soon running parallel to Durdidwarrah Rd, for about 200m. Cross the gravel road and follow a fire trail, also parallel to the road, for about 100m, then bear left along a track. This descends for almost 1km to *Old Mill Camping Ground* (two hours from Grahams Creek). The toilet and water tank are about 50m southwards uphill.

Day 2: Old Mill Camping Ground to Little River

4½ hours, 17km

Set out along the 4WD trail leading east from the creek crossing to soon pass Pine Track on the right. About 250m farther on, turn right along Geebung Track. This track climbs gently up a broad ridge. About 40 minutes from Old Mill, bear right along a minor fire trail that leads south for 1.3km to Sawpit Gully Rd. Turn left here and continue for a short distance to the Geelong–Ballan road (about 1½ hours from Old Mill).

Walk south-east beside the road for 1km then turn off along a 4WD track; swing left at a junction 100m on, then pass a barrier and Redbeak Track on the right. Continue

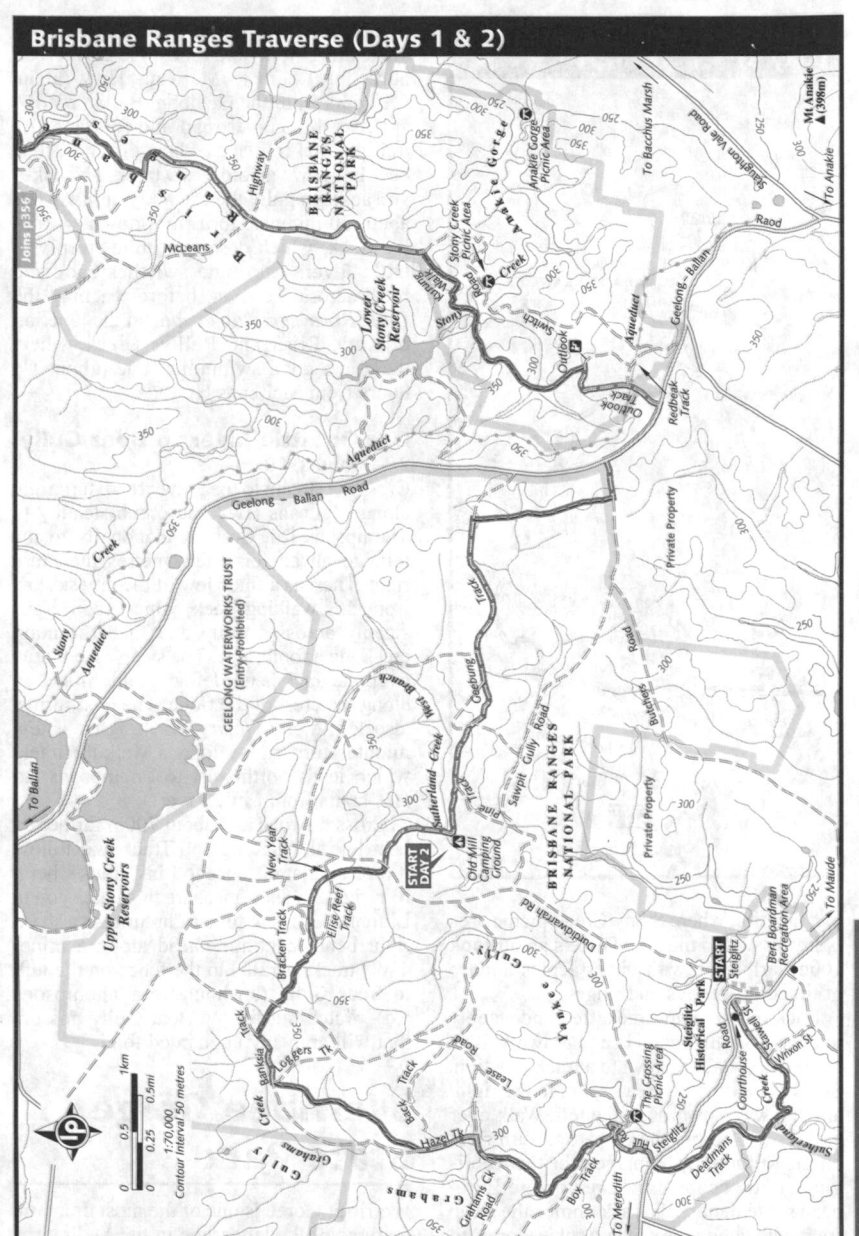

Brisbane Ranges Traverse (Days 1 & 2)

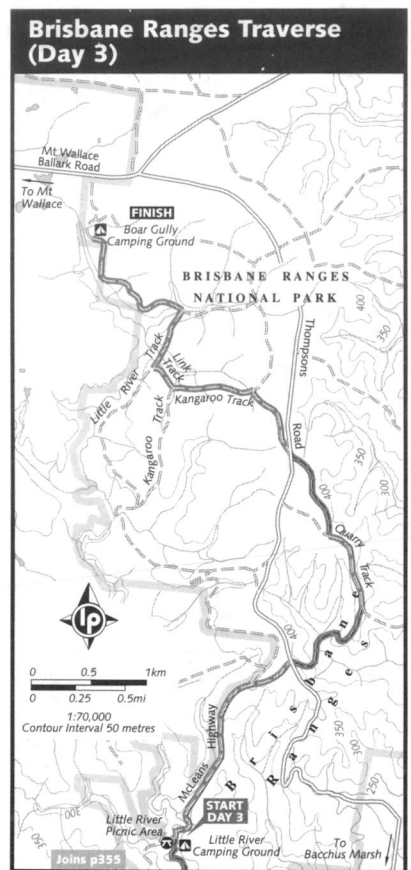

Brisbane Ranges Traverse (Day 3)

Switch Rd. Turn left at this point (leaving the Kurung Walk) and follow the gravel road north for 1.8km to McLeans Hwy (about 1½ hours from the Geelong–Ballan road).

Cross this gravel road and follow a fire trail parallel to it for a short distance, then bear left down an old 4WD track. This takes you across a gully then steadily uphill. After about 20 minutes, turn right down a walking track, which descends quite steeply to **Little River**. The route switches back and forth across the river, before reaching the *Little River camping ground* at the junction of Little River and Reillys Creek, where there is a good swimming hole (about 1½ hours from McLeans Hwy).

Day 3: Little River to Boar Gully
2½–3 hours, 10km

Cross the stream to the gravel road, turn right along McLeans Hwy and climb steadily to Thompsons Rd. Cross it diagonally to the left, go ahead for a few metres then turn right. There is a fine view of the city skyline from this walking track, which soon drops steeply across a gully and then the main creek via a footbridge. The steep ascent now over, the track bends left at a minor junction along the crest of the ridge. The next turn is also left, along Quarry Track. After a few minutes turn right along a walking track, which leads north-west to Thompsons Rd (1½ hours from Little River).

Cross the road and about 700m farther on bear left along Kangaroo Track and follow it for a similar distance to Link Track – here, turn right. In short measure this takes you to Little River Track for a right turn. At a sharp right bend, continue ahead along a minor 4WD track, parallel to the fence on the left, to **Boar Gully** (an hour from Thompsons Rd). Watch out for the Boar Gully possum that will grab any unguarded food.

Werribee Gorge State Park

to a junction where Stony Creek picnic area is signposted to the left. There's an **outlook** 100m farther on with views across a maze of timbered valleys and ridges.

Back on the main track, descend steeply to cross a small creek via a boardwalk, then go over a spur and down to a track junction. Stony Creek picnic area is 50m to the right, and the way onwards to the left. Walk over an old wall across the creek and turn right on the **Kurung Walk**, named for the Aborigines who occupied the area before European settlement. This track climbs the steep spur, with good views over Anakie Gorge, to

Werribee Gorge is one of the most dramatic features of the landscape in the Melbourne region, a deep incision through rocks of complex and ancient lineage. Although the geological importance of the gorge was recognised early in the 20th century it wasn't until 1975 that the state park was created, taking in the gorge and the surrounding bushland. The park, 61km west of Melbourne, now covers 443 hectares.

Skilfully built walking tracks and the remains of a water race, built in 1928 to take water to the town of Bacchus Marsh, make the gorge accessible to walkers. On warm days you can take a refreshing dip in one of the pools in the gorge.

NATURAL HISTORY

The oldest rocks exposed in the gorge are sediments deposited in a sea bed about 450 million years ago. These were squashed and bent by upheavals in the earth's crust and later invaded by shafts of granitic material from inside the earth. South-eastern Australia was frozen under a vast ice sheet about 250 million years ago; evidence of this in Victoria was first found in Werribee Gorge where rocks bear the scratches caused by movement of the glaciers. Much later, about four to six million years ago, lava from nearby volcanoes spread across the surrounding lands. Most recently, more unrest along a fault in the earth's crust opened the way for the Werribee River to slice through.

Along the river you'll find manna gums, with smooth grey-white bark – look out for koalas. Grey box, red stringybark and white cypress pine cling to the steep rocky slopes above. The cliffs provide ideal nesting sites for wedge-tailed eagles, unmistakable with their 2m wing spans, and peregrine falcons, most likely to be seen during the August to November breeding season.

PLANNING

The spring display of wild flowers, especially wattles, makes this the best season for this park; in early summer, the pools in the gorge are just right for refreshing swims. Footwear with good tread is essential for rock hopping and scrambling through the gorge. Carry all the drinking water you'll need – the river water can't be trusted.

Maps & Books

Meridian Productions' *Lerderderg & Werribee Gorges* map folder has background information and a 1:35,000 topographical map showing the walking tracks and access to the park. The Vicmap 1:25,000 *Ingliston* sheet covers the Werribee Gorge area but is way out of date.

Jack's Track Notes: Day Walks in Werribee Gorge by Jack Myers is a rich source of information about the whole district; it's available from the newsagent in Bacchus Marsh.

Parks Victoria provides a park notes map for Werribee Gorge State Park, with brief notes and a good map, but it's not easy to track down – try the Anakie office (see Information Sources in the introduction to the Brisbane Ranges National Park).

Regulations

You are not permitted to camp or light fires in the park.

NEAREST TOWN

For a description of accommodation and other services in Bacchus Marsh, see Nearest Towns in the introduction to the Brisbane Ranges National Park.

Werribee Gorge

Distance	10km
Duration	3½–4 hours
Standard	medium
Start/Finish	Quarry car park
Nearest Town	Bacchus Marsh
Public Transport	no

Summary Variety is the keynote of this very scenic walk, with sections of eucalyptus woodland, views of farm paddocks and a long rock hop through the sheer-walled Werribee Gorge.

The highlight of this walk is the rock hop and scramble through the gorge, a distance of roughly 1.5km. Several sections of the walking track are separated by small bluffs. It's necessary to negotiate some cliffs where there are good hand and footholds, but you do need to have confidence in what you're doing. The cliffs are very unstable and rock falls are fairly common, especially during and immediately after wet weather. The rocks can be very slippery after rain.

The route down to and up from the gorge is generally via well-defined tracks – follow the orange arrowheads. Although the time taken for this walk indicates that it's just a half-day outing, an hour or three can easily be added on a warm day for swims in the gorge pools. If you're really pressed for time, the Short Circuit walk leads down to the lower end of the gorge.

GETTING TO/FROM THE WALK

Leave the Western Fwy via the Pentland Hills Rd exit, 5km west of Bacchus Marsh, and turn right at a T-junction along the Pentland Hills Rd, which goes under the freeway then parallels it for about 2km to another underpass. Turn left along sealed Myers Rd and continue steeply downhill past the park entrance to the Quarry car park (6km from the freeway).

THE WALK

Standing at the information shelter near the car park, you'll see the first marker on the wall of the toilets. The walking track climbs through an old quarry to a minor vehicle track; turn right and continue to the bus parking area. Go along the sealed road for about 25m and then turn left through a small gate in the fence. Follow the clearly defined track through open woodland, past the turn-off to the Short Circuit walk and on to the **Eastern Lookout**, about 100m to the right. This lookout gives expansive views to the north and east, where Melbourne may be visible on a clear day. Back on the main track, continue to a T-junction and turn left. Roughly 1km from Eastern Lookout, you come to **Western Lookout**, from which the contrast between cleared land and the bush is particularly striking.

On the nearby rocky knoll, don't be tempted to descend to the right but continue down the very narrow spur. Swing left, well

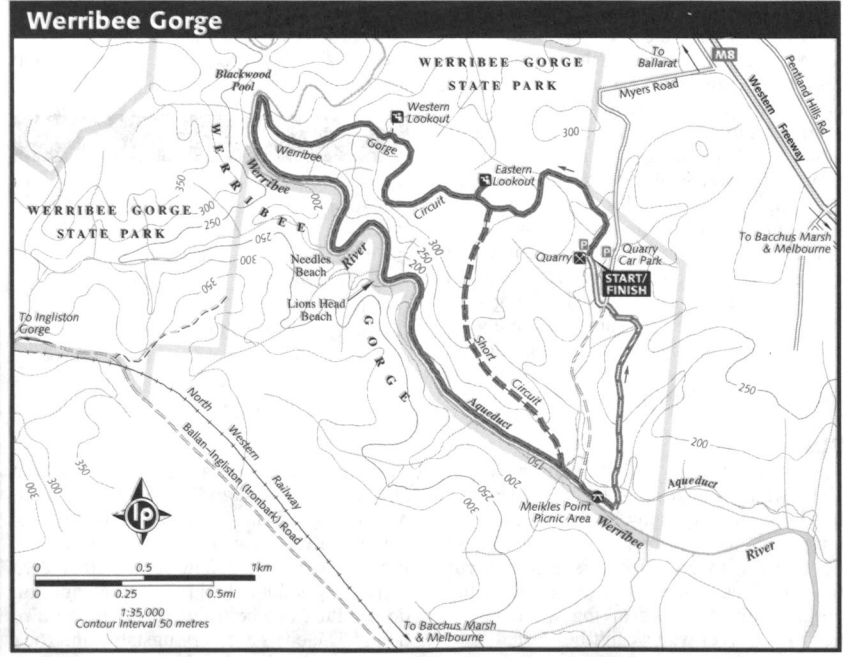

Werribee Gorge

down, to descend gradually to Werribee River and **Blackwood Pool** (about one hour from the start).

Walk along the river bank, following a track and narrow rock ledges. After about 15 minutes you come to **Needles Beach**, then there's a low bluff to be negotiated. A track leads on to **Lion's Head Beach**, beyond which is a trickier scramble round jutting cliffs – the way is clear enough as a worn route over the rocks. After that, it's plain sailing along the track beside the old water channel. About 1km farther on, pass the Short Circuit walk turn-off to the left and bear right down some steps to Meikles Point picnic area (45 minutes from Needles Beach). Go through to the far end of the area, then left up some steps, past the toilets and follow the marked track steeply up a spur. Bear left on the crest, then left again to cross a gully and continue on to an old hut at a sharp bend on the road; the car park is a little farther on (30 minutes from the river).

Macedon Ranges

From higher points around Melbourne the Macedon Ranges dominate the north-western skyline. Right on the Great Dividing Range, the central part of the range forms a horse-shoe around the Turitable Creek system and falls largely within the Macedon Regional Park. The dominant features of the park are Mt Macedon and Camels Hump, both topping the 1000m mark – the highest summits within 50km of Melbourne. Tall messmate (eucalyptus) forest covers the lower and middle slopes, while snow gum woodlands cling to the higher ground. The Macedon Ranges Walking Trail, a round trip from Macedon train station, takes in major features of the park. The walk described here is the core of this route, from near the town of Mt Macedon and back.

HISTORY

The forests on the mountain were plundered for timber during the early decades of settlement around Melbourne, so much so that in the 1870s the government established a

nursery at the town of Macedon to promote reforestation of the ranges. Great swathes of radiata pine were planted, although these days they're being largely replaced with indigenous species. Mt Macedon became a fashionable retreat for wealthy Melbourne families during the late 19th century, and to some extent still plays that role.

In 1935 William Cameron, a Melbourne businessman and Mt Macedon resident, was present at the dedication of a huge cross that he'd had built near the summit of Mt Macedon as a memorial to servicemen killed during WWI. Cameron, whose son had died during the war, also had the road to the cross built and gardens planted, mainly with exotic trees and shrubs. The cross was damaged by lightning in 1975, and the devastating bushfires that ravaged Mt Macedon on Ash Wednesday 1983 spared neither the cross nor the gardens. The cross was demolished in 1995 and rebuilt in a style faithful to the original by a leading Melbourne construction company.

PLANNING

This is a good summer walk through country mostly above 600m. Even so, it can be cold on Macedon in midsummer; when the walk was researched for this book, a fleece jacket and hat were very welcome. You'll need to carry water as there are no reliable water sources along the way.

The whole walk can be done in a long day from Melbourne; otherwise it's possible to stay locally overnight (although camping isn't permitted in the regional park).

Maps

Royal Australian Survey Corps' 1:50,000 *Lancefield* topographical map covers the walk but does not show all the walking tracks. Parks Victoria provides a *Walking Trail* brochure with a detailed topographical map showing the route of the walk and adequate track notes. The distance of the walk is misleadingly given as 29.1km. This is actually the total distance of the round walk from Macedon train station via Camels Hump, Clyde Track and Alton Rd (20.4km), plus the alternative and preferable route

What's in a Name?

Within the parks featured in this chapter are places bearing Aboriginal names (Werribee, Dandenong), British names (Brisbane, Gellibrand) and others which don't seem to fit either tradition.

The Macedon Ranges are a good example of the last, their title carrying echoes of the Balkans. Explorer Major Thomas Mitchell, who left his mark on Victoria in many places, was responsible. He climbed the ranges in 1836 hoping to see Port Phillip Bay, and used his knowledge of Greek history to name the mountain in honour of Philip of Macedon, who unified Macedonia in the southern Balkans and the Greek city-states into a mighty empire in the 4th century BC.

Then there's Sanatorium Lake, also in the Macedon Ranges. Tuberculosis was a common affliction in the late 19th century, the treatment for which was confinement to an institution far from the pestilent atmosphere of Melbourne. A sanatorium, or convalescent hospital, was established south of Mt Towrong in 1899, but burnt down in 1910.

Steiglitz Historic Park, next to Brisbane Ranges National Park, commemorates Charles Augustus von Steiglitz, a member of a noted German family who owned property in the area, including the site of the mining town.

Dandenong is believed to come from an Aboriginal word *banyenong* (meaning 'burning' and 'the past'), possibly of the Wurundjeri people, who visited the ranges in summer to collect plants for tools, medicines and food.

from Camels Hump to Mt Macedon town via Sanatorium Lake and Mt Towrong (8.7km). There are also Park Victoria notes for the regional park as a whole and for the Sanatorium Lake Eco Trail, available from the Parks Victoria office in Macedon.

Information Sources

The nearest visitor centre is in the town of Woodend (☎ 03-5427 2033), about 12km north-west of the Mt Macedon turn-off via the Calder Fwy. The Macedon Ranges Information Service (☎ 1800 244 711) offers advice and help with accommodation. It's open weekdays. Parks Victoria has an office in Macedon (see Nearest Towns).

NEAREST TOWNS
Mt Macedon

This small town, 65km from Melbourne via Calder Fwy, is overlooked by the Macedon and Towrong mountains. *Mount Macedon Trading Post and General Store*, on Mt Macedon Rd, is open daily for snacks, drinks and local wines. There are also a couple of *tearooms* and the more formal *Mountain Inn Hotel (☎ 03-5426 1755, 351 Mt Macedon Rd)* for accommodation and reasonable bar meals.

Macedon

Macedon lies at the foot of the Macedon Ranges. Parks Victoria has an office (☎ 03-5426 1866) in Nursery Rd, open weekdays.

Places to Stay & Eat On the corner of McBean Ave and Old Calder Hwy, *Macedon Caravan Park (☎ 03-5426 1528)* has plenty of well-grassed tent sites for $13, on-site vans for $33 for two people and en suite cabins from $47. A barbecue picnic shelter serves as a basic campers' kitchen.

Moran's Macedon Family Hotel (☎ 03-5426 1231), on Smith St, serves lunch and dinner in its bistro from Monday to Saturday (lunch only on Sunday); steaks are $17 and pasta $13. For self-caterers, Macedon has a small *supermarket*, *butcher* and *baker*.

Getting There & Away Macedon is 60km from Melbourne via the Calder Fwy; use either the Mt Macedon exit and signposted streets to reach the town, or the Macedon exit 4km farther north.

The V/Line train service (☎ 13 6196) to Kyneton stops at Macedon several times daily, more frequently on weekdays than on weekends. The journey takes an hour and costs $15 ($10.60 during off-peak times).

Macedon Ranges Trail Highlight

Distance	18.4km
Duration	5½–6 hours
Standard	medium
Start/Finish	Douglas Rd car park
Nearest Towns	Mt Macedon, Macedon
Public Transport	no

Summary A walk steeped in history, visiting sites associated with European exploration and settlement, and a memorial to WWI soldiers.

This walk starts and finishes nearly 2km west of the town of Mt Macedon where the Macedon Ranges Walking Trail crosses a road, and so leaves out the least interesting section of the official trail (from Macedon train station). From Camels Hump, at 1011m about 10m higher than Mt Macedon, the route to Mt Macedon town is via Sanatorium Lake and Mt Towrong (804m), rather than following the other official route via minor roads. The climb to Mt Macedon is steep but the walking track is generally well graded. The walking tracks and fire trails are well signposted, except between Mt Towrong and Mt Macedon town, although the route is easy enough to follow with the help of the Parks Victoria map.

GETTING TO/FROM THE WALK

From Mt Macedon township drive 1.7km westwards along Douglas Rd to a small parking area about 150m west of the end of the sealed road.

If you arrive by train at Macedon train station, you can walk to the trailhead, one hour and 3.4km away. Head east from the station briefly then turn left along Smith St and follow it north past Nursery Rd (the Parks Victoria office is a short distance along) to the site of the old scouts camp. Continue from here along a gravel fire trail towards Memorial Cross (as signposted); Bawden Rd is 1km away.

THE WALK

Climb the steps from the road near the Douglas Rd car park; the track soon begins the as-cent in a series of fairly long zigzags. Pass the turn-off to Clyde Track and Alton Rd (Hoods Track); higher up, the track climbs steeply through some tree ferns. A short side track leads to a scenic view; soon snow gums replace the tall forest – a sign that the top is near. After about 45 minutes, you reach the wide sealed path midway between the car park at Harbison picnic ground (near Mt Macedon summit) and the **Memorial Cross**, and close to **Major Mitchell Lookout**. Both the cross and the lookout are well worth visiting, especially for the views; there's also the **memorial** to the *Kurana* (a plane that crashed on the mountain in 1948), 200m east of the sealed path and near the car park.

To continue, follow the foot track from the south-western corner of the car park. After about five minutes, a short track leads left to **Western Lookout** for fine views of the town of Woodend and the countryside southwards. Walk north along the edge of the escarpment for a short distance and return to the main track. It contours the forested slope, past the track to Cameron picnic ground, and several minutes later crosses a fire trail.

About 50 minutes from Mt Macedon, turn right at a junction and walk up a 4WD track to McGregors picnic ground. Skirt its northern edge and follow a signposted track back into the forest. In a few minutes, turn right at a junction up to a car park, from where Camels Hump Track leads up to the **summit lookout** (30 minutes from McGregors). A topograph identifies surrounding features. From another lookout nearby there are better views to the south-west.

Return to the car park and go back down to the track junction encountered earlier and head towards Days picnic ground. This track skirts the Hump and leads up to Mt Macedon road; cross it diagonally left to a walking track signposted to Days picnic ground and Sanatorium Lake (see the boxed text 'What's in a Name?'). Continue to this spacious picnic ground and bear right, past the toilets and information board, across the access road and head towards the start of a walking track, signposted to Sanatorium Lake. Keep to the walking track for about

Macedon Ranges Trail Highlight

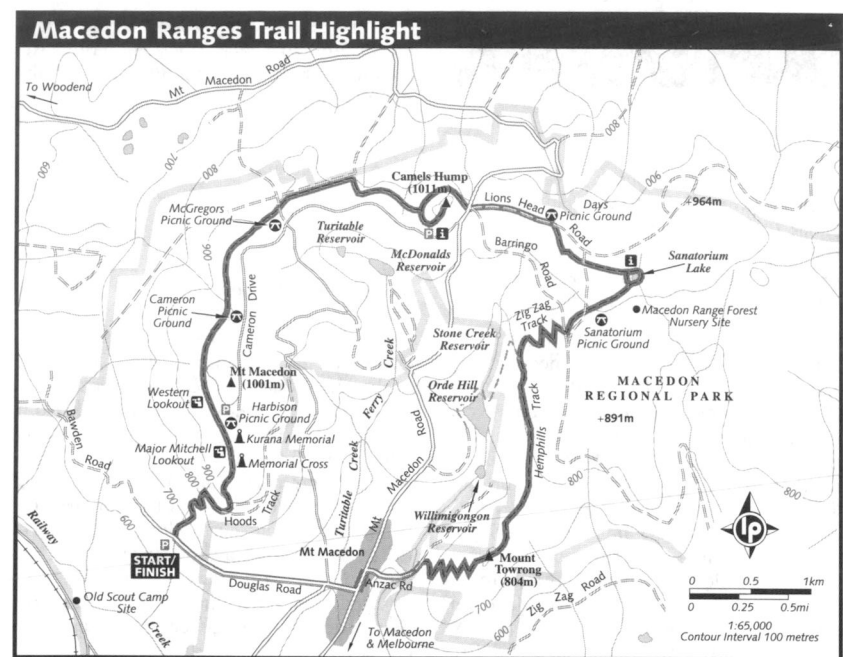

500m and bear left to the **lake** (where the track to the right goes to the picnic ground), a similar distance farther on. You could spend quite some time here reading the detailed information about the natural and human history of the area, and wandering around the hauntingly beautiful lake.

To continue, walk towards Sanatorium picnic ground, passing a short side track to the site of the old Macedon Range Forest Nursery, marked now by huge rhododendron bushes. At the picnic ground, walk down the gravel access road to Barringo Rd and cross it diagonally left to Zig Zag Track, an aptly named fire trail which descends to a junction with Hemphills Track. Follow this southwards to a broad saddle (about 50 minutes from the lake).

Leave this track to follow the signposted Mt Towrong walking track, which climbs steadily to the **summit** with a large cairn and limited outlook. The descent starts straight away and soon you emerge into open ground with fine views of Mt Macedon (town and peak). The rocky track descends steeply to a fire trail – turn left here and continue down, across Willimigongon Creek and up to Mt Macedon Rd (about 40 minutes from Mt Towrong). To return to the start, walk down the road for 150m to Douglas Rd; the car park is 1.7km along.

Woodlands Historic Park

The threshold of Melbourne's busy international airport seems an unlikely location for a walk, but Woodlands Historic Park, 2km to the north, provides just that. The gently undulating grasslands and open river red gum woodland around Moonee Ponds Creek, culminating in Gellibrand Hill (204m) and the historic Woodlands homestead, provide the setting for an easy walk along good tracks. Among the red gums are some magnificent specimens more than 200 years old.

HISTORY

People of the Woiworung Aboriginal tribe occupied the area around Moonee Ponds Creek and Gellibrand Hill. They used the bark of the river red gums to build shelters and canoes and to fashion small shields; several trees still bear witness to their skilful use of natural resources.

Woodlands homestead is a rare and nationally important example of an 1840s kit house, prefabricated in Britain. In 1843 William Greene arrived in Melbourne from Ireland with his large family. He purchased about 270 hectares of land around Moonee Ponds Creek, becoming the first European settler in the area. The timber homestead was shipped to Melbourne and erected, and sheep and cattle put to graze. The property changed hands several times and the homestead was extended and altered, but many of the original features survived intact.

In 1977 the property was purchased and taken over by the then National Parks Service. The homestead has since been restored inside and out, and excellent displays describe its history. During the 1980s, 400 hectares in the southern section of the park were fenced to provide a protected habitat for the threatened eastern barred bandicoot. This area, known as the Back Paddock, is also being managed to restore the open woodland and grassland as it would have been before European settlement. Elsewhere in the park are the ruins of two other homesteads, built in the 1860s and 1870s: Dundonald near Gellibrand Hill, and Cumberland near the southern boundary.

PLANNING

Just about any time of the year is suitable for walking in Woodlands, although the grasslands do become rather dry during summer. The Somerton Rd car park is open from 8.30 am to 4.30 pm daily (6 pm weekends and public holidays). Woodlands homestead is open to the public from noon to 4 pm on Wednesday, weekends and public holidays,

and guided tours are provided by members of the Friends of Woodlands Historic Park (☎ 03-9304 2788).

Maps & Books

The Friends' leaflet for the park has a better map than that on the Parks Victoria heritage notes sheet. See also the Department of Crown Lands and Survey 1:25,000 *Keilor* and *Broadmeadows* maps.

Red Gums & Riders by Jane Lennon, describing the fascinating history of the area within the park, is available at the homestead.

NEAREST TOWN

The closest suburb to Woodlands is Greenvale, about 3km to the east. Drive east along Somerton Rd for 2.5km, then south along Mickleham Rd for 500m to a small shopping centre where you'll find a *milk bar*, *fish and chip shop* and *supermarket*.

The Somerton Rd picnic area has free electric barbecues, picnic tables and toilets.

Gellibrand Hill

Distance	10km
Duration	3–3½ hours
Standard	easy
Start/Finish	Somerton Rd picnic area
Nearest Town	Greenvale
Public Transport	yes

Summary An easy walk featuring magnificent river red gums, a historic homestead dating from the 1840s, and eastern grey kangaroos, all close to Melbourne's international airport.

This easy walk takes in the major features of the park – Woodlands homestead, red gum woodlands, Gellibrand Hill and the Back Paddock. It starts and finishes at the Somerton Rd picnic area. If you diverge from the route described here, be sure to find the gates in and out of the Back Paddock – the high fence is electrified to keep out predators.

GETTING TO/FROM THE WALK

Woodlands is 22km from the city centre via the Tullamarine Fwy and Sunbury, Oaklands and Somerton Rds (see Getting Around at the

MELBOURNE REGION

beginning of the chapter for information on eTags for tollways). The walk starts and finishes at the picnic area adjacent to Somerton Rd, which borders the park to the north.

THE WALK

From the information shelter on the southern side of the picnic area, cross the bridge over Moonee Ponds Creek and follow the track to the right signposted to Woodlands homestead. Go through a gate along a wide track lined with river red gums, bear right at an intersection, then left beside a grove of these big trees and continue to the homestead (25 minutes from the picnic area).

Leave the homestead from the front garden by the path that bends around left through a small gate, past the toilets on the left and through another gate. Cross a gravel road and follow a track across low grassy **Woodlands Hill**. Among the many features of the wide view from here is Mt Macedon to the north.

Head eastwards down a vehicle track for about 300m (passing a sign pointing left to the picnic area). At a vague junction turn right and go through a gate, then right again at a track junction, towards Gellibrand Hill. This is Boundary Track, which leads south then east between the eucalyptus plantation on the left and Back Paddock on the right. About 500m after turning east, the buildings of the former Greenvale geriatric hospital can be seen through the trees to the left. The track dips then climbs to a junction. Turn right through a tall gate into Back Paddock and continue up a wide track to the summit of **Gellibrand Hill**, with its air navigation installation and a topograph to pinpoint the features in the panoramic view (1¼ hours from the homestead). The ruins of **Dundonald homestead** are beyond the fence about 200m to the east.

Drop down from the summit westwards and take the first turn to the left along a gravel track. Turn right, descending gradually; pass

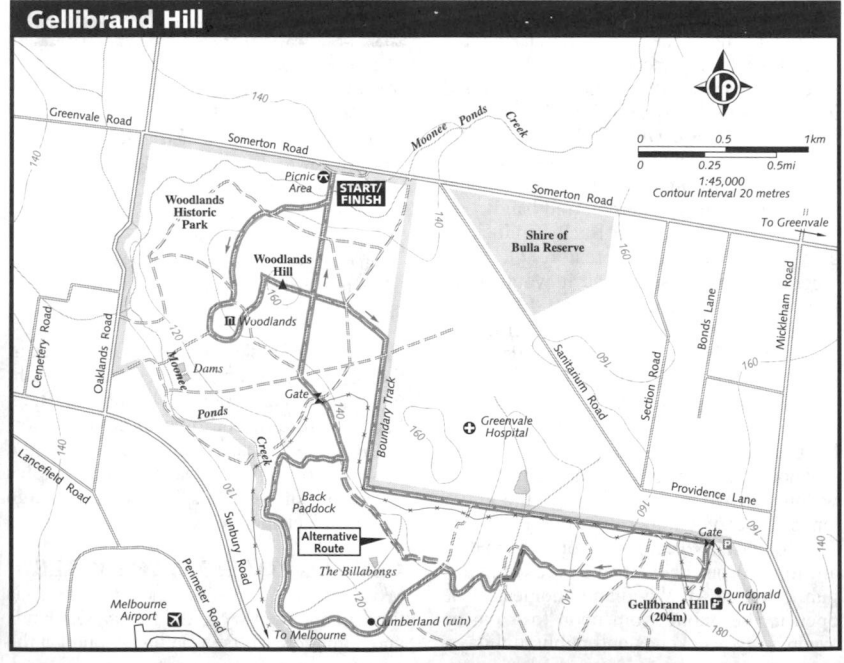

a junction on the right and continue in the direction of the homestead and Somerton Rd. The track loses more height and bends to the left to parallel a small creek, then crosses it and winds round a low hill on the right. At the next junction, you have a choice. If you go left, you'll pass the **Cumberland homestead** ruins and the **Billabongs**, following the track generally westwards, then north, close to Moonee Ponds Creek, and east to a track junction – turn left and go on to the Back Paddock gate. Alternatively, continue straight on for about 1.3km to an information shelter and the Back Paddock gate.

Head for Somerton Rd past one of the most imposing red gums in the entire park. Cross a gravel road, then climb over a stile at the gateway and continue straight ahead along a mown track. Cross another road, pass through a small gateway and go down to the picnic area (about 1¼ hours from Gellibrand Hill).

Dandenong Ranges National Park

The Dandenong Ranges have been a place of escape since the late 1860s for Melburnians drawn to the magnificent forests of towering eucalyptuses and luxuriant fern gullies, only 35km east of the city. Despite vigorous exploitation of the forests for timber until the 1930s, and ever-spreading suburbia, relatively large tracts of bushland have survived. Five areas make up the 3215-hectare Dandenong Ranges National Park, established in 1987. Each of these areas caters for walkers with varied opportunities for short strolls or longer outings. The walk described in detail is in beautiful Sherbrooke Forest, on the southern slopes.

NATURAL HISTORY

The Dandenong Ranges are mainly volcanic in origin, the result of ancient sub-surface eruptions of lava exposed by the removal of overlying sedimentary material.

The upper southern and eastern slopes support open forest of mountain ash up to

100m high, and cool temperate rainforest of sassafras, tree ferns and kangaroo ferns in deep gullies. Open eucalyptus forest, made up mainly of box and stringybark, clothes the more exposed drier northern and western slopes of the park.

The superb lyrebird is the most treasured of the 130 species of birds known in the park. Although they're difficult to spot in the dense undergrowth, you'll almost certainly hear their enthralling concerts – mimicking several birds in an unbroken song, usually punctuated by unbirdlike sounds reminiscent of squeaking doors and rasping chain saws. It's more likely you'll see crimson rosellas, raucous sulphur-crested cockatoos and eastern whipbirds.

PLANNING

It's not often too hot or too cold for comfortable walking in the Dandenongs, although spring and early summer are the best times. There's a kiosk about halfway along the walk described, so you won't need to carry refreshments.

Maps & Books

The Vicmap 1:25,000 *Lysterfield* map covers the area of the walk. Better, though, is the Parks Victoria park notes sheet (with map) for Sherbrooke. *Sherbrooke Forest* by the Friends of Sherbrooke Forest is an excellent little book with background on the forest and its plant communities, and a detailed plant identification guide.

Information Sources

Park notes and other information on Dandenong Ranges National Park are available from the Parks Victoria office (☎ 03-9758 1342), near the Ferntree Gully picnic ground, Upper Ferntree Gully, or the more accessible Dandenong Ranges & Knox Visitor Information Centre (☎ 03-9758 7522), 1211 Burwood Hwy, Upper Ferntree Gully, which is open daily.

NEAREST TOWN

Dandenong Ranges & Knox Visitor Information Centre (see Information Sources) can provide a list of local accommodation – the

Dandenong Ranges are well supplied with B&Bs and self-contained cottages.

Belgrave

The walk starts and finishes in this bustling outer suburb. In the shopping centre along Main St, just west of the train station, are *hot bread shops*, *takeaway food outlets*, a *fish and chip shop* and *cafes*. The *Puffing Billy Cafe* along here serves eat-in or takeaway hot food and drinks. In a quieter setting, a short distance east of the train station in Bayview Rd, is the *Grapevine Café* (☎ 03-9754 1004), open for coffee, cakes and lunch.

Getting There & Away Belgrave is about 35km east of Melbourne via the Burwood Hwy. To park the car, drive through the Main St shopping centre and across the bridge to the car park, just ahead on the left.

Belgrave train station (Metcard Zone 3) is at the end of the Belgrave railway line; the journey from the city takes one hour and 10 minutes.

Sherbrooke Forest

Distance	9km
Duration	3½–4 hours
Standard	easy-medium
Start/Finish	Belgrave train station
Nearest Town	Belgrave
Public Transport	yes

Summary Good walking tracks through magnificent towering mountain ash forest and luxuriant fern gullies, the haunt of the elusive lyrebird.

The Sherbrooke section of the national park contains probably the finest mountain ash forest and the most luxuriant fern gullies in the Dandenongs. The walk includes a climb of nearly 300m from Belgrave, hence the grading, but the tracks are well designed and it's rarely very steep. For many people, Belgrave is synonymous with Puffing Billy (☎ 03-9757 0710), one of the world's best preserved steam railway lines. It runs daily from Belgrave to Gembrook, a distance of around 25km.

THE WALK

To avoid crossing a busy road from the train station platform, follow the footpath towards the **Puffing Billy train station**, but go up and round to the right just before reaching it. Walk past the car park to Old Monbulk Rd and follow it across Clematis Creek and steeply up, over the Puffing Billy line and round to the right, along the gravel road to the park entrance. Head uphill along Coles Ridge Track, through magnificent mountain ash forest towards Grants picnic ground. The broad fire trail climbs comfortably to a sealed road with a picnic area close by. A little way along the road, turn right along a sealed path – the **Margaret Lester Walk**, Victoria's first bushland track for people with disabilities. Several illustrated sign boards describe aspects of local history. The walk brings you to the *Sherbrooke Forest Kiosk* (one hour from Belgrave), open from 9 am to around 5.30 pm daily, where you can buy a range of snacks, drinks (ginger beer

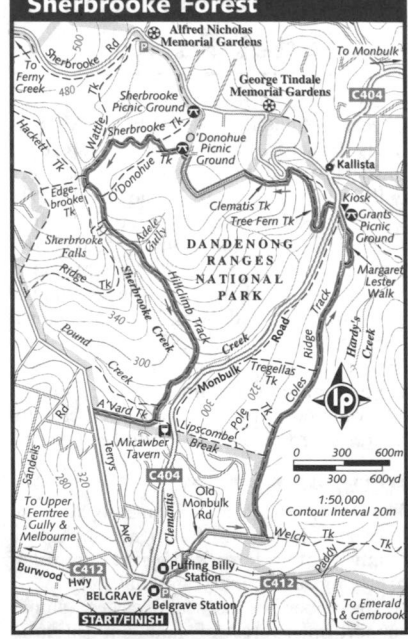

Sherbrooke Forest

connoisseurs shouldn't miss the Olde Stoney, brewed in Grafton, New South Wales) and light meals.

Cross the road from the kiosk and bear left along Tree Fern Track, which drops down across **Clematis Creek** through luxuriant tree ferns. Follow the creek upstream and turn left along Clematis Track, which climbs quite steeply to a gravel road (30 minutes from the kiosk). Turn left and walk past private houses on the right to O'Donohue picnic ground. Either go left round the edge of the picnic ground to a track on the other side, or along a well-worn track round the outside of the fenced-off area to the same track. Follow it for a short distance and turn right, then shortly left along Sherbrooke Track. Here you're in the midst of the finest stand of mountain ash, truly magnificent trees with trunks up to 2m wide. Pass a wide bridge then Edgebrooke Track, both on the right, and at the next junction go left towards **Sherbrooke Falls** along Hillclimb Track, and left again a few steps farther on.

The waterfalls, rather slender in summer, are in a beautiful setting, surrounded by ferns and mountain ashes. Continue down the Hillclimb Track and across Sherbrooke Creek (about an hour from O'Donohue picnic ground). Pass a minor track on the right and at the next one, turn right. Climb steeply to a sealed road (Terrys Ave), turning left onto it. Traffic along the shady avenue isn't particularly busy, and it's possible to keep to the grassy road edge. A footpath on the left provides safe passage down the steep descent; with busy Main St in view, cross again for the last 100m. To reach the train station, cross Main St and the road bridge and turn right (one hour from Sherbrooke Creek).

Mornington Peninsula National Park

Conservation of the environment was largely neglected on the Mornington Peninsula until the 1970s when the state government began to buy back private land and local campaigners campaigned for the creation of parks. From its small beginnings as Cape Schanck Coastal Park in 1975, Mornington Peninsula National Park (2686 hectares) now takes in the ocean coast between Point Nepean and Bushranger Bay and from Stockyard Creek east to Flinders, plus the western side of the valley of Main Creek up through Greens Bush. As part of the long-planned 30km Peninsula Coast Walk from Dromana to Cape Schanck, the walk described in this section takes you from the leafy woodlands and fern gullies around Main Creek to the dramatic coastal cliffs of Cape Schanck.

PLANNING

Just about any time of the year is suitable for this walk; in summer it's rarely too hot for too long. There are no reliable sources of fresh water along the walk, so carry all you'll need for the day. On warm days, be on the lookout for snakes – two were met when we researched this walk on a partly cloudy, mild day.

Maps & Books

The Vicmap 1:25,000 *Cape Schanck* topographical map covers the area of the walk and shows most walking tracks. Parks Victoria produces park notes for the national park generally, and for Cape Schanck and other specific areas. The Meridian Productions *Mornington Peninsula & Arthurs Seat Map Guide* comprises a 1:25,000 topographical map of the ocean coast and Greens Bush, maps of Point Nepean and Arthurs Seat State Park (1:20,000), practical information and walk descriptions. *Peninsula Perspectives* by Winty Calder is a good introductory text to the natural history of the area.

Information Sources

The helpful staff at the Peninsula Visitor Information Centre (☎ 03-5987 3078), Point Nepean Rd, Dromana 3936, can advise about accommodation on the Mornington Peninsula; it's open daily. The centre also stocks copies of the park notes.

Permits & Regulations

Camping is not permitted in the park. Phytophthora is a problem in the park, so keep to the defined walking tracks (see the boxed text 'Phytophthora' earlier in this chapter).

NEAREST TOWN
Flinders

This large town, 11km east of the Boneo and Cape Schanck Rds junction, is a good place to head after the walk. ***Flinders Bakehouse Cafe*** *(☎ 03-5989 0091)*, on Boneo Rd, is open from 9 am to 5 pm Friday to Sunday; sample the famous Flinders bread – no additives and genuinely home-baked. The cafe is licensed and BYO (Bring Your Own), and offers pies ($7), soup, bread ($5.50) and other treats. The bread is also sold at the ***general store*** nearby.

Flinders Village Cafe *(☎ 03-5989 0700)*, on Cook St, is open daily until around 5 pm and does particularly good scones, as well as salads, quiches and sandwiches.

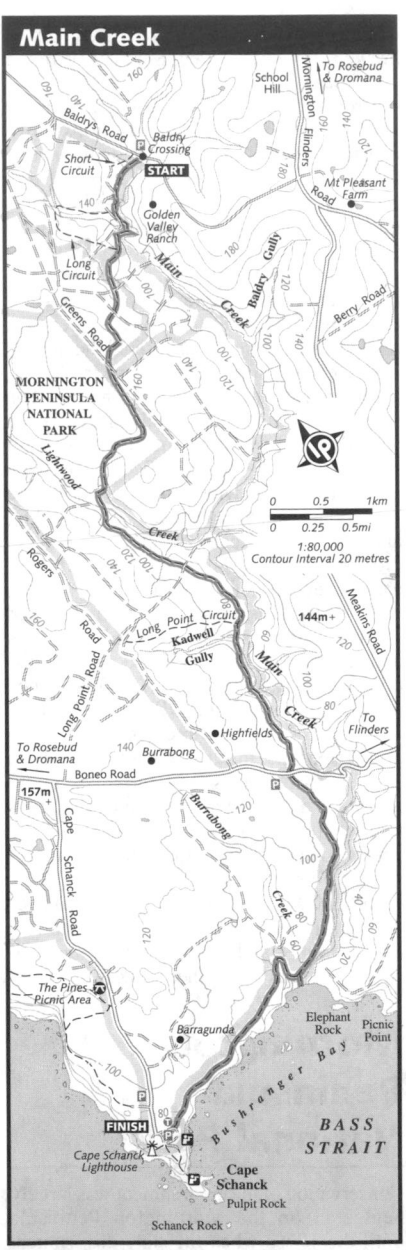

Main Creek

Distance	14km
Duration	4–4½ hours
Standard	medium
Start	Baldry Crossing
Finish	Cape Schanck
Nearest Town	Flinders
Public Transport	no

Summary A varied walk through eucalyptus woodland, down the open valley of Main Creek to Bushranger Bay and along the cliff tops to dramatic Cape Schanck.

This walk, on a good track marked with orange arrowheads, unites the best features of the Mornington Peninsula National Park: open eucalyptus woodlands, lush fern glades, rugged coastal scenery, the Cape Schanck lighthouse and a secluded sandy beach.

There are several alternatives to the through walk if organising transport is a problem. From Baldry Crossing, two circuits sample the eucalyptus woodland and the fern gullies; the Long Circuit is 3.6km. Farther south, the Long Point Circuit leads through woodland and grassland down to Main Creek and back. It starts at the junction of Rogers and Long Point Rds (Long Point Rd leads north-east from Boneo Rd, about 200m south-east of the Cape Schanck Rd junction). The third option is to start at Boneo Rd and walk to Cape Schanck and back, a distance of 11km.

GETTING TO/FROM THE WALK
To the Start
The walk starts at Baldry Crossing on Baldrys Rd, Main Ridge; there is a small parking area on the northern side of the road. The most direct approach from Melbourne is via Nepean Hwy and Mornington Peninsula Fwy. Take the Jetty Rd exit and continue south to Browns Rd, then Baldrys Rd.

From the Finish
To reach Cape Schanck, turn south (left) at the end of the Mornington Peninsula Fwy along Boneo Rd and follow this generally south for about 10km to Cape Schanck Rd. The car park is 4km farther on at the end of the sealed road. During summer there is a $3.50 parking fee.

THE WALK
Cross Baldrys Rd from the car park and follow the walking track into open eucalyptus bushland, beside Main Creek for a while, then overlooking its deep valley. The trail soon passes track junctions for the Long and Short Circuits on the right, crosses a side creek and then climbs well above Main Creek. Go past the second turn-off for Long Circuit on the right and continue along the ridge. Beyond a broad swathe of grassland (about 30 minutes from the start) it's back into the woodland and some dense clumps of

grass trees. The track descends across a shallow gully and then ferny Lightwood Creek (an hour from Baldry Crossing). Continuing generally southwards now, the track passes a junction on the right (to Rogers Rd) and follows Lightwood Creek for nearly 1km to a turn-off for Long Point Circuit, then returns to the deeper valley of Main Creek. A little way past the next junction (with the Long Point Circuit), banksias make their appearance. Having crossed Kadwell Gully the track leads on for 2km to Boneo Rd (1¼ hours from Lightwood Creek).

Cross the road and, on the far side of the rough parking area, follow the track beyond the barrier. Sandy surfaced, it passes through banksia thickets and clumps of wattle, with good views down steep-sided Main Creek to the ocean. About 45 minutes from Boneo Rd you reach a junction where a track descends steeply to **Bushranger Bay beach** – a good place for lunch. Although the surf may look inviting, bear in mind that cross rips (undertows or currents) can make swimming hazardous. Nevertheless there is much fun to be had poking about Elephant Rock and Picnic Point, at the eastern end of the beach.

Back up on the main track, the way is across Burrabong Creek and through teatree thickets and open grassland with good coastal views. About an hour's walking from the beach brings you to the Cape Schanck car park; continue along the access road to the kiosk. From near here, it's well worth taking 30 minutes or more to go down the boardwalk and steps towards the cape – the views, especially towards Bushranger Bay, are great.

Operating since 1859, **Cape Schanck Lighthouse** (☎ 03-9568 6411) is open daily for tours ($6 adults, $4 children).

Victoria

Victoria has more than 100 national and state parks and other conservation reserves, protecting and making accessible high mountain ranges and subalpine summits, mountain forests, almost unspoiled coastlines, rocky peaks in the west and the fascinating waterways and semiarid 'deserts' of the north-west. There are thousands of kilometres of walking tracks, from short informative nature trails to major long-distance routes. There's also space for wilderness treks in the north-western dry country and in the remote ranges and valleys of the east and north-east.

Most parks have camping grounds with facilities and there are plenty of comfortable places to stay in nearby towns. The parks are generally easily reached; major roads with good cross-country links radiate from the state's capital, Melbourne, and many parks are accessible from interstate. This chapter covers the state's most popular walking areas, with descriptions of a number of one-day and extended trips and suggestions for others.

INFORMATION
Maps

For general route planning, road maps published by HEMA and Gregory's are adequate and are widely available in specialist map shops (see the section on Buying Maps under Information in the Melbourne Region chapter), larger bookshops and newsagents. The Melway *Greater Melbourne* street directory, published annually, has superlative maps of the city and environs, and useful state-wide coverage.

Topographical maps for walkers are published by the state government's mapping agency, Geospatial Information, in the Vicmap series. All but the far north-west corner is covered at 1:25,000, while several Outdoor Leisure Map sheets (also Vicmap) focus on popular areas such as the Grampians, with maps at various scales. The whole state is also covered by the 1:100,000 map series published by the national mapping agency, Auslig, but these are less suitable for walking.

Highlights

The craggy Mt Difficult Range – scenery typical of Grampians National Park

- Wandering among majestic river red gums beside the Murray River in Hattah–Kulkyne National Park

- Visiting places of immense significance to Aboriginal people in Grampians National Park

- Exploring the towering cliffs and seal colonies of Cape Bridgewater on the Great South West Walk

- Trekking in Victoria's highest mountains with their wonderfully scenic exposed peaks, pretty snow plains, rocky crags and tall forests

- Charting the wild, unspoiled beaches of Croajingolong National Park

More up-to-date and useful topographical maps are also produced privately by Meridian Productions and by SR Brookes.

For maps covering individual walks, see Planning in the introduction to each section.

Victoria

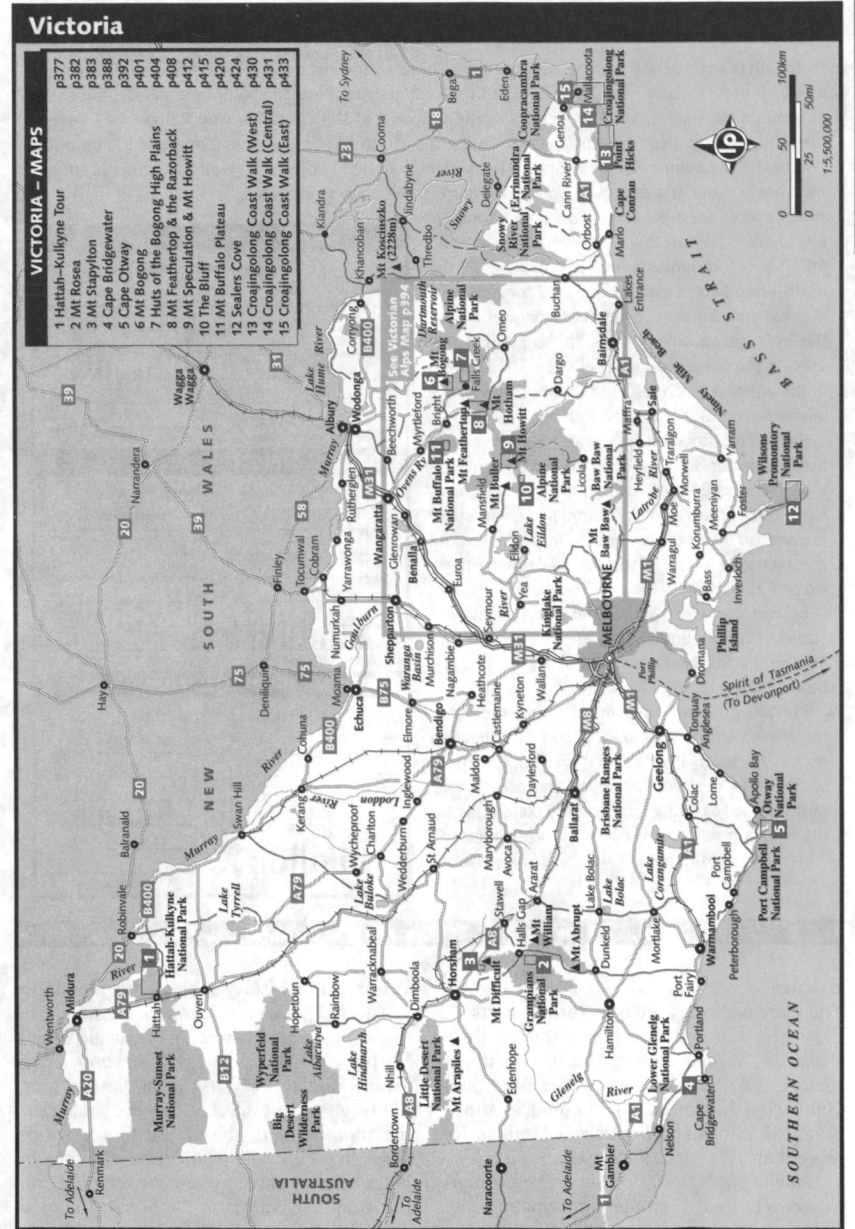

VICTORIA

The Climate of Victoria

Victoria has a temperate, four-seasons climate, although the distinctions between seasons are often upset by unpredictable weather. There are three climatic regions: the south and coasts, the alpine or mountainous areas, and the country north and west of the Great Dividing Range. As a general rule, the south and coastal areas have a similar climate to Melbourne (see Climate in the introduction to the Melbourne Region chapter), the Victorian Alps are colder and wetter, and the north and west are warmer and drier with conditions more stable than elsewhere.

In summer, the average daily maximum temperatures are in the low 20s along the coasts, around 18°C in the mountains and up to 33°C in the north-west. Except along the coastal fringes, summer sunshine averages eight hours daily. In winter, the average maximum along the coast is 12°C, 15°C in the north-west and between 3°C and 9°C in the alpine areas. Frosts occur almost anywhere inland during most winter months.

Rainfall is distributed fairly uniformly throughout the year in the south and in parts of eastern Victoria. The north-west, west and exposed coasts have wet winters and dry summers. The wettest areas are in the north-eastern mountains and some coastal slopes, where annual rainfall can sometimes exceed 2500mm.

Between June and September, snow usually lies above 1500m. Snowfalls between 500m and 1000m are fairly common but are more unusual below 500m.

Prevailing winds come mainly from the west, but there can be marked differences in direction north and south of the Great Divide. Generally, southerlies and south-westerlies, and occasionally north-easterlies, bring rain; hot, dry conditions are often accompanied by north to north-westerly winds. During summer, coastal areas enjoy cooling afternoon sea breezes.

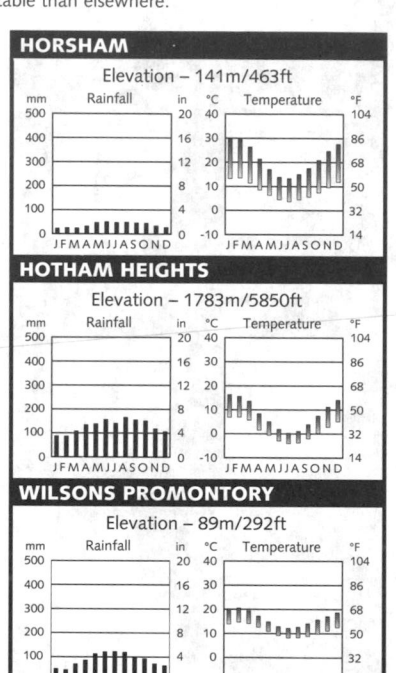

Books

There are walking guides to various parts of the state, but only Tyrone Thomas' *120 Walks in Victoria* covers the whole state. *Victoria's National Parks* by See Australia Guides has lots of excellent colour photos, practical information and basic guides to more than 120 parks and reserves.

Camping in Victoria: National Parks (and) Reserves has good summary information and is especially useful if you have a 4WD.

For natural history subjects, the plentifully illustrated *Trees of Victoria & Adjoining Areas* by Leon Costermans is unsurpassed. Barbara Triggs' *Tracks, Scats and Other Tracks* is also very useful as you're more likely to see the tracks than the makers of the footprints. In the Green Guide series, *Birds* by Peter Rowland and *Parrots* by Peter Lindsey have good photos and are not too weighty. Numerous regional guides to wild flowers are available.

Lonely Planet has the state well covered with *Victoria*, *Melbourne* and *Out to Eat – Melbourne*. For coastal enthusiasts, the Lonely Planet Pisces series includes *Diving & Snorkeling Victoria Australia*.

Information Sources

The Tourism Victoria Web site (🖳 www.tourism.vic.gov.au) includes a state-wide accommodation list; alternatively, call ☎ 13 2842. Local visitor centres, which should be able to provide more comprehensive information, are detailed under individual park sections later in this chapter.

Parks Victoria (☎ 13 1963) manages the state's parks; the Web site at 🖳 www.park web.vic.gov.au provides a good introduction. The telephone call line is helpful only for basic inquiries; for detailed queries, you'll be given the number for the park in question. Parks Victoria also produces a Web site, Stepping Out (🖳 www.tracks.vic.gov.au), which provides practical information for walkers on areas right across Victoria.

The Victorian National Parks Association (☎ 03-9650 8296, fax 9564 6843, 📧 vnpa @vicnet.net.au, 🖳 www.vnpa.org.au), 10 Parliament Place, East Melbourne, Victoria 3002, is a leading conservation organisation with a very active walks program.

The Federation of Victorian Walking Clubs (☎ 03-9455 1876, fax 9457 5438, 📧 vicwalk @vicnet.net.au, 🖳 www.vicnet.net.au/~vic walk), Banyule St, Viewbank, Victoria 3084, represents more than 70 clubs in the state and maintains a very useful Web site.

Detailed weather charts and reports are published in the *Age* and *Australian* newspapers; less detailed reports are given on the evening TV news. Tide table can be accessed over the Internet on 🖳 www.fish net.com.au/weather/tidesvic.html or 🖳 www.ntf.flinders.edu.au/cgi-bin/tides.

For information on Melbourne's visitor centres, map shops and outdoor gear shops, see Melbourne in the introduction to the Melbourne Region chapter.

Permits & Regulations

Regulations vary from park to park across Victoria. As a general rule, however, permits are required to stay in most national and other park camping grounds. These are available on site, where you have to pay by cash, or from park offices; fees for walk-in camp sites are lower. Bookings are necessary at some parks during busy holidays.

In the great majority of parks, fires must be lit in the fireplaces provided. Fuel stoves are preferred, to minimise the impact on the fragile bush environment. During days of Total Fire Ban, all fires are forbidden, even fuel stoves. If you are caught with an open fire on these days, you are not only endangering yourself and the environment, but you can also cop a hefty fine and/or prison sentence.

In some national parks (including Wilsons Promontory), fires are completely banned at all times, so a stove is essential.

Off-track walking certainly isn't prohibited in Victoria's parks, but some areas are more sensitive than others, so discuss your plans with park staff first. For more information on how to minimise your impact on the environment, see the section on Responsible Walking in the Facts for the Walker chapter.

GATEWAY

See the introduction to the Melbourne Region chapter for information on accommodation and other services available in Melbourne.

Hattah–Kulkyne National Park

There's nowhere else in Victoria quite like Hattah–Kulkyne National Park in the far north-west, with its network of lakes and creeks, filled occasionally by floodwaters from the Murray River, part of Australia's longest river system (the Murray–Darling). Beyond the confines of these waterways, sharply defined by fringing river red gums, sandy plains and low dunes miraculously support mallee eucalyptuses and native pines. A wide-ranging web of walking and 4WD tracks make the park and neighbouring Murray–Kulkyne Park very accessible to walkers. There's plenty of scope for day outings and extended treks – opportunities to become attuned to the unique feeling of space, timelessness and peace that pervades the park. The 2½-day walk described here can be adapted to individual preferences and provides a good introduction to the area.

HISTORY

For at least 5000 years, Aboriginal people spent considerable time along the Murray River, judging by the large middens (mounds of discarded shells and bone fragments) and scars on trees where bark has been removed to make canoes and implements.

European settlers arrived in the 1840s, and a large part of the Hattah–Kulkyne area was taken up for grazing. The Aboriginal population declined quickly and had disappeared by the early 20th century.

The scientific importance of Hattah Lakes was recognised early when a sanctuary was declared in 1915 to protect flora and fauna. A national park was set up in 1960 after a lengthy campaign by conservation groups, and extended to become Hattah–Kulkyne National Park in 1980; at the same time, Murray–Kulkyne Park was established. The combined area of the parks is nearly 50,000 hectares, including 32km along the Murray River.

In 1982 Unesco designated the two parks as a World Biosphere Reserve, recognising that they protect a quite unusually unspoiled semiarid environment.

NATURAL HISTORY

Hattah–Kulkyne's landscape consists entirely of sands, which accumulated a few million years ago and have been sculpted into subtle lines of dunes and low ridges, oriented generally east-west, by the prevailing winds.

Chalka Creek is a branch of the Murray River which leaves and then rejoins the river in an arc from south to north through a cluster of linked lakes. At the time of research, the creek had last flooded in 1996 and the locals were confidently predicting another flood 'very soon'.

Magnificent river red gums line the creek, lakes and the Murray River, shading its sandy beaches, with the more sparse

The Meaning of Mallee

Popularly known as Victoria's Outback, or Dry Country, the Mallee is in far north-western Victoria, north of Warracknabeal and west of Swan Hill. Much of the original vegetation has been cleared from the eastern half of the Mallee since European settlement, but the greater part of the western half has remained almost unchanged. More than one million hectares are now protected in Murray–Sunset, Wyperfeld and Hattah–Kulkyne National Parks, Big Desert Wilderness Park and several smaller reserves, including Murray–Kulkyne.

The term 'mallee' also refers to about 20 species of many-stemmed eucalyptuses and to the community of plants in which they're dominant. Mallee eucalyptuses are remarkably well adapted to the harsh environment: along with a spreading root system and tough, leathery leaves to minimise water loss, they are able to sprout new shoots from the root stock if stems are burnt or broken off. Mallees can live for hundreds of years.

blue-grey black box (another eucalyptus) beyond. Both depend on periodic flooding to germinate, so the creek bed fills with the dense growth of young trees after the water has receded. Belying the desert stereotype, the dunes and plains are largely covered with yellow and white mallee eucalyptuses, colourful wattles, mallee tea trees, hardy dark green native cypress pines and needle-leaved bulokes (a casuarina similar to the she-oaks found elsewhere). In total, almost 1000 plant species have been found in the park. Wild flowers are very plentiful.

Among more than 200 species of birds, you can't fail to hear raucous parrots, rosellas and Major Mitchell cockatoos. The parks are an important breeding ground for water birds, and the amazing malleefowl breeds here.

Western grey, eastern and red kangaroos live in the park. 'Roos' became a controversial issue when their numbers grew to such an extent in the 1980s that there wasn't enough feed to go around. An area known as the Mournpall Block was fenced to keep them away from water, but culling (shooting) met with strong opposition even though starvation was threatening. The population now is still large, but more in harmony with the food supply.

PLANNING
When to Walk
The best seasons for the park are during winter and spring (May to November), when the weather is generally fine and mild with cold nights and clear days. It's usually too hot for safe and enjoyable walking during summer and autumn when daily temperatures well above 30°C are common.

What to Bring
You'll need to carry drinking water on any walk in the park. Water is available at the park camping grounds, but if you camp by the Murray River a water purifier should be used. Rather than depend on a campfire, you should also take a fuel stove (see Permits & Regulations later).

Any walk in the park will inevitably pass through grassland where large burrs are an unavoidable discomfort, so gaiters or long trousers are highly recommended.

For experienced walkers, the park offers the chance to do some cross-country walking with a map and compass for route finding. Discuss your plans with the rangers first, however; they know the area as well as their own back yards.

Maps & Books
The Meridian Productions *Hattah–Kulkyne Map Guide* has topographical maps of the two parks and adjacent areas at 1:75,000, and of both Lake Hattah and Lake Mournpall at 1:30,000, plus background and practical information. The maps are generally very good, although the tracks along the Murray River between Messengers and Cantala Track come and go and are difficult to pinpoint.

Of the government map series, Vicmap's 1:50,000 *Hattah Lakes* map in the Outdoor Leisure Map series is too out of date (1990),

Warning

River red gums (ominously known as widow-makers) can unload branches without warning, so choose your tent site carefully, well clear of these large trees.

while the Auslig 1:100,000 *Nowingi* map is less useful than the Meridian guide.

Parks Victoria's park notes sheet, *Touring, Walking, Camping*, has basic information about the park and a dreadful map. A good general guide to the area is *Discover Victoria's Mallee* by Margaret Kelly. For wildflower identification, IR McCann's profusely illustrated *The Mallee in Flower* is excellent.

Information Sources
The visitor centre (☎ 03-5029 3253) is 2km along the sealed access road to the park. It's generally open daily and park staff should be there most mornings from 8.30 am for a couple of hours. Information displays provide interesting background on the park's history and environment.

Permits & Regulations
You need a permit to camp at either of the two camping grounds (Lake Hattah and Lake Mournpall) in Hattah–Kulkyne, but not for camping in Murray–Kulkyne Park. The cost is $9 per night per site for up to six people. Permits are available at the visitor centre (see Information Sources earlier) or from the box at the park entrance on the Hattah Robinvale Rd. To simplify paying camping fees, bring cash or a cheque book – a credit card will be useless.

In the national park, fires may only be lit in the fireplaces provided. In Murray–Kulkyne Park there aren't any fireplaces, so clear a wide space around the fire and douse it completely before striking camp

NEAREST TOWN & FACILITIES
Ouyen
About 40km south of the national park, Ouyen (pronounced o-yin) is the nearest town of any size to the park. The Mallee Tourism Association (☎/fax 03-5029 1000),

Oke St, Ouyen 3490, has a small office open weekdays and Saturday morning, with basic information about accommodation and knowledgeable locals on hand.

Mallee Building & Electrical Supplies, 51 Oke St, sells large gas bottles and small camping gas canisters. Neither of the two banks has an ATM.

Places to Stay & Eat The *Ouyen Caravan Park (☎/fax 03-5092 1426, 10 Calder Hwy)* is a friendly place where you can pitch a tent for $12.50 per night (two people), or stay in a double en suite cabin for $50. The facilities include a small, well-equipped campers' kitchen.

There are also three motels and the *Victoria Hotel (☎ 03-5092 1550)*, an old-style country pub and one of the places to go for a meal – standard pub fare or Chinese.

Otherwise, there are the *roadhouses* attached to the petrol stations, and the *Mallee Deli*, beside the Calder Hwy, open daily for takeaways (serving pizzas on weekends).

There are two *supermarkets* and the unmissable *Mallee Bakery*, the home of the Victorian Vanilla Slice Championship. Even if you're staying elsewhere, call at Ouyen to sample this treat – thin, flaky pastry with creamy custard and just the right thickness of pink icing.

Getting There & Away Ouyen is on the Calder Hwy (route A79), 450km north-west of Melbourne and 100km south of Mildura.

The V/Line bus (☎ 13 6196) between Melbourne and Mildura stops in Ouyen (this is the same bus that will take you directly to the park – see Getting There & Away under Hattah–Kulkyne National Park).

Hattah–Kulkyne National Park

The Lake Hattah *camping ground* near the visitor centre is rather bare, while the Lake Mournpall *camping ground*, 8km north along a reasonable gravel road, is more spacious and shady. Both have pit toilets and a limited water supply.

The unsealed River Track (branching from the Hattah Robinvale Rd 22km east of Hattah) gives access by car to *camp sites*

along the Murray River; it is suitable for 2WDs, although very corrugated in places.

The nearest telephone is at *Hattah Lakes Store*, near the Calder Hwy junction. This amazing place, open daily, is decked out with politically very incorrect jokes and sells fuel, takeaways, basic supplies, beer and wine, and even has a fax machine and shower.

Getting There & Away The entrance to the park is 4km along the Hattah Robinvale Rd (C252), east of the settlement of Hattah on the Calder Hwy (35km north of Ouyen, 65km south of Mildura).

The V/Line (☎ 13 6196) Melbourne to Mildura bus service offers a rare opportunity to use public transport to visit a national park; the one-way fare to Hattah is $49.20 for the seven-hour journey.

Hattah–Kulkyne Tour

Duration	3 days
Distance	56km
Standard	easy-medium
Start/Finish	national park visitor centre
Nearest Town	Ouyen
Public Transport	yes

Summary Easy walking through the heart of the peaceful park, beside creeks and lakes that depend on the life-giving floodwaters of the Murray River.

This three-day walk follows Chalka Creek eastwards to the Murray River from Lake Hattah. It then wanders downstream beside the Murray River for several kilometres, before returning across dunes and plains to Lake Mournpall, then back to the start along part of the historic Camel Pad Track. Each day can, with minor adaptations, stand alone as a day walk from bases at Lake Mournpall or beside the Murray River (see Other Walks at the end of the chapter for suggestions).

Some parts of the walking tracks, old 4WD tracks and short sections of the River Track are sandy, making for fairly slow going, but at least there aren't any steep ups or downs. Generally, walking is pretty easy and the daily distances pass surprisingly comfortably. Parts of the walk route, mainly around Lake Mournpall, are track marked with orange arrowheads.

GETTING TO/FROM THE WALK

The walk starts and finishes at the visitor centre. It is accessible by public transport if you are prepared to walk in along the Shingle Back Track (7km), which starts 200m north of the bus stop at the Hattah Lakes Store.

THE WALK
Day 1: Lake Hattah to Ki Bend

6½ hours, 25km

From the visitor centre, follow the gravel road to Lake Hattah camping ground. The road then becomes more of a 4WD track as it skirts the northern side of the lake bed. Continue along signposted Bugle Ridge Track leading eastwards between Hattah Lake and the nearby **Little Lake Hattah** via the regulator (low dam), which controls the water flow during flood times. Soon the track crosses open grassland, with Lake Bulla just to the south. The next line of river red gums marks the location of Lake Brockie; then, at an acute-angled track junction, turn

sharp left (an hour from the start). The track crosses grassland and areas of black box to swing around between Lakes Tullamook and Nip Nip. About 30 minutes from the junction, turn left along Nip Nip Track to reach a gate in the stockyard fence.

Climb over it carefully and continue ahead for about 150m, then turn left along Stockyard Track through lush grassland. Crossing low dunes, the track gives good views of the colourful landscape: red sand, green clumps of wattles and patches of black box. About 30 minutes from the gate, there's a well-preserved sample of **old stockyards** on the left, showing the skilful use of timber without wire or nails. Pass Roonki Track on the left and merge with another track coming in from the left; go right at a fork to another junction and continue ahead along Chalka Creek Track.

The walking is easy for about 6km, close to **Chalka Creek**, through black box, then back to the creek. The track then turns south-east to follow a power transmission line for 1km. Leaving the line behind, it's another 2km to River Track at Messengers Crossing (2¾ hours after joining Chalka Creek Track). Here the creek leaves the

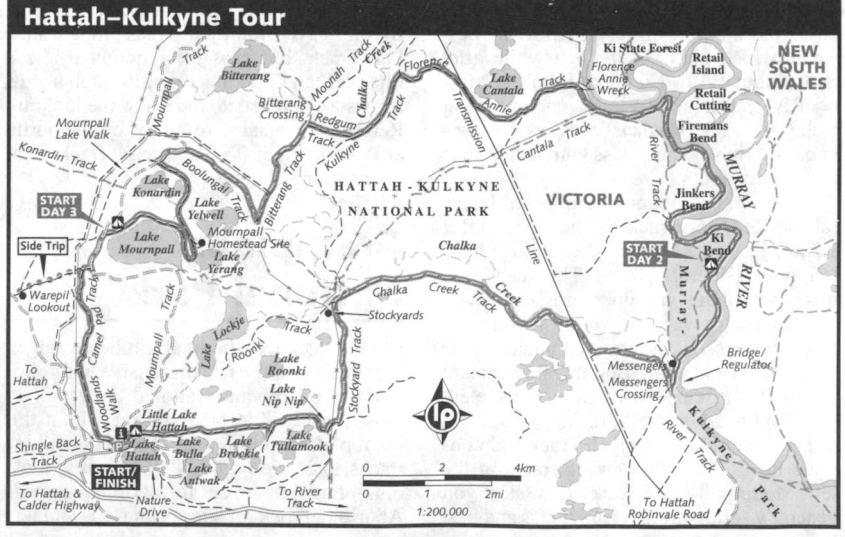

Hattah–Kulkyne Tour

broad **Murray River**. Cross the creek regulator and follow River Track for nearly 1km to a junction opposite a house (Messengers) on the left and continue along the right-hand track to Ki Bend. The best *camp sites* are about 2km farther on, above a sandy beach.

Day 2: Ki Bend to Lake Mournpall
5¾–6¾ hours, 24km

Follow the track round Ki Bend and back to River Track; turn off again after 1km along a track signposted to Jinkers Bend. It's difficult to accurately describe the route for the next 5km through a maze of tracks; the best advice is to keep as close as comfortably possible to the river, following 4WD tracks round Jinkers Bend, past Firemans Bend and Retail Cutting. Eventually you should reach a junction with River Track, with a sign pointing to Retail Bend. A 20-minute walk along River Track brings you to Florence Annie Track; turn left here, leaving the river behind (the wreck of the *Florence Annie* nearby isn't exactly prominent).

Soon you're walking across grassland dotted with bulokes; pass a junction on the left. With Lake Cantala nearby to the north, continue across open grassland to relatively hilly red sand dunes. The track then passes beneath a power transmission line and leads on across a string of very shallow depressions, which hold water for a while after rain. About 1½ to 1¾ hours from the Murray River, turn left at a track junction along Kulkyne Track. **Chalka Creek** soon closes in on the right – much less entrenched than it is farther south.

At the next junction (30 minutes later), follow Redgum Track to the right. After 1.2km, just past Bitterang Crossing, head left along Bitterang Track. This leads into black box plains and open grassland, with low dunes for variety. About 40 minutes from the crossing, go through a gate in the fence, turn right along Boolungal Track and follow it for 3km, mostly across shadeless grassland to Mournpall Track.

Turn left onto Mournpall Track and continue for 750m to a walking track on the left: Mournpall Lake Walk. This takes you generally south through woodlands and past

Lake Konardin. Look out for a short side track on the left to the site of the second **Mournpall homestead**. A little farther on, the track swings sharply right and leads on to **Lake Mournpall**. The track keeps well inland from the sandy shore through river red gums for a few hundred metres, then leads down to the beach and on to the extensive *camping ground* just past a low dune (one hour from Mournpall Track).

Day 3: Lake Mournpall to Lake Hattah
1¾–2¾ hours, 7km

Follow the 4WD track generally west to Mournpall Track and walk south along it for about 1km to a junction, where you turn right. Continue along the signposted **Camel Pad Track**, bearing left at a junction 200m farther on. Follow it south for 3km through black box plains, sandy grassland and dunes dotted with native pines. Turn left at the next junction to reach the visitor centre, 2.6km away, mainly through black box woodland.

Side Trip: Warepil Lookout
1¾–2¾ hours, 7km return

A few kilometres west of Lake Mournpall, this lookout gives panoramic views across the Mallee country and towards the Murray River. Leave Mournpall Track along Camel Pad Track, but pass the junction where it turns left and continue west through a gate, across a gravel road and on to the **lookout**. Return by the same route (or by the northern circuit track to Mournpall Track, near the camping ground).

Grampians National Park

From a distance, the long, timbered ridges, precipitous slopes and massive unbroken cliffs of Grampians National Park look almost inaccessible on foot. Yet within this great park are more than 160km of walking tracks to a wide variety of features: lookouts, fantastic rock formations, age-old Aboriginal rock art sites, waterfalls and fern

VICTORIA

gullies. Rising suddenly from the plains of western Victoria, the 167,000-hectare park, known as Gariwerd (meaning 'Big Mountain') to local Aboriginal people, protects nearly 900 native plant species and numerous mammals and birds. The history of European occupation spans gold mining, grazing, quarrying, timber harvesting, water storage and tourism.

Two walks are described in detail: the ascent of imposing Mt Rosea, one of the highest peaks in the park and, on the northern edge, a walk to Mt Stapylton through fantastic rock formations. Other walk suggestions (see Other Walks at the end of the chapter) include an overnight trip from Halls Gap.

NATURAL HISTORY

The Grampians extend for 80km north-south and 50km east-west at the western end of the Great Dividing Range. They comprise a long central, almost continuous spine of peaks through Mt Difficult and Serra Ranges, Victoria Range in the west and Mt William Range in the east. Mt William (1167m) is the highest summit in the Grampians.

The greater part of the ranges is built of hard, quartz-rich sandstone formed over hundreds of millions of years in cycles of accumulation and erosion. The characteristic ridges, with a long gentle western slope and steep eastern escarpment (cuesta), are the result of differing rates of erosion of hard and softer rock. Outcrops of granite in the Grampians are most obvious as narrow bands in the Wonderland (an area west of Halls Gap), where vegetation is taller and relatively luxuriant.

Botanically, the Grampians are rich and complex, but it's easy to recognise four of the vegetation types. Tall open forests of brown stringybarks, manna gums and blackwoods are most extensive near Halls Gap, while sheltered gullies harbour luxuriant tree ferns. Low woodlands with stringybarks, peppermints, banksias, tea-trees and hosts of wild flowers are widespread on the slopes. On more exposed ground along the ridges, low, prickly heaths with banksias, she-oaks, grevilleas and smaller shrubs form nearly impenetrable scrub.

The Grampians are internationally famous for their springtime displays of wild flowers, probably best seen in the open woodlands. More than 900 species of native flora have been recorded, including up to 19 that don't occur naturally anywhere else.

PLANNING
When to Walk

The Grampians' season is almost year-round; the best time for wild flowers is from September to late November, although there are almost always some in bloom. Midsummer temperatures can climb well above 30°C, when streams can run dry.

What to Bring

During winter, weather conditions can be much cooler and snow can fall, so be prepared with a warm jacket. You'll also need to carry water for the day. For walks anywhere in the park, a fuel stove is preferable (to help conserve timber), although fireplaces are provided at most camping grounds.

Maps & Books

The Friends of Grampians–Gariwerd and Parks Victoria have produced several guides: *Southern Grampians Walks*, *Wonderland Walks* and *Northern Walks*, which are indispensable. Each contains brief descriptions of numerous day walks and some overnight expeditions and basic maps.

Parks Victoria's free *Visitor Guide* includes maps showing approach roads and the location of camping and picnic grounds. The *Grampians National Park Touring Guide* is aimed mainly at car-borne visitors.

The People of Gariwerd by Gib Wettenhall is a beautifully illustrated presentation of the Aboriginal heritage of the area (available at Brambuk Aboriginal Cultural Centre – see Information Sources).

For wildflower identification, IR McCann's profusely illustrated *The Grampians in Flower* is excellent, although *Common Native Plants of the Grampians* by Rodger Elliot & Trevor Blake is a handier size. *Introducing Grampians Geology* by GW Cochrane, GW Quick & D Spencer-Jones should answer all your rock questions.

Information Sources

The National Park Centre (☎ 03-5356 4381), Grampians Tourist Rd (PO Box 18, Halls Gap), 2.5km south of Halls Gap, is open daily. It has excellent displays about the park's natural and cultural history and a good bookshop; an audiovisual presentation on the park is screened regularly. Friendly staff can provide information about walking and camping.

The Brambuk Aboriginal Cultural Centre (☎ 03-5356 4452, fax 5356 4455), Grampians Tourist Rd, is a short walk from the National Park Centre and open daily. It houses displays about the history and culture of the Koori peoples of south-western Victoria, and Gariwerd (Grampians) in particular, and organises displays of dancing and art site tours. There's a craft shop stocked with works by Koori people, and the excellent Bush Tucker Cafe (see Places to Eat). Two leaflets about Aboriginal rock art sites in the Northern and Southern Grampians dispel myths about these places, with explanations by Koori people.

Permits & Regulations

Payment of camping fees ($8.30 per site, paid on location) is mandatory at all the national park camping grounds. Bush camping is permitted elsewhere, except in some specific areas, including the Major Mitchell Plateau, Wonderland Range and part of the Victoria Range; check at the national park visitor centre in Halls Gap for full details.

NEAREST TOWN
Halls Gap

This large town is the traditional capital of the Grampians and has all the services you're likely to need.

In the centre of Halls Gap, the visitor centre (☎ 03-5356 4616), Grampians Tourist Rd, is open daily and can help with accommodation and bookings, and keeps basic walks information.

The National Park Centre and Brambuk Aboriginal Cultural Centre are a short way out of town on the Grampians Tourist Rd (for details, see Information Sources earlier).

There isn't a bank in Halls Gap, but you'll find an ATM in the petrol station, which sells camping supplies, including Primus gas canisters.

Places to Stay The *Halls Gap Caravan Park* (☎ *03-5356 4251, fax 5356 4421,* ✉ *hgcp@netconnect.com.au)*, Grampians Tourist Rd, is the most central of the local camping-caravan parks, although less shady and peaceful than those farther out. Unpowered sites cost $16 for two and the tariff for the simplest of the cabins is $45. There is a barbecue and plenty of individual fireplaces.

***Brambuk Backpackers** (☎ 03-5356 4250, fax 5356 4455)*, 2.5km south of Halls Gap

---

Gariwerd & Brambuk

To learn the meaning of these names, it's necessary to spend some time at the Brambuk Aboriginal Cultural Centre, in the area most people now know as Grampians National Park.

This building is designed to reflect the mountains' contours and a cockatoo (an important totemic symbol) in flight. It incorporates five circles, one for each Koori (Aboriginal) community with links to the centre; each has ancient connections with Gariwerd (Big Mountain), the Koori name for the area long before white settlers called it the Grampians. The materials used in the centre, including mud bricks and timber, have special cultural significance for each community.

Brambuk means belonging to the Bram brothers, key figures in the legendary creation of the mountains. For the Kooris, Brambuk symbolises their renewal after nearly two centuries under European domination. Here Kooris teach visitors about their cultural practices, stories, beliefs and management of the land. Gariwerd has some of the finest evidence of Koori existence in south-eastern Australia, especially in the rock art sites, now known by Koori rather than inappropriate European names.

A highlight of a visit to the centre are indigenous foods prepared and served in the Bush Tucker Cafe – modern Aboriginal cuisine could feature on restaurant menus worldwide.

and across the road from the Brambuk Aboriginal Cultural Centre, opened early in 2000. All bedrooms are en suite doubles, costing $18 per person; facilities include a kitchen and an Internet cafe.

YHA's *Halls Gap Eco-Hostel* (☎ *03-5356 4544, fax 5356 4543,* **℮** *hallsgap@yhavic .org.au)*, on the corner of Buckler St and Grampians Tourist Rd, also opened in early 2000. Tariffs start at $15 for a bed in a small dorm, $20 per person in a double or twin and $55 per family room. The building incorporates many admirable energy and water conservation features.

Places to Eat In Halls Gap, *Cafe Rosea* (☎ *03-5356 4511)*, at Stony Creek Stores, has huge pizzas that will defeat all but the most ravenous – the steak and chips ($15) is also pretty hefty. The cafe is BYO (Bring Your Own) and well placed for the free entertainment put on by a local flock of raucous and acrobatic corellas – but guard your plate from the tame kookaburras!

The *Bush Tucker Cafe*, in the Brambuk Aboriginal Cultural Centre (see Information Sources), offers the rare chance to try gourmet bush tucker, including emu kebabs ($10), crocodile salad ($12) and delicious wattle tea and coffee; the cafe is licensed.

The *supermarket* in the main street is rather pricey, but does stock liquid fuel and gas for camping stoves. The nearby *bottle shop* stocks local and many other wines.

The *bakery* in Stony Creek Stores makes excellent bread and won the Victorian Vanilla Slice Championship in 1998, but your diligent cake assessment team voted Ouyen's slices the best; Halls Gap is better at caramel slices.

Getting There & Away By road, Halls Gap is about 260km from Melbourne via the Western Hwy (A8) to Ararat and then via Moyston (C222), or via Stawell on the Western Hwy (C216).

V/Line (☎ 13 6196) operates a daily train and coach service from Melbourne to Halls Gap via Ballarat, Ararat and Stawell. The one-way fare is $38.90 for the 4½-hour journey. Tickets can be purchased in Halls Gap from the large newsagent in the main street (which also sells stamps, phonecards and local guidebooks).

Mt Rosea

Duration	3–3½ hours
Distance	7km
Standard	medium
Start/Finish	Rosea camping ground
Nearest Town	Halls Gap
Public Transport	no

Summary This is the best high mountain climb in the Grampians, to a summit with superb panoramic views. It makes an easy day walk or part of an extended trek from Halls Gap through the Wonderland and back.

Mt Rosea (1009m) is the most rewarding of the high peaks in the park. Mt William is about 160m higher, but the presence of a communications tower and sealed road minimise any feeling of naturalness. D'Alton Peaks, the only other peaks in the park above 1000m, are slightly higher than Rosea, but only reached by fighting through dense, trackless and prickly scrub. To climb Mt Rosea, you follow marked walking tracks virtually the whole way to the top with its superb view (a height gain of 409m). Around the summit is a stand of unusual Grampians gums found nowhere else in Victoria. A low, rather stunted tree, it has glossy dark green leaves and large knobbly fruit.

The walk is described as an out-and-back journey. As part of an overnight expedition (see Other Walks at the end of the chapter), you could descend instead to Borough Huts camping ground, beside Grampians Tourist Rd, following walking and old 4WD tracks.

PLANNING
For a description of when to walk and what to bring, see Planning in the introduction to the Grampians National Park.

Maps
The most convenient topographical map is Vicmap's 1:50,000 *Northern Grampians* map in the Outdoor Leisure Map series,

VICTORIA

which includes some 1:25,000 maps of the Wonderland covering the walk. In Vicmap's 1:25,000 series, you'll need *Moora Moora* and *Halls Gap*.

GETTING TO/FROM THE WALK

Rosea camping ground, at the junction of Silverband and Stony Creek Rds, can be reached by either of two routes from Halls Gap. The southern approach via Grampians Tourist Rd and Silverband Rd is an easier drive (14km) than via the winding Mount Victory Rd and Silverband Rd (9.5km).

Halls Gap Taxis (☎ 019 943 691 mobile) provides a drop-off and pick-up service.

THE WALK

From Rosea camping ground, walk along Stony Creek Rd for 30m and turn left along a track signposted to Mt Rosea. The wide track climbs steadily, soon generally paralleling the cliffs of Mt Rosea, visible through the trees. Nearly 30 minutes from the start, the track turns towards the ridge and climbs to open expanses of rocks, bends left – follow cairns here – and arrives rather abruptly on a clearly defined ridge (40 minutes from the camping ground).

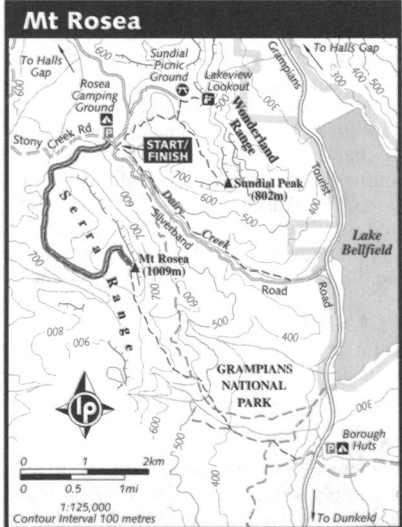

Turn sharp left and continue along the side of the valley below on the right, then cross it and climb towards a wooded ridge. Follow the track beneath a rock overhang, between large boulders and on to the crest of the ridge; the trail soon joins an older track with orange arrowhead markers. The way is then a tight squeeze between large boulders and on to a metal bridge spanning a small chasm. Continue past several rock overhangs and out into the open. From a track junction on a wooded spur (where the track to Borough Huts takes off), it's only a couple more minutes to the **summit** of Mt Rosea (an hour from the first ridge). The truly panoramic view extends from Mt Arapiles in the west to Mt Napier far to the south and the Langi Ghiran Range near Ararat in the east. A topograph, shaky on its rusty base, may help to identify surrounding features.

To return to the Rosea camping ground, simply retrace your steps. For Borough Huts camping ground, return to the nearby track junction and head towards the huts, carefully following track markers steeply downhill to a gap. The track soon improves and descends steadily through tall forest, crossing and recrossing an old 4WD track several times. You should reach the *camping ground* about 1¾ hours after leaving the top.

Mt Stapylton

Duration	4½–5 hours
Distance	12.2km
Standard	medium-hard
Start/Finish	Stapylton camping ground
Nearest Towns	Wartook, Halls Gap
Public Transport	no

Summary A spectacularly exciting and dramatically scenic walk with plenty of rock hopping, to a fine mountain summit in the northern Grampian range.

The Mt Stapylton climb, close to the northern tip of the Grampians, is one of the most exhilarating and scenic walks in the park. Between sections of well-made walking track, there's plenty of rock hopping, some moderate scrambling and a traverse of an exceptionally long rock ramp. The weird and wonderful rock formations include a very lifelike bird poised to take flight. The walk starts and finishes at Stapylton camping ground, a good base for other walks in the Northern Grampians and close to Ngamadjidj Aboriginal shelter.

Mt Stapylton was named by explorer Major Thomas Mitchell in 1836 after his second-in-command, Granville Stapylton.

PLANNING
For a detailed description of when to walk and what to bring, see Planning in the introduction to the Grampians National Park.

Maps
Vicmap's 1:50,000 *Northern Grampians* sheet in the Outdoor Leisure Map series covers only part of the Mt Stapylton walk. In the 1:25,000 Vicmap series, the *Stapylton* map is the best option.

GETTING TO/FROM THE WALK
From Grampians Rd (C222), turn east along Plantation Rd at a junction 25km south of the Western Hwy or 43km north-west from Halls Gap. The sealed surface ends 3.8km along; Stapylton camping ground is 2.2km farther on. For a drop-off and pick-up service from the trailheads, call Halls Gap Taxis (☎ 019 943 691 mobile).

THE WALK
The walk starts at the western end of the camping ground car park. A short gravelled walking track leads to a fire trail junction; continue directly ahead (do not turn right) and follow the track through open bushland and across a boardwalk to Pohlner Rd. Cross the gravel road and follow a clear path through bushland for about 100m to a junction and bear right. The gradient sharpens as you begin to climb via many short flights of stone steps. The track reaches a broad ridge and climbs more gently through pine, banksia and stringybark woodland. At a track junction, continue towards Mt Stapylton and soon emerge onto open rocky ground (1½ hours from the start) with superb views of the rugged Mt Difficult Range to the south.

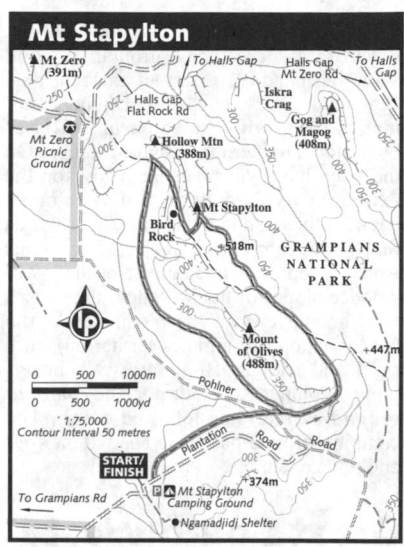

For the next 15 minutes or so, the route alternately crosses rock ribs and open ground, then leads through a eucalyptus woodland. At the edge of a deep cleft, descend steeply and turn sharp left at the bottom, go down a gully for about 50m, then bear right along a narrow path. This takes you back to open rock; a little farther on, look up to the left to spot an orange triangle, indicating the line upwards along a sandstone terrace below a high cliff. Then it's down a rock ramp, left then right, generally skirting the cliffs, to a succession of ramps, bushland and terraces to a deep gully. Climb to a track junction (one hour after reaching open ground) and turn right to Mt Stapylton. The trail continues up to a ridge, but then promptly loses some of this height; go along the base of the cliffs and through a narrow gap to a long ramp rising to the left. Climb this steep rock slab, skirting the beautifully fretted sandstone on the mountain's western face. Then comes a slightly awkward scramble up a 2m chimney, an airy traverse and the **rocky summit**. The magnificent panorama takes in Mt Zero and Hollow Mountain nearby, the Victoria and Mt Difficult Ranges, and many distant features.

Return to the last track junction and head towards Mt Zero picnic ground. Beyond some bushland, you start an amazing descent down a broad band of rock hundreds of metres long, with the colourful walls of Stapylton's western face soaring above. On the way, have your camera ready for the extraordinary **Bird Rock**. A few minutes back into bushland, turn left towards Stapylton camping ground (45 minutes from the top). The track traverses the lower wooded slopes of the Mt Stapylton massif, with good views of the mountain. At the next junction (40 minutes farther on), turn right and another 10-minute walk brings you to Pohlner Rd. Return to the *camping ground* by the route followed earlier. The camping ground has some shady tent sites and a water supply.

Great South West Walk

The 250km-long Great South West Walk (GSWW), in the south-western corner of the state, is one of the finest long-distance walking tracks in Australia. The walk is immensely varied, featuring lovely eucalyptus forests, pockets of cool temperate rainforest, the serenely beautiful Glenelg River lined with limestone cliffs, the nearly unbroken 60km-long beach of Discovery Bay, spectacular Cape Bridgewater headland, glorious Bridgewater Bay, the cliffs and heaths of Cape Nelson and the foreshores of Nelson, Grant and Portland Bays. Virtually all this is on public land, in national and coastal parks, state forest, and coastal and road reserves.

Hundreds of people have completed the GSWW since it was opened in 1981 and many more have enjoyed short sections. The boxed text 'Planning the Great South West Walk' provides practical information about the full walk. A day walk along the spectacular section near Cape Bridgewater is described in this section and an outline of a day beside the Glenelg River is given in Other Walks at the end of the chapter.

HISTORY
The GSWW was developed as a cooperative effort between enthusiastic and dedicated volunteers, Parks Victoria and its predecessors, and local businesses. The idea for the GSWW came from the local chief district ranger, Sam Bruton, who found in high school principal Bill Golding a match for his enthusiasm and determination. National parks staff, high school students and volunteers were drawn together to prepare camp sites, cut tracks, build bridges and mark the route; it was first walked in November 1981. The Friends of the Great South West Walk was established at roughly the same time; the group continues to make improvements to the trail, provides support and information to walkers and promotes the walk widely.

Cape Bridgewater

Duration	4¾–5 hours
Distance	18km
Standard	easy-medium
Start	Bridgewater Lakes
Finish	Bridgewater Bay
Nearest Towns	Cape Bridgewater, Portland
Public Transport	no

Summary Coast walking second to none along superb cliff-top tracks, past natural springs, blowholes, spectacular headlands, a seal colony and over Victoria's highest coastal cliff.

The Cape Bridgewater headland separating Discovery and Bridgewater Bays has the highest coastal cliffs in Victoria (at 130m) and is a major highlight of the GSWW. The walk takes you right round the headland from Bridgewater Lakes to Bridgewater Bay on an excellent walking track, often quite close to the cliff's edge. (The limestone cliffs are inherently unstable, so think twice before trying to get a better photo from near the edge.)

Several solidly built lookouts provide exciting views of the cliffs and of the Australian fur seal colony – about 650 youngsters on the eastern shore.

PAUL SINCLAIR

PAUL SINCLAIR

RICHARD I'ANSON

Top: Sunset over tranquil Lake Mournpall in the dry, Mallee country, Hattah–Kulkyne NP, Victoria.
Middle: Taipan Wall, popular with rock climbers, Mt Stapylton, Grampians National Park, Victoria.
Bottom: Petrified forests create an eerie landscape at Cape Bridgewater, near Portland, Victoria.

PETER PTSCHELINZEW

ALISTAIR PATON

PAUL SINCLAIR

GREG CAIRE

GREG CAIRE

GREG CAIRE

Exploring Victoria's coast. **Top Left:** Footprints, Cape Otway NP. **Top Right:** A stunning view of the Cathedral, Wilsons Promontory NP. **Middle Left:** Wave-worn boulders at Waterloo Bay, Wilsons Promontory NP. **Middle Right:** Wading Thurra River, Croajingolong NP. **Bottom Left:** Winter clouds, Croajingolong NP. **Bottom Right:** Dawn light catches the spray, Seal Cove, Croajingolong NP.

While most of the route is within Cape Bridgewater Coastal Reserve, the 500m of track south-west of Cape Bridgewater town crosses private land.

The Springs Camp, one of the GSWW camp sites, 6.5km from Bridgewater Lakes, could serve as a base for a leisurely exploration of the headland, lakes and beaches.

NATURAL HISTORY

Most of the headland consists of limestone, resting on a base of black volcanic basalt and scoria. When rainwater percolating through the limestone meets the basalt, it can't go any farther and escapes through the rock 'junction' to form springs. On the western side of the cape, these springs were used to water cattle.

Another intriguing feature is the so-called petrified forest near Cape Duquesne. With the less colourful but correct name of rhizo concretions, these fragile (and protected) empty tubular formations are actually the outlines of ancient roots, plant remains and hollows in the soil which were filled with lime-rich material; this set – like concrete – and has been exposed by erosion of the surrounding material.

PLANNING

For a description of when to walk and what to bring, see the boxed text 'Planning the Great South West Walk'.

Maps

The Vicmap 1:25,000 *Cape Bridgewater* map shows the route of the walk, although there have been some changes since it was researched and published.

NEAREST TOWNS
Cape Bridgewater

Cape Bridgewater, a handful of holiday houses and permanent homes, is tucked into a corner of idyllic Bridgewater Bay, a lovely arc of white-sand and rolling surf.

Places to Stay & Eat At the *Cape Bridgewater Holiday Camp (☎ 03-5526 7267)*, on Bridgewater Rd, you can stay in one of the self-contained double cabins for $40, or for $17 per night in a backpacker dorm with the use of a large kitchen.

Sea View Lodge (☎ 03-5526 7276), on Bridgewater Rd, is an old-style friendly place overlooking Bridgewater Bay. There's a budget double with private facilities for $60 with B&B; the more luxurious doubles start at $90. You can prepare your own meals in a small kitchen or have a barbecue. Hosts Sue and Phil can provide transport to local walks.

Just up the hill from the beach, *Spindrift Tea Rooms (☎ 03-5526 7264)* is open from 10.30 am to 6 pm Thursday to Monday and on all public and school holidays. The Devonshire teas are second to none; more substantial meals cost around $9.50. The tea rooms has a BYO licence.

Bridgewater Bay Kiosk, by the beach, is open daily until 5 pm for takeaways and cold drinks.

Getting There & Away Cape Bridgewater is 21km west of Portland via Bridgewater Rd (C193). There is no public transport.

Portland

Portland is Victoria's oldest town and the gateway to the GSWW. The Visitor Information Centre (☎ 03-5523 2671, fax 5521 7287, ✉ portlandvic@glenelg.vic.gov.au), in the Maritime Discovery Centre, Lee Breakwater Rd, Portland 3305, on the shore of Portland Bay, is open daily. Here you can pick up local accommodation information and maps and guides for the walk.

Portland Disposals (☎ 03-5523 1441), on 13 Julia St, stocks general camping gear, including small gas canisters.

Places to Stay & Eat Overlooking the bay, *Centenary Caravan Park (☎ 03-5523 1487)*, in Bentinck St, has cabins from $42, powered sites at $15 per double and tent sites at $13 per double. The park's backpacker accommodation is very popular and often booked out; the tariff is $16 per person in twin rooms, with shared facilities including a kitchen. Otherwise, Portland is well supplied with hotels and motels – contact the visitor centre for full details.

Planning the Great South West Walk

Before embarking on the Great South West Walk (GSWW), an unforgettable trekking adventure, some planning and preparation is necessary; the information here is a useful starting point.

The best time to undertake the GSWW is in autumn (between March and May) or September and December. Although long, the GSWW is generally a fairly easy walk, mostly on tracks or fire trails and with minimal distances on roads. The total trail distance is 225km by the Discovery Bay beach route or 247km by the inland alternative. It can be completed in 12 to 14 days.

Passing only through the small towns of Nelson (near the South Australian border) and Cape Bridgewater (between Nelson and Portland), a good deal of the GSWW is through quite remote country, where walkers need to be well prepared. Walkers are encouraged to make entries in the logbooks at camp sites, mainly to keep track of people in the event of bushfires. Streams in the Cobboboonee Forest may be drinkable, but the Glenelg River is usually brackish. There's very little surface water along the coast.

What to Bring
A fuel stove is essential as firewood is extremely scarce or nonexistent at the coast camp sites. The walk involves long sections with no shelter from sun, wind or rain, so good protective clothing is vital. Remember that it can be very hot and dry in the forest during summer and wet in normal winters.

You'll need to be prepared to carry food and fuel from Portland to Nelson and from there back to Portland. Parcels can be sent to the Nelson post office (☎ 08-8738 4061). The Friends of the GSWW *may* be able to deliver food parcels to walk camp sites (see Information Sources later for contact details).

Maps & Books
The Great South West Walk, a booklet of planimetric 1:100,000 maps, provides practical information and a basic description of each stage between the camp sites. *Short Walks on and Around the Great South West Walk* is a booklet by David Huxtable describing 20 outings.

The walk (except the short section through South Australia) is covered by 11 Vicmap 1:25,000 topographical maps, most showing its route. Parks Victoria's *Lower Glenelg National*

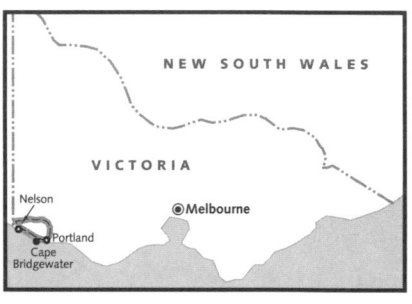

There are plenty of pubs, fish-and-chip shops and good restaurants. For good value you could try the BYO *Pino's Pizza House* (☎ *03-5521 7388, 8 Julia St)* for pizza, pasta and steak; expect to pay around $12.

Canton Palace (☎ 03-5523 3677, 7 Julia St) offers a Chinese smorgasbord for around $14; it is BYO and licensed.

Percy St has a *supermarket* (open daily), *butcher, fish shop, greengrocer* and *bakery*.

Getting There & Away Portland is 365km by road from Melbourne via the Princes Hwy (A1), or 453km via the Great Ocean Rd (B100).

V/Line (☎ 13 6196) has a daily train and coach service from Melbourne via Geelong and Warrnambool to Portland; the one-way fare is $44.20 for the 4¾-hour journey.

GETTING TO/FROM THE WALK
The walk starts at Bridgewater Lakes. From Portland, turn off Bridgewater Rd 18km west of Portland, then follow the Bridgewater Lakes road to the car park and picnic area overlooking the lakes. If you're staying

Planning the Great South West Walk

Park: Discovery Bay Coastal Park visitor guide includes a useful map and basic information about facilities and features.

Information Sources
The Friends of the Great South West Walk group (✉ fgsww@hotmail.com.au), PO Box 192, Portland 3305, is a useful first contact for walkers. Members can give trail advice, provide a drop-off and pick-up service and may be able to deliver food parcels to camp sites. Descriptions of the walk are available on Portland's Web site (💻 www.portlandnow.net.au). There's a Lower Glenelg National Park office (☎ 08-88738 4051) in Nelson, open daily, which distributes national park camping permits.

Permits & Regulations
Use of the camp sites along the GSWW is free for anyone doing a section of the walk. Otherwise, for camp sites in Lower Glenelg National Park you'll need to obtain a permit ($9.50 per night during peak periods and $6.90 at off-peak times) from the park office in Nelson (see Information Sources). Each camp site has a toilet and fireplace and water should be available.

Getting To/From the Walk
As the walk starts and finishes in the town of Portland (see Nearest Towns in the Cape Bridgewater walk), access by public transport isn't a problem.

The Walk
Days 1 to 4 (75.7km) take you from Portland north to Cobboboonee Forest, then generally west to the Glenelg River. Three days (53.2km) of spectacular walking downstream lead you to the small town of Nelson. A pleasant place to break the journey, Nelson has a well-stocked *shop*, the *Nelson Hotel (☎ 08-8738 4011)* for a square meal and accommodation, and the *Kywong Caravan Park (☎ 08-8738 4174)*.

From here, the biggest challenge unfolds: Discovery Bay. Few people go all the way along the sand, which can be very soft. The inland alternatives include crossing Mt Richmond National Park down to the eastern end of the bay and on towards Cape Bridgewater (five days, 71.8km), with accommodation and places to eat (see Nearest Towns in the Cape Bridgewater walk). The next stage is from the village of Cape Bridgewater to a camp just inland from Bridgewater Bay (15km). Another two days (31.5km) will bring you back to Portland.

locally, it may be possible to arrange a lift for the 8.5km from Cape Bridgewater town to the start of the walk.

THE WALK
On the southern side of the Bridgewater Lakes picnic area, go through a stile in the fence where a sign indicates the distance to the Blowholes. Follow an old 4WD track for about 150m, then climb another stile on the left and continue generally south. After several minutes, pass a turn-off to Discovery Bay and bear left towards the Blowholes.

The track overlooks **Bridgewater Lakes** as it crosses undulating dunes lying along the narrow valley cradling the lakes. Cross an informal track leading to the beach; a little farther on, a gravel walking track leads up to the low cliff tops overlooking Descartes Bay and the rocky coast. About 1.5km farther on, steps lead down to secluded **Whites Beach**.

Pass the turn-off to the Amos Rd car park and after 2.5km you come to the Springs Camp (1½ hours from Bridgewater Lakes). Continue across the limestone pavement, past some 'petrified forest' and on to a lookout

VICTORIA

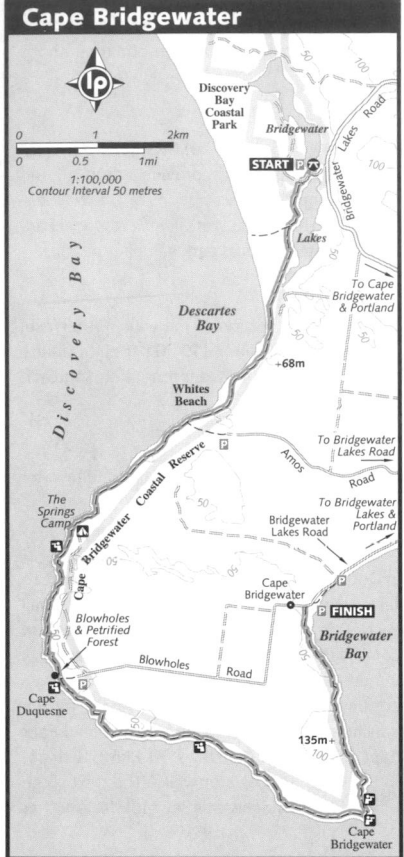

Cape Bridgewater

Discovery Bay Coastal Park
Bridgewater
START
Lakes
To Cape Bridgewater & Portland
Descartes Bay
+68m
Whites Beach
To Bridgewater Lakes Road
Amos Road
The Springs Camp
To Bridgewater Lakes & Portland
Bridgewater Lakes Road
Cape Bridgewater
FINISH
Bridgewater Bay
Blowholes & Petrified Forest
Blowholes Road
Cape Duquesne
135m+
Cape Bridgewater

0   1   2km
0   0.5   1mi
1:100,000
Contour Interval 50 metres

Discovery Bay

Bridgewater Coastal Reserve

Springs). With Discovery Bay now out of sight, you reach **Cape Duquesne** and head eastwards along a superb cliff-top track. The track leads on, mostly above the cliffs, to **Cape Bridgewater** and its lookout (1¼ hours from Petrified Forest). From here, you can look straight down to the rock platform where seals usually bask. Another nearby lookout gives even more dramatic views of a sea cave.

The track then climbs to Victoria's **highest coastal cliff** (130m); the panorama takes in Discovery Bay, the beautiful crescent of Bridgewater Bay and Cape Nelson to the east. Descend steadily to the shore, then climb over a low cliff and down to a car park beside the road. From here, steps lead down to the bay foreshore (one hour from the cape).

Otway National Park

Its wild and spectacular coast, temperate rainforest and tall eucalyptus forests make Otway National Park, declared in 1981, one of the most diverse parks in Victoria. An elongated, mainly narrow coastal strip stretches from the estuary of the Gellibrand River near Princetown almost to Cape Otway; a large forested block extends into the rugged Otway Ranges for up to 12km from the coast between Point Franklin and Shelly Beach (near Apollo Bay). The total area is 12,876 hectares, including 60km of beautiful coastline.

There are several shortish walking tracks along the coast and some in the forests to the east; the magnificent Great Ocean Walk, traversing the entire park, is well on the way to completion. The walk described is an adaptable one linking Aire River and Parker River beach via Cape Otway – some of the finest coast walking in the state.

platform where a sign explains the phenomenon of freshwater pools on the rocky shore. About 200m farther on, another sign describes the volcanic origins of the twin rock pools below; from here, it's a good kilometre to the next vantage point, where the geology of Cape Bridgewater is revealed.

A side track leads to **Blowholes Lookout** (2km from the Springs Camp), where the view of Discovery Bay is always spectacular and the blowholes sometimes also. Follow the circuit track south back to the main track and you will soon arrive at the official **Petrified Forest** (45 minutes from the

HISTORY

The Katabanut Aboriginal people spent time on the Otway coast, the many middens revealing their enjoyment of rich harvests from the sea.

The Cape Otway Lightstation began operation in 1848 to help guide ships round the treacherous coast. Even so, ships still foundered and the vestiges of wrecks can be seen on the beaches; graves in the tiny Cape Otway cemetery testify to the hazards of early sea travel. The 'old light' was extinguished in 1994 and replaced with a small, automatic, solar-powered beacon.

The dense forests and rugged terrain have to some extent impeded settlement; however, the Otways are also a rich source of timber and the forests have been extensively harvested since the late 19th century. Logging in the Otways is still a controversial issue.

NATURAL HISTORY

The park is in one of the wettest areas in Victoria, so vegetation everywhere away from the coast is luxuriant. Among the eucalyptus species in the forests blanketing the steep southern slopes of the Otway Ranges are mountain ash (Australia's tallest hardwood tree) and the handsome blue gum. Many sheltered gullies are filled with dense cool temperate rainforest of myrtle beech, ferns and satinwood, a white-flowering shrub found nowhere else in Victoria. In striking contrast, coastal cliffs and dunes can support only low wind-pruned shrubs, mainly coastal tea-tree, coastal wattle and coast heath.

PLANNING

November to April is the best time to be in the Otways; it's usually cooler than other parts of Victoria during the summer. The rest of the year can be cold, wet and windy and gales can sweep the coast, although fine spells are not unknown.

If you plan to camp at one of the national park camping grounds, you will definitely need a fuel stove and/or you own firewood from outside the park (see Permits & Regulations later). You'll also need to carry drinking water – there are very few reliable sources along the coast.

Maps & Books

Vicmap's 1:50,000 *The Otways & Shipwreck Coast* map in the Outdoor Leisure Map series covers a huge area from Port Campbell to Angahook. It shows some walking tracks, although not the current park boundaries. It's available locally at various outlets. Of the Vicmap 1:25,000 series, you'll need the *Glenaire* and *Cape Otway* maps for this walk.

Walking the Otways compiled by Geelong Bushwalking Club has descriptions of 38 day walks and two extended treks in the area, each with an extract from the Vicmap 1:50,000 sheet. Some walks cross private property, but owners change, so seek permission first before setting out. Consult the park office about walks using tracks described as 'rough' – they may have become impassable.

Plant Identikit Otway Ranges by Rodger Elliot & Trevor Pescott is a good general natural history guide. *Beacons of Hope* by Donald Walker includes the early history of Cape Otway, and several titles by Don Charlwood about local maritime history will help pass a wet day enjoyably. Trevor Pescott's *The Otway Ranges* covers both the human and natural history of the area.

Parks Victoria has produced a comprehensive brochure about the park, including camping information.

Information Sources

The Apollo Bay Parks Victoria office (see Apollo Bay later in this section for details) is a useful contact for park information.

Permits & Regulations

A fee is charged for camping permits at any of the six national park camping grounds, however basic; it should be collected by a ranger visiting the area. For vehicle-based camping at Aire River East and West, Johanna Beach and Blanket Bay, it's $8.30 per site per night for up to six people; at Point Franklin and Parker Hill, the fee is $3.50 per site. For car-free walkers, the fee at Parker Hill and Point Franklin is $0.60 per person per night and $1.40 at Aire River, Johanna Beach and Blanket Bay.

It's necessary to book a site at the popular Blanket Bay camping ground during Christmas and Easter holidays; call the Apollo Bay office (see Apollo Bay later).

Warning

On one of the wildest, windiest places on the Victorian coast, this walk can include extensive stretches along beaches and the rocky shore. Before setting out, assess the state of the tide (ask at the Visitor Information Centre in Apollo Bay); if it's on the way in, use the inland alternatives and return along the shoreline. Always be on the alert for freak waves, especially if there's a good swell running.

Collection of firewood is prohibited in the park. You can buy a bag of wood from the Mobil petrol station on the Great Ocean Rd at the eastern end of Apollo Bay; during busy periods, Parks Victoria may provide wood at busier camping grounds.

NEAREST TOWNS & FACILITIES
Lavers Hill

This small settlement, spread along the Great Ocean Rd 49km north-west of Apollo Bay and 35km from Cape Otway, is prone to enveloping mists.

Places to Stay & Eat The *Lavers Hill Roadhouse Caravan Park (☎ 03-5237 3251)*, on the Great Ocean Rd, provides tent sites ($12), powered sites ($15), on-site caravans ($30) and small, simple doubles ($40) with shared facilities. Next door is a tavern where dinner is served from 6 until 8 pm Monday to Saturday. There's a handy *bottle shop* next door.

Blackwood Gully Tea Rooms (☎ 03-5237 3290), on the Great Ocean Rd, is open daily for daytime meals and takeaways, its speciality being Billabongs – a damper (type of scone) with fillings ($10.50) – maps are sold as well.

Gardenside Manor Tea Rooms (☎ 03-5236 3391), Great Ocean Rd, is open from 8 am till early evening. It comprises a tearoom, takeaway food service, the local post office and a small shop, which sells maps and books, fresh meat, bread and stove fuel.

Details of other accommodation in the area are available from the Great Ocean Rd Visitor Information Centre (see Apollo Bay).

Getting There & Away Lavers Hill is 242km from Melbourne via the Princes Fwy and Princes Hwy (M1) to Geelong, the Surf Coast Hwy (B100) to Torquay and the scenic Great Ocean Rd (B100).

A V/Line bus (☎ 13 6196) stops at Lavers Hill on Friday only, en route from Melbourne, Geelong and Lorne to Warrnambool (117km west of Lavers Hill). The one-way adult fare to Lavers Hill is $34.20 for the 5¾-hour journey.

Apollo Bay

Pretty Apollo Bay is a popular summer resort. The Visitor Information Centre (☎ 03-5237 6529, fax 5237 6194, @ gorvic @colacotway.vic .gov.au), Great Ocean Rd, Apollo Bay 3233, can tell you all you need to know about facilities around Apollo Bay. It's open daily and stocks a good range of local guides and maps, including the Parks Victoria brochure on the park.

The Parks Victoria office (☎ 03-5237 6889, fax 5237 7495) is on the corner of Oak Ave and Montrose St (about 2km north of the Great Ocean Rd) and is open weekdays.

True Value Hardware, 43 Great Ocean Rd, sells Primus gas and stove fuel.

Places to Stay & Eat Of the caravan parks in the area, *Apollo Bay Recreation Reserve (☎ 03-5237 6577, 121 Great Ocean Rd)*, beside the Barham River, has both powered and unpowered sites from $20.

Surfside Backpackers YHA (☎03-5237 7263, @ apollobay@yhavic.org.au), on the corner of Great Ocean Rd and Gambier St, has a great outlook over the beach. It has a range of rooms, from small dorms to doubles and family rooms – prices start at $13 a night.

Eateries are thick on the ground and range from takeaways to sophisticated restaurants. Several offer imaginative menus with main courses from $16 to $18, including *Buffs Bistro (☎03-5237 6403, 51 Great Ocean Rd)* and *Bay Leaf (☎ 03-5237 6470, 131 Great Ocean Rd)*.

For self-caterers there are two *supermarkets*, a good *bakery*, *health food shop*, *butcher* and an *ice-cream shop* with 40 different temptations.

Drop in to *Nautigals Café (☎ 03-5237 6058)*, on the Great Ocean Rd, any time after 8 am for breakfast while you check emails ($2) and surf the Net ($5 for 30 minutes).

Getting There & Away Apollo Bay is 189km from Melbourne (see Lavers Hill earlier for details).

V/Line (☎ 13 6196) runs a daily bus service from Melbourne via Geelong (four hours); the adult one-way fare is $27.

Cape Otway

Run by a pioneering local family, *Bimbi Park (☎/fax 03-5237 9246)*, Lighthouse Rd, in a peaceful bushland setting, has cabins for $60, on-site vans from $32, tent sites for $15 per double, and a backpacker lodge with bunkrooms and a communal kitchen where the tariff is $15. During summer, films are shown in a marvellous open-air cinema.

Cape Otway Lightstation (☎ 03-5237 9240) has double studio apartments at $245 for a weekend; you'll need to take only your own food. It's open daily for tours from 10 am to 5 pm, costing $6 to have a look round or $10 for a guided tour.

Getting There & Away The Otway Lighthouse Tourist Rd (C157) branches from the Great Ocean Rd 25km west of Apollo Bay. Bimbi Park is 7km along the road and 5km north of Cape Otway. The road goes all the way to the Cape Otway Lightstation.

Cape Otway

Duration	2 days
Distance	33km
Standard	medium
Start/Finish	Aire River East camping area
Nearest Towns	Lavers Hill, Apollo Bay
Public Transport	no
Summary	A magnificent coast walk along cliff tops and beaches, past an unusual waterfall and historic Cape Otway to sheltered coves and a bush camp site.

This is a superbly scenic and varied walk taking in cliffs, beaches, rock platforms, a

waterfall and a secluded river estuary. It can be done as an overnight walk from Aire River through to Parker Hill camping area and back (33km return), or as two out-and-back journeys: from Aire River to Cape Otway (22km return) and from Cape Otway to Parker River (11km return).

Yet another possibility is to start both day walks from Cape Otway. To get there, follow the Otway Lighthouse Tourist Rd to the car park 12km from the Great Ocean Rd. You'll be following marked walking tracks nearly all the way: the route, sandy in places and rocky in others, is generally well defined and marked with orange arrowheads. By the time you read this, the route of the walk eastwards from Cape Otway car park to the coast may have been realigned; it should be clearly signposted.

If the Aire River mouth is closed, which it usually is, the sand on the seaward side can be very soft and treacherous.

GETTING TO/FROM THE WALK
To reach Aire River East camping area, turn off the Great Ocean Rd 24km from both Lavers Hill and Apollo Bay along a narrow sealed road signposted 'Hordern Vale access'. Keep on the bitumen (past a junction) towards Otway National Park, where you turn right to Aire River East camping area; it's 2km down the gravel road.

THE WALK
Day 1: Aire River East Camping Area to Parker Hill
4½–5 hours, 16.5km

There are two possible alternative routes for the first section of the walk from Aire River to Rainbow Falls. It's possible to walk from *Aire River East camping area* (with toilet, water and simple fireplaces) to the coast via the sandy 4WD track close to the river. At low tide, it takes about 30 minutes to negotiate lowish bluffs and boulders to 'Cormorant Rock', a favourite perch for these black sea-going birds to dry their wings. From there it's the sands of **Station Beach** all the way to **Rainbow Falls** (8km from the start). Note, however, that this route along the beach can be rather soft.

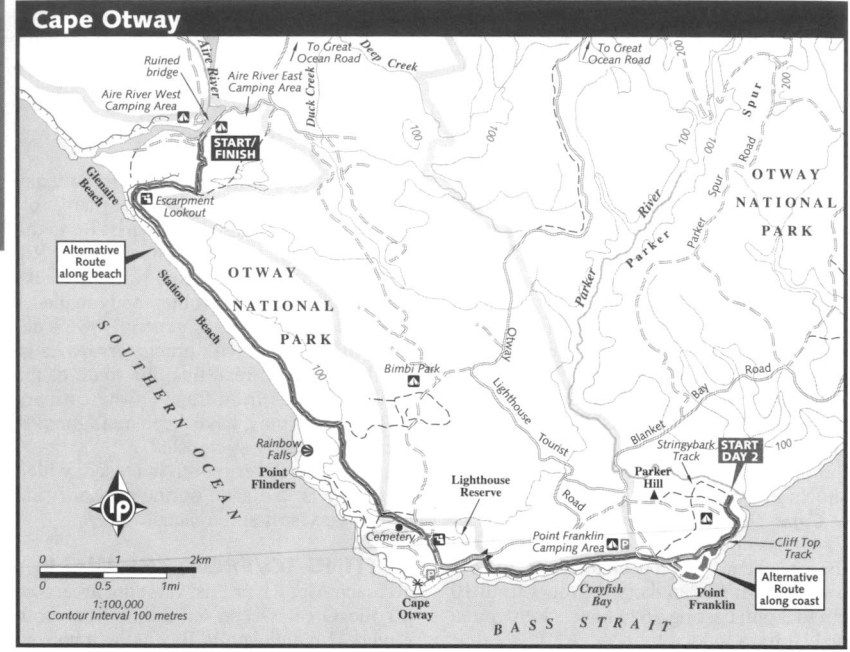

For the main route (and second alternative), follow a short path from the camp site to the shore, emerging not far from the ruinous bridge across Aire River. Walk down the 4WD track for 100m and turn left up a track (signposted to Escarpment Track and the lightstation) for 50m then go left again along a sandy foot track. Heading in the general direction of the coast, it burrows through dense coast wattle. About 40 minutes from the start you come to the short side track to **Escarpment Lookout**, with fine views of Station Beach and the coast westwards. Back on the main track, you soon emerge onto open and rocky ground; some cairns and occasional arrows mark the route. About 40 minutes after reaching open ground, the route crosses a sandy 4WD track and 10 minutes farther on you come to a delightful **spring** with cold clear water bubbling out of the ground.

Continue to a track junction where you can diverge down to the beach to have a look at **Rainbow Falls** – in good years, there's quite a cascade over the rocks covered with multicoloured algae and mosses.

Rejoin the track and continue past a turn-off to Bimbi Park on the left, then start to climb as the track leads away from the coast, partly in the open, partly through clumps of tea-tree and wattle. After 40 minutes you come to tiny **Cape Otway Lighthouse Cemetery** with the graves of lightstation staff and children, and seamen who drowned in the Blanket Bay disaster of 1896. A short distance beyond the cemetery, turn right along a wide track and follow it to Cape Otway car park (20 minutes from the cemetery); on the way it's worth taking a side track to a good **lookout** over the lightstation and grounds.

Walk across the car park and along the road for 400m to the grid and gateway. On the coastal side of the grid, negotiate the fence on the right and follow a narrow walking track gently uphill through the grass, soon crossing another east-west fence. Then bear left, paralleling the fence on your left, still on a narrow track. After about 250m in this direction, the track heads for the low cliff top, which it generally keeps to, apart from an inland stretch past a small point on the western side of Crayfish Bay.

About 40 minutes from the road, you come to a rough path leading down to **Crayfish Bay**; you can either go down to the shore and follow it all the way to Parker River, or stay high for a while, along what is now a clearly defined, occasionally sandy track. Along the upper track, you soon reach a parking area. Walk through it to a cluster of signs pointing to Parker River and follow the **Cliff Top Track** through bushland. This leads to the *Parker Hill camping area* and, a short distance farther on, the secluded inlet where the river flows towards the sea.

Here you join the coastal approach to Parker River by going down the steps from the parking area to the beach. The rusted remains of the anchor of *Eric the Red*, which sank near here in 1880, are set into a rock beside a small gully nearby. About 15 minutes' walking brings you to Point Franklin (about 40 minutes from Crayfish Bay), where the coastline changes direction more markedly than at Cape Otway. Around the corner, the view is north-east to the steep timbered ridges reaching down to the shore.

Continue along the shoreline rock platform, at the base of low cliffs, round the beautiful honeycomb rocks of the headland on the western side of the **Parker River estuary** and on to the small beach (25 minutes from Point Franklin). To reach the track up to Parker Hill, walk upstream beside the river (the water here should be drinkable) and find a narrow track leading west into the scrub. It soon climbs the hillside to a junction where signs indicate the way to Point Franklin by Cliff Top Track, the coast and Stringybark Track. Continue up to the *Parker Hill camping area* in trees near the end of a 4WD track (about 15 minutes from the beach). Water from the Parker River, about 500m down the hill to the beach, may be slightly brackish but it's drinkable.

Day 2: Parker Hill to Aire River
4½–5 hours, 16.5km
If you arrived at Parker Hill via the shoreline route, you could start the return along the Cliff Top Track. From near the end of the 4WD track here, bear left across an open grassy area along a narrow track (Cliff Top Track), past another sign to Point Franklin. With the lightstation in view, bear right along an old 4WD track and continue to a parking area. Here you can, of course, choose to walk along the shore to Crayfish Bay, then up to the cliff top and the track followed on the outward journey.

Alternatively, keep inland across the car park, past the Point Franklin camping area and along an old 4WD track to the walking track, which leads to the road and the Cape Otway car park (1½ hours from Parker Hill). Join the track signposted to Rainbow Falls and Aire River, and follow it back, with as much or as little beach walking as you want.

Victorian Alps

The Victorian Alps begin roughly 100km north-east of Melbourne, continuing to the Victoria–New South Wales (NSW) border. They include all of the highest peaks in the state. Much of the mountain range is protected in Australia's largest national park, the Alpine National Park (646,000 hectares). Other smaller but equally important parks are Baw Baw National Park and Mt Buffalo National Park.

Like Kosciuszko National Park, many rare and endangered species of fauna survive in the Victorian Alps, and the region is covered in a diverse variety of vegetation, some of it only found in isolated localities.

The Victorian Alps are a tourist attraction year-round. Pretty towns can be found in the valleys around the area, each catering for the traveller and offering a good base from which to explore the mountains. In winter, downhill skiers flock in large numbers to the major ski resorts of Falls Creek, Mt Buller and Mt Hotham, and to smaller areas at Mt Baw Baw and Mt Buffalo. Cross-country skiing is also popular, the

VICTORIA

Victorian Alps

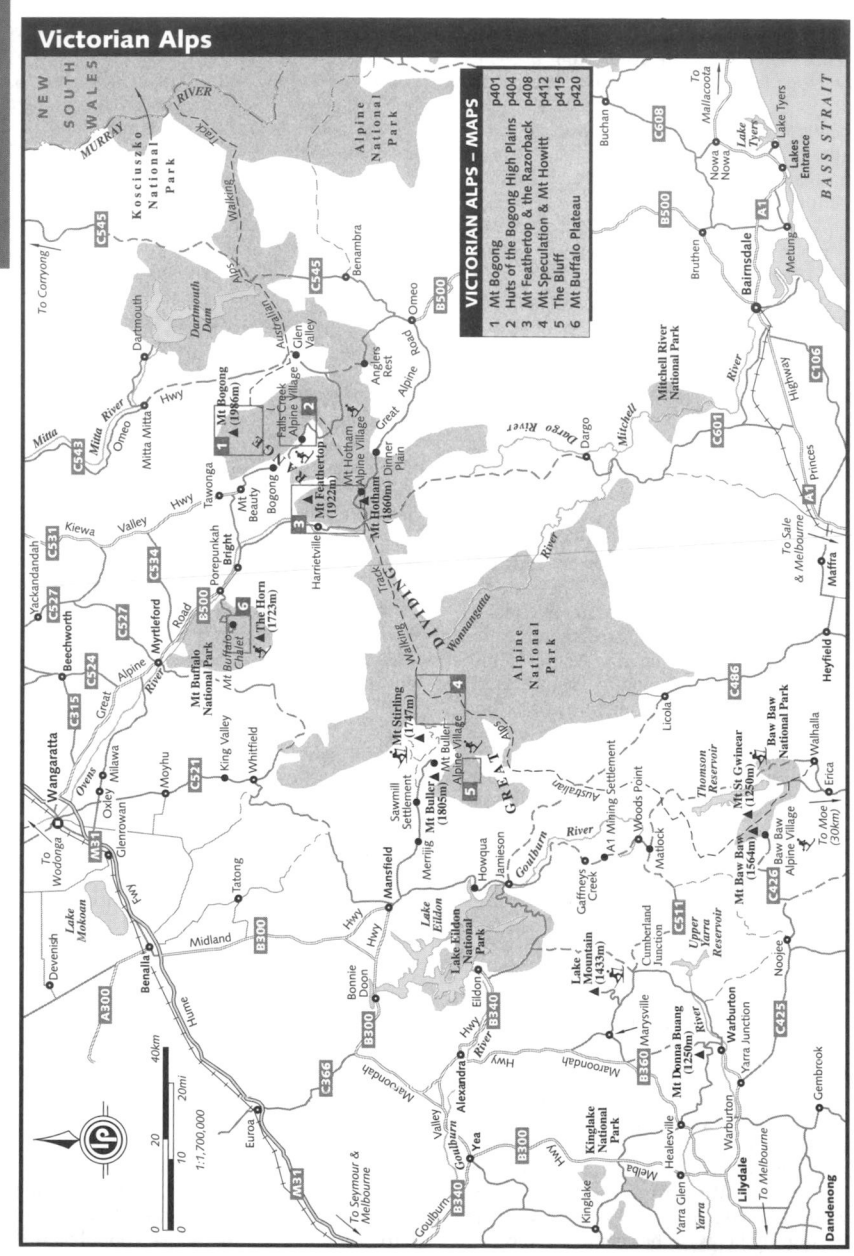

rolling plains and rounded summits being ideal for this sport, while bush camping, 4WD driving and fishing are popular in the summer months.

But by far the best way to see the most attractive and isolated parts of the Victorian Alps is on foot. This huge area is well covered by a network of walking tracks and old 4WD roads, giving access to most of the scenic country. Unfortunately, there is little in the way of true wilderness, but you can still get a feel for the 'wilderness experience' and a sense of isolation during the walks described here. The most popular areas for walking in the Victorian Alps are in the Bogong High Plains region (incorporating the summits of Mts Bogong and Feathertop) and the Wonnangatta–Moroka region (particularly between Mt Speculation and the Bluff). There are five walks described in these two areas, both of which are within the boundaries of the Alpine National Park. One walk is described in Mt Buffalo National Park, an area strikingly different from any other part of the Victorian Alps.

HISTORY

As with all the Australian High Country, the region was first visited by Aborigines about 5000 years ago. They gathered on the mountain plains during the summer months to feed on the Bogong moths, which they found in cracks and fissures in rocks. By the 1860s there were only four local Aborigines left in the area.

In 1843 John Mitchell approached the mountains up the upper Kiewa Valley, but one of the first visits to the highest areas was made by two graziers, Jim Brown and Jack Wells, who traversed the Bogong High Plains in 1851. They also named many of today's well-known features, including Mt Feathertop, Mt Fainter and Pretty Valley, and cut the area's first stock routes.

The botanist, Baron von Mueller, reached north-east Victoria in 1853 and climbed both Mt Buller and Mt Buffalo. The following year, his botanical surveys brought him to the Bogong High Plains.

By the 1880s and 1890s, there was an influx of graziers and, with the discovery of large gold deposits in the valleys, miners. Gold prospectors pushed far up the valleys, and some even high onto the mountains. While most sources of gold eventually ran dry, the Red Robin mine (near Mt Hotham), founded in 1941, is still a viable, small-time operation today.

Locals, appreciating the scenic beauty of the mountains, began promoting the area with brochures and guided walks. Residents from the town of Bright formed the Bright Alpine Club in 1887 and members led excursions to the mountains in both summer and winter; Mts Buffalo and Feathertop being two of their most visited areas. Roads were gradually cut to the heads of the valleys, then over the Alps at Mt Hotham, so that a large section of the mountains became readily accessible to travellers.

The government funded the construction of many accommodation houses in the mountains, such as 'Hotham Heights' at Mt Hotham (1925) and the Chalet on Mt Buffalo (1910). In the early 1920s Hilda Samsing, the lessee of the Chalet, imported a number of pairs of Norwegian skis to facilitate travel around the snow-covered plateau in winter for Chalet guests. Skiing soon became a recognised sport, and the Chalet staff began to offer guided tours of the plateau. Mt Buffalo had, by 1936, laid claim to Australia's first ski lift, but was soon followed by fully fledged resorts at Mt Buller, Mt Hotham and Falls Creek in the 1950s.

The Victorian Railways took over management of the Chalet in 1924. They enlarged and refurbished it so that the Chalet became what was considered at that time the best tourist accommodation house in Australia.

NATURAL HISTORY
Geology

While now relatively low in stature – only 1986m at their highest point – the Victorian Alps were once much higher after a period of uplift and folding between about 95 and 70 million years ago. Since this time, extensive erosion has produced the valleys, plains and rounded mountain tops that we see today. Differential weathering of sediments has produced some quite dramatic and spectacular landscapes, such as the escarpment that can be seen running west from Mt Howitt to the Bluff, with the tilted beds of sedimentary layers clearly visible.

The area within Mt Buffalo National Park was formed by a vastly different process. Around 250 million years ago molten rock pushed upwards into the bedrock before cooling; the surrounding sediments eroded to form the fantastic granite rock outcrops that we now see on the plateau. Some areas of the Alpine National Park have also been intruded by lava flows, and igneous rocks can be seen in isolated locations such as Mt Jim on the Bogong High Plains.

While there is no direct evidence of glaciation in the Victorian Alps, as there is in Kosciuszko National Park, there are some 'periglacial' features resulting from the freeze-thaw process, including solifluction terraces and block streams (boulders of granite and basalt that once flowed downhill and look like rivers of grey rock).

Flora

The flora of the area is generally divided into five main sequences according to altitude. On the valley floors grows savanna woodland, with forests of white and yellow box, black sallee and white manna gum, often with an understorey of low grasses.

Above the woodland dry sclerophyl forest with scribbly gum, peppermint, stringybark and messmate dominates. Between about 900m and 1450m, wet sclerophyl forest harbours tall and slender mountain ash, mountain gum and alpine ash; the understorey consists of ferns, grasses and the native cherry bush.

Higher again, from 1450m to 1800m, is the subalpine zone of predominantly snow gum – tall and straight at lower elevations and short and gnarled near the tree line. Commonly there is a thick understorey of tussock grass and shrubs, purple hovea, royal grevillea, yellow kunzea and the pink grass trigger plant.

Above 1800m is the alpine zone, where the climate is generally too cold and severe for any tree growth at all, except in isolated locations. This region of low plants consists mainly of heaths, grasses, herbs and snow-patch vegetation. Sphagnum bogs occupy wet sites, absorbing water and releasing it slowly throughout the year. Alpine plants are extremely fragile and are slow to recover when damaged.

Fauna

There is also a rich variety of fauna in the Victorian High Country. Some of the more commonly seen animals include the kangaroo, wombat, echidna, native bush rat and marsupial mice. In rivers and streams you might be fortunate enough to see platypuses, water rats and many species of fish.

Birds frequently seen include gang gang and yellow-tailed cockatoos, wedge-tailed eagles, pied currawongs and ravens, colourful flame robins and, deep within alpine ash forest, the elusive lyrebird.

Lizards and skinks are common, but there are also some venomous reptiles, such as black, brown and tiger snakes, that you should avoid. Unfortunately, many feral animals now inhabit the region, including rabbits, foxes, cats and deers. In some areas you may even see brumbies (wild horses).

CLIMATE

The Victorian Alps climate is very similar to that of the range over the border in NSW. For a description of weather conditions in the mountains, see Climate in the introduction to Kosciuszko National Park in the New South Wales chapter.

PLANNING
When to Walk

Winter is really the only season when walking is out of the question, either because of the deep snow that covers many parts of the walking areas described here, or because of the road closures affecting access to some places (contact the Parks Victoria offices mentioned under Information Sources for further information). For the large part of the Victorian Alps, you can walk any time between October and April, although you may find some snowdrifts lingering on the highest peaks of Mts Bogong and Feathertop. The most popular months are January to

Australian Alps Walking Track

This spectacular long-distance walk traverses about 680km of alpine country and summits Australia's highest peaks. The track is an extension and revision of the much older Alpine Walking Track, which traversed the Victorian High Country. It begins in the tiny village of Walhalla in Victoria and ends at the Namadgi Visitor Centre near the outskirts of Canberra in the Australian Capital Territory (ACT).

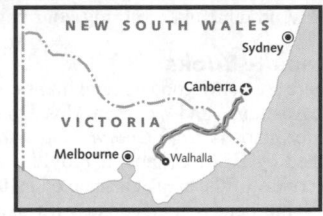

When the original plan for a Victorian Alpine Walking Track was mooted in the 1940s it was met with much disdain by walkers who wanted to keep the mountains free of marked trails. However, in the 1950s and 60s, with logging and tourist roads pushing further into the Victorian mountains and slowly eroding the wilderness value of popular walking destinations, the idea of an Alpine Walking Track became increasingly popular. Work started on the trail in 1970 and was finally completed in 1976, covering a 400km section from Walhalla to the Victorian border at Tom Groggin (near Thredbo).

For many years it was argued that the track should be pushed over the border into New South Wales (NSW) and the ACT, but it was not until the early 1990s that the three governments came to their senses and proposed the Australian Alps Walking Track. The completed track, most of which is clearly marked, follows much of the original route of the Alpine Walking Track, then crosses the mountains of NSW and the ACT, taking in challenging peaks and breathtaking vistas all the way.

It takes about eight weeks to walk the whole track, but most walkers tend to complete sections of the track as shorter, less demanding tours. If you are interested in walking the entire track remember that no major towns are passed (only a few ski villages), so it is necessary to store food caches at designated points beforehand.

The best source of information on the track is John Siseman's *Australian Alps Walking Track*. This excellent guide includes detailed track notes, as well as background information on history, environment, climate, flora and fauna, camping, and maps.

Walks in this book that follow sections of the Australian Alps Walking Track are Mt Bogong, Huts of the Bogong High Plains, and Mt Speculation & Mt Howitt in the Victoria chapter, and Mt Kosciuszko & the Main Range in the NSW chapter.

March, as days are usually warm, weather is generally stable, wild flowers put on their best displays and frosts are least likely.

What to Bring

You should be prepared for mountain weather in all areas visited by the described walks, although some protected areas, such as the Mt Buffalo Plateau, are less severe. Even during optimum walking months, carry wet-weather gear and warm clothing. You can wear runners (training shoes) but proper walking boots offer better foot support and protection against the elements. Lightweight gloves also come in handy in cool, damp conditions, and a warm hat is a must.

For the overnight walks described, a good waterproof tent (strong enough to withstand powerful winds) is essential. A warm, high-quality sleeping bag is also a good idea, especially in the highest areas or during autumn and spring when the nights are frosty.

Fuel stoves are another essential item on the overnight walks, particularly on Mts Bogong and Feathertop where no campfires are allowed. Water points are described in the walk descriptions, but some may dry up on occasions, so it is imperative that you carry at least one large (1L) water bottle per person, and have it full when you commence your walk. There is an increased risk of sunburn, especially in summer and at altitude, so apply sunscreen liberally and frequently, plus lip balm to prevent dry and cracked lips. And remember to bring your compass!

Maps & Books

There are many good general maps covering the Australian and Victorian Alps. One of the better maps is *High Country Victoria*, published by HEMA Maps. It provides a good overview of the area at a scale of 1:300,000.

Some handy guidebooks with extensive walking notes and other information to the region include *Victoria's Alpine National Park* by John Siseman and *70 Walks in Victoria's Bright & Falls Creek Districts* by Tyrone Thomas. *Australian Alps Walking Track*, also by John Siseman, has detailed track notes on this long-distance track as it meanders through the region. *Australian Alps – Kosciuszko, Alpine & Namadgi National Parks* by Deirdre Slattery has some track notes, but also contains loads of other information on the environment, history and development of the Victorian Alps and Snowy Mountains region.

There are some good historical books on the Victorian High Country, but they may be hard to find; these include *Cattleman & Huts of the High Plains* by Harry Stephenson and *Cattlemen of the High Country* by Tor Holth. *The Scroggin Eaters* by Graeme Wheeler gives a good insight into the history of bushwalking in Victoria, and particularly the Victorian Alps.

If you are interested in the flora and fauna of the region, two books worth a look are *Wildlife of the Australian Snow-Country* by Ken Green & William Osborne and *Wildflowers of the Snow Country – A Field Guide to the Australian Alps* by Ian Fraser & Margaret McJannett, with watercolours by Helen Fitzgerald.

Information Sources

The best places for information on the region, including accommodation, transport, maps and books, are local visitor centres. The most convenient centres are listed under the Nearest Towns heading for each walk.

Information can also be sought at local newsagents, some local petrol stations and outdoor gear stores (including those in the major cities).

The Australian Alps National Parks Web site (🖳 www.australianalps.environment .gov.au) is a useful source of background information on the Alps region.

Permits & Regulations

There are no camping fees for bush camping in the Alpine National Park, although there is a charge for using a site at the established camping ground in Mt Buffalo National Park. Mt Buffalo National Park also has a park entrance fee.

One major restriction to be aware of is that no campfires are permitted in the areas surrounding the summits of Mts Bogong and Feathertop – these places are fuel-stove-only areas.

Mt Bogong

Duration	2 days
Distance	26.5km
Standard	medium-hard
Start/Finish	Mountain Creek Camping Area
Nearest Towns	Mt Beauty, Tawonga South
Public Transport	no

Summary A long, steep ascent to Victoria's highest summit, then an exposed ridge to Camp Valley. As well as great views, the trail passes an old stone hut and an isolated mountain waterfall.

For many years Mt Bogong was familiar only to local cattlemen. They drove their cattle to the mountain tops each summer to graze on the sweet herbs and grasses which grow in profusion. Over the years the cattlemen gradually cut paths on which they drove their cattle. By the early 1900s Mt Bogong had been discovered by bushwalkers and cross-country skiers, and a series of huts slowly appeared on the mountain. These added to Maddison's 'Aertex' hut (now in ruins), constructed by the Maddison family in the lower reaches of Camp Valley. Summit Hut (now destroyed) and Michell Hut were constructed as refuges on the two most popular access routes to the mountain, and the popular Cleve Cole Hut was built in memory of a pioneer skier of the region who died on the mountain (see the boxed text 'The Death of Cleve Cole').

The two side trips, to West Peak and Howmans Falls, could easily be completed from a base camp at Cleve Cole Hut, extending the trip to three days on the mountain.

PLANNING

For a detailed description of when to walk and what to bring, see Planning in the introduction to the Victorian Alps. It should be noted that as this is a very exposed walk in sections, you must have a strong weatherproof tent, wet-weather gear, good sleeping bag, warm clothes and a fuel stove.

Maps

The Vicmap 1:50,000 *Bogong Alpine Area* map in the Outdoor Leisure Map series is the best option for this walk. Also by Vicmap are the 1:25,000 sheets titled *Nelse* and *Trappers Creek*, but these show no more detail than *Bogong Alpine Area*.

Permits & Regulations

The walk is within a fuel-stove-only area. No campfires are permitted, so you must carry a fuel stove for cooking.

NEAREST TOWN & FACILITIES
Mt Beauty & Tawonga

At the head of the Kiewa Valley, Mt Beauty (and its twin town of Tawonga South) is an excellent base for walks on Mt Bogong and the Bogong High Plains. Confusingly, Mt Beauty is not a mountain, but a small country town that survives on tourism and the nearby Kiewa Hydroelectric Scheme.

On the left as you come into town along the Kiewa Valley Hwy (C531) is the Australian High Country Visitors Centre (☎ 03-5754 3172). It is open daily and has an accommodation booking line (☎ 1800 808 277). Also on the highway, but a little farther back in Tawonga South, is a Parks Victoria office (☎ 03-5754 4693).

There's an ATM in the shopping centre in Hollonds St.

Places to Stay There are several accommodation options in Tawonga South. *Mt Beauty Holiday Centre & Caravan Park (☎ 03-5754 4396)* has tent sites from $13 per night and on-site vans and cabins from $44. *Carver's Log Cabins (☎ 03-5754 4863)*, in Buckland St, has basic cabins sleeping up to six people from $75 to $110 per night.

Valley View Lodge/Motel (☎ 03-5754 1033), in Allamar Court, has doubles from $90, including breakfast.

For pub-style accommodation, try the *Bogong Hotel (☎ 03-5754 4482)*, on the Kiewa Valley Hwy in the small town of Tawonga, 4km north of Tawonga South. It has rooms with shared bathrooms from $30 a night.

Closer to the trailhead is *Tawonga Caravan Park (☎ 03-5754 4428)*, which has tent sites for $12 per night, on-site vans from $40 and cabins from $45. You'll find it 1km from Tawonga on Mountain Creek Rd.

Places to Eat You can get a good pizza at *Tuscany on Kiewa (☎ 03-5754 4084)*, on the main road in Tawonga South, beside Pyles Coaches & Service Station.

For a more upmarket meal, try *Roi's Diner (☎ 03-5754 4495)*, on the highway into Tawonga South. Good for a feed after the completion of the walk is the *Bogong Hotel* (see Places to Stay), where lunchtime and evening counter meals are served.

Just off the main road in Mt Beauty is the shopping centre on Hollonds St, where you'll find a *supermarket* and a few *cafes* and *takeaway outlets*.

Getting There & Away Mt Beauty is 365km from Melbourne via Myrtleford. From Albury, 95km away, drive through Wodonga, then along the Kiewa Valley Hwy.

By public transport, take a train to Wangaratta and then a bus to Mt Beauty ($45 one way); call V/Line (☎ 13 6196) for reservation details. Pyles Coaches (☎ 03-5754 4024), in Tawonga South, runs a bus between Albury and Mt Beauty ($16.50 one way).

Camping Grounds

The closest camping option to the walk is at the *Mountain Creek Camping Area*, right at the trailhead. There are plenty of flat camp sites, toilets and a few picnic tables; water is also handy.

GETTING TO/FROM THE WALK

Mountain Creek Camping Area is about 15km from Mt Beauty. Drive north for 4km from Mt Beauty to the small town of Tawonga. Turn right (east) opposite the Bogong Hotel and follow Mountain Creek Rd for 10.5km to the trailhead at the Mountain Creek Camping Area.

If you require a ride from Mt Beauty, contact the Mt Beauty Taxi Service (☎ 03-5754 4739, 0409 573 909).

THE WALK
Day 1: Mountain Creek Camping Area to Cleve Cole Hut via Mt Bogong
5–7 hours, 12.5km

Follow a 4WD track east into the forest from the camping area. Within 15 minutes you'll come to a grassy area and gate; it is possible to drive 2WDs to this point, so you could start the walk here. Continue along the track, negotiating five creek crossings, until you reach the sixth crossing. Fill your water bottles here as this is the last reliable water supply until you reach Cleve Cole Hut.

Ten minutes later, the signposted track up the Staircase Spur leaves the main track on your right. The track climbs steeply over the series of flat sections that give the spur its name, until you reach *Bivouac Hut* at 1440m and about two hours (5.5km) from the start. It is possible to *camp* by Bivouac Hut, but you will have to rely on a rainwater tank for drinking water. The hut itself offers shelter and has a small potbelly stove, but there are no bunks.

The track continues easily for a short distance beyond the hut before climbing steeply again. About an hour from the hut, the track unexpectedly climbs out of the forest and onto the windswept grassy moors of the upper mountain. Snow poles now accompany the route as you pass below two small knolls named Castor and Pollux, soon reaching Gorge Gap where the final ascent to the summit begins.

A steep climb ensues, but you are rewarded with increasing views as you climb higher. On the distant north-east horizon you can see the Snowy Mountains, Australia's highest mountain range. Farther up you will pass a **memorial cairn** marking the place where three skiers died in a 1943 blizzard. A while later you may notice the scattered ruins of **Summit Hut**, which was destroyed by an unknown arsonist in 1978. (There is a small semipermanent spring a few metres above the ruins.) Another 300m brings you to a T-junction at the top of the high, treeless ridge that forms the summit plateau of Mt Bogong. At this point, marked by a snow pole and signpost, turn right (west) and follow the track for five minutes to the huge cairn at the summit of **Mt Bogong** (1986m). It will take you about four to five hours to cover the 8.5km from the start of the walk.

Return to the T-junction mentioned above and follow the track east to Hell Gap. The route swings slowly round to the south from here, then gradually east again as it passes over Rocking Stone Saddle, Lendenfeld Point and Tadgell Point. The track then descends into the forest before reaching the grassy *camping area* at *Cleve Cole Hut*, 4km and one hour from the summit. With eight beds, a sink, running water and stove, the hut is luxurious compared to most mountain huts but is often full.

Alternative Camp Site
The Horseyards If the camping area at Cleve Cole Hut is crowded, consider camping about 400m north of the hut across an open valley. The pleasant grassy camp sites, near some old yards, can be seen from the hut, and water can be obtained from a small creek 100m before reaching the camp site.

Side Trip: West Peak
1½ hours, 6km return

From the summit of Mt Bogong, a faint track leads west down the broad ridge and into a shallow saddle. Here the track becomes poorly defined, but walk slightly south of west to the top of Hooker Plateau. A few old snow poles are scattered along

VICTORIA

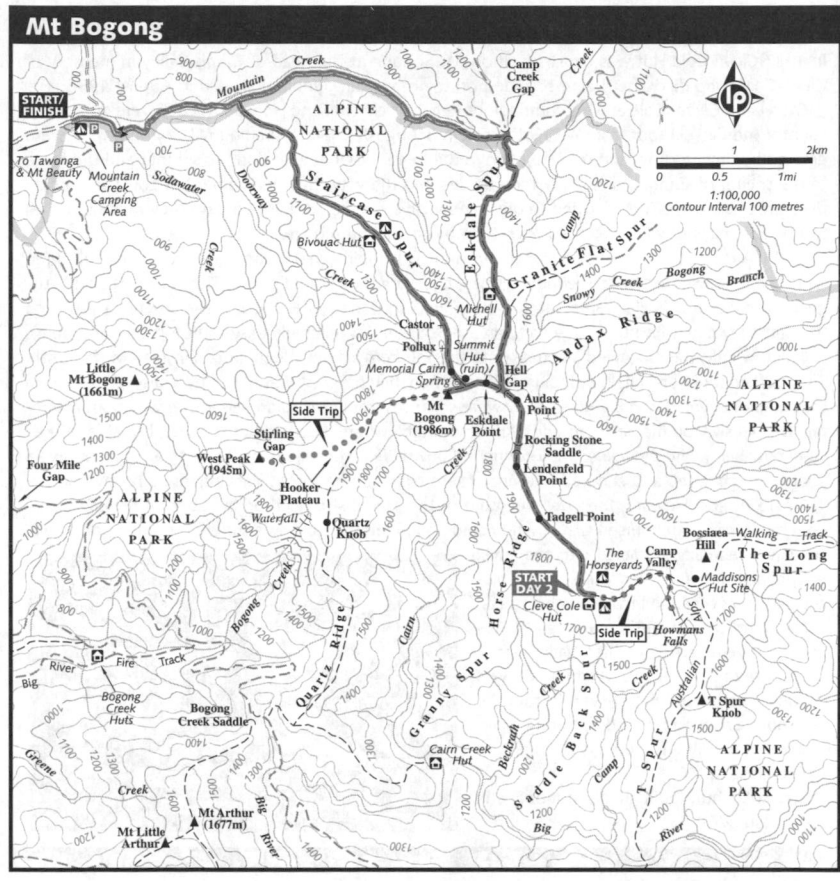

Mt Bogong

the route. From the western edge of Hooker Plateau, descend west into a saddle and locate a foot pad, which will bring you to **West Peak** (1945m). Excellent views, particularly down into the Kiewa Valley, are to be had from here. Return to the summit along the same route.

Note that this trip should not be undertaken in foggy conditions by inexperienced walkers, as it is easy to become disoriented on the featureless Hooker Plateau. Also, if you have allocated a third day for your walk, this side trip can easily be done from the overnight camp near Cleve Cole Hut.

Day 2: Cleve Cole Hut to Mountain Creek Camping Area
4–5 hours, 14km

From the hut, return along the track towards Mt Bogong. At Hell Gap, a track bears north and skirts the east side of Eskdale Point to join the Eskdale Spur, 500m away. The path heads down the spine of the narrow spur to a track junction where the spur flattens out. The main track heads left (north-west) and descends into the forest, soon arriving at **Michell Hut**, which is capable of comfortably sleeping four people, but relies on an often mouse-infested small tank for water.

The Death of Cleve Cole

In 1937 Cleve Cole Hut was constructed on Mt Bogong at the head of Camp Valley in memory of Cleve Cole, who died after being stranded on the mountain during a blizzard in August 1936.

Cleveland 'Cleve' Cole and his companions Percy 'Mick' Hull and Howard Michell were on a cross-country (nordic) ski tour from Mt Hotham. On 8 August, while ascending Mt Bogong, they were greeted by driving snow and thick fog above the tree line. Unable to find the summit and the route to the shelter of Camp Valley, they tried to descend the way they had come, but could not locate the start of the spur. They decided to dig a snow cave for shelter. For two days they made searches for the summit, but were defeated each time by the raging blizzard.

By 11 August, with little food remaining and with their general condition worsening, all three wrote final farewell letters to their loved ones, believing they would perish. They decided on 12 August to make one final attempt at the summit. Surprisingly, they found the summit cairn, and thought they could find their way to Staircase Spur (and a relatively easy route off the mountain).

Unknowingly, they followed a course onto the southern side of the mountain instead of the north. They battled for hours, finally stopping at 2 am when their progress was halted by a large creek, which they later discovered was Big River. They were still miles from civilisation and a long way from Mountain Creek valley on the northern side of the mountain, where they had hoped to be, but at least they were now below the snow line. They continued down Big River valley on 13 and 14 August, but were unable to light a fire and endured two unpleasant nights in the forest, sleeping inside hollow logs.

On 15 August Howard, the fittest member of the group, struggled on in search of help. Mick set up a rough camp and nursed Cleve, who could no longer walk and was suffering from hypothermia.

Howard eventually stumbled into the small gold-mining town of Glen Valley, and a rescue party was organised to collect the others.

Mick and Cleve were rescued on 18 August and were carried to Glen Valley, arriving in town late on 19 August. Cleve's condition had deteriorated even further; he was now unconscious and suffering from extreme frostbite. He died that night in Omeo Hospital.

The solid hut, built in his honour, still stands today.

GLENN VAN DER KNIFF

The route from the hut descends deeper into the forest, levels out for a little, then drops steeply to a small stream, which is reliable in all but the driest of times. Below the stream, follow the track down to the major saddle of Camp Creek Gap. Here there is a track junction, with the route heading west into a gully (the headwaters of Mountain Creek). During wet times it can be a battle to avoid leeches along the next 700m of track. Fortunately, it is only about 15 minutes until you reach a scrub-free 4WD track. Once on the 4WD track it is pleasant walking for 6km to the end of the walk at the *Mountain Creek*

Camping Area, passing the track that leads up the Staircase Spur along the way.

Side Trip: Howmans Falls
1 hour, 4km return
The short trip to Howmans Falls is highly recommended. From Cleve Cole Hut follow the walking track, and snow poles, east into the forest. The track soon descends to the treeless Camp Valley, then follows alongside Camp Creek, crossing it twice before swinging round to the south. After passing a few cascades, the path ends at the top of the main **waterfall**. Return along the same route.

If you have allocated a third day for your walk, this side trip can easily be done from the overnight camp near Cleve Cole Hut, possibly combining it with the West Peak side trip mentioned above for a long day walk.

Huts of the Bogong High Plains

Duration	3½–4½ hours
Distance	14.5km
Standard	medium
Start/Finish	Langford Gap
Nearest Town	Mt Beauty, Tawonga South
Public Transport	no

Summary This pleasant walk gives an insight into the history of European activity on the Bogong High Plains. There's a few easy ascents, but most of the walking is over gentle snow plains, rolling countryside and through snow gum glades.

For over 100 years local families have grazed their cattle on the Bogong High Plains in the summer. Two of these families, the Kellys and Fitzgeralds, had constructed huts nearby on the plains to serve as a base when they were mustering cattle. While their original shelters are no longer standing, huts of more recent vintage occupy the sites and preserve the families' names. The Johnston and Edmondson families also erected huts, which today are popular camp sites in both summer and winter.

The described walk starts high on the plains and climbs gently through scattered forest to the open plains at an area known as the Park. The main walk heads east from here, but a side trip can be made to Edmondsons and Johnstons Huts first. Then, back on the main route, an open plain is crossed to its eastern edge. Here you will find, hiding among the picturesque woodlands, Kellys and Fitzgeralds Huts. The walk culminates with a casual stroll of a few hours beside an aqueduct.

PLANNING
For more detail on when to walk, what to bring and permits and regulations, see Planning in the introduction to the Victorian Alps.

Note that this walk cannot be accessed in winter as the Bogong High Plains Rd is closed by snow beyond Falls Creek.

Maps
The Vicmap 1:50,000 *Bogong Alpine Area* map in the Outdoor Leisure Map series is the best map for this walk. The 1:25,000 *Nelse* and *Mt Wills* maps, also by Vicmap, are useful but show no more detail than *Bogong Alpine Area*.

NEAREST TOWNS & FACILITIES
Mt Beauty & Tawonga South
For a description of accommodation and other services in Mt Beauty and Tawonga South, see Nearest Towns & Facilities in the Mt Bogong walk earlier.

Falls Creek
This small town is actually a thriving ski resort during the winter months, but in summer it is very laid-back and quiet. There is a tourist information office (☎ 1800 033 079) on the main road as you enter the town, which can help you find accommodation.

Places to Stay & Eat Lodges offering accommodation during summer include *Alpha* (☎ 03-5758 3488), with bunk beds starting from about $17, and *Viking* (☎ 03-5758 3247), which has beds from $28. Both lodges are on Parallel St.

Quick, basic snacks can be purchased at the *Wombat Cafe*, part of the Snowland Centre. Some food items can be purchased in the small *general store* at Falls Creek (in the Snowland Centre), but prices and the range of products are better in larger towns.

Getting There & Away Falls Creek is 30km south of Mt Beauty along the sealed Bogong High Plains Rd, but there is no public transport available except during the winter ski season.

GETTING TO/FROM THE WALK
Continue along the road beyond Falls Creek until the bitumen ends, then continue for a farther 6km to the start of the walk at Langford Gap. The road is navigable by 2WDs.

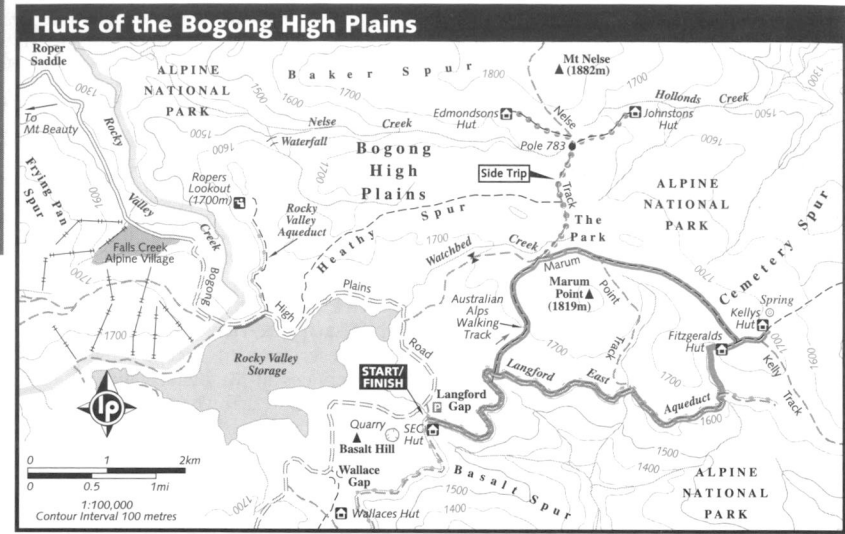

Huts of the Bogong High Plains

THE WALK

From Langford Gap, a path crosses Langford East Aqueduct and joins the Australian Alps Walking Track. This track parallels the aqueduct, almost immediately passing a small hut. Within 30 minutes you'll pass a small dam, which looks more like a swimming pool than a reservoir. A little farther on, after a major bend in the aqueduct, a signpost indicates a track heading north towards Marum Point.

This faint track climbs gently through snow gum glades and small plains, wending its way higher before joining a closed 4WD track at a large snow plain named the Park. About 50m ahead, Marum Point Track veers to the right (east) towards Kellys and Fitzgeralds Huts. At this point you have the option to take the side trip described later.

Marum Point Track, and its accompanying snow pole line, head east to a broad saddle, where the track turns more to the south-east. Stay with the snow poles and walking track. After about 40 minutes you'll reach a signpost at the eastern edge of the plain, pointing to Kellys Hut (north) and Fitzgeralds Hut (south). Walk towards Kellys Hut first, taking a footpath past some grand snow gums, then passing left through an old

stockyard, before following an old 4WD track to the hut, only 10 minutes from the signpost. Ignore the signposted Kelly Track, which heads east from near the old stockyard.

Kellys Hut, originally built in 1901 but later rebuilt in 1958, sits in an attractive forest of aged snow gums, providing a pleasant ***camp site*** for overnight walkers (the hut itself is rather grotty); there is a creek north of the hut for water. Return to the signpost and continue 300m to ***Fitzgeralds Hut***.

The original Fitzgeralds Hut, built in 1903, was one of the oldest huts on the plains until it was burnt to the ground by an out-of-control campfire in the early 1990s. The new hut is on the same site and has been built in a similar design to the original.

The next 1km from the hut is along untracked terrain, but navigation is not difficult. Walk west for a few hundred metres alongside a fence, then bear south across grasslands until you reach a small creek. You should find a cattle pad on the eastern side of the creek and this will lead you down to Langford East Aqueduct.

The track along the aqueduct heads generally west and provides easy walking. Water is plentiful and you may even notice

VICTORIA

Bogong High Plains Short Walks

There is much more to see of the Bogong High Plains than simply the major summits, spurs and valleys. Here are a few short walk options that will give you a taste of what the area has to offer.

Ropers Lookout
(1½ hours, 4km)

Starting from the eastern end of the Rocky Valley Storage dam wall, follow the track alongside the Rocky Valley Aqueduct north for 25 minutes to where the aqueduct ends. A track climbs straight up the hill, then loops to the south to end at the interesting basalt outcrop of Ropers Lookout (1700m).

Mt Nelse
(3 hours, 11km)

While not particularly 'short', this walk is nonetheless quite easy with good tracks for most of the route. Nelse Track (labelled Big River Fire Track on Vicmap's *Bogong Alpine Area* map) leaves the Bogong High Plains Rd 5km from Falls Creek. Follow the track north-east to the Park, then generally north to where it levels off north-west of Mt Nelse. Leave the track here and walk across the open, grassy plain to the summit of Mt Nelse (1882m). Return via the outward route.

Wallaces & Cope Huts
(2 hours, 8km)

The walk starts where a 4WD track heads east away from the Bogong High Plains Rd about 10km from Falls Creek. Follow this track east for 15 minutes to Wallaces Hut, the oldest hut on the Bogong High Plains. Continue down the main track (east) as it descends gently to meet Langford West Aqueduct. Turn right and you'll soon reach Rover Lodge, a large building used by the Rover Scouts, 25 minutes from Wallaces Hut. Beyond Rover Lodge, the route follows the aqueduct, then veers briefly onto a foot track before joining a 4WD track that leads west to Cope Hut. Past the hut, the track soon rejoins the Bogong High Plains Rd, which you follow north for 800m. Take the snow pole line (and accompanying track) north-east, which soon brings you back to Wallaces Hut. Return to your vehicle.

Rocky Knobs
(1½ hours, 4km)

While not on tracks, walking to Rocky Knobs does not present too many problems except in foggy conditions. The walk starts about 11km past Falls Creek on Bogong High Plains Rd at a point where a snow pole line veers east away from the road. Strike out west, then northwest across a mixture of snow plains and forested hills to the summits of Rocky Knobs (1790m).

Mt Cope
(1 hour, 3km)

The start of this track is at a signpost (to 'Mt Cope') on the Bogong High Plains Rd, 13km beyond Falls Creek. The faint track heads south-west and over the plains to the foot of Mt Cope, before climbing to the peak. The boulder-covered summit of Mt Cope (1837m) provides a great vantage point from which to view the Bogong High Plains and, particularly, west to Pretty Valley.

GLENN VAN DER KNIJFF

Wallaces Hut, a cattlemen's hut built in 1889, sits among pretty snow gums

some small trout in the aqueduct. The journey from Fitzgeralds Hut to the trailhead is 6.5km and will take 1½ to two hours.

Side Trip: Edmondsons & Johnstons Huts
2 hours, 8km return

The short trip to these huts is recommended and can be incorporated into the main walk to make a long day trip. From the junction of the Nelse Track (marked Big River Fire Track on Vicmap's *Bogong Alpine Area* map) and Marum Point Track, walk north along Nelse Track for 2km. Soon after passing the side track (on your right) to Johnstons Hut, the track to Edmondsons Hut (1km away) can be seen heading west. *Edmondsons Hut* has a sleeping platform at one end of the hut and is well used by walkers and cross-country skiers, who like to use it as a base from which to explore the snow-covered plains in the Mt Nelse area.

Retrace your steps as far as the turn-off to Johnstons Hut and follow the track east down into the grove of snow gums surrounding the hut. While *Johnstons Hut* is open to the public, one section remains locked. Pleasant *camp sites* exist in the vicinity of the hut; water can be fetched from a creek to the north if you plan to stay overnight. The return to the main walk is made along the outward route.

Mt Feathertop & the Razorback

Duration	2 days
Distance	36km
Standard	hard
Start/Finish	Harrietville
Nearest Towns	Bright, Harrietville
Transport	no

Summary A steady ascent to Federation Hut, then a climb to the summit of Mt Feathertop. An unusual hut, excellent views along the spectacular Razorback ridge, and a beautiful eucalyptus forest are some of the walk's highlights.

Mt Feathertop, named for the appearance of lingering snowdrifts in spring, has attracted walkers for decades. And for good reason!

It is arguably one of Victoria's most attractive and impressive mountains, as well as the state's second highest; it is cut off from the High Country to the east by the deep valley of the Kiewa River; and it stands proudly aloof at the head of the Ovens Valley, dominating the skyline. Snaking away from Mt Feathertop to the south is the Razorback – a mecca for walkers and skiers since the 1930s and one of Australia's most scenic ridge walks. In winter, cross-country skiers and budding mountaineers are drawn to the area's snowy slopes, ridges and crags. But beware: in winter the mountain's slopes are prone to ice and Mt Feathertop has claimed many lives.

PLANNING

For a detailed description of when to walk and what to bring, see Planning at the start of the Victorian Alps section.

Be aware that as most of this walk is along dry ridges and spurs, there are few places to collect water – make sure you carry plenty. As well, the springs and small streams high on the mountain can cease flowing during very dry periods and the water tanks at Federation and Bon Accord Huts cannot be relied upon during the height of summer.

Maps

Probably the best and most useful map for this walk is the Vicmap 1:50,000 *Bogong Alpine Area* sheet in the Outdoor Leisure Map series. Vicmap's 1:25,000 *Feathertop* and *Harrietville* maps cover the area, but they show no more detail than *Bogong Alpine Area*.

Permits & Regulations

Mt Feathertop and its immediate surrounds, including much of the Razorback, has been classified a fuel-stove-only area.

NEAREST TOWNS
Bright

In the upper reaches of the Ovens Valley, Bright is a pretty tourist town that has a wide range of facilities, activities and services of use to bushwalkers.

The Alpine Information Centre (☎ 03-5755 2275), 119 Gavan St, is open daily and has heaps of information for travellers. It also operates an accommodation booking service (☎ 1800 500 117). There's also a Parks Victoria office (☎ 03-5755 1577), at 46 Bakers Gully Rd, which has a range of brochures on the nearby national parks.

The main shopping centre is on Ireland St, where there's an outdoor gear shop that sells a wide range of camping equipment.

Places to Stay & Eat There are a number of caravan parks in and around Bright; the largest is *Bright Caravan Park (☎ 03-5755 1141)*, Cherry Lane, which has tent sites from $17 and on-site vans and cabins from $48.

Bright also has two hostels. One is in the Bright Caravan Park, while *Bright Hikers Backpackers' Hostel (☎ 03-5750 1244, 4 Ireland St)* is right in the main shopping street and offers Internet access. Both have dorm beds from around $16.

For pub-style accommodation try the *Alpine Hotel (☎ 03-5755 1366)*, opposite the clock tower, sandwiched between Barnard and Anderson Sts. It has basic double rooms from $45 or motel-style doubles from $50.

Elm Lodge (☎ 03-5755 1144, 2 Wood St) has rooms from $47 per double, with discounts for backpackers and hostellers. There are numerous other accommodation options, so contact the tourist centre for further details.

There are plenty of takeaway food outlets in town, including two *bakeries*. For a pub meal try the *Alpine Hotel*, but for a little more ambience head to the trendy *Caffe Bacco (☎ 03-5750 1711)*, opposite the Caltex petrol station. Also worth checking out is the *Tin Dog Café & Pizzeria (☎ 03-5755 1526)*, on the corner of Gavan and Barnard Sts.

There are two *supermarkets* in the Ireland St shopping centre.

Getting There & Away Bright is 306km north-east of Melbourne by road, first along the Hume Fwy to near Wangaratta, then along the Great Alpine Rd.

By public transport, take a train to Wangaratta and then a connecting bus to Bright. Call V/Line (☎ 13 6196) to make a booking.

Harrietville

At the foot of Mt Feathertop is the pretty town of Harrietville. Some maps can be bought at the small general store, but you'll need to buy groceries in Bright.

Places to Stay & Eat The *Harrietville Caravan & Camping Park (☎ 03-5759 2523)* has tent sites from $5 and on-site vans from $30. The *Alpine Lodge Inn (☎ 03-5759 2525)* has units from $60 per double, while *Cas Bak Holiday Flats (☎ 03-5759 2531)* has self-contained cabins (also from $60 for a double).

Motel-style accommodation can be found at the *Snowline Hotel (☎ 03-5759 2524)*, which has double rooms from $50. The hotel also offers counter lunches and dinners, and the balcony is a popular place for a drink after a hard walk.

Getting There & Away Harrietville is 24km south of Bright along the Great Alpine Rd. Although there is no regular public transport, the Bright Taxi Service (☎ 0408 589 370) will take passengers to Harrietville.

GETTING TO/FROM THE WALK

From Harrietville, turn east onto Mt Feathertop Rd just north of the 'school bridge' (near the small general store and riverside park). Follow this road for 1km to where the bitumen ends at a small information board.

THE WALK
Day 1: Harrietville to Federation Hut

5–6 hours, 13km

Follow the broad track into the forest for a few hundred metres until you cross a small stream. Fill your drinking bottles here as there may be no water at the trackside springs farther up the mountain. The trail ascends steadily, soon narrowing into a good foot track. After 2km, you cross a major gully which, during spring, carries a good supply of water. Continue climbing, passing the signposted Picture Point (although there is nothing to see here) and Tobias Gap, eventually reaching the top of the spur at Wombat Gap (two hours and 6km from the start).

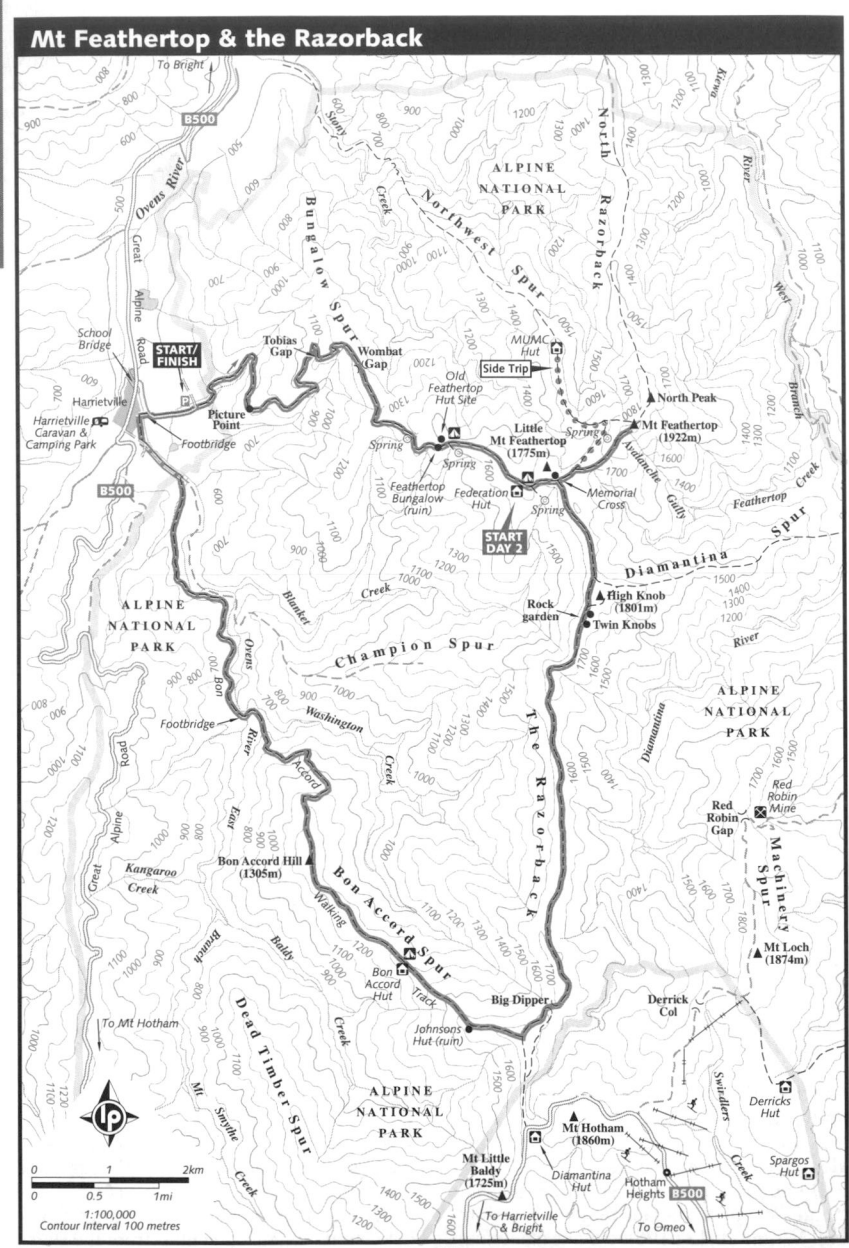

Soon after entering alpine ash forest, you pass a small spring (generally reliable for most of the year). Another kilometre along the track, the forest changes to feature shorter and more twisted snow gums. Soon you pass the ruins of the **Feathertop Bungalow** – a large structure built in the 1920s for use by skiers, but destroyed by wildfire in January 1939 – on your left; then comes a signpost indicating water a few hundred metres to the right (east). This is the last reliable water point along the main track. To the left of the signpost is the site of the **Old Feathertop Hut**. While there is nothing left of the hut, there are a some flat, grassy *camp sites* here, with a nearby water supply. The area is protected by the snow gum forest. Camping here, however, is really only an option if you plan to end Day 2 at Bon Accord Hut.

About 10km from the start, the track breaks out from the forest to arrive at a grassy clearing and *Federation Hut*. There are sheltered *camp sites* among the trees near the hut.

The summit cannot be seen from the hut, but a short stroll of a few minutes to a small knoll south of the hut provides a fine view. There is a rainwater tank by the hut (although during dry periods this may be empty) and a spring 30 minutes to the east (this is not as reliable as the one near the Feathertop Bungalow ruins).

It is worth making the two-hour return trip to the summit now to shorten the walk on Day 2. The track leads north-east from the hut to a track junction in a saddle just to the east of Little Mt Feathertop. Take the left-hand track, then, shortly afterwards at another junction, a right-hand track; continue along the exposed ridge top to the **summit**. The views are impressive indeed, with very steep slopes dropping away in most directions; you'll feel as though you're on top of the world. Observant walkers will notice the shiny blob on a ridge below and to the west of the summit. This is the Melbourne University Mountaineering Club (MUMC) Hut (see the boxed text 'Mt Feathertop UFO'), the route to which is described in the side trip.

Mt Feathertop UFO

The first geodesic structure of its kind built in Australia, the Melbourne University Mountaineering Club (MUMC) Hut was constructed in the 1960s by a group of active climbers keen to create a base from which they could practise their mountaineering skills in winter. Mt Feathertop was their ideal choice; its steep, snowy slopes are prone to ice (especially on the mountain's steep southeast face) and there is plenty of terrain to hone telemarking, snow camping, cramponing and self-arrest techniques.

Tragically, a car accident on the way to the mountain during construction claimed the lives of three club members, and memorial plaques can be seen in the hut. So prominent was the hut's shiny reflection that Ovens Valley residents, convinced it was distracting to drivers at certain times of day, insisted that the club paint it; every few years the dark green paint job is stripped away by the harsh alpine weather and must be renewed.

Side Trip: MUMC Hut
2 hours, 6km return
A visit to MUMC Hut is a pleasant return journey from the camp site. Take the track from Federation Hut towards Mt Feathertop, but then take the left-hand track at the junction 200m from the saddle east of Little Mt Feathertop. The path initially cuts across the steep west face of Mt Feathertop (crossing a reliable spring) before joining the Northwest Spur for the final section to the hut. Return along the outward route.

Day 2: Federation Hut to Harrietville
8–9 hours, 23km
Return to the first track junction above Federation Hut and follow the south-east track as it sidles round the west side of a hill to the Razorback ridge, soon coming to yet another junction. The track heading east leads to Diamantina Spur and a very steep descent to the Kiewa River West Branch. Take the right-hand track, which sidles round the west side

of High Knob, bypassing a climb to the summit, and you'll shortly arrive at a magnificent **rock garden** wedged into the side of the Twin Knobs. During summer, this area is likely to be carpeted with wild flowers.

Beyond Twin Knobs, the track gains the ridge again and generally follows the spine of the **Razorback**, at times passing through glades of snow gum forest for another 7km, to eventually pass into a deep saddle known as the **Big Dipper**. A short but steep climb to the head of the **Bon Accord Spur** follows, where you'll be rewarded with panoramic views and the knowledge that from this point onwards the walk is basically downhill!

Bear west from the top of the hill, marked with a few old snow poles, and follow the Bon Accord Walking Track. It descends gently at first, but then more steeply, into a tall alpine ash forest to reach *Bon Accord Hut*, on a large flat area 40 minutes from the head of the spur. If there is clean water in the tank, or you have carried plenty with you, *camping* here for the night could be a pleasant option. The hut has no beds, but you could roll out a sleeping mat on the floor. It would also make for a short Day 2 and an easy walk to Harrietville on a third day.

The first 2km beyond the hut are an easy ramble. Soon another descent begins, but the track is in good condition, not particularly steep, and before long you reach the depths of the valley at the junction of the Ovens River East Branch and Washington Creek. Cross the river on a new footbridge and follow the track downstream on the west side of the river.

Not far from the river crossing, the track improves and follows a course just above an **old aqueduct** for a while. Not always obvious, the aqueduct was constructed by gold miners around the turn of the 20th century. The track provides relaxed walking.

About 4km from the river crossing (and 10km from Bon Accord Hut), the foot track joins a dirt road and this is followed west for a short distance to join a minor sealed road on the fringe of Harrietville. Turn right, then right again after another 100m and follow a foot pad beside the river for 500m to a footbridge over the Ovens River.

On the far side is Mt Feathertop Rd, which will lead you back east to the beginning of the walk.

Mt Speculation & Mt Howitt

Duration	2 days
Distance	24.5km
Standard	medium-hard
Start/Finish	Howitt Spur
Nearest Town	Mansfield
Public Transport	no

Summary A steep climb leads to the Crosscut Saw (a highlight of Victorian bushwalking), then to one of the best camp sites in Victoria on Mt Speculation. Traversing the scenic summit of Mt Howitt, the route then drops steeply again to the Howqua River.

Since the 1920s the Wonnangatta Wilderness, which includes the summits of Mt Howitt, Mt Speculation and the Crosscut Saw, has been one of the most sought-after walking areas in the Victorian Alps; the spectacular summits, ridges and spurs in the area have drawn walkers like moths to a flame. Fortunately, in 1982 the area was given the protection of national park status, but logging of the superb alpine ash forests in the lower areas has all but ruined much of the once pristine river valleys. Many of the old logging roads are now being left to nature and are becoming increasingly overgrown, but a few major ones remain, giving relatively easy access for bushwalkers and other mountain enthusiasts. In the 1980s many of the peaks in this area, including Mt Howitt, were used for horse-riding sequences during the filming of the popular Australian films, *The Man From Snowy River* and *The Man From Snowy River 2*.

PLANNING

For a description of when to walk and what to bring, see Planning in the introduction to the Victorian Alps.

Be aware that between June and October the vehicle access road is closed to traffic at Telephone Box Junction (near Mt Stirling).

It is essential that you carry enough drinking water for each day as few water points are passed. There is, however, a reliable water source near the camp on Mt Speculation.

Maps

Vicmap's 1:50,000 *Howitt-Selwyn* map covers the entire walk and is the best choice for geographic and contour information. The Victorian Mountain Tramping Club (VMTC) 1:50,000 *Watersheds of the King, Howqua & Jamieson Rivers* map, which is specially produced for bushwalkers, could make a useful additional reference.

NEAREST TOWN & FACILITIES
Mansfield

A popular stopping point for campers and 4WD enthusiasts, Mansfield is a major gateway to the Alpine National Park.

The Mansfield Visitor Information Centre (☎ 03-5775 1464, ✉ infocent@mansfield .net.au), on High St, opens daily and offers a helpful accommodation booking service (☎ 1800 060 686). Mansfield also has a Natural Resources & Environment (NRE) office (☎ 03-5733 0120), at 33 Highett St.

The Maroondah Hwy, named High St in town, is the main road on which you will find an array of shops, including an outdoor gear shop.

Places to Stay & Eat The *James Holiday Park* (☎ 03-5775 2705), on Ultimo St, has tent sites from $14 and on-site vans from $35. *Mansfield Backpackers' Inn* (☎ 03-5775 1800, 112 High St) has dormitory-style beds from $15 and double motel-style rooms from $60.

Pub-style accommodation can be found at the *Mansfield Hotel* (☎ 03-5775 2102) and the *Delatite Hotel* (☎ 03-5775 2004). Both are on High St and offer rooms from about $25 per person. The *Mansfield Motel* (☎ 03-5775 2377, 3 Highett St) has rooms from $61 for a double.

High St has numerous *cafes*, *takeaways* and a *supermarket*.

Getting There & Away Mansfield is 192km north-east of Melbourne via the Melba Hwy (to Yea), Goulburn Valley Hwy and Maroondah Hwy. If coming from the north, follow the Hume Fwy to near Benalla, then turn south along the Midland Hwy to Mansfield.

While it is possible to take a V/Line bus (☎ 13 6196) from Melbourne to Mansfield, there is no public transport from Mansfield to the trailhead, so your best option is to use a private vehicle or hire car.

Howitt Spur

If you only require a few tent sites, you could camp at the small grassy clearing at the trailhead (at the base of Howitt Spur). Although the sites are limited, water is handy, and it is most convenient if you want an early start the next morning.

GETTING TO/FROM THE WALK

From Mansfield, follow the Mt Buller Rd east for 40km (past the villages of Merrijig and Sawmill Settlement) to a road junction at Mirimbah. Turn left onto the Stirling Rd and this leads, in 8km, to Telephone Box Junction. Follow the right-hand road (Circuit Rd) from the junction for 19km over Howqua Gap to an intersection where Bindaree Rd leaves Circuit Rd on the south side.

Bindaree Rd zigzags its way down to meet the Howqua River, about 10km from the turn-off; avoid any minor side tracks that branch from the main road. In the valley, the increasingly rough road heads east, changes its name to Upper Howqua Rd and arrives at the base of Howitt Spur (the trailhead) in 4km. A track junction and clearing mark the starting point.

THE WALK
Day 1: Howqua River to Mt Speculation via the Crosscut Saw

4–5 hours, 12km

From the clearing at the foot of Howitt Spur, cross to the north side of the Howqua River and follow the continuation of Upper Howqua Rd, here called Queen Spur Rd, up the southern slopes of Stanleys Name Spur. The track provides easy walking as it climbs steadily for 3.5km (one hour) to a saddle on the crest of the spur. Turn right

Mt Speculation & Mt Howitt

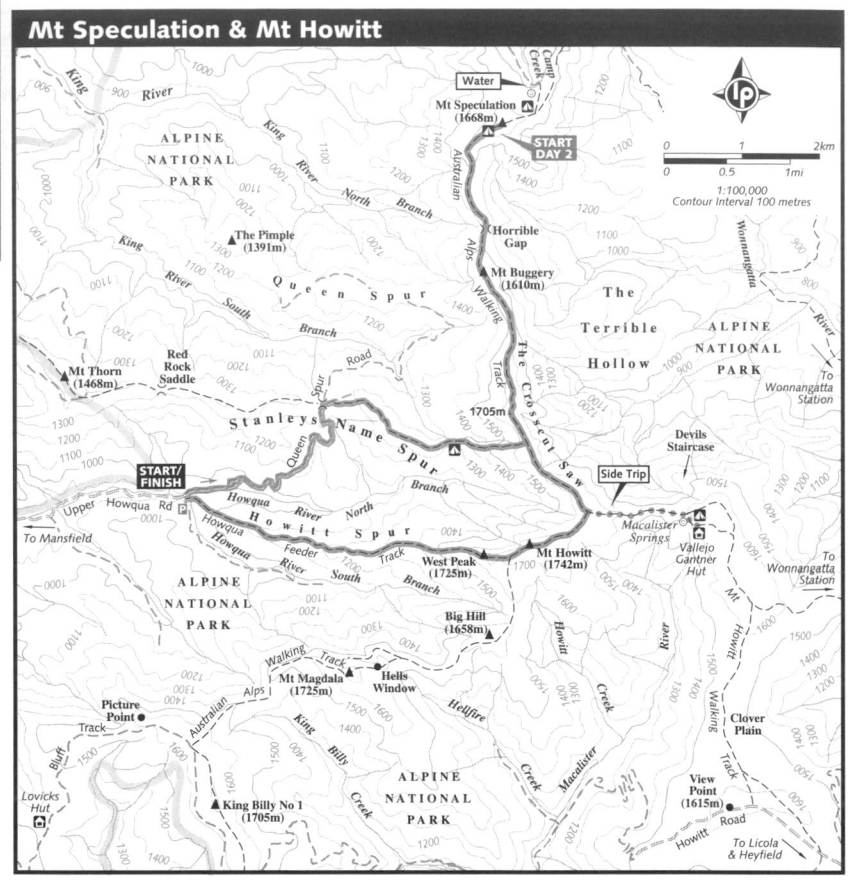

(east) at the saddle and follow an old, indistinct, 4WD track for 200m to where a yellow marker on a tree indicates the faint walking track (on your right) along the crest of Stanleys Name Spur. The track climbs a little, then undulates until it reaches a pleasant *camp site* at the foot of the Crosscut Saw. There is usually water in a creek 100m to the north (except in the driest times).

Continue east very steeply up the spur; there are a few rocky bluffs to negotiate that are not for the faint-hearted. After about 1km, the track cuts to the left, sidling across the steep slope, and eventually tops out in a

saddle at the southern end of the Crosscut Saw. Turn north here and follow the obvious path, the Australian Alps Walking Track, for about 15 minutes as it climbs to the highest summit of the **Crosscut Saw** (1705m). The terrain along this part of the Alps and the views to be had along the way are among the most dramatic in the Victorian High Country.

The track undulates generally northwards over many of the knolls that make up the teeth of the Crosscut Saw, then descends into forest. About 2km from the Crosscut Saw high point, a short steep climb brings you to the top of **Mt Buggery** (1610m), which is soon followed by an even steeper descent of 200m into Horrible Gap. Beyond this saddle, the route climbs north through thick forest to more open country near Mt Speculation. Approaching the mountain top the track climbs a few rocky bluffs before arriving at the summit of **Mt Speculation** (1668m) and one of Victoria's most spectacular *camp sites*. The view south from the summit, particularly in autumn when fog often fills the upper Wonnangatta Valley early in the morning, is nothing short of breathtaking. To the east lie the craggy summits of the Razor and Viking, seemingly close at hand, and beyond these on the distant horizon you can make out Mts Bogong and Feathertop and other peaks of the Bogong High Plains.

There are plenty of flat, grassy *camp sites* on the summit ridge, and if the weather is fine it is recommended that you stay here for the night. Farther to the east, and about 100m below the summit, there are more excellent *camp sites* (still with stunning views), but these are more sheltered and are better in adverse conditions. Water can be found at the head of Camp Creek, about 1km north-east of the summit, along a well-defined track. It's about a 45-minute return trip.

Day 2: Mt Speculation to Howitt River via Mt Howitt
4–5 hours, 12.5km
Return along yesterday's route to the saddle where Stanleys Name Spur track joins the southern end of the Crosscut Saw; the views are quite different walking south. From the

The Wonnangatta Murders

Wonnangatta Station, a cattle farm built in 1861 by Oliver Smith, was established in one of the most isolated places in Victoria, the upper Wonnangatta Valley. The Bryce family joined Smith in partnership, but eventually bought the farm outright; they eventually sold it in 1914 to two Mansfield graziers by the name of Phillips and Ritchie. James Barclay was hired as manager, and it was at this point that one of the most mysterious stories of the Victorian Alps unfolded.

Barclay had run the station for a few years before deciding to hire an extra person to do the cooking and assist with jobs around the farm. He employed John Bamford, a fellow known to have a strong, fierce temper and a nervy demeanour.

Only two months after Bamford began his employment, Harry Smith, from the nearby town of Eaglevale, visited the property and was surprised to find the place seemingly deserted. He notified the owners in Mansfield, who arrived at the station in late January 1918. There was no sign of the manager or cook so they began a search of the property. Noticing some drag marks on a field and some cuts in a fence nearby, they followed the clues to discover the partially decomposed and mutilated body of Barclay near a creek bed. Barclay's remains were taken on horseback to Mansfield, where it was found that he had been shot. Bamford was an obvious suspect, especially as he was nowhere to be found. And Bamford's horse, which should have been at the station, was found roaming the slopes of Mt Howitt.

After the winter snows had melted, another search was conducted by a police constable, Harry Smith, and two local cattlemen. To their surprise they found Bamford's body, also murdered, partially hidden under a log near the Howitt Plains. He had been shot in the head.

Who then murdered Bamford? It had been thought all along that Bamford had murdered Barclay, but with this latest discovery new questions arose. One of the detectives assigned to the case surmised that Bamford had, indeed, killed Barclay in one of his fits of rage, then a friend of Barclay's had taken the law into his own hands and killed Bamford.

Whatever the case, the murders remain unsolved. Sadly, Wonnangatta Station was destroyed by fire in 1957 and there are only the remains of the station's cemetery to remind us of the fascinating, if macabre, past of the valley.

saddle (2½ hours from Mt Speculation), continue walking along the Australian Alps Walking Track. It passes another saddle, then climbs onto the exposed plateau north-east of Mt Howitt. Here you'll find a track junction, the left (east) track heading to Macalister Springs, Vallejo Gantner Hut and Howitt Rd (see the Macalister Springs side trip described later). Continue south-west over the plains for 1km to **Mt Howitt** (1738m). Here you're greeted by a sweeping panorama of the surrounding High Country and one of the finest view points in Victoria.

The route now heads west and is less obvious across the summit plateau. At a T-junction, the Australian Alps Walking Track heads south, but keep right and follow the minor track west as it descends to a slight saddle before climbing to the head of Howitt Spur at **West Peak** (1725m). Howitt Spur plummets from this high point; the track negotiates the very steep upper section by way of a series of rock scrambles and zigzags. Once down in the forest, the route eases off considerably and becomes a pleasant ramble all the way to the trailhead beside the Howqua River (about 1½ hours from West Peak).

Side Trip: Macalister Springs
1 hour, 3km return
The short trip to Macalister Springs is worth the effort, even if just for the slightly different perspective it gives to the depths of Terrible Hollow and the Crosscut Saw. From the track junction 1km north-east of Mt Howitt, a well-defined foot track heads east along a narrow ridge, which provides fine views to the north. Leaving the ridge the track contours round to a spring, the headwater of the Macalister River, and to the peculiarly shaped *Vallejo Gantner Hut*, with space for four on a sleeping platform. Return along the same route.

There are two camping options in the vicinity of Macalister Springs. The most scenic, but also most exposed, *camp sites* are on the ridge a few hundred metres north-east of the spring, while more protected *camp sites* are just above the spring near the hut.

The Bluff

Duration	5–6 hours
Distance	13km
Standard	medium
Start/Finish	Refrigerator Gap
Nearest Town	Mansfield
Public Transport	no

Summary A steep climb up the craggy face of the Bluff, then an easy exploration of the unusual summit area. Traverse another high peak, visit an old cattleman's hut, then return along easy paths beneath soaring cliffs.

From many angles the Bluff appears to be like many of the peaks in this part of the Victorian Alps, comprising a series of seemingly impenetrable crags and high grassy moors. From the north, the mountain seems protected by the huge escarpment, but there is a way through the cliffs which makes for an exciting walk. While this track is too steep for cattle, they have grazed on the alpine grasses of the summit areas for many years, particularly those of the Stoney and Lovick families (from the Mansfield area), who accessed the Bluff by a longer and considerably easier route. Bluff Hut, to the east of the mountain, was built and used for many years by them when mustering or tending to their cattle. The hut has since been enlarged and is now popular with walkers and 4WD enthusiasts.

PLANNING
For a more detailed description of when to walk, what to bring and permits and regulations, see Planning in the introduction to the Victorian Alps.

Maps
The Vicmap 1:50,000 *Howitt-Selwyn* topographic map covers the eastern half of the walk, while Vicmap's 1:25,000 *Buller North* map covers the rest of the Bluff's summit area. Also able to be used, in addition to the two Vicmap sheets, is the VMTC 1:50,000 *Watersheds of the King, Howqua & Jamieson Rivers* map, which is produced specially for bushwalkers.

NEAREST TOWN

For a description of Mansfield, see Nearest Town & Facilities for the Mt Speculation & Mt Howitt walk earlier in this section.

GETTING TO/FROM THE WALK

From Mansfield, take the Mt Buller Rd east for 18.5km to the small settlement of Merrijig. Two kilometres beyond Merrijig, a good dirt road to the right (Howqua Track) leads over Timbertop Saddle for 16.5km to Sheepyard Flat.

The road continues beyond this large camping area, changes its name to Brocks Rd and deteriorates into a rougher road, still easily navigable by 2WDs. It follows the river for a while before climbing to Eight Mile Gap, 19km from Sheepyard Flat.

Turn left at the gap onto Bluff Link Rd and continue for 6km to Refrigerator Gap. The start of the walk is 800m farther up the road at a small car park, where the walking track to the Bluff is signposted.

There is no public transport to the start of the walk.

THE WALK

The way to the Bluff is initially along an old 4WD track, which becomes progressively steeper and deteriorates into a foot track. The route zigzags a little, passes close to a few damp bogs, then reaches a rocky escarpment at a large boulder. This is a good place to rest and prepare yourself for the stiff climb ahead.

While not far to the top, the way is slow and tedious as the route negotiates a number of rocky buttresses, eroded gullies and twisted snow gums. Almost without warning, you break free from the clutches of the crags and arrive on the meadows of the summit plateau. Here, the track eases off and swings to the east to attain the summit of the **Bluff** (1725m), which is marked by a rock cairn.

Be aware that it could quite easily take you two hours to come to grips with the

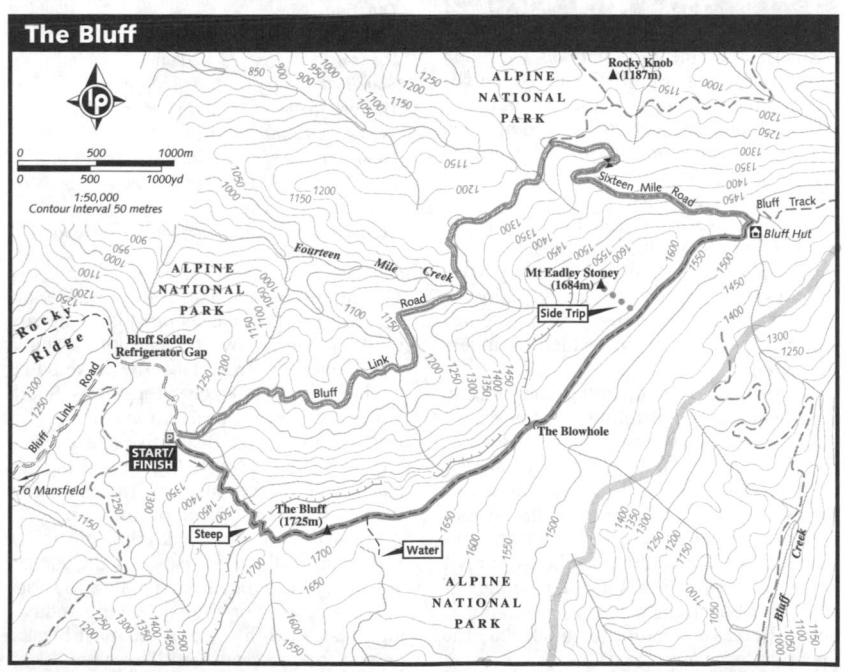

Bogong Moth

The Bogong moth (Agrotis infusa) is a brown moth that grows to a length of about 5cm. It's a migratory creature that breeds and lives in the lowlands of NSW during autumn, winter and spring. However, during summer, when the food in the lowlands is exhausted and it gets too hot, the moth migrates to the High Plains.

At the Bluff, Mt Buffalo and other places in the alpine region, it hides in the cracks and crevices of rocks. Once the sun sets, the moths leave their hiding spots and fly around, becoming easy prey for ravens, kestrels and pied currawongs. The Aborigines also used to follow the moth to the High Country as it was considered a delicacy. It was commonly roasted and the wings and legs were separated from the body. Usually the body was made into a paste with a nutty flavour. At the end of summer the moths return to lower country to lay eggs and the cycle begins again.

northern escarpment of the Bluff and reach the summit. Because of the interesting geography and geology of the mountain, if you have time to spare, it is recommended that you spend some of it exploring the crags and wild-flower gardens of the Bluff's upper ramparts.

The track heads east from the summit and drops a little. About 300m from the top, bear south, following a faint foot pad in places, and descend into a large snow plain for water. The plain is scattered with snow gums and bisected by a stream, which meanders through it.

Back on the ridge top east of the summit, turn right (east) and follow the track as it gradually descends into a saddle known as the **Blowhole**. From here, the foot track sidles across the rock slabs on the south-east slopes of Mt Eadley Stoney (1684m). About 1.5km from the Blowhole, it is worth embarking on a quick climb to the top of **Mt Eadley Stoney**, which is about 15 minutes' walk directly up the slope. The walking is not difficult, the scrub not thick and the views are excellent.

Returning to the track, the route continues east a little more before dropping into the forest and to a saddle beside **_Bluff Hut_**. Once a small shack, the hut has been enlarged and modified over the years; until quite recently, commercial cross-country ski tours were conducted from here. Allow about two hours to cover the 4km (and Mt Eadley Stoney side trip) from the Bluff to Bluff Hut.

From the hut, Sixteen Mile Rd descends initially west for 2km to an intersection where it meets Bluff Link Rd, deep within the alpine ash forest. Turn left and follow the road for 4km to the end of the walk, passing a few small streams along the way. While you may see some 4WD traffic along this section of the route, fortunately Bluff Link Rd is not too busy and there are some interesting views to be had above you of the cliffs of Mt Eadley Stoney and the Bluff.

Mt Buffalo Plateau

Duration	5–6 hours
Distance	16km
Standard	medium
Start/Finish	Camp Plain
Nearest Towns	Bright, Porepunkah
Public Transport	no

Summary A wonderful day walk, with only a few short climbs, giving an overview of the Buffalo Plateau with its attractive snow plains, snow gum and alpine ash forests, and shapely tors.

Mt Buffalo National Park, one of Australia's first national parks, celebrated its centenary in 1998. Named by early explorers Hume and Hovell in 1824 (see the boxed text 'Hume & Hovell Track' in the New South Wales chapter for a description of their journey) because of its distinctive shape when viewed from the west, Mt Buffalo has arguably some of the most varied and attractive scenery found anywhere in Australia.

Formed by a geological uplift of molten rock many millions of years ago, the plateau has since been eroded heavily along a series of weaknesses, or faults, leaving today's high plateau with some of the most bizarre granite rock outcrops you'll ever see.

Top Left: The Cathedral and the Hump, Mt Buffalo NP, Victoria. **Top Right:** The Cathedral soars above the grassy plains, Mt Buffalo NP. **Middle:** Mt Feathertop from Twin Knobs on the Razorback, Alpine NP. **Bottom Left:** Sunrise on Mt Speculation, with the Bluff in the distance, Alpine NP. **Bottom Right:** Looking north-east to the Viking from Mt Howitt, Alpine NP.

SANDRA BARDWELL

SANDRA BARDWELL

SANDRA BARDWELL

Top: Wild flowers and rocky outcrops near Smiths Beach, Leeuwin–Naturaliste NP, WA.
Middle: Waves pound the coastline at Rame Head, Walpole–Nornalup NP, WA.
Bottom: The Stirling Range, misty with distance, seen from Toolbrunup Peak, Stirling Range NP, WA.

Historically, Mt Buffalo has been popular with nature lovers and bushwalkers since it was first climbed by local miners and farmers in the 1850s. So popular did the area become that in 1910 the Victorian government built the large, rambling Chalet, which has provided accommodation for many visitors to the plateau. Australia's first ski lift was constructed on the plateau in 1936, creating an all-season resort.

Mt Buffalo's subalpine environment has a diverse range of flora and fauna; some plants are endemic to the park, including the Buffalo sallee, Buffalo wattle and fernleaf baeckea. Many creeks drain the plateau along a series of faults, plummeting off the plateau's rim in a spectacular series of cascades and waterfalls. Best viewed from the lookouts and tracks near the Chalet (see the boxed text 'Mt Buffalo Short Walks'), Crystal Brook and Eurobin Creek are two of these major watercourses.

PLANNING

For a detailed description of when to walk, what to bring and permits and regulations, see Planning in the introduction to the Victorian Alps. Remember that the soil of the Buffalo Plateau is fragile and particularly prone to erosion, so be careful not to stray off the defined tracks.

Maps & Books

The Vicmap 1:25,000 *Buckland* and *Eurobin* maps cover the entire walk. However, if you are interested in walking more of the park, you will need to get the 1:25,000 *Dandongadale* and *Nug Nug* maps as well.

A useful guidebook for the Mt Buffalo area is the Algona Publications guide, *Mt Buffalo National Park*, but it is out of print and difficult to find.

Information Sources

There is a Parks Victoria office (☎ 03-5755 1466) on Mt Buffalo Rd, 100m north of the trailhead, which has maps and brochures.

Permits & Regulations

Walking permits are not required, but it is a good idea to book a camp site if you wish to camp on the plateau at the Lake Catani Camp Ground (which is usually full during holiday periods). There is also a park entry fee of $8 per car, payable at the entrance station to the park.

NAT WEBB

The Chalet around 1920. In the summer of 1985, bushfires burnt much of the plateau and guests at the Chalet were evacuated as flames licked at the building; only the supreme efforts of firefighters saved the historic establishment. Tourists today can still experience the historic charm of the now-privatised hotel, an excellent base from which to explore the Buffalo Plateau.

Mt Buffalo Short Walks

There is so much to see in Mt Buffalo National Park that you should try and allow a little extra time (you don't need much) for some of its finest sights; here are just a few.

Eurobin Falls

(45 minutes, 2km)

About five minutes' drive from the Entrance Station, on the left of the road is the well-marked track to Ladies Bath Falls and Eurobin Falls. These are seen to best advantage in winter or after heavy rain.

The north wall of the Gorge, from near the Chalet

Rollasons Falls

(1¼ hours, 4km)

About halfway to the plateau from the Entrance Station is the signposted track to Rollasons Falls. Near the falls, the track divides – left to the upper fall and right to the lower fall. It is worth visiting both.

The Gorge

(1 hour, 3km)

Immediately in front of the Chalet, at the western edge of the car park, a track leads to the point where Crystal Brook plummets over the rim of the Gorge. Nearby are numerous excellent lookouts, which will keep you awe-struck for some time. All tracks are well marked and easy to follow.

The Monolith

(45 minutes, 2km)

Opposite the Parks Victoria office on Mt Buffalo Rd, near the start of the Mt Buffalo Plateau walk (described here), is a track that ascends east to the perilous-looking balancing tor of the Monolith (1419m). While the track itself is not too steep, the final climb to the top of the boulder is up a stairway.

The Hump

(30 minutes, 1.5km)

At a high saddle between the small ski areas of Dingo Dell and Cresta, a track heads west and climbs a fire-scarred hill to another saddle between the Hump and the huge outcrop of the Cathedral. Follow the track south from the saddle to the summit of the Hump (1695m), where there are impressive views of the surrounding countryside.

The Horn

(30 minutes, 1.5km)

The track to the highest point on the plateau begins at the very end of the road across the plateau, about 3km from the Cresta ski area. There is a fine lookout at this point. The track climbs round the western and northern edges of the Horn (1723m), getting steeper near the top, where the path is protected by wire fences. As expected, the views are more than impressive.

NEAREST TOWNS & FACILITIES

For a detailed description of Bright, see Nearest Towns for the Mt Feathertop & the Razorback walk earlier in the Victorian Alps section.

Porepunkah

Six km west of Bright along the Great Alpine Rd is the small town of Porepunkah. The V/Line bus (☎ 13 6196) from Wangaratta stops near the pub on its way to/from Bright.

Rush-Inn Caravan Park (☎ *03-5756 2292)*, on the Great Alpine Rd, has tent sites from $13 and cabins starting at $50. On the Mt Buffalo Rd, 300m west of the roundabout, is *Porepunkah Caravan Park* (☎ *03-5756 2380)*, which offers tent sites from $6 per person and on-site vans and cabins from $40.

Pub-style accommodation is possible at the *Porepunkah Hotel & Motel* (☎ *03-5756 2391)*, which has double rooms from $40 and also offers counter meals.

Takeaway food can be found at the shop that is part of the Mobil petrol station (and post office), and the *Porepunkah General Store* sells food items.

Lake Catani Camp Ground

The most convenient place to stay near the trailhead is on the plateau at the *Lake Catani Camp Ground*, which has camp sites for $14 per night. Bookings are essential during holiday times; contact the Entrance Station (☎ 03-5756 2328) during normal working hours. The camping area is 2km from the start of the walk.

Chalet

An interesting accommodation option, albeit a more expensive one, would be to stay at the historic and rustic *Chalet* (☎ *03-5755 1500, 1800 037 038,* ✉ *buffaloc@netc.net.au)*. The cheapest option is to stay in a 'Guesthouse' room (using a share bathroom), starting at $119 per person. Prices increase according to the level of accommodation, but standard charges include an a la carte dinner, breakfast, lunch, park entry and some activities. There is also a snack bar in the Chalet.

GETTING TO/FROM THE WALK

The trailhead is reached by following Mt Buffalo Rd from Porepunkah into Mt Buffalo National Park. Once on the plateau, 25km from Porepunkah, keep right at an intersection (the left-hand road leads to the Chalet) and continue for about 500m (just past the Parks Victoria office) to Reservoir Rd and the start of the walk.

There is no public transport from Bright to Mt Buffalo, except during the winter ski season. An expensive option is to take a taxi to the plateau; contact Bright Taxi Service (☎ 0408 589 370).

THE WALK

Reservoir Rd leaves the Mt Buffalo Rd adjacent to a snow clearing depot and crosses Camp Plain before following the pretty valley of **Crystal Brook** upstream. The walking is easy, and the track almost flat, for a little over 3km (45 minutes) to an intersection. Turn right (west) and follow Mt McLeod Fire Track up the slope for a few hundred metres to a signposted walking track on the left, which heads toward the triple rock formations of Og, Gog and Magog. The walking track leads above a small reservoir before climbing to a T-junction; turn left and walk 300m to **Og, Gog and Magog** (1490m) for fine views of the surrounding terrain and many of the high peaks of the Victorian Alps.

Return to the T-junction and proceed around the flanks of **Jessies Lookout**. Keen observers may notice wombats, or even the elusive lyrebird, in the forested sections of this walk. The track soon descends to the south and arrives at another T-junction. The described walk will return to this point later, but now follow the right-hand track as it skirts around the northern extremity of **Five Acre Plain**. Twenty minutes' walking will bring you to an intersection and a signpost indicating the way 500m south-west to Eagle Point (two hours, 7.5km from the start). Like many other rocky lookouts in the park, **Eagle Point** (1470m) can only be ascended by climbing a series of ladders; those of you with a fear of heights may wish to err on the side of caution and remain at the base of the summit boulders. The view south from the top includes Mts Cobbler, Howitt, Stirling and Buller. This is also a fine place to enjoy lunch.

Return to the T-junction south of Og, Gog and Magog and head along the walking track signposted 'The Chalet'. Leading past the head of Five Acre Plain, the track swings to the north-east, then south-east to meet up with Rocky Creek Track on **Wild Dog Plains**. Turn left and follow the track

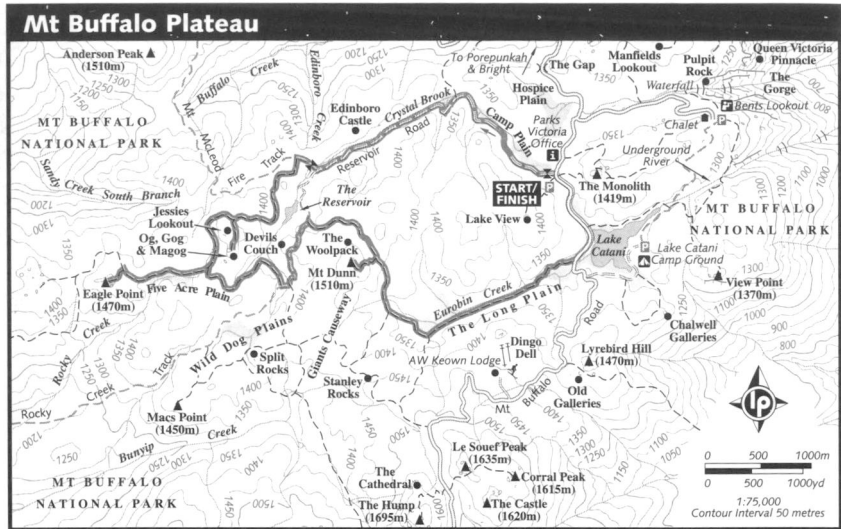

Mt Buffalo Plateau

north to cross the headwaters of Crystal Brook. Continue up the track, soon passing the side track to Devils Couch (which can be easily climbed if desired). A little farther on, around 15 minutes from the Crystal Brook crossing, is the signposted turn-off (right) to Mt Dunn.

The track to Mt Dunn heads east then south-east for 1km to a T-junction east of the peak, where a sign indicates the short side trip to **Mt Dunn** (1510m); again, ladders are required for the ascent. The return journey will take about 30 minutes, but is well worth the effort, particularly as Mt Dunn's central location on the plateau ensures extensive views in all directions.

Back at the intersection east of Mt Dunn, follow the main route south towards Eurobin Creek and the Long Plain, keeping left when passing two signposted side tracks along the way. Once on the **Long Plain** the main track swings to the north-east and stays close to **Eurobin Creek**, paralleling its south bank for a little over 1km before crossing to the north bank for the final section of track to the Mt Buffalo Rd. To complete the walk, a stroll north along the road for 1km brings you back to Camp Plain.

Wilsons Promontory National Park

Known affectionately as 'the Prom', Wilsons Promontory is a 40,000-hectare majestic combination of forest, granite mountains and secluded, sandy bays. With 130km of uninterrupted coastline, a rich variety of wildlife and coastal habitats, and an ancient, almost timeless quality to its landscape, it is little wonder that the Prom is one of Victoria's most treasured national parks.

Swimming in the tranquil waters of Refuge Cove on a summer weekend, it is easy to forget that the Prom juts out into one of Australia's most tempestuous ocean stretches. Yet storms in Bass Strait can be awe-inspiringly ferocious; the sheltered coves on its lee side are a well-known sanctuary for small yachts seeking shelter from the westerly gales.

Visitors to the park will find excellent camping facilities and an extensive network of well-maintained walking trails. Walks vary from short nature trails out of Tidal River to overnight walks in more remote areas. With a carefully managed permit system, trails on the east coast rarely feel crowded.

HISTORY

More than 6500 years before maritime explorer George Bass sighted the promontory in 1797, the Aboriginal Brataualung and Boonerwrung peoples had populated the Prom. The Prom (called Yirruk or Wamoom) was a rich source of seasonal food and resources, and a place of powerful spiritual significance.

George Bass first sighted the Prom on an epic journey to chart the south-east coast of Australia in an open whale boat called the *Reliance*. On returning with Matthew Flinders in 1798, the pair named it Wilsons Promontory. There followed a succession of ultimately failed sealing, whaling, logging, grazing and tin-mining ventures, which heavily taxed the area's natural resources and dispossessed the Brataualung and Boonerwrung of their land. At the height of the timber extraction, Sealers Cove supported a population of 58 people.

The unique ecological value of the promontory did not go unnoticed, and naturalists, spearheaded by the Field Naturalists Club of Victoria, campaigned tirelessly for its protection. In 1898, 36,800 hectares were set aside as a temporary national park, a status later made permanent. Almost nothing remains now of the early European settlements. Since 1898 new proposals for commercial development have periodically threatened to detract from the park's wild areas – while these have been met with widespread and so far successful community opposition, the pressure for development continues.

NATURAL HISTORY

Like many 'wild' areas in Australia, the Prom's environment has, in fact, been substantially modified by humans. Extensive resource exploitation, cattle grazing, human habitation and a succession of major fires (that of 1951 burnt 75% of the park) have all left slow-to-heal scars on the landscape. One particularly curious and ill-fated ecological experiment involved the release, like a mini-Ark, of a number of nonlocal native animals to increase the Prom's wildlife count; few survived.

Wilsons Promontory National Park today contains the largest coastal wilderness area in Victoria. It sustains an astonishing diversity of coastal habitats with 740 species of flora some of which are found nowhere else on the mainland. The route of the Sealers Cove walk passes through a diverse range of distinct plant communities: open forest, woodland, rainforest, wetland, sand dunes, coastal scrub and heathland.

Each community supports its own rich mix of animal life (with more than 30 mammal species). Most visible in the open grassland around Tidal River are populations of wombats and eastern grey kangaroos. In the open forests and woodlands, brushtail and ringtail possums cohabit with less common species such as tiny eastern pygmy possums, while in the heathlands, swamp rats and swamp antechinuses, among a host of other small animals, scamper about under a tangle of hakeas, kunzeas and coastal tea-trees. About 230 bird species (about half of Victoria's quota) visit or breed in the area. Almost decimated by the 19th-century sealing trade, Australian fur seals are occasionally seen on the coast and breed on outlying islands.

PLANNING
When to Walk

With an average minimum daily temperature in winter of 11°C, walking at the Prom is feasible, even enjoyable, year-round. This despite the fact that the Prom is notorious for its changeable weather, strong prevailing westerlies and the wild storms which blow in from Bass Strait. Camp sites along the trail are well sheltered.

Summer is more suited to walkers keen on swimming (with an average maximum daily temperature in January of 20.7°C), but this time of year can also be very crowded, especially during school holidays. The heathlands flower most brilliantly during winter.

It's advisable to time your walk so that you arrive at the Sealers Creek crossing (Day 1) at low tide – you may otherwise be in for a deep wade. Ask at the Tidal River visitor centre for tide details.

What to Bring

You'll need to pack camping equipment, including a fuel stove (open fires are banned).

Always pack rain and warm-weather gear, whatever the forecast, as the Prom's weather is notoriously unpredictable, but don't forget your swimmers.

Maps & Books

Vicmap's 1:50,000 *Wilsons Promontory National Park* map in the Outdoor Leisure Map series is detailed and accurate – although the text on the reverse side is outdated, having been last updated in 1991. *Wilsons Promontory: Marine and National Park Victoria* by Geoff Westcott is an excellent book with detailed notes on the history, geology, and flora and fauna of the park. *Discovering the Prom*, also by Geoff Westcott, is a very useful, pocket-sized guide to the many walks around the promontory. A series of park notes published by Parks Victoria on the park and its walks can be picked up from the Tidal River visitor centre.

Information Sources

The park visitor centre (☎ 1800 350 552, fax 5680 9555, @ wprom@parks.vic.gov .au) is based at Tidal River, 30km south of the park entrance along the access road. It has a range of publications, audio-visual presentations and an extensive information display. The centre oversees accommodation at Tidal River and distributes camping permits for the trails.

Permits & Regulations

Entry to the park costs $9, while camping out of Tidal River costs $4.90 per person per night. Camping is restricted to approved camping sites, for which permits are required (restrictions are also imposed on the number of nights you can spend at each camp site). Permits are regularly checked by the park's rangers and you cannot vary your itinerary. Out of peak season it's possible to pick up a permit either at the entrance to the park or from the visitor centre at Tidal River. During holidays, but particularly over Christmas and Easter, book well ahead. Booking forms are available from Parks Victoria (☎ 13 1963).

Campfires are banned throughout the park.

NEAREST TOWN & FACILITIES
Foster

The busy rural service town of Foster, on the South Gippsland Hwy, is a very convenient place to break the journey to the Prom and buy supplies. Once a thriving town of the Victorian gold rush, it retains something of its old charm. The visitor centre is next door to Foster's historical museum on Main St; the Commonwealth Bank and post office are nearby.

Places to Stay & Eat The *Foster Caravan Park* (☎ 03-5682 2440), on Nelson St, has sites for $14.30 (two people) and on-site cabins for $44 ($49.50 with bathroom) in a shady ground with laundry facilities.

Foster Backpackers Hostel (☎ 03-5682 2614, 17 Pioneer St) offers comfortable doubles ($50) and dorm accommodation ($17). The owner provides bus transport to Tidal River on request (see Getting There & Away under Tidal River) and hires out camping equipment at $10 per night.

Rose Cabin (☎ 03-5682 2628, 21 Victory Ave), five minutes from the centre, has cosy self-contained twin cabin accommodation at $30 person. Linen is provided.

Black Cherry Cafe (☎ 03-5682 2110), on the main street, serves simple but filling fare. It becomes the town's only restaurant on Saturday night (closed in winter).

Around the corner, the bistro at the *Exchange Hotel* (☎ 03-5682 2377) has a daunting selection of dishes and generous serves.

The well-stocked *supermarket* is on the main street.

Getting There & Away V/Line (☎ 13 6196) has a daily bus service departing Melbourne at 4.30 pm and arriving in Foster at 7.15 pm. The return service leaves Foster at 7.49 am daily except Sunday; the Sunday bus departs Foster at 3.25 pm. An extra service departs Melbourne on Friday at 6.40 pm. Tickets cost $44.60 return (discounted tickets are available mid-week).

Tidal River

Tidal River camping ground, at the start of the walk, is a mecca for campers seeking the escape of bush and ocean on a budget. It has a range of accommodation, with prices dependent on the season, the number of people and the length of stay.

As a guide, during peak season *camp sites* cost $17.60 for up to three people and a car, $3.80 for each additional camper and $5.50 per additional vehicle. *Huts* cost from $49.50 per night, motel-style *units* from $93.50 (for up to two people) and luxury, solar-powered *cabins* from $129.50. For more information and bookings, contact the visitor centre (☎ 1800 350 552), which is on the left side of the Ring Rd as you enter Tidal River.

There's also a small *shop* with a limited range of groceries, camping supplies and *takeaway* food. Outside are public telephones and a petrol and LP gas pump.

Getting There & Away If driving from Melbourne, get onto the South Gippsland Hwy in Dandenong and continue until the signed turn-off for the Prom at Meeniyan (148km). Tidal River is 87km south-east from Meeniyan via Fish Creek.

There's no public transport to Tidal River, but Foster Backpackers Hostel (see Places to Stay & Eat under Foster) will drop off and pick up people from the Prom on request. The owner charges a maximum of $20 one way per person, depending on how many people are on board.

Sealers Cove

Duration	2 days
Distance	44.5km
Standard	medium
Start/Finish	Tidal River visitor centre
Nearest Town	Foster
Public Transport	yes

Summary A two-day circuit through a lush and variable coastal landscape. Both days are long, but with gentle gradients and tucked-away beaches, this is an excellent introduction to bushwalking in a safe environment.

This coast-to-coast (and back) walk through the heart of the national park leaves behind the crowds at Tidal River to explore the less accessible east coast. As well as sheltered, gem-like coves ideal for swimming, walkers have a chance to explore a fascinating array of coastal environments.

While we've described this walk as a two-day trip, possible over a weekend, the stages are long and there's a lot to see along the way. If you have the time, think about taking an extra day by camping at Sealers Cove and Little Waterloo Bay.

Alternatively, if you can arrange transport (see Getting To/From the Walk), it's possible to do a shorter circuit that begins and ends at Mt Oberon car park (36km). On the second day, continue north up the Lighthouse Track rather than taking the left turn-off to Oberon Bay.

Before setting out, check tide times with the Tidal River visitor centre. While never impassable, at high tide the Sealers Cove crossing can rise to a chilling waist height. Tide tables can be accessed over the Internet (see Information Sources in the introduction to this chapter).

GETTING TO/FROM THE WALK

For those wanting to begin the walk from Mt Oberon car park, there is no public transport. However, at the busiest times of the year Parks Victoria operates a free minibus to shuttle walkers between Tidal River (leaving from outside the visitor centre) and Mt Oberon car park. Check with the Tidal River visitor centre for first and last bus times.

THE WALK
Day 1: Tidal River to Refuge Cove
4½–6½ hours, 20km

This is a long day with one long (300m) ascent to Windy Saddle and several tantalising beaches en route, so start early. Take plenty of water with you.

The day begins from Tidal River with a somewhat tedious 3.5km road-walk up to Telegraph Saddle and Mt Oberon car park. Leaving Tidal River along the main access road (in the direction of the park entrance), turn right 1km from the visitor centre onto

Sealers Cove

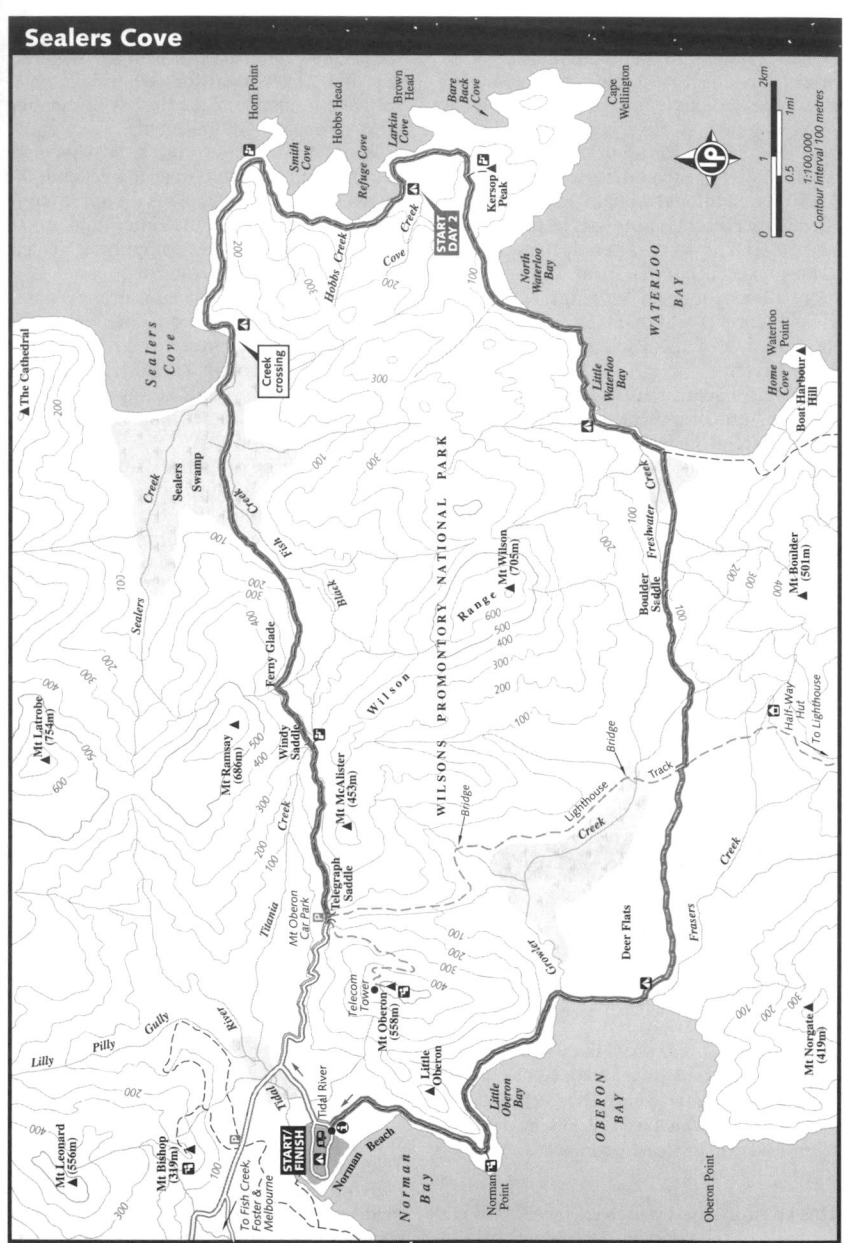

the Mt Oberon road. From the eastern end of Mt Oberon car park, follow the sign pointing east to 'Refuge Cove 4½ hours, 16.4km'. The sandy track heads out through eucalyptus forest, contouring gently round Mt McAllister and up the southern slope of Titania Creek valley to Windy Saddle (30 to 45 minutes). To the west you can see right across the Prom to Norman Island.

From here the track continues roughly east for the next 7km, descending 300m through sassafras, myrtle and beech to **Sealers Cove**. The last 2km section is through a primordial-looking swampland, much of it along a boardwalk. The water flowing beneath is rust-coloured from the tannin leached from surrounding tea-trees.

Once you hit the beach (a good place for a picnic if you can fend off the seagulls), turn right and walk 600m to the Sealers Creek outlet for your first wade. The Sealers Cove *camping ground* (with piped water and toilets) is just beyond.

Continue through the camping ground following the trail signed 'Refuge Cove, Coastal & Hill Track'. At the far side, it turns left (north) and crosses a creek, climbing for 45 minutes up and around the headland to Horn Point (3km). The **lookout** has uninterrupted views of Five Mile Beach to the north and the Seal Islands to the east.

Turning south-east, the path angles round Smith Cove, cuts across the 'neck' of Hobbs Head and descends through stringybarks and banksias to North Refuge Beach, 30 minutes from the lookout. Stay on the track as you make your way above the rocks along the foreshore to the next sandy bay, a popular mooring point for yachts. Walk down onto **Refuge Cove** beach past the camping ground reserved for 'yachties'. The walkers' *camping ground* (also with water and toilets) is 100m inland on a path up the true left bank of Cove Creek.

Day 2: Refuge Cove to Tidal River

8–10 hours, 24.5km

Signs point the way out of the camping ground as the track climbs around the scrubby headland over slabs of exposed granite, turning south above Larkin Cove. After a steep zigzagging ascent, you should reach the side track (on the left) to **Kersop Peak** (214m), 45 minutes to an hour after starting. The summit (10 minutes return) has fantastic views south to the lightstation and the hump-backed Rodondo Island.

Back on the main path, descend 200m to North Waterloo Bay through a shady stringybark forest. Walk south-west along the beach to the first set of rocks; a sign points right to where the track begins again. The next section of path along the rocky foreshore is narrow and eroded in places, requiring some care. Two to three hours (6.5km) from Refuge Cove, the northern end of Little Waterloo Bay appears. The *camping ground*, through which the track passes, is in the trees on the other side of the brackish creek.

Continue south through the next headland. As you come out onto **Waterloo Bay** beach, the signed trail crosses Freshwater Creek and turns right (west) after 50m, making its way up through wetlands and hakea-studded heathland to the large boulders on Boulder Saddle. Mt Wilson (705m) rises impressively to the north-west. The tops of the boulders to the left of the track below the saddle make for a scenic picnic spot.

Beyond the saddle is a series of giant granite **tors**. The path contours beneath them and descends through banksias, tea-trees and gnarled she-oaks to the junction with Lighthouse Track, roughly 1½ to two hours (5.7km) from Waterloo Bay.

Turn right (north) up the track for 100m before turning left onto a trail signed 'Oberon Bay', a mere 3.5km away. Two kilometres long and bordered by an extensive system of sand dunes, the beach is stunningly beautiful. Walk north along the sand to the final crossing of the day, Growlers Creek. The last stage of the walk contours round the coastline to Little Oberon Bay and then up to **Norman Point** lookout, before descending the final kilometre to Norman Beach. You can either reach the Tidal River camping ground along the beach or stay on the path through the stand of tea-trees behind.

Croajingolong National Park

Croajingolong National Park protects a magnificent stretch of rugged Victorian coastline, some 100km in length, extending from Bemm River in the west to Cape Howe in the east, on the NSW state border. It is a wild tangle of swamps, forests, and heathlands, fringed by remote, windswept beaches and tidal estuaries. The area covers 87,500 hectares of East Gippsland wilderness. As the majority of Australians live on or near the relatively narrow strip of the country's south-eastern coastal margin, enormous pressure is placed on fragile coastal environments, and very little still exists in its pristine, original condition. Croajingolong represents some of the only surviving untouched coast remaining along the south-east coast of Australia.

In keeping with the Parks Victoria policy to preserve the area's continued high conservation value, two large areas of the park are being allowed to revert back to a wilderness state. For walkers, this will mean some tracks will become gradually more indistinct. In the light of this, parties should be proficient in bush navigation, carry first-aid kits and be fully self-sufficient.

HISTORY

Aboriginal occupation dates back more than 40,000 years. The coast provides an amazing array of food sources, including birds, fish, marsupials and aquatic plant life, and as a result, Croajingolong was a favoured residence of the local Krautungulung tribe (meaning 'People of the East'). The name Croajingolong is a corruption of this. Evidence of their long occupation is given by the many shell middens encountered. Exposed by wind and wave action, they occur at various points along the sandy coast – more than 60 are known to exist.

Point Hicks was the first section of Australian coast spotted by James Cook's *Endeavour* crew in 1770, and George Bass also sheltered in Wingan Inlet for 10 days in 1797. Sealers had arrived by 1820, and went on to all but wipe out the local Australian fur seal population (happily seals have since returned).

The coast has been responsible for 40 known shipwrecks, including the *Sydney Cove* (near Cape Howe in 1797) and the *Shah* (off Rame Head in 1837); the tragic sinkings of *Monumental City* (in 1853) and *Iron Prince* (in 1942), both off Gabo Island, led to the loss of 37 lives on each. Debris from the catamaran *Windsong* is still visible around Petrel Point, where it was dashed against rocks in 1984 with three people perishing.

During WWII, the area that is now Mallacoota Aerodrome was a strategic defence base from which Hudson bombers patrolled the waters of Bass Strait looking for Japanese submarines. The threat was taken so seriously that all shipping was generally routed away from the strait and round the coast of Tasmania. Japanese sub crews are known to have come ashore on the remote beaches to take on water supplies. The current Old Coast Road, now used as part of the coast walking track, was once a military supply and telegraph line, connecting an observation post on Little Rame Head with the Operations Headquarters at Mallacoota.

NATURAL HISTORY

Croajingolong is recognised as one of the most significant conservation reserves in Victoria, and is one of three listed World Biosphere Reserves in the state.

Vegetation is extremely diverse, ranging from subtropical vines, ferns, mosses, native orchids and stands of warm temperate forest to banksia forest and heathland on the coastal fringe. The seed pods of the banksia have a characteristic, open-mouthed appearance and are often referred to as 'banksia men'. Inland there are pockets of rainforest, as well as woodlands, plains and low-lying swamps.

The bird life here is rich, with the park sheltering half of Victoria's and one-third of Australia's bird species. Pelicans, lyrebirds, satin bowerbirds, parrots, cockatoos, oystercatchers along the coast, sea-eagles, hawks and migrating sea birds are all present. Many small mammals, such as possums and sugar gliders, and reptiles such as snakes and giant lace monitors are found here. The Skerries islands, just off the coast at Wingan Inlet, support a colony of Australian fur seals, and if you are lucky you may see migrating whales heading up and down the coast.

The coastal landscape is diverse, with enormous sand dunes near Thurra River and behind Sandpatch Point. The beautiful beaches, broken only by the occasional inlet, lie between rocky promontories and occasional cliffs.

PLANNING
When to Walk

Croajingolong is enjoyable at any time of the year. Severe storms and strong winds are common along this coast, so be prepared for all seasons, even in summer. Winter can be cold, wet and windy; however, the region seems to enjoy a lot of sunshine.

Parks Victoria strictly controls the number of visitors to the park, so in quiet periods (especially in winter) it's possible to complete the route without seeing another soul.

What to Bring

Take sunscreen and a broad-brimmed hat, as the beach sections are exposed to a lot of UV light, especially in summer. Take along warm clothes and wet-weather gear, and keep everything in a waterproof backpack liner (or garbage bag), in case your backpack becomes immersed on a river crossing. Gaiters are advisable and can protect against prickly coastal scrub and the numerous snakes.

Weather conditions leading to flooded rivers and heavy seas can mean waiting at the source of the problem until conditions improve, so take an extra day or two of food for emergencies. Pack a good first-aid kit.

A fuel stove and enough fuel for the five days is essential. A water filter is also a very useful piece of equipment as it allows you to use the water from small streams and pools from bogs and freshwater soaks that would otherwise have to be boiled.

Maps & Books

Natmap's 1:100,000 *Mallacoota* and *Cann* maps adequately cover the walk, but are a bit low on detail. The *Map of the Croajingolong*

Warnings

High Tides & Heavy Seas

Three things can transform your Croajingolong walk from a pleasant coastal stroll into a hard and serious undertaking: high seas, high tides and stormy, southerly weather. These conditions will make crossing the many inlets difficult, and make walking over the rocky points unsafe. Around the rivers and inlets, fast-flowing water can sweep you off your feet, pack and all, and push you into the breakers.

As a general rule, if you're in any doubt about the safety of a crossing, wait. Wingan Inlet can be particularly deep and difficult, and should only be tackled when it's as close to low tide as possible.

The Victorian Tide Tables, obtainable from the Australian Government Publishing Service or over the Internet (see Information Sources in the introduction to this chapter) will help you plan your arrival at crossing points. Fishing tackle shops may also supply tide charts of some description. Also check with Parks Victoria for information on the status of crossings.

Snakes

Snakes are very common throughout the park, so care is required (particularly near scrubby areas around water courses where they may be foraging for food). Wearing gaiters can provide a small measure of protection, and watch out for snakes warming themselves in the sun in the early morning.

Ticks

Paralysis ticks, a particularly nasty form of tick, are extremely common in this area, and it is wise to check yourself and your companions each night for unwelcome visitors. (For a discussion of ticks and how to remove them, see Bites & Stings in the Health & Safety chapter.) Bites from paralysis ticks have on rare occasions been known to be fatal if the attached tick is left undiscovered for a long period, but no problems will be encountered if you remove it early.

National Park sketch map by SR Brookes is a very useful supplement to the maps above, indicating the location of signposts, water sources and camp sites. The Vicmap

1:50,000 *Mallacoota* map in the Outdoor Leisure Map series is useful for the Wingan Inlet to Mallacoota stretch, and covers a similar area to the 1:100,000 *Mallacoota* map mentioned above. *Walking the Wilderness Coast* by Peter Cook & Chris Dowd is an excellent little book. It covers walks extending west and east of the area dealt with here, and provides much useful and accurate information regarding camp sites and the area's history, flora and wildlife.

Information Sources
There are Parks Victoria Information Centres in Mallacoota and Cann River (see Nearest Towns & Facilities in the walk section for details). These can supply information on the Croajingolong Coast Walk, maps and track notes. For further information, you can also ring the Parks Victoria Information Line (☎ 13 1963).

Permits & Regulations
In an effort to protect the wilderness coastline, Parks Victoria and the NSW National Parks & Wildlife Service (NPWS) have adopted a permit system for overnight walkers. A maximum of two nights' camping is allowed at each camp site, with a maximum group size of eight people. There is a maximum number of overnight walkers permitted in each section of the park.

Permits can be arranged at the Mallacoota or Cann River Parks Victoria Information Centres (see Nearest Towns & Facilities), as well as the NSW National Parks & Wildlife Service in Merimbula. The permit cost is $5 per person per night.

The park is very busy in holiday periods (ie, Christmas and at Easter), so if you are planning to walk at these times it's advisable to obtain an advance booking form several months in advance (which can be posted or faxed to the Parks Victoria offices). The permit will be forwarded to you when the booking is confirmed. Pre-bookings for Easter and Christmas open three months prior to the holiday period.

An intentions form should be completed and returned to the Mallacoota Information Centre before you set out.

Croajingolong Coast Walk

Duration	5 days
Distance	59km
Standard	easy-medium
Start	Thurra River camping area
Finish	Mallacoota Aerodrome
Nearest Town	Mallacoota, Cann River
Public Transport	yes

Summary This walk follows the wild, rugged coast of far eastern Victoria, across some of the most unspoilt beaches in the state. It is a wilderness walk, and sweeping deserted stretches of sand, rocky headlands, coastal dunes and tidal inlets are all features.

This five-day walk within Croajingolong National Park extends from Thurra River to the coastal hamlet of Mallacoota in Victoria. The walk features a variety of scenery ranging from wide, open beaches to small coves with rocky headlands, river estuaries and coastal heathlands. The walk provides an opportunity for people to experience remote bush camping in a coastal wilderness area of spectacular beauty.

While it's possible for a fit and gung-ho walking party to traverse this route in good weather in as little as three long days, it's worth taking the time to absorb and explore the region at a leisurely pace.

Water can be an issue, particularly at the height of summer. Very high tides can inundate the estuaries of the freshwater rivers and make their water salty and undrinkable for many kilometres upstream.

Take plenty of water with you from Mallacoota, at least for the first night's camping and the first day's walk. Especially in summer, where you camp will largely depend on where you can stock up on reliable fresh water. Water sources are detailed in the walk description.

NEAREST TOWNS & FACILITIES
Mallacoota
The Parks Victoria Information Centre (☎ 03-5158 0219, fax 5158 0583), on the corner of Allan and Buckland Drives, has excellent

information on Croajingolong, and brochures about walking tracks around Mallacoota.

There's a fishing shop opposite the caravan park, which has some very basic camping gear, and a petrol station across the road from the supermarket in the centre of town.

Places to Stay & Eat The *Mallacoota Foreshore Caravan Park (☎ 03-5158 0362)* has unpowered sites at $12 for two adults plus $5 for each adult thereafter. (Summer prices are $20 per unpowered site and $6.60 per extra adult.)

The *Mallacoota Hotel/Motel (☎ 03-5158 0455)*, in Maurice Ave, has units from $45. *Mallacoota Lodge YHA (☎ 03-5158 0455)* is run through the pub on Maurice Ave and has singles, doubles and dorm beds from $15 per person.

The several small cafes and restaurants include *Barnacles Seafood Bistro*, with mains from $10 to $16, *The Tide Restaurant (☎ 03-5158 0100)*, specialising in expensive seafood, and the *Waterfront Cafe (☎ 03-5158 0064)*, which opens daily for lunch and breakfast.

Two *supermarkets* are right in the centre of town for food and last-minute supplies.

Getting There & Away Twenty-three kilometres off the Princes Hwy, Mallacoota is 500km east of Melbourne and 500km south of Sydney.

While buses stop at Genoa, on the Princes Hwy, there is no scheduled transport from Genoa down to Mallacoota. Accommodation places may be able to arrange transport from Genoa if you ring in advance.

Cann River
The closest town to the start of the walk, Cann River is only a small town on the Princes Hwy, where the basics such as food and fuel can be stocked up on.

The Parks Victoria Information Centre (☎ 03-5158 6351, fax 5158 6435), on the Princes Hwy, is a Parks Victoria office. The staff here can arrange permits and receive payment of your camping fees.

Accommodation is provided at *Hop Inn Motor Inn (☎ 03-5158 6331)*; *Pelican Point*

Coffee Lounge, on the Princes Hwy, features country cooking and a sandwich bar.

Thurra River Camping Area
At the trailhead, *Thurra River camping area* costs $13.50 per person per night. It is recommended for the first night of the walk as the car shuttle will usually take place in the evening. If you leave a vehicle at Thurra River, ensure it is left in the area designated for walker vehicles.

Inquiries and bookings for Thurra River camping area can be directed to the Parks Victoria Information Centres at Mallacoota and Cann River, or to the camping ground managers at the Point Hicks Lighthouse (☎/fax 03-5158 4268). You can also pay on site, depositing the money in an honesty box.

GETTING TO/FROM THE WALK
To reach the Thurra River trailhead, take the Tamboon Rd southwards from Cann River (15km), then turn left onto Point Hicks Rd (25km). Point Hicks Rd may be closed after heavy rain.

As there is no public transport to either end of the trail, you'll need to organise a car shuttle – leaving a car at the Mallacoota Aerodrome, the end of the walk, then driving back to Thurra River, at the start.

A car shuttle to Thurra River can be arranged through Tony Gray (☎ 0408 516 482, 03-5158 0472). He runs a shuttle service from Mallacoota, and has a comfortable 4WD for the purpose. He charges $150 for up to five people and $170 for five to seven people, for transfers to Thurra River camping area. Your car is left at the Mallacoota Aerodrome, at the end of the walk.

THE WALK
Day 1: Thurra River Camping Area to Gale Hill Camp Site
4 hours, 10km
Follow the dirt road from the camping ground east, take a right turn at the fork and head out to the beach via several other camp sites. Head east along the beach, and you'll soon come to the outflow of the Thurra River. This crossing is usually a fairly straightforward wade; however, heavy rains

VICTORIA

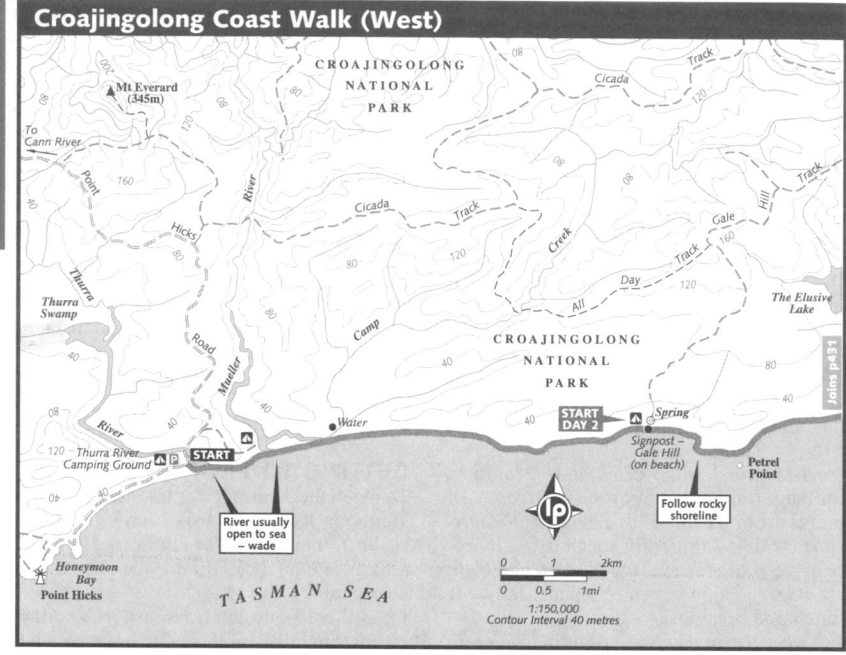

Croajingolong Coast Walk (West)

Joins p431

may increase the river flow considerably. Occasionally flow will be blocked altogether by a sand bar.

Continue east along the beach for 1.5km to the crossing of the Mueller River, which at the time of research was significantly deeper and faster than the Thurra River crossing. Water can be found behind the dunes on the eastern side of the inlet, 300m up from the crossing.

Continue along the beach, which provides great swimming in summer, but can be exposed to strong southerly winds and blown sand in winter. Head for the visible rocky section of beach, cross this and continue up to **Petrel Point**. A rocky prominence becomes visible on the beach: here lies the entrance between the dunes to Gale Hill. This entrance used to be difficult to find, but Parks Victoria has now installed a single-pole sign that is clearly visible.

Follow the track over the dunes, across a small wooden bridge and into the tea-tree

for five minutes to the *camp site*. Water is available from a small soak here, but this may dry up in hot weather.

Day 2: Gale Hill Camp Site to Wingan Inlet
4 hours, 12km

Leaving the dunes, continue east along the beach and head towards rocky Petrel Point, visible close by. Continue over the rocks around the point, keeping slightly inland towards the grassy patches in bad weather. Bits of fibreglass hull from the catamaran *Windsong* lie scattered here. If the wind is really strong and the sea is rough, there is a rough track through vegetation higher up the hill.

Drop down onto the second small beach when the end of the rocks is reached and head east, passing many small rocky outcrops for about 3km. A high dune here comes close to the sea, and can be an obstacle at high tide or in rough seas. Cross the rock bar and another signpost appears

Croajingolong Coast Walk (Central)

Broome Creek

CROAJINGOLONG
NATIONAL
PARK

To Cann River Road

Jungle Creek

Wingan River

West Wingan Creek

Rocky Creek

The Elusive Lake

CROAJINGOLONG
NATIONAL
PARK

Wingan Inlet

START DAY 3

Permanent fresh water

Signpost "Red River Walking Track"

START DAY 4

Water beside steps

Gulches along coast

Sandpatch Point

Deep crossing – often impassable

Wingan Point

Fly Cove

The Skerries

TASMAN SEA

Rame Head

0   1   2km
0   0.5   1mi
1:150,000
Contour Interval 40 metres

marked with red arrows, heading left up into the sand hills. This section of track avoids the cliffs of **Rame Head** by going inland through melaleuca scrub. Rock hopping round Rame Head is not recommended as large waves and tides may prevent access and rocks may be slippery or unstable.

After an hour, a track junction to Rame Head is marked. A brief but quite steep walk gets you to the **lookout** here, and is worth visiting. Back on the track, which is marked by red arrows as it continues north-east, the forest becomes more dense and is very pretty. The track then drops into Fly Cove, just before Wingan Inlet.

Head along the sand north-east and pick up the vague track visible on the lower section of sand dunes. This leads to the *camping area* via a wooden boardwalk around the inlet lagoon. The camping area is accessible by car on a gravel road. A designated overnight camping area is available for wakers, along with a supply of water.

Day 3: Wingan Inlet to Benedore River
5–6 hours, 15km

Wingan Inlet is one of the larger estuaries on the coast and has a fast outflow. Only attempt this crossing at low tide. At the time of writing, it was possible to wade across, keeping an eye out for deep holes in the sand (the current is strong, so be careful). If the inlet is very deep, ask around in summer and you may be able to arrange a lift across in a boat with fishermen camped here. In winter, however, the place is a little deserted, especially mid-week.

A small track continues on the other side (another *camp site* is located here) and heads up the hill; it is signposted 'Easby Track', and after 15 minutes drops back down to the beach. Follow these round to meet the Easby Walking Track. Head towards Easby Creek with a lot of rock hopping, passing a small soak on the way that is a good source of freshwater. Water in

The Ravages of Bushfires

After a protracted drought that parched Croajingolong from 1980 to mid-1983, the park and surrounding areas were ravaged by fierce bushfires. This culminated in a huge firestorm, which pushed along the coast from Cann River to Point Hicks and Mallacoota, destroying 80% of the park in one hit and sparing only the marshes of Thurra Swamp. All in its path was reduced to ashes. The size of the fire meant few birds, reptiles or other animals survived.

From this destruction, the park has regenerated very well, almost back to its former glory. Another fire started by a lightning strike near Cann River in 1998 burnt out a large section of heathland across the Thurra River, but was not nearly as destructive as the 1980 blazes.

Easby Creek in not suitable for drinking; there is a *camp site* here, however.

Continue rock hopping along the coast for about 4km, after which **Red River** is reached. The estuary here is wide and deep, but the crossing point near the sea is usually an easy wade across. Walk along the mouth of Red River across the beach. A signpost, about 100m past the river entrance, points left and is marked 'Red River Walking Track'.

Turning left into the sand dunes at the signpost, continue steeply up and over the first and second dunes, descending wooden steps to the Red River *camp site*, perched above the beautiful estuary and nestled among tea-trees and banksias. The water here is brackish. An alternative water supply is about 30 minutes away along the overgrown 4WD track (turning left at a junction). It's also possible to camp here as an alternative to Benedore River if the weather is windy.

From the junction, head right and follow the overgrown 4WD track north-east, up the hill and through progressively thicker forest and sword grass to a second track junction. Watch for ticks here. Take the right fork (signposted 'Sand Patch Track') and follow it through thick forest to where the track narrows and drops to the beach. Water can

be found near where the track exits – fill up here if possible. Continue for 15 minutes along the beach to Benedore River. *Camp sites* are located on both sides of the inlet, but the west side is best as it's higher and not as swampy as the east side.

Day 4: Benedore River to Shipwreck Creek
3½ hours, 10km

Cross the inlet. It can be a little deep, but is easy to wade across. Pick up the track beside the lagoon that heads north for 150m to the *camp site* on this side. An old 4WD track continues inland from here and over the dunes behind Little Rame Head to Seal Cove (about 8km and two hours from Benedore River). Take the side track to Little Rame Head and back for an interesting diversion on the way.

Seal Creek has a pretty *camp site* right near the beach. On the east side of Seal Creek, a track starts near another small creek, on the ridge that separates the two, and heads off into the scrub. It continues uphill through forest towards the west, then swings east to cross Seal Creek over fallen trees. Continue along an old 4WD track until a gate marked 'Walkers Only' is reached – pass through the gate and continue on the track through heathlands bordered by forest. The trail crosses a section of boggy, wet ground for roughly 30 minutes before descending through the trees to pretty Shipwreck Cove. Walk up wooden steps and continue 500m to the *camping area*. Camp in the forest just south of the numbered car camping spots. Water is available from Shipwreck Creek upstream.

Day 5: Shipwreck Creek to Mallacoota Aerodrome
4 hours, 12km

Pick up the track marked 'To Heath Track 200m'. Follow this to a track which is part of the Old Coast Rd (but has been closed to vehicles for some time). You leave the forest quickly and continue through heathland, skirting the cliffs of the rocky coastline. From time to time glimpses of small coves emerge through the heath. Continue along the track

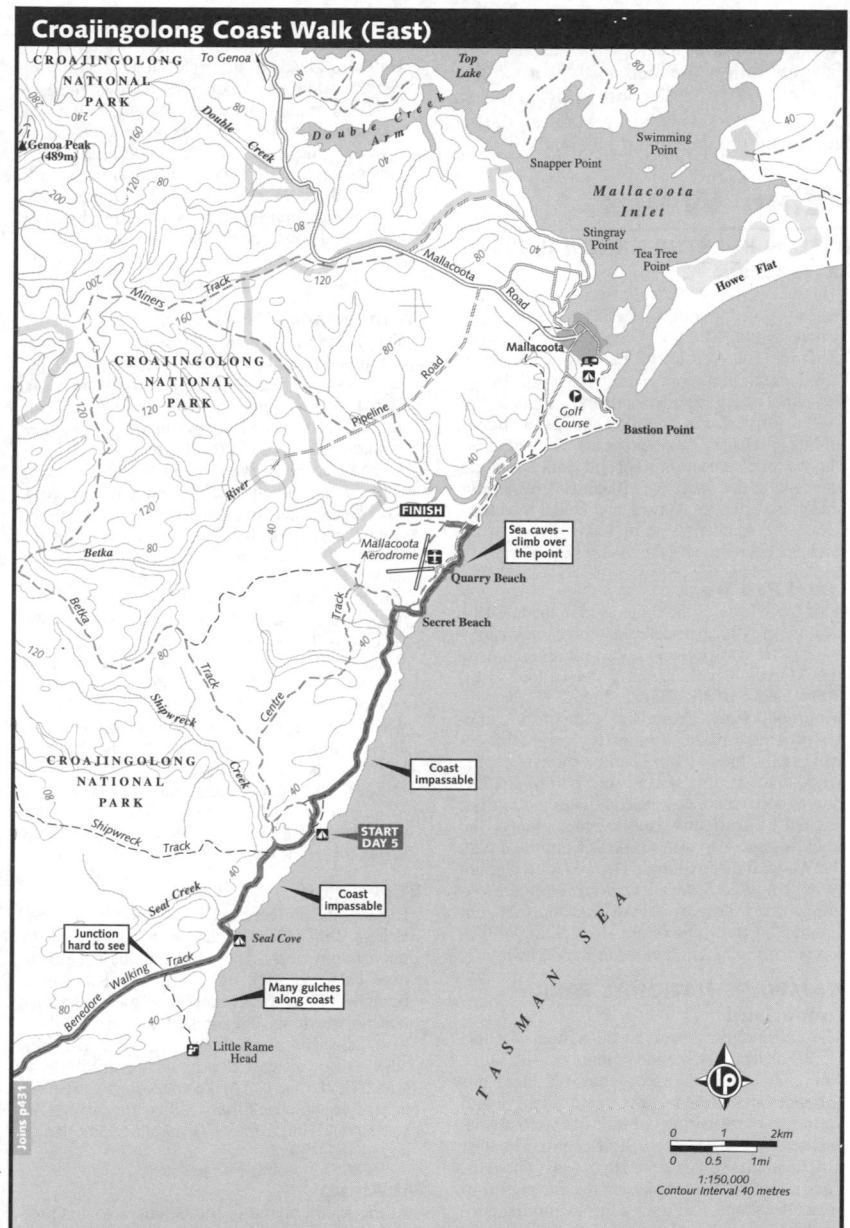

Croajingolong Coast Walk (East)

CROAJINGOLONG NATIONAL PARK

To Genoa

Top Lake

Genoa Peak (489m)

Double Creek

Double Creek Arm

Snapper Point

Swimming Point

Mallacoota Inlet

Stingray Point

Tea Tree Point

Howe Flat

Miners Track

Mallacoota Road

CROAJINGOLONG NATIONAL PARK

Road

Pipeline

Mallacoota

Golf Course

Bastion Point

River

Betka

Betka

FINISH

Mallacoota Aerodrome

Sea caves – climb over the point

Quarry Beach

Secret Beach

Track

Centre Creek

Shipwreck

Track

CROAJINGOLONG NATIONAL PARK

Shipwreck Track

Coast impassable

START DAY 5

Coast impassable

Seal Creek

Track

Junction hard to see

Benedore Walking Track

Seal Cove

Many gulches along coast

Little Rame Head

T A S M A N   S E A

Joins p431

0   1   2km

0   0.5   1mi

1:150,000
Contour Interval 40 metres

VICTORIA

until you reach an intersection with Centre Track, which leads to Shipwreck Creek. Turn right and follow the road north as it turns to bitumen. Skirt Mallacoota Aerodrome to pick up the cars where they were left during the car shuttle, thus ending the walk.

Other Walks

HATTAH–KULKYNE NATIONAL PARK
Lakes Circuit

This 12km, four-hour walk from Lake Hattah is an easy-going tour of several lakes of the Chalka Creek system. Follow Day 1 of the Hattah–Kulkyne Tour (described earlier) to the acute-angle track junction. Turn right and follow Brockie Track generally south and west to Hattah Nature Drive Track. To follow the eastern circuit of this interesting drive (notes are available from the visitor centre), turn right and walk anticlockwise along the track, past Black Box Waterhole and close to Lakes Arawak and Bulla, then back along the southern side of Lake Hattah to the park access road near the visitor centre.

Camel Pad Track

This track follows the route used in the late 19th century by Afghan traders and their camels carrying salt (from Spectacle Lake) for shipment via the Murray River. Linking the Calder Hwy, 200m north of the Hattah Lakes Store, with Mournpall Track, about 1km south of the camping ground, it passes through typical mallee eucalyptus, black box and cypress pine woodlands. It also skirts a salt pan (a shallow depression where salt accumulates naturally), fringed by distinctive salt-tolerant plants. The track is generally well marked. Combined with the Woodland and Shingle Back Tracks, it could provide a full day's walk (20km). From the visitor centre, follow Woodland Track north to join Camel Pad Track and return along Shingle Back Track from a junction close to the highway.

GRAMPIANS NATIONAL PARK
Wonderland

The extraordinary rock world of the Wonderland is deservedly the most popular walk in the Grampians, winding its way past the Elephants Hide, through Grand Canyon and Silent St and up to the breathtaking summit of the Pinnacle, perched high above the visitor centre. The best way to do the walk is from Halls Gap, where the track starts on the far side of the car park, opposite the shops, and passes the swimming pool then the caravan park on the left. The track is well marked all the way. For the return, about 50m below the Pinnacle a track signposted to Halls Gap leads to the right along the cliff top for several hundred metres, then down the eastern flank of the Wonderland Range. Well down, take care at a sharp right bend to keep the arrowhead markers in sight and continue down a series of zigzags to the edge of the caravan park. Allow about four hours for this 9.6km walk. The *Wonderland Walks* map folder produced by the Friends of Grampians–Gariwerd and Parks Victoria is useful (see Maps & Books in the Grampians National Park section earlier).

Wonderland–Rosea Tour

The Wonderland and Mt Rosea walks can be combined to make a varied and quite challenging two- or even three-day walk from Halls Gap. From the Pinnacle, go down to Devils Gap and on to Rosea camping ground via Lakeview Lookout, above Lake Bellfield.

The *camping ground* (about 10km from Halls Gap), at the junction of Silverband and Stony Creek Rds, has fireplaces and a toilet but no water, so you will have to carry all you'll need. Having climbed Mt Rosea the next day, you then have a choice. The quicker return to Halls Gap is to go back almost to the Pinnacle and descend as described earlier for the Wonderland walk. Alternatively, continue from Mt Rosea down to Borough Huts camping ground, where there is water (11km from Rosea camping ground). Next day, return to Halls Gap via the Bellfield Track, which wanders up and down through forest above the eastern shore of Lake Bellfield, beside Fyans Creek and on to the Grampians Tourist Rd bridge – Halls Gap is less than 2km farther on. You will need Vicmap's 1:50,000 *Northern Grampians* map in the Outdoor Leisure Map series for this walk.

Briggs Bluff

Right at the northern end of Mt Difficult Range, Briggs Bluff (619m) is a spectacular peak with outstanding views. The starting point is the Bee-hive Falls car park by Roses Gap Rd, which branches from the Grampians Tourist Rd just north of Wartook. The marked track passes Bee-hive Falls and climbs very steeply to the cliff edge. Allow at least five hours for this 10.6km walk. Thick mist can make conditions extremely hazardous, so check the weather forecast before setting out. The *Northern Grampians* tourist map covers the walk.

Mt Abrupt

At the southern end of the Grampians, this precipitous peak is well named, and gives some of the best views of the ranges, valleys and surrounding plains. A good track climbs, steeply in places, through eucalyptus woodland to a rocky ridge and then up to the summit. It starts from a car park beside the Grampians Tourist Rd, 57km south of Halls Gap or 8km north of the town of Dunkeld. This small town has a caravan park, hotel and takeaway places; the Dunkeld visitor centre (☎ 1800 807 506) can provide full details.

GREAT SOUTH WEST WALK
Glenelg River Gorge
From the junction of North Nelson Rd (6km from Nelson town) and River Track, the walk downstream to Nelson through the extremely scenic gorge, makes a very pleasant day's outing; allow 4½ to five hours for the 18km walk. The route is well marked and easy to follow. As well as fine river and gorge views, there's plenty of attractive stringybark woodland with banksias, wattles and grass trees to wander through. It's almost guaranteed that you'll see emus; the female's presence is betrayed by her unusual guttural drumming call.

VICTORIAN ALPS
Bogong High Plains Circuit
This six-day walk covers the best of the Bogong High Plains in a distance of about 85km; much of the walking is along the Australian Alps Walking Track. The route starts at Bogong Village, 16km south of Mt Beauty, and climbs steadily west – steeply at times – to Mt Fainter, then heads south through snow plains and scattered forests as it traverses the Niggerheads, the Bogong High Plains and Mt Nelse. The route makes a very steep descent to Big River, then an equally steep ascent to Victoria's highest peak, Mt Bogong. Crossing the mountain on the west side, the track then descends south to Bogong Creek Saddle, before turning west along Big River Fire Trail. Lower down, an old tramway is followed for much of the distance back to Bogong Village. Regarded as a walk of medium standard, it is an ideal introduction to walking in the Bogong High Plains area.

Viking Circuit
An extremely popular and scenic walk for experienced walkers, this circuit walk starts on the High Plains about 86km north of Licola (which is 54km north of Heyfield). While only about 45km in length, allow four days for this walk as there is much climbing involved, tracks are poorly defined in some places, and the terrain is rough. Fortunately, the attractive scenery more than compensates for the slow walking.

The route starts at the Howitt Plains car park, on Howitt Rd, and heads north over Clover Plain before turning east along a faint track to reach Wonnangatta Spur. The faint track joins Zeka Spur Track lower down, eventually reaching the Wonnangatta River. The route then climbs a ridge north-west to the Viking; a faint foot pad exists in places. Here the route joins the Australian Alps Walking Track and heads west as it traverses the summit of the Razor and Mt Despair before climbing to Mt Speculation. (The poorly marked route over the Razor can be difficult to follow.) The route then crosses the Crosscut Saw to Mt Howitt, before leaving the main track and bearing east to Macalister Springs. A 5km walk south leads back to the Howitt Plains car park.

Lake Tali Karng
This medium-grade two-day walk brings you to one of the most popular walking destinations in the Victorian Alps. Formed by a massive landslide a few thousand years ago, Lake Tali Karng has the appeal of an oasis deep within a rugged mountain environment.

Starting on the plains at McFarlane Saddle, 61km north-east of Licola, the route initially heads south on a foot track before joining an old vehicle track that leads to Moroka Saddle. Bear east here on a walking track to the summit of Mt Wellington, then walk south along a 4WD track to Millers Hut. The route then heads generally north-west to the edge of the plateau, before dropping steeply down Riggalls Spur to the lake and a pleasant camp site.

Next day, follow a track along the north shore, then climb steeply up Gillios Track to the plateau. On top, a track heads north across Spion Kopje to join the 4WD track followed on the previous day. Retrace your steps to McFarlane Saddle.

CROAJINGOLONG NATIONAL PARK
Point Hicks Lighthouse
A short 4.5km walk heads out to Point Hicks Lighthouse from Thurra River. A display board at the lightstation recounts details of the area's history, including shipwrecks and the nearby Aboriginal middens.

Thurra Dunes
Thurra River is a region containing enormous sand dunes. A 4km return walk starts from the Thurra River camping area, and reaches the 30m dunes via a track through banksias and heathland.

Genoa Peak
Starting from the Genoa Peak car park, a 1.5km walk (two hours return) climbs to the top of the granite tor of Genoa Peak and offers great views over the wilderness coast and Gabo Island just off the coast.

Western Australia

Australia's largest and most sparsely populated state, Western Australia (WA) is remote both geographically and in outlook from the relatively crowded eastern states. For walkers this means widely spaced, scenically magnificent walking areas of great natural interest, and friendly locals.

This chapter concentrates on the accessible south-west region of the state. The national parks of the north-western Kimberley region (Purnululu and Windjana Gorge) and of the central western Pilbara (Karijini and Millstream–Chichester) are the places to go for adventurous walking in remote, rugged areas of great beauty.

In the south-west, towering karri, jarrah and tingle forests (unique to WA), long, almost pristine coasts, mountain ranges and wild flowers are the themes in several national parks and conservation reserves (there are more than 70 state-wide). Australia's second-longest walking track, the Bibbulmun Track, extends for 964km from the outskirts of Perth through forest, heathland and along the coast to Albany, and is central to exploring the area. Other tracks open up the Leeuwin–Naturaliste coast in the extreme south-west, and several of the imposing peaks of the Stirling Range. Facilities are generally excellent in the parks and in the colourful, welcoming towns throughout the area. Four day walks and an overnight walk are described in detail, with suggestions for several others.

INFORMATION
Maps

Australia Quality Publishing's 1:170,000 *South West Corner* and 1:268,000 and 1:533,000 *South Coast East to Cape Arid* maps are widely available and simple to use. They include tourist information, road distances and major walking tracks.

Walkers are less well served with large-scale topographical maps than elsewhere in Australia. The south-west is covered by Auslig's 1:100,000 maps, but these are generally

Highlights

JASON EDWARDS

Overlooking a river-eroded gorge in Walpole–Nornalup National Park

- Walking across limestone cliffs, flowering heathlands and outstanding rocky points in Leeuwin–Naturaliste National Park

- Standing inside towering tingle trees in Walpole–Nornalup National Park

- Climbing the rugged, cliff-lined peaks of the Stirling Range

- Wandering along the south coast's beautiful wild beaches and rocky shores to Cosy Corner or Peaceful Bay

- Sampling the long, long Bibbulmun Track, through majestic karri and jarrah forests

ancient. The Royal Australian Army Survey Corps (Army) 1:50,000 coverage is useful but patchy. Conservation & Land Management (CALM) publishes 1:50,000 topographic maps, especially for forested areas, while the Department of Land Administration (DOLA) publishes black-and-white topographic maps.

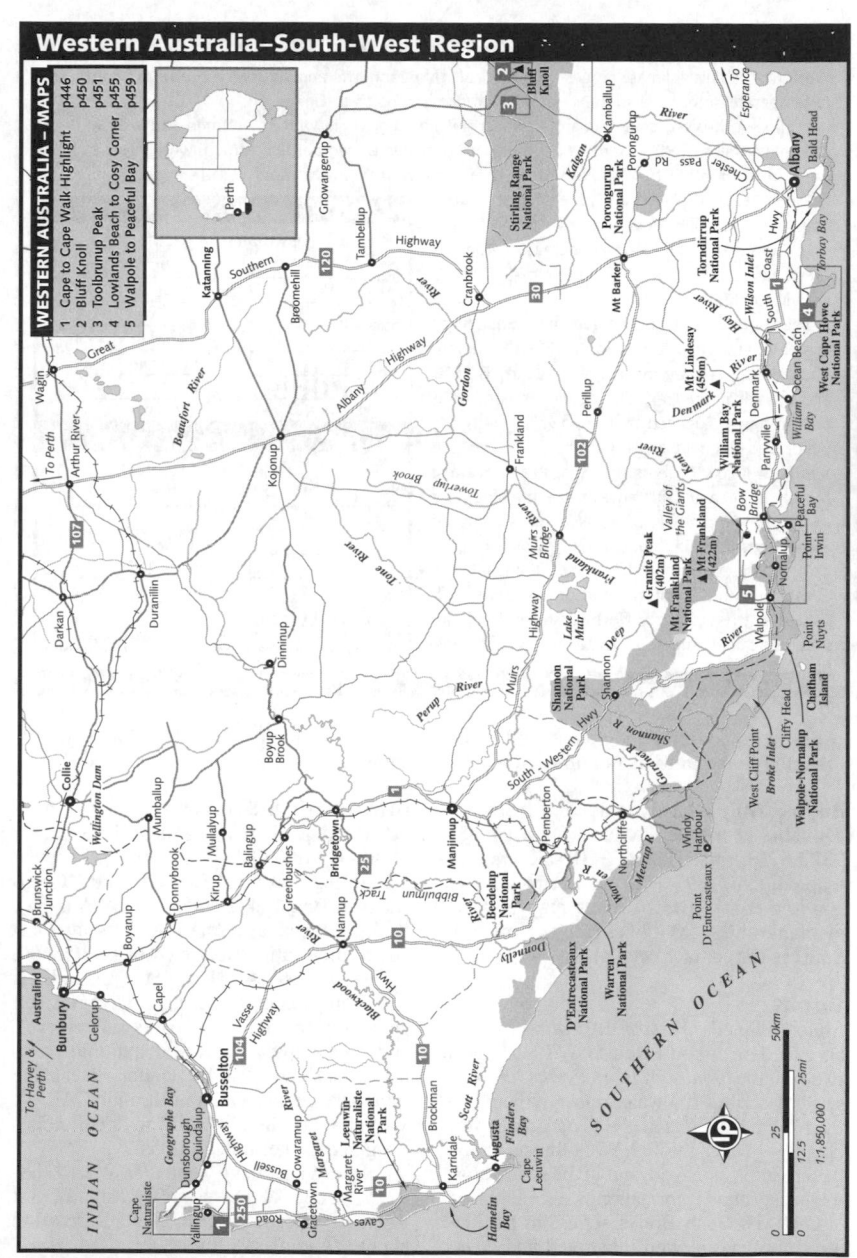

WESTERN AUSTRALIA–South-West Region

WESTERN AUSTRALIA

The Climate of Western Australia

Western Australia's climate ranges from tropical in the far north, arid across the centre and south-east, to temperate in the area south-west of Esperance and north to Geraldton.

In the south-west, summers are warm to hot and dry, while winters are mild and wet. In Perth, daily maximums of 30°C or more are the norm between December and March, with February being the hottest month. The minimum rarely drops below 10°C at this time. Perth's average maximum is barely 16°C in July, which is the coldest month. Rain is scarce from November to April with less than 20mm monthly. Rainfall increases dramatically between May and October when 75% of the annual total falls.

The southern coastal strip generally experiences cooler weather than the inland part of the region. The average January maximum in Albany is 25°C and the minimum 15°C. During winter, conditions are strongly influenced by the prevailing westerly winds and frequent gales that charge in from the Southern Ocean. July is the coldest and wettest month in Albany with an average maximum of 16°C and 126mm of rain. Frosts are fairly common away from the coast, but snow can be expected only on the highest peaks of the Stirling Range. Westerly winds continue through summer, although with less ferocity. North-easterlies bring hot weather, often tempered by afternoon sea breezes.

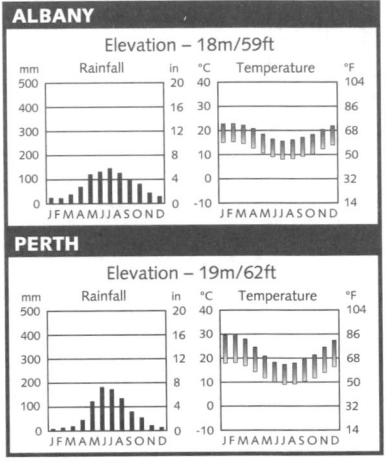

For maps covering individual walks, see Planning in the introduction to each walk.

Buying Maps Auslig and Army maps are available at the Perth Map Centre (☎ 08-9322 5733, fax 9322 5673, ✉ sales@perth map.com.au), 891 Hay St, Perth. CALM and sometimes DOLA maps may also be available at CALM offices (see Information Sources for contact details).

Books

Lonely Planet's *Western Australia* provides an excellent introduction to WA. CALM's two-volume *Family Walks in Perth Outdoors* series describes 104 walks, most of them less than 10km long. *Bushwalks in the South-West* details 49 walks through WA's forests, along the coast to Cape Arid, and in the mountains; the background information is excellent.

CALM's Bush Books series, in pocket-sized format, are well illustrated and cover mammals, orchids, trees, birds of the forests and wild flowers.

Information Sources

CALM's head office and service centre (☎ 08-9334 0333, fax 9334 0466, 💻 www .calm.wa.gov.au) is at 50 Hayman Rd, Como (Locked Bag 104, Bentley DC, WA 6983). It's open weekdays. The WA Naturally Outdoors Information Centre (☎ 08-9430 8600, fax 9430 8699), 47 Henry St, Fremantle, is open daily except Tuesday. Here you can gather information about parks and reserves, and buy maps, guides and national parks passes (see Permits & Regulations later). The same services are available through CALM's Web site. Details of CALM regional offices are given in the walk sections.

The Environment Centre of WA (☎ 08-9225 4103, ✉ ecwa@ecwa.asn.au), 1st floor, 10 Pier St, Perth, has information about WA conservation issues.

A few walking clubs are based in Perth, including Perth Bushwalkers (☎ 08-9362 1614). Nonmembers who are active members of an Australian bushwalking club are welcome on club walks, which take place every Sunday and on many weekends.

Weather charts and forecasts are published in the the *West Australian* daily newspaper, and on the evening TV news.

Permits & Regulations

An entry fee is charged at some national parks; in the south-west these include Leeuwin–Naturaliste, Stirling Range and Porongurup. A day pass costs $8 per vehicle and is valid for as many parks as you visit on a single day. A holiday pass is a far better investment – $20 for four weeks, visiting an unlimited number of parks. Passes are available from CALM offices and through its Web site (see Information Sources earlier).

Fees are charged at national park camp sites and range from $8 to $11 per site, depending on facilities. Campfires are generally banned or restricted during the fire danger period from November to March. During days of Total Fire Ban, all fires are forbidden, even fuel stoves. If you are caught with an open fire on these days, you are not only endangering yourself and the environment, but you can also cop a hefty fine and/or prison sentence. Check with the local CALM office for up-to-date information.

GETTING AROUND

Easyrider Backpackers (☎ 08-9226 0307, ✆ tours@easyriderbp.com.au), 158 William St, operates jump-on, jump-off circuits including one from Perth to Dunsborough, Margaret River, Augusta, Walpole, Denmark and Albany. A ticket costs $159 and is valid for three months.

Realistically, a car is the most practical form of transport in WA. Roads are excellent and traffic generally light. Road trains (trucks), measuring up to a daunting 36.5m long, roar along specially designated road train routes. However, drivers are generally very courteous, so passing them isn't the nightmare you might fear.

GATEWAYS
Perth

The WA capital has two-thirds of the state's 1.8 million population. Free of the turmoil of many large cities, Perth is cosmopolitan and friendly.

Information At the Western Australian Tourist Centre (☎ 1300 361 351, 🖳 www .tourism.wa.gov.au), Forrest Place, Perth, you can pick up a comprehensive guide to accommodation and information about major attractions. It's open daily.

The Free Backpackers Guide to WA, widely available at tourist offices and outdoor gear shops, is a mine of information about accommodation, travel, car hire and much more.

Cybercafes are concentrated on Wellington St; typical rates are $3 per 30 minutes and discounts are usually available to YHA members and student card holders.

Supplies & Equipment A few of the major national chains of outdoor gear shops have branches near the centre. Mountain Designs (☎ 08-9322 4774) and Paddy Pallin (☎ 08-9321 2666) are at the western end of Hay St; Snowgum (☎ 08-9321 5259) is at the western end of Murray St. For gear hire, try Aussie Camping Hire (☎ 08-9300 3172), 2/44 Winton Rd, Joonolup.

Places to Stay Perth has accommodation for all tastes and budgets. Your first stop should be the Western Australian Tourist Centre (see Information earlier).

The ***Britannia International YHA*** *(☎ 08-9328 6121, fax 9227 9784, ✆ britannia @yhawa.com.au, 253 William St)* is the larger of the YHA's two hostels, both in lively Northbridge. It has a range of rooms costing from $16 in small dorms to $70 for the family room. Email access is available.

The Royal Hotel *(☎ 08-9324 1510, 1800 249 124, fax 9321 2443),* on the corner of Wellington and William Sts, is one of the YWCA/YMCA group and has singles for $64 and doubles/twins for $60; tariffs for rooms with private facilities are slightly higher. There's a restaurant in the hotel.

Places to Eat The popular *Down Under Food Hall*, near the corner of William St and Hay St in the city centre, has dishes from $6.

Northbridge boasts a cornucopia of ethnic tastes. Try *Hare Krishna Food for Life (200 William St)* for a $5 all-you-can-eat vegetarian lunch Monday to Friday, or a $2 meal between 5 and 6 pm. Also on William St is a string of Asian restaurants, including *Sri Melaka* (Malaysian) at No 313 and *White Elephant Thai* at No 323. For first-rate Italian food, head to *Mamma Maria's (105 Aberdeen St)*.

There is a *Foodland* supermarket *(556 Hay St)* in the city and a *Coles* on the corner of Fitzgerald and View Sts, North Perth.

Getting There & Away Perth is around 4400km from Sydney by road, across the arid expanse of the Nullarbor Plain. It is accessible via the Eyre and Great Eastern Hwys from the east, and via the Great Northen Hwy from the north.

Air Perth is well served by international flights, particularly from South-East Asia and Europe. Qantas (☎ 13 1313) and Ansett (13 1300) operate flights to Perth from all Australian state capitals and many regional centres. The flight time from Sydney is about four hours, but in summer the three-hour time difference means you can leave Sydney at 5 pm and arrive in Perth at 6 pm.

Qantas, Ansett and their partner airlines serve many country centres within WA. Skywest Airlines (☎ 08-9334 2288, **e** info @skywest.com.au) flies to Albany, Esperance and many other places; Maroomba Airlines (☎ 08-9478 3850, **e** maroomba @iinet.net.au) flies to Margaret River.

Bus Greyhound (☎ 13 2030) provides bus services to Perth from Adelaide, Darwin, Melbourne and Sydney. The 3565km journey from Melbourne via Adelaide, for example, takes about 48 hours ($244 one way). Buses arrive and depart from the terminal in Wellington St, East Perth.

Train The *Indian-Pacific* railway line (☎ 13 2147, **e** salesagent@gsr.com.au) runs from Sydney to Perth via Broken Hill and Adelaide, with connections from Melbourne and Alice Springs. The one-way Sydney–Perth fare starts at $439 coach class (meals are extra) and the trip takes three days.

Country passenger train services in WA are confined to Perth–Busselton and Perth–Kalgoorlie. Westrail (☎ 13 1053) operates a wide-ranging network of bus services to regional centres from the East Perth Terminal. South-West Coachlines (☎ 08-9324 2333) operates from Perth City Bus Port in Mounts Bay Rd to several towns in the south-west. Details are given in the walks sections.

Car Rental All the major car hire companies have offices in Perth and numerous regional centres. Smaller companies, such as Delta (☎ 13 1390) and Sunset (☎ 08-9245 2466) may offer competitive rates.

Getting Around Perth's central public transport organisation, Transperth, operates buses, trains and ferries. There are Transperth information offices (☎ 13 6213) in the Plaza Arcade, the City Bus Port on Mounts Bay Rd at the foot of William St, and at the Wellington St train station.

To/From the Airport Perth's international and domestic airports are separate but close together, 10km east of the city. Perth Airport Bus Service links the terminals; the fare is $6. Transperth (☎ 13 2213) operates regular daily services from St George's Terrace to the domestic airport (40 minutes; around $3).

Albany

The oldest settlement in WA and the largest town in the south-west, Albany is well worth a day or more in its own right, before or between walks in the Stirling Range and along the south coast.

Information The helpful tourist bureau (☎ 1800 644 088, fax 9842 1490), Proudlove Parade, Albany 6330, is open daily. It provides an accommodation booking service and sells Bibbulmun Track maps and some local guides; while you're there, pick up a free town guide.

The CALM office (☎ 08-9842 4500), 120 Albany Hwy (near McDonald's), is open weekdays. It provides local national park and Bibbulmun Track information.

You can check and send emails at Compu-games (☎ 08-9842 2229), 373 Middleton Rd; it's open normal office hours and charges $5 for 30 minutes. Yak Yak Bar (☎ 08-9842 9399), 39 Stirling Terrace, is open from 9 am until late and also charges $5 per half-hour; coffee and snacks are available.

Supplies & Equipment For camping supplies, including all types of fuel, try Trail-blazers (☎ 08-9841 7859), 184 Albany Hwy, and the Great Outdoors Centre (☎ 08-9841 6818), 151 Albany Hwy, both open daily.

Places to Stay & Eat There are several caravan parks in and near Albany. *Middleton Beach Caravan Park (☎ 08-9841 3593, fax 9842 2088)*, at Middleton Beach 3km east of town, has grassed tent sites for $17 a double; there's a campers' kitchen, free gas barbecues and a small shop.

Emu Beach Holiday Park (☎ 08-9844 1147), on Medcalf Parade, Emu Beach, is about 9km out and very peaceful. Shady tent sites cost $13 for two; the campers' kitchen is well set up and there are free barbecues.

Four backpacker places are clustered around the southern end of the town. *Albany Bayview YHA (☎/fax 08-9842 3388, 49 Duke St)* has twins, doubles and family rooms or dorms from $14.

You could eat out every night for a fort-night at a different place in Albany. Among the more colourful options is *Shamrock Cafe* (☎ 08-9841 4201, 184 York St), open daily from early until late for Guinness pie ($11), Dublin Bay pasta ($11) and much else.

Al Fornetto Ristorante (☎ 08-9841 1061), in York St, is open daily from 6 pm for pizzas from a wood-fired oven (from $13) and pasta (from $12) using genuine Italian products; the restaurant is licensed and BYO (Bring Your Own).

There's a huge *Coles* supermarket by the Albany Hwy near the northern end of York St, and the *Foodland* supermarket at the southern end of York St is open daily.

Getting There & Away Albany is 409km from Perth via the Albany Hwy.

Skywest Airlines (☎ 08-9841 6655, 9334 2288 in Perth) flies daily to Albany from Perth airport (65 minutes). The one-way seven-day advance booking fare is $115.

Westrail's (☎ 13 1053) most direct bus service, The Southerner (via the town of Williams), departs Perth daily (six hours; $35.10 one way).

Budget and Avis have offices in Albany; Albany Car Rentals (☎ 08-9841 7077) offers small vehicles for $30 per day for a hire of more than five days.

Leeuwin–Naturaliste National Park

Long-distance walking tracks linking distinct geographical features are particularly satisfying, and the Cape to Cape Walk in Leeuwin–Naturaliste National Park is a first-class example. It extends for 136km between Cape Naturaliste, one of the most prominent features in the far south-west, and Cape Leeuwin, the south-western extremity of the continent, where the west-facing coast ends and the shore turns east to confront the Southern Ocean. It's a walk with much variety: cliffs, beaches, coves, limestone pinnacles and caves, stands of wind-combed heath and woodland, wild flowers, lighthouses, a few small seaside settlements and some quite remote country. There are six camp sites along the walk and at least three others nearby. However, the walk isn't only for the hardy – several coast access roads make day walks possible if you have suitable transport arrangements. The northernmost section of the walk is described here and an outline given of the other sections.

HISTORY

Evidence has been found of Aboriginal people occupying this south-westernmost corner for many millennia before Europeans arrived. French explorers named prominent features at the beginning of the 19th century and small parcels of land were taken up from about 1828. The first homestead in the area, Ellenbrook, a few kilometres south of Gracetown, dates from 1854 and is on the route of the walk. However, settlement did not really get started until logging of the forest began in the 1890s. After several shipwrecks during the later 19th century, lighthouses were built at Cape Leeuwin in 1895 and Cape Naturaliste in 1903. The national park was established in the 1970s and now protects 19,700 hectares.

Long, Dark & Slithery

Both venomous and harmless snakes are as much a part of the bush as kookaburras and kangaroos. They are an important item in the diet of many birds, especially the kookaburra, and in turn feed on small rodents.

Any time from late September until mid- to late autumn, you may well meet more than one or two during walks anywhere in the bush.

Two venomous species are common in south-west Western Australia. The dugite, which is up to 1.5m long, has a small head and is coloured grey, olive or brown with a scattering of brown-red. It's at home in coastal dunes, heaths and forests. The extremely venomous tiger snake is on the small side, stretching to 1m, and is dark brown or black with lighter blotches; it inhabits swamps and wetlands.

Reptiles suffer from a largely undeserved bad reputation. Snakes will be generally more afraid of you – with your large, heavy feet – than you need be of them. As soon as they detect your footfall, they'll slither away to safety. You will be at risk of an attack only if you provoke a snake or if you disturb one early in spring, when they're sluggish after their winter sleep and likely to feel more vulnerable.

If you're really unlucky the treatment for snake bite is outlined in the Health & Safety chapter. In a few words: don't panic, move the victim as little as possible, apply a firm bandage over the affected limb and seek immediate medical help.

NATURAL HISTORY

The dominant feature of the national park is the elongated granite-based and limestone-capped ridge. The granite is around 600 million years old, but the limestone, comprised of solidified sandy materials, is a relative newcomer during the last two million years. The ridge rises sharply from the shore up to 200m and tapers gently inland to undulating hills.

The two main vegetation types are woodlands of aromatic peppermint gums and colourful banksias, and low heathland with wattles, honey-myrtles (bottlebrush), coastal daisy bushes, pimelias and many more. There are also small areas of jarrah and marri eucalyptus forest, and at Boranup is the western-most occurrence of karri forest; this forest, less than 100 years old, is regrowth after clear felling between the 1880s and 1913.

Dieback is a problem in parts of the park; tracks may be closed to try to limit its spread (see the boxed text 'Phytophthora').

PLANNING
When to Walk

The time to be in the Leeuwin–Naturaliste area is late September to early November, when wild flowers are at their best. During summer, apart from crowded accommodation, especially during the February grape harvest, you'll also find plenty of snakes (see the boxed text 'Long, Dark & Slithery' earlier for a description of common species).

You'll need a hat and sunglasses, a 2L water bottle and a fuel stove if you're going to camp.

Maps & Books

The Auslig 1:100,000 *Busselton* and *Leeuwin* maps are useful for an overall picture of the area and for access roads, although the maps are almost historic – published in 1981. The leaflets published by CALM, one for each of the five sections of the walk, are outstanding value, with a 1:100,000 map, brief track notes and background information. For even more detail, there's CALM's newspaper-format *A Guide to Leeuwin–Naturaliste National Park*. All these are available from local CALM and tourist offices.

Phytophthora

Phytophthora cinnamomi, or cinnamon fungus, is probably responsible for more plant deaths than almost any other disease in the world today. This subtropical fungus attacks the roots of plants (including trees), causing the plant to starve. Banksias and dryandras are the most susceptible among the 900 species of vulnerable plants, many of which are rare or endangered. Not only are the plants affected, but also the mammals, birds and insects that rely on them for food and shelter.

The war against dieback is being waged on several fronts. In national parks and nature reserves, CALM is upgrading roads (to gravel surface) and closing and revegetating those that are not needed. Dieback-free areas with high conservation value are protected by access restrictions on vehicles and walkers. During wet weather, Special Protection Areas and tracks are closed to stop the fungus from spreading further.

At the beginning of tracks in the south coast parks, you'll find large, lidded metal trays equipped with a stiff brush, where you should thoroughly clean your boots at the start and finish of your walk. In fact, walkers are encouraged to clean their footwear (and vehicles) before and after *any* walk in the bush. By doing the right thing, you can help to ensure that dieback is controlled and that it does not invade disease-free areas.

It's not only on the ground that the war is being waged. There's good evidence in Stirling Range National Park that spraying with phosphite (derived from phosphoric acid buffered with potassium hydroxide to prevent acid damage) bolsters plants' immune systems and drastically reduces or halts the fungus in its path, although it isn't actually eradicated from the soil. In 1998 a three-year campaign was launched to attack dieback with aerial spraying each autumn, starting in the eastern ridge of the Stirling Range and around Mondurup Peak.

CALM's *Bushwalks in the South-West* includes descriptions of six shortish walks in the national park. On top of all this are three more leaflets: CALM's *Cape Naturaliste Walk Network*, which covers four linked short walks at the Cape, including the Whale Lookout Track; *Margaret River Walk/Cycle Trails*, including the 15km return Ten Mile Brook Trail; and *Yallingup-Smiths Beach Walk Trails*, covering five short walks in the area about 15km south of Cape Naturaliste. All are available from local tourist outlets.

Published late in 1999, the beautifully illustrated *Walking the Capes* by Jane Scott & Patricia Negus describes 21 circular walks in and near the national park. *Native Flora of the Cape Naturaliste Region* produced by the Toby Inlet Catchment Group identifies about 200 native plants and is aimed at the enthusiastic amateur. Both are available from local tourist offices.

Permits & Regulations

National park entry fees are charged at Leeuwin–Naturaliste; season passes can be purchased from the CALM offices in Busselton or Margaret River.

A fee of $5 per person per night is charged for the camp sites along the Cape to Cape Walk – the Ranger will (probably) call during the evening. Although solidly built fire places are provided, CALM urges walkers to stick to fuel stoves – camp fires are usually prohibited during summer anyway.

NEAREST TOWNS
Dunsborough

This seaside town 10km south-east of Cape Naturaliste could serve as a base for walks in the northern section of the national park.

Warning

Freak or king waves and swells can surge in from an apparently peaceful sea, so when walking along beaches and rocky shores, keep an eye out to sea, and take extra care when the wind is blowing strongly (which is often).

WESTERN AUSTRALIA

The tourist office (☎ 08-9755 3299, fax 9756 8065, ⓔ bsntb@highway1.com.au), on Seymour Blvd, is on the eastern side of Dunsborough Park shopping centre and is open daily. Here you can obtain Cape to Cape Walk and local accommodation information.

Outdoor Sports, on Dunn Bay Rd, adjacent to the shopping centre, sells Coleman gas canisters.

Places to Stay & Eat The YHA hostel, *Three Pines Resort (☎/fax 08-9755 3107, 285 Geographe Bay Rd, Quindalup),* is on the beachfront 1km south-east of the town centre. The tariff starts at $15 a night for a bed in a family room; there are also twins and doubles. The hostel has a kitchen, barbecues and a shop.

Green Acres Beachfront Caravan Park (☎ 08-9755 3087, 77 Gifford Rd, Dunsborough) has tent sites for $14 and cabins from $35 for a double.

There aren't many places to go for an evening meal; you could brave the Dunsborough Bay Village Resort, on Dunn Bay Rd, where the *Golden Bay Chinese Restaurant* provides eat-in and takeaway service.

In the shopping centre you'll find *greengrocers*, a *bakery*, *butcher* and *supermarket*.

Getting There & Away Dunsborough is 255km south of Perth and 24km west of Busselton via Caves Rd.

South-West Coachlines (☎ 08-9324 2333) and Westrail (☎ 13 1053) run daily services from Perth to Dunsborough (about $22 one way; four hours).

Dunsborough is on an Easyrider Backpackers bus circuit (see Getting There & Away under Gateways earlier).

Margaret River

This prosperous, rather trendy and central town could make a base for all walks in Leeuwin–Naturaliste National Park.

The tourist bureau (☎ 08-9757 2911, fax 9757 3287, ⓔ amrta@netserv.net.au), Bussell Hwy, is open daily. It can book local accommodation, and sells walking maps and local and natural history books. The CALM office is 1km north of town on the Bussell

Hwy; it's open weekdays. Here you can buy national park passes and obtain up-to-date information about local walking tracks.

Lloyds The Old Tin Shed, in the main street, is open daily and stocks gas canisters, liquid fuel and camping equipment. The CyberCorner Cafe (☎ 08-9757 9388), behind the Challenge Bank in the main street, is open daily.

Places to Stay & Eat Close to the centre of town, *Riverview Caravan Park (☎ 08-9757 2270),* on Willmott Ave, has grassed and shady tent sites for $15.

Closer to the Cape to Cape Walk is *Gracetown Caravan Park (☎ 08-9755 5301, fax 9755 5508),* on the corner of Caves and Cowaranup Bay Rds, 5km from Margaret River. Bushland tent sites cost $16 a double; there's a pleasant, open campers' kitchen and gas barbecue. Cabins for four adults cost $45. A small on-site shop has basic supplies.

Of the local backpacker places, *The Margaret River Lodge (☎ 08-9757 9532, fax 9757 2532, ⓔ stay@mrlodge.com.au, 220 Railway Terrace)* has variously sized rooms, some with en suite, from $15.

For an evening meal, one of the best bets is *Goodfellas*, opposite the tourist bureau. It's open nightly from 6 pm for pizzas from a wood-fired oven (from $10) and pasta ($15), and is both BYO and licensed.

For self-caterers the large *Supa Valu* supermarket is open daily. There's a popular *bakery* in the shopping arcade. If you're lucky enough to strike the Sunday *market*, you'll be able to buy local honey, fruit and vegetables; don't miss *Sunday's Ice Cream Shop* in the plaza where the market is held.

Getting There & Away Margaret River is on the Bussell Hwy 277km from Perth.

South-West Coachlines (☎ 08-9324 2333) operates a daily service to Margaret River via Bunbury and Busselton ($23 one way; five hours). Westrail's (☎ 13 1053) daily bus service takes a little longer ($24.50). The Easyrider Backpackers bus goes through Margaret River.

Margaret River Taxis can be contacted on ☎ 08-9757 3444.

Cape to Cape Walk Highlight

Duration	5½–6 hours
Distance	20km
Standard	medium
Start	Cape Naturaliste
Finish	Wyadup
Nearest Town	Dunsborough
Public Transport	no

Summary Along paths and tracks across heathland above the scenic, rocky coastline, with two short sections of beach walking and sweeping coastal views.

This section of the Cape to Cape Walk provides plenty of walking along specially built tracks. The route is well marked with timber posts bearing a walking figure logo. Yallingup and Smiths Beaches are almost guaranteed to be tougher going on soft sand, whatever the state of the tide – there's little variation between high and low tides.

As an end-to-end walk, this section depends on transport being available at each end, but there are alternatives. The walk could be split into two easy outings, especially suitable for families with young children; by making use of good access to the coast at Yallingup Beach, 14km from Cape Naturaliste, the section to Wyadup could be a shorter there-and-back walk of 12km. Another possibility is to make a base at the unnamed camp site 11km south of the cape and 3km north of Yallingup.

Before starting the walk, it's well worth having a good look around Cape Naturaliste, using the well-organised network of paths from the car park to a lookout over the cape and to a whale-watching lookout. Humpback whales frequent the area from October to December and southern right whales from June to September. The Cape Naturaliste Lighthouse is open daily – call ☎ 08-9755 3955 for details.

GETTING TO/FROM THE WALK
To the Start
From the major road junction on Caves Rd, on the western edge of Dunsborough, drive north-west along the clearly signposted Cape Naturaliste Rd to the car park at the end, a distance of 13km.

From the Finish
To reach the end of the walk at Wyadup, turn off Caves Rd 13km south of Dunsborough along Wyadup Rd; at a junction 4km on, turn right for the parking area at the end of the road.

THE WALK
From the car park at Cape Naturaliste, walk along the road towards the lighthouse; just past the Maritime Museum, turn left (where there is a large water tank) and a few metres along, go right at a fork, on a sandy track. After 180m turn left at the start of the Cape to Cape Walking Track.

The track, sandy in places, heads south through scrub then lower heathland where wild flowers in springtime make a great display. After about 45 minutes cross Sugarloaf Rd, about 500m inland from the shore, with **Sugarloaf Rock** close by; this is a prominent feature throughout the walk. Long views southwards to Cape Clairault now open up. The track soon reaches the edge of the low, fretted limestone cliff and generally follows it to the car park above **Three Bears Beach** (about an hour from Sugarloaf Rd).

A long flight of timber steps descends to the beach, famous for its good surf but perhaps notorious among walkers for the soft sand. About 75m from the end of the beach, walk up a wide sandy track past the northern end of a line of cliffs to a 4WD track. Follow it south for about 500m; where it turns east to climb away from the coast, go right along a wide sandy track. About 45 minutes from Three Bears Beach, the track goes through some tall tea-trees where an unnamed *camp site* is set back from and just east of the track, close to a low cliff.

The track meanders on to Rabbits Car Park (30 minutes from the camp site), where there's a framed map of the local walk trails. From here, go to the right for about 15m then down a sandy path to the **beach** and its soft sand. The superb, even lines of breakers can take your mind off the

Cape to Cape Walk Highlight

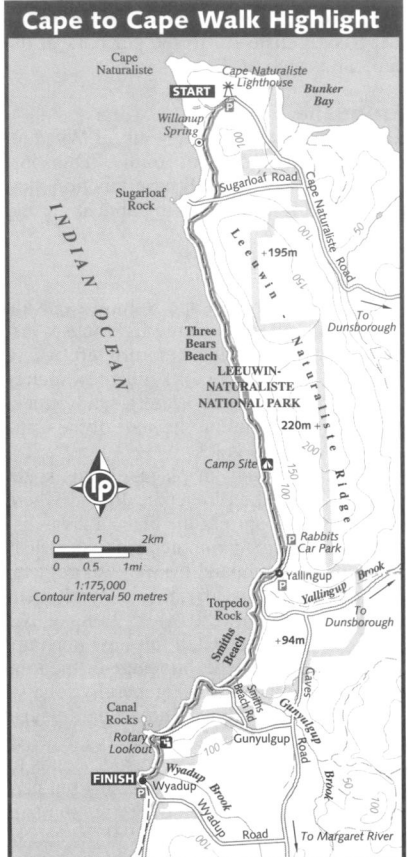

one to follow, past **Torpedo Rock** on the shoreline. A little farther on, bear right down Quenda Trail to **Smiths Beach**, about half soft and half firm sand (about 30 minutes from Yallingup). A path on the edge of the fringing bushland passes some unusual conglomerate boulders with very large granite stones in the limestone matrix. Paddle across a small stream a little farther on.

At the end of the beach, climb to a road and turn right and follow it to a car park. From here the track snakes through some large boulders, maintaining its height. Climb slightly to the ridge to join a clear track that passes above a rocky cove and leads up to a car park. Turn left, cross a sealed road and climb the steps to **Rotary Lookout**, which gives first-class views northwards to Cape Naturaliste. Then follow the markers carefully down through low scrubby vegetation to the steps to the shore, about 200m before the end of the ridge. At sea level, cross a stream and follow a grassy path to the end of a road at Wyadup (1¾ hours from Smiths Beach).

Stirling Range National Park

If you're feeling deprived of mountain walking and need a change from the long, flat coast, Stirling Range National Park is the place to go. Just within sight of the sea and between the undulating coastal plain and the flat inland, this 115,661-hectare park has plenty of spectacular, rugged peaks, dominated by Bluff Knoll (1073m), the highest peak in the state's south-west. Good walking tracks make the ascents relatively easy and there are some opportunities for off-track walking.

slow going, and after barely 500m, opposite a quiet natural pool, steps lead up to a grassed, shady area next to a car park (there are toilets nearby). This is **Yallingup**. A small open shelter has a display about the whales that frequent the coast between July and September. Another information board describes the features of Yallingup Reef just offshore. Nearby, the *Surfside Klosk* sells drinks, ice creams, sandwiches and burgers.

From the south end of this grassed area, follow a hard-surfaced path that soon parallels the road for a few hundred metres to a car park. The signposted Torpedo Trail is the

The Stirling Range is internationally renowned for its springtime displays of wild flowers – more than 1000 species have been recorded. The range was named in 1835, after Captain James Stirling, WA's first Governor. Although the surrounding country was taken up from the earliest years of European settlement, the rocky, wooded range was avoided. The national park, WA's third, was dedicated in 1913 to protect its flora and mountain landscape. Tourist roads were built in the 1920s but it wasn't until the 1960s that walking tracks were developed to the peaks both east and west of the main through road, Chester Pass Rd.

Two short walks are described in this section. For a rundown on the challenging Stirling Ridge Walk, see the boxed text later). Dieback is a serious problem; CALM has introduced strict control measures to try to limit its spread. Special Protection Areas, including the area around Yungermere Peak and a tract south of Stirling Range Drive, are out of bounds (see the boxed text 'Phytophthora' earlier).

NATURAL HISTORY

The range consists of a 65km-long east-west block of tough sandstone, quartzite and slate, rising very steeply from the surrounding plains up to 300m in the west and 850m in the east.

Summers are warm and dry and winters cool and wet, although wet in the northern fringes means an annual rainfall of less than 400mm. This moderate climate and the intricate topography have produced the abundant wild flowers. More than 1100 species of flowering plants have been recorded in the park, including about 80 that are endemic to the range. Woodlands of jarrah, marri and several other eucalyptuses are widespread on the slopes and in the deep valleys. On upper slopes and highest ground are mallee (multistemmed) eucalyptuses, banksia scrub and abundant wild flowers. Mountain bells are among the most beautiful. They have clusters of bell-shaped flowers enclosed by brightly coloured leaves (or bracts). When killed by fire, they regenerate from seed lying in the soil.

Several of the 35 species of mammals in the park are nocturnal, although there's a chance you'll see eastern grey kangaroos and brush (or red-necked) wallabies.Of the numerous species of birds, which include cockatoos and parrots, the smaller, colourful honeyeaters, wrens and robins are usually the most prominent.

PLANNING
When to Walk

Without doubt the best time for this park is spring, for the renowned wild-flower displays and for reasonably good weather. Summer is generally too hot and dry for comfortable walking, although winter, in between bursts of wild southerly weather, isn't out of the question.

What to Bring

It's essential to carry plenty of water on any walk in the park; boots are the recommended footwear for the rougher, less-used tracks.

Even if the plains, foothills and lower peaks are bathed in sunshine, the summit of Bluff Knoll can be mist-shrouded, or mist and cloud can drop down with little warning. The temperature there is usually much cooler than at the sheltered car park so be prepared with protective clothing.

Maps & Books

In the Natmap 1:100,000 series, the *Borden* and *Toombullup* maps cover the park and are particularly useful for identifying the various peaks; walking tracks are not shown. In the DOLA 1:50,000 series, the *Ellen Peak* and *Chester Pass* maps cover the walks described; for walks farther to the west you'd need the *Mondurup* and possibly *Tenterden* maps. A special DOLA 1:15,000 *Stirling Range East Ridge* map, is published for Stirling Ridge walkers (see the boxed text 'Stirling Ridge Walk').

Mountain Walks in the Stirling Range Part 1: The Peaks to the West of Chester Pass and *Part 2: The Peaks to the West of Chester Pass* (*Part 2* actually covers the eastern range) by AT Morphet are invaluable companions for walking in the park. These distinctive guides are organised around accurate, detailed sketches and profiles of the peaks on which walking routes are superimposed; no reference is made to published maps. Check with park rangers about access to the more remote peaks because of the problems with dieback.

CALM's national park leaflet gives an introduction to the park and shows the location of the main walks. Its *Mountains of Mystery:*

Stirling Ridge Walk

Just 19km separates Ellen Peak (1012m), at the eastern end of the Stirling Range, and Bluff Knoll (1073m) – a fair distance for a normal day's walk. However, this involves several steep ups and downs along the crest of the ridge via Pyungoorup Peak (1061m), Bakers Knob, Mirlpunda's spires and Isongerup Peak. There's plenty of scrambling and potentially tricky route finding through thick bush – there is no marked track, just the pads created by walkers. The Stirling Ridge Walk usually takes three days, with two nights' camping or bivouacking in sheltered caves, and demands considerable fitness and experience in walking over rough ground.

Although camping in the national park is restricted to Moingup Spring, CALM goes along with ridge walkers camping along the route as the only practical way of completing this wilderness walk. The provisos are that fuel stoves must be used for cooking and all rubbish must be carried out. Water is scarce and the ridge is exposed to frequent onslaughts of mist, low cloud and strong winds.

Unless your group has two cars, you'll need to arrange transport to the start or from the finish of the walk (see the Stirling Range Retreat under Nearest Town & Facilities later in this section). At the eastern end, access is usually via Sandalwood Rd into Glenelg Estate, and a 4WD track south towards the park boundary. Walkers are strenuously urged to leave their vehicle at the stop sign on this track. Many vehicles get bogged at creek crossings over the next 2km to the trailhead, and the owner of the property through which the track passes is none too happy about being asked to extricate cars.

The eastern section of the park has been designated as a wilderness area. Within the next few years, to protect the fragile natural environment of the ridge increasingly at risk from the trampling of many hundreds of booted feet each year, and to preserve walkers' solitude, CALM may introduce a registration system. Meantime, walkers are asked to enter details of their walk in a register at the ranger station at Moingup Spring or at the information shelter beside Bluff Knoll Rd near the Chester Pass Rd junction (see Information Sources in this section)

A shortened version of the walk, the Stirling Circuit or Half Ridge Walk, from Mirlpunda to Bluff Knoll, provides a healthy taste of ridge walking without the necessity of staying out overnight. This and the full ridge walk are described in detail in AT Morphet's guide (Part 2) to the eastern range (see Maps & Books in this section).

Bluff Knoll – the highest peak of the Stirling Range

A Natural History of the Stirling Range and the companion *Flora List* are mines of information about the park. They're available from CALM and from Stirling Range Retreat (see Nearest Town & Facilities). Of the wild-flower guides, *Wild Flowers of the Stirling Range* by B Fuhrer & N Marchant is good value.

Information Sources

The ranger station is at Moingup Spring, 23km to the north of the junction between Woogenilup Rd and Chester Pass Rd (driving from Mt Barker). Information about track conditions is available from the office. There is also an information shelter beside the Bluff Knoll Rd near the Chester Pass Rd junction.

Permits & Regulations

The standard $8 per day national park entry fee is charged; there's an honesty box at a roadside shelter on the north side of Bluff Knoll Rd, east of Chester Pass Rd. Camping is allowed only at the official park site.

Walkers are strongly urged to leave details of any walks off recognised tracks at the ranger station at Moingup Spring or at the Bluff Knoll Rd information shelter (see Information Sources earlier).

Dieback control measures are in force, so you'll find boot-cleaning trays at the start of the Toolbrunup Peak and other walks.

NEAREST TOWN & FACILITIES

For a description of accommodation and other services in Albany, see Gateways in the introduction to the chapter.

Mt Barker

This is the largest convenient town when approaching the range from the south-west.

The excellent tourist bureau (☎ 08-9851 1163, fax 9851 1919, ✉ mtbarkwa@comswest.net.au), Albany Hwy, is open daily and provides comprehensive local information.

Near the town centre, Barker Home Video (☎ 08-9851 1880), 61 Lowood Rd, is open daily. The friendly owner provides email access ($2.50 per 30 minutes) and an outgoing fax service ($1.50 to $2).

Places to Stay & Eat On Albany Hwy at the northern end of town, *Mount Barker Caravan & Cabin Accommodation (☎ 08-9851 1691, fax 9851 2691)* has shady tent sites for $13 (there's a campers' kitchen) and park cabins at $35 for a double.

The distinctive A-framed backpacker place, *Chill Out (☎ 08-9851 2798, 79 Hassell St)*, parallel to the highway at the southern end of town, has singles, twins and doubles from $15 per night in spacious, almost hotel-standard rooms. The spacious kitchen and living area are well furnished and the hosts are very welcoming.

For a meal, there's *Henry Plantaganet's Cafe (☎ 08-9851 2233, 17 Lowood Rd)*, open from 6 to 8 pm Tuesday to Sunday for pasta ($7.50) and anything with chips ($5 to $7.50). *Mount Barker Hotel (☎ 08-9851 1477, 39 Lowood Rd)* serves a variety of pizzas ($12) and a range of meat-based main courses ($13 to $17).

The *Supa Valu* supermarket, open Monday to Saturday, sells liquid fuel for camp stoves. There's also a *butcher* and the excellent *Lockwood's Bakery*.

Getting There & Away Mt Barker is 359km from Perth via the Albany Hwy. There are daily Westrail (☎ 13 1053) bus services from Perth.

Stirling Range

Moingup Spring camp site (☎ 08-9827 9230), beside Chester Pass Rd, 78km north of Albany and within Stirling Range National Park, operates on a first-come, first-served basis for bushland tent sites. The fee is $8 per night for one or two people. There are gas barbecues, toilets, water and picnic tables. The ranger in charge of the national park is based nearby.

Just outside the northern boundary of the park, 12km farther along Chester Pass Rd in Borden, is *Stirling Range Retreat (☎ 08-9827 9229, fax 9827 9224, ✉ stirlingrangeretreat@bigpond.com)*. Tent sites, many with uninterrupted views of the western Stirling Range, cost $12 a double. There is a large campers' kitchen and gas barbecues; a Total Fire Ban is in force from November to the end of March. Caravans, cabins and chalets start from $35 for two in a small van, to $79 or more for two in a spacious chalet. Several books about the national park are on sale (or loan) at the office; details of the Kanga and Ongirup Creek local walks are available. The friendly hosts can provide transport for Stirling Ridge walkers; booking is essential and the charges are $30 for Ellen Peak and $10 for Bluff Knoll.

Across the road from the Stirling Range Retreat is *Bluff Knoll Cafe (☎ 08-9827 9293)*, open daily. The menu includes steaks, fish, chops and a vegetarian omelette (meals from $12 to $22). The cafe is licensed – a great chance to try the local, limited production wine ($17 to $42 per bottle). You can also have a beer or glass of wine without buying a meal. Takeaway food, a small range of groceries and drinks are available. In March 2000, the cafe's lease was for sale so these details may change.

Drive 9km north from Moingup Spring along Chester Pass Rd and you'll come to

Amelup Service Station (☎ 08-9827 9222), open daily for burgers, pies and sandwiches to eat in or take away; basic groceries and fuel are also on sale.

If you arrive at your camping area and find you've forgotten the beer and/or wine, the nearest source is *Kamballup Roadhouse*, 35km south of Stirling Range Retreat; it's open from 8 am to 7 pm Monday to Saturday and 8 am to 6 pm on Sunday.

Getting There & Away Stirling Range National Park is 330km south-east of Perth and 75km north of Albany. From Mt Barker, drive along Woogenilup Rd for 39km to Chester Pass Rd, then turn north (left) to reach the park boundary. Albany is directly south along Chester Pass Rd.

Bluff Knoll

Duration	3–3½ hours
Distance	6.2km, 634m ascent
Standard	medium
Start/Finish	Bluff Knoll car park
Nearest Town	Stirling Range
Public Transport	no

Summary A well-graded track lined with a rich array of seasonal wild flowers rises to the broad, open summit of south-west WA's highest peak, with magnificent all-round views.

With towering grey sandstone cliffs on its northern face, Bluff Knoll dominates the eastern section of the range. Its Aboriginal name Bullah Meudal, meaning 'Great, Many-Face Hill', is most appropriate. Although it looks unassailable from the car park near the base of the cliffs, a clearly defined track leads up through a wide, well-hidden break in the cliffs to the summit plateau. The highest point is easy to find near the cliff edge, but is undistinguished by a cairn. The 360-degree view is superb. The climb is straightforward and free of any scrambling and should not present any great difficulty for reasonably fit walkers.

During spring and early summer, the track is a veritable wild-flower avenue, so a field guide is worth carrying.

GETTING TO/FROM THE WALK

The clearly signposted Bluff Knoll Rd leads south-east from Chester Pass Rd, 12km north of Moingup Spring and 200m south of the entrance to Stirling Range Retreat. The car park is 8km along this sealed road.

THE WALK

The path initially leads down, but soon begins climbing, not too steeply, straight towards the cliffs. The track steepens as you near the cliffs, briefly parallels a tiny stream, then gradually turns south-westwards to find the break in the cliffs at the gap between Bluff Knoll and Coyanarup Peak to the south-west. Here the woodland gives way to heathland, dotted with grass trees and clumps of she-oaks and low eucalyptuses. Then, it's up beside a frog-filled gully to the summit plateau, where the path is on the exposed southern flank of the knoll. A short path leads to a good vantage point for views south across the plains to the coast. There are plenty of sheltered spots around the **summit** from which to take in the awesome views east to Ellen Peak and west right across the range.

The return is simply a matter of retracing your steps.

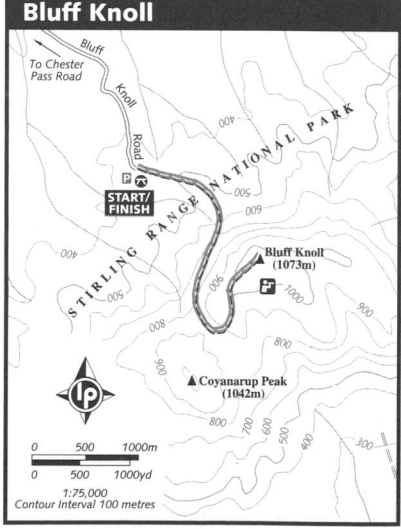

Bluff Knoll

Toolbrunup Peak

Duration	3 hours
Distance	4km, 600m ascent
Standard	medium-hard
Start/Finish	Toolbrunup car park
Nearest Town	Stirling Range
Public Transport	no

Summary A steep, mainly rocky ascent with some scrambling to a superb panoramic vista from the second-highest summit of the range.

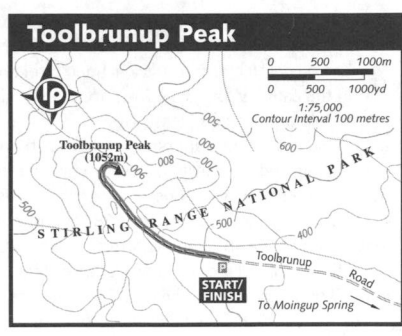

At 1052m, this peak is a much more challenging climb than Bluff Knoll. All but the first kilometre of track is steep and rocky and you need to be fit, agile and confident in scrambling over rocks in order to make it to the small summit. The views are magnificent and here you feel you are in the heart of the range, surrounded by rugged peaks and ridges.

Toolbrunup Peak is in a dieback risk area, so you must clean your boots before and after the walk at the tray near the car park.

A bushfire swept through this area in 1996 and there is plenty of evidence of strong eucalyptus recovery, with new growth on burnt trees surrounded by new saplings.

The peak is one of the best places in the Stirling Range to see examples of ripple marks on the sandstone boulders – clear evidence of the origins of the rock in an ancient sea. Wild flowers are plentiful in season, especially in the woodland and the lower scrub; look out for Baxter's banksia, white-flowering southern cross and boronia.

GETTING TO/FROM THE WALK

Access from Chester Pass Rd is along the signposted Toolbrunup Rd, 12.5km south of Stirling Range Retreat or 200m north of Moingup Spring camp site. The car park is at the end of the 4km-long gravel road.

THE WALK

For the first 15 minutes the track rises gently through low marri woodland, then steepens and, from a drift of scree across the track, gets serious about climbing. With a deepish gully on the right, the forest becomes more open and gives way to thicket. About 40 minutes from the start you reach the foot of a long run of scree composed of large boulders. From here, the Porongurup Range to the south comes into view. The way up is clear enough, with yellow- or white-topped stakes helping to show the route. A short, almost level section of track provides brief respite, then it's up again, with cliffs closing in on the right. A steep climb brings you to the main ridge, with wider views to the west (about 1½ hours from the start). Make your way up a narrow defile, along a wide ledge and up left to the **summit**, with its comfortably flat rock slabs (about 1¾ hours from the start). Allow about 1½ hours for the descent.

West Cape Howe National Park

Although relatively small in area (3500 hectares), this national park has spectacular coastal cliffs, culminating in Torbay Head, the most southerly point of WA. Midway between Albany and Denmark, it is readily accessible from both towns and is traversed by a section of the Bibbulmun Track (which, however, bypasses the track to West Cape Howe headland near Torbay Head).

The walk described starts at Lowlands Beach slightly west of the park and finishes at Cosy Corner, just outside the park. Bibbulmun Track camp sites offer the chance to spread the walk over a couple of days.

Bibbulmun Track

The original Bibbulmun Track, named after an Aboriginal group from the Albany area, was opened in the early 1970s. The 650km route extended from Kalamunda on Perth's south-eastern fringe to Walpole on the south coast. However, it touched too many of the wrong places (mines, logging areas) and missed the right ones – wild country and small country towns.

Rerouting and the construction of camp sites and walking tracks began in the late 1980s. The new 964km Bibbulmun Track, one of Australia's longest walking tracks, from Kalamunda to the historic town of Albany, was opened in 1998. The track largely uses existing 4WD tracks and purpose-built walking trails. The 48 camp sites are at roughly 20km intervals and each has a three-sided timber shelter with sleeping platforms, a picnic table, fireplace (when regulations permit), tent sites, toilets and water. For the time being these facilities are free, and are available on a first-come, first-served basis.

The route is marked with a stylised symbol of the Waugal, a mythical being from the Dreaming of the indigenous peoples of the south-west. For the Noongar people (of whom the Bibbulmun are a subgroup), the Waugal is profoundly significant in the formation of landscape features.

The track passes through several small towns including Dwellingup, Pemberton, Northcliffe and Walpole, all useful for supplies, accommodation and public transport. One coastal inlet is crossed by boat, another by canoe and two must be waded.

From Kalamunda, the route goes through varied forests and over granite peaks to Dwellingup, near the 200km mark. There follows 50km through the forested Murray River valley, then karri and jarrah forests continue southwards for more than 350km to near Northcliffe. Islands of forest, rivers and plains (liable to flooding between July and November) lead down to the coast at Mandalay Beach and on to Walpole (another 130km). The track then heads up tingle forest and back to the coast at Conspicuous Beach for the final section of nearly 160km to Albany. Many people have done the track end to end, taking seven to eight weeks, and many more do sections at a time.

The track is managed by CALM (☎ 08-9334 0265, @ bibtrack@calm .wa.gov.au) with abundant help from The Friends of the Bibbulmun Track, a nonprofit community organisation.

CALM has published eight 1:75,000 topographical maps of the track and two superb pocket guides for the northern and southern sections, with succinct track notes and practical and background information. These are available at CALM offices and visitor centres.

The Friends (☎ 08-9481 0551, fax 9481 0546, @ friends@bibbul muntrack.org.au, 🖳 www.bibbulmuntrack.org.au), PO Box 7605, Cloisters Square 6850, maintain an information-packed Web site. It's especially useful for accommodation and contacts with operators providing transport and luggage transfer for walkers. The Friends issue a free information pack and run a busy program of activities.

WESTERN AUSTRALIA

Perth

Walpole

HISTORY

Almost within living memory, people of the Minang Aboriginal tribe maintained the tradition of spending summer on the coast. The name West Cape Howe was adopted in 1801 to distinguish the cape from one of the same name on the New South Wales–Victoria border. The karri forests inland were logged in the late 19th and early 20th centuries, partly to provide timber for the Great Southern Railway from Albany to Beverley. The park was established in 1985, and is popular with walkers, hang-gliders, rock climbers and anglers.

NATURAL HISTORY

Most of the park consists of granites and limestones, so the black dolerite rock of the

Cape stands out in marked contrast. Along the cliff top here, up to 75m above the surging sea, hardy, salt-tolerant plants thrive in the spray. Wind-pruned heathlands are widespread, interspersed with banksias, dryandras (similar in appearance to banksias but with domed flower heads), clumps of peppermint gums, melaleucas and wattles. Among the many wild flowers, masses of pink coastal banjine are particularly striking.

PLANNING

Spring is the best time for this walk, although almost any time would be suitable, provided the weather isn't too wild.

Surface water between camp sites is extremely scarce, so carry all you'll need for the day. Sections of the walk, especially on the cape, are exposed to the weather – be prepared with windproof and waterproof gear. You'll also need to carry a fuel stove as campfires are banned in the park.

Maps & Books

You'll need CALM's *A Guide to the Bibbulmun Track: Southern Half* and the 1:75,000 *Denmark-Albany* track map. DOLA's 1:50,000 *Torbay* map has more topographic information but doesn't show the track. If you can find a copy in Albany, CALM's small book *Coastal Walks around Albany* by John Watson has a description of this walk. In the CALM Bush Books series, *Wildflowers of the South Coast* is useful.

Permits & Regulations

Entry to the park is free. Open fires are strictly banned at the Bibbulmun Track camp sites on this walk. Dieback control measures are in force, with several boot-cleaning stations along the walk.

NEAREST TOWNS

For a description of accommodation and other services in Albany, see Gateways in the introduction to the chapter.

Denmark

The park is roughly halfway between Denmark and Albany (see Gateways earlier for information on Albany). Denmark is very popular with people seeking an alternative to city living.

The tourist bureau (☎ 08-9848 2055, fax 9848 2271), 60 Strickland St, is open daily. It has information about local accommodation, Bibbulmun Track maps and local and natural history books.

The Environment Centre & Bookshop (☎ 08-9848 1644), 25 Strickland St, is open Monday to Saturday. As well as being the resource centre for local and regional environmental issues, it has Bibbulmun Track information and an extraordinary range of environment books.

At the Shire of Denmark's Telecentre (☎ 08-9848 2842), near the tourist bureau, you can send and check emails for $8; it's open weekdays.

Liquid fuel and gas canisters are available from the large hardware shop on the highway, Jack E Ricketts & Co.

Places to Stay & Eat Of the three caravan parks in the area, *Rivermouth (☎ 08-9848 1105)*, on Inlet Drive beside Wilson Inlet, is the closest to town. It has grassed tent sites at $11 for a double, small simple cabins ($36) and on-site vans ($30). At the small shop you can buy fresh local fruit and vegetables and basic supplies.

Denmark Waterfront Backpackers (☎ 08-9848 1147, fax 9848 1965, 63 Inlet Drive) is 3km from the highway. You'll pay from $15 for a bed in a spacious double or quad; the facilities are excellent. The nearby BYO restaurant features ostrich fillet or fish ($18.50) and a vegetarian dish ($12.50).

Less expensive, *Blue Wren Café (☎ 08-9848 1365, 21 South Coast Hwy)* is open Thursday to Saturday, with a curry night on Thursday. *Bandaleros Mexican Restaurant (☎ 08-9848 2188, 18 Holling Rd)* serves enchiladas ($14.50) and tortillas ($15); this BYO place occupies a 1920s corrugated iron building.

For self-caterers there's the *Denmark Co-Op*, on the corner of Strickland St and South Coast Hwy, the unmissable *Denmark Baker* in Strickland St, and *Denmark Fresh Fruit & Vegetables*, on the highway, for organic and bulk produce.

WESTERN AUSTRALIA

Getting There & Away Denmark is on the South Coast Hwy 53km west of Albany and 66km east of Walpole. The daily Westrail (☎ 13 1053) Perth–Manjimup–Albany bus service stops in Denmark (around $30 one way).

There is a taxi service (☎ 08-9848 2295) in Denmark.

Lowlands Beach to Cosy Corner

Duration	5¾–6¼ hours
Distance	23km
Standard	medium
Start	Lowlands Beach
Finish	Cosy Corner
Nearest Towns	Albany, Denmark
Public Transport	no

Summary A magnificently varied and scenic walk through heathland and woodland, along a limestone ridge and across granite boulders; optional side trip to West Cape Howe, near WA's most southerly point.

The route follows walking tracks and old 4WD tracks where conditions underfoot vary but the sandy sections are not long. Numerous junctions are well signposted.

If organising the necessary transport for a one-way walk is a problem, you could spend two days doing this walk, staying at the Torbay camp site on the first night and returning from there the following day – the views are always completely different on the way back. Alternatively, the informal camp site at Cosy Corner has gas barbecues and toilets.

GETTING TO/FROM THE WALK
To the Start
Drive east along the South Coast Hwy to Lower Denmark Rd. Follow it for 6km and turn right towards Tennessee South and Lowlands Beach. The sealed road ends 3.4km along. Turn left at a junction with Thompson Rd (on the right); the car park at the end of the road is 2.5km from the end of the sealed road. The Bibbulmun Track crosses the road 200m north of the car park.

From the Finish
To reach Cosy Corner, continue along Lower Denmark Rd 8.1km from the Lowlands Beach turn-off. Turn right along the road clearly signposted to Cosy Corner; the car park and camping area are 4.2km farther, at the end of the sealed road.

THE WALK
The track climbs from the road through low thicket and gives good views west to Wilson Inlet near Denmark, and as it gains height, of Lowlands Beach. After about an hour or more, the track turns towards the coast and soon reaches West Cape Howe *camp site* (1¼ hours from the start), with a great view south-east to its namesake. This is a fine spot for a rest.

The track continues its sinuous course through thickets and stands of peppermint gums, across some open ground and around gullies. About an hour from the camp site, the track crosses a succession of fairly shallow gullies, in places following old 4WD tracks. Several junctions are clearly marked. About 2½ hours from the camp site you come to a track junction where a sign indicates the turn-off to the right for West Cape Howe and Dunsky (Beach).

The broad track gains some height then descends and crosses a 4WD track at an angle; white-topped posts mark the route. Cross another sandy track and climb slightly. After about 15 minutes emerges into the open and starts to descend. Pass a turn-off to Dunsky Bay and continue on a 4WD track. At a fork, turn right then immediately left along a very sandy track. Fortunately the surface hardens after several minutes; at another fork turn left to a large informal car park. Continue past the barrier for stunning views of the cliffs of the **West Cape Howe** (about 45 minutes from the main track). Return to the main track by the same route.

A steady climb leads to a limestone ridge, with fine views eastwards, and on to a boardwalk, part of the Bruce Tarbotton Memorial Walk. About 30 minutes after rejoining the track, pause at a boot-cleaning station at a road crossing, where Shelley Beach is to the right. There's another station

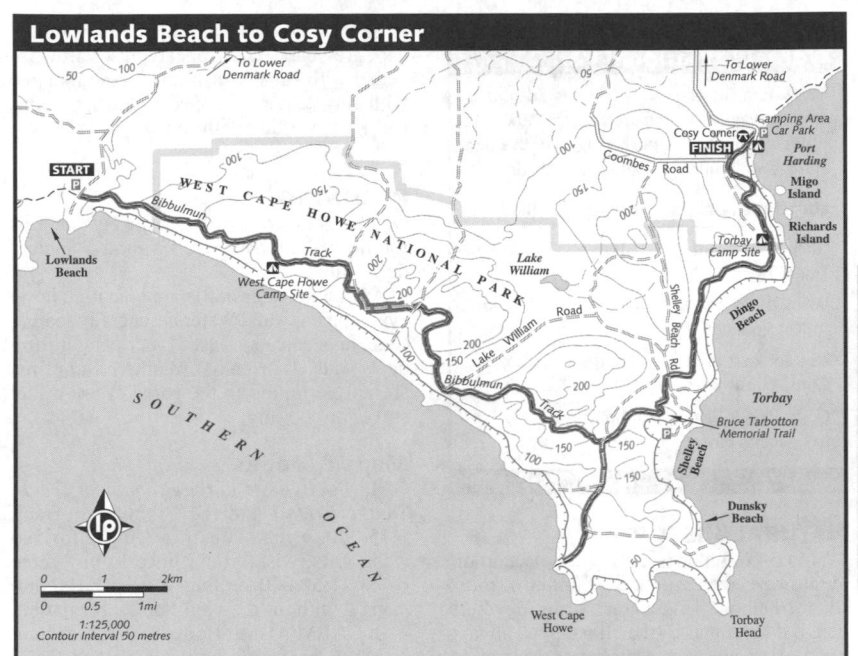

Lowlands Beach to Cosy Corner

a little farther on, then the route goes up and over some granite slabs, through a stand of melaleucas with fine views of Dingo Beach, and across a sandy 4WD track. Continue through some banksia then eucalyptus woodland to the Torbay *camp site* (one hour from the boot-cleaning stations).

Along the final stretch to Cosy Corner, the track passes another boot-cleaning station and goes through stands of marri, crosses a tiny stream and descends to the car park, picnic area and camping area via a long flight of steps (40 minutes from Torbay camp site).

Walpole–Nornalup National Park

Majestic forests of tingle trees and karri, remote beaches, peaceful inlets, windswept heathlands and headlands all make this a park of great variety and superlative beauty. It adjoins D'Entrecasteaux National Park in the west and extends east from Mandalay Beach for 40km along the coast to Point Irwin and the shores of Foul Bay. Established in 1911, the park's 18,100 hectares include the hilly forested interior around the Frankland River.

The Bibbulmun Track crosses the park with a generous sample of the forest and coast. The small town of Walpole is located in the centre of the park and serves as a base for walks in the area. The four-day walk described here starts at Walpole and takes in tingle forest, the amazing Tree Top Walk in the Valley of the Giants, and the coast from Conspicuous Beach to the hamlet of Peaceful Bay (see the boxed text 'Forest Giants' later in this chapter). Bibbulmun Track camp sites are spaced at reasonable distances, making for easy stages. Day 4 is only 10.5km.

A brief guide to some alternative day trips is provided in the boxed text 'Short Walks in Walpole–Nornalup National Park' later in this section.

Short Walks in Walpole–Nornalup National Park

Below is a list of worthwhile easy day trips around Walpole–Nornalup National Park. The walks take in some of the highlights of the area and are well-suited to parties with children.

start/finish points	duration	distance
Walpole to Giant Tingle Tree	3 hours	10km
Valley of Giants to Nut Lookout	2 hours	7km
Nut Lookout to Conspicuous Beach	2 hours	7km
Conspicuous Beach to Peaceful Bay	4 hours	14km

NATURAL HISTORY

Walpole–Nornalup is the wettest place in the south-west, with an annual rainfall of more than 1000mm. Tingle trees grow nowhere else but here, and as the climate has always been warm and wet, they have survived 65 million years. Red tingles grow to 70m and are the only eucalyptus with buttressed trunks, reaching up to 20m across. This makes them one of the largest living things on the planet. Many trees in the forest are multiple centenarians, and some are even 400 years old. Wildfires can burn through the heart of the trees, leaving a huge hollow. The tree survives because its growth is concentrated in the outer layers of the trunk. Yellow and Rate's tingles are also confined to the area and differ only subtly from red tingles.

Karri is another eucalyptus confined to the south-west of WA, in a long strip between Albany and Cape Leeuwin. Very different in appearance from the tingle, it has a slender white trunk, turning pinkish in autumn, soaring 30m straight to the lowest branches then up to 90m. Karri is highly prized for its timber, and its continuing exploitation is an extremely controversial issue in WA.

Two other WA eucalyptuses are found here. Jarrah has grooved, reddish-brown to grey bark, and marri is distinguished by its large fruits and splashes of red gum on the dark grey bark. These eucalyptuses grow together with karri oaks, a small, pine-like tree with tiny leaves wrapped round its stems, and karri wattles with masses of very pale yellow flowers in spring.

PLANNING

October and November are the best months for this walk, when there's a good chance of dry weather.

A hat and water bottle are essential, however long the walk. Water is generally scarce, so always carry at least 1L per person for a day's walk or 2L in hot weather. Campfires are not permitted in the park, so use a fuel stove for cooking.

Maps & Books

CALM's *A Guide to the Bibbulmun Track: Southern Half* and the Bibbulmun Track 1:75,000 *Walpole* map are ideal for the walk. Otherwise, you'd have to buy three RASC 1:50,000 or four Auslig 1:100,000 maps – without the vital track information.

In CALM's Bush Books series, *Common Trees of the South-West Forests* and *Common Wildflowers of the South-West Forests* are very useful. A small CALM booklet, *Saving the Giants*, describing the redevelopment of the Valley of the Giants, is available from the Giants visitor centre, as is *Discovering the Valley of the Giants and Walpole–Nornalup National Park*. Another CALM publication, the newspaper-format *A Guide to the Karri Country* includes a feature on the Valley of the Giants. Look out for a comprehensive rundown on the history of the park in *In Praise of a National Park* by Lee & Geoff Fernie.

Information Sources

For advice on things to do in Walpole–Nornalup National Park, drop in to the Walpole visitor centre or the district CALM office. For details of both, see Walpole under Nearest Towns.

NEAREST TOWNS

For a description of accommodation and other services in Denmark, see Nearest

Warnings

- On fine sunny days, you're likely to meet the odd snake or two; these will usually slither off into the bush out of sight.

- Along the coast, 'king waves' (ie, really big ones) can surge in without warning from a seemingly calm sea, so think twice about straying far from the track.

- Blister bush, with shiny green leaves, grows near Kingie Rock (last day en route to Peaceful Bay). It can cause blisters, so steer clear.

Towns in the introduction to West Cape Howe National Park.

Walpole

Walpole is a very small town on the South Coast Hwy.

The tourist bureau (☎ 08-9840 1111, fax 9840 1355), off the highway in the Pioneer Park, is open daily. The friendly staff provide accommodation information and sell tickets for the Tree Top Walk. You can buy Bibbulmun Track maps and guides and natural history references. Pick up a copy of the handy, free *Visitor Guide*, available outside the office when it's closed.

The local CALM office (☎ 08-9840 1027), on the highway 200m west of the bureau, is open weekdays and is a good contact for information about the track.

The BankWest branch is open only on Wednesday morning. The Pioneer Store is a bank agency and can handle withdrawals from card-based accounts; it's open daily. Check email at the Top Deck Cafe (see Places to Stay & Eat).

Places to Stay & Eat The friendly *Coalmine Beach Caravan Park* (☎ 08-9840 1026, fax 9840 1346) is on the shore of Nornalup Inlet; the track passes through it about 3km from Walpole. A tent site costs $13 for a double; there's a clean, spacious campers' kitchen and small shop.

At the eastern end of Walpole *Tingle All Over Budget Accommodation* (☎ 08-9840 1041, 61 Nockolds St)* has a range of rooms for $17.

At *Top Deck Cafe* (☎ 08-9840 1344), in the centre of town, Wednesday is pizza night ($16) and on Friday night it's fish and chips ($5 to $10). The cafe is licensed and the list includes local wines.

Both supermarkets are open daily, and the town also has a *butcher*, *bakery* and *health food shop*.

Getting There & Away Walpole is on the South Coast Hwy, 112km south of Manjimup and 62km west of Denmark. The town is on the daily Westrail (☎ 13 1053) Perth to Albany bus service (around $30 one way; seven hours).

Peaceful Bay

Peaceful Bay Caravan Park (☎ 08-9840 8060) is close to the beach and the track. Shaded grassy sites cost $12 for a double; on-site vans are $36 per double; barbecues are provided. The nearby small shop carries a survival-level range of supplies. At the time of research the park was for sale, so some details may have changed.

Peaceful Bay Chalets (☎ 08-9840 8169), on Peppermint Way, is 400m from the track. The tariff is $15 in doubles or small dorms.

Getting There & Away Turn off the South Coast Hwy 43km west of Denmark or 23km east of Walpole. There's a car park at the end of the sealed road at Peaceful Bay (9km).

Walpole to Peaceful Bay

Duration	4 days
Distance	57.3km
Standard	medium
Start	Walpole
Finish	Peaceful Bay
Nearest Towns	Walpole, Peaceful Bay
Public Transport	start only

Summary All the best of the south coast: magnificent forests of red tingle and karri, an unspoilt river, wild and rocky coast and sandy beaches. The walk can be split into eight shorter outings.

This walk starts near the swampy shores of Nornalup Inlet, climbs to the magnificent red tingle and karri forests, then returns to the coast and its limestone cliffs and sandy beaches, following the Bibbulmun Track all the way. The recommended duration makes for an easy-going trip; fit walkers can easily do it in 2½ days.

Walpole is on a bus route, but Peaceful Bay is not, so you'll need to arrange to be picked up at the end of the walk. Local accommodation hosts may be willing to help. The table accompanying this walk summarises the possibilities for dividing the long walk into several shorter ones, which can be done one way (with transport at each end), or there and back.

Generally, conditions on the track are excellent, making for good progress. The amount of ascent overall isn't great, but the several shortish ups and downs during each day's walk are a factor to be considered.

THE WALK
Day 1: Walpole to Frankland River
4½–5 hours, 17.6km

From the highway at the western end of Walpole, walk south along Boronia Ave. After 300m turn right down a gravel track for a short distance then left and continue almost to the shore. Turn left, in tea-tree scrub, walk across a car park and parallel the shore, then go through another car park at a jetty. A few hundred metres farther on, turn left at a T-junction then right at a fork. Then, after 500m, turn right and shortly right again and go down **Coalmine Beach Heritage Trail** through wetlands to cross Collier Creek on a boardwalk. Continue through thick melaleuca; cross the sealed Knoll Drive, then a gravel road; turn left along a walking track close to the shore and in 100m walk through the caravan park.

About 200m beyond the office, turn right along signposted **Delaney Walk**, through a narrow strip of bush between Nornalup Inlet and the road. Beyond a lookout, turn left and almost immediately right along an old 4WD track. Continue to the highway and cross over; 300m farther on, turn right. At the next junction go left and start climbing. About 40 minutes from the road, the track passes below Hilltop Lookout, with good inlet and ocean views. Continue gaining height; about 800m farther on, turn right for a short distance along a 4WD track, then continue on a walking track.

At the next junction (30 minutes from Hilltop Lookout), with a car park to the left, continue on an excellent track to the giant tingle trees boardwalk (see the boxed text 'Forest Giants' later). Continue on the track, past a junction on the left, across a gravel road and slightly uphill. About 25 minutes from the **Giant Tingle Tree**, cross the forested summit of Douglas Hill, then generally descend to cross a creek. Turn right along a wide 4WD track and keep heading down past a track to the right. A good hour from Douglas Hill, leave the road and follow a walking track; cross the gravel Creek Rd then two small creeks. In a few more steps you reach the beautifully located Frankland River *camp site* (20 minutes from Creek Rd).

Day 2: Frankland River to Giants Camp Site
3½–4 hours, 14.3km

The first short stretch is beside the river; the track then crosses a spur. Just beyond a steep flight of steps, turn right along a gravel track then shortly left. The track wanders up and down and arrives at **Sappers Bridge** across the Frankland River (30 minutes from the camp site). Cross it and turn right along Brainy Cut Off and climb to a right turn along a walking track. Then it's through karri and jarrah forest down to and across **Boxhall Creek**. The track then undulates across a couple of tracks and small creeks. Turn left beyond the second bridge, then descend to cross a creek; turn sharp left almost immediately and go up to cross Twin Creek Rd (about 1½ hours from Sappers Bridge).

The next kilometre can be rather boggy, then there's an ascent to cross a gravel road diagonally right. About 1km farther on, cross the sealed Valley of the Giants Rd and veer left; ascend to cross a gravel road. Continue to the **Tree Top Walk** car park (1½ hours from Twin Creek Rd).

Go past the walk entrance, down steps to a boardwalk. Then swing left across a

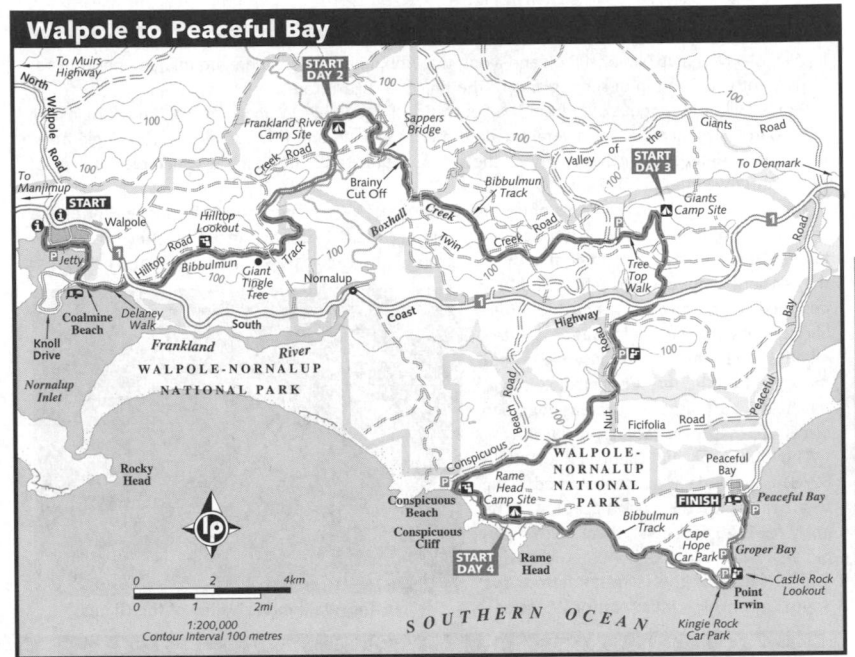

Walpole to Peaceful Bay

gravel track and climb to a junction; turn sharp left. The track descends steadily to Giants *camp site*, deep in the forest (25 minutes from the car park).

Day 3: Giants Camp Site to Rame Head Camp Site

4–4½ hours, 15.6km

Head east along a 4WD track and after 200m bear right and climb past some fine tingle trees. The route crosses a gravel road, several small creeks, another road, then descends through a mixture of tingles and karri trees. Cross the South Coast Hwy (about 45 minutes from the camp site). Continue to the right along the formation of the old Denmark to Nornalup railway line. Beyond a swamp you are confronted by a wall of scrub; here, turn sharp left (25 minutes from the highway). Cross a creek and keep to the right of a barbed-wire fence, climbing through forest before soon emerging into a stand of tea-trees and grass trees. Cross a

track and shortly afterwards bear right along a sandy track, then right again after 50m to **Nut Lookout**, near a car park (approximately 30 minutes from the rail formation).

The track descends through heath, with superb views eastwards, then mixed woodland, with a short section on a wider track, to cross Nut Rd. Continue down through heath – the wild flowers here are brilliant – then turn left and descend to the gravel Ficifolia Rd. Follow this road to the right for 400m and then leave it along a walking track (one hour from Nut Lookout). This leads through heathland for about 600m; from here, turn right. The sandy track wanders up and down through woodland. About 2km farther on, a steep descent leads to the edge of a **small lake** (not mentioned in CALM's guidebook). Continue through woodland to the swampy lake fringe, then climb to a long sandy ridge. At a T-junction, turn left (Conspicuous Beach car park is to the right). At the next junction not long afterwards you

WESTERN AUSTRALIA

Forest Giants

In Walpole–Nornalup National Park and along the Bibbulmun Track, there are unique opportunities to walk into and on top of some giants of the tingle and karri forest.

Beside Hilltop Rd, about 5km from the South Coast Hwy near Walpole, at the Giant Tingle Tree site, boardwalks meander for several hundred metres around and through a cluster of tingle trees. Interpretive signs explain the history of these fascinating trees, including a venerable survivor of devastating wildfires in 1937 and 1951.

The Tree Top Walk, in the Valley of the Giants, is one of WA's major tourist stops. The centrepiece is an amazing aerial walkway through the tingle and karri trees. Six linked inverted suspension bridges, made of steel, rise to 40m above the ground in a circuit walk of about 400m. There's also the Ancient Empire Walk with beautifully designed interpretive signs and the Tingle Shelter with yet more information. All this might sound intrusive and insensitive, but the impact on the forest is incredibly slight, much less so than the severely degraded picnic site that these facilities replaced.

The Valley of the Giants (☎ 08-9840 8263) is open daily and only closed if the weather makes the walk hazardous. The entry fee is $5 for adults; there's also a picnic area with barbecues. Access is via the sealed Valley of the Giants Rd from the South Coast Hwy, 14km east of Walpole.

Tree Top Walk in the Valley of the Giants

TREVOR CREIGHTON

---

can diverge left to a **whale-watching platform** with a fine view of the beach. After this, follow the track to the right, then go down some flights of steps and along a boardwalk. Farther on, cross or bypass a small stream (depending on its depth) and walk along **Conspicuous Beach** (an hour from Ficifolia Rd).

At the far end, a pole marks the exit along a sandy track. Follow it inland for about 300m then turn right and climb steeply. About 25 minutes from the beach, you reach a **high point** with magnificent views to the east and west. Continuing south then east, good views of the rugged west side of Rame Head unfold; Baxter's banksia is plentiful around here as are white-tailed black-cockatoos. Descend slightly, turn left along an old 4WD track for a short distance, then right, and another 100m brings you to the turn-off to Rame Head *camp site*, with fantastic views east to West Cape Howe (50 minutes from the beach).

Day 4: Rame Head Camp Site to Peaceful Bay
3–3½ hours, 10.5km

Rejoin the main track, which rises and falls through heath and woodland. Descending towards the beach, cross a track and follow another to the beach (25 minutes from the camp site). For the next 6km to Point Irwin the route is along several sandy beaches and bouldery shorelines separated by low rocky or scrubby headlands. The beaches provide good walking, except perhaps at high tide. The track is generally along well-marked walking or sandy 4WD tracks. You will reach **Castle Rock** car park above Point Irwin 1½ hours from the first beach.

Walk around the car park and follow cairns across a granite dome scattered with boulders – the views here are excellent. A short section along a 4WD track leads down to Kingie Rock car park. Continue down across some streamlets and merge with a 4WD track to reach Cape Hope car park.

Then, a sandy track leads north across heathland; walking tracks drop down to **Groper Bay** beach. Beyond the beach cross rocks to some tiny shelly beaches and small headlands. About 300m from Groper Bay, fork right at a junction on a headland for 150m along a sandy track to the end of another beach, which may be rather soft. Cross marram-grassed dunes to a firmer beach. At the far end, climb wooden steps to a concrete path leading to a car park; follow more concrete to the car park near the Peaceful Bay shop (one hour from Castle Rock).

Other Walks

LEEUWIN–NATURALISTE NATIONAL PARK
Cape to Cape Walk

Section 2 of the Cape to Cape Walk (see the Leeuwin–Naturaliste National Park section earlier for section 1), 27km from Wyadup to Cowaramup, passes through a very narrow section of Leeuwin–Naturaliste National Park, nearly all along cliff-top walking tracks interspersed with short beach strolls. The views are superb. There is a *camp site* about halfway along, just south of the main intermediate vehicle access from Caves Rd along Moses Rock Rd. Cowaramup Bay is a short distance from Gracetown Caravan Park (see Nearest Towns in the Leeuwin–Naturaliste National Park section).

The 31km stretch from Cowaramup to Redgate Beach is partly along the coast, taking in the spectacular Cape Mentelle, and partly inland via Ellenbrook House and the coastal settlement of Prevelly Park. The walkers *camp site* is near Ellenbrook.

Redgate Beach to Hamelin Bay (29km) features fantastic limestone cliffs, shady marri forest and Hamelin Bay. Coastal walking tracks and forest 4WD tracks make for easy walking, but the soft sands of Hamelin Bay are hard work. There are *camp sites* at Contos Field, 8km south of Redgate Beach (accessible from Caves Rd via Contos Rd), and beside Point Rd, 1km south of Contos, accessible by car. Access roads to near Contos and Boranup provide opportunities for short walks. There's a caravan park at Hamelin Bay, but no shops.

The final section to Cape Leeuwin (29km) has 3km along soft sand and some scrambling over low cliffs, inland bush tracks, magnificent views and a final easy section to the lighthouse. The town of Augusta is 8km along the road

from the lighthouse. The *camp site* is about 7km south of Hamelin Bay.

Augusta has a youth hostel, caravan park, hotel and shops. Westrail (☎ 13 1053) and South-West Coachlines (☎ 08-9324 2333) run daily bus services from Perth.

STIRLING RANGE NATIONAL PARK
Mt Trio

This 856m peak stands slightly apart from the Stirling Range and gives superb views, especially of Toolbrunup Peak. The name refers to its three separate summits, the westernmost being the highest. Dieback control is necessary here, with a boot-cleaning tray at the start. Allow up to three hours for the 2km walk, which involves a 500m ascent on a clear track.

To reach the start, turn off Chester Pass Rd 4.6km north of Moingup Spring or 7.5km south of the Bluff Knoll Rd junction, along Formby South Rd. Follow it for 3.7km to the gravel Mt Trio Rd; the car park is 1.5km along this rather rough road.

Mt Hassell

Between Toolbrunup and Mt Trio another short walk (2km return) involves a steep final climb to the Mt Hassell summit (847m) and its panoramic views. The walk starts 4km west along Stirling Range Drive from Chester Pass Rd.

Talyuberlup Peak

This 783m peak stands in the heart of the western range; from the picnic area beside Stirling Range Drive (21km from Chester Pass Rd), a track leads to some scrambling along rocky ledges. Allow about two hours for the 2km return walk.

Mt Magog

Close to Talyuberlup, this is a longer walk (7km return, about four hours) to a double summit (856m). It starts from Mt Magog picnic area beside a short circuit road off Stirling Range Drive, about 27km west of Chester Pass Rd.

DONNELLY RIVER

In the heart of the karri forest country, the beautiful Donnelly River valley contains some very fine stands of these magnificent trees. The Bibbulmun Track follows the valley for about 65km. The 27km section between the old timber town of Donnelly River (also known as Wheatley) and One Tree Bridge follows good walking tracks and old 4WD tracks, so the distance can be covered in one day if transport can be arranged at both ends. Alternatively, Tom Rd *camp site*, overlooking the river 16km south of

Donnelly River, could serve as a base or staging point on a longer walk.

At Donnelly River the original timber cottages from the days when it was a timber milling town now provide accommodation; further information is available by phoning ☎ 08-9772 1244 or emailing ✉ donnelly@karriweb.com.au. The traditional *Donnelly River Store* is a lifeline to track walkers; as well as supplies, it stocks track information and a map of two local walks. To reach Donnelly River, turn off the South West Hwy at Bridgetown towards Nannup; the town is 31km farther on via Brockman Hwy and Sears Rd.

One Tree Bridge is on Graphite Rd about 23km west of the modern timber town of Manjimup on the South West Hwy. The Manjimup tourist bureau (☎ 08-9771 1831) can help with local accommodation (including two caravan parks); there's also a CALM office (☎ 08-9771 7988) for track information and its informative *Guide to the Karri Country*. There are plenty of supermarkets, shops, an Internet cafe and a few places to eat in the town.

This section of the Bibbulmun Track is covered by CALM's *Pemberton* map and *A Guide to the Bibbulmun Track. Southern Half*, also by CALM.

PORONGURUP NATIONAL PARK

Just a few kilometres south of the Stirling Range, this park is completely different, featuring huge domes of granite and luxuriant karri forest. The Nancy's Peak Circuit Walk starts at the Tree in the Rock picnic area, 3km from the town of Porongurup and, with a side trip to Marmabup Rock, takes in the main features of the park (3½ hours, 7km). CALM's leaflet for the park has a basic map and background information, although its *Porongurup National Park: A Range of Attractions* is more detailed and is available at *Porongurup Tearooms* (☎ 08-9853 1110). Here

you can enjoy lunch or afternoon tea, purchase basic supplies and stay at the adjoining *YHA hostel* (doubles and a dorm for $14). Transport can be arranged for guests from Mt Barker or Albany. There's also *Porongurup Range Tourist Park* (☎ 08-9853 1057) nearby, where you can pitch a tent for $14 or stay in a cabin ($40). The Mt Barker tourist bureau (see the Stirling Range National Park section earlier) can provide details of other local accommodation.

An entry fee is charged for the park, payable on site ($8). Camping is not permitted, and dieback control measures are in force. Access is via Porongurup Rd from Mt Barker or from Chester Pass Rd 40km north of Albany.

TORNDIRRUP NATIONAL PARK

This small park protects most of the rugged headland of Flinders Peninsula on the southern side of King George Sound, just south of Albany. A walking track traverses the narrow eastern half of the park to Bald Head and makes for a highly scenic day's walk (about 5½ hours, 12km). The track starts from a car park near Isthmus Hill, reached from Albany via Frenchman Bay and Salmon Holes Rds, and roads to Misery Beach and Isthmus Hill. It's narrow in places and inclined to be overgrown with prickly scrub, so long trousers are recommended.

Entry to the park is free; camping is prohibited. A map is scarcely necessary but the Auslig 1:100,000 *Albany* and *Mount Barker* maps are useful for identifying the many features in the panoramic views. The CALM book *Coastal Walks around Albany* describes the walk.

The nearest place for refreshments is the *Frenchman Bay kiosk* which does takeaway food and Devonshire teas. The adjacent *caravan park* (☎ 08-9844 4015) has tent sites for $15 and modern cabins at $45 for a double.

Glossary

Visitors from abroad who think Australian is simply a weird variation of English/American may quickly find themselves lost in a strange collection of Australian words. The meaning of some words in Australia is completely different from that in other English-speaking countries, while others are derived from Aboriginal languages, or from the slang used by early convict settlers. This includes many words pertaining to the landscape, flora and fauna that are relevant to the walker. The list that follows focuses primarily on words that walkers may come across, whether it be in the bush or down the pub. Lonely Planet also publishes an *Australian phrasebook*, which is an introduction to both Australian English and Aboriginal languages, and the Glossary of the *Australia* guidebook has a comprehensive list of words and phrases.

anabranch – branch stream that turns out of a river and re-enters it downstream
arete – narrow ridge, particularly between glacial valleys
arid – having little or no rain
ATM – Automated Teller Machine; machine for extracting cash from a bank
Auslig – Australian Surveying & Land Information Group; national mapping agency

barbie – barbecue (BBQ)
billabong – ox-bow bend in a river cut off by receding waters
billy – small cooking pot
billy lifter – utensil used to lift a hot billy
bitumen – tarred road surface (tarmac)
bivouac or **bivvy** – makeshift shelter used in the open; large waterproof sleeping sack used for this purpose
bloke – man
boardwalk – walkway made of timber planks; *duckboards*
bombora – offshore reef
bore – artesian well
bottle shop – liquor shop
brumby – wild horse

bush, the – undeveloped areas away from the city
bushbash – to force your way through pathless bush
bushfire – fire in bushland
bush tucker – indigenous foods, found naturally in the bush
bushwalking – hiking, tramping, walking; walking for pleasure in the bush
buttress – pillar-like rock formation protruding from a hillside
BYO restaurant – restaurant to which you can Bring Your Own alcohol

cable crossing – tensioned wires strung across a creek (should not be crossed when flooding)
cairn – pile of stones marking a walking route, a summit or a prominent geographical feature
CALM – Department of Conservation and Land Management in Western Australia
camp site – area suitable for camping, often without facilities
camping ground – designated camping area with facilities
canyon – gorge or ravine, usually formed by a river
cascade – small waterfall
cask – large cardboard box containing an aluminium bag full of wine
Centre, the – the arid region in Australia's centre
circuit – walk that starts and ends at the same point
CMA – Central Mapping Authority of New South Wales; now *LPINSW*
contour – line on a topographic map connecting points of the same altitude; to move across a slope along the same level
cooee – call used to locate people over long distances; shouting distance, close ('to be within cooee of…')
counter meal – pub meal
creek – small watercourse or stream
cuesta – long low ridge with a steep *escarpment* and a gentle back slope

cyclone – violent tropical storm, confined to northern Australia

damper – bread traditionally made of flour and water and cooked in the ashes of a campfire
deli – delicatessen and/or milk bar
dieback – microscopic fungus called *Phytophthora cinnamomi*, which attacks, and usually kills, some species of native plants
dolerite – coarse-grained volcanic rock
Dreamtime – the time for Aboriginal people when totemic ancestors formed the landscape, made the laws and created the people who would inherit the landscape
Dry, the – dry season in northern Australia (April to October)
duckboards – boards forming a pathway over wet or muddy ground; *boardwalk*

ECD – Emergency Call Device; solar powered phones installed along walking trails
Eftpos – Electronic Funds Transfer at Point of Sale; electronic means of making retail purchases with a debit or credit card
escarpment – line of cliffs along the edge of a ridge

fire trail – *4WD* track, usually in national parks, built for fire-fighting vehicles
ford – to cross a river by wading
fork – point where a path splits into two
4WD – four-wheel drive; also 4x4
freshie – freshwater crocodile (usually harmless)
fuel stove – cooker, usually portable, using liquid fuel or gas canisters
fuel-stove-only area – area where campfires are banned

gap – saddle or pass; low point on a ridge or between peaks
Gondwanaland – ancient supercontinent that included modern Australia, Africa, Antarctica, South America and the Indian subcontinent
gorge – large, steep-sided valley, usually surrounded by cliffs
GPS – Global Positioning System; an electronic means of accurately fixing location using microwave satellite signals

granite – light-coloured, coarse-grained lava rock
grid reference – method of fixing location by using the numbered horizontal and vertical lines (grid) on topographical maps
GST – Goods and Services Tax
gully – small valley
gum tree – eucalyptus tree

HI – Hostelling International
homestead – residence of property owner (or manager) in the bush
hut – simple building used for accommodation, mainly in national parks, generally unsupervised and without facilities

inlet – indentation in the coast, usually with a narrow opening to the sea
ISIC – International Student Identity Card
isthmus – narrow stretch of land connecting two larger landmasses
IYHF – International Youth Hostels Federation

jumper – sweater or pullover

king tide – unusually high tide

lead – narrow opening through thick bush
limestone – sedimentary rock composed mainly of calcium carbonate
logbook – book or register at the start and finish of a walk to record walkers' movements; also in huts as a visitors' book
lookdown – lookout or viewpoint
loop – see *circuit*
LPINSW – Land & Property Information New South Wales; state government mapping agency

mallee – a group of eucalyptuses with multiple stems; the north-west of Victoria
management track – 4WD track in national park used by park rangers
mangrove – coastal tree genus that grows in salt water
midden – mound of discarded shells and bone fragments

NPWS – National Parks & Wildlife Service; state-based national park agency

Outback – remote, sparsely inhabited interior areas of Australia
outlet – of a lake, an opening that permits water to flow away

pad – indistinct informal track, usually made by animals, also by walkers
paddock – fenced area of land, usually for livestock
Parks Victoria – Victoria's state-based national park agency
plateau – elevated area of land that is almost level
potbelly stove – wood or coal-burning stove used for heating in some older huts
pound – broad-basin valley created by the uplifting and sinking of land

ranger – on-site park management official
ridgeline – crest of a ridge, often used for travel through alpine areas
road train – large goods truck towing several trailers
runoff – rainfall running into creeks and rivers as surface water

saddle – pass or gap; low point on a ridge or between summits
saltie – saltwater crocodile (dangerous)
sandblow – large, unstable dune of sand which is slowly driven forward by a prevailing wind
sandstone – sedimentary rock comprised of sand grains
scree – weathered rock fragments at the foot of a cliff or on a hillside
scrub – low dense vegetation
sealed road – tarred road
semiarid – characterised by low rainfall and scrubby vegetation
Shellite – liquid fuel derived from petroleum and used in camp stoves
sidle – to *contour*
snow line – level below which snow seldom falls or lies on the ground
snow plain – open grassed area in alpine country, usually surrounded by snow gums

snow poles – route markers used in alpine areas
spot height – altitude of minor features, marked on topographical maps
spur – small ridge that leads up from a valley to a main ridge
station – large sheep or cattle farm
swimming hole – large pool on a creek or river, safe for swimming
switchback – route that follows a zigzag course up or down a steep incline

tarn – small alpine lake
Top End – northern part of the Northern Territory
topographic – showing the surface configuration of a region; with *contours*
Total Fire Ban – prohibition of all open flames on days of extreme fire danger
tor – high, bare, rocky hill
track – formed route for use by walkers (walking track) or vehicles (*4WD* track)
tree line – highest natural level of tree growth
trig point – Australian/New Zealand term for triangulation point; point used in triangulation as a basis for mapping
tucker – food
true left/true right bank – side of a riverbank as you face downstream
2WD – two-wheel drive; also 2x4
TWS – The Wilderness Society

Unesco – United Nations Educational, Scientific and Cultural Organisation

waterhole – small pool or lake
weatherboard – timber cladding on house
Wet, the – rainy season in the north (December to February)
wildfire – bushfire out of control
World Heritage Area – (WHA) area included on a list of places deemed by *Unesco* to be of world significance

yabbie – freshwater crayfish
YHA – Youth Hostels Association

LONELY PLANET

Guides by Region

L onely Planet is known worldwide for publishing practical, reliable and no-nonsense travel information in our guides and on our Web site. The Lonely Planet list covers just about every accessible part of the world. Currently there are 16 series: Travel guides, Shoestring guides, Condensed guides, Phrasebooks, Read This First, Healthy Travel, Walking guides, Cycling guides, Watching Wildlife guides, Pisces Diving & Snorkeling guides, City Maps, Road Atlases, Out to Eat, World Food, Journeys travel literature and Pictorials.

AFRICA Africa on a shoestring • Cairo • Cairo City Map • Cape Town • Cape Town City Map • East Africa • Egypt • Egyptian Arabic phrasebook • Ethiopia, Eritrea & Djibouti • Ethiopian (Amharic) phrasebook • The Gambia & Senegal • Healthy Travel Africa • Kenya • Malawi • Morocco • Moroccan Arabic phrasebook • Mozambique • Read This First: Africa • South Africa, Lesotho & Swaziland • Southern Africa • Southern Africa Road Atlas • Swahili phrasebook • Tanzania, Zanzibar & Pemba • Trekking in East Africa • Tunisia • Watching Wildlife East Africa • Watching Wildlife Southern Africa • West Africa • World Food Morocco • Zimbabwe, Botswana & Namibia
Travel Literature: Mali Blues: Traveling to an African Beat • The Rainbird: A Central African Journey • Songs to an African Sunset: A Zimbabwean Story

AUSTRALIA & THE PACIFIC Auckland • Australia • Australian phrasebook • Australia Road Atlas • Bushwalking in Australia •Cycling New Zealand • Fiji • Fijian phrasebook • Healthy Travel Australia, NZ & the Pacific • Islands of Australia's Great Barrier Reef • Melbourne • Melbourne City Map • Micronesia • New Caledonia • New South Wales & the ACT • New Zealand • Northern Territory • Outback Australia • Out to Eat – Melbourne • Out to Eat – Sydney • Papua New Guinea • Pidgin phrasebook • Queensland • Rarotonga & the Cook Islands • Samoa • Solomon Islands • South Australia • South Pacific • South Pacific phrasebook • Sydney • Sydney City Map • Sydney Condensed • Tahiti & French Polynesia • Tasmania • Tonga • Tramping in New Zealand • Vanuatu • Victoria • Walking in Australia • Watching Wildlife Australia • Western Australia
Travel Literature: Islands in the Clouds: Travels in the Highlands of New Guinea • Kiwi Tracks: A New Zealand Journey • Sean & David's Long Drive

CENTRAL AMERICA & THE CARIBBEAN Bahamas, Turks & Caicos • Baja California • Bermuda • Central America on a shoestring • Costa Rica • Costa Rica Spanish phrasebook • Cuba • Dominican Republic & Haiti • Eastern Caribbean • Guatemala • Guatemala, Belize & Yucatán: La Ruta Maya • Healthy Travel Central & South America • Jamaica • Mexico • Mexico City • Panama • Puerto Rico • Read This First: Central & South America • World Food Mexico • Yucatán
Travel Literature: Green Dreams: Travels in Central America

EUROPE Amsterdam • Amsterdam City Map • Amsterdam Condensed • Andalucía • Austria • Baltic States phrasebook • Barcelona • Barcelona City Map • Berlin • Berlin City Map • Britain • British phrasebook • Brussels, Bruges & Antwerp • Brussels City Map • Budapest • Budapest City Map • Canary Islands • Central Europe • Central Europe phrasebook • Corfu & the Ionians • Corsica • Crete • Crete Condensed • Croatia • Cycling Britain • Cycling France • Cyprus • Czech & Slovak Republics • Denmark • Dublin • Dublin City Map • Eastern Europe • Eastern Europe phrasebook • Edinburgh • Estonia, Latvia & Lithuania • Europe on a shoestring • Finland • Florence • France • Frankfurt Condensed • French phrasebook • Georgia, Armenia & Azerbaijan • Germany • German phrasebook • Greece • Greek Islands • Greek phrasebook • Hungary • Iceland, Greenland & the Faroe Islands • Ireland • Istanbul • Italian phrasebook • Italy • Krakow • Lisbon • The Loire • London • London City Map • London Condensed • Madrid • Malta • Mediterranean Europe • Mediterranean Europe phrasebook • Moscow • Mozambique • Munich • the Netherlands • Norway • Out to Eat – London • Paris • Paris City Map • Paris Condensed • Poland • Portugal • Portuguese phrasebook • Prague • Prague City Map • Provence & the Côte d'Azur • Read This First: Europe • Romania & Moldova • Rome • Rome City Map • Russia, Ukraine & Belarus • Russian phrasebook • Scandinavian & Baltic Europe • Scandinavian Europe phrasebook • Scotland • Sicily • Slovenia • South-West France • Spain • Spanish phrasebook • St Petersburg • St Petersburg City Map • Sweden • Switzerland • Trekking in Spain • Tuscany • Ukrainian phrasebook • Venice • Vienna • Walking in Britain • Walking in France • Walking in Ireland • Walking in Italy • Walking in Spain • Walking in Switzerland • Western Europe • Western Europe phrasebook • World Food France • World Food Ireland • World Food Italy • World Food Spain
Travel Literature: Love and War in the Apennines • The Olive Grove: Travels in Greece • On the Shores of the Mediterranean • Round Ireland in Low Gear • A Small Place in Italy • After Yugoslavia

LONELY PLANET

You already know that Lonely Planet produces more than this one guidebook, but you might not be aware of the other products we have on this region. Here is a selection of titles that you may want to check out as well:

Watching Wildlife Australia
ISBN 1 86450 032 8
US$19.99 • UK£12.99 • 149FF

Cycling Australia
ISBN 1 86450 166 9
US$21.99 • UK£13.99 • 169FF

Australian phrasebook
ISBN 0 86442 576 7
US$5.95 • UK£3.99 • 40FF

Australia
ISBN 1 86450 068 9
US$24.95 • UK£14.99 • 180FF

Outback Australia
ISBN 0 86442 504 X
US$21.95 • UK£13.99 • 170FF

Healthy Travel Australia, NZ & the Pacific
ISBN 1 86450 052 2
US$5.95 • UK£3.99 • 39FF

Sean & David's Long Drive
ISBN 0 86442 371 3
US$10.95 • UK£5.99 • 90FF

Diving & Snorkeling Australia's Great Barrier Reef
ISBN 0 86442 763 8
US$17.95 • UK£11.99 • 140FF

Tasmania
ISBN 0 86442 727 9
US$16.95 • UK£10.99 • 130FF

Australia Road Atlas
ISBN 1 86450 065 4
US$14.99 • UK£8.99 • 109FF

Sydney Condensed
ISBN 1 86450 045 X
US$9.95 • UK£5.99 • 59FF

Sydney
ISBN 0 86442 724 7
US$15.95 • UK£9.99 • 120FF

Available wherever books are sold

 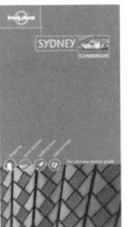 

Index

Text

For a list of walks, see the Table of Walks (pp4–7)

Bold indicates maps.

Bold indicates maps.

Bold indicates maps.

Boxed Text

MAP LEGEND

BOUNDARIES

	International
	Regional
	Disputed

HYDROGRAPHY

	Coastline
	River, Creek
	Lake
	Intermittent Lake
	Salt Lake
	Canal
	Spring, Rapids
	Waterfalls
	Swamp

ROUTES & TRANSPORT

	Freeway
	Highway
	Major Road
	Minor Road
	Unsealed Highway
	Unsealed Major Road
	Unsealed Minor Road
	Track
	Lane
	Tunnel
	Train Route & Station
	Chairlift/Ski Lift
	Described Walk
	Alternative Route
	Side Trip
	Walking Track
	Ferry Route

AREA FEATURES

	Park (Regional Maps)
	Park (Walk Maps)
	Beach
	Cemetery
	Reef
	Urban Area

MAP SYMBOLS

✪ CAPITAL	National Capital	Airport	Parking
◉ CAPITAL	Regional Capital	Bus Stop	Pass/Saddle
● CITY	City	Cave	Picnic Area
● Town	Town	Church	Police Station
● Village	Village	Cliff or Escarpment	Post Office
		Contour	Shopping Centre
		Fence or Boundary	Ski Area
	Camping Area	Gardens	Spot Height +100m
	Hut	Gate	Stately Home
	Lookout	Hospital	Toilet
	Place to Eat	Lighthouse	Tourist Information
	Place to Stay	Mine	Transport
	Point of Interest	Mountain or Hill	Trigonometric Point △
	Shelter	National Park	Zoo

Note: not all symbols displayed above appear in this book

LONELY PLANET OFFICES

Australia
Locked Bag 1, Footscray, Victoria 3011
☎ 03 9689 4666 fax 03 9689 6833
📧 talk2us@lonelyplanet.com.au

USA
150 Linden St, Oakland, CA 94607
☎ 510 893 8555 or ☎ 800 275 8555 (toll free)
fax 510 893 8572
📧 info@lonelyplanet.com

UK
10a Spring Place, London NW5 3BH
☎ 020 7428 4800 fax 020 7428 4828
📧 go@lonelyplanet.co.uk

France
1 rue du Dahomey, 75011 Paris
☎ 01 55 25 33 00 fax 01 55 25 33 01
📧 bip@lonelyplanet.fr
🖥 www.lonelyplanet.fr

**World Wide Web: 🖥 www.lonelyplanet.com *or* AOL keyword: lp
Lonely Planet Images: 📧 lpi@lonelyplanet.com.au**